THE
ARMED CONFLICT SURVEY
2022

The worldwide review of
political, military and humanitarian
trends in current conflicts

published by

for

The International Institute for Strategic Studies

The International Institute for Strategic Studies
Arundel House | 6 Temple Place | London | WC2R 2PG | UK

THE ARMED CONFLICT SURVEY 2022

First published November 2022 by **Routledge**
4 Park Square, Milton Park, Abingdon, Oxon, OX14 4RN

for **The International Institute for Strategic Studies**
Arundel House, 6 Temple Place, London, WC2R 2PG, UK

Simultaneously published in the USA and Canada by **Routledge**
52 Vanderbilt Avenue, New York, NY 10017

Routledge is an imprint of Taylor & Francis, an Informa business

© 2022 The International Institute for Strategic Studies

DIRECTOR-GENERAL AND CHIEF EXECUTIVE Dr John Chipman
EDITOR Dr Irene Mia
ASSOCIATE EDITOR Jack May
CONSULTING EDITOR FOR SUB-SAHARAN AFRICA Dr Benjamin Petrini
GRAPHICS COORDINATOR Flora Bell
EDITORIAL Flora Bell, Gregory Brooks, Christopher Harder, Michael Marsden, Nicholas Woodroof
DESIGN AND PRODUCTION Alessandra Beluffi, Ravi Gopar, Jade Panganiban, James Parker, Kelly Verity, Loraine Winter
CONFLICTS Adam Weinstein (Afghanistan and Pakistan), Dr Ryan Berg (Brazil), Mohamed Diatta (Central African Republic), Kyle Johnson (Colombia), Douglas Farah and Marianne Richardson (El Salvador and Honduras), Iris Madeline (Great Lakes Region), Michael Deibert (Haiti), Dr Alex Waterman (India), Tamer Badawi (Iraq), Noa Shusterman (Israel–Palestinian Territories), Dr Mohd Tahir Ganie (Kashmir), Dr Andrea Carboni (Lake Chad Basin and Nigeria), Dr Umberto Profazio (Libya), Rodrigo Aguilera (Mexico), Samuel Ratner (Mozambique), Morgan Michaels (Myanmar), Richard Giragosian (Nagorno-Karabakh), Michael Hart (Philippines and Thailand), Constantin Gouvy (The Sahel), Dr Francesco Milan (Somalia), Dan Watson (South Sudan), Tsion Belay Alene (Sudan), Dr Samir Puri (Russia–Ukraine), Dr Gregory Johnsen (Yemen)
REGIONAL ESSAYS Juan Pablo Medina Bickel, Dr Irene Mia (Americas), Dr Samir Puri (Asia), Dr Nigel Gould-Davies, Dr Thornike Gordadze (Europe and Eurasia), Dr Gregory Johnsen (Middle East and North Africa), Dr Benjamin Petrini (sub-Saharan Africa)
GLOBAL TRENDS Alec Crawford (The Aftermath of War in a Changing Climate: Aligning Solutions for Climate Security and Peacebuilding), Dr Irene Mia, Erica Pepe (Climate Change and the Instrumentalisation of Natural Resources in the Continuum of War: the Role of Non-state Armed Groups and International Responses), Laura Birkman (Transition in Turbulence: Geostrategic Implications of Climate Change and the Energy Transition)
THE CHART OF ARMED CONFLICT Erica Pepe, Juan Pablo Medina Bickel
RESEARCH CONTRIBUTIONS Emily Hardesty, Victoria von Stein (Armed Conflict Global Relevance Indicator), Shiloh Fetzek, Dr Benjamin Petrini, Dr Sandra Ruckstuhl (The Aftermath of War in a Changing Climate: Aligning Solutions for Climate Security and Peacebuilding), Caroline Emmett, Dr Catherine-Lune Grayson, Irénée Herbet, Vanessa Murphy, Michael Nest, Dr Sandra Ruckstuhl, Dr Erika Weinthal (Climate Change and the Instrumentalisation of Natural Resources in the Continuum of War: the Role of Non-state Armed Groups and International Responses), Douglas Farah, Vanda Felbab-Brown, Mónica Serrano, Paulo José dos Reis Pereira (Americas Regional Analysis), Henry Boyd, Emile Hokayem, Antoine Levesques, Dr Maria Shagina, Viraj Solanki

COVER IMAGES Getty

All rights reserved. No part of this book may be reprinted or reproduced or utilised in any form or by any electronic, mechanical, or other means, now known or hereafter invented, including photocopying and recording, or in any information storage or retrieval system, without permission in writing from the publisher.

British Library Cataloguing in Publication Data
A catalogue record for this book is available from the British Library

Library of Congress Cataloguing in Publication Data

ISBN 978-1-032-30442-7
ISSN 2374-0973

A soldier surveys a camp for displaced people in Jubaland, Somalia, 14 April 2022

Contents

Editor's Introduction	5
Notes on Methodology	11
Global Trends	17
The Aftermath of War in a Changing Climate: Aligning Solutions for Climate Security and Peacebuilding	18
Climate Change and the Instrumentalisation of Natural Resources in the Continuum of War: the Role of Non-state Armed Groups and International Responses	25
Transition in Turbulence: Geostrategic Implications of Climate Change and the Energy Transition	32
Conflict Reports	39
1 Americas	**40**
Regional Analysis	40
Mexico	44
Colombia	56
Brazil	66
Haiti	76
El Salvador	86
Honduras	94
Regional Outlook	100
2 Europe and Eurasia	**102**
Regional Analysis	102
Russia–Ukraine	106
Nagorno-Karabakh	118
Regional Outlook	127
3 Middle East and North Africa	**130**
Regional Analysis	130

French President Emmanuel Macron speaks at a conference in Baghdad, 28 August 2021

Syria	134
Iraq	144
Israel–Palestinian Territories	154
Yemen	164
Libya	174
Egypt	186
Turkey	192
Regional Outlook	198

4 Sub-Saharan Africa — 200

Regional Analysis	200
The Sahel	204
Lake Chad Basin	220
Central African Republic	230
South Sudan	240
Ethiopia	252
Somalia	262
Great Lakes Region	270
Nigeria	282
Cameroon	292
Mozambique	302
Sudan	310
Regional Outlook	320

5 Asia — 322

Regional Analysis	322
Afghanistan	326
Kashmir	338
Myanmar	350
Pakistan	362
India	372
Thailand	382
Philippines	390
Regional Outlook	399

Data Appendix — 400

Index — 414

Editor's Introduction

In February 2022 – as the world was still reeling amid the disastrous legacy of the coronavirus pandemic – Russia's invasion of Ukraine brought about the most consequential inter-state armed conflict since the Second World War, hitting the global economy with yet another major shock by disrupting agricultural-goods and energy supply chains.[1] By adding to pre-existing inflationary pressures (through its impact on staple cereals, fertilisers and energy prices), the war fuelled poverty, inequality and food insecurity – the latter already at record highs following the pandemic.[2] Inevitably, these trends will exacerbate root causes of conflict and instability in fragile countries – particularly in those dependent on food and energy imports. Furthermore, the unprecedented humanitarian crisis and reconstruction needs created by the war in Ukraine will limit the international humanitarian aid and development funding available to many conflicts and crises in other parts of the world.

Worsening food insecurity is a visible manifestation of how the global shocks of the coronavirus pandemic and the war in Ukraine intersect with the long-standing and accelerating climate-change emergency. Climate change and conflict appear to be increasingly connected in a vicious circle, with the former indirectly contributing to conflict dynamics (by aggravating their drivers and amplifying or creating tensions and grievances) and the latter reducing states' ability to mitigate the impact of climate change through adaptation strategies.

Figure 1: Prevalence of moderate or severe food insecurity as a percentage of the total population, by region, 2014–21

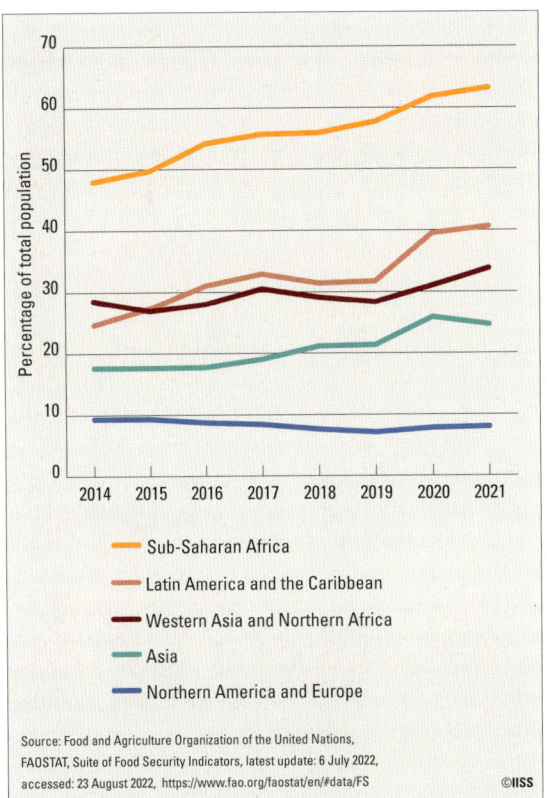

Source: Food and Agriculture Organization of the United Nations, FAOSTAT, Suite of Food Security Indicators, latest update: 6 July 2022, accessed: 23 August 2022, https://www.fao.org/faostat/en/#data/FS ©IISS

Geopolitics is centre stage

The Armed Conflict Survey has been monitoring and making sense of the global conflict landscape since the inception of the series in 2015, documenting the increasing complexity of conflict drivers, actors and dynamics, as well as the related intractability challenge evident in most ongoing conflicts.

One important source of complexity noted by *The Armed Conflict Survey* since its inception has been the increasing internationalisation of armed conflicts. While most contemporary wars are internal in their essence, a growing number and range of regional and global powers have been intervening in conflicts – in more or less overt forms – in pursuit of their strategic interests, further complicating internal dynamics that often already have a transnational character (e.g., jihadist Islamism) and multiple, complex drivers.[3]

While geopolitical competition had returned to the fore of the global armed-conflict landscape in the years prior to Russia's large-scale invasion of Ukraine, this development escalated this trend to a new level, with profound repercussions for great-power competition, geopolitical alignments and the sustainability of the current rules-based international system. Notably, the war seems to have marked an inflection point in the recent trend of Western countries' intervention fatigue and lack of strategic clarity on intervention, reconstruction and foreign policy – a trend that had provided opportunities for middle powers (including Russia) to assume greater roles in conflicts and peacemaking processes in recent times. The West's intervention fatigue was evident during the reporting period of *The Armed Conflict Survey 2022*, culminating with the full withdrawal of foreign troops from Afghanistan in July and August 2021 following two decades of involvement in the country. By threatening security in Europe, the Russia–Ukraine war strengthened the West's cohesion (apparent in the concerted imposition of sweeping economic sanctions on Russia), prompting NATO and European countries to undertake a reassessment of their strategic priorities while also triggering a rearmament process in many of the latter. The new approach – to continental and global security, among other issues – adopted by Western actors will likely have wide-ranging implications for many ongoing civil wars.

Global energy-transition and climate-change-mitigation strategies are also becoming a kernel of geopolitical competition – a trend that is sure to grow in significance in the coming decades. Disagreements over mitigation responsibilities and competition for control of green-transition-critical resources and technologies will likely become increasingly important sources of inter-state tension and exacerbate current geopolitical divides. Notably, control of green-transition-critical minerals might drive increasing third-party intervention in civil wars in resource-rich, fragile countries and become a key consideration in non-state armed groups' (NSAGs') calculations.

The Armed Conflict Survey 2022 aims to provide our audience of experts, practitioners and policymakers with a strategic assessment of the contemporary global conflict landscape, shedding light on its domestic, regional and global drivers, making sense of current developments and anticipating future trends (including political risks and potential hotspots for conflict). In an effort to unpack the complex nexus between the domestic and geopolitical dimensions of most active conflicts, it maps conflict parties and their regional and transnational interlinkages in detail, focusing on ever-proliferating NSAGs as well as direct and proxy third-party state interventions and global influences. Our Armed Conflict Global Relevance Indicator (ACGRI) provides an additional filter for strategic analysis and prioritisation. In line with the International Institute for Strategic Studies' global character and strategic and geopolitical research focus, it benchmarks the global relevance of conflicts based on their geopolitical impact and repercussions in addition to their intensity and human impact. Our Regional Analysis chapters, covering trends of strategic importance, provide further insights regarding important regional dynamics. Trends included range from de-escalation in the Middle East and geopolitical dimensions of conflicts in sub-Saharan Africa to the regional repercussions of the Russia–Ukraine war in Eurasia, the geopolitics of fentanyl in the Americas and China's intervention modalities in Asia's conflicts. This edition also features Regional Outlook sections that outline prospects for peace, escalation and possible regional spillovers, as well as key political risks and likely areas of fragility to watch in the year ahead.

Climate and conflict

As in previous editions, *The Armed Conflict Survey 2022* includes a section dedicated to selected current or emerging global trends of particular relevance for the global conflict landscape. Given the increasingly urgent need to understand the complex interlinkages between climate change, climate vulnerability and conflict amid accelerating global warming, this edition includes a special feature on climate security. The section delves into three important aspects of the climate–conflict nexus, selected for their strategic importance in shaping the conflict landscape going forward.

The essay 'The Aftermath of War in a Changing Climate: Aligning Solutions for Climate Security and Peacebuilding' investigates the interrelations between peacebuilding and climate resilience and the considerable opportunities for aligning the peacebuilding and climate-resilience agendas in fragile and conflict-affected countries. Peacebuilding programmes that are designed to be climate resilient can support the mitigation of climate risk and build local and national resilience to a variety of shocks and stressors – including environmental ones – thereby also strengthening their sustainability. At the same time, well-designed climate programming in contexts of fragility can also reinforce peacebuilding processes by offering a less politically sensitive platform for dialogue, cooperation and confidence-building among parties. However, certain challenges will have to be overcome if the two agendas are to be brought together, including divisions among those working in the humanitarian, development and peacebuilding space and different timescales for peacebuilding and climate programming (the former usually being more short term and the latter more long term). Furthermore, to make peacebuilding increasingly climate resilient, more climate finance is needed from donors. This may be achieved by raising their awareness of the challenges that climate change poses to stabilisation efforts.

'Climate Change and the Instrumentalisation of Natural Resources in the Continuum of War: the Role of Non-state Armed Groups and International Responses' explores how increasing scarcity of natural resources raises their intrinsic value as a tool for military and political leverage during war and its aftermath, resulting in further environmental degradation and human insecurity. NSAGs' recourse to natural resources as an instrument of warfare and political power is a particularly worrisome development negatively impacting counter-insurgency efforts and conflict and post-conflict interventions, as well as efforts in environmental preservation and activities geared towards tackling structural fragilities. The many shortcomings of international rules (including international humanitarian law, international human-rights law and international environmental law) – in terms of applicability, compliance and enforcement, where NSAGs are concerned – call for innovative ways to engage with NSAGs on protecting natural resources and, more generally, ensuring the respect of basic international principles. Developments in the international-law architecture and the work done by several multilateral actors to engage with NSAGs are reasons for hope. The development of data-driven early-warning frameworks that can identify where conflicts involving resources are most likely to occur will also be an important step to reduce risks, strengthen resilience and prioritise action.

The last essay in this section, 'Transition in Turbulence: Geostrategic Implications of Climate Change and the Energy Transition', considers the geopolitical dimensions and repercussions of climate-mitigation efforts and the related global transition from fossil-fuel-based to low-carbon energy systems. Willingness and ability to respond and collaborate on climate change will differ between states depending on their emission levels, development stage, strategic priorities, resource dependencies, technological progress and ability to absorb the resulting social, political and economic shocks. It will also depend on geopolitical realities, relative geo-economic leverage and some sort of agreement between the developing and developed world – notably on who bears more responsibility to act and pay (and how quickly). At the same time, the urgent need to decarbonise will likely result in increased competition to control and dominate the resources and technologies needed for the green-energy transition, with important repercussions for the geopolitical balance of power and the global conflict landscape. This context will exacerbate the multiplier effect that intensifying climate change is already having on inter-state and internal tensions over scarce natural resources, especially in climate-vulnerable countries. The essay argues that addressing the climate emergency will require de-politicising the climate challenge, reducing energy dependencies and driving sustained, coherent and timely action, notably by creating strong incentives for great powers to collaborate.

Visualising conflict and instability

The data-rich analysis throughout *The Armed Conflict Survey 2022* is visually complemented by multiple graphic elements, including regional and conflict-specific maps, charts and tables, illustrating core conflicts trends during the reporting period and related data (including military events, interventions and data on humanitarian impact and forced displacement), as well as regional and global links and spillovers. An exhaustive categorisation and analysis of conflict parties, together with timelines of key military and political events for the period under review, provide invaluable background information on the conflicts reviewed.

In addition, the accompanying Chart of Armed Conflict provides a visual snapshot of climate-vulnerability and food-security trends in the 33 active conflicts covered in *The Armed Conflict Survey 2022*, complementing the insight generated in the Global Trends section and specific conflict chapters. In an effort to bring to life the complex nexus between climate vulnerability and conflict, the chart maps violent events for the countries in which conflicts take place together with the ACGRI's human-impact pillar and indicators of climate vulnerability and sustainability, food risk and food inflation.

A look into the future: regional outlooks for conflict

The Armed Conflict Survey 2022 complements its strategic assessment of conflict drivers and domestic, regional and global conflict trends with analysis of future evolutions in the global conflict landscape, exploring prospects for peace and escalation, political risks and potential flashpoints to monitor. This 'horizon scanning' exercise aims to provide forward-looking insights to inform the strategies of our audience of policymakers, practitioners and corporate actors operating in or near conflict-affected countries.

The outlook for conflict in the **Americas** remains bleak amid intractable root causes, the increasing political clout and transnational reach of criminal groups and rising regional and international demand for illicit drugs. However, a number of political developments have the potential to lead to some modest pacification in the region in the medium term, including a possible revival in negotiations between Venezuela's government and opposition and steps towards a full implementation and extension of the peace agreement in Colombia under the leadership of the newly elected president, Gustavo Petro. However, much deteriorated socio-economic conditions following the coronavirus pandemic, coupled with rising inflation and food insecurity, will provide yet more opportunities for criminal groups to entrench themselves in local communities while challenging state institutions' legitimacy and ability to govern. In fragile countries particularly vulnerable to climate change, such as Haiti or those in Central America's Northern Triangle, increasing inflation and food insecurity will result in heightened domestic instability and drive uncontrolled migration flows, with negative repercussions for regional security. The constant optimisation and reconfiguration of criminal groups' business according to profit margins and demand will drive contestation and violence around drug-trafficking routes (including ports) and markets, reaching countries largely spared from drug-related violence until recent years, such as Costa Rica and Panama in Central America (where drugs seizures are on the rise) and Ecuador in South America, where gang rivalries have produced large-scale prison massacres in recent years. Mexican drug-trafficking organisations' focus on fentanyl will continue, driving conflict as they reconfigure their business and areas of control accordingly. Although cocaine will remain part of their portfolio in the near term, a move to mainly fentanyl is a possible scenario in the medium term, with important implications for regional drugs-trafficking dynamics.

In **Europe and Eurasia**, the outcome of the Russia–Ukraine war, the largest inter-state armed conflict in Europe since the Second World War, will have far-reaching implications. While Russia's attempt to impose a pro-Moscow regime in Ukraine has failed, the outcome of the war remains highly uncertain amid risks that it could escalate to even more intense or destructive forms of conflict. Even Russia's minimalist military goals of occupying the entire Donbas plus two southern *oblasts* – Kherson and Zaporizhzhia – will not be easy to achieve given Kyiv's determination to continue fighting, Western military aid to Ukraine, widespread insubordination within the occupied regions and inherent flaws in Russia's planning and conduct of the offensive. Ukraine's success (and ability to decide when to start negotiations on a durable ceasefire on its own terms) will depend on the swift delivery of weapons from the West, as well as on financial and economic support provided by the European Union and the United States. Against the backdrop of little progress towards a peace settlement to stabilise the ceasefire ending the 2020 conflict between Armenia and Azerbaijan over Nagorno-Karabakh, the weakening of Russia following the conflict in Ukraine has increased Azerbaijan's room for manoeuvre, bolstered by Turkey's support. Although Armenia does not seem to have recovered fully from the defeat in 2020, lacking the resources necessary for a new round of hostilities, the risk of renewed conflict remains significant, especially amid signs that Azerbaijan may seek to gain control of further territory. The flare-up of tensions between Tajikistan and Kyrgyzstan in April 2021, which saw more than 50 people lose their lives, highlighted not only the difficult bilateral relationship but also the larger issue of undemarcated borders in Central Asia. While several incidents (including explosions and a rocket attack in April 2022) have taken place in Transnistria since February, the odds of the war in Ukraine spilling over there are slim. Moreover, for as long as the war in Ukraine continues, it is unlikely that Transnistria's separatist forces and the relatively small contingent of Russian forces there will be able to launch a major offensive on their own. Georgia's Russia-occupied breakaway provinces – Abkhazia and South Ossetia – have remained calm so far. However, Russian success in Ukraine would reinforce Georgia's drift into Moscow's orbit, creating internal tensions between the government on one hand and the pro-EU opposition and part of the population on the other. Moscow's defeat in Ukraine would also carry risks for Tbilisi: if Russia turns to Georgia as a consolation prize, the latter would not be able to offer much resistance due to its much-reduced military budget and capabilities.

Most of the conflicts in the **Middle East and North Africa** are likely to remain in a state of protracted stalemate over the next year. However, the potential for escalation in Yemen and Syria remains high, despite a truce in the former and a military stalemate in the latter. A number of different scenarios could spark a renewal of fighting. President Recep Tayyip Erdoğan continues to suggest that Turkey will launch a new offensive in northern Syria targeting the Syrian Democratic Forces (SDF). The SDF has said that it may make common cause with President Bashar al-Assad if Ankara launches the operation, potentially reshaping and reinvigorating the conflict. Russia, which had been upset with Turkey's decision to block its warships in the Black Sea following its invasion of Ukraine, also urged Turkey not to launch the assault. The escalation potential also remains high in the Israeli–Palestinian conflict, even as Israel's growing relationship with the Arab Gulf states means that it will likely receive less criticism for its actions. The Russia–Ukraine war's impact on global food prices could be disproportionate for the region, especially in the event of a global recession, worsening food insecurity and exacerbating current conflicts and fault lines of instability.

After two decades of sustained growth, the double shock of the coronavirus pandemic and the Russia–Ukraine war has complicated the outlook for **sub-Saharan Africa**, especially for fragile and conflict-affected countries. Conflicts in the Sahel, the Lake Chad Basin and the Great Lakes region, fuelled by transnational conflict dynamics and porous borders, pose the greatest escalation risks. The radical Islamist groups active in these conflicts, which are affiliated to either the Islamic State or al-Qaeda, aim to progressively expand violence and their reach in the region. A trend of violence spillover from the Sahel to some of West Africa's coastal countries was evident during the reporting period, with attacks in Benin, Côte d'Ivoire and Togo. Further, the complex set of conflict drivers in the region – including chronic deficit of governance in the peripheries (e.g., in the Central African Republic and Sudan), multiple concomitant conflicts (e.g., Ethiopia and Nigeria) and overlapping local insurgencies and transnational jihadism (e.g., Mozambique and Somalia) – will continue to prevent decisive progress towards durable peace. The increasing number of inter-state disputes in the region are also contributing to instability: Ethiopia and Sudan engaged in deadly border clashes in the al-Fashaga Triangle in June 2022 in a dispute that intersects with the Grand Ethiopian Renaissance Dam issue, which also involves Egypt. Tensions between the Democratic Republic of the Congo and Rwanda have also risen due to the presence of NSAGs in border regions. On a more positive note, some possible progress on peace and security could result from the ceasefire and upcoming negotiations between Ethiopia and the Tigray People's Liberation Front. Moreover, under the newly elected President Hassan Sheikh Mohamud, Somalia will hopefully repair some of its internal fractures. A new phase in the struggle against al-Shabaab is also beginning with the transition from the African Union peacekeeping operation – active for 15 years – to the AU Transition Mission in Somalia, which aims to transfer responsibilities to the Somali National Army by 2024.

Few of **Asia's** intra-state armed conflicts offer firm prospects for peace in the short term. Myanmar poses a severe escalation risk amid an insurgency in the central plains and the ascendancy of the People's Defence Force and its clashes with the military junta. Uncertainties over the rule of the Afghan Taliban and its influence on regional security loom over the outlook for peace in Afghanistan and Pakistan. Although the former has not relapsed into outright war following the Taliban takeover in 2021, the group has struggled to provide healthcare, education and financial services amid a deepening humanitarian crisis caused by food insecurity. Violence in the country has also been rife, involving groups such as the Islamic State Khorasan Province (ISKP), National Resistance Front, Afghanistan Freedom Front and the High Council for Resistance, among others. A deterioration of security in Afghanistan is possible in the short term, while increased insecurity in the country would likely spill over to Pakistan, where an emboldened Tehrik-e-Taliban Pakistan, Baloch separatists and ISKP remain active. The India–Pakistan relationship also remains a potential threat to Asia's stability. In Kashmir, militant violence is unlikely to subside in the foreseeable future, while it is unlikely that Pakistan's Prime Minister Shehbaz Sharif will be able to productively engage Indian Prime Minister Narendra Modi on the Kashmir issue given the latter's hardline stance. Deepening tensions between the US and China over Taiwan also pose a major risk for Asia's security. Conversely, in Thailand, some room for optimism is afforded by the April 2022 agreement between the Thai government's Peace Dialogue Panel and the Patani Malay National Revolutionary Front, which provides the basis for further talks. Moreover, in the Philippines, security forces appear ascendant, placing Islamist militant groups under pressure in western Mindanao. Although this situation may not lead to a stable peace, a reduction in violence may be possible.

Notes

[1] Russia and Ukraine are among the largest producers of agriculture and staple cereals in the world. In 2021, together they accounted for 30% of global wheat exports. The two countries provide at least 30% of 50 countries' wheat-import needs. Russia is also among the largest exporters of fertilisers, oil and gas globally. It is the third-largest oil producer, with a 12% market share. See Food and Agriculture Organization of the United Nations (FAO), 'Impact of the Ukraine–Russia Conflict on Global Food Security and Related Matters under the Mandate of the Food and Agriculture Organization of the United Nations', 8 April 2022; and Carlos David Carrasco Muro, 'Ukraine–Russia War: How Will It Affect Latin America and the Caribbean?', World Economic Forum, 29 March 2021.

[2] According to the FAO, 2.3 billion people (or just under 30% of the world's population) globally were moderately or severely food insecure in 2021, an increase of over 350 million people since 2019. The prevalence of severe food insecurity increased by 2.4 percentage points – to 11.7% – in the same period, with an additional 207m suffering from severe food insecurity. See FAO, IFAD, UNICEF, WFP and WHO. 2022. *The State of Food Security and Nutrition in the World 2022. Repurposing food and agricultural policies to make healthy diets more affordable*. Rome, FAO. https://doi.org/10.4060/cc0639en.

[3] Third-party intervention has tripled over the last decade and reached record levels. See 'The Long Aftermath of Armed Conflicts', in IISS, *The Armed Conflict Survey 2021* (Abingdon: Routledge for the International Institute for Strategic Studies, 2021), pp. 22–8.

Notes on Methodology

The Armed Conflict Survey 2022 reviews and analyses events, dynamics and trends related to active armed conflicts around the world. We define an armed conflict as a sustained military contest between two or more organised actors making purposive use of armed force. The inclusion of a conflict in the book is based on this definition and the methodology detailed below.

Armed conflicts in 2021–22

The Armed Conflict Survey 2022 includes 33 armed conflicts that were ongoing between 1 March 2021 and 30 April 2022 (the 'reporting period'), organised across five regional sections covering the Americas, Asia, Europe and Eurasia, the Middle East and North Africa, and sub-Saharan Africa.[1] Each section comprises individual conflict chapters (longer Conflict Reports and shorter Conflict Summaries, depending on a conflict's global relevance as assessed by IISS analysis) introduced by a Regional Analysis that explores a trend of regional strategic relevance. It is closed by a Regional Outlook that examines the short-term prospects for active armed conflicts in the region – and the implications for regional and international security – and identifies future hotspots and political risks that should be monitored.

The review of conflicts is complemented by a special feature section covering selected aspects of climate security, reflecting the increasingly urgent need to understand and tackle the multiple impacts of accelerating climate change on conflict and security.

We have introduced a number of changes with respect to last year's edition in order to refine our methodology and ensure our coverage is up to date. Given the marked degeneration of political and security conditions in Haiti following the assassination of president Jovenel Moïse in July 2021, *The Armed Conflict Survey 2022* covers the conflict in the country for the first time. We have also made some adjustments to our treatment of conflicts in sub-Saharan Africa to fully capture their increasing regionalisation and internationalisation (see sub-Saharan Africa Regional Analysis on page 200). In this sense, we have extended the regional unit of analysis used in the previous edition for the Sahel and Lake Chad Basin conflicts to the Great Lakes Region in order to put more emphasis on regional dynamics. The regional lens allows for a better understanding of the strategic motives and behaviours of great powers and external actors whose operations are mostly transnational. Uganda is also included for the first time in the book, as part of the Great Lakes Region conflict, because its territory was targeted by Islamic-State-affiliated groups in late 2021.

Finally, to reflect changes in the relative global relevance of conflicts in the reporting period, we have consolidated our coverage of the India–Northeast, India–Central (Maoist), Philippines (NPA) and Philippines (ASG & Moro) conflicts into single chapters for India and Philippines respectively. Further, the Mozambique and Pakistan chapters, which were previously Conflict Reports, have been streamlined, becoming Conflict Summaries. Conversely, our chapter on Cameroon has been extended, becoming a Conflict Report.

Criteria for inclusion and removal

Defining armed conflict as a military or violent phenomenon means *The Armed Conflict Survey 2022* does not aim to determine the applicability of international humanitarian law to different conflict situations (as in the Geneva Conventions or the Rome Statute).

The Armed Conflict Survey includes armed confrontations that meet our thresholds in terms of *duration*, *intensity* and *organisation* of the conflict parties.

We require an armed conflict to run for at least three months and feature violent incidents on a weekly or at least fortnightly basis. *The Armed Conflict Survey*'s definition of armed conflict does not involve a numerical threshold of battle-related deaths, contrary to conflict datasets such as the Uppsala Conflict Data Program. For wars between states – which feature substantial levels of military mobilisation, simultaneous and numerous armed clashes, or significant fatalities – the duration threshold may be relaxed.

The organisation of the conflict parties refers to their ability to plan and execute military operations or violent attacks. The scale of such attacks is not a factor in this determination – for the purpose of inclusion in *The Armed Conflict Survey 2022*, for example, planting improvised explosive devices (IEDs) is equivalent to battlefield clashes. For armed conflicts that involve state parties, the deployment of armed forces or militarised (not regular) police is required. Non-state armed groups (NSAGs) must demonstrate some logistical and operational capacity, such as access to weapons and other military equipment, or an ability to devise strategies and carry out operations, coordinate activities, establish communication between members and recruit and train personnel. Territorial control or a permanent base in an area is not required. *The Armed Conflict Survey 2022* also remains agnostic about the type of organisational structure adopted by armed groups. Not all NSAGs have a distinct and effective chain of command – such as many of those operating in sub-Saharan Africa – but can be highly decentralised, maintain an amorphous structure, rely on a transnational network or have a global reach. A hierarchical military structure is therefore not an inclusion criterion. In each conflict chapter, the Conflict Parties table lists the main organisational capabilities of the actors involved.[2]

The Armed Conflict Survey 2022 excludes cases of protests and riots when happening in isolation. Instances of government repression, ethnic cleansing or genocide that occur outside of a conflict situation are also not included, regardless of their scale, unless the population develops a capacity to fight back through an armed, organised resistance, or another state intervenes – as in the case of the Khmer Rouge regime in Cambodia when Vietnam invaded in 1979.

Taking into account the extraordinary complexity of contemporary conflicts, our definition does not discriminate based on the nature of their drivers. *The Armed Conflict Survey 2022* includes conflicts motivated by political, socio-economic, ideological, religious and criminal reasons – or a combination of these elements. This approach allows us to cover conflicts in the Americas, which involve a mixture of organised crime and political violence, often perpetrated by actors with elusive political or ideological motives.

The Armed Conflict Survey applies two criteria for removal. Armed conflicts that have lost the above-defined characteristics for inclusion are removed after two years. An armed conflict terminated through a peace agreement also ceases to be included if it is followed by military demobilisation of all conflict parties.

Classification and categorisation of armed conflicts: scope and actors

The unit of analysis in *The Armed Conflict Survey 2022* is the conflict itself (the military or violent confrontation between armed actors). In most cases, conflicts take place within the boundaries of a state and are therefore listed under those country names. This applies for single conflicts but also for instances of overlapping distinct insurgencies occurring within the boundaries of a single country. Concomitant insurgencies ongoing in India, Iraq, Nigeria or the Philippines, to mention a few, are combined in single-country chapters for the purpose of our analysis. As mentioned, other conflicts have a regional scope, unfolding across multiple states. This is the case for the insurgency in the Lake Chad Basin – which involves parts of Cameroon, Chad, Niger and Nigeria – or the multifaceted and interrelated conflicts in the Sahel, spanning Burkina Faso, Mali and Niger. Conflicts that have elements of inter-state confrontation either take the name of the disputed region (Nagorno-Karabakh, Kashmir) or the parties involved (Russia–Ukraine, Israel–Palestinian Territories).

Conflicts may involve state or non-state actors. According to the types of actors involved and the interactions between them, armed conflicts have been grouped into one (or more) of the three following categories: inter-state (or international) conflicts, internal conflicts and internationalised-internal conflicts.[3]

An *inter-state* conflict involves two or more states (or a group of states) and takes place on the territory of one or several states, as well as in the global commons. This is the least common modality of conflict in the current landscape. However, inter-state conflicts are often among the most globally significant, as exemplified by the Russia–Ukraine war.

An *internal* conflict takes place in the territory of one state and is fought either by a government (and possibly allied armed groups) against one or more NSAGs, or between two or more NSAGs without the direct participation of state forces. Within this category, we include the sub-categories of localised insurgencies (such as the one ongoing in southern

Thailand), intercommunal conflicts (such as the one in Sudan) and organised crime (such as most of the conflicts in the Americas). However, these groupings are not necessarily mutually exclusive and many internal conflicts feature characteristics of two or more sub-categories.

Lastly, *internationalised-internal* conflicts are confrontations in which the kernel of the dispute remains domestic, but which feature the military intervention of one or more external states. Such involvement may include training, equipping or providing military intelligence to a conflict party or participating in the hostilities, either directly or through local proxies and sponsored actors.

The Armed Conflict Global Relevance Indicator (ACGRI)

The Armed Conflict Survey 2022 features the second edition of our Armed Conflict Global Relevance Indicator (ACGRI) as an additional tool of analysis and prioritisation to complement IISS qualitative expertise. The ACGRI assesses and benchmarks the global significance of conflicts across the world based on three pillars – or drivers – of significance, covering the following dimensions:

- The **human impact** of conflicts, in terms of human losses and hardship. The rationale for including this dimension stems from the nexus between conflict-related fatalities, forced displacement and further domestic social, economic and political instability with spillover effects on regional and global stability.
- The **incidence** of conflicts, as a measure of intensity and related security implications and potential negative externalities on neighbouring countries and beyond.
- The **geopolitical impact** of conflicts, measured by several variables we created to capture the involvement of third parties and interventions by the international community, based on IISS proprietary data and other international sources.

Given data availability and comparability challenges at the conflict level, the ACGRI uses the country in which a conflict happens as the unit of analysis rather than the conflict itself. This methodological choice is justified by the fact that most of the armed conflicts covered are internal (internationalised or not), meaning the conflict can be assimilated to the country in which it takes place. Where there are multiple insurgencies taking place at once in a country, the country score encompasses all of them. This means it will not be possible to differentiate the global significance of each domestic insurgency in isolation. In a similar fashion, conflicts that spill over national borders and affect several countries (such as those in the Sahel and Lake Chad Basin) are not given a regional score, with global relevance assessed instead at the level of each country involved.

In contrast, for the Russia–Ukraine, Nagorno-Karabakh and Israel–Palestinian Territories conflicts, the unit of analysis is the conflict itself.[4] India and Pakistan are treated separately in the case of the conflict in Kashmir due to the presence of other localised insurgencies ongoing in both countries. Geopolitical indicators relevant to Kashmir (such as the number of United Nations Security Council (UNSC) resolutions) are attributed to both countries to ensure that the final score reflects the geopolitical impact of the inter-state conflict.

The indicator is composed of a total of eight variables (see Table 1), which are good proxies of the dimensions of global relevance we seek to cover, considering the availability of reliable data.

As a preliminary step to combine variable scores into pillar and ACGRI scores, data for each variable is normalised on a 0–10 scale, through the following approach:

Eq.1 (indicator data−0)/(y−0) × 10 = variable score

where the indicator data refers to continuous data, y refers to the maximum value from the target countries and 0 is used as the minimum value.[5]

Each pillar score is the arithmetic mean of the composing variable, multiplied by 10, giving a pillar score between 0 and 100.

The scores of the ACGRI composing pillars are displayed throughout the book in a continuous colour progression (using conditional formatting) in order to respect the (cardinal instead of ordinal) distance between countries and to reflect more precisely the differentiation of conflicts' global relevance based on the continuum of the ACGRI scores for the full sample.

Table 1: ACGRI pillars and variables

Pillar	Variable	Description	Source
Human impact	Fatalities	Number of fatalities due to violent events, by country, 1 March 2021–30 April 2022[6]	Armed Conflict Location & Event Data Project (ACLED), www.acleddata.com
	Refugees	Number of refugees (total), counted by country of origin, as of 31 December 2021[7]	UN High Commissioner for Refugees, UN Relief and Works Agency for Palestine Refugees in the Near East
	Internally displaced persons (IDPs)	Number of IDPs (total), by country, as of 31 December 2021[8]	Internal Displacement Monitoring Centre, UN High Commissioner for Refugees, International Organization for Migration
Incidence	Violent events	Number of violent events, by country, 1 March 2021–30 April 2022[9]	Armed Conflict Location & Event Data Project (ACLED), www.acleddata.com
Geopolitical impact	Foreign countries' involvement[10]	Number of foreign countries 'involved' in the conflict, by country, as of 30 April 2022[11]	IISS analysis, Military Balance+, Arianna Antezza, Andre Frank, Pascal Frank, Lukas Franz, Ekaterina Rebinskaya and Christoph Trebesch, 'The Ukraine Support Tracker: Which countries help Ukraine and how?', Kiel working paper, no. 2218, 2022
	Deployments by major geopolitical powers	Number of military personnel deployed by major geopolitical powers in conflict-affected countries, by country, as of 30 April 2022[12]	Military Balance+
	UNSC resolutions	Number of UNSC resolutions concerning conflicts under review, by country, 1 March 2021–30 April 2022	UNSC
	Peacekeeping and other multilateral missions	Number of operational peacekeeping, special political and military missions and other multilateral missions concerning conflicts in countries under review as of 30 April 2022[13]	Military Balance+, Stockholm International Peace Research Institute (SIPRI),[14] UN,[15] regional organisations, ad hoc coalitions

Data for all the variables included in the ACGRI is listed in the Data Appendix, along with detailed source information, definition and the underlying calculation methodology for each variable.

Selected data from the ACGRI is also featured in the 'Key Conflict Statistics' boxes in Conflict Reports and Conflict Summaries along with other background variables relevant to the context under analysis, such as the Gini index, GDP per capita (based on purchasing power parity in constant prices–international dollars) and the functioning of government pillar of the Economist Intelligence Unit's Democracy Index.

Full data for all these background variables is also contained in the Data Appendix.

The Chart of Armed Conflict

The Chart of Armed Conflict provides relevant data and information for the 33 conflicts included in *The Armed Conflict Survey 2022*, including key humanitarian and climate-security data.[16] The Chart provides a visual snapshot of the incidence (conflict-related violent events) and human impact (ACGRI's pillar including conflict-related fatalities, refugees and IDPs) of covered conflicts.

The interlinkages of climate vulnerability and security risks and other stressors are also visualised, complementing the book's special feature on climate security. Food-insecurity patterns are notably depicted for conflict-affected countries, given their relevance as a driver of instability and conflict and the current spike in food prices that has followed the coronavirus pandemic and the outbreak of the Russia–Ukraine war.

Multilateral missions included are conflict-related multilateral peace and stabilisation operations (either conducted under the aegis of the UN or regional organisations, or ad hoc coalitions of states authorised by the UN) that support the peace process and/or facilitate peacebuilding and conflict prevention. Civilian and political missions, which do not involve armed forces, are also listed at the bottom of the Chart.[17] Data is obtained from the Military Balance+, SIPRI's Map of Multilateral Peace Operations and the official websites of the UN, regional organisations and ad hoc coalitions.[18]

Notes

1. Although the reporting period for the conflicts included in *The Armed Conflict Survey 2022* ends on 30 April 2022, we have covered important events that happened after this date in an effort to make the publication as timely as possible. Such events include presidential elections in the Philippines (May) and Colombia (June). Given the global relevance and magnitude of the ongoing Russia–Ukraine war, we have extended its reporting period to 31 July 2022. In all other cases, events after the end of April 2022 will be covered in the 2023 edition of *The Armed Conflict Survey*.
2. Unless otherwise stated, all figures related to military strength and capability, defence economics and arms equipment in the Conflict Parties tables are taken from Military Balance+.
3. The nature of the conflicts in Afghanistan and Ukraine significantly evolved over the reporting period. We have therefore changed the name, typology of conflict and starting date for the latter to reflect the new reality of the conflict, which passed from being an internationalised-internal confrontation to a fully fledged inter-state conflict. For Afghanistan, we have revised the typology of conflict but not its starting date given that the new phase began with the full withdrawal of foreign troops and the Taliban's takeover in 2021 remains rooted in the previous phase.
4. For the Russia–Ukraine war, the indicator is primarily informed by data for Ukraine as the latter is the theatre of fighting.
5. The normalisation formula is partially adjusted for the 'Deployments by major geopolitical powers' to account for the presence of clear outliers. In this sense, Ukraine is excluded from the normalisation formula and assigned the highest score, together with the second-highest value in the sample (Syria).
6. Conflict fatalities include those that result from battles, explosions/remote violence and violence against civilians.
7. Data for Ukraine is as of 4 May 2022, as the most recent data available. This exception is motivated by the extension of the reporting period for the Russia–Ukraine war.
8. Most recent available data for Egypt and El Salvador were from 2020 and 2018 respectively. Data for Ukraine is as of 3 May 2022.
9. Violent events include battles, explosions/remote violence and violence against civilians.
10. Our methodology includes the following definition of 'involvement' for third parties in conflict. For internal conflicts, foreign countries are considered 'involved' if they are either present through the deployment of military capabilities (outside of a multilateral mission as defined in the ACGRI) or they meet all the following criteria: presence of intelligence assets; provision of military financial support; role in an advisory or operational command-and-control capacity; and sale or transfer of military equipment. For inter-state conflicts, third-party countries are considered 'involved' if they are either present through the deployment of military capabilities (outside of a multilateral mission as defined in the ACGRI) or they meet two or more of the following criteria: presence of intelligence assets; provision of military financial support; role in an advisory or operational command-and-control capacity; and sale or transfer of military equipment.
11. Data for Ukraine is as of 1 July 2022, as most recent data available.
12. Calculated based on the number of military personnel deployed into conflict-affected countries by main geopolitical powers within the G20 (including unilaterally, as part of a combat coalition or a mission under the aegis of an international organisation and excluding deployments that are not conflict related).
13. These include missions undertaken by the UN, regional organisations or ad hoc groups related to UN sanctions/UNSC resolutions or endorsed by the UN and other international organisations. Data refers to active missions as of 30 April 2022 that fulfil the two following criteria: 1) objective (relating to multidimensional peace and conflict resolution) and 2) geographical scope (relating to the analysed conflicts in the countries under review).
14. SIPRI, 'SIPRI Map of Multilateral Peace Operations, 2022', May 2022, https://www.sipri.org/publications/2022/sipri-map-multilateral-peace-operations-2022.
15. UN, 'UN Special Political Missions and Other Political Presences 2022', 1 March 2022.
16. See the Data Appendix for full details.
17. The estimated strength of the mission refers to the military strength, unless otherwise stated. An asterisk indicates international civilian staff. The list of multilateral missions is updated as per the cut-off date of 30 April 2022.
18. For more details on variables included, see the Data Appendix.

GLOBAL TRENDS

A village chief in Garissa county, Kenya, surveys his community's dead cattle, 8 December 2021

The Aftermath of War in a Changing Climate: Aligning Solutions for Climate Security and Peacebuilding

There is significant overlap between conflict-affected, fragile states and the countries and regions most vulnerable and exposed to climate change. In states experiencing violence or transitioning from war to peace, the drivers of climate risk and vulnerability are often similar to those that drive conflict risk and vulnerability: multi-dimensional poverty, social and economic inequality, political marginalisation, food insecurity and histories of violence, among others. Poor governance and weak state institutions magnify each of these drivers, creating the crucial foundation for shared vulnerabilities to climate change and conflict. Geography also conspires against these countries, with many located in regions projected to experience the most severe climate extremes in the coming decades, including the Horn of Africa, the Sahel and the Middle East.

The strong link between climate and conflict vulnerability means that climate-change resilience is often lower for populations living in conflict-affected contexts.[1] In fragile states recovering from or experiencing conflict, many livelihoods are climate dependent and precarious: a harvest or herd can be lost with a sudden flood, a prolonged drought or the onset of violence. The institutions and governance systems that should be in place to protect populations from climate-related shocks and stresses are often missing or overwhelmed. Governments, with limited staffing and resources, must make difficult decisions regarding domestic budget allocations, while investments to build climate resilience are often difficult to justify in the face of immediate public-service needs, such as water, food security, energy, health, job creation and education. Some governments may be too dysfunctional or mired in conflict to even contemplate climate considerations. Yet a failure to protect their populations from increasingly dire climatological change can further weaken governments' authority. As such, climate change increasingly makes it even more difficult for governments and their populations to recover from violence or address conflict fault lines.

The nexus between climate and fragility risks

Climate and fragility risks are often mutually reinforcing; conflict and violence can erode adaptive capacities of both the state and the population, as well as the state's ability to address climate impacts, while climate impacts can exacerbate conflict drivers, pushing existing tensions and grievances towards violence or creating new ones. In northern Iraq, years of conflict and persecution against Yazidi communities at the hands of the Islamic State (ISIS) have left a region once heavily dependent on agriculture on the precipice: conflict-related neglect of the land, alongside a changing rainfall regime and higher temperatures, meant that wheat production was expected to fall by 70% by the end of 2021.[2] In Yemen, the destruction and weaponisation of water infrastructure during the ongoing conflict has greatly increased water scarcity for a population struggling in an already semi-arid landscape.[3] In Africa, increasingly erratic and declining rainfall rates are threatening the agriculture sector, with climate change expected to lead to a loss of agricultural output of between 17% and 28% on the continent, compared to 3–16% globally.[4] This reduced output is expected to significantly increase food insecurity, constrain livelihoods and push migration, indirectly contributing to conflict dynamics in particularly hard-hit regions, such as the Sahel. The increased volatility of global food prices, particularly those increases relating to Russia's war in Ukraine and disrupted global supply chains, will only exacerbate these domestic and regional food-security challenges. And while it should not be assumed that climate stress will automatically push groups and people towards conflict over land, water, food or resources, the unprecedented changes in climate within fragile contexts will likely complicate efforts to prevent conflict and establish or maintain peace and security in many parts of the world.

The energy transition adds a new dimension to economic and political instability in fragile states. Firstly, the global transition away from fossil fuels will create winners and losers. For conflict-affected states that rely on revenues from oil, gas and coal for a considerable proportion of their budget, the switch to renewables will impact national revenues; without necessary economic diversification, the switch could undermine governments' abilities to deliver public services and meet basic needs. Secondly, rapidly scaled-up investments in renewable-energy technologies and the necessary infrastructure to deliver low-carbon energy to growing populations will require decisions about how climate finances are spent, who benefits from the investments and how this might impact conflict. Finally, the low-carbon-energy transition could create new sources of revenue for strategic-mineral-producing countries (including those needed to build wind turbines, solar panels, batteries and electric vehicles). Many governments are eagerly watching this transition, and the anticipated rapid growth in demand for critical minerals, with an expectation of windfall revenues. However, care must be taken to ensure that mineral-exploration and -extraction processes are responsible and well governed, and that the revenues are properly managed. Such an approach would help to ensure that efforts to mitigate climate change do not unintentionally lead to environmental degradation, resource-rent capture, human-rights abuses, social conflict and a new resource curse.

Climate change presents a significant and increasing challenge to peacebuilding and the ways conflicts are addressed from diplomatic, security and development standpoints. Climate impacts may threaten and undo progress towards peace in areas that have stabilised. At the same time, peace agreements and development strategies in conflict-affected states often do not consider climate impacts and projections, nor how these impacts can influence future social and power dynamics. This is not necessarily a wilful omission: immediate suffering must be addressed, institutions built and basic needs restored. Furthermore, the climate data and information needed to inform effective climate policies and strategies are often missing, insufficient or too high level to be applied to the local context, hampering the ability of policymakers to understand local climate dynamics and their relationship to the conflict.

Peacebuilding and climate resilience: opportunities to align

The many shared drivers of climate and conflict vulnerability in fragile states provide considerable opportunities for aligning peacebuilding and climate-resilience agendas and for designing and implementing interventions that address both challenges. In contexts of ongoing, protracted conflict, the political will and institutions required to bring together climate and conflict responses may not be present or functional, and the path to peace may not be clear. The government may not even have complete control over its territory, limiting its ability to act in those areas where the rule of law is weak or missing. For partners working in these contexts, including humanitarian organisations, alignment of local and national peacebuilding and climate objectives may be more realistic.

Peacebuilding interventions and programmes that are designed to be climate resilient can support the mitigation of climate risk and build local and national resilience to a variety of shocks and stressors – including environmental ones – thereby strengthening the sustainability of these efforts. Designing these interventions to specifically address climate-risk drivers can also promote peace and reduce the drivers of instability by supporting livelihoods, reducing food and water security, and strengthening governance. At the same time, well-designed climate programming in contexts of fragility can also bolster peacebuilding processes – by offering a less politically sensitive platform for dialogue, cooperation and trust-building around the shared challenge of a changing climate among parties that would otherwise have difficulty finding common ground.

Climate-resilient peacebuilding programming is crucial, as is conflict-sensitive climate programming. Programmes and projects focusing on climate mitigation and adaptation must be designed in a way that is cognisant of the broader conflict context, including its dynamics, causes and actors. Programme designers will need a thorough understanding of the groups that potentially stand to gain from climate programming, as well as those that might lose, and will have to craft projects accordingly to eliminate these imbalances. Such an approach ensures that, at the very least, interventions do not exacerbate existing tensions and grievances and instead align with and enhance the peacebuilding agenda.

Governments rebuilding their laws, policies, institutions and systems in the aftermath of conflict (including those that govern the use of natural resources, land tenure and conflict management) should embrace the opportunity to adopt and implement practices that benefit the environment and promote resilience. For example, the Central African Republic's peacebuilding plan includes as a central pillar a commitment to renewing the social contract between the state and the population through strengthened governance, enhanced food security, improved water services and greater climate resilience.[5] Going further, countries can bring conflict sensitivity and peacebuilding considerations into national policy and planning processes, such as by following the National Adaptation Plan (NAP) process, through which countries identify and implement priority climate-adaptation actions.[6] The NAP process represents an effort by governments to address climate risks in a systematic way while aligning their adaptation activities and priorities with their medium- and long-term development planning. Aligning the NAP with a country's peacebuilding agenda makes sense: both take a holistic approach to addressing vulnerabilities; are or should be built around participative, inclusive decision-making; deal with medium- and long-term timelines; and must be country-owned, designed and driven in order to succeed. Significant institutional support is also available to countries developing their NAPs, including growing international expertise on climate–conflict links. Finally, the NAP process is backed by considerable political will and international financing that could support shared adaptation and peacebuilding objectives, such as institution-building and strengthened governance.[7]

Conflict sensitivity should also be better integrated into international climate finance. A 2020 evaluation of environmental programming by the Global Environment Facility (GEF) found that one-third of its global portfolio was invested in countries affected by major armed conflicts.[8] The GEF does not currently have a definition, policy or procedures in place for investing in such contexts, though the evaluation found that conflict and fragility have a significant impact on the likelihood that a project will be cancelled or delayed.[9] The evaluation recommended that to address this shortcoming the GEF Secretariat should develop guidance for conflict-sensitive programming throughout the programme lifecycle.[10]

Somalia offers an interesting case study. The federal government – with international partners and its implementing partner, the United Nations

Table 1: Number of weather stations in selected countries, 2021

Country	Fragile States Index ranking (2021)	Land area (km²)	Population, millions (2020)	Number of land surface climate stations	People per station	Stations per km²
Yemen	1	527,970	29.8	N/A	N/A	N/A
Somalia	2	637,660	15.9	N/A	N/A	N/A
Syria	3	185,180	17.5	12	1,458,333	15,431
South Sudan	4	633,907	11.1	N/A	N/A	N/A
Democratic Republic of the Congo	5	2,344,860	89.6	13	6,892,307	180,373
Central African Republic	6	622,980	4.8	17	282,352	88,997
Chad	7	1,284,000	16.4	14	1,171,428	91,714
Sudan	8	1,854,105	43.8	28	1,564,285	66,218
Afghanistan	9	652,860	38.9	4	9,725,000	163,215
Zimbabwe	10	390,760	14.9	20	745,000	19,538
Norway	178	625,222	5.4	461	11,713	1,356
Finland	179	338,450	5.5	922	5,965	367

Sources: Global Historical Climatology Network; World Bank DataBank; Fund for Peace Fragile States Index

Development Programme (UNDP) – integrated conflict considerations into its proposal to the Green Climate Fund for support in developing its NAP, recognising throughout the document the role that climate change does and will likely play in exacerbating conflict drivers and undermining Somalia's peacebuilding efforts.[11] Furthermore, in the country's NAP framework, the government laid out its vision for its adaptation planning process, underscoring the need to align its NAP process with its peacebuilding efforts and highlighting conflict sensitivity as a key guiding principle for all adaptation actions in the country.[12]

The way forward

Climate-resilient peacebuilding and conflict-sensitive climate programming need to coexist and mutually reinforce each other, while both need to be informed by a strong understanding of the conflict and climate contexts. Practitioners and policymakers operating in these fields must develop a deeper understanding of how climate change and other environmental factors can and do influence power and security dynamics in conflict-affected contexts to ensure that peacebuilding responses are comprehensive and built on sound analysis. Moreover, they will need a greater appreciation for expected future changes in climate and – with regard to adaptation measures and their design – what works best at the local, national and regional levels. This analysis can be further enhanced by detailed stakeholder mapping to identify entry points for action.[13]

Developing such an understanding – already a complex task – will be much more difficult in fragile contexts. Investments in the systems and infrastructure necessary to generate and store climate data, including weather stations and databases, are often limited in fragile states prior to the onset of violence, while existing equipment can be destroyed or fall into disrepair during conflict. The staff needed to maintain, interpret and use this information may have fled or been killed, while training and recruitment programmes understandably will have been halted. For example, the Taliban disbanded Afghanistan's meteorological authority, fired its staff, banned weather forecasting and burned the country's climate-data archives upon initially seizing power in 1996. In Rwanda, the number of reporting rain-gauge stations plummeted from 100 in 1990 to nearly zero following the 1994 genocide.[14] Adaptation programmes and projects are often delayed or cancelled with the onset of conflict, with international organisations and donors frequently withdrawing due to concerns around staff and partner safety. Climate financing also typically decreases or dries up altogether.[15]

Governments and their national and international partners, including in the private sector, must work together to rebuild this infrastructure and these capacities. Beyond allocating domestic and international funding to the rebuilding of weather stations and the training of staff, the governments of fragile states and their partners should access open-source databases and global climate information to fill some of these gaps. Promising efforts in this space are under way. For example, the Complex Risk Analytics Fund, established in 2021 by the UN and its partners, is a new multilateral financing instrument specifically designed to support increased and improved data generation and is used to 'anticipate, prevent, and respond to complex risks in fragile and crisis-affected settings'.[16] There is also increased use of satellite imagery to track land-use change, freshwater resources and livestock movements, among other potential climate–conflict factors, to augment on-the-ground information and serve as a tool for early warning.[17]

Governments must also try to strengthen the institutional arrangements in place for both peacebuilding and climate change. While their own internal capacities may continue to be constrained, they should try to adopt more comprehensive approaches to address risk and make more concerted efforts to avoid duplicating effort or promoting maladaptive practices. The burden of accomplishing this should not lie just with the government; it must be supported by increased coordination, resourcing and communication across stakeholders working on climate and peacebuilding, including civil society, international organisations, the donor community and the private sector.

Outstanding challenges

In contexts defined by conflict and fragility, divisions between those working in the humanitarian, development and peacebuilding space often persist and questions around mandates and remits can block collaboration across each of these pillars. For example, humanitarians may resist working on peacebuilding for fear of compromising their independence, neutrality and impartiality.[18] The UN and the donor community have explored improved coordination across these pillars and identified environmental factors – including climate change – as possible areas of convergence and collaboration, given their potential impacts on conflict, human migration and natural disasters.[19] The UN's Climate Security Mechanism (CSM) was established in 2018 to help the UN address climate-security challenges in a more systematic way, through collaboration between the Department of Political and Peacebuilding Affairs, UNDP and the UN Environment Programme.

Donor governments are also announcing additional relevant commitments and policies. The Canadian government has committed to creating a NATO Climate Change and Security Centre of Excellence, while the United States government, through its 2019 Global Fragility Act, has reaffirmed the links between state fragility, violent conflict and climate change and restated its commitment to conflict prevention and the promotion of peace.[20] The United Kingdom's government – which hosted a high-level open debate on climate and peacebuilding at the UN Security Council (UNSC) in February 2021 – has placed risk and resilience at the core of its country programmes.[21] Germany worked to elevate climate concerns in UN security policy during its two-year term on the UNSC (2019–20) and partnered with Niger to establish a new Informal Expert Group on Climate and Security to act as a forum for detailed discussions of these matters among UNSC members.[22] It also plans to use its 2022 G7 presidency to launch a Climate, Environment, Peace and Security Initiative. These efforts, among many others, point to an encouraging, and hopefully lasting, trend to widen the scope of peacebuilding, both as a concept and as a practice, to reflect the increasingly close ties between climate, peacebuilding and development.

A further challenge, mentioned earlier, is timescales. Within conflict-affected contexts, there is an urgent and understandable need to relieve immediate suffering and restore basic services. It can be very difficult for actors operating within these contexts to prioritise actions targeting future – and often uncertain – risks. However, this situation is changing; whereas previously the impacts of a changing climate were sometimes abstract and far off, they are now experienced around the world, while the modelling of future risks has become more detailed, complex and alarming. As such, it is no longer a choice of immediate versus future priorities. Rather, programmes and projects geared towards immediate

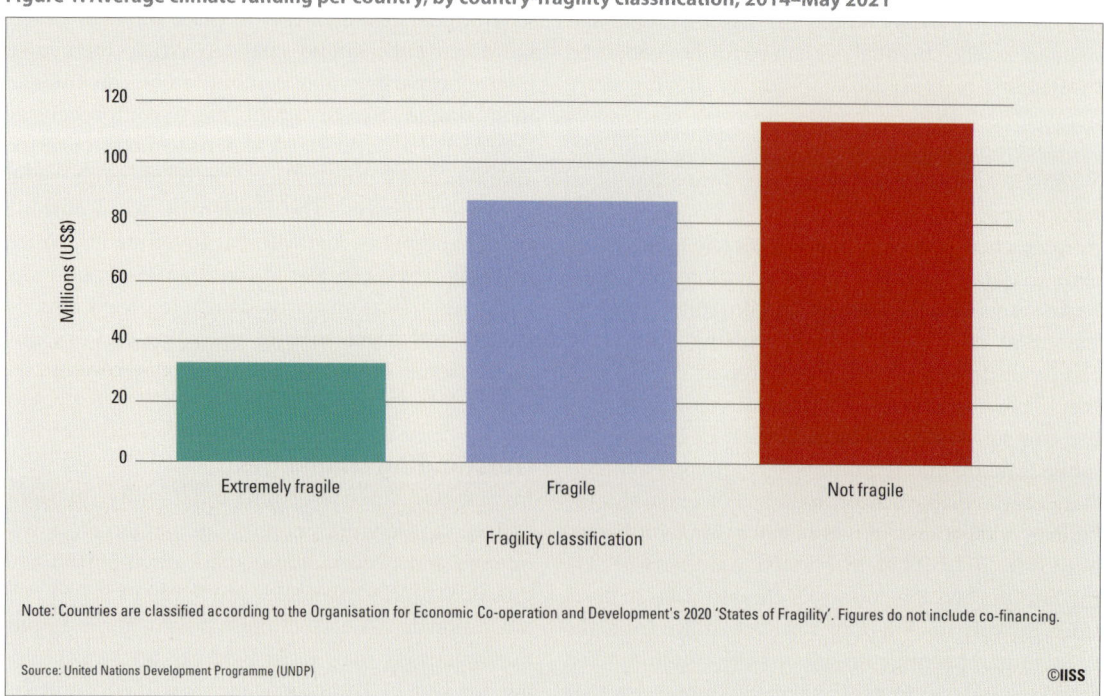

Figure 1: Average climate funding per country, by country-fragility classification, 2014–May 2021

Note: Countries are classified according to the Organisation for Economic Co-operation and Development's 2020 'States of Fragility'. Figures do not include co-financing.

Source: United Nations Development Programme (UNDP)

needs and actions must integrate longer-term climate considerations or risk becoming undermined and unsustainable. Flood risks must be integrated into the design and placement of refugee settlements, for example, while drought projections should be considered in decisions around agricultural-livelihood programmes. Organisations working in conflict-affected and fragile contexts must take a longer-term view to building peace.

Finally, while development assistance to fragile countries is increasing – according to the Organisation for Economic Co-operation and Development, more net bilateral assistance went to fragile contexts in 2018 than ever before (US$76 billion) – climate financing remains risk averse and more is needed.[23] In Somalia, for example, peacebuilding efforts following decades of conflict have been complicated by a prolonged, catastrophic drought that has pushed the country towards famine, decimated livelihoods, displaced millions and exacerbated fighting among clans over pasture and water. A US$1.46bn humanitarian appeal was launched by the UN for the country in December 2021, with 79% of the funding received by mid-August 2022.[24] However, more broadly, a review by the UNDP and the CSM found that climate financing is not getting to the most vulnerable; the amount delivered to countries considered 'extremely fragile' between 2014 and May 2021 averaged just US$2.1 per person, compared to US$10.8 in fragile states and US$161.7 in non-fragile states, including small island developing states.[25]

To make peacebuilding more climate resilient, donors must increasingly recognise the challenges and resource demands that climate change poses for stabilisation efforts in general. The needs of fragile states should be elevated in international policy discussions, in the same way that the unique challenges faced by small island developing states have drawn significant attention.[26] Changes in approach are required, including establishing more flexibility and longer timescales for peacebuilding financing to better reflect the changing context. Attempts should be made to quantify the co-benefits or dividends of adaptation and mitigation actions for peacebuilding, to help incentivise increased investment. Progress in this area may also require the establishment of new funding mechanisms, backed by donor countries, that specifically target projects and programmes that address both climate and conflict.[27] Aligning peacebuilding and climate action would help to get more desperately needed money – from sources such as the Green Climate Fund and Adaptation Fund – to fragile states.

Notes

[1] Resilience here is taken to mean 'the ability of a system, community or society exposed to hazards to resist, absorb, accommodate to and recover … in a timely and efficient manner, including through the preservation and restoration of its essential basic structures'. See United Nations Office for Disaster Risk Reduction, 'Resilience'.

[2] Erol Yayboke, Catherine Nzuki and Anastasia Strouboulis, 'Going Green while Building Peace: Technology, Climate, and Peacebuilding', Center for Strategic and International Studies, 3 March 2022.

[3] Ibid.

[4] Ahmadou Aly Mbaye and Landry Signé, 'Climate Change, Development and Conflict–Fragility Nexus in the Sahel', Brookings Institution, 2022, p. 16.

[5] Government of the Central African Republic, 'Plan National de Relèvement et de Consolidation de la Paix (2017–2021)' [National Recovery and Peacebuilding Plan], 2016.

[6] Alec Crawford and Clare Church, 'The NAP Process and Peacebuilding', International Institute for Sustainable Development, February 2020.

[7] Ibid.

[8] Global Environment Facility, 'Evaluation of GEF Support in Fragile and Conflict-affected Situations', 2020.

[9] Ibid.

[10] Ibid.

[11] Green Climate Fund, 'Readiness Proposal: With United Nations Development Programme (UNDP) for Somali Republic', 2019.

[12] Federal Government of Somalia, 'Somalia's National Adaptation Plan (NAP) Framework', Directorate of Environment and Climate Change, 2022.

[13] All peacebuilding and climate-change policy and programming in conflict-affected states must also be designed and implemented in a gender-responsive and socially inclusive way. Achieving this goal will require more than being sensitive to gender differences; policy and programming should actively address marginalisation and gender norms, roles and inequalities, including by identifying specific actions that will empower women and marginalised groups within projects, their households and communities, and policy and planning processes. See Angie Dazé and NAP Global Network, 'Gender in National Adaptation Plan (NAP) Processes', June 2019.

14 Tony Dokoupil, 'Send in the Weathermen', NBC News, 2015; and Alec Crawford et al., 'Accessing and Using Climate Data and Information in Fragile, Data-poor States', International Institute for Sustainable Development, 2015.
15 Alec Crawford et al., 'Promoting Climate-resilient Peacebuilding in Fragile States', International Institute for Sustainable Development, 2015; and Crawford and Church, 'The NAP Process and Peacebuilding'.
16 'What Is CRAF'd?', The Complex Risk Analytics Fund (CRAF'd).
17 Yayboke, Nzuki and Strouboulis, 'Going Green While Building Peace: Technology, Climate, and Peacebuilding'.
18 Elizabeth Ferris, 'The Humanitarian–Peace Nexus', Research briefing paper, UN Secretary-General's High-Level Panel on Internal Displacement, 2020.
19 See Paul Howe, 'The Triple Nexus: a Potential Approach to Supporting the Achievement of the Sustainable Development Goals?', *World Development*, vol. 124, December 2019.
20 Yayboke, Nzuki and Strouboulis, 'Going Green While Building Peace: Technology, Climate, and Peacebuilding'.
21 Sarah Dalrymple, 'Donors at the Triple Nexus: Lessons from the United Kingdom', Development Initiatives, 2019.
22 International Crisis Group, 'Can the UN Security Council Agree on a Climate Security Resolution?', 2021.
23 Organisation for Economic Co-operation and Development, 'States of Fragility 2020', 2020; and UN Development Programme (UNDP), 'Climate Finance for Sustaining Peace: Making Climate Finance Work for Conflict-affected and Fragile Regions', 2021.
24 UN Financial Tracking Services, 'Somalia 2022: Country Snapshot for 2022'.
25 UNDP, 'Climate Finance for Sustaining Peace: Making Climate Finance Work for Conflict-affected and Fragile Regions', p. 3.
26 *Ibid.*
27 *Ibid.*

Climate Change and the Instrumentalisation of Natural Resources in the Continuum of War: the Role of Non-state Armed Groups and International Responses

An important effect of accelerating climate change is its impact on the availability of key natural resources, including water, food, energy and land. While their increasing scarcity can exacerbate or drive conflict, it can also raise their intrinsic value as a tool for military and political leverage in the continuum of war, including in its aftermath, with major negative implications for environmental sustainability and human security.[1] Such a trend is very apparent in the context of internal confrontations, which comprise the majority of active conflicts globally and are often intractable amid a proliferation of actors and motivations. Non-state armed groups' (NSAGs') recourse to natural resources as an instrument of warfare and political power is a particularly alarming development with far-reaching implications for counter-insurgency efforts and conflict and post-conflict interventions, as well as for environmental preservation and efforts to address structural fragilities.[2]

In trying to address this issue, the existing shortcomings in international rules – in terms of applicability, compliance and enforcement where NSAGs are concerned – represent a major challenge.[3] Given this context, a strategic investigation of the dynamics of the phenomenon is needed to identify priorities for action and explore solutions, including possible preventative measures, adjustments to the legal framework and multilateral solutions. The fact that across the world between 60 million and 80m people live under the quasi-state governance of NSAGs adds to the urgency of the matter.[4]

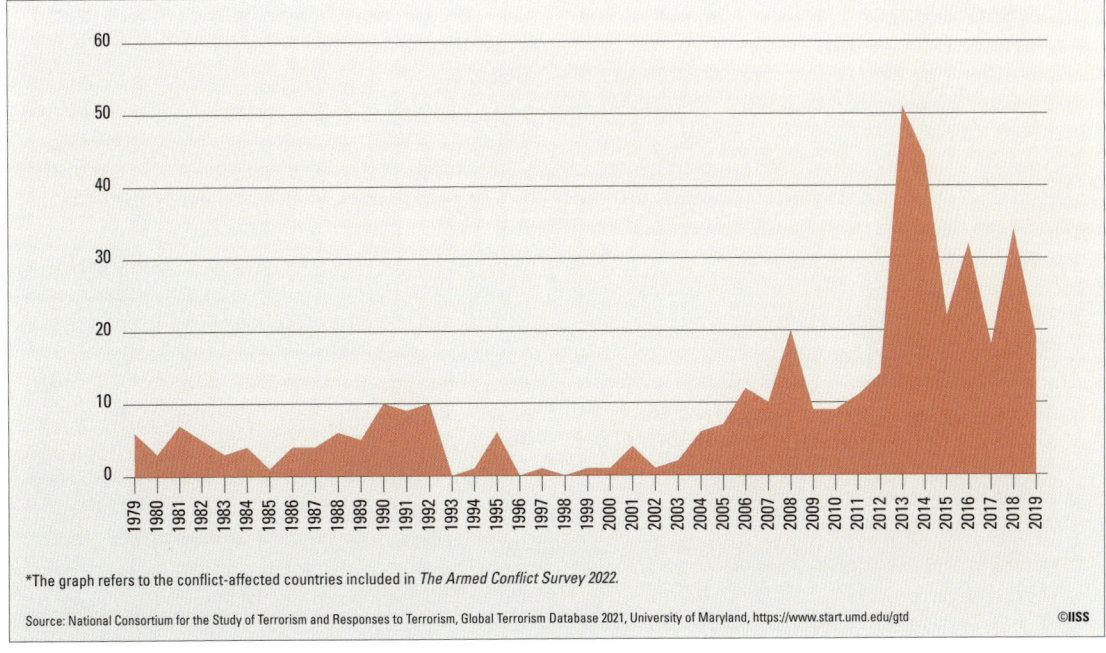

Figure 1: Number of armed assaults and infrastructure attacks on food or water supply and utilities by NSAGs in conflict-affected countries, 1979–2019*

*The graph refers to the conflict-affected countries included in *The Armed Conflict Survey 2022.*

Source: National Consortium for the Study of Terrorism and Responses to Terrorism, Global Terrorism Database 2021, University of Maryland, https://www.start.umd.edu/gtd ©IISS

Understanding instrumentalisation of natural resources: our framework

In recent decades, conflicts have become increasingly protracted and blurred in their active and stabilisation/reconstruction phases. Actors' strategies and motivations have adapted accordingly – as seen in their instrumental use of natural resources to prevail over the enemy but also to reinforce their political leverage and legitimacy in the post-conflict phase.

In light of these developments, our classification of the different ways that natural resources can be weaponised differs from prevalent literature on the topic: while the latter focuses mostly on the active phase of conflicts, we focus instead on a conflict's continuum. Our framework is therefore focused on the main motivation behind a resource's instrumentalisation and the conflict phase in which instrumentalisation takes place.

Military weaponisation

Military weaponisation occurs when natural resources are exploited as a target or weapon of warfare during an active conflict either to secure strategic goals or for tactical purposes. This typology includes situations where resource control is used to intimidate and coerce opposing parties (and/or civilian populations), including through psychological warfare (for example, by threatening to attack a key water infrastructure or to deprive an enemy of access to a given key natural resource).

Natural resources have notably become an integral part of NSAGs' military strategies and campaigns, providing them with the ability to inflict targeted damage without necessarily directly attacking, occupying or controlling areas (see Box 1). They also enable NSAGs to gain greater military capacity than they would otherwise have in conventional warfare.

Box 1: Military weaponisation of water

Control (or poisoning/destruction) of water resources and infrastructure (including dams and wells) has often been leveraged by NSAGs to exert pressure on the general population and opposing parties in warfare. For example, severe water scarcity (due to years of drought and water mismanagement) has not only intensified Iraq's and Syria's instability and ongoing violence in recent times but has also been systematically leveraged by different NSAGs to reach their goals, with catastrophic consequences for civilians.

The Islamic State (ISIS) was responsible for about half of the water-weaponisation incidents in the two countries from 2012–15.[5] The group's systematic use of water resources as a weapon was on a scale unprecedented in modern warfare.[6] It sought control over dams and used water as a strategic tool to weaken opponents and create hardship in water-stressed areas by diverting rivers and flooding lands. Some examples are discussed below:

- In 2013, the capture of Syria's largest dam, Tabqa, gave ISIS control of approximately 60% of the country's fresh and drinkable water resources and was a very effective defensive tool to slow the advance of the enemy (by threatening to destroy the dam, cut power to Damascus and flood 90,000 residents in the surrounding lands).
- In October 2014, ISIS diverted the Khalis tributary river of the Tigris River, flooding 781 acres of agricultural land and parts of Mansouriya in Iraq's Diyala province.[7]
- In 2014, the group seized control of Iraq's largest dam, Mosul, which prompted US airstrikes in support of a combined Kurdish–Iraqi offensive mobilised to retake it and prevent its use as an instrument of war by ISIS.[8]

On several occasions ISIS militants also used water resources to gain tactical advantages on the battlefield, including by diverting rivers in Iraq's Shirwain Basin area to thwart the advance of Iraqi security forces.

The damage (and disruption of access) to water services and facilities since the start of the war in Syria has resulted in a 40% reduction in the availability of drinking water, impacting access to safe water for 14.6m people while also causing mass migration and displacement.[9]

The conflicts in the Sahel and Somalia have also seen the military instrumentalisation of water by NSAGs. In the Lake Chad Basin, where some 40m people across Cameroon, Chad, Niger and Nigeria compete for dwindling water supplies,[10] Boko Haram has often used natural resources as a military tool in its strategy of violence. The poisoning of wells and rivers in offensive operations against the Nigerian Army has been the most egregious example.[11] Al-Shabaab has also used water as a strategy of coercion. The group's destruction of the water wells of Garbaharey, a strategically crucial city in southern Somalia, and its seizure of the river basins in the surrounding areas in 2014 deprived the local population living in government-controlled areas of access to water supplies and inflicted hardship on government forces without even occupying the town.[12]

Political weaponisation
Political weaponisation occurs when natural resources are instrumentalised for political leverage and/or to reinforce legitimacy with local populations (through incentivisation). This modality is not limited to the active conflict phase but can be observed along the continuum of war, including in the instability phases that could precede it and in its aftermath.

While military weaponisation is normally centred around 'negative' instrumentalisation of natural resources (in an offensive or defensive way), political weaponisation can include 'positive' elements, including the protection of specific natural resources or provision of land and water infrastructure to incentivise support or cooperation from a local population or other parties. In fragile states, where climate vulnerability often overlaps with and exacerbates root causes of conflict or instability, NSAGs' control of scarce natural resources has proven an effective tool to strengthen their territorial control and legitimacy with the general population – by filling voids left by overstretched and inefficient states (see Box 2).

Box 2: Natural resources for political leverage

There are many examples of the ways in which NSAGs have replaced the state by providing local populations with access to key natural resources under their control, thereby building legitimacy and strengthening their hold on territory.

In Somalia, al-Shabaab wielded water and food supplies not only as a critical part of its strategy against the Somali government but also as an instrument to gain legitimacy with the local population. Building on its widely publicised food-aid campaign during the 2017 famine, the group has since acquired a quasi-state role, imposing taxes on the use of water resources, agricultural products and livestock.

In the 'Middle Belt' states in north-central Nigeria, increasing water scarcity and environmental deterioration in recent years have driven displacement and prompted pastoralists from the Lake Chad Basin area and other West African Sahel countries to seek alternative pasture routes, fertile land and water supplies. This has not only led to disputes and violent conflicts with local farmers but also played a significant role in enabling Nigeria's jihadi insurgencies. Boko Haram and the Islamic State West Africa Province (ISWAP) have skilfully leveraged existing vulnerabilities to position themselves as alternative providers of safe pasture for herders, thereby strengthening their territorial control and influence over vast areas surrounding Lake Chad.[13]

In Afghanistan, which is among the countries most vulnerable to climate change globally, natural resources have been instrumentalised often by the Taliban in pursuit of political gains and to bolster its legitimacy. In particular, competition over the limited land for opium production, long a source of conflict, has offered the group an opportunity – by allowing opium cultivation in remote areas under its control – to secure farmers' political support and consolidate economic and political power in rural areas.

Similarly, in Syria and Iraq, control over access to water and lands allowed ISIS to gain and maintain political support for its efforts to establish a 'caliphate'. The group positioned itself as the legitimate provider of basic services to the population, including water, energy and food supply, while extracting economic value from the natural resources it controlled via taxes.

In Colombia, the left-wing Revolutionary Armed Forces of Colombia (FARC) guerrilla group took advantage of the state's absence from peripheral territories and widespread discontent around land distribution to exert territorial control and entrench itself in local communities, becoming the de facto government in much of the country's rural areas.

Figure 2: The nexus between climate change, natural resources and their weaponisation

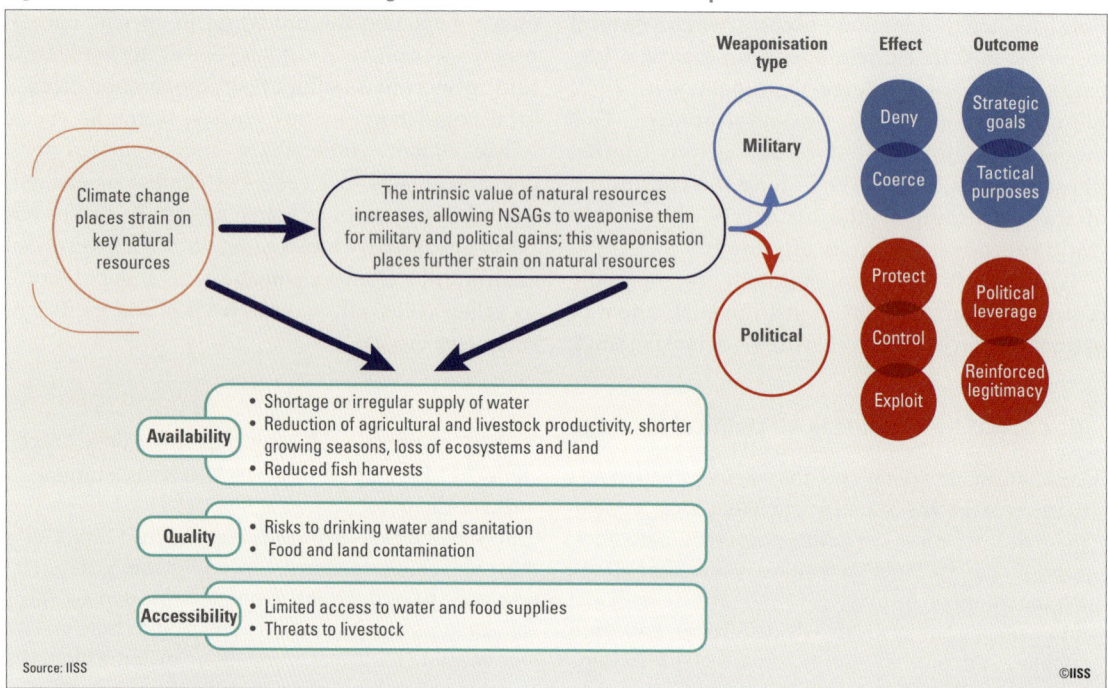

Source: IISS

The international regulatory framework and its shortcomings

The accelerated trend of instrumentalisation of natural resources highlighted above is even more concerning given the many challenges related to their protection in the context of internal armed conflicts. While international humanitarian law (IHL) – complemented by international human-rights law (IHRL) and international environmental law (IEL) principles – does provide a regulatory framework for preventing instrumentalisation, shortcomings abound with respect to the laws' scope, effective enforcement and applicability to the non-state actors that, crucially, represent the majority of perpetrators in the present conflict landscape.

In terms of the regulatory framework, general IHL rules protecting civilian objects in the conduct of hostility apply to natural resources, including the prohibition to target these indiscriminately, and the principles of proportionality (and precaution to avoid or minimise any environmental damage) whenever they can be considered legitimate military objectives.[14] Moreover, in the aftermath of the Vietnam War and its horrific environmental damages, new and specific IHL rules were established, including the Convention on the Prohibition of Military or Any Other Hostile Use of Environmental Modification Techniques (ENMOD); Article 8 of the Statute of the International Criminal Court (ICC); and Protocol I of the Geneva Conventions, relating to the prohibition of methods and means causing damage to the environment during warfare. The IHRL and IEL, which continue to apply during conflicts, add an extra layer of defence, the former through its protection of minorities and right to an effective remedy, the latter through most of its provisions.

Worryingly, the existence of this strong body of rules does not seem to be preventing conflict parties from weaponising natural resources. Besides implementation challenges relating to the scope and meaning of certain provisions (i.e., how to assess when a given natural resource is a legitimate military target and how to judge proportionality), mechanisms to enforce the regulatory framework have been lacking or proven ineffective: the ICC's 2009 indictment of then Sudanese president Omar al-Bashir for crimes against humanity (including the poisoning of wells and water pumps by the army under his control) has been the only attempt (so far unsuccessful) to sanction military instrumentalisation of natural resources to date.

The situation is further complicated by the fact that NSAGs are not technically bound to international law in the same way as state actors and international organisations, creating an additional limitation relating to compliance with and enforcement of the international framework protecting natural resources in conflict.[15] However, there have been encouraging developments in the international legal architecture with respect to engaging with and regulating non-state actors, acknowledging their increasingly significant role in modern conflicts. Such efforts have included the 2019 UN International Law Commission's Draft Principles on the Protection of the Environment in relation to Armed Conflicts (PERAC), which aimed to ensure better protection of the environment during and after armed conflicts and in situations of occupation. PERAC should be adopted by the UN General Assembly in 2022, once UN stakeholders have submitted their comments. Another encouraging development came in 2020 when the International Committee of the Red Cross (ICRC) updated its Guidelines on the Protection of the Natural Environment in Armed Conflict, which largely cover obligations for NSAGs.[16] On a related note, the non-profit organisation Conflict and Environment Observatory (CEOBS) was created in 2018 to increase awareness and understanding of the environmental and derived humanitarian consequences of conflicts and military activities. The organisation is also exploring ways and tools to monitor the implementation of the PERAC principles once they are approved.

Despite the above, ensuring compliance by NSAGs remains a major concern and a continued priority for the international community given how instrumentalisation of scarce resources, including water and land, has become an integral part of NSAGs' warfare and strategies to assert and retain power in the continuum of war. Efforts must be made to further engage with these actors, promote their accountability and raise their awareness of the significant costs associated with reckless use of the environment in war. Finding a common denominator between their doctrines (including agreements with opponents, unilateral declarations and internal rules and regulations) and international legal principles – and building accountability based on commonality – appears the best possible strategy in current circumstances. Analyses of available NSAG doctrines show that even if very few address environmental questions, most include specific commitments to abide by the ICRC's Geneva Conventions and/or IHL – in the case of the latter, presumably by its principles on environmental protection.[17] Wherever environmental protection is addressed in these doctrines, at times it is arguably more absolute than that provided for by IHL, sometimes justifying attacks in the name of environmental preservation – which incidentally could be problematic with regard to IHL.

Irrespective of an explicit commitment to abide by IHL rules on environmental protection in conflict, many questions remain regarding the actual ability and willingness of NSAGs to ensure compliance in practice. The issue is not only that sometimes doctrines can be driven primarily by propaganda motivations or international pressures, but also that if they are not translated into internal rules, and disseminated and used to inform training for the given NSAG's rank and file, they may have little impact in practice. Having acknowledged these limitations, NSAG doctrines are a starting point for building consensus on common rules with actors that must be part of the solution.

Possible solutions

The search for better solutions to protect scarce natural resources from malicious instrumentalisation in the continuum of war – with a focus on prevention and NSAGs – is rendered all the more urgent by accelerating climate change.

The international momentum to address climate change has led to greater attention being paid to the environmental repercussions of armed conflict (and related activities) within the UN system. This focus is evident in ongoing debates on climate, water security, conflict and environmental damage (despite the UN Security Council's vetoes on related resolutions)[18] and in the International Law Commission's draft principles on PERAC. Such developments provide hope that consistent progress towards a more effective international framework is possible in the short to medium term.

The role played by the non-governmental organisation Geneva Call, which has engaged NSAGs to improve their protection of civilians during armed conflicts according to international humanitarian norms, notably by countersigning and monitoring compliance with deeds of commitments, appears a promising strategy to ensure that such actors are better aligned and compliant with (and enforce) IHL environmental regulations. Geneva Call is already focusing on aspects of environmental protection in conflict: in 2021, it adopted a deed on conflict-related food insecurity. A similar instrument, by which NSAGs commit not to weaponise natural resources, could help to raise visibility of the issue while also holding signatories accountable for commitments undertaken. Moreover, such a measure would build pressure on NSAGs to better socialise and disseminate commitments among their members, which it is hoped would result in increasing compliance.

The ICRC has developed contacts with approximately three-quarters of the over 600 armed groups identified worldwide, a number that includes the approximately 100 NSAGs that can be 'legally classified as parties to non-international armed conflicts', and has been trying to facilitate the implementation of the Guidelines on the Protection of the Natural Environment in Armed Conflict.[19] The ICRC has proposed concrete actions to this effect, arguing that areas of particular environmental importance or fragility should be identified and designated demilitarised zones.[20]

NSAGs' external sponsors are another important lever that should be utilised to increase their engagement and compliance. A large majority of internal conflicts are internationalised and see the intervention or involvement (often through local NSAGs as proxies) of third-party states. Efforts to promote third parties' commitment to the protection of natural resources in conflict could translate to additional pressure on NSAGs to comply with the international legal framework and to ensure their doctrines and practice implement it.

Finally, the requirement for metrics and data that can enable effective monitoring of natural-resource scarcity – and how conflicts aggravate it – cannot be overstated given the need to prioritise efforts and adopt evidence-based policies and strategies. A particularly important aspect will be the design of early-warning methods and frameworks to identify areas and states most at risk of resources weaponisation (based on conflict intensity, climate vulnerability, presence of natural resources and key infrastructure, governance, and economic and political factors, among others), reduce risks and strengthen resilience. A data-driven assessment of where conflicts involving resources are most likely to take place in the short to medium term would help focus decision-makers' attention and better facilitate targeted action (including via prioritisation for adaptation financing).

Notes

[1] This is all the more concerning in the current context of growing global food insecurity amid the impact of the coronavirus pandemic – and Russia's war on Ukraine – on socio-economic conditions and the functioning of supply chains. The war in Ukraine not only exacerbated pre-existing inflationary pressures (through its impact on food and energy prices) but also restricted the global supply of agricultural products – including wheat, barley, corn and sunflower oil (through Russia's blockade of Ukrainian ports) – for import-dependent countries, several of which are among the least developed countries globally. For instance, Eritrea's wheat imports in 2021 were derived entirely from Russia (53%) and Ukraine (47%). See Food and Agriculture Organization of the United Nations, 'Impact of the Ukraine–Russia Conflict on Global Food Security and Related Matters under the Mandate of the Food and Agriculture Organization of the United Nations (FAO)', 8 April 2022.

[2] On such groups' use of natural resources as instruments of warfare and political power, see, for example, Marcus D. King and Julia Burnell, 'The Weaponization of Water in a Changing Climate', in Caitlin E. Werrell and Francesco Femia (eds), *Epicenters of Climate and Security: The New Geostrategic Landscape of the Anthropocene* (Washington DC: Center for Climate and Security, 2017), pp. 67–73.

[3] See, for example, Thibaud de La Bourdonnaye, 'Greener Insurgencies? Engaging Non-state Armed Groups for the Protection of the Natural Environment During Non-international Armed Conflicts', *International Review of the Red Cross*, no. 914, December 2021.

[4] International Committee of the Red Cross (ICRC), 'ICRC Engagement with Non-state Armed Groups: Why, How, for What Purpose, and Other Salient Issues', ICRC Position Paper, 4 March 2021, p. 2.

[5] Marcus D. King, 'The Weaponization of Water in Syria and Iraq', *Washington Quarterly*, vol. 38, no. 4, 2015, p. 159.

[6] See Marwa Daoudy, 'Water Weaponization in the Syrian Conflict: Strategies of Domination and Cooperation', *International Affairs*, vol. 96, no. 5, September 2020.

[7] King, 'The Weaponization of Water in Syria and Iraq'.

[8] Alex Milner, 'Mosul Dam: Why the Battle for Water Matters in Iraq', BBC News, 18 August 2014.

[9] ICRC, 'Syria Water Crisis: Up to 40% Less Drinking Water After 10 Years of War', 1 October 2021; and UN International Children's Emergency Fund, 'Water Sanitation and Hygiene'.

[10] UN Educational, Scientific and Cultural Organization, 'Lake Chad: Monitoring Water Quality Through Satellite Earth Observation', 21 April 2022.

11 'Boko Haram Poisoning Water Sources: Nigerian Army', AA News, 1 October 2015.
12 'Al-Shabaab's "Water Terrorism" Is Yielding Results and Tragedy in Somalia's Civil War', *World*, 12 August 2014.
13 Paul Carsten and Ahmed Kingimi, 'Islamic State Ally Stakes Out Territory around Lake Chad', Reuters, 30 April 2018.
14 These principles have been further clarified by the ICRC's updated 2020 Guidelines on the Protection of the Natural Environment in Armed Conflict. See ICRC, 'Guidelines on the Protection of the Natural Environment in Armed Conflict', 25 September 2020.
15 While as a general rule international law applies only to states and international organisations, it is now broadly accepted that IHL (and IHRL and IEL to different extents) also applies to NSAGs with sufficient organisational structure and control of territory, as well as those involved in armed conflicts of sufficient intensity.
16 See endnote 18 for more details.
17 See Jonathan Somer, 'Environmental Protection and Non-state Armed Groups: Setting a Place at the Table for the Elephant in the Room', Conflict and Environment Observatory, 4 December 2015; and de La Bourdonnaye, 'Greener Insurgencies? Engaging Non-state Armed Groups for the Protection of the Natural Environment During Non-International Armed Conflicts'.
18 In December 2021, the Security Council failed to adopt draft resolution S/2021/990 on the adverse effects of climate change on security due to the veto of Russia (and non-permanent member India). China abstained. The draft resolution aimed to integrate climate-related security risk into conflict-prevention strategies – in particular in affected countries and regions. The proposal was drafted along the lines of a German-drafted resolution that was not voted for in 2020 due to resistance from China, Russia and the United States. See UN, 'Security Council Fails to Adopt Resolution Integrating Climate-related Security Risk into Conflict-prevention Strategies', SC/14732, 13 December 2021.
19 Jelena Pejic, Irénée Herbet and Tilman Rodenhäuser, 'ICRC Engagement with Non-state Armed Groups: Why and How', ICRC blog, 4 March 2021; and ICRC, 'ICRC Engagement with Non-state Armed Groups', 4 March 2021.
20 Vanessa Murphy and Helen Obregón Gieseken, 'Fighting without a Planet B: How IHL Protects the Natural Environment in Armed Conflict', ICRC blog, 25 May 2021.

Transition in Turbulence: Geostrategic Implications of Climate Change and the Energy Transition

Dubbing the climate crisis a 'code red for humanity', United Nations Secretary-General António Guterres cautioned in March 2022 that 'continued reliance on fossil fuels puts the global economy and energy security at the mercy of geopolitical shocks', as evidenced by Russia's war in Ukraine.[1] In 2021, the World Bank projected that more than 216 million people will be displaced or forced to migrate as a result of climate-related risks by 2050.[2] More than ever before, states must find ways and means to collaborate on addressing climate change.

The Glasgow Climate Pact reached at the 2021 UN Climate Change Conference (COP26) showed an unprecedented political will to address the global climate emergency. However, experts agree that the gap between aspiration and action remains too large. According to the 2022 Intergovernmental Panel on Climate Change report, the national determined contributions (NDCs) agreed at the 2015 climate summit in Paris have proven difficult to enforce, will result in average global-warming levels exceeding 1.5°C by the end of the twenty-first century and do little to prevent increases in weather extremes globally.[3] Limiting warming remains possible but will require an acceleration of mitigation efforts as well as stronger adaptation and financial measures to cope with current and emerging extreme-weather trends.[4]

The willingness and ability to respond to and collaborate on climate change will differ between states depending on their emission levels, strategic priorities, resource dependencies, technological progress and ability to absorb the resulting social, political and economic shocks. Strong and sustained reductions in emissions of carbon dioxide (CO_2) and other greenhouse gases could quickly improve air quality, stabilising global temperatures in 20–30 years.[5] Ambitious climate action can yield significant results, but it will need to be accompanied by a global energy transition and take into account new geopolitical realities.

Inter-state tensions, geopolitical stressors and climate-mitigation responses

The debate on climate-change mitigation currently focuses (and will continue to do so) on who bears more responsibility to act and pay, and how quickly. According to the United States' 2021 National Intelligence Estimate on Climate Change, the top ten emitters of greenhouse gases in 2018 were responsible for 70% of global emissions (with China, the US, the European Union, India and Russia making up the top five).[6] These top emitters underscore that population and economy size are major national-emissions drivers. By virtue of their size, these countries and regions also play a role in shaping geopolitical trends and developments. Current tensions between top emitters therefore pose a significant challenge to developing a coherent response to global warming.

The top five emitters of greenhouse gases provide a useful lens to assess the potential for effective international action on climate change. China and the US are the two largest economies and highest emitters in the world, accounting for almost 40% of global emissions.[7] Both invest heavily in green-energy technologies and will likely set important standards for the rest of the world. Despite these common interests, serious collaboration between China and the US on climate change is unlikely to materialise in the near term. Bilateral tensions on geopolitics, human rights, trade and security have risen to an all-time high, leaving potential joint efforts wrought with uncertainty.

Current geopolitical developments are creating new energy partnerships and related dependencies. Russia's large oil and gas reserves provide it with important levers for geostrategic power. Weeks before its invasion of Ukraine, Russia concluded a series of agreements with China, including a 30-year deal to supply the latter with ten billion cubic metres of gas per year via a new pipeline.[8] Russian–Chinese strategic collaboration is further reinforced by plans to develop a Polar Silk Road in the Russian Arctic and further exploit untapped oil and natural-gas reserves in the region with the support of Chinese investment.

Table 1: Top ten global greenhouse-gas emitters

		Share of global greenhouse-gas emissions (2018)	GDP (2022, US$)	Population (2020)	Climate mitigation targets (2021)	Renewable-energy investments (2021, US$)
	China	26.1%	19.9trn	1.4bn	At least 65% below 2005 levels by 2030	266bn
	US	12.7%	25.3trn	329m	50–52% below 2005 levels by 2030	114bn
	EU	7.5%	17.2trn	488m	55% below 1990 levels by 2030	219bn
	India	7.1%	3.5trn	1.4bn	33–35% below 2005 levels by 2030	14bn
	Russia	5.4%	1.8trn	144m	80% below 1990 levels by 2050	N/A
	Japan	2.5%	4.9trn	125m	46% below 2013 levels by 2030	26bn
	Brazil	2.2%	1.8trn	212m	43% below 2005 levels by 2030	12bn
	Indonesia	2.0%	1.3trn	273m	41% (conditionally) below business-as-usual scenario by 2030	1.5bn
	Iran	1.7%	1.7trn	83m	4% below business-as-usual scenario by 2030	N/A
	Canada	1.5%	2.2trn	38m	40–45% below 2012 levels by 2025	964m

Sources: The Hague Centre for Strategic Studies; IMF World Economic Outlook database, April 2022

In addition to its strategic relationship with Beijing, Moscow is also looking to develop new economic partnerships in the Global South. Following US and EU announcements that they will discontinue their energy collaborations with Russia, the latter signed long-term oil- and gas-delivery agreements with India at record-low prices.

Misaligned incentives for the energy transition

The actions required to remain within critical global-warming thresholds necessitate a transition from the old fossil-fuel-based energy system to a new low-carbon one. Whilst even the most advanced economies will struggle to transition to greener energy sources, it will be very difficult for countries like China and India to satisfy their energy demands with low-carbon alternatives.[9] The International Energy Agency projects that even in a net-zero future, the world will still use 50% of the gas and 25% of the oil used in 2021.[10] The carbon transition will therefore likely be a phased reduction rather than a sudden elimination.[11] Some fossil fuels are more polluting than others and different schedules will need to be considered for their elimination. In order to meet global-warming thresholds, coal use must be eliminated, oil use must decline immediately and natural-gas consumption must diminish by 2030.[12]

Sudden geopolitical shocks can be important catalysts for change. The Russia–Ukraine war and partial boycotts of Russian fossil fuels have led to a surge in international oil and gas prices, and will lead to fundamental shifts towards cleaner energy consumption, especially in Europe and the US, in the longer term. This will force oil and gas producers to find alternative markets at lower prices. In the next decade, the Western transition to a low-carbon economy may paradoxically result in increased consumption of fossil fuels in developing countries as they become cheaper alternatives to renewable energy sources, for which the required research and development (R&D) investment will come with high technological and infrastructure costs. In the short term, oil and gas consumers in the Global South could benefit from the lower market prices resulting from reduced demand in the EU and US, which will strengthen their energy security and aid job creation and economic growth.[13] In the medium term, as renewables become more competitive in the world market, new trade patterns will emerge, presenting new sources of geopolitical clout for those well positioned in green-energy markets.

Depending on their ability to adapt to these dynamics, state actors will likely split into three camps: those that embrace the global green-energy transition; those that continue oil and gas production and consumption; and those that explore both options until it becomes more opportune to forgo one for the other. China will be one to watch: as the world's largest carbon emitter and biggest investor in energy renewables, it currently sets the global pace for phasing down fossil-fuel production and increasing renewable-energy use. China's innovation potential would benefit from more strategic partnerships with other green-technology leaders. However, many of its recent energy agreements are with oil- and gas-producing countries like Russia and Iran. Closer collaborations on green-energy technologies between the US, the EU and other industrialised nations could undermine China's dominant position in the future.

A decisive shift in the Global South to clean energy would challenge the development model and economic sustainability of oil- and gas-exporting countries. As the physical impacts of climate change are projected to hit poor countries the hardest, there will be a strong incentive for them to transition to renewables. However, given their equally pressing development challenges, the pull of cheaper fossil-fuel resources may still be irresistible without the financial and technological support of the energy-transition leaders. Moreover, the pressing need to decarbonise the global economy could lead to the use of penalties to push countries to net zero, which would result in further tensions between states.

Geostrategic competition over renewable resources

The urgency to decarbonise will likely result in increased competition to dominate the resources and technologies needed for the green-energy transition. These include critical minerals such as copper and zinc (essential for wind and solar infrastructure), lithium and nickel (essential for electric vehicles) and cobalt. Copper, lithium and nickel, in particular, are projected to account for over 80% of the market value of critical minerals in 2050.[14]

If current conditions continue, the undisputed leader in the global renewable economy will be China. The country currently dominates the global production of critical minerals, plays a key role in their value-chain process and is a key market for them.[15] Today, 72% and 61% of the world's cobalt and lithium respectively are processed in China.[16] Moreover, China has been the largest global investor in renewable energy in the last decade, capturing 35% of the market in 2021 alone with US$266bn, more than double the US investment in the same year.[17] As the energy transition to net zero will require a formidable increase in wind- and solar-power generation, China will have insurmountable leverage over countries aiming to meet their NDCs.

China has already used its dominance in the supply chain for critical minerals to exert geopolitical power, though with limited success. In 2010, it stopped exporting rare-earth elements to Japan during a dispute over the Senkaku/Diaoyu islands. Japan responded by expanding research and development to improve domestic production of rare-earth elements (REE), causing China's global market share to drop from over 95% in 2010 to around 70% in 2018.[18] In May 2019, amid the US–China trade war, China threatened to cut off all exports of REE to the US. The Biden administration pushed back in early 2021 by expanding its domestic REE supply chains, aiming to break the US dependency on critical minerals from China and boost sustainable practices.[19]

Despite these setbacks, China is likely to continue to leverage its dominant position on the global renewable market for geopolitical gains, especially in Asia. Historical trends suggest that the conflictive US–China trade relationship may spill over into the issue of climate change in general, and the energy transition in particular. Therefore, security of supply – of critical materials and other resources needed for the global energy transition – should remain a priority for the US, EU and other leaders in green technology moving forward.

At the same time, other countries will have increased potential to strengthen their geostrategic position in the global renewables market. The top producers of copper are currently Chile, Peru and China, while the top producers of lithium are Australia, Chile and China.[20] The US and Germany are currently the second- and third-largest investors in clean energy and R&D and may join forces to reduce China's dominance in the future.[21] Meanwhile, Norway is the global leader in carbon-capture and -storage technologies.[22] China will therefore have to contend with

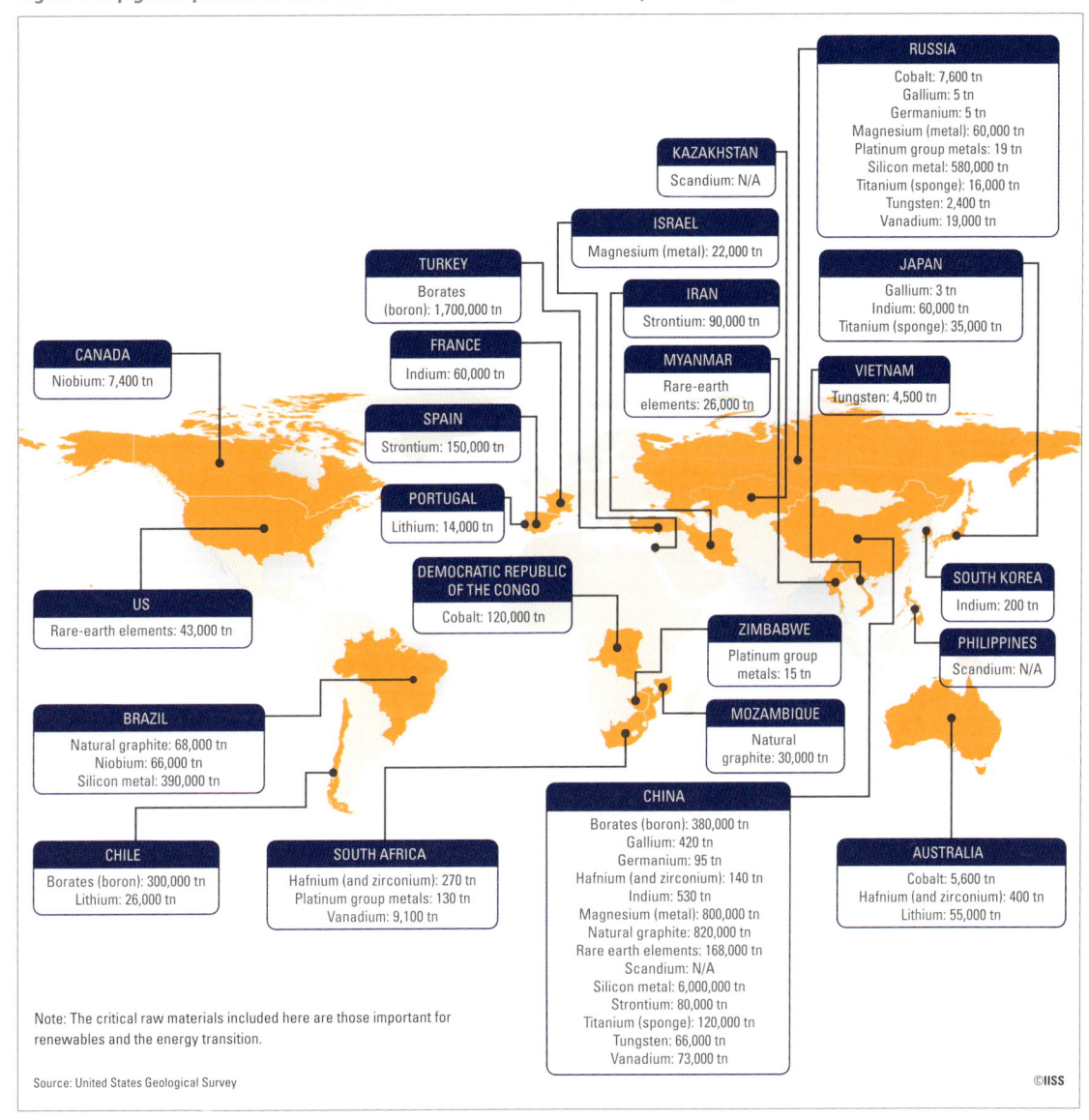

Figure 1: Top global producers of selected critical raw materials (tonnes produced), 2022

RUSSIA
Cobalt: 7,600 tn
Gallium: 5 tn
Germanium: 5 tn
Magnesium (metal): 60,000 tn
Platinum group metals: 19 tn
Silicon metal: 580,000 tn
Titanium (sponge): 16,000 tn
Tungsten: 2,400 tn
Vanadium: 19,000 tn

KAZAKHSTAN
Scandium: N/A

ISRAEL
Magnesium (metal): 22,000 tn

JAPAN
Gallium: 3 tn
Indium: 60,000 tn
Titanium (sponge): 35,000 tn

TURKEY
Borates (boron): 1,700,000 tn

IRAN
Strontium: 90,000 tn

FRANCE
Indium: 60,000 tn

MYANMAR
Rare-earth elements: 26,000 tn

VIETNAM
Tungsten: 4,500 tn

CANADA
Niobium: 7,400 tn

SPAIN
Strontium: 150,000 tn

PORTUGAL
Lithium: 14,000 tn

SOUTH KOREA
Indium: 200 tn

US
Rare-earth elements: 43,000 tn

DEMOCRATIC REPUBLIC OF THE CONGO
Cobalt: 120,000 tn

ZIMBABWE
Platinum group metals: 15 tn

PHILIPPINES
Scandium: N/A

BRAZIL
Natural graphite: 68,000 tn
Niobium: 66,000 tn
Silicon metal: 390,000 tn

MOZAMBIQUE
Natural graphite: 30,000 tn

CHINA
Borates (boron): 380,000 tn
Gallium: 420 tn
Germanium: 95 tn
Hafnium (and zirconium): 140 tn
Indium: 530 tn
Magnesium (metal): 800,000 tn
Natural graphite: 820,000 tn
Rare earth elements: 168,000 tn
Scandium: N/A
Silicon metal: 6,000,000 tn
Strontium: 80,000 tn
Titanium (sponge): 120,000 tn
Tungsten: 66,000 tn
Vanadium: 73,000 tn

CHILE
Borates (boron): 300,000 tn
Lithium: 26,000 tn

SOUTH AFRICA
Hafnium (and zirconium): 270 tn
Platinum group metals: 130 tn
Vanadium: 9,100 tn

AUSTRALIA
Cobalt: 5,600 tn
Hafnium (and zirconium): 400 tn
Lithium: 55,000 tn

Note: The critical raw materials included here are those important for renewables and the energy transition.

Source: United States Geological Survey ©IISS

increased competition in the markets driving the green-energy transition.

Emerging geopolitical flashpoints in climate-vulnerable regions: from Tibet to the Arctic

The intensifying physical effects of climate change will act as a multiplier of geopolitical risks, accelerated by the increasing competition for control of the scarce natural resources essential for human survival. These risks are especially acute in climate-vulnerable regions where the extremes of climate change are already leading to inter-state tensions over water and food. The resources needed to power the renewable-energy economy are also increasingly contributing to inter-state and regional tensions that may alter the geopolitical landscape in the future.

The exploitation of water for hydropower in Tibet is a case in point. China has complete control over ten major river systems flowing out of the Tibetan Plateau. Tibet is still a virgin territory: less than 0.6% of its water resources are used for development purposes.[23] However, this situation is changing rapidly due to China's ambitious plans for hydropower investment, which include the world's largest hydropower project in the Yarlung Tsangpo Grand Canyon, not far from the Indian border.[24] To service this project, China has been constructing dams on the Brahmaputra – a major river flowing out of the Tibetan Plateau. The resulting diversion of water has the potential to irreversibly damage India's agricultural land in Arunachal Pradesh and represents a serious risk to Bangladesh, either through floods or reduced water flow. Water therefore has the potential to be used as a strategic weapon in the region, with Chinese control of waterways translating into geo-political leverage.

Regional tensions over water are not new. India has been building its own dams on the Siang, a tributary river of the Brahmaputra, since 2009, relocating and scaling down these plans due to concerns of flooding upstream in China. Under conditions of peace, water disagreements may be managed collaboratively. However, as the populations of China and India increase and the former continues to industrialise its southwestern provinces, bilateral tensions are set to grow over regional territorial claims, resource sovereignty and natural resources. Although tensions over water may escalate into unrestrained competition, and even risk developing into a fully fledged conflict, hydropower expansion is set to continue.[25] China's hydropower plans also affect Bhutan, Cambodia, Laos, Nepal, Pakistan, Thailand and Vietnam, meaning water disputes between China and India could spill over into the broader region.

The Arctic is another emerging geopolitical flashpoint, in terms of both its vulnerability to the physical effects of climate change and the opportunities it presents for further oil, natural-gas and mineral extraction. The Arctic is warming at two to three times the average global rate, while its melting ice caps are a key driver of rising sea levels globally. The region presents what scholars call 'a strategic ambiguity', insofar as the Arctic has a history of concomitant peaceful multilateral cooperation and geostrategic competition.[26] A few developments have rapidly changed the geopolitical environment in the Arctic in the last decade. The first concerns Russia's increasing assertiveness in the region, which started with its territorial claims of the entire Northern Sea Route in 2007. The second relates to the widespread build-up of Russian and NATO forces, military bases and hardware, which reached a new high following Russia's invasion of Ukraine in February 2022.[27] A third is the increased involvement of non-Arctic states in the region.[28]

These developments point to the direct link between geopolitics and climate change. Melting ice caps open new maritime trade routes that could considerably shorten travel distances between Asia and Europe.[29] They also open the seas for military activities and exercises, enhancing the possibility of violent confrontations. Moreover, the Arctic harbours up to 13% of the world's undiscovered oil and 30% of its natural gas respectively, which could be of special interest to Asian markets.[30] China achieved non-observer status in the Arctic Council, an intergovernmental forum promoting cooperation, coordination and interaction in the region, in 2013. Increased tensions between Russia and the West following the former's 2014 annexation of Crimea presented an opportunity for China to expand its activities in the Arctic via the development of a so-called Polar Silk Road, a regional extension of its Belt and Road Initiative. Ultimately, the Polar Silk Road seeks to connect three large economic zones – East Asia, North America and Western Europe – through the Russian part of the Arctic. Other non-Arctic states are supporting these efforts with their own investments, potentially pushing an already climate-fragile region to its breaking point and undermining efforts to reduce global warming.

While it is unlikely that states would engage in direct conflict in the Arctic in the near term, there are increasing concerns that the re-emergence of great-power competition and related tensions in Europe between Russia and NATO members and allies, as well as on the global level between China and the US, could spill over into the region. Specifically, the Russia–Ukraine war is worsening Arctic relations and highlighting critical fault lines between Russia and NATO members and allies. Finland and Sweden have successfully applied to join NATO, potentially leaving Russia as the only non-member in the Arctic Council. As developments in the region affect Russia's vital security interests, it may seek to transform its geostrategic relationship with China in the region into a military partnership – a development that would make regional cooperation on the Arctic's climate challenges even more difficult.

Towards a realist approach to climate-change mitigation

Responding to climate change requires a long-term commitment and mindset that overrides short- and medium-term state interests. In order to manage state responses to climate change in a more strategic manner, action will need to be taken at different levels. Firstly, international diplomacy should be further geared towards a better understanding of national and regional needs and ambitions, and 'coalitions of the willing' should be built accordingly. While these coalitions may function as traditional alliance systems and will likely take shape according to complementary interests, more can be done to develop an objective case for global climate action. Multilateral high-level agreements can be supplemented by regional partnerships, based on shared vulnerabilities or complementary strengths, to align incentives, develop joint operational plans and mobilise action.

Secondly, comprehensive strategies need to be developed to support climate-mitigation and -adaptation efforts and reduce fossil-fuel dependencies, especially in the Global South. While climate change is a worldwide phenomenon, specific climate conditions vary by region. Adaptation plans will need to be supplemented by resilience-building measures and financing mechanisms to limit the direct impacts of extreme weather on water, food and energy systems. Designing tailor-made early-warning tools that capture the causal pathways between climate change, development and security would support the design of smarter policy interventions.[31] Fragile countries require greater attention so that climate risks do not develop into national-security risks (which may, in turn, become regional security risks). Much more needs to be done to develop and implement energy-transition plans. Care must be taken not to undermine trust and cooperation by enforcing penalties to push countries to net zero. Efforts should focus on mapping the impacts of fossil-fuel use and defining the required capabilities to replace current energy sources with greener alternatives. On a regional level, smaller states can support one other in defining joint mitigation goals. Regional trade and investment schemes can aid the development and deployment of green technologies, providing a collective answer to mitigation and reducing state-level vulnerabilities in securing energy supply.

Thirdly, stronger incentives are required to limit inter-state competition over natural resources. Currently, NDCs are the global instruments for developing climate action plans. They are developed at state level without consideration of regional-level dynamics, policy coherence and desired outcomes. They lack enforcement power and do not adequately consider broader sustainability and development goals, good practice and resource pooling. If NDCs are to remain the standard for developing national climate action plans, they need to be more transparent, operational and comparable. To monitor and measure progress, they should be subject to certified adaptation-based approaches. The Organisation for Economic Co-operation and Development has developed guiding principles on managing sustainable-development results that could serve as a model for NDCs.[32]

As climate-related risks impact all states' vital security and economic interests, the stakes to collaborate have never been higher. However, geopolitical tensions can hinder progress. A realist framework is therefore needed to manage climate change and the energy transition. While climate change remains a global challenge, actions to reduce or mitigate global warming will lie foremost with states and their societies. Addressing climate change is a formidable task that requires depoliticising the climate challenge, reducing energy dependencies and driving sustained, coherent and timely action. In a world where great-power interests continue to dominate international relations, there are no guarantees that states will follow a collaborative approach unless they are provided with strong incentives.

Despite these uncertainties, current geopolitical developments may ultimately support climate-change mitigation. Russia's invasion of Ukraine and China's increasing assertiveness in international renewable markets have pushed the US, EU and others to reduce oil and natural-gas dependencies, accelerate green-energy technologies and rethink supply security. To manage global warming, it will be critical to monitor the top greenhouse-gas emitters and see how and with whom they align themselves. In the next decade, all roads lead to China. Whilst in the short term its interests will be served by fossil-fuel extraction, as the lead investor, producer and supplier of renewables, China has everything to gain from a faster transition to clean energy. The question then becomes not if the global energy transition will materialise, but who will control the standards that set the rules of the game.

Notes

1. United Nations, 'Secretary-General Calls Latest IPCC Climate Report "Code Red for Humanity", Stressing "Irrefutable" Evidence of Human Influence', Press release, 9 August 2021.
2. World Bank, 'Millions on the Move in Their Own Countries: The Human Face of Climate Change', 13 September 2021.
3. Intergovernmental Panel on Climate Change, 'Climate Change 2022: Impacts, Adaptation, and Vulnerability', Contribution of Working Group II to the Sixth Assessment Report of the Intergovernmental Panel on Climate Change, 2022, p. 2.
4. Climate-change mitigation focuses on avoiding and reducing emissions of heat-trapping greenhouse gases into the atmosphere to prevent the further warming of the planet. Climate adaptation means altering behaviour, systems and lifestyles in a way that protects societies, economies and ecosystems from the most severe impacts of climate change. Finally, climate resilience concerns the ability to anticipate, prepare for and respond to future risks. See World Wildlife Fund for Nature, 'What's the Difference Between Climate Change Mitigation and Adaptation?'.
5. Intergovernmental Panel on Climate Change, 'Climate Change Widespread, Rapid, and Intensifying – IPCC', 9 August 2021.
6. National Intelligence Council, 'Climate Change and International Responses Increasing Challenges to US National Security through 2040', National Intelligence Estimate, 21 October 2021, p. 2.
7. Emma Newburger, 'China's Greenhouse Gas Emissions Exceed Those of U.S. and Developed Countries Combined, Report Says', CNBC, 6 May 2021; Ivana Kottasová, 'China Submits New "Disappointing" Emissions Pledge to UN', CNN World, 28 October 2021; and International Institute for Sustainable Development, 'US Sets Target to Reduce Emissions by 50–52% Below 2005 Levels in 2030', 28 April 2021.
8. Kandy Wong and Laura Zhou, 'China, Russia Enhance "Growing Energy Partnership" with Gas Deal during Xi Jinping, Vladimir Putin Meeting', *South China Morning Post*, 4 February 2022.
9. Alongside renewables, hydrogen will become an increasingly important energy source, especially for aviation and maritime transport and industry, which cannot be electrified.
10. Luke O Callaghan-White, 'The Geopolitical Implications of the Energy Transition', The Institute of International and European Affairs, 14 December 2021.
11. Coal can be replaced with natural gas because they are largely used for the same purposes (for example, electricity and heat), but oil has a specific purpose (transport) and cannot meaningfully be replaced with natural gas, but rather with renewable sources needed for the production of electric cars, and with hydrogen for aviation and maritime transport.
12. Coal is the most polluting fossil fuel with the largest carbon footprint, followed by oil then natural gas. See International Energy Agency, 'World Energy Outlook 2021: Executive Summary', December 2021.
13. Simone Tagliapietra, 'The Geopolitical Implications of the Global Energy Transition', Bruegel, 7 March 2019.
14. Nikos Tsafos, 'Safeguarding Critical Minerals for the Energy Transition' Center for Strategic & International Studies, 13 January 2022.
15. Ibid.
16. O Callaghan-White, 'The Geopolitical Implications Of The Energy Transition'.
17. Govind Bhutada, 'Ranked: the Top 10 Countries by Energy Transition Investment', Visual Capitalist, 7 February 2022.
18. Cary Huang, 'China's Ban On Rare Earths Didn't Work on Japan and Won't Work in the Trade War With the US', *South China Morning Post*, 5 June 2019.
19. China supplied up to 80% of the United States' rare earth imports in 2019, according to the US Geological Survey. See Nikos Tsafos, 'Safeguarding Critical Minerals for the Energy Transition'.
20. Ibid.
21. Bhutada, 'Ranked: the Top 10 Countries by Energy Transition Investment'.
22. Ian Havercroft and Christopher Consoli, 'Is The World Ready For Carbon Capture and Storage?', *Global CSS Institute*, 2018.
23. Tibetan Policy Institute, 'Tibetan Perspectives on Tibet's Environment', 2021, p. 46.
24. Sayanangshu Modak, 'Spotlight on Planet's Largest Hydropower Project by China on Yarlung/Brahmaputra', Observer Research Foundation, 12 December 2020.
25. Along the Chinese part of the Brahmaputra alone, the 13th five-year plan (2016–20) refers to six hydroelectric plants already in operation, three under construction and eight more planned for the near future. See Central Committee of the Communist Party of China, 'The 13th Five-Year Plan For Economic and Social Development of the People's Republic of China', Chapter 30, article 1, 2016.
26. Robin Allers, András Rácz and Tobias Sæther, 'Dealing With Russia In The Arctic: Between Exceptionalism And Militarization', German Council on Foreign Relations, 26 October 2021, p. 3.
27. 'How Russia's Future With NATO Will Impact The Arctic', *Foreign Policy*, 25 February 2022.
28. The Arctic Council comprises eight Arctic States: Canada, Denmark (including Greenland), Finland, Iceland, Norway, Russia, Sweden and the US, and 13 non-Arctic observer states: China, France, Germany, India, Italy, Japan, the Netherlands, Poland, Singapore, Spain, South Korea, Switzerland and the UK.
29. Dmitry Yumashev et al., 'Towards a Balanced View of Arctic Shipping: Estimating Economic Impacts of Emissions From Increased Traffic on the Northern Sea Route', *Climate Change*, vol. 143, 2017, p. 143.
30. Jackie Grom, 'Arctic May Boost Oil and Gas Reserves', *Science*, 28 May 2009.
31. Tim Sweijs, Marleen de Haan and Hugo van Manen, 'Unpacking the Climate Security Nexus: Seven Pathologies Linking Climate Change to Violent Conflict', *The Hague Centre for Strategic Studies*, March 2022.
32. Organisation for Economic Co-operation and Development, 'Managing For Sustainable Development Results', 2021.

CONFLICT REPORTS

Protesters sing the Ukrainian national anthem outside the Russian embassy in Kyiv, 22 February 2022

1 Americas

Regional Analysis		Brazil	40	Honduras		94
Conflict Reports		Haiti		Regional Outlook		100
Mexico		**Conflict Summaries**	44			
Colombia		El Salvador	56		86	

Members of the Honduran National Anti-Gang Force guard an alleged Mara Salvatrucha (MS-13) gang leader, Tegucigalpa, 27 July 2021

Overview

The Americas' conflict landscape remains dominated and driven by a mixture of organised crime and political violence. Criminal groups fight against one another for control of illicit economies (notably drug trafficking). In the process, they challenge the state's territorial control and monopoly on the use of force. Although by and large they do not have political or ideological motivations, these criminal groups are growing as political actors in their own right. Not only do they strive to infiltrate institutions and influence political developments in their favour, they also increasingly play a quasi-state role in areas under their control, providing essential services and governance to local populations, further cementing their legitimacy vis-à-vis the latter. The coronavirus pandemic accelerated these trends; its disastrous socio-economic legacy is likely to reinforce criminal groups' power and political role against a backdrop of ever more limited government resources and effectiveness, high poverty levels and lack of opportunities for young people.

Another trend strengthened by the pandemic has been the increasing internationalisation of organised crime's supply chain, partnerships and operations. This development has elevated the region's importance for global stability and security. The fast-growing business of the synthetic drug fentanyl, largely controlled by Mexican drug-trafficking organisations (DTOs), is also drawing international attention to the region given the drug's role in driving a major and deadly epidemic in the United States and China's prominent position in its supply chain.

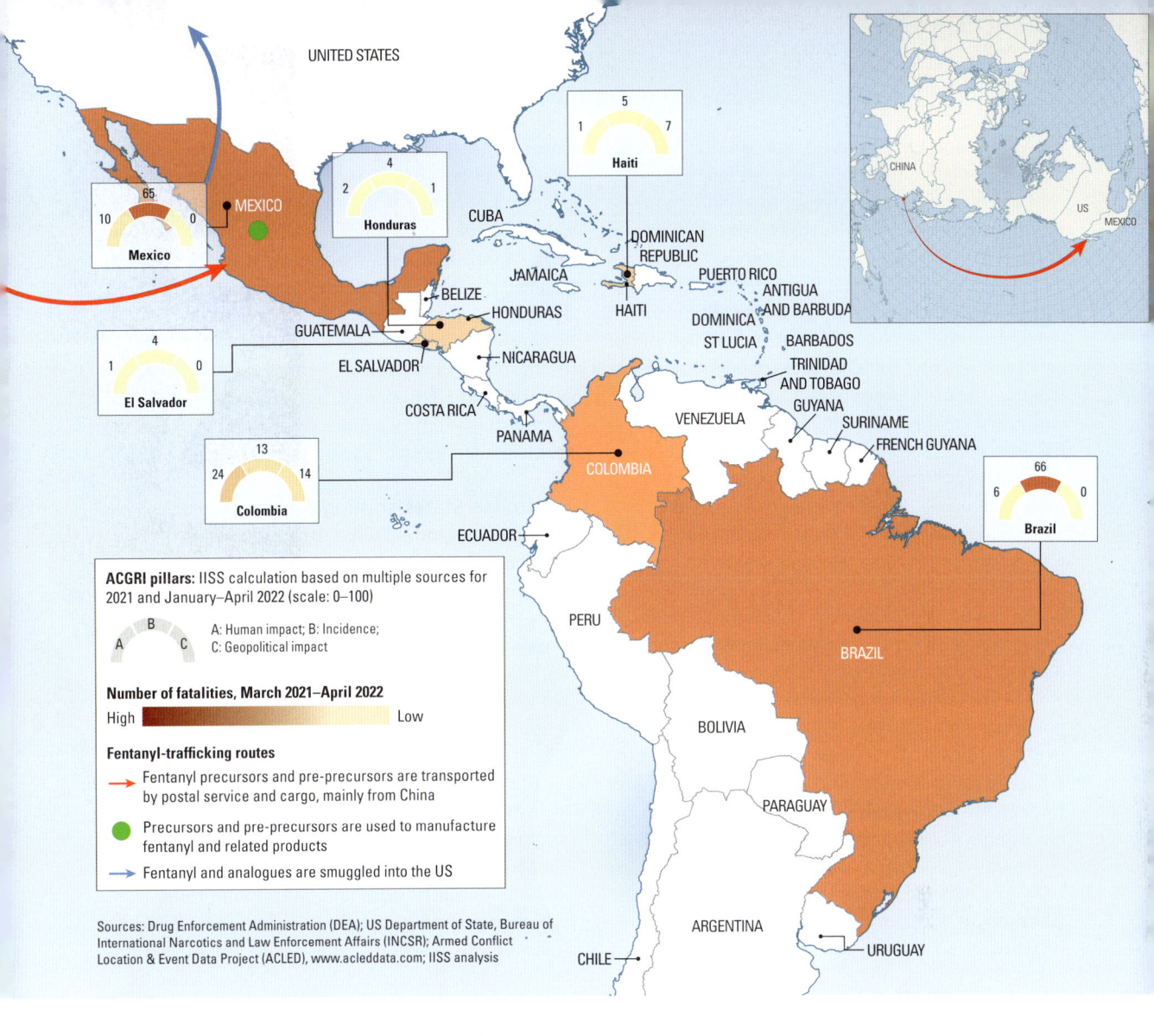

In Focus: the Rise of Fentanyl, Geopolitical Drivers and Security Spillovers

In recent years, opioid consumption and related overdose deaths in the US have evolved into a national epidemic and major health emergency. The crisis follows over two decades of unregulated prescription of pharmaceutical drugs to treat severe pain. Increased scrutiny on the matter in turn fuelled demand for illegal drugs, first heroin and then fentanyl – the latter being 50 times more potent than the former.[1]

In 2021, the US registered a record high of 107,000 overdose deaths, of which nearly two-thirds corresponded to synthetic opioids (primarily fentanyl).[2] In the 2021 fiscal year, US authorities seized 133% more fentanyl (by volume) than in the same period in 2020.[3] Counterfeit-pill seizures, which represented one-fourth of fentanyl seizures in 2021, notably registered a dramatic 50-fold increase between 2018 and 2021.[4]

Mexican DTOs enter the business

Motivated by the expanding business opportunities in illegal fentanyl and the shrinking returns of the illicit marijuana trade, Mexican DTOs, led by the Cartel Jalisco New Generation (CJNG) and the Sinaloa Cartel, consolidated the country's role as a regional hub for fentanyl production and distribution. Mexico was the origin of 98% of all fentanyl-related seizures in the US in the 2021 fiscal year.[5]

Fentanyl precursor and pre-precursor chemicals manufactured in Asia (mainly China) are now processed and trafficked to the US by Mexican DTOs.[6] The latter also press fentanyl into pills to be sold as counterfeit prescription medicine and even mix it with other drugs, such as white heroin and cocaine.

High returns make the illegal fentanyl business exceptionally lucrative. A 2017 US Drug Enforcement Administration analysis reported that a kilogram of 99% pure fentanyl could be sold for US$1.3 million–US$1.9m in the US, compared to US$80,000 for an equivalent amount of heroin.[7] Moreover, the business has low entry barriers and a relatively unsophisticated supply chain. Fentanyl's active ingredient is not of natural origin, allowing drug cartels to skip processing in rural areas – a stage required for cocaine and heroin production (for coca leaves and poppy seeds respectively). Instead, the active ingredient can be produced in rudimentary laboratories, often in facilities already in use for methamphetamine production in urban centres.

The partial reconfiguration of the largest DTOs' portfolios towards the fentanyl trade is driving peaks in localised violence in Mexico, a country where – according to President Andrés Manuel López Obrador, speaking in March 2022 – criminal groups are responsible for 75% of homicides.[8] Although overall homicides have declined since 2019, key states linked to the production and distribution of synthetic drugs have seen a drastic increase in homicides and massacres over recent years. Michoacán, home of Mexico's largest port, Lázaro Cárdenas, from which a significant amount of fentanyl and precursors enter the country from China, has seen a 63% surge between 2018 and 2021.[9] Colima, which has Mexico's second-largest port, Manzanillo, was the state that registered the greatest increase in homicides nationwide between the last quarter of 2021 and the first of 2022.[10] Similarly, clashes between organised-crime groups in the bordering state of Sonora, key for manufacturing and smuggling fentanyl across the US border, have led to a more than 100% increase in homicides between 2018 and 2021.[11]

The United States' shifting counter-narcotics focus and regional spillovers

The fentanyl emergency provided additional impetus for changes to the Mérida Initiative – the framework that had governed US–Mexico security cooperation for over a decade. Signed in 2007 after the launch of the 'war on drugs' against DTOs in Mexico, the initiative had failed to curb violence. Despite some success in securing the arrest of key drug kingpins (one of its aims, together with disrupting illicit supply chains), homicide rates increased by over 90% between 2008 and 2021 amid DTOs' fragmentation.[12] Against such a backdrop, the US and Mexico agreed the Bicentennial Framework for Security, Public Health, and Safe Communities (or Bicentennial Framework) in October 2021. Besides a greater emphasis on public health and economic development, the agreement strengthens joint regulation and law-enforcement capacity to tackle synthetic-drug trafficking, including regulatory mechanisms to prevent dual-use substances from being used in fentanyl production. It also seeks to improve oversight and coordination to curb and prevent trafficking in parcels and e-commerce via air post and maritime cargo.

As the opioid crisis in North America is expected to worsen, US regional counter-narcotics policies will likely begin to prioritise fentanyl over cocaine – a development expected to have knock-on effects on security policies across the region. For decades the US has been the region's greatest ally in fighting drug trafficking, especially with regard to cocaine production and distribution in South and Central America. If Washington does opt to prioritise fentanyl, countries involved in the cocaine business may see declining US support for their counter-narcotics efforts. Such a development

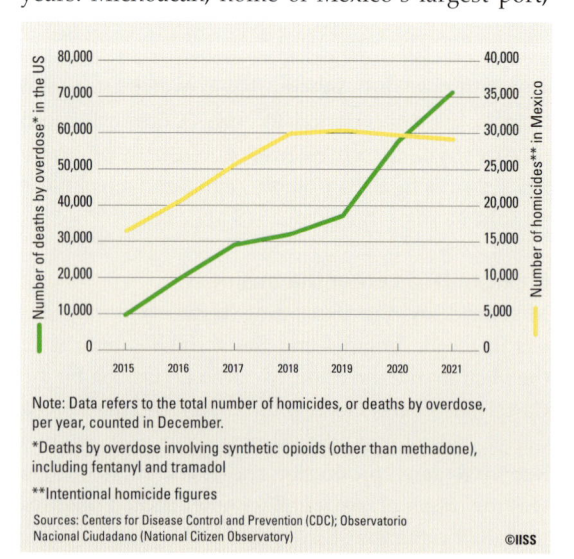

Note: Data refers to the total number of homicides, or deaths by overdose, per year, counted in December.
*Deaths by overdose involving synthetic opioids (other than methadone), including fentanyl and tramadol
**Intentional homicide figures
Sources: Centers for Disease Control and Prevention (CDC); Observatorio Nacional Ciudadano (National Citizen Observatory)   ©IISS

Figure 1: Homicides in Mexico and deaths by overdose involving synthetic opioids in the US, 2015–21

would create significant challenges for cocaine powerhouse Colombia but also for Brazil, where criminal groups will continue to thrive amid a rising appetite in the domestic market (Brazil is second only to the US for cocaine consumption) and in export markets in South America, Europe, West Africa and Asia.[13] Shifting US priorities may also facilitate a review of current drugs policies and a move towards alternative counter-narcotics strategies in the region, as advocated by Colombian President Gustavo Petro.

China and the geopolitics of fentanyl

Fentanyl analogues and precursors are mostly produced in China. As a result, regional and international security cooperation is incomplete without Beijing's engagement. During the reporting period, ongoing US–China tensions suggested that it is unlikely any substantial progress on this issue will be achieved in the short to medium term.

China scheduled all types of fentanyl-like substances in 2019 following years of diplomatic pressure from the US.[14] Nonetheless, traffickers rapidly switched to producing fentanyl in Mexico, importing precursors – and pre-precursors not yet controlled – from China.[15] Criminal groups' ability to swiftly reconfigure supply chains highlights the need for continued, fluid cooperation among countries to adapt their regulation and enforcement accordingly. However, China has made no effort to establish significant regulations since 2019. Moreover, incipient cooperation between Mexico and China presents new challenges since the latter does not accept responsibility for the illegal fentanyl production happening in the former.[16] Moreover, the dark web further enables Chinese producers to sell their products to more diverse illegal actors in Mexico, fuelling fragmentation in the fentanyl business there, as well as violent confrontation among DTOs for its control.

Notes

[1] United States Government Publishing Office, 'Fentanyl: The Next Wave of the Opioid Crisis: Hearing Before the Subcommittee on Oversight and Investigations of the Committee on Energy and Commerce, House of Representatives, One Hundred Fifteenth Congress, First Session', serial no. 115–16, 21 March 2017.

[2] US, National Center for Health Statistics, 'US Overdose Deaths in 2021 Increased Half as Much as in 2020 – But Are Still Up 15%', Centers for Disease Control and Prevention, 11 May 2022.

[3] Bureau of International Narcotics and Law Enforcement Affairs, US Department of State, '2022 International Narcotics Control Strategy Report – Volume I: Drug and Chemical Control (As submitted to Congress)', 1 March 2022, p. 68.

[4] National Institutes of Health, US Department of Health and Human Services, 'Law Enforcement Seizures of Pills Containing Fentanyl Increased Dramatically Between 2018–2021', 31 March 2022.

[5] Bureau of International Narcotics and Law Enforcement Affairs, US Department of State, '2022 International Narcotics Control Strategy Report – Volume I: Drug and Chemical Control (As submitted to Congress)', p. 68.

[6] Vanda Felbab-Brown, 'China and Synthetic Drugs: Geopolitics Trumps Counternarcotics Cooperation', Brookings Institution, 7 March 2022.

[7] Steven Dudley et al., 'Mexico's Role in the Deadly Rise of Fentanyl', Wilson Center, February 2019.

[8] Roberto Garduño and Fabiola Martínez, 'El 75% de homicidios, relacionados con narcotráfico: AMLO' [75% of Homicides Related to Drug-trafficking: AMLO], *Jornada*, 3 March 2022.

[9] See Observatorio Nacional Ciudadano's [National Citizen Observatory's] Plataforma de Incidencia Delictiva [Criminal Incidence Platform], 'Homicidio doloso tasa por cada 100,000 Habitantes, Michoacan' [Intentional homicide rate per 100,000 people, Michoacan]; and President Andrés Manuel López Obrador, '31.03.22 Versión estenográfica de la conferencia de prensa matutina del presidente Andrés Manuel López Obrador' [Stenographic Version of the Morning Press Conference of President Andrés Manuel López Obrador], 31 March 2022.

[10] Sibylline, 'Sibylline Data Analysis – Mexico', 17 May 2022.

[11] Omar Brito, 'Aumento de violencia en Sonora y BC se debe a tráfico de fentanilo: AMLO' [Increase in Violence in Sonora and BC is Due to Fentanyl Trafficking: AMLO], *Milenio*, 24 August 2021; and Observatorio Nacional Ciudadano's [National Citizen Observatory's] Plataforma de Incidencia Delictiva [Criminal Incidence Platform], 'Homicidio doloso tasa por cada 100,000 Habitantes, Sonora' [Intentional homicide rate per 100,000 people, Sonora].

[12] See Observatorio Nacional Ciudadano's [National Citizen Observatory's] Plataforma de Incidencia Delictiva [Criminal Incidence Platform], 'Homicidio doloso Tasa Por Cada 100,000 Habitantes, Nacional' [Intentional homicide rate per 100,000 people, National], data collected on 23 June 2022.

[13] United Nations Office on Drugs and Crime, 'Global Overview: Drug Demand Drug Supply', World Drug Report 2021, June 2021, p. 24.

[14] US, Drug Enforcement Administration (DEA), 'Fentanyl Flow to the United States', DEA Intelligence Report, DEA-DCT-DIR-008-20, January 2020, p. 3.

[15] Bureau of International Narcotics and Law Enforcement Affairs, US Department of State, '2022 International Narcotics Control Strategy Report – Volume I: Drug and Chemical Control (As submitted to Congress)', p. 69.

[16] Vanda Felbab-Brown, 'China and Synthetic Drugs Control: Fentanyl, Methamphetamines, and Precursors', Foreign Policy at Brookings, March 2022, p. 25.

MEXICO

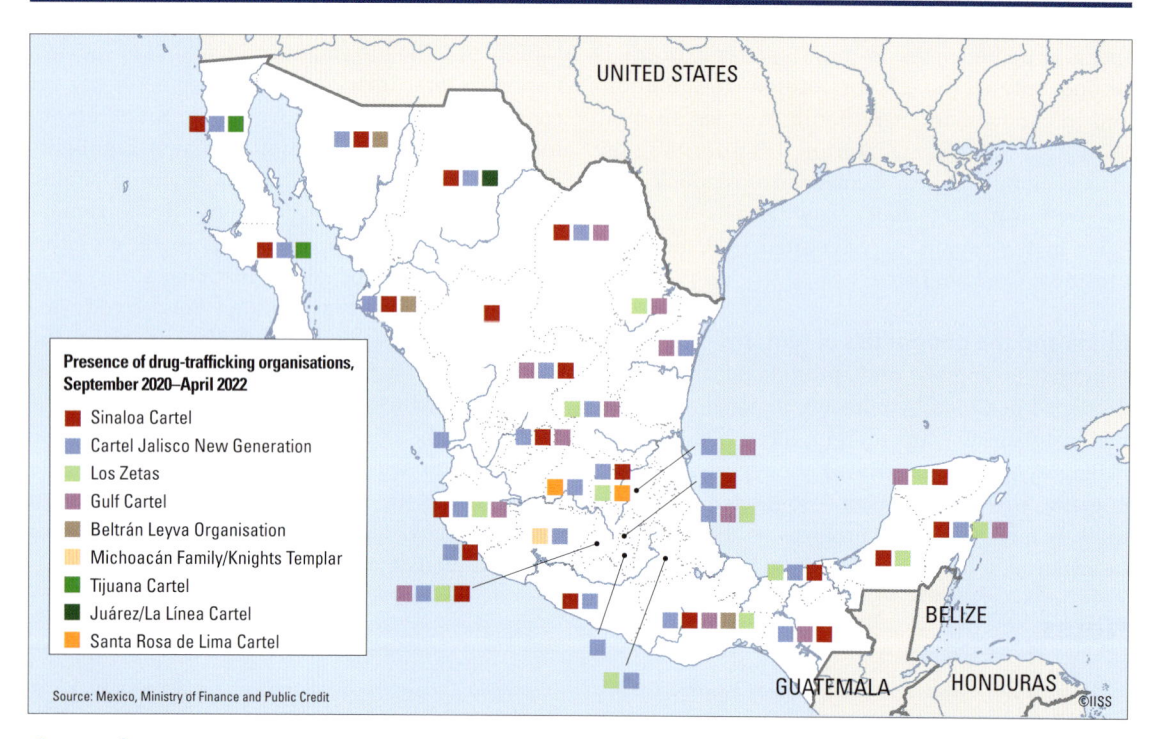

Presence of drug-trafficking organisations, September 2020–April 2022
- Sinaloa Cartel
- Cartel Jalisco New Generation
- Los Zetas
- Gulf Cartel
- Beltrán Leyva Organisation
- Michoacán Family/Knights Templar
- Tijuana Cartel
- Juárez/La Línea Cartel
- Santa Rosa de Lima Cartel

Source: Mexico, Ministry of Finance and Public Credit

Overview

Mexican drug-trafficking organisations (DTOs) originated in the 1970s, serving both as intermediaries, trafficking cocaine from South America to the United States, and as local producers of drugs (primarily marijuana). At the time, operations were largely controlled by the Guadalajara Cartel, led by Miguel Ángel Félix Gallardo. After his arrest in 1989 – following the murder of a Drug Enforcement Administration (DEA) agent in Mexico – the territory that the cartel had controlled was split between four major DTOs run by Félix Gallardo's closest associates, namely the Sinaloa, Juarez, Tijuana and Sonora cartels. This arrangement largely persisted for the next 15 years. Drug-related violence began escalating after the electoral defeat of the Institutional Revolutionary Party (PRI) in 2000, which had previously ruled continuously for seven decades. Its defeat undid many existing unofficial agreements between the DTOs and the government. Numerous high-profile acts of violence led then-president Felipe Calderón (2006–12) to launch the war on drugs in December 2006, triggering a full-scale confrontation between state security forces and the DTOs that is ongoing today.

Of the 19 DTOs identified by the government, 11 operate in more than one state and two – the Sinaloa Cartel and the Cartel Jalisco New Generation (CJNG) – have a presence in every state of Mexico, as well as strong international operations. The DTO landscape in Mexico changes constantly and is increasingly fragmented, with even the once-dominant Sinaloa Cartel now split into large factions. This leaves the CJNG as the only major cartel in Mexico with a relatively cohesive structure (although it too has suffered some internal divisions). The rest of Mexico's DTOs are remnants of larger organisations that have split over the past decade, usually following the arrest or killing of their leaders. Although these DTOs do not have the same strength or influence as their predecessors, their large number raises the probability of heightened regional competition for local drug markets and trafficking routes, which are the main drivers of violence.

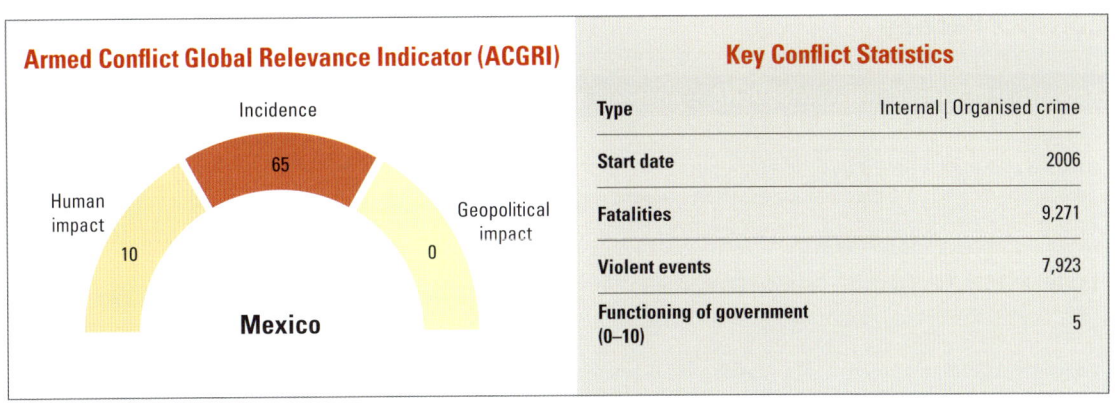

Armed Conflict Global Relevance Indicator (ACGRI)

- Incidence: 65
- Human impact: 10
- Geopolitical impact: 0

Mexico

Key Conflict Statistics

Type	Internal | Organised crime
Start date	2006
Fatalities	9,271
Violent events	7,923
Functioning of government (0–10)	5

ACGRI pillars: IISS calculation based on multiple sources for 2021 and January–April 2022 (scale: 0–100). See Notes on Methodology and Data Appendix for further details on Key Conflict Statistics.

Mexico recorded 29,246 homicides during 2021, a rate of 22.8 per 100,00 people, which represented a decrease of 1.8% compared to the previous year (when homicides fell by 2.1%).[1] These two consecutive annual decreases suggest that the spike in violence that began in 2015 may have plateaued, though there is still little evidence to suggest that this reflects the start of a sustained decline over the next few years. In contrast to 2020, Mexico had minimal coronavirus restrictions for much of 2021 (particularly after the end of the country's second wave in February) and the reduction in homicides therefore occurred in a context much closer to the pre-pandemic normal.

Despite the decline in homicides in 2021, violence over the past few years has remained high by historical comparison and the government of President Andrés Manuel López Obrador (who will remain in office until 2024) appears unwilling to change the fundamentals of its existing strategy to combat DTOs. This strategy uses the military as well as the National Guard (GN), a nominally civilian gendarmerie-style force created in 2019 that in practice is under the operational control of the military. Efforts to professionalise Mexico's poorly trained and underfunded police forces (which are organised at a sub-national level) have been slow; this will continue to compromise Mexico's security strategy given the inability of the military and the GN to effectively police the entirety of the country's vast territory. Stemming the flow of illegal weapons from the US will also remain a problem given the long and porous border between the two countries. In an attempt to do so, the government has resorted to more unconventional methods, including filing a US$10 billion lawsuit against six large US gunmakers for their alleged negligence in preventing these guns from being trafficked into Mexico.

The US is Mexico's main partner in the war against DTOs. Since the implementation of the Mérida Initiative in 2008, the US has supplied Mexico with considerable security assistance, including weapons procurement, training and intelligence, amounting to an estimated US$3.3bn.[2] The Mérida Initiative is currently being reworked into the broader Bicentennial Framework for Security, Public Health, and Safe Communities, which is expected to be finalised in 2022. The US–Mexico security relationship has had its frictions in the past and there is some degree of domestic resistance in Mexico to US involvement in national affairs. However, there is broad cross-party support in both countries for maintaining the security relationship given the perceived reciprocal benefits, despite the current strategy having largely failed to curtail violence in Mexico or to prevent large inflows of narcotics into the US.

Given its broad impact across Mexican society, crime remains the country's primary public concern. Additionally, DTOs have not been afraid to influence local politics and electoral processes through the intimidation and even murder of political candidates and public officials. While this has had an impact on governability in the country's most turbulent regions, the overall risk from DTOs to political stability at a national level remains low.

Conflict Parties

Secretariat of National Defence (SEDENA) – army and air force

Strength: 165,500.

Areas of operation: Across the whole country but concentrates its forces in the north and the Pacific region: in Baja California, Chihuahua, Coahuila, Jalisco, Guerrero, Michoacán, Sonora and Tamaulipas.

Leadership: Gen. Luis Crecencio Sandoval (head of SEDENA); Gen. Manuel de Jesús Hernández González (head of the air force).

Structure: SEDENA forms one branch of Mexico's two defence ministries. The army is divided into 12 military regions and 46 military zones. The air force is divided into four air regions. The General Staff of National Defence is divided into eight sections, of which the second section (intelligence) and the seventh section (combatting drug trafficking) focus on DTOs.

History: The Ministry of War and the Navy was created in 1821 to supervise the army and navy. In 1939 it was divided to create SEDENA and the Secretariat of the Navy (SEMAR).

Objectives: Provide internal security and fight drug trafficking.

Opponents: DTOs.

Affiliates/allies: SEMAR, GN and special-forces combat group GAIN (Drug Trafficking Information Analysis Group), which is in charge of capturing DTO leaders. Also supported by the National Intelligence Centre (CNI) and the Attorney General's Office, as well as foreign governments through cooperation programmes (e.g., the Bicentennial Framework for Security, Public Health, and Safe Communities with the US and, previously, the Mérida Initiative).

Resources/capabilities: Infantry, armoured vehicles and combat helicopters. 2021 budget: US$5.5bn (MXN 112.6 bn).[3]

Secretariat of the Navy (SEMAR)

Strength: 50,500.

Areas of operation: The country's coasts, divided into the Pacific and Gulf of Mexico–Caribbean zones.

Leadership: Adm. José Rafael Ojeda Durán.

Structure: Divided into General (70%) and Naval Infantry Corps (marines; 30%), which operate in eight naval regions and 18 naval zones (12 in the Pacific and six in the Gulf and Caribbean). The marines' special forces also combat criminal groups in the country's interior.

History: Created in 1821. SEMAR separated from SEDENA in 1939.

Objectives: Defend Mexico's coasts, strategic infrastructure (mainly oil platforms in the Gulf of Mexico) and the environment at sea, and fight piracy.

Opponents: DTOs, particularly those that traffic people along the coasts, from South and Central America, and those that transport drugs via the sea from Colombia and Venezuela.

Affiliates/allies: SEDENA, GN and CNI. Cooperates with US Coast Guard at the border.

Resources/capabilities: Fast vessels for interception, exploration and intelligence; supported by naval aviation. 2021 budget: US$1.8bn (MXN 37.5bn).

National Guard (GN)

Strength: 102,600.

Areas of operation: Across the whole country. The states of Guanajuato, Jalisco, Mexico, Michoacán, Oaxaca and Sinaloa had the highest number of operational coordination regions at the end of 2020.

Leadership: Alfonso Durazo (secretary of public security and citizen protection, SSPC); Gen. (Retd) Luis Rodríguez Bucio (commander).

Structure: The planned 266 coordination regions across the country were operational as of the end of 2021. A total of 213 GN bases were also operational with an additional 35 under construction and 246 planned for 2022–23.[4]

History: Began operating in May 2019, by presidential order. The law gave GN personnel the authority to stop suspected criminals on the streets.

Objectives: Reduce the level of violence in the country and combat DTOs.

Opponents: DTOs and medium-sized criminal organisations.

Affiliates/allies: SEDENA, SEMAR, and local and municipal police.

Resources/capabilities: Acquired resources from the defunct Federal Police, including their helicopter teams and equipment such as assault rifles. Relies on intelligence from SEDENA, SEMAR and the CNI.

Sinaloa Cartel (CPS)

Strength: Unknown.

Areas of operation: Headquartered in Culiacán, Sinaloa, but with a presence in all 32 states of Mexico and particularly in the Pacific (the cartel is also known as the Cartel del Pacífico or Cartel del Pacífico–Sinaloa). Outside Mexico, it is active in Asia, Canada, Central America and Europe. In the US, it has an important presence in California, Colorado, Texas and New York.

Leadership: Historical leader since the mid-1990s, Joaquín 'El Chapo' Guzmán, was captured in 2016 and imprisoned for life in the US in 2019. His number two, Ismael 'El Mayo' Zambada García, is in a leadership struggle with El Chapo's sons, Ovidio and Iván Archibaldo.

Structure: Hierarchical organisation, with three subdivisions: finance/business, logistics for drug transportation and military structures. In recent years, the cartel has associated with numerous smaller DTOs such as Los Salazar and Los Talibanes.

History: Preceded by the Guadalajara Cartel, co-founded in the late 1970s by leader Rafael Caro Quintero. In the 1990s, following the peace processes in Central America, the large-scale ground transit of cocaine began. In the mid-1990s, El Chapo became leader of the Sinaloa Cartel, opened routes from Guatemala to Mexico and the Tijuana route, and forged alliances with the Medellín Cartel in Colombia. Focused for 20 years on cocaine, but now diversifying into heroin, methamphetamine and fentanyl.

Objectives: Control all drug markets (for cocaine and methamphetamine in particular), including production networks in Colombia, distribution in Central America and Mexico, and consumption in the US. Recover its position as the dominant DTO in Mexico.

Opponents: Other DTOs, particularly the CJNG. SEMAR, SEDENA's intelligence section and special forces. The US DEA and Defense Intelligence Agency (DIA).

Affiliates/allies: Many subordinate medium-sized and small DTOs at the regional level, including cocaine-producing partners in Colombia. Partners with many corrupt Mexican government officials, particularly in its home state of Sinaloa and other regions where it operates.

Resources/capabilities: High-powered weapons, such as the Barrett M107 sniper rifle and anti-aircraft missiles, and a large fleet of drug-transport planes.

Cartel Jalisco New Generation (CJNG)

Strength: Unknown.

Areas of operation: Headquartered in the state of Jalisco, with a presence in most states, particularly Colima, Guanajuato, Guerrero, Jalisco, Michoacán and Nayarit. It also controls the Pacific ports of Manzanillo and Lázaro Cárdenas, where chemicals from China enter Mexico. It has rapidly expanded in the US, where it is thought to have a presence in 35 states and in Puerto Rico.

Leadership: The main leader is Nemesio Oseguera Cervantes, commonly known as 'El Mencho'.

Structure: El Mencho successfully co-opted all regional leaders of the Michoacán Family and the Knights Templar to control the laboratories in the Michoacán mountains.

History: Formed in 2011 in Guadalajara, Jalisco, CJNG initially produced methamphetamine in rural laboratories in Jalisco and Michoacán. In 2012–13, it expanded to Veracruz. Since 2015–16 its influence has grown throughout the country, thanks in part to gaps left after the government successfully targeted other DTOs (such as the Michoacán Family, the Knights Templar, Los Zetas and the Sinaloa Cartel).

Objectives: Fully replace the Sinaloa Cartel at the helm of Mexico's criminal networks.

Opponents: Other DTOs, particularly the Sinaloa Cartel. SEMAR, SEDENA's intelligence section and special forces. The US DEA and DIA.

Affiliates/allies: Demobilised members of the Michoacán Family and the Knights Templar, as well as large numbers of collaborating peasants.

Resources/capabilities: Estimated capital of US$1bn from the sale of methamphetamine and fentanyl as well as the extortion of merchants and money-laundering activities in Guadalajara. Known to possess high-powered weapons and has used drones to attack government forces.

Los Zetas

Strength: Unknown. Hit hard by the government between 2012 and 2016.

Areas of operation: Tamaulipas State, mainly along the border with Texas, as well as Coahuila, Nuevo León, Veracruz, Tabasco and the area along the border with Guatemala.

Leadership: Founded by Heriberto Lazcano, former member of the Mexican army. Since 2013, 33 of its main leaders (including Lazcano) have been arrested or killed in combat by military forces. Its Cartel del Noreste splinter group is believed to be led by Juan Gerardo Treviño-Chávez 'El Huevo'.

Structure: Originally a horizontal, decentralised structure that worked as a large business with multiple criminal activities. Less successful at drug trafficking, its cells were involved in extortion, kidnapping, the collection of criminal taxes from businesses and migrant trafficking from Central America to Texas. Currently split into two main groups, Zetas Vieja Escuela and the Cartel del Noreste. Another group known as Los Talibanes operates in north-central Mexico in association with the Sinaloa Cartel.

History: Began as the armed wing of the Gulf Cartel, drawing most of its members from the Mexican and Guatemalan

Los Zetas

armies. Notorious for perpetrating mass violence against the civilian population and migrants. Between 2010 and 2012, a major SEMAR offensive to dismantle the 'Gulf Corridor' weakened the group significantly. It is the DTO against which the Mexican government has been most successful.

Objectives: Control criminal activity in the Gulf of Mexico states.

Opponents: CJNG, Gulf Cartel and the special forces of SEMAR.

Affiliates/allies: Criminal networks in Tamaulipas State.

Resources/capabilities: Migrant smuggling and criminal taxes on merchants.

Gulf Cartel

Strength: Unknown.

Areas of operation: Operates and controls territory in Tamaulipas State, particularly the border area with Texas, including strategic border cities, such as Nuevo Laredo, Reynosa and Matamoros.

Leadership: The Gulf Cartel was led by Osiel Cárdenas Guillén at the peak of its power in the early 2000s but has suffered from high turnover of leadership since his capture in 2003. Numerous Gulf Cartel leaders have been arrested or killed by government forces in recent years.

Structure: Unstable, with fragmented leadership. Splinter groups include Los Ciclones, Los Metros, Panteras and Grupo Sombra.

History: The second-oldest DTO in the country, smuggling alcohol, weapons and drugs across the US border since the 1940s. After forging a partnership with the Colombian Cali Cartel in the 1990s, the group focused on introducing cocaine to the US market. Los Zetas violently separated from the group in 2010.

Objectives: Smuggle drugs on the Texas–Tamaulipas border and control drug trafficking in northeast US.

Opponents: Los Zetas, CJNG and the special forces of SEMAR and SEDENA.

Affiliates/allies: Closely linked to Tamaulipas State's governors (three former governors have been charged in Texas) and criminal networks.

Resources/capabilities: Many Tamaulipas businessmen help the cartel to launder money.

Beltrán Leyva Organisation (BLO)

Strength: Unknown.

Areas of operation: Mainly in the states of Guerrero and Morelos, and the Mexico City–Acapulco highway. The group controls poppy production and the export of heroin from Iguala (Guerrero) to Chicago, IL.

Leadership: Founded by brothers Arturo, Alfredo, Carlos and Héctor Leyva. Arturo was killed in 2009 and the other three were imprisoned, with Héctor dying in 2018. The organisation is now split into various groups.

Structure: Based around vertically organised cells. After the death or imprisonment of the four brothers, the organisation fragmented into different groups which primarily operate in the state of Guerrero. The two largest are Los Rojos and Guerreros Unidos, the latter of which also traces its origins to splinter cells of the Knights Templar cartel. Both groups have been identified as being responsible for the 2014 Ayotzinapa massacre and are also believed to be in conflict with each other.

History: A breakaway group of the Sinaloa Cartel formed in 2008 in Sinaloa before moving to the South Pacific–Acapulco (Guerrero State), Morelos and Mexico State. The groups are among the most important DTOs operating in the highly violent region known as 'Tierra Caliente', which covers parts of the states of Guerrero, Michoacán and Mexico State.

Objectives: Control heroin trafficking in the South Pacific and from Mexico to Chicago.

Opponents: Sinaloa Cartel, CJNG and the special forces of SEDENA.

Affiliates/allies: An estimated 100,000 peasants who grow poppies in Guerrero.

Resources/capabilities: Profits from the sale of heroin in the US and from criminal activities such as extortion and kidnapping in Mexico.

Michoacán Family / Knights Templar (Cárteles Unidos)

Strength: Unknown.

Areas of operation: The surviving criminal cells moved to Guanajuato, Guerrero and Mexico State.

Leadership: Fragmented following the 2015 arrest of Servando Gómez Martínez. The current organisation, known as Cárteles Unidos, is led by Juan José Farías Álvarez 'El Abuelo'.

Structure: Organised into independent groups – including the Cartel del Abuelo and Los Viagras – that in recent years banded together under the name Cárteles Unidos. Many of these groups are notable for having begun as vigilante-style autodefensa (self-defence) groups but later branched out into criminal activities.

History: Gained power by producing methamphetamine, importing chemical precursors from China. Founded by Nazario Moreno Gonzalez in 2005, the organisation's initial recruitment was based on a religious discourse. Between 2006 and 2012, the group built a broad network of collaborators among the population, bribed a large number of

Michoacán Family / Knights Templar (Cárteles Unidos)

local politicians on the Pacific coast of Michoacán and ran methamphetamine laboratories in the mountains. However, the group was practically dismantled by Mexican government forces between 2013 and 2016. Following the capture of its first leaders, the Michoacán Family became the Knights Templar in 2013–14, under the leadership of Servando Gomez. The organisation known as Cárteles Unidos was created in 2019 as a response to CJNG activity in Michoacán.

Objectives: Control mining and agricultural production (of avocados for export to the US) in Michoacán state; control the port of Lázaro Cárdenas (for smuggling the chemical base for producing methamphetamine); and steal fuel in Guanajuato State.

Opponents: Sinaloa Cartel, CJNG and the special forces of SEDENA.

Affiliates/allies: A large number of collaborating peasants.

Resources/capabilities: The revenue from criminal taxes on many economic activities.

Tijuana Cartel (also known as Arellano Felix Family Organisation)

Strength: Exact numbers unknown, but thought to have regained some strength since 2018.

Areas of operation: A bi-national, cross-border organisation operating between Tijuana, Baja California and San Diego, CA; Los Angeles, CA.

Leadership: Its original leaders, Benjamin Arellano Felix and his brothers Ramón, Eduardo, Luis Fernando, Francisco, Carlos and Javier, are all imprisoned in Californian jails. The cartel is currently led by their sister, Enedina Arellano Felix.

Structure: Groups of young people become either gunmen or cocaine exporters (middle-class youth who have visas to cross the border). Their leaders are family members. A splinter group associated with the CJNG is known as the Cartel Tijuana New Generation.

History: During the 1980s and 1990s, the Arellano Felix brothers controlled the north of the country and transported drugs across the border using tunnels and people crossing the border, as well as migrants. The arrest of the Arellano Felix brothers led to the cartel's decline amid the Sinaloa Cartel's dominance in the region. However, the latter's troubles in recent years have led to a resurgence of the Tijuana Cartel.

Objectives: Control drug trafficking from Baja California to California, US.

Opponents: Sinaloa Cartel, the special forces of SEDENA and US intelligence services cooperating with Mexican authorities at the border.

Affiliates/allies: Many people cross the border daily with small amounts of drugs.

Resources/capabilities: Revenue from the cross-border cocaine trade.

Juárez Cartel

Strength: Unknown.

Areas of operation: A bi-national, cross-border organisation active in North Chihuahua and North Sonora in Mexico and southwest Texas; Las Cruces and Albuquerque, NM; and Tucson, AZ in the US.

Leadership: Founded by Amado Carrillo Fuentes in the 1990s and later led by his brother, Vicente Carrillo Fuentes, until the latter's arrest in 2014. The cartel is now split into various smaller groups with fragmented leadership.

Structure: There are at least seven different splinter groups operating in Ciudad Juárez and the state of Chihuahua. Of these, the largest group is known as La Línea. Other groups include Los Aztecas and the New Juárez Cartel.

History: Amado Carrillo Fuentes, the 'Lord of the Skies', orchestrated the smuggling of drugs in small planes at low altitude, which went undetected by radars. In 2009, the group began to fight with the Sinaloa Cartel for control of the Central Mexican and the US-highway trafficking routes. Although the Juárez Cartel has regained strength since, it continues to fight with Sinaloa Cartel cells across the state of Chihuahua.

Objectives: Control drugs crossing from Ciudad Juárez to El Paso, into New Mexico and Arizona, and to northeast US.

Opponents: Sinaloa Cartel, the special forces of SEDENA and the DEA.

Affiliates/allies: Groups of young people become either gunmen or drug exporters (middle-class youth who have visas to cross the border).

Resources/capabilities: The proceeds from drug trafficking.

Santa Rosa de Lima Cartel (CSRL)

Strength: Exact numbers unknown but experienced large-scale arrests in 2019–20.

Areas of operation: Guanajuato; minor operations in neighbouring states including Queretaro and Hidalgo.

Leadership: Founded by David Rogel Figueroa 'El Güero' in 2014 and from 2017 led by José Antonio Yépez Ortiz 'El Marro' until his capture in 2020. His successor, Fernando Emmanuel 'El Panther', was captured in October 2021.

Structure: Organised into numerous regional cells. One cell known as the 'Shadow Group' was previously associated with the Gulf Cartel. Many high-level operatives (including financial operatives) are relatives of El Marro.

History: Formed in 2014 as a huachicolero (fuel theft) gang in the state of Guanajuato and grew to a fully fledged DTO after 2017 when El Marro assumed leadership, expanding its operations to include drug trafficking, retail drug trade, kidnapping and extortion. Significantly weakened since 2019 because of the government's campaign against fuel theft as well as conflict with the CJNG, which has contested its dominance in the state.

Objectives: Control the fuel-theft market in Bermuda Triangle area of Guanajuato as well as supplementary resources through drug trafficking (mainly cocaine) and other illegal activities in that area.

Opponents: CJNG, GN, other SEDENA and SEMAR forces.

Affiliates/allies: Local fuel-theft gangs.

Resources/capabilities: The proceeds from fuel theft and other drug-trafficking revenues. Fuel-theft income has fallen significantly since 2019 and it is believed the group is severely weakened, having possibly lost around 40% of its manpower.

Conflict Drivers

Geopolitical and geostrategic influences
US demand and policy:
The market conditions driving the prevalence of DTOs in Mexico stem from the US demand for illegal drugs (annual spending reached an estimated US$150bn in 2016).[5] DTOs are also easily able to obtain assault rifles and other weapons in the US and smuggle them across the border to Mexico, usually in small but steady quantities that are difficult to detect, a method known as 'ant trafficking'. US drug policy has largely supported the military strategies adopted by successive Mexican governments to combat DTOs. This, in turn, has precluded discussion of potential alternative approaches such as a more widespread legalisation of drugs (including some hard drugs), or negotiations between government and the DTOs.

Political
Institutional corruption and impunity:
Mexico has traditionally suffered from high levels of corruption and impunity, enabled by a political culture that tolerates them as well as lax law enforcement. In Transparency International's 2021 Corruption Perceptions Index, Mexico ranked 124th (out of 180) worldwide and second worst (only above Venezuela) among Latin America's seven largest economies.[6] Impunity is a particularly problematic element of Mexican corruption: it is estimated that 93.3% of all crimes go unreported or are not investigated by authorities.[7] Police inefficiency has also been a long-standing factor in Mexico's institutional weakness when it comes to fighting crime, and many police forces (particularly at the municipal level) are known to be infiltrated by DTOs or other organised-crime groups. Additionally, the number of police is very low, with an estimated level of just 0.9 police officers per 1,000 residents, well below international standards of 2.8 police officers per 1,000 residents.[8]

Economic
Poverty and precarity:
Widespread poverty and precarious labour conditions among Mexico's youth (around one-quarter of the population) contribute to a constant supply of manpower for DTOs. An estimated 43.9% of Mexico's population (55.7 million people) lived under the national poverty line in 2020,[9] a figure that has not improved significantly since the 1990s, and labour informality is high at 56.5% of the labour force.[10] These factors, along with limited social mobility, highlight the poor future prospects for many young people as the potential income from joining a DTO far outstrips that offered by most legal employment, despite the risk of death or imprisonment.

Geography:
Mexico's location, situated between the main source of cocaine production (South America) and the main consumption market for all drugs (the US), triggered its emergence as a major drug-trafficking centre. Mexico is also a major drug producer in its own right, as the largest producer of opium in the Western Hemisphere (it accounts for an estimated 9% of global

supply, only behind Afghanistan and Myanmar) and an important producer of marijuana.[11] Mexico has also established itself in recent years as a major producer of synthetic drugs such as methamphetamine and fentanyl, the latter made from precursor chemicals imported from China.

Key Events in 2021–22

POLITICAL EVENTS

6 June 2021
Mexico holds midterm elections. The ruling party, Morena, and its allies lose their congressional supermajority but remain the dominant political force.

8 June
US Vice President Kamala Harris visits Mexico for talks on migration and other bilateral issues.

4 August
Mexico files a US$10bn lawsuit in a Massachusetts court against six US gunmakers over negligence in stopping gun trafficking.

19 August
Official deaths from COVID-19 in Mexico reach 250,000.

8 October
Mexico and the US begin dialogue on the Bicentennial Framework for Security, Public Health, and Safe Communities, which will replace the Mérida Initiative.

8 November
The US–Mexico border reopens for non-essential crossings after being closed for 19 months due to the coronavirus pandemic.

22 November
President Andrés Manuel López Obrador signs a controversial decree to give key infrastructure projects national-security status. Critics say the move could impact transparency.

2 December
Mexico and the US agree to restart the Trump-era 'Remain in Mexico' policy for asylum seekers.

28 January 2022
An investigation over potential influence peddling by one of López Obrador's sons with a US oil services firm is published.

5 February
The government restates its intention to incorporate the GN into the military.

10 March
The European Parliament condemns the level of violence against journalists in Mexico, drawing a sharp rebuke from the government.

MILITARY/VIOLENT EVENTS

5 March–6 June 2021
An estimated 102 political candidates and public officials are murdered over the course of the midterm election campaigns.

19 June
A Gulf Cartel convoy murders at least 15 people, mostly civilians, in the border city of Reynosa.

8 October
CSRL leader Fernando Emmanuel 'El Panther' is captured.

15 November
Rosalinda González Valencia, wife of CJNG leader Nemesio Oseguera Cervantes and allegedly an important financial operative, is captured.

1 December
Esteban Méndez, presumed leader of the Unión Tepito DTO based in Mexico City, is captured.

9 December
A road accident results in the death of 54 migrants as migration to the US through Mexico intensifies.

20 February 2022
An administrative reform of SEDENA gives the Mexican army a separate command.

27 February
A shoot-out between warring factions of the CJNG leaves 17 people dead during a funeral in Michoacán.

4 March
A journalist is murdered – the seventh since the start of the year.

Responses to the Conflict

Security
There were no major changes to security policy in 2021, as the government proceeded to consolidate the reforms enacted earlier in the term, particularly those related to the GN. In 2021, the GN finished setting up its territorial structure (organised around 266 regional commands), with further recruitment and the construction of over 200 new GN installations across the country planned in 2022–23. López Obrador intends to transform the GN into a separate branch of the military (under SEDENA), which runs contrary to its original conception as a civilian force. This has proven controversial and will likely meet stiff opposition in congress. In early 2022, a major reorganisation of SEDENA took place in which a separate Army Command was established. Previously, the secretary of defence was also the head of the army. This change is intended to improve the administrative and operational efficiency of the army as one of the three main branches of SEDENA (which also includes the air force and territorial commands).

Economic/development
The Mexican economy bounced back from the coronavirus pandemic, growing by 5% in 2021.[12] However, GDP per capita remains at approximately the same level as in 2014, highlighting the persistent stagnation of living standards, which is one of the root causes of high criminality. Mexico was among the G20 countries that devoted less coronavirus-related fiscal assistance to individuals and businesses (just 0.7% of GDP).[13] This illustrates the government's fixation on fiscal austerity, exacerbated by low tax intake, which provides limited resources for development and security spending. These limitations are partly alleviated by the budgetary priority given towards the government's key policies, such as the establishment of the GN and other projects that could have a positive impact on violence in the longer term. One of these projects is a flagship youth scholarship programme that is partly intended to keep young people (who are most prone to criminality) off the streets. Nevertheless, the government's lack of interest in significantly increasing its revenue base means that efforts to combat violence will always fall short. The government has also significantly increased the minimum wage in the past three years but overall, wages remain low and job quality is still poor for most Mexicans (especially outside larger cities). This will remain an incentive for many people to join criminal organisations.

Diplomacy
Mexico's bilateral relationship with the US remains key in terms of security. After frictions during the Trump administration, considerable progress has been made under US President Joe Biden to revamp security cooperation, primarily through the Bicentennial Framework for Security, Public Health, and Safe Communities. The new framework is based on a more holistic approach to addressing bilateral security challenges, which includes placing greater emphasis on prevention of substance abuse, providing economic and educational opportunities, and professionalising criminal justice and police agencies. It also places a greater focus on attacking DTOs' finances and cyber crime, arms trafficking and the synthetic drugs trade, which now provides a larger share of DTO financing. Some elements of this have already been put into practice, such as the increased seizures of fentanyl and methamphetamine under the current administration.

Humanitarian aid
Although data on internal displacement is difficult to verify, it is estimated that as many as 357,000 people may have been displaced by drug-related violence in Mexico since the war on drugs began in 2006, with 9,700 of these displacements occurring in 2020. The states of Guerrero and Chiapas, which are also marred by high levels of poverty, were the most affected in 2020.[14] Although each state in Mexico has

Figure 1: Mexican military deployments (as of January 2022)

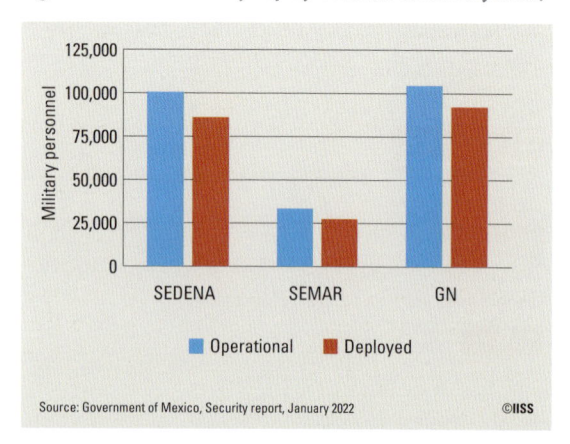

Source: Government of Mexico, Security report, January 2022

a commission for supporting victims of violence, long-term support is lacking. Another important humanitarian concern is the human-rights abuses committed by security services. Over the course of 2021, the National Human Rights Commission received 345 human-rights complaints relating to the GN, 339 relating to SEDENA and 109 relating to SEMAR.[15] These complaints relate to arbitrary detentions, excessive use of force, intimidation, prevention of access to justice, cruel and degrading acts, torture and forced disappearances. Despite promises from López Obrador to end these abuses, it is likely that they will persist given the poor levels of training on human-rights issues.

Conflict Outlook

Political scenarios

In the midterm elections in June 2021, the ruling party, Morena, and its allies retained a solid majority in both houses but lost their congressional supermajority. Although the government will now need the opposition's support to pass constitutional reforms, it will still be able to pass most other types of legislation, including budget legislation and executive decrees. Given that most substantive security policies have now been passed (including the creation of the GN), its lack of a supermajority will not significantly inhibit the government from pursuing its existing security agenda until the end of its term in 2024.

López Obrador's expansion of the military's role in civilian activities (such as in the construction and administration of infrastructure projects) throughout his term has proven highly controversial, fuelling concerns about its impact on democracy and political stability. Unlike most Latin American countries, however, Mexico has had nearly a century of uninterrupted political transitions under civilian rule and it is therefore less likely that the military will attempt to step outside the bounds set by the executive and attempt to involve itself in politics.

Escalation potential and conflict-related risks

The reduction of homicides in 2021 offers some hope that a downward trend in violence may be on the way. However, the dynamics of the drug war make this impossible to predict as it will depend on the balance of power between different DTOs, as well as the fragmentation of many of these groups (often following the arrest or killing of their leaders), which leads to power vacuums or escalations in violence. The predominance of two large DTOs (the Sinaloa Cartel and the CJNG) marks a change from recent years, and the close geographical proximity of the two groups raises the risk of significant violence in Mexico's Pacific region if competition intensifies.

The more fragmented nature of the Sinaloa Cartel following the arrest of its former leader, Joaquín 'El Chapo' Guzmán, in 2016 has also led to conflicts among its multitude of factions, while many smaller cartels have emerged from the remnants of formerly more powerful organisations. This fragmentation, along with the absence of a single dominant cartel, will also reduce the likelihood of a more sustained decline in violence like there was during the so-called 'Pax Sinaloa' of 2011–14 when the Sinaloa Cartel was dominant.

Prospects for peace

The persistence of widespread poverty and lack of economic opportunities for large segments of the Mexican population, combined with the inability of successive governments to establish a security policy that demonstrably reduces violence, suggests that the conflict against DTOs will not end any time soon. At best, the consolidation of the multitude of smaller, warring DTOs into a few large ones could reduce competition between them and thereby violence. The impact of the government's efforts to combat financial crime and synthetic drugs on DTOs' finances could either reduce their capacity for violence or, alternatively, lead them to expand their reach into other criminal, or even some non-criminal, activities.

Strategic implications and global influences

Although Mexico's security relationship with the US has not been without complications in the past few years, there appears to be a concerted effort on both sides to establish a bilateral security agenda under the Bicentennial Framework that appeals to each country's respective priorities. One sign that suggests better cooperation going forward was Mexico's agreement with the US in December 2021 to restart the controversial 'Remain in Mexico' programme for asylum seekers while their asylum claims are processed; this programme had been introduced (under some duress) during the Trump administration. Nevertheless, the overall success of the Bicentennial Framework will largely depend on the ability of Mexican authorities to overcome their institutional deficiencies and produce more satisfactory results in their fight against DTOs, all the more considering they have already received substantial US assistance over the years in the form of intelligence sharing, weapons procurement and training. Other aspects of the framework, such as reducing the illegal flow of arms, will be complicated by the reluctance of many US states along the border to tighten gun laws; studies have shown a correlation between an increase in gun sales along the border and homicides in Mexico.[16]

Notes

[1] Observatorio Nacional Ciudadano's [National Citizen Observatory's] Plataforma de Incidencia Delictiva [Criminal Incidence Platform], 'Homicidio doloso Tasa Por Cada 100,000 Habitantes, Nacional' [Intentional homicide rate per 100,000 people, national], data collected on 23 June 2022.

[2] Congressional Research Service, 'Mexico: Evolution of the Mérida Initiative, FY2008–FY2021', 20 September 2021, p. 1.

[3] Ministry of Finance of Mexico, 'Informes sobre la Situación Económica, las Finanzas Públicas y la Deuda Pública' [Report on the Economic Situation, Public Finance and Public Debt], 2021.

[4] Ibid.

[5] RAND Corporation, 'Americans' Spending on Illicit Drugs Nears $150 Billion Annually; Appears to Rival What Is Spent on Alcohol', 20 August 2019.

[6] Transparency International, 'Corruption Perceptions Index'.

[7] National Institute of Statistics and Geography (INEGI), 'Encuesta Nacional de Victimización y Percepción Sobre Seguridad Pública (Envipe) 2021' [National Survey on Victimisation and Perception of Public Security 2021], 22 September 2021, p. 1.

[8] National Institute of Statistics and Geography (INEGI), 'Censo Nacional de Seguridad Pública Estatal 2021: Presentación de resultados generales' [National Census of State Public Security 2021: Presentation of general results], p. 9.

[9] Coneval, 'Medición de la Pobreza 2020' [Measurement of Poverty 2020], 2020.

[10] National Institute of Statistics and Geography (INEGI), 'Principales Resultados de la Encuesta Nacional de Ocupación y Empleo (nueva edición) (ENOEN) de Diciembre de 2021' [Main Results of the National Survey on Occupation and Employment (New Edition) (ENOEN) December 2021], December 2021, p. 4.

[11] United Nations Office on Drugs and Crime, 'World Drug Report 2021: Drug Market Trends: Cannabis, Opioids', June 2021, p. 86.

[12] IMF, 'World Economic Outlook Database', July 2022.

[13] IMF, 'Fiscal Monitor Database of Country Fiscal Measures in Response to the COVID-19 Pandemic', October 2021.

[14] Internal Displacement Monitoring Centre (IDMC), 'Mexico: Displacement Associated with Conflict and Violence', p. 1.

[15] National Human Rights Commission (CNDH), 'Consejo Consultivo Informe mensual Diciembre 2021' [Consultive Advice Monthly Report December 2021], December 2021, p. 7.

[16] David Esparza, Shane Johnson and Paul Gill, 'Why Did Mexico Become a Violent Country?', *Security Journal*, vol. 33, no. 1, June 2020, pp. 1–31.

COLOMBIA

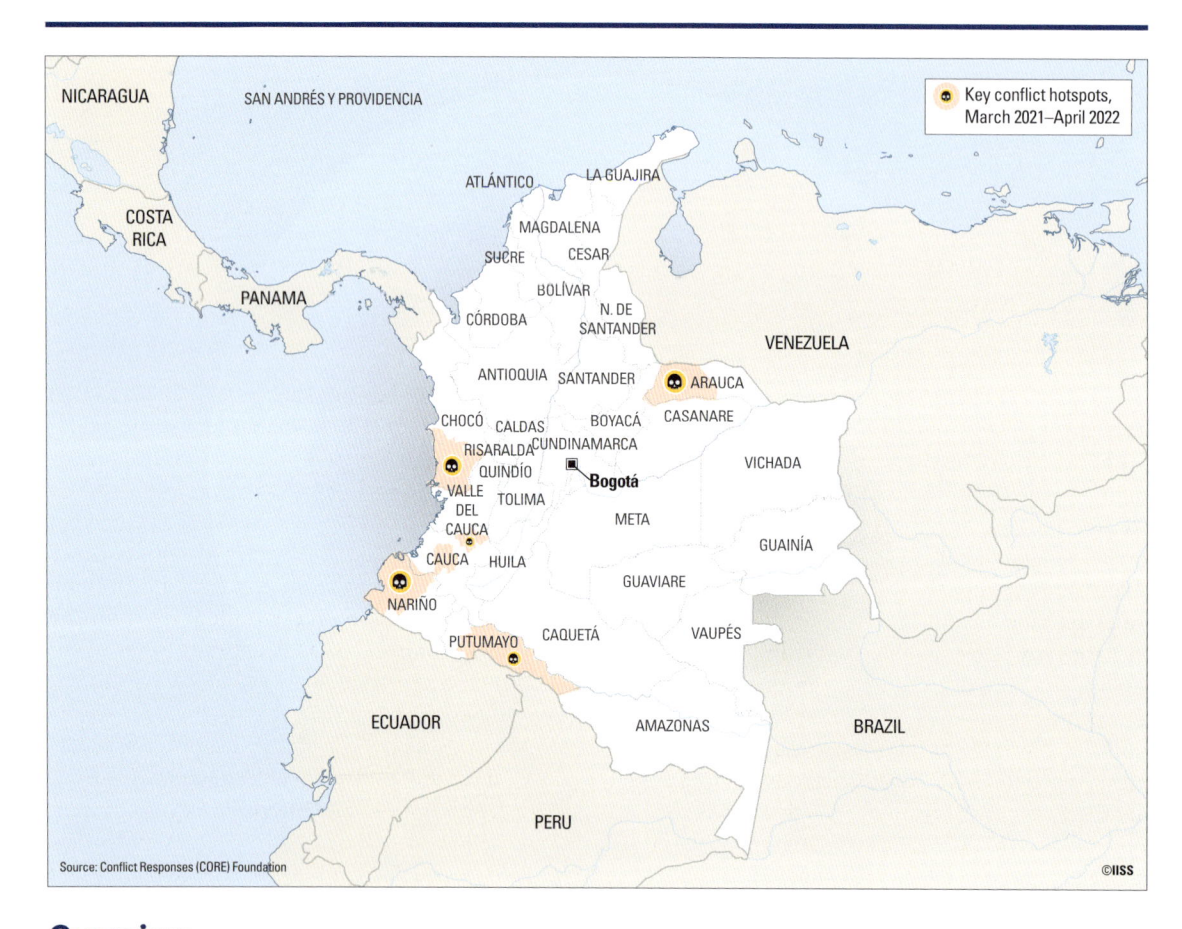

Overview

Colombia has been ravaged by violence since its independence in 1810. A civil war in 1948–58 – known as La Violencia – between the country's only two political parties at the time evolved in the 1960s to include multiple Marxist guerrilla groups fighting the state. Paramilitary groups emerged in the 1980s, supported by state authorities, drug traffickers and private actors. Since the early 1990s, economic incentives, especially drug trafficking, have played an increasing role in the conflict, bolstering armed groups like the Revolutionary Armed Forces of Colombia (FARC) and paramilitaries organised under the United Self-Defense Forces of Colombia (AUC), as well as splinter groups that have appeared more recently following the negotiation processes with these two armed actors. However, political ideology has not completely disappeared from the conflict.

By the early 2000s, the AUC controlled the majority of northern Colombia, while the guerrillas controlled most of southern and eastern Colombia. Between 2002 and 2006, the AUC engaged in negotiations with the government, leading to a disarmament, demobilisation and reintegration (DDR) process that culminated in 2006. Design and implementation setbacks during this process led to the emergence of criminal groups, labelled by the government as *bandas criminales* (criminal gangs). The largest of them, known as the Gulf Clan, still operates today, mainly in northern Colombia.

The Colombian state, with support from the United States under Plan Colombia (2000–15), was able to weaken FARC significantly throughout the 2000s, pushing the group into peace talks in 2012 that resulted in the signing of a peace agreement

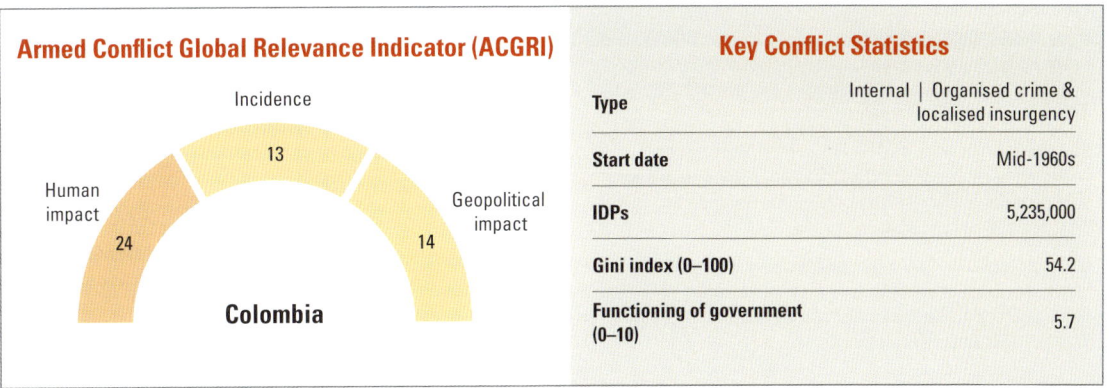

Armed Conflict Global Relevance Indicator (ACGRI)

- Incidence: 13
- Human impact: 24
- Geopolitical impact: 14

Colombia

Key Conflict Statistics

Type	Internal | Organised crime & localised insurgency
Start date	Mid-1960s
IDPs	5,235,000
Gini index (0–100)	54.2
Functioning of government (0–10)	5.7

ACGRI pillars: IISS calculation based on multiple sources for 2021 and January–April 2022 (scale: 0–100). See Notes on Methodology and Data Appendix for further details on Key Conflict Statistics.

in 2016. Since then, the guerrillas have handed over their weapons and the group has turned into a political party. Nonetheless, armed FARC dissident groups, led by former guerrilla commanders, continue to operate.

These groups, along with the National Liberation Army (ELN), which was not part of the peace process, have reshaped conflict dynamics in recent years in various regions of the country. In 2021, the Gulf Clan was the non-state armed group (NSAG) with the widest territorial presence and most significant military capabilities, followed closely by the ELN. However, two FARC dissident groups strengthened and became better organised, the first led by Miguel Botache Santillana (alias 'Gentil Duarte'), who – until his death in May 2022 – coordinated numerous FARC dissident units, and the second – known as 'Second Marquetalia' – led by a former FARC negotiator, alias 'Iván Márquez'. Since 2020, the Gulf Clan has also expanded its operations in northern Colombia.

Competition on former FARC-controlled territories and illicit economies continued to cause high levels of violence in 2021. In total, 96 massacres were registered, a steep escalation from the eight in 2015, and just above the 91 registered in 2020.[1] Homicides in areas affected by the armed conflicts reached levels slightly higher than those in 2012, when peace talks began.[2] Mass forced displacement also increased by 181% compared to 2020, to 74,000 people, and another 66,000 people were unable to move from their communities at some point in time due to violence.[3] Attacks against the civilian population also jumped by 37% in 2021 compared to 2020, to 2,435.[4] In addition, 135 armed confrontations between NSAGs were reported, up from 107 in 2020. By contrast, combat between state forces and NSAGs dropped to 203 cases, down from 267 in 2020.[5] Although state forces captured or killed some important NSAG commanders during the reporting period, these did not lead to a decrease in violence.

Violence against and between NSAGs intensified within Venezuela during 2021 and early 2022. With attacks against FARC dissidents and the death of three Second Marquetalia commanders in Venezuela, the country no longer seemed to be the brazen safe haven for all Colombian NSAGs that it once was.

The Biden administration continued to see Colombia as its main partner in the region, although it applied more pressure than the Trump administration had for the full implementation of the 2016 peace agreement, while still supporting Colombia's efforts against NSAGs and in dealing with the Venezuelan refugee emergency.

Conflict Parties

Colombian armed forces

Strength: Army: 185,900; navy: 56,400; air force: 13,650; National Police (PONAL): 172,400.

Areas of operation: Across the country, but limited presence in some rural areas such as the Catatumbo, Urabá, Eastern Plains, Pacific coast regions and border areas.

Colombian armed forces

Leadership: President Iván Duque (commander-in-chief); Diego Molano (minister of defence); Luis Fernando Navarro Jiménez (general commander).

Structure: Army, navy and air force. PONAL oversees public and civil security. PONAL has been controlled and administered by the Ministry of National Defence and has included militarised units since 1953.

History: Originated in the late eighteenth century as the Liberating Army of the independence movement against the Spanish Empire. The military forces were formally created with the 1821 Cúcuta Constitution.

Objectives: Defend national sovereignty, militarily attack and defeat NSAGs, and maintain rule and order.

Opponents: ELN, FARC dissidents, the Gulf Clan and other criminal organisations.

Affiliates/allies: PONAL.

Resources/capabilities: 2021 defence budget of US$5.91bn (excluding the PONAL budget). Overall capabilities and professionalisation have improved in recent decades.

Gentil Duarte's FARC dissidents

Strength: Approximately 3,500 members.[6]

Areas of operation: Presence in at least 15 of Colombia's 32 departments: Amazonas, Arauca, Bolívar, Caquetá, Casanare, Cauca, Guainía, Guaviare, Meta, Nariño, Norte de Santander, Putumayo, Valle del Cauca, Vaupés and Vichada.

Leadership: Miguel Botache Santillana (alias 'Gentil Duarte'; top commander and coordinator, until his death in May 2022). 1st Front: Néstor Gregorio Vera Fernández (alias 'Iván Mordisco'); 28th Front: Omar Pardo Galeano (alias 'Antonio Medina'); Western Coordinating Command: unknown after death of Euclides España Caicedo (alias 'Jonier').

Structure: Replicates the former FARC operational structure with fronts and mobile columns. However, leadership only coordinates how individual structures operate.

History: The group brought together multiple FARC units that rejected the 2016 peace agreement. Other units have emerged between 2018 and 2021. They all claim to be the 'true' FARC.

Objectives: Rebuild the old FARC, recover the areas of the old FARC and fight the state and 'establishment'.

Opponents: Colombian armed forces; the Gulf Clan in Bolívar and Nariño; the ELN in Cauca, Arauca and Bolívar; and Second Marquetalia units in Cauca, Nariño and Putumayo.

Affiliates/allies: ELN in Catatumbo; Mexican drug-trafficking organisations, mainly the Sinaloa Cartel and the Cartel Jalisco New Generation (CJNG).

Resources/capabilities: Inherited FARC's former economic structures and rent-seeking activities (including extortion, drug trafficking and illegal mining). Makes income through drug trafficking or tax collection on drug distribution in its areas of influence.

Second Marquetalia (FARC dissidents)

Strength: Around 2,000 members.[7]

Areas of operation: Border areas with Venezuela, mainly in the departments of Guainía, Norte de Santander and Vichada, and Cauca, Meta, Nariño and Putumayo.

Leadership: The main commanders include Luciano Marín Arango (alias 'Iván Márquez'); José Aldinever Sierra Sabogal (alias 'Zarco Aldinever'); and Géner García Molina (alias 'Jhon 40').

Structure: Has incorporated other groups under a claimed unified command. Its organisational structure includes a 'National Direction'.

History: Created in 2018 when a group of senior FARC commanders abandoned the reincorporation process and resumed fighting; its existence was publicly announced in August 2019.

Objectives: Recreate the original FARC, take over the state or initiate a new negotiation process.

Opponents: Colombian armed forces and Gentil Duarte's dissidents in Cauca, Nariño and Putumayo.

Affiliates/allies: The ELN, especially on a political level, but also on a local level in Cauca and Apure state, Venezuela.

Resources/capabilities: Its sources of financing include former undeclared assets of FARC, drug trafficking and illegal gold mining. Renewed weaponry with more modern rifles.

National Liberation Army (ELN)

Strength: Approximately 2,500 members in arms; 1,100 in Venezuela;[8] and an unknown number of part-time militia members.

Areas of operation: Operates in at least 13 of Colombia's 32 departments and some cities, including Cali, Cúcuta, Medellín and very limitedly in Bogotá.[9] Retains a particularly strong presence along the border with Venezuela, especially in the departments of Arauca and Norte de Santander, and, to a lesser extent, in Cesar, La Guajira and Vichada. It has also expanded greatly within Venezuela.

Leadership: Eliécer Erlington Chamorro Acosta (alias 'Antonio García'; commander).

National Liberation Army (ELN)

Structure: The Central Command directs strategy and is composed of four publicly recognised commanders and a larger 35-person National Direction. The ELN has seven regional war fronts, including the Camilo Torres Restrepo National Urban War Front.

History: Founded in 1964 by a group of left-wing intellectuals and students embracing liberation theology, who directly studied the Cuban Revolution.

Objectives: On paper, overthrow the Colombian government and create a socialist state; operationally, local 'armed resistance'.

Opponents: Colombian armed forces; the Rastrojos in Catatumbo (during 2021); the Gulf Clan in Antioquia, Bolívar, Chocó and Norte de Santander; and Gentil Duarte's dissidents in Arauca, Bolívar and Cauca.

Affiliates/allies: The Second Marquetalia politically and territorially in Cauca, Norte de Santander and Apure state, Venezuela.

Resources/capabilities: Extortion, illegal mining and gasoline trafficking are important sources of income. Imposes taxes on and regulation over the drug trade in Cauca, Chocó and Norte de Santander.

The Gulf Clan (also known as Gaitanistas Self-Defence Forces of Colombia (AGC) or the Urabeños)

Strength: Approximately 1,600–1,700 members, though estimates vary.[10]

Areas of operation: Presence in at least 17 departments in Colombia, as well as in Panama and Venezuela.[11] Based in the Urabá region, in northwest Colombia. Has an extensive presence in the city of Medellín and departments of Antioquia, Atlántico, Bolívar, Cesar, Chocó, Córdoba, La Guajira, Magdalena, Nariño, Norte de Santander, Santander, Sucre and Valle del Cauca.

Leadership: Jobanis de Jesús Ávila Villadiego (alias 'Chiquito Malo') and José Gonzalo Sánchez Sánchez (alias 'Gonzalito') after the capture of Dairo Antonio Úsuga David (alias 'Otoniel'), in October 2021.

Structure: Various local fronts are directly commanded by the leadership in Urabá, while the other local criminal organisations are subcontracted and expected to provide services and follow strategic orders when requested.

History: Emerged from the demobilisation of AUC paramilitaries in 2006. Some of its leaders were former Popular Liberation Army (EPL) combatants who demobilised in 1991, but later joined the AUC.

Objectives: Drug trafficking. Using the name Gaitanistas Self-Defence Forces is a way of legitimising itself as a group with political goals.

Opponents: Colombian armed forces; ELN in Bolívar, Chocó and Norte de Santander; Gentil Duarte's dissidents in Nariño; and the Caparros in Antioquia.

Affiliates/allies: Corrupt elements of the Colombian armed forces.

Resources/capabilities: Financing mainly comes from transnational drug trafficking, providing services for independent drug traffickers and illegal mining. Multiple group members, including leaders, run their own international trafficking routes.

Conflict Drivers

Geopolitical and geostrategic influences

Venezuela's support for NSAGs:
Venezuela continues to be an important ally for NSAGs, who have used the country to support their operations in Colombia. Venezuela, though, is no longer the safe haven for all NSAGs that it historically has been. In April 2020, conflict broke out between Venezuelan state forces and the 10th Front FARC dissident group, while three top Second Marquetalia FARC dissident commanders were killed in Venezuela in May and December 2021. It appears that only the ELN can still count on consistent, high-level support from the Venezuelan regime.

Security

Ineffective security policy:
Security policy in Colombia has focused on killing or capturing leaders of NSAGs to provide protection to local populations and apply the rule of law, and on the drug trade to undermine NSAGs' finances. These policies, however, have not led to a decrease in violence. Given the complex landscape of multiple NSAGs, attacking one often means strengthening another.

Political

Limited state presence and legitimacy:
The state does not respond to local needs in the areas affected by armed conflicts in Colombia. Its presence is often limited to military and police forces, and local authorities' ability to act is extremely restricted by budgetary constraints. As a result, the state lacks legitimacy among these populations. In areas such as Arauca and Tumaco, state institutions are stronger but corruption, insecurity and a lack of funding undermine their effectiveness.

The 2016 peace agreement looked to address these issues by building peace and strong institutions at the same time, but it has suffered from piecemeal implementation under the Duque administration. The killing of social leaders and ex-combatants, as well as the poor implementation of security aspects of the peace accord, have both contributed to and been a result of worsening armed conflict.

Economic

Socio-economic inequalities:
Long-lasting socio-economic inequalities continue to fuel the conflict. The United Nations Development Programme classifies Colombia in the 10th percentile of the most unequal countries in terms of human development.[12] This inequality is most visible when comparing urban and rural areas, with urban multidimensional poverty at 12.5% compared to 37.1% in rural areas.[13] Job opportunities and security in rural areas are also extremely low, as are job quality and pay.

Land ownership is also extremely unequal: Colombia's Gini index for land distribution as of 2016 was 0.9 (on a scale from zero to one, where one is the highest possible inequality).[14] Land ownership and armed conflict form a vicious cycle in which the former fuels the latter by promoting illicit crops, while the latter causes increased concentration of land ownership in fewer hands.

Illegal economies:
Coca cultivation (and cocaine production) and illegal mining are economic drivers of conflict, providing NSAGs with most of their financial resources. NSAGs either tax these economies or participate directly in them. Some areas of armed dispute among NSAGs, such as Cauca, Nariño and Putumayo, are also home to some of the largest coca crops and highest levels of drug trafficking.

Key Events in 2021–22

POLITICAL EVENTS

26 January 2021
Colombian minister of defence Carlos Holmes Trujillo dies of COVID-19-related pneumonia.

28 April
Nationwide protests against a proposed tax-reform bill begin, lasting three months in numerous cities across Colombia.

MILITARY/VIOLENT EVENTS

21 March 2021
Fighting breaks out between Venezuelan state forces and 10th Front FARC dissidents in Apure state, Venezuela.

April
The government downgrades the EPL, also known as Los Pelusos, from an 'organised armed group' to an 'organised criminal group'.

17 May
Second Marquetalia dissident ideologue Seuxis Hernández (alias 'Jesús Santrich'), is killed in Venezuela. Second Marquetalia publicly recognises his death the next day.

28 May
Thirteen people are killed in one day in ongoing protests in the city of Cali.

31 May
Eight Venezuelan soldiers kidnapped by 10th Front FARC dissidents are released, putting an end to the conflict between the group and Venezuelan forces.

25 June
The ELN announces that Antonio García is its new leader, after the resignation of former top commander Nicolás Rodríguez Bautista (alias 'Gabino'), due to health issues.

26 August
Duque enacts into law the 16 special congressional districts 'Special Circumscriptions for Peace', after the Constitutional Court ruled that they had in fact been approved by Congress in 2017.

1 October
The Constitutional Court rules that the Truth Commission's mandate (from the 2016 peace agreement) is to be extended by seven months.

23–24 November
UN Secretary-General António Guterres visits Colombia to commemorate the five-year anniversary of the signing of the 2016 peace agreement.

Early December
Aliases 'El Paisa' and 'Romaña' are killed in Apure state, Venezuela, apparently by mercenaries hired by Gentil Duarte.

19 January 2022
Colombia's Constitutional Court rules that the process to restart aerial fumigation of coca crops violates communities' rights to effective participation in the decision.

2 January 2022
The conflict between the ELN and the 10th, 28th and 45th FARC dissident fronts begins in Arauca and Apure state, Venezuela.

23–26 February
The ELN declares a national 'armed strike', aiming to blockade the areas where the group operates as a way to protest against the Duque government.

5 March
A delegation of senior US officials visits Venezuela for talks with members of the Maduro government to discuss energy security, among other things. Duque, who was not consulted on the move, reacts with outrage.

13 March
Congressional elections are held throughout Colombia, including votes for the 16 Special Circumscriptions for Peace, on one of the most peaceful congressional election days in Colombia in decades.

28 March
A military operation in Putumayo against FARC dissidents kills 11, allegedly including four civilians.

19 April
The Colombian Congress holds a debate on a censorship motion against the minister of defence, Diego Molano, after a military operation on 28 March in Putumayo allegedly killed four civilians.

4 May
Otoniel, former head of the Gulf Clan and one of Colombia's biggest drug traffickers, is extradited to the US.

25 May
Miguel Botache Santanilla (alias 'Gentil Duarte') is killed by an explosive attack in the camp in which he was hiding in Venezuela.

19 June
Gustavo Petro from the leftist Historical Pact coalition wins the presidential run-off election.

Responses to the Conflict

Security

Colombian security policy has prioritised capturing or killing important NSAG leaders and a coercive approach to the drug trade. The government made some progress towards these goals in 2021. Various NSAG leaders were killed or captured, most famously the commander of the Gulf Clan, Otoniel, considered to be perhaps Colombia's biggest drug trafficker. Colombia also recorded near-record levels of coca-crop eradication and record cocaine seizures. However, these successes have not translated into a decrease in violence.

Against this backdrop, the armed forces and police experienced legitimacy losses among the general population amid a series of corruption scandals involving the armed forces and widespread outrage against the police for its violent repression of major protests in 2021. Among the most egregious corruption scandals to be revealed were links between the armed forces' former commander, retired General Leonardo Barrero, other retired military leaders, and alias 'Matamba', a drug trafficker and commander of the Gulf Clan in Nariño. Furthermore, in June members of the army were removed from their posts for likely involvement in a car bombing inside a military base in Cúcuta, on the border with Venezuela. Legitimacy was also undermined by a lack of effective oversight on public forces, with the Ministry of Defence closing 211 out of 231 investigations against police officers (for abuses during the 2021 protests) and imposing only nine punishments.[15]

The 2016 peace accord with FARC included six points: comprehensive rural reform; political participation; the end of the conflict, including ceasefires and demobilisation; addressing the problem of illicit drugs, including an alternative development programme; victims, with transitional-justice mechanisms negotiated; and implementation. It also contained useful tools for addressing ongoing violence. Its implementation, however, has been piecemeal. The National Commission for Security Guarantees was meant to create a policy to dismantle NSAGs, but it has not produced such a policy yet, and it is unlikely to do so. Additionally, the Special Jurisdiction for Peace – the restorative-justice tribunal created by the accord – recently argued that the government has no clear policy for protecting ex-combatants.

Economic/development

Of the goals of the 2016 peace agreement, rural-development reforms and illicit-crop substitution have lagged the most. The implementation of the rural reform envisaged by the agreement to close economic and land inequality gaps in the country – among the main conflict drivers – has been slow and fragmentary: between December 2016 and October 2021, 69% of stipulations did not progress sufficiently to be completed within their designated time frames and another 14% were not initiated.[16] The illicit-crop substitution programme is also unlikely to be completed as expected, if at all in some areas.

Additionally, after the economic downturn caused by the coronavirus pandemic, and in an effort to shield the incomes of the most vulnerable segments of the population from rising inflation, the government adopted a new unconditional cash-transfer policy, 'Ingreso Solidario', which reached four million vulnerable households that were not already covered by a socio-economic protection programme.[17] Nonetheless, policy results are deficient: despite decreasing last year, the monetary poverty rate in rural areas remains higher than

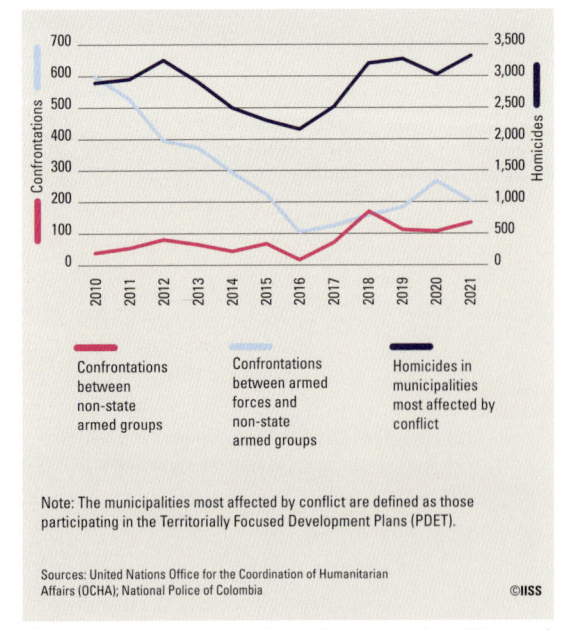

Figure 1: Homicides in conflict-affected municipalities and confrontations with non-state armed groups, 2010–21

the national average.[18] Similarly, national unemployment is yet to recover from the labour-market shock induced by the pandemic.

Diplomacy

The US government's recent push for a comprehensive implementation of the peace agreement, coupled with existing European Union support, may lead Colombia to make more rapid progress than it has done previously on the issue. Additionally, the recent removal of the former FARC from the US Foreign Terrorist Organization list on 30 November 2021 will allow US economic and political support to play a wider, and perhaps more effective, role in supporting peace-agreement implementation. Before this, support for ex-combatant reintegration and the illicit-crop support programme had been minimal to none. In parallel, the US continued to support anti-narcotics efforts including forced manual eradication of coca crops and interdiction efforts.

Conflict Outlook

Political scenarios

Gustavo Petro, a leftist candidate and former guerrilla fighter who demobilised in the 1990s, defeated Rodolfo Hernández, an independent candidate and former mayor of Bucaramanga, in the presidential run-off election in June 2022. His victory will likely mark an inflection point in current security policies, with a shift away from hardline narcotics policies and the so-called 'war on drugs' approach, as well as from automatic alignment with the US.

Petro will probably have a difficult relationship with some factions in the armed forces, given his history as a guerrilla member. He has also committed to continue the implementation of the 2016 peace agreement, while signalling his willingness to seek a fast negotiation with the ELN. During his campaign, he also said that he would explore negotiations with other armed groups such as the Gulf Clan and FARC dissidents. Yet there is no guarantee that negotiations would be successful, especially with the ELN, as its horizontal structure and the autonomy of its local units will likely hinder a cohesive approach to peace talks.

Escalation potential and conflict-related risks

Escalation is possible, if unlikely, for different local conflicts in Colombia. If Gentil Duarte's FARC dissidents look to attack the Second Marquetalia wherever they find them, conflict could break out in places like Norte de Santander and Caquetá. If the ELN's current conflict with the FARC dissident fronts in Arauca becomes a confrontation between all ELN units and all FARC dissidents connected to Gentil Duarte, conflict could spread to Casanare, northern Cauca and Nariño.

Conflicts could de-escalate if one of the NSAGs involved achieves control over disputed areas. Nonetheless, in almost all these conflicts, victory for any NSAG is far off, except perhaps for the ELN against FARC dissidents in Arauca.

Local humanitarian initiatives, through which communities create proposals that try to pressure armed actors to act according to international humanitarian law, could mitigate the effects of armed conflict on local communities. However, these initiatives had little success both before and during the reporting period. NSAGs have often rejected them, and direct dialogue between NSAGs and local communities has only been successful in the unique case of Catatumbo.

Strategic implications and global influences

The US is heavily invested and interested in Colombia's stability, as is made clear by the Biden administration's continued support for the fight against drug trafficking and NSAGs, and in the full implementation of the 2016 peace agreement.

Maintaining stability in Colombia also has implications for great-power competition in the region, given the country's alignment with the US and its role in containing Venezuela and, through this, Russia's influence in the region. It is also an important partner for the US in mitigating the Venezuelan migration crisis and related regional instability, having welcomed and hosted 1.8m Venezuelan refugees and migrants, the vast majority since 2018 (for which the US has also provided economic support).[19]

Moves by the US to negotiate access to cheaper Venezuelan oil in the aftermath of Russia's invasion of Ukraine could hint at a possible weakening or lifting of sanctions against the Maduro regime and some rapprochement between the two countries in the short to medium term. The re-establishment of US–Venezuela relations may improve stability, as it will likely increase pressure on Nicolás Maduro to fight Colombian NSAGs operating in Venezuela. Improved US–Venezuela relations will also likely mitigate uncontrolled migration flows to neighbouring countries, including Colombia. Petro's willingness to re-establish diplomatic relations with Caracas will probably add momentum to a new regional approach to tackle the Venezuela crisis.

Notes

[1] Indepaz, 'Masacres en Colombia durante el 2020, 2021 y 2022' [Report of Massacres in Colombia During 2020, 2021 and 2022], 5 March 2022; and Indepaz, 'Posacuerdo traumático: Coletazos en la transición desde el acuerdo de paz al posconflicto' [Post-agreement Trauma: the Transition from the Peace Agreement to Post-conflict], 2020.

[2] Statistics from the National Police, 'Estadistica delectiva' [Criminal Statistics], 2010–21, homicide statistics cross-checked against the 170 municipalities included in the Territorially Focused Development Programmes (PDETs).

[3] Humanitarian Advisory Team, 'Colombia: Impacto y tendencias humanitarias entre enero y diciembre de 2021' [Colombia: Humanitarian Impact and Trends Between January and December 2021], 8 February 2022.

[4] United Nations Office of the Coordinator for Humanitarian Affairs (OCHA), 'Monitor: Colombia', 2020–21.

[5] Ibid.

[6] Indepaz, 'Los focos del conflicto en Colombia' [The Areas of Conflict in Colombia], September 2021, p. 7.

[7] Ibid.

[8] Ibid.; and 'Así delinquen en Venezuela 1.500 integrantes del Eln y las disidencias' [This Is How 1,500 Members of the ELN and Dissidents Operate in Venezuela], El Tiempo, 24 May 2021.

[9] Conflict Responses (CORE) Foundation conflict monitoring.

[10] Indepaz, 'Los focos del conflicto en Colombia'.

[11] Conflict Responses (CORE) Foundation conflict monitoring.

[12] United Nations Development Programme (UNDP), 'Human Development Report 2019: Beyond Income, Beyond Averages, Beyond Today: Inequalities in Human Development in the 21st Century', 2019, pp. 300–3.

[13] National Administrative Statistical Department (DANE), 'Pobreza multidimensional' [Multidimensional Poverty], 2 September 2021.

[14] 'El 64 % de hogares rurales no cuentan con acceso a la tierra' [64% of Rural Homes Do Not Have Access to Land], El Tiempo, 26 November 2016; and Fabio Alberto Pachón Ariza, 'Distribución de la propiedad rural en Colombia en el siglo XXI' [Distribution of Rural Property in Colombia in the 21st Century], 2021, p. 3.

[15] Juan Pappier (@JuanPappierHRW), tweet, 8 February 2022.

[16] Kroc Institute, 'Five Years of Peace Agreement Implementation in Colombia: Achievements, Challenges, and Opportunities to Increase Implementation Levels: December 2016–October 2021', December 2021.

[17] National Planning Department (DNP), 'Ingreso Solidario se fortalece: cambian montos, cobertura y periodiciad de pagos' [Ingreso Solidario Is Strengthened: Change in Amount, Coverage and Payment Frequency], 22 February 2022.

[18] National Administrative Department of Statistics, 'Comunicado de prensa: Pobreza monetaria 2021' [Press Release: Monetary Poverty 2021], 26 April 2022.

[19] Paula Rossiasco and Greta Granados De Orbegoso, 'Waking Up to a New Reality: Latin America's Response to the Venezuelan Exodus', World Bank Blogs, 7 April 2022.

BRAZIL

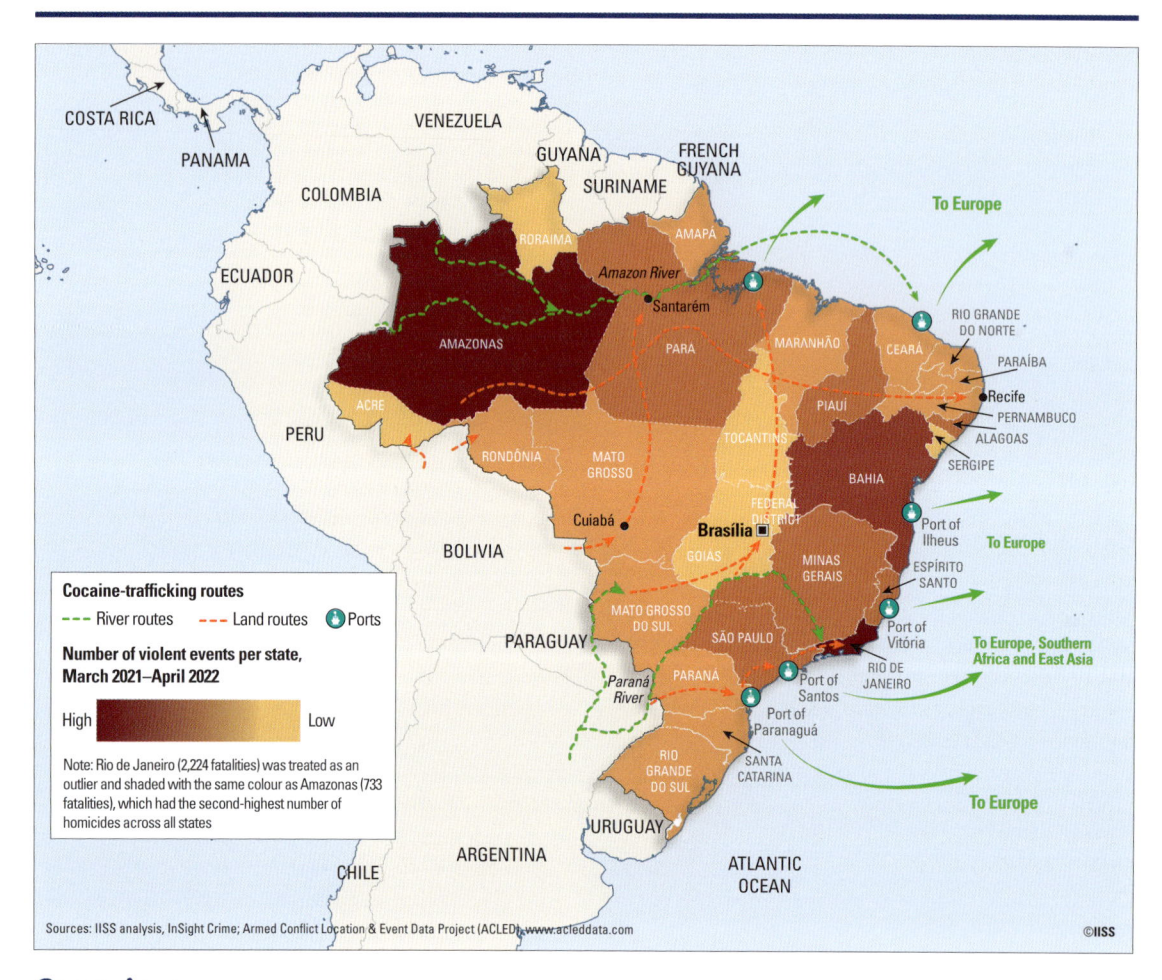

Overview

Brazil's battle against armed groups and drug trafficking has been ongoing for decades. Criminal gangs have long controlled territory, challenged the state's rule and provided socio-economic goods to those who live in their areas of control. Higher levels of incarceration have not led to greater peace. Rather uniquely, Brazil's criminal groups are largely prison-based organisations. Brazil's three most fearsome criminal organisations were born, nurtured and continue to thrive in the country's broken prison system, justifying their purpose as fighting for the rights of the downtrodden and jailed populations. The Red Command (CV), Brazil's oldest organised-crime group, started in 1979 in the Candido Mendes prison on Rio de Janeiro's Ilha Grande. The First Capital Command (PCC) is the CV's main rival, formed after a riot in Taubaté prison in São Paulo in the early 1990s. The Family of the North (FDN), based in the Amazon region and headquartered in Manaus, has experienced major setbacks in the last few years.

Contests between criminal organisations have been punctuated by the presence of powerful militia groups in states like Rio de Janeiro. These groups, comprised of police officers and members of the state security services (both former and current), often operate in a similar fashion – controlling territory, extorting businesses and increasingly competing over the drug-trafficking business. Brazilian President Jair Bolsonaro's proximity to many police unions, well-known affinity for the Brazilian armed forces and hardline security policies have given the impression

Armed Conflict Global Relevance Indicator (ACGRI)

Incidence: 66
Human impact: 6
Geopolitical impact: 0

Brazil

Key Conflict Statistics

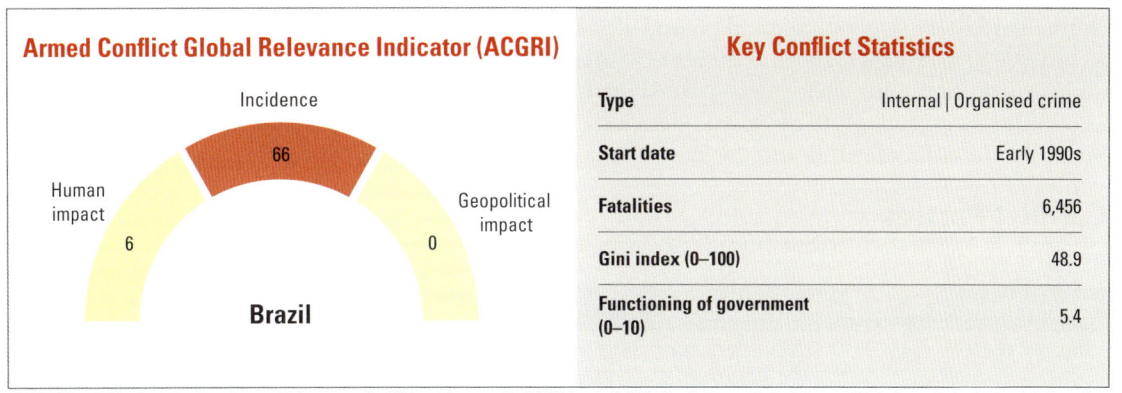

Type	Internal | Organised crime
Start date	Early 1990s
Fatalities	6,456
Gini index (0–100)	48.9
Functioning of government (0–10)	5.4

ACGRI pillars: IISS calculation based on multiple sources for 2021 and January–April 2022 (scale: 0–100). See Notes on Methodology and Data Appendix for further details on Key Conflict Statistics.

that, at best, the current administration tolerates the presence of militias and, at worst, actively works to provide them with political protection.

In the reporting period, three major trends stood out in Brazil's armed conflict. Firstly, criminal groups not only fought one another in contested territory but sought to make gains in areas hitherto dominated by rival factions. For instance, the PCC fought the CV and made incursions on the latter's home turf in Rio – a prospect that would have been unthinkable just a few years ago. This is a testament to shifting alliance structures and the desire to take advantage of opportunities where they exist in a contested landscape, but it also highlights an increasingly intense fight for territory in Brazil. Likewise, both the PCC and the CV have challenged the FDN on its home turf in the Amazon. Criminal organisations can no longer take their home bases for granted.

Secondly, competition for Amazonas State (and, to a lesser extent, Acre State) intensified. The state has grown in strategic significance because of its distinctive geographic features and vastness, making it simultaneously an excellent state to traffic illicit products through and a very difficult terrain to patrol. The region borders Colombia and Peru, which are both major coca producers. Facilitated by a lack of border control, the flow of illicit products from both countries across the borders is constant and easy. The presence of Venezuelan refugees in Roraima State, who are actively recruited by both the PCC and the CV, also partially enables criminal groups' activities in the Amazon. By some estimates, the state's population has increased by around 25%, driven largely by Venezuelans. The PCC has also fortified ties with Venezuela's criminal organisations, especially the Tren de Aragua, and amassed a greater arsenal of weapons by smuggling them across the porous border with Venezuela.

Thirdly, groups continued their drive to 'internationalise' their operations. In past years, Paraguay and Bolivia have received the bulk of attention, especially from the PCC and the CV. In 2021, there were signs that Brazilian criminal groups had begun to turn their attention toward Argentina, which had previously been spared much of the violence characteristic of the competition between the PCC and the CV in Paraguay and Bolivia. Currently, the PCC and the CV seem to have only an incipient presence in Argentina, but further expansion, driven by economic and business dynamics, cannot be ruled out. Shipping costs from traditional Brazilian ports, such as Santos in São Paulo, have increased. This has made ports such as the Port of Rosario in Argentina attractive alternatives as they are capable of serving similar international markets and have similar logistics operations. Economic challenges and poorly paid customs and police officers also make Argentina an attractive target for groups like the PCC, which excel at co-opting security officials.

In 2021, Brazil registered 41,100 homicides, a rate of 18.5 per 100,000, marking a slight decline from 2020.[1] While this is still a higher number of homicides than in Colombia, Mexico and Venezuela, these numbers compare favourably to the high-water mark for homicides in Brazil in 2017, when nearly 60,000 and a nationwide rate of 30.8 per 100,000 were registered.[2]

The reduction in homicide numbers also coincided with a number of police-inflicted killings owing partly to the hardline security policies favoured by many politicians, including Bolsonaro.

During the first three months of 2021, police killed a record 453 people, showing that despite a Supreme Court ban on such raids, police were granted many 'extraordinary exceptions' to carry out operations.[3] By far the most discussed security incident in 2021 was the early May police raid on the Jacarezinho *favela* in Rio de Janeiro. The raid, which lasted a full day and took place under the Supreme Court ban, left at least 27 suspects and one police officer dead, marking one of the deadliest police raids in history.[4]

Conflict Parties

Military Police of Rio de Janeiro (PMERJ/PM)

Strength: 41,024 members.[5]

Areas of operation: Rio de Janeiro State.

Leadership: Col. Rogério Figueiredo de Lacerda (commander-in-chief).

Structure: Accountable to the Rio State government. Its hierarchy resembles that of the army and its members are reserves for the armed forces.

History: Created in May 1809. Current structure introduced in July 1975.

Objectives: Fight organised-crime groups.

Opponents: Organised-crime groups and militias.

Affiliates/allies: Unofficially, some militias and gangs, such as the Pure Third Command (TCP).

Resources/capabilities: Weapons currently used include IMBEL *ParaFAL* 7.62mm battle rifle and the IMBEL IA2 assault rifle.

Red Command (CV)

Strength: 5,000 members in Rio de Janeiro State, and an estimated 30,000 associates in Amazonas State (and some in Acre State).[6]

Areas of operation: Rio de Janeiro, Acre, Amapá, Alagoas, Ceará, Federal District, Pará, Rio Grande do Norte, Rondônia, Roraima, Mato Grosso and Tocantins. Traditionally headquartered in the Alemão *favela* complex in the northern zone of Rio de Janeiro. Also present in Bolivia, Colombia and Paraguay.

Leadership: Márcio Santos Nepomuceno (alias 'Marcinho VP'), and Elias Pereira da Silva (alias 'Elias Maluco'), lead the group from jail. Gelson Lima Carnaúba (alias 'Gê'), one of the founders of the FDN, switched sides in 2018 and now leads the CV in Amazonas.

Structure: Decentralised structure with 'area leaders' in charge of neighbourhoods and favelas, 'managers' responsible for drug-dealing spots, which are secured by 'soldiers' who fend off threats by other dealers or the police. 'Scouts' keep watch for potential risks and warn 'soldiers'.

History: The oldest and largest gang in Rio de Janeiro, which formed around 1979 in a maximum-security prison in Ilha Grande, off the southern coast of Rio de Janeiro. Involved in transnational drug trafficking since the 1980s, importing cocaine from Colombia and exporting it to Europe. Its activity declined after a police pacification programme in the Alemão favela complex in November 2010, but the group has since regained prominence and spread throughout Brazil and beyond.

Objectives: Maintain and enlarge its operating area to other neighbourhoods in Rio de Janeiro and other Brazilian states to expand its drug-trafficking market and extortion practices.

Opponents: In Rio de Janeiro: PMERJ, TCP, Friends of Friends (ADA), militia groups, PCC. In Brazil: 13 Tram (B13), Guardians of the State (GDE), Crime Syndicate (SDC), Tocantins Mafia (MF), Class A Command (CCA), 30 Tram (B30), Northern Union (UDN), PCC.

Affiliates/allies: In Rio de Janeiro: None. In Brazil: First Group of Santa Catarina.

Resources/capabilities: Revenue sources include drug trafficking, extortion of small businesses, kidnapping for ransom and weapons smuggling. Members are equipped with large numbers of handguns, AK-47s, bazookas and grenades.

First Capital Command (PCC)

Strength: Approximately 30,000.[7]

Areas of operation: Based in São Paulo State but maintains operations throughout much of Brazil, except the states of Goiás, Maranhão and Paraná. Also in Argentina, Bolivia, Colombia, Mozambique, the Netherlands, Paraguay, Peru, Portugal, South Africa and Venezuela.

Leadership: Marcos Willians Herbas Camacho (alias 'Marcola'), took over the leadership in 2002, although he has been imprisoned since 1999.

First Capital Command (PCC)

Structure: Highly organised, with a CEO and strategic Deliberative Council (13 members); board of directors (three members), Administrative Board; Legal Board; State Board; Economic Board; Institutional Relations Board; and Human Resources. These groupings are referred to as 'sintonias'. The structure on the street is comprised of 'managers', 'soldiers', 'scouts' and 'killers'.

History: Created by eight inmates on 31 August 1993 in a prison in Taubaté. In May 2006, after Marcola and 760 other prisoners were transferred to another prison, inmates rebelled in 74 state prisons and there were coordinated attacks on police officers, vehicles, jails and public buildings. More than 500 people were killed within a week.

Objectives: Deepen and entrench its position of power in Brazil and beyond.

Opponents: In Rio de Janeiro: PMERJ, TCP, ADA, CV. In Amazonas state: CV, FDN.

Affiliates/allies: In Rio de Janeiro: TCP, ADA.

Resources/capabilities: Revenue sources include drug trafficking, bank and cargo robbery, money laundering, illegal gambling and kidnapping for ransom. The average revenue of the PCC is US$100 million per year.[8] The gang uses pistols, rifles, bazookas and grenades.

Pure Third Command (TCP)

Strength: Unknown.

Areas of operation: Rio de Janeiro.

Leadership: Fernando Gomes de Freitas, Alvaro Malaquias Santa Rosa (alias 'Peixão').

Structure: Decentralised structure with 'area leaders' in charge of neighbourhoods and favelas, 'managers' responsible for drug-dealing spots, which are secured by 'soldiers' who fend off threats by other dealers or the police. 'Scouts' keep watch for potential risks and warn 'soldiers'.

History: Created from the 2002 union of dissidents from ADA and the now-defunct Third Command (formed in the 1980s) after the death of Uê (who had been expelled from the CV for treason) and the arrest of Celsinho da Vila Vintém (head of ADA). Has acquired partial control over several *favelas* since 2016, establishing itself as the second-most powerful criminal organisation in Rio after the CV (excluding the vigilante militias). During 2017 and 2018, the rapid decline of ADA led many of its members to switch their allegiance to the TCP. The TCP's evangelical Christian members have been known to attack and expel followers of Afro-Brazilian religions from their areas.

Objectives: Maintain areas currently under its control and expand its operating area to other neighbourhoods in Rio de Janeiro and other states.

Opponents: CV, ADA, militias, PMERJ.

Affiliates/allies: PCC.

Resources/capabilities: Revenue sources include drug trafficking and extortion. Weapons include pistols, rifles, bazookas and grenades.

Friends of Friends (ADA)

Strength: Unknown, although numbers have been waning for several years.

Areas of operation: Rio de Janeiro.

Leadership: Celso Luis Rodrigues (alias 'Celsinho da Vila Vintém'), one of the gang's founders.

Structure: Decentralised structure with 'area leaders' in charge of neighbourhoods and favelas, 'managers' responsible for drug-dealing spots, which are secured by 'soldiers' who fend off threats by other dealers or the police. 'Scouts' keep watch for potential risks and warn 'soldiers'.

History: Created in 1998, in recent years ADA has suffered heavy losses in clashes with the CV and, to a lesser extent, the TCP.

Objectives: Maintain its few areas of control in Rio de Janeiro city and expand operations to other neighbourhoods, especially outside the Rio metropolitan area where there is less competition.

Opponents: CV, TCP, militias, PMERJ.

Affiliates/allies: PCC.

Resources/capabilities: Main revenue source is drug trafficking. Weapons include guns, pistols, rifles, bazookas and grenades.

Militias (various)

Strength: Unknown.

Areas of operation: Ninety-six of 163 neighbourhoods around Rio de Janeiro city, particularly in the western neighbourhoods of Campo Grande, Paciência and Santa Cruz, as well as areas to the north of the city, such as Seropédica and Nova Iguaçu in Baixada Fluminense.

Leadership: The Justice League, the largest and most organised of the Rio militias, is led by Wellington da Silva Braga, also known as 'Ecko'. Brothers Jerominho and Natalino Guimarães, the League's founders, remain influential. The leadership of other smaller militia groups is unclear.

Militias (various)

Structure: Similar structure to gangs, with area leaders, managers and soldiers, although at a different scale. Leaders control more than one neighbourhood or region and managers are responsible for a region or neighbourhood. Unlike in drug groups, soldiers operate from privileged positions (such as police stations). 'Killers' are responsible for executions.

History: Expanded rapidly during the 2000s. Comprised of former or current police officers (mostly from the PMERJ), firefighters and prison guards. The militias claim to provide security, but also traffic drugs, and extort, abduct and kill locals.

Objectives: Expand control over licit and illicit business and gain political influence, including by directly holding public offices in municipalities.

Opponents: ADA, CV, occasionally the PMERJ.

Affiliates/allies: TCP.

Resources/capabilities: Revenue sources include both licit and illicit business, such as drug trafficking, extortion, murder-for-hire operations, oil theft and sale, money laundering, real-estate transactions, and internet and TV services. Since militia members are often law-enforcement agents, they have access to the same weapons as those agencies, especially .40-calibre pistols and various types of rifles.

Family of the North (FDN)

Strength: Possibly the second-largest criminal group in the country with as many as 13,000 members.[9]

Areas of operation: Amazonas, Acre and Ceará states.

Leadership: José Roberto Barbosa (alias 'Zé Roberto da Compensa'), and his son Luciano da Silva Barbosa (alias 'L7').

Structure: Decentralised structure with 'area leaders' in charge of neighbourhoods and favelas, 'managers' responsible for drug-dealing spots, which are secured by 'soldiers' who fend off threats by other dealers or the police. 'Scouts' keep watch for potential risks and warn 'soldiers'.

History: Created by Carnaúba and Barbosa between 2006 and 2007, it became widely known after prison massacres in Manaus in 2015. That year, the FDN, together with the CV, carried out murders of PCC leaders; efforts by the state to broker a truce failed. The FDN competes for the treasured 'Solimões route', used to transport cocaine produced in Colombia and Peru through rivers in the Amazon region.

Objectives: Expand and consolidate control of drug-trafficking routes in the Amazon region; survive the onslaught from the CV in Amazonas.

Opponents: PCC, ADA, GDE, Primeiro Grupo Catarinense, CV.

Affiliates/allies: Okaida.

Resources/capabilities: Revenue sources include drug trafficking and money laundering. Members use pistols, rifles, bazookas and grenades.

Family of the North–Pure (FDN–P)

Strength: Unknown.

Areas of operation: Amazonas State.

Leadership: João Pinto Carioca (alias 'João Branco').

Structure: Decentralised structure with 'area leaders' in charge of neighbourhoods and favelas, 'managers' responsible for drug-dealing spots, which are secured by 'soldiers' who fend off threats by other dealers or the police. 'Scouts' keep watch for potential risks and warn 'soldiers'.

History: Created in 2019 by João Branco, a former senior member of FDN, who was dissatisfied with the group's waning influence inside prisons and decreasing drug sales following the end of its alliance with the CV. From a federal prison in Paraná, Branco gathered FDN members loyal to him in Amazonas to eliminate FDN leadership inside the prisons. This command leaked, sparking a war between FDN and FDN–P that led to the deaths of over 55 prisoners.[10]

Objectives: Eliminate FDN.

Opponents: FDN.

Affiliates/allies: Unknown.

Resources/capabilities: Revenue sources include drug trafficking and money laundering. Members use pistols, rifles, bazookas and grenades.

Other conflict parties

There are many other relevant criminal organisations whose territory is more circumscribed, such as the 13 Tram (B13) and Ifara. They became more relevant throughout 2021, precisely by allying themselves with Brazil's largest criminal organisations and playing an active role in achieving territorial expansion. Like their larger allies, they are mostly prison-based criminal organisations.

Figure 1: Selected weapons seizures, May–November 2021

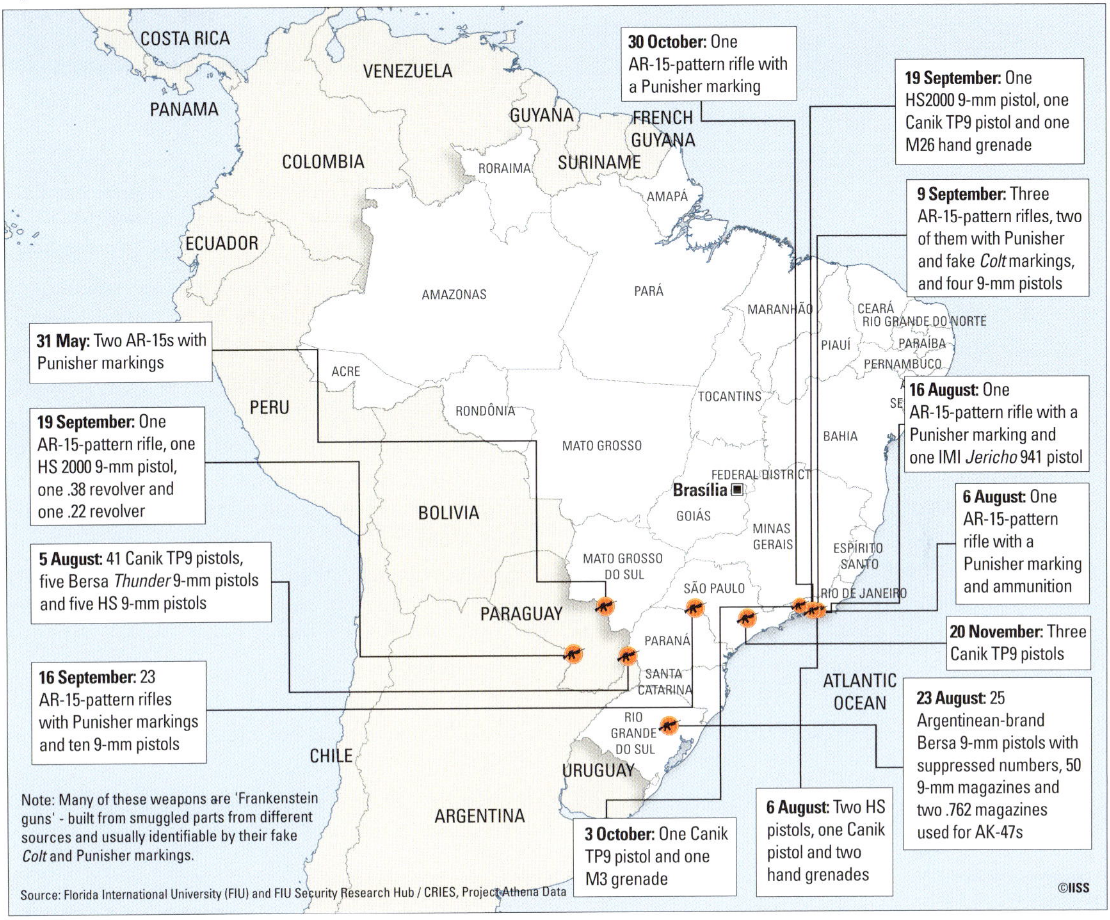

30 October: One AR-15-pattern rifle with a Punisher marking
19 September: One HS2000 9-mm pistol, one Canik TP9 pistol and one M26 hand grenade
9 September: Three AR-15-pattern rifles, two of them with Punisher and fake Colt markings, and four 9-mm pistols
31 May: Two AR-15s with Punisher markings
19 September: One AR-15-pattern rifle, one HS 2000 9-mm pistol, one .38 revolver and one .22 revolver
16 August: One AR-15-pattern rifle with a Punisher marking and one IMI Jericho 941 pistol
6 August: One AR-15-pattern rifle with a Punisher marking and ammunition
5 August: 41 Canik TP9 pistols, five Bersa Thunder 9-mm pistols and five HS 9-mm pistols
20 November: Three Canik TP9 pistols
16 September: 23 AR-15-pattern rifles with Punisher markings and ten 9-mm pistols
23 August: 25 Argentinean-brand Bersa 9-mm pistols with suppressed numbers, 50 9-mm magazines and two .762 magazines used for AK-47s
3 October: One Canik TP9 pistol and one M3 grenade
6 August: Two HS pistols, one Canik pistol and two hand grenades
COSTA RICA
PANAMA
VENEZUELA
GUYANA
FRENCH GUYANA
SURINAME
COLOMBIA
RORAIMA
AMAPÁ
ECUADOR
AMAZONAS
PARÁ
MARANHÃO
CEARÁ
RIO GRANDE DO NORTE
PIAUÍ
PARAÍBA
PERNAMBUCO
ACRE
PERU
RONDÔNIA
TOCANTINS
BAHIA
MATO GROSSO
FEDERAL DISTRICT
Brasília
GOIÁS
MINAS GERAIS
BOLIVIA
ESPÍRITO SANTO
MATO GROSSO DO SUL
SÃO PAULO
RIO DE JANEIRO
PARAGUAY
PARANÁ
SANTA CATARINA
ATLANTIC OCEAN
RIO GRANDE DO SUL
CHILE
URUGUAY
ARGENTINA
Note: Many of these weapons are 'Frankenstein guns' - built from smuggled parts from different sources and usually identifiable by their fake Colt and Punisher markings.
Source: Florida International University (FIU) and FIU Security Research Hub / CRIES, Project Athena Data
©IISS

Conflict Drivers

Security

Steady supply of weapons:

The PCC, the CV and even the FDN have found ways to ensure a steady supply of high-powered weapons. In the wake of *Operation Patagonia Express*, the United States' nickname for the plot that eventually foiled the shipment of weapons from south Florida to Argentina (where they were smuggled through the tri-border area and into Brazil) in June 2019, the PCC had to retool efforts to gain reliable access to powerful semi-automatic weapons, such as AR-15s. To do so, it began smuggling weapons parts from different sources, assembling 'Frankenstein guns' in Brazil and relying in particular on Airsoft parts to complete the weapons, drastically reducing their traceability (they are usually identifiable by their fake Colt and Punisher markings). This route is also used to traffic pistols imported into Paraguay and then redistributed to Brazil. Open-source intelligence (i.e., pictures of captured weapons) analysed by small-arms experts has revealed upper portions of AR15s combined with lower portions of replica Airsoft weapons made cheaply in China.[11] While the gun lifespan is reduced, the inter-operability of AR15 uppers with lower Chinese Airsoft guns fulfils the PCC's three principal priorities: an arsenal of weapons for territorial defence and conquest, cheaper overall operating costs and less traceability by Brazilian and international authorities.

Political

Endemic corruption:

Corruption is a major driver of Brazil's armed conflict and a feature of life in Brazil. Bolsonaro himself remains ensnared in several anti-corruption investigations, along with his sons. Since 1998, no governor of Rio de Janeiro State has finished their term without an arrest for alleged corruption.[12] As a result, faith in government has declined precipitously. In Transparency International's 2021 Corruption Perceptions Index, the country ranked 96th out of 180, several places below its position in 2020.[13]

Economic
Intensifying competition for new markets:
The largest internal driver of Brazil's conflict is the desire by different groups to expand control of drug-trafficking routes established and consolidated throughout the country, including those serving domestic drug consumption (Brazil is home to one of the largest drug markets in the world) and the lucrative routes serving international markets, mostly in Europe and to a lesser extent in lusophone Africa. Control over these routes depends upon alliances, the maintenance of corruption networks amongst officials and power projection beyond prison walls. A breakdown in tacit understandings between groups and officials can lead to intense territorial rivalry and gruesome violence. Furthermore, as the global pool of drug users expanded during the first two years of the pandemic, facilitated by the ease of buying drugs over the internet and on the dark web, criminal organisations extended their fight to control the new share of the global drug market.

Global supply-chain breakdown:
The PCC, CV, FDN and even smaller criminal organisations within Brazil understand that their future survival relies on their successful 'internationalisation' to serve the aforementioned lucrative drug markets outside Brazil. The coronavirus pandemic, coupled more recently with Russia's war in Ukraine, has badly disrupted global supply chains, causing a ripple effect throughout the global shipping industry. This has had important implications for drug shipments to international markets. Firstly, the disruption has meant a marked increase in shipping prices globally. Secondly, there are fewer container ships, in which illicit products are often creatively hidden, operating globally. To ensure the reliability of drug deliveries for end users abroad, criminal organisations increasingly need to consolidate their control over several maritime ports at the same time to provide themselves with a range of options.

Key Events in 2021–22

POLITICAL EVENTS

8 March 2021
Supreme Court Justice Edson Fachin annuls former president Luiz Inácio 'Lula' da Silva's conviction in the *Operation Car Wash* investigation, clearing the way for him to run in the 2022 presidential elections.

16 April
Brazil's Supreme Court begins a two-day public hearing on police raids to construct a new plan to reduce human-rights violations and killings.

11 May
Rio de Janeiro's Public Prosecutor's Office establishes a task force to examine the details of the Jacarezinho raid and how many police operations ignore the Supreme Court ban.

10 August
President Bolsonaro attacks Brazil's electronic voting system, stating that it is likely to lead to fraud. Congress rejects a proposal to return the country to a paper-ballot system.

7 September
Bolsonaro holds raucous rallies in Brasília and São Paulo on Brazil's Independence Day, hinting at a possible rejection of the 2022 presidential results.

MILITARY/VIOLENT EVENTS

24 March 2021
Sixteen members of the PCC are caught at Patio de Seccional Colorada in Pedro Juan Caballero, Paraguay, including a high-level member of the PCC's international team.

6 May
At least 28 people, including one police officer, are killed in Jacarezinho after a police raid.

31 October
Brazilian police kill a group of 25 suspected PCC bank robbers in Varginha, Minas Gerais State.

26 December
Bolsonaro takes credit for a reduction in Brazil's homicide rates, attributing it to his hardline security policies.

6 February 2022
Bolsonaro gets the Senate to reconsider an earlier bill to loosen gun access and increase the number of legal-carry permits (previously implemented through an executive order).

8 April
Lula selects centre-right former governor of São Paulo Geraldo Alckmin as his running mate.

March/April 2022
A series of massacres in the Compensa neighbourhood of Manaus indicates that the battle for the Amazon – involving competing criminal organisations – remains far from settled.

Responses to the Conflict

Security

2021 was characterised by a flouting of the Supreme Court's June 2020 ban on police raids and a return to a policy that emphasised 'confrontation'. Predictably, this led to police killings of innocent bystanders and suspected criminals. Between June 2020 and March 2021, Rio's police killed nearly 800 people.[14] Similar trends played out in other Brazilian states. Brazilian security policy continues to suffer from a predominant focus on short-term tactical operations while neglecting to address the aforementioned, long-standing drivers of violence. There is currently no sustained effort to create viable political and social institutions in *favelas*, ensure better access to and provision of basic services, and offer state presence in neglected neighbourhoods.

Economic/development

Despite limited fiscal space, Bolsonaro's government acted decisively to support the most vulnerable segments of the population (particularly in the informal sector) during the coronavirus pandemic, increasing the monthly payments of the long-lasting cash-transfer programme. This effort notwithstanding, poverty and food insecurity increased significantly. The socio-economic deterioration is further aggravated by the rising inflation caused by the Russia–Ukraine war. Brazil's GDP grew by 4.6% in 2021 but is forecast to fall into recession this year as the effects of large fiscal stimulus wear off, against the backdrop of a deteriorating fiscal and macro-economic position.[15]

Diplomacy

Brazil has often blamed neighbouring countries for organised crime, in particular Bolivia and Paraguay. The Maduro regime in Venezuela serves as another convenient excuse. While it is certainly true that Brazilian criminal organisations utilise Bolivia and Paraguay as hubs for their transnational operations, and the Maduro regime is actively involved in illicit activity that amplifies regional instability, it is Brazil that lacks the ability to patrol its vast borders effectively. Groups such as the PCC operate seamlessly across these porous borders. With PCC ranks swelling with Venezuelan refugees, and strong recruitment campaigns in Bolivia and Paraguay in past years, the domestic and international conditions are ripe for an enduring PCC presence.

Conflict Outlook

Political scenarios

With the elections approaching, the domestic political scene remains fragmented and volatile. The overturning of Luiz Inácio 'Lula' da Silva's conviction for corruption in March 2021 made him eligible to run for president in October 2022. At present, the presidential race appears to be a contest between the latter and the incumbent Bolsonaro, which will make for a highly divisive campaign. Bolsonaro has already threatened further instability in the event of an electoral outcome he deems unfair, which could well materialise judging from the polls, which register a preliminary (although shrinking) lead for

Lula. On 7 September 2021 (Independence Day in Brazil), Bolsonaro presided over massive rallies and threatened the other branches of the constitutional government. Desperate to further close the gap in polls, Bolsonaro could reprise his polarising rhetoric on security issues and, more specifically, return to some of the phraseology he employed in his 2018 campaign.

Security is likely to be an important issue in the election, even if not the most important issue. During the first Lula presidency (2003–10), Brazil, and specifically Rio de Janeiro State, undertook a wide-ranging and ambitious security policy called 'pacification'. The strategy featured an attempt to strengthen the state in hitherto neglected areas, and could resurface as an idea Lula promotes on the campaign trail.

Escalation potential and conflict-related risks

Militias in Rio de Janeiro have expanded their territory in recent years, driven by a major weakness in Brazil's security strategy. Indeed, only a small percentage of police operations occur in neighbourhoods with a strong presence of militias, whereas a much higher percentage occur in territory controlled by Rio's other criminal groups.[16] It appears as though the politically connected nature of the militias has helped focus security operations on more traditional criminal organisations. Organised-crime groups have even accused the police of advancing militia interests. Violence is likely to escalate as long as Rio's police prove incapable of arresting the growth and potency of the militias, which increasingly operate in a manner similar to the traditional commands.

There is also potential for further escalation in the Amazon region, as groups vie for control of the coveted Solimões River for drug trafficking. In this region, erstwhile logic about traditional alliances has broken down, as evidenced by rumours of a potential alliance between the PCC and the FDN – which are traditional rivals – with the aim of rolling back recent gains made by the CV. There is also a growing interest in the northeastern states, such as Ceará, as points of embarkation for drug shipments. While the tectonic plates of alliances shift, there is potential for an upswing in violence in 2022.

Strategic implications and global influences

Brazilian criminal organisations are operating in a way that is more globally minded than ever before. Brazilian security forces have tracked and arrested members of the PCC far from home. For instance, Gilberto Aparecido dos Santos (alias 'Fuminho'), on Brazil's 'most wanted' list, was arrested in Mozambique, 5,000 miles from São Paulo State, in April 2020.[17] For the PCC, lusophone Africa and its permissive environment for drug trafficking has become an incipient focus of its international operations. The CV also maintains strong international links and sees transnational expansion as crucial to its survival. Likewise, weapons trafficking and the aforementioned 'Frankenstein guns' assembled by groups like the PCC have become increasingly internationalised. Thus, a confluence of factors means the competition to expand domestically will intensify, just as international expansion becomes crucial to the continued survival of many criminal organisations.

Supply-chain disruption and global shipping prices are also highly relevant for the future of Brazil's transnational organised-crime groups. Supply-chain challenges and a slowdown and bottleneck in global shipping means that criminal groups are unable to reliably ship products to their end users, and that the control of ports is an increasingly important area of contestation.

Notes

[1] Monitor da Violência, 'Número de assassinatos cai 7% no Brasil em 2021 e é o menor da série histórica' [Number of Murders Drops 7% in Brazil in 2021 and is the Lowest in the Historical Series], 21 February 2022; and InSight Crime, 'InSight Crime's 2021 Homicide Round-Up', 1 February 2022.

[2] 'Murders in Brazil Fall to Lowest in 14 Years', *Brazilian Report*, 22 February 2022.

[3] Terence McCoy, 'Rio Police Were Ordered to Limit Favela Raids During the Pandemic. They're Still Killing Hundreds of People', *Washington Post*, 20 May 2021.

[4] Ibid.

[5] 'Sem Concurso, PMERJ Tem 30 Mil Soldados a Menos que Previsto em Lei' [Without Competitions, PMERJ Has 30 Thousand Soldiers Fewer Than Provided for by Law], *Folha Dirigida*, 7 October 2019.

[6] Robson Bonin, 'Comando Vermelho vira preocupação do Governo Bolsonaro – Entenda' [Comando Vermelho Becomes the Concern of the Bolsonaro Government – Understand], *Veja*, 22 August 2020.

[7] 'PCC', *Americas Quarterly*; and InSight Crime and American University's Center for Latin American & Latino Studies, 'The Rise of the PCC: How South America's Most Powerful Prison Gang Is Spreading in Brazil and Beyond', CLALS Working Paper Series, No. 30, 6 December 2020, p. 23.

[8] Angelika Albaladejo, 'PCC Files Document Gang's Explosive Growth in Brazil and Beyond', InSight Crime, 5 June 2018.

[9] 'The Rise of the PCC', p. 52.

[10] 'FDN x FDN Pura: Conflito entre João Branco e Zé Roberto Motivou mortes' [Family of the North vs Pure Family of the North: Conflict between João Branco and Zé Roberto Motivated Deaths], acrítica.com, 28 May 2019; and Chris Dalby, 'Brazil Prisons Become Battlegrounds for Família do Norte Civil War', InSight Crime, 29 May 2019.

[11] Andrei Serbin Pont (@SerbinPont), tweet, 19 January 2021.

[12] The architect of Rio's pacification and security strategy, former governor Sérgio Cabral, was sentenced to 14 years in prison in 2017. More recently, former governor Wilson Witzel was impeached in April 2021, after being suspended for corruption. At the national level, in 2018, former president Luiz Inácio 'Lula' da Silva was convicted of money laundering and corruption and sentenced to nearly ten years in prison. In 2019, former president Michel Temer was also arrested on charges of corruption.

[13] Transparency International, '2021 Corruption Perceptions Index'.

[14] Flávia Milhorance, 'Police Kill Hundreds in Rio de Janeiro Despite Court Ban on Favela Raids', *Guardian*, 18 April 2021.

[15] International Monetary Fund, 'World Economic Outlook Database', April 2022.

[16] Leandro Resende, 'Apenas 6.5% das Operações Policiais no Rio Foram em Area de Milícia, Diz Estudo' [Only 6.5% of police operations in Rio were in militia areas, says study], CNN Brazil, 30 October 2020.

[17] Ryan Berg, 'Reports of the PCC's Demise Are Greatly Exaggerated', *Americas Quarterly*, 27 April 2020.

Americas

HAITI

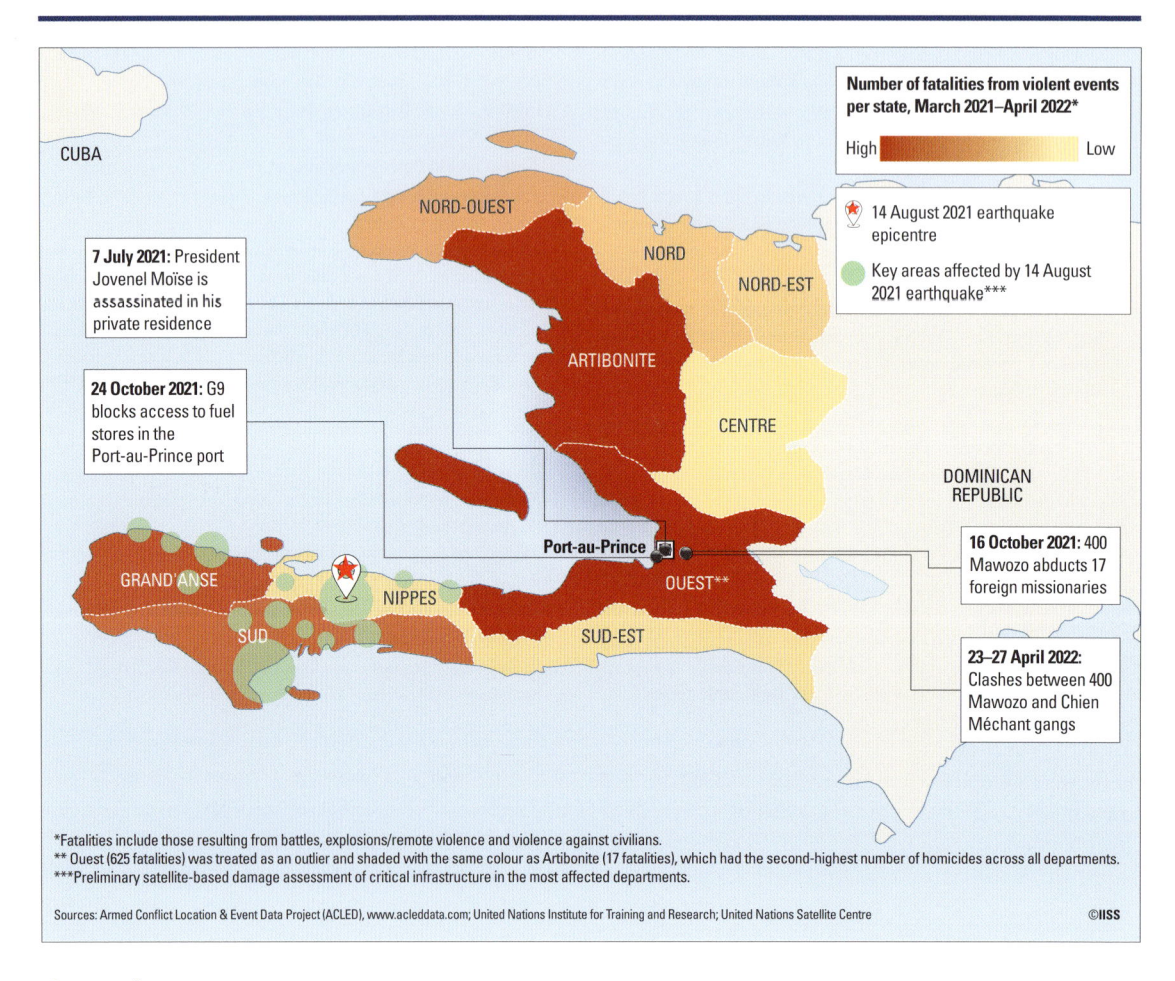

Number of fatalities from violent events per state, March 2021–April 2022*

High — Low

★ 14 August 2021 earthquake epicentre
● Key areas affected by 14 August 2021 earthquake***

7 July 2021: President Jovenel Moïse is assassinated in his private residence

24 October 2021: G9 blocks access to fuel stores in the Port-au-Prince port

16 October 2021: 400 Mawozo abducts 17 foreign missionaries

23–27 April 2022: Clashes between 400 Mawozo and Chien Méchant gangs

*Fatalities include those resulting from battles, explosions/remote violence and violence against civilians.
** Ouest (625 fatalities) was treated as an outlier and shaded with the same colour as Artibonite (17 fatalities), which had the second-highest number of homicides across all departments.
***Preliminary satellite-based damage assessment of critical infrastructure in the most affected departments.

Sources: Armed Conflict Location & Event Data Project (ACLED), www.acleddata.com; United Nations Institute for Training and Research; United Nations Satellite Centre

©IISS

Overview

Since the Duvalier family dictatorship was overthrown in 1986, after ruling for 29 years, Haiti has experienced a fitful and incomplete transition to representative democracy, buffeted by *coups d'état*, political violence, contested elections and interim governments. During this period, only one elected president – René Préval (1996–2001; 2006–11) – has handed over power to an elected successor. While the form of democracy – regular elections – has taken hold in the country, the fact of democracy – a government that is able to respond to the needs of its people and a 'loyal opposition' acknowledging its defeat – has not. The assassination of president Jovenel Moïse on 7 July 2021 marked the most recent development in Haiti's ongoing political struggle and has resulted in a constitutional vacuum that, coupled with spiralling insecurity, has sent the country into an unprecedented crisis.

Moïse, an agribusinessman who ran as the candidate of the centre-right Haitian Tèt Kale Party (PHTK), became president in 2016, promising an aggressive infrastructure programme to help revive the economy, which was still struggling from a devastating earthquake in January 2010 and Hurricane Matthew in October 2016. Moïse oversaw several important road-infrastructure projects and began to attempt to restructure Haiti's faltering energy grid. However, he found it very difficult to govern amid allegations of corruption (which he denied)

Armed Conflict Global Relevance Indicator (ACGRI)

Haiti

- Incidence: 5
- Human impact: 1
- Geopolitical impact: 7

Key Conflict Statistics

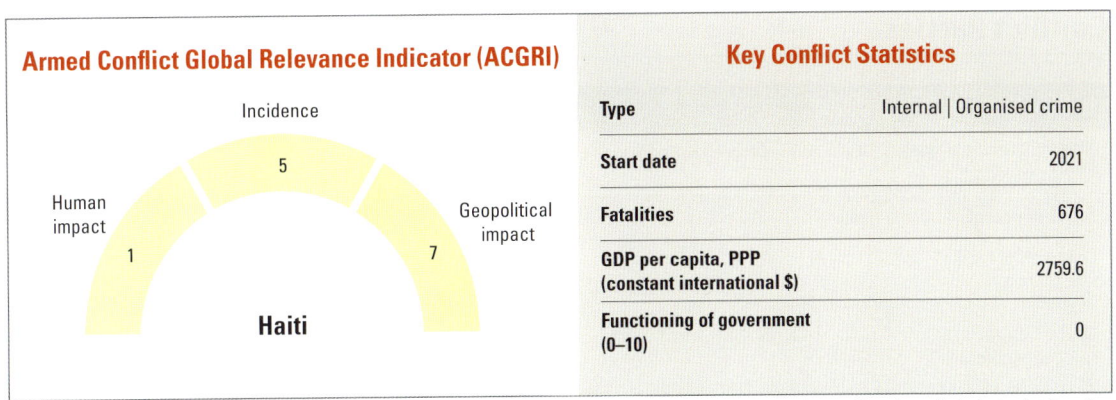

Type	Internal | Organised crime
Start date	2021
Fatalities	676
GDP per capita, PPP (constant international $)	2759.6
Functioning of government (0–10)	0

ACGRI pillars: IISS calculation based on multiple sources for 2021 and January–April 2022 (scale: 0–100). See Notes on Methodology and Data Appendix for further details on Key Conflict Statistics.

and an extremely obstructive opposition. During his presidency he was also trailed by allegations that he was linked to politically aligned armed gangs that have a stronghold over the poorest areas of the Haitian capital, Port-au-Prince. These armed groups emerged during the presidency of Jean-Bertrand Aristide (2001–04) and today most groups have armed cadres (known as *baz* – 'base' in Creole).

In January 2020, the terms of most members of parliament expired, leaving the country in yet another constitutional crisis. When the electoral council resigned the following July, Moïse created a new electoral council and unilaterally appointed its members, tasking them with organising local and federal elections, and overseeing a commission to rewrite Haiti's 1987 constitution. This was to be approved by a plebiscite, a move that many called unconstitutional and dictatorial. Several constitutional experts also argued that the year Moïse had spent as an interim president should be deducted from his five-year term, but Moïse refused to step down before February 2022.

Prior to his assassination in July 2021, Moïse had survived an attempted coup in February that year. While the conspiracy leading to Moïse's death has not been fully ascertained, it seems linked to Haiti's political and business elites, shady security agencies based in Florida and a host of Colombian former military personnel; around two dozen Colombian private security contractors were believed to be involved in the attack.[1] The head of the president's personal security detail, Dimitri Hérard, was also arrested. Three judges have been assigned to and resigned from the case thus far. Little over a month after the assassination, on 14 August 2021, southern Haiti was rocked by a devastating earthquake that killed over 2,000 people and caused widespread structural damage to buildings in southern towns such as Les Cayes and Port Salut.[2]

The new prime minister–designate, Ariel Henry, secured the backing of various international actors in Haiti and was sworn in as prime minister on 20 July 2021 despite controversy about the legitimacy of his appointment, given that it had not been confirmed before Moïse's death. His appointment has since become even more controversial amid revelations that he had been in close contact with Joseph Felix Badio, a former Ministry of Justice official currently at large and sought for possible involvement in the killing. Since assuming office, Henry has ruled in an uneasy cohabitation with the opposition party, the Democratic and Popular Sector. Another group, known as the Montana Accord and made up of veteran Haitian politicians and some civil-society actors, has also made a claim to executive power. The group, which is named after the Montana hotel in Port-au-Prince where it meets, has called for a five-member presidential college and elected a provisional president and prime minister (a former head of Haiti's central bank and a former senator, respectively).

Meanwhile, Haiti's security situation has grown ever more dire. The southern suburb of the capital, Martissant, has been the site of brutal gang warfare and mass displacement for more than a year, while to the capital's east, a kidnapping gang known as 400 Mawozo make travelling to and from the Dominican Republic or Haiti's Central Plateau a dangerous prospect.

Conflict Parties

Haitian National Police (PNH)

Strength: Officially around 16,000, believed to be around 13,000 working.[3]

Areas of operation: Countrywide.

Leadership: Frantz Elbe (director general).

Structure: Several branches including:
- The Central Directorate of the Administration and General Services (DCASG)
- The Central Directorate of the Administrative Police Force (DCPA)
- Intervention and Maintenance of Order Corps (CIMO)
- The General Security Unit of the National Palace (USGPN)
- Departmental Operation and Intervention Brigade (BOID)
- Central Directorate of the Judicial Police (DCPJ)
- The Controlling of Narcotics Trafficking Brigade (BLTS)

In addition, each of Haiti's ten administrative departments has a specific police force.

History: Created in June 1995 following the demobilisation of the Haitian army in April that year.

Objectives: With the motto 'Protéger et Servir' (Protect and Serve), the PNH is the main law-enforcement body in Haiti, with ancillary bodies tasked with providing a wide range of security duties, from guardian to the president and drug interdiction to protecting the environment.

Opponents: The Grand Ravine *baz*, the 5 Segonn gang in Village de Dieu, 400 Mawozo.

Affiliates/allies: Some elements of the PNH are believed to have at least a modus vivendi with the G9 gang coalition headed by Jimmy Chérizier (alias 'Barbecue') and especially the Baz Pilate.

Resources/capabilities: Despite its role as an official security force, the firepower of the PNH is believed to be met if not exceeded by that of the various armed groups operating in the Port-au-Prince metropolitan area.

G9 Family and Allies (G9)

Strength: Several hundred.[4]

Areas of operation: Lower Delmas (approximately Delmas 2 to 24), Boston and Belekou sections of Cité Soleil, La Saline, most of the neighbourhood of Bel Air, Ti Bois section of Martissant, lower Rue Bolosse 4ème and 5ème Avenue and 1ère and 2ème Avenue in Martissant.

Leadership: Jimmy Chérizier (alias 'Barbecue'), a former officer in the PNH's Departmental Unit for Maintenance of Order (UDMO), who went rogue following a November 2017 PNH raid against a gang in the hillside slum of Grand Ravine during which at least two police officers and ten civilians died.

Structure: Confederation of gangs in the metropolitan Port-au-Prince area controlled from the capital's lower Delmas region. In addition to Chérizier's cadre, the G9 also claims the armed groups in the following areas as its members:
- The Boston section of the seaside Cité Soleil slum, currently led by Mathias Saintil
- The Belekou section of Cité Soleil, currently led by Andrice Iscard (alias 'Iska')
- The neighbourhood of La Saline, currently led by Serge Alectis (alias 'Ti Junior')
- Most of the neighbourhood of Bel Air north of the National Palace; the group is allied with the Krache Dife (Fire Spitters) gang led by James Alexander (alias 'Sonson')
- The Ti Bois section of the Martissant neighbourhood in the capital's south, currently led by Chery Christ-Roi (alias 'Cristla')
- Rue Bolosse 4ème and 5ème Avenue and 1ère and 2ème Avenue in Martissant; the gang, known as the Baz Pilate, is believed to have close links to the police; its leadership is unclear.

History: Chérizier announced the existence of the G9 coalition in June 2020, in a video-taped address surrounded by dozens of armed, masked men, saying a 'major revolution' was beginning in Haiti.

Objectives: Elements of the G9 have engaged in politically laced rhetoric from time to time, but it is currently unclear whether this is just rhetorical or part of a more genuine attempt to begin encroaching on political power.

Opponents: Village de Dieu gang and Grand Ravine *baz*.

Affiliates/allies: Some elements of the PNH are believed to be sympathetic.

Resources/capabilities: Extensive, derived from the control of some of the docks in the capital area and the looting of stores and businesses.

400 Mawozo

Strength: Believed to comprise at least 200 individuals and an unknown number of ancillary supporters.[5]

Areas of operation: The Port-au-Prince suburb of Croix-des-Bouquets, Thomazeau, some areas of the Central Plateau.

Leadership: Until May 2022, 400 Mawozo was led from prison by Germine 'Yonyon' Jolly, who has since been extradited to the United States. Now it is led by Joseph Wilson, also known as 'Lanmò' (Death), who is assisted by several deputies.

400 Mawozo

Structure: The group's leadership is believed to be based in Croix-des-Bouquets with other cells operating east and north of the capital.

History: Founded by Germine 'Yonyon' Jolly, who led the gang from prison until his May 2022 deportation to the US.

Objectives: Generate income through extensive kidnapping activities.

Opponents: The PNH, G9, Chen Mechann.

Affiliates/allies: Smaller gangs in Canaan, Tabarre and Tirobu areas.

Resources/capabilities: Profits from kidnapping are believed to provide many millions of US dollars; control over a wide swathe of territory in eastern Haiti.

5 Segonn

Strength: Several dozen, probably approaching 100 members and supporters.[6]

Areas of operation: Village de Dieu neighbourhood of Port-au-Prince.

Leadership: Izo (leader).

Structure: Izo is assisted by several deputies and many foot soldiers.

History: The 5 Segonn gang in its current incarnation emerged after the killing of former Village de Dieu gang leader Arnel Joseph in February 2021.

Objectives: Beyond criminal enrichment, unclear. Izo has tried to start a career as a rapper.

Opponents: Ti Bois *baz* and the PNH.

Affiliates/allies: Closely allied with the Grand Ravine *baz*.

Resources/capabilities: Extensive, mostly derived from kidnapping.

Grand Ravine *baz*

Strength: Believed to comprise around 200 under arms.

Areas of operation: Rue Bolosse 4ème and 5ème Avenue, Pont Breya and the area commonly known as *zòn pwojè*.

Leadership: Renel Destina (alias 'Ti Lapli'; leader).

Structure: The overall leader Ti Lapli is assisted by several subordinates, including aliases 'Bougoy' and 'Killy'. Fighting between these three leaders within Grand Ravine in April 2021 makes the current structure somewhat uncertain.

History: Grand Ravine has been a stronghold of armed groups for much of the last 25 years. The current orientation under Ti Lapli has existed since roughly 2018.

Objectives: Increase income through kidnapping, hijacking of trucks and other criminal activities.

Opponents: Ti Bois *baz* and the PNH.

Affiliates/allies: 5 Segonn.

Resources/capabilities: Extensive kidnapping network.

Ti Bois *baz*

Strength: Believed to comprise approximately 60 men.[7]

Areas of operation: Area of Martissant demarcated by Fontamara 23, Martissant 7 and the *zone denwi*.

Leadership: Chery Christ-Roi (alias 'Cristla'; leader).

Structure: Cristla is assisted by several deputies.

History: Emerged in its current formation under the leadership of Cristla roughly 20 years ago.

Objectives: Control its area of Martissant.

Opponents: Grand Ravine *baz* and 5 Segonn.

Affiliates/allies: The Ti Bois *baz* is part of the G9 coalition of gangs.

Resources/capabilities: Income raised through taxes on trucks bringing supplies to and from the mountainous area as well as those traversing to a quarry within the territory; nightclubs, bars, restaurants and various other businesses. Despite being outnumbered by other gangs, the Ti Bois *baz* has managed to defend its stronghold for many years.

Baz Pilate

Strength: Believed to comprise approximately 50 men.	**History:** Unknown.
Areas of operation: Lower areas of Martissant, including the lower parts of Rue Bolosse 4ème and 5ème Avenue and 1ère and 2ème Avenue up to the Port-au-Prince cemetery, as well as the roads leading to the Portail de Léogâne police station.	**Objectives:** Unclear.
	Opponents: Believed to be hostile to the Grand Ravine *baz*.
Leadership: Unclear, but the PNH is believed to have some control over it.	**Affiliates/allies:** Historically affiliated with some elements of the PNH.
Structure: Unknown.	**Resources/capabilities:** Robbery, extortion and occasional contract killing.

Conflict Drivers

Political

Investigation into Moïse's murder:
The investigation into Moïse's murder remains the political third rail in Haiti and one which goes to the heart of the current government and many of its collaborators. The ongoing arrests and extraditions to the United States of some that were allegedly involved in the killing provide hope that the investigation – which was widely seen to be hamstrung by the Haitian government – may progress. The Haitian human-rights organisation Réseau National de Défense de Droits Humains (RNDDH) has repeatedly called for Henry to explain his phone calls with alleged conspirator Joseph Félix Badio on the night of Moïse's murder. Many in Haiti remain convinced about the involvement of members of the interim government in the plot. Revelations about the crime and the possible involvement of members of the Henry government are likely to continue to destabilise the country's political situation and lead to increased conflict with political and civil-society actors as the government's already weak legitimacy further erodes.

Elections:
Haiti has not held presidential or parliamentary elections since November 2016. There are currently only a handful of elected senators and no elected deputies or local officials. The lack of a government that has been elected by popular mandate, however flawed it may be, further erodes the legitimacy of the non-elected powers currently vying for control. There is a consensus among many diplomatic and civil-society figures in the country that the government will delay holding elections for as long as possible.

Economic

Gangs:
Over the last year, the gangs in the Port-au-Prince metropolitan area have expanded their areas of influence to the point where both the southern and western suburbs of the capital are under the control of illegal armed groups. The economic impact of this situation has been severe. In the Port-au-Prince suburb of Croix-des-Bouquets, for example, a stronghold of the 400 Mawozo gang, roiling violence significantly aggravated the food-insecurity crisis. In Martissant, the gangs completely control traffic on the country's main north–south road and can open or close it at will.

Social

Earthquake recovery:
Various groups in southern Haiti have sharply criticised Henry for what they view as the government's insufficient response to the August 2021 earthquake, which has further eroded the government's legitimacy. Earthquakes continue to occur on a daily basis in southern Haiti, and the situation remains very difficult for residents, with roads damaged or strewn with earthquake-related debris and some residents living in precarious conditions. This context, combined with the interruption of travel between the capital and the south caused by the violence in Martissant, continues to drive violent eruptions, as shown by the violent protest that took place at the airport in Les Cayes in March 2022.

Key Events in 2021–22

POLITICAL EVENTS

7 February 2021
Failed coup attempt against president Jovenel Moïse. A number of people are arrested in connection with the attempt, including Supreme Court Justice Yvickel Dabresil, PNH official Marie Louise Gauthier and physician Marie-Antoinette Gauthier, who had historically been associated with the Fanmi Lavalas party of former president Jean-Bertrand Aristide.

5 July
Moïse appoints Ariel Henry as prime minister.

20 July
Henry is sworn in as prime minister.

30 August
Political and civil-society groups sign the Montana Accords.

September
Images of Haitians at the US–Mexico border being mistreated and chased by US Border Patrol officials prompt outrage over the Biden administration's handling of the migration crisis.

23 September
US Special Envoy for Haiti Ambassador Daniel Foote resigns, citing the mass deportation of Haitian migrants and asylum seekers by the US.

25 October
G9 leader Chérizier publicly demands the resignation of Henry after the G9 blocks access to fuel stores, causing fuel and electricity shortages.

MILITARY/VIOLENT EVENTS

12 March 2021
A police raid against the 5 Segonn gang operating in Village de Dieu ends in disaster, with six police officers killed.

7 July
Moïse is shot dead in his private residence in Port-au-Prince by an armed commando (composed of Colombian mercenaries) in an overnight raid.

16 October
400 Mawozo abducts 17 foreign missionaries, including 16 US citizens and one Canadian citizen, and demands US$1m ransom per hostage.

6 December
The Grand Ravine *baz* and Village de Dieu gang take over the Martissant police commissariat.

24–31 December
Two attacks on the Port-au-Prince neighbourhood of Bel Air by gangs allied with the G9 coalition of armed groups kill at least ten people, amid accusations from human-rights organisations that the government funnels money from the metropolitan area's sanitation programme to the G9.

27 December
Seven minibus passengers are killed by gunfire as they try to cross Martissant.

1 January 2022
Henry and his delegation are forced to flee the northern city of Gonaïves under fire following a shoot-out between armed groups and security forces.

15 January
Former Haitian senator John Joël Joseph is arrested in Jamaica, suspected of involvement in Moïse's assassination.

20 February
The Dominican Republic begins the construction of a controversial wall along its frontier with Haiti.

1–2 March
Henry suggests that the Caribbean Community (CARICOM) should help facilitate dialogue in Haiti. CARICOM welcomes the suggestion but little further action is taken.

21 March
Henry controversially renews the mandates of 58 judges despite criticism that his interim role does not give him the power to do so.

6 January 2022
Two journalists are killed by a gang operating in the mountains of Laboule 12, Port-au-Prince.

1 February
Haitian police kill sidekick of Village de Dieu gang leader Izo; gangs retaliate by shooting at motorists.

29 March
Thousands join protests in Port-au-Prince and other cities against insecurity and violence on the 35th anniversary of Haiti's 1987 constitution. Manifestations remain peaceful in most cities but end in violence in Les Cayes with the burning of a US aid aircraft.

April
A feud within the Grand Ravine *baz* in Martissant erupts, causing yet more violence in the neighbourhood.

23–27 April
Fighting between 400 Mawozo and Chen Mechann gangs paralyses the area north of Port-au-Prince.

24–26 April
At least 20 people are killed and hundreds are displaced in Croix-des-Bouquets due to clashes between gang members.

29 April
Dominican diplomat Guillen Tatis is kidnapped in Croix-des-Bouquet, presumably by 400 Mawozo. He is released on 4 May.

Responses to the Conflict

Security

The gangs outnumber the Haitian police in terms of both members and capabilities in the capital and elsewhere. PNH Director Frantz Elbé has called for police training on crisis and emergency situations, rescue operations and civil protection, as well as on fighting human smuggling and trafficking, and money laundering. The government's efforts to support the police have been perceived as half-hearted at best, consisting mostly of after-the-fact measures such as a possible law mandating support for the families of killed police officers. In the Artibonite Valley in northern Haiti, residents have begun to form paramilitary groups to battle the insecurity of the gangs there, sometimes with lethal results.

In July 2021, the Biden administration announced that it was sending experts from the Transportation Security Administration and the Cybersecurity and Infrastructure Security Agency to work with their Haitian counterparts to improve aviation and critical-infrastructure security. The US is also deploying advisers to the Haitian judicial police and Inspector General to assist in processing alleged cases of corruption, human-rights abuses and police misconduct. However, faced with several thousand armed gang members in the capital alone, these measures seem unlikely to change the dynamic of insecurity.

Economic/development

During fiscal year 2021, USAID's Bureau for Humanitarian Assistance provided around US$92m in assistance to Haiti and, following the August 2021 earthquake, an additional US$55.5m in emergency funding to support affected populations in the departments of Grand'Anse, Nippes and Sud.[8] In March 2022, the World Bank approved funding support for Haiti's agricultural sector and road infrastructure totalling US$132m.[9]

Blackouts continue to impact Haiti's economy, with even some areas of the capital going without electricity for over a week at a time.[10] Between February and April 2022, for example, the southern city of Jérémie was without electricity for two months. The earthquake, reduced harvests, income losses related to low rainfall and insufficient food assistance are driving food insecurity in the country. In April 2022, the Famine Early Warning Systems Network reported that up to 2.5m people are expected to face crisis levels of acute food insecurity by October 2022.[11]

Diplomacy

Thus far, the international community has presented a more or less united front in its support of the Henry government, despite initial and now increasing doubts about its legitimacy and efficacy. On 12 March, US Assistant Secretary of State for Western Hemisphere Affairs Brian A. Nichols met with Henry to discuss security and economic stability and 'emphasized the need for Haitians to forge a strong consensus on a political way forward'.[12] The current United Nations mission in Haiti, the Bureau intégré des Nations Unies en Haïti (BINUH) – the successor to the 2004–17 Mission des Nations unies pour la stabilisation en Haïti (MINUSTAH) – was previously considered by many to be overly deferential to the Moïse regime. Since his killing, however, it has been increasingly sidelined as the Haitian factions fight among themselves.

Humanitarian aid

At the height of its mission in southern Haiti after the August 2021 earthquake, the US government had 19 helicopters, eight transport aircraft, six ships and approximately 1,200 personnel mobilised to support the relief effort.[13] Many in the region subsequently complained that little aid – national or international – reached the region with any degree of efficacy.

Concurrent with the situation in the south, many people are displaced and struggling in Port-au-Prince. Gang violence displaced 19,000 people in the capital between June 2021 and February 2022, with many in Martissant still living in temporary accommodation in areas such as the Centre Sportif in the nearby neighbourhood of Carrefour.[14]

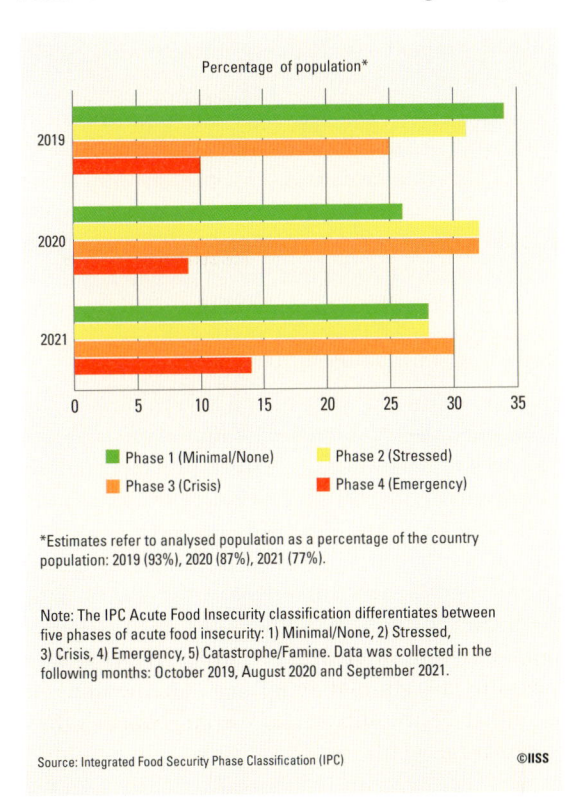

Figure 1: Acute food insecurity rates in Haiti, 2019–21

*Estimates refer to analysed population as a percentage of the country population: 2019 (93%), 2020 (87%), 2021 (77%).

Note: The IPC Acute Food Insecurity classification differentiates between five phases of acute food insecurity: 1) Minimal/None, 2) Stressed, 3) Crisis, 4) Emergency, 5) Catastrophe/Famine. Data was collected in the following months: October 2019, August 2020 and September 2021.

Source: Integrated Food Security Phase Classification (IPC)

Conflict Outlook

Political scenarios
The investigation into Moïse's murder continues to cause controversy, with local human-rights groups alleging that the Henry government is blocking a thorough investigation into the crime. In early 2022, the arrest in Panama and subsequent extradition to the US of Antonio Palacios, one alleged member of the squad of Colombian private security contractors said to be responsible for the president's killing, provided hope that more information about the tangled case of the president's death will come to light. This was further buttressed by the arrest in the Dominican Republic and extradition to the US of Rodolphe Jaar, a convicted drug trafficker and businessman also allegedly linked to the case. Although Henry continues to claim to want to organise an election in 2022, he has so far been unable to even organise an electoral council to oversee the preparation and oversight of any potential poll. Relations between the prime minister and the remainder of the Senate are extremely poor, with Senate President Joseph Lambert frequently saying that Henry is the 'biggest obstacle' to resolving the country's political crises.[15] Some of the prime minister's own erstwhile allies have also made a habit of bad-mouthing him to the press. The government's lack of legitimacy, combined with the roiling violence in the capital, make it highly unlikely that viable elections will be held in 2022.

Escalation potential and conflict-related risks
The continued lack both of clarity about the president's death and of a democratically elected government, coupled with the expansion of gang-controlled zones in the capital and elsewhere, bodes a bloody and unsettled remainder of 2022. The areas of gang-controlled territory in and around the capital expand month by month, while the gangs themselves, once largely dependent on political patronage, have developed vibrant flows of criminal revenue independent from their former masters in the political and economic elite. It will likely be more difficult than it previously was to rein them in come election time, and the security forces currently lack the means and the morale to defeat them. In effect, the state has ceded much of the territory in the Ouest department to the gangs, leading to a situation of quasi-criminal governance.

Although Haiti's drug trade is generally dominated by wealthier political and business actors, there is some evidence to suggest that the operations of the US Drug Enforcement Administration (DEA) have been compromised in the country. One of several men arrested in connection with the president's assassination was a Haitian-American man who had previously been a DEA informant. For years, there have been reports of unethical and perhaps illegal behaviour on the part of DEA officials investigating drug trafficking in Haiti. This dynamic may well continue in the chaotic and unstable atmosphere of Haiti's current government.

Strategic implications and global influences
The Biden administration's approach to the illegal immigration of migrants of Haitian origin to the US via its southern border with Mexico – often involving summarily shipping Haitians back to Port-au-Prince, sometimes handcuffed or otherwise restrained – will likely inflame an already delicate and potentially explosive situation, as the Henry regime, like the Moïse government before it, is seen by Haitians to push its people to such desperate measures. The immigration crisis could also occur closer to home as well, with people travelling from Haiti to the US directly by sea. Between October 2021 and January 2022, the US Coast Guard rescued more than 800 Haitians at sea between Haiti and the US, in contrast to 3,900 in total over the five previous years.[16]

The continued work by the government of the neighbouring Dominican Republic on a series of barriers and walls to further prevent Haitian migration to the eastern two-thirds of Hispaniola will almost certainly also increase pressure within Haiti itself. Drug and weapons trafficking, though hardly new phenomena, appear to still percolate through the upper echelons of Haiti's political culture. With the central government's authority barely extending beyond the walls of its offices, both will likely continue unabated in the near term.

Notes

1 Sophie Reardon, 'Colombian Man Allegedly Involved in Murder of Haitian President Jovenel Moïse Arrested in U.S.', CBS News, 4 January 2022.
2 'Haïti-Séisme-Sud: Le bilan partiel atteint 2,189 morts, dont 1,832 dans le département du Sud, et plus de 12,000 blessés' [Haiti-earthquake-south: The Partial Toll Reaches 2,189 Dead, Including 1,832 in the Sud Department, and More Than 12,000 Injured], AlterPresse, 19 August 2021.
3 Author interviews, January–February 2022.
4 Author interviews, 2019–22.
5 Author interviews, January–March 2002.
6 Author interviews, March 2022.
7 Ibid.
8 USAID Bureau for Humanitarian Assistance, 'Haiti Assistance Overview', January 2022.
9 World Bank, 'The World Bank Approves US$132 Million Package to Improve Haiti's Food Security and Road Infrastructure', press release, 17 March 2022.
10 'Sévère rationnement de l'énergie électrique' [Severe Rationing of Electrical Energy], Radio Métropole, 29 March 2022.
11 USAID, 'Haiti – Complex Emergency', Fact Sheet, 4 May 2022.
12 Brian A. Nichols (@WHAAsstSecty), tweet, 12 March 2022.
13 Caleb Becker, 'In the Face of Tragedy, the United States Comes to the Aid of a Partner in Need in Haiti', US Department of State, 29 March 2022.
14 Jess DiPierro Obert and Paula Dupraz-Dobias, 'In Haiti, Gang Violence Strains Aid Operations and Demands New Approaches', New Humanitarian, 7 February 2022; and 'Les déplacés de Martissant entre l'enclume et le marteau' [The Displaced People of Martissant Between a Rock and a Hard Place], Radio Métropole, 30 July 2021.
15 'Le premier ministre Henry est un obstacle à la résolution de la crise, selon le sénateur Lambert' [Prime Minister Henry Is an Obstacle to Resolving the Crisis, According to Senator Lambert], Radio Métropole, 22 March 2022.
16 'U.S. Coast Guard Intercepts 191 Haitians Aboard Sailing Vessel off Bahamas', Reuters, 27 January 2022.

EL SALVADOR

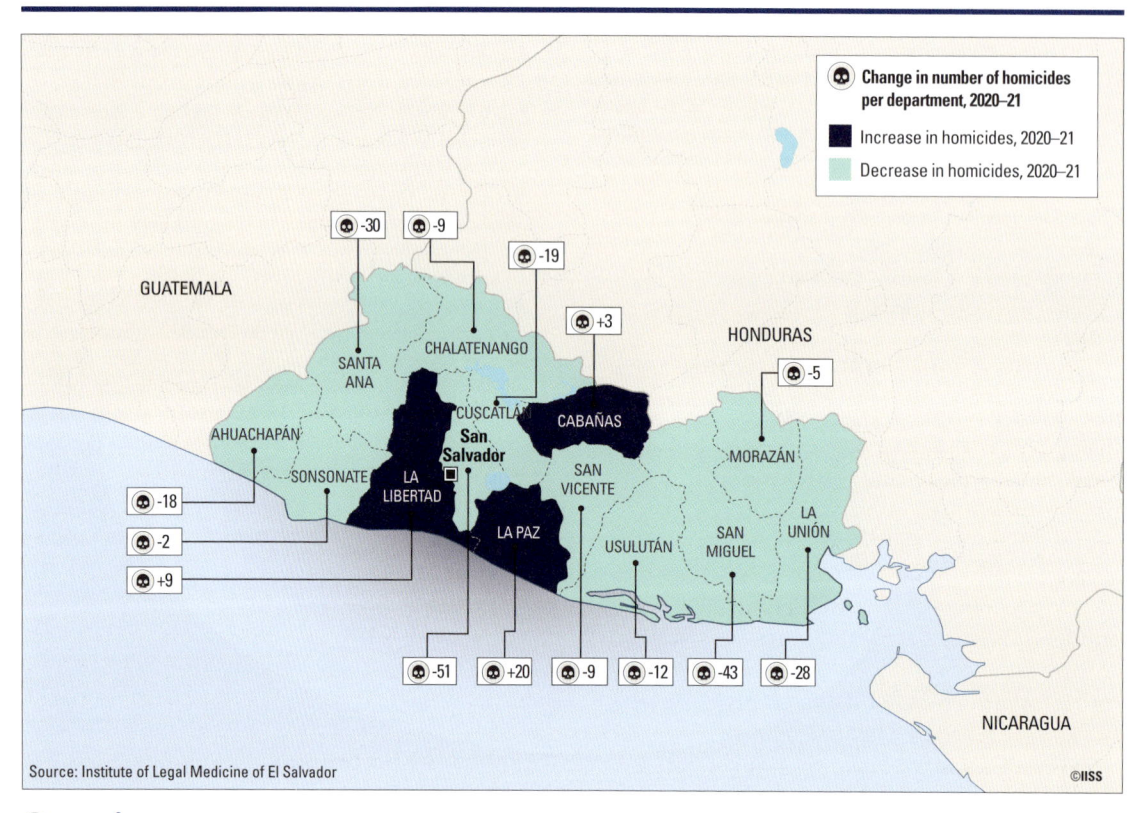

Change in number of homicides per department, 2020–21
■ Increase in homicides, 2020–21
□ Decrease in homicides, 2020–21

Source: Institute of Legal Medicine of El Salvador ©IISS

Overview

The conflict between the Salvadoran state and the Mara Salvatrucha (MS-13) gang has been a multi-phased battle for territorial control, political legitimacy and economic resources. The MS-13 was established in the mid-1990s by members deported from California, mainly Los Angeles, and by the early 2000s had evolved into a military force that challenged the state, thriving in the weak economic and legal structures of post-civil-war El Salvador. Over time it consolidated territorial control across the country and developed revenue streams from extortion, kidnapping, assassinations and the sale of marijuana, crack cocaine and cocaine. As it became entrenched in local communities, the MS-13 attracted new members with combat experience from El Salvador's civil war (1979–92). Despite attempts by successive administrations, repressive strategies failed to stem the gang's expansion. By 2012, the MS-13 had over 12,000 members in El Salvador and its main rival, the Barrio 18 gang, had 8,000–10,000 members.[1] At that time, El Salvador's homicide rate was also among the highest in the world. This situation prompted the government to engage the gangs in the first formal negotiations that year, resulting in a 'truce', where the gangs reduced visible homicides in exchange for government concessions and payments. However, the pact collapsed in 2014, with the gangs realising the true scope of their political leverage. Since then, the MS-13 has consolidated its territorial control and grown its military capabilities, using spikes in violence as leverage in negotiations with the government, while the Barrio 18 has suffered from internal divides and lost territory.

In 2021, secret negotiations between the MS-13 and the administration of President Nayib Bukele were publicly exposed, showing that the conflict between the state and the gang has moved from

Armed Conflict Global Relevance Indicator (ACGRI)

- Incidence: 4
- Human impact: 1
- Geopolitical impact: 0

El Salvador

Key Conflict Statistics

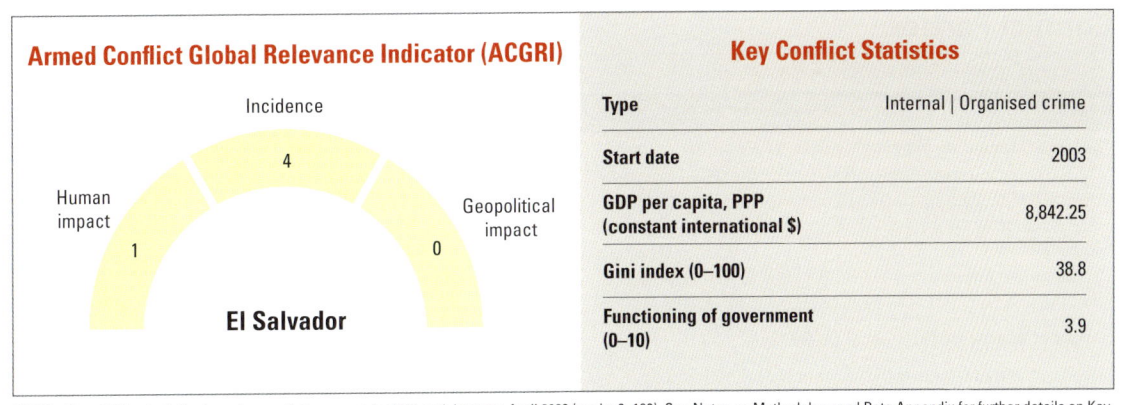

Type	Internal | Organised crime
Start date	2003
GDP per capita, PPP (constant international $)	8,842.25
Gini index (0–100)	38.8
Functioning of government (0–10)	3.9

ACGRI pillars: IISS calculation based on multiple sources for 2021 and January–April 2022 (scale: 0–100). See Notes on Methodology and Data Appendix for further details on Key Conflict Statistics.

a primarily military confrontation to a series of negotiated non-aggression pacts.[2] The pacts seem to include the exchange of votes in gang-controlled areas and a reduction in homicide rates for legal protection and growing incorporation into the country's formal political structure, as well as access to state resources.[3]

The ongoing relationship between the MS-13 and the Bukele administration has fundamentally shifted the nature of the conflict away from historical fighting between the two main gangs and by both gangs against the state.

Multiple sources attribute the decrease in homicides in 2020 and 2021 to the non-aggression pacts.[4] However, the official homicide statistics should be considered incomplete, as they do not include the high number (488 in 2021) of 'disappeared' persons and other types of violent deaths.[5] The discovery of multiple clandestine cemeteries across the country, containing dozens of bodies that were not counted in the official statistics, also underscores the incomplete nature of the official statistics.[6]

In 2021, the MS-13 continued to employ several tactics to assert its dominance – including executions, public beatings, extortion and forced displacement – which further took a toll on economic growth and community cohesion. Although the coronavirus pandemic limited some of its activities, the group pursued a multi-pronged strategy to expand its power while transporting cocaine, upgrading its weapons, increasing its political activities and diversifying its financial holdings. As vaccination rates rose and COVID-19 cases dropped, El Salvador lifted all vaccination requirements to enter the country, allowing the MS-13 to return to its more traditional activities (including human trafficking and smuggling), with greater legitimacy as a semi-state actor.

The negotiations between the Salvadoran government and the MS-13, and the Biden administration's willingness to publicise information about them, caused a significant deterioration in El Salvador's bilateral relations, which added to its international isolation from historical allies such as the European Union.

Bukele continued to use the electoral successes of his New Ideas party – which swept the legislative elections on 28 February 2021 – to consolidate power. On 1 May 2021, the day that the newly elected New Ideas legislators were seated in the Legislative Assembly, Bukele removed five Supreme Court justices from the Constitutional Chamber and fired the attorney general. The new Legislative Assembly, controlled by Bukele's New Ideas party, appointed five new justices to the Supreme Court in late June, in violation of El Salvador's constitutional process.[7] In August 2021, the Supreme Court reversed a ruling that the previous court had made to extradite a senior leader of the MS-13 wanted for several murders in the United States.

Conflict Parties

El Salvador armed forces

Strength: According to official reports, 24,500 active military (20,500 army, 2,000 air force, 2,000 navy). President Nayib Bukele has made repeated statements to the press that he intends to grow the size of the armed forces, including public statements from July 2021 that he intends to add 1,000 people to the armed forces every six weeks.[8] It is therefore possible that the armed forces now include as many as 28,000.

Areas of operation: Throughout El Salvador.

Leadership and structure: René Francis Merino Monroy (minister of defence).
Six brigades across the country; three infantry battalions; one special military-security brigade with two military-police and two border-security battalions; one artillery brigade; one mechanised cavalry regiment; special-forces command with one special-operations group and an anti-terrorist command.

History: Held a long-standing monopoly on the government, contributing to the civil war from 1979–92. The 1992 Peace Accords introduced key reforms to the relationship between the military and civil society, in particular establishing civilian oversight of the military and creating a civilian police force.

Objectives: Responsible for defence against external threats. Works with the police for internal-security purposes, including fighting the MS-13. Plays a primary role in counter-narcotics operations and continues to play a law-enforcement role alongside the police (despite this being ruled unconstitutional by the Supreme Court).

Opponents and affiliates/allies:
Opponents: The MS-13, Barrio 18, cocaine-transport groups and other smaller criminal groups in El Salvador.
Allies: The National Civil Police (PNC) and some civilian paramilitary groups.

Resources/capabilities: Special-operations command; high-mobility multi-purpose wheeled vehicles; light armoured vehicles; M113 armoured personnel carriers and multiple other armoured vehicles; eight UH-1H helicopters; two UH-1M helicopters and assorted other helicopters.

The National Civil Police (PNC)

Strength: Approximately 26,000. The coronavirus pandemic and the ensuing budget crisis prevented the proposed increase.

Areas of operation: Throughout El Salvador.

Leadership and structure: Mauricio Antonio Arriaza Chicas (director general).
The security force tasked with countering the MS-13 is comprised of three anti-gang units of approximately 600 special-forces troops and 400 PNC officers.[9] This is separate from the counter-narcotics and organised-crime units.

History: Founded as a result of the 1992 Peace Accords, in an effort to repair civil society's relationship with the security forces. The PNC has faced intractable challenges since its foundation, most notably organised crime led by the MS-13 and other groups.

Objectives: Primarily responsible for internal threats, including combatting gangs, organised crime and drug trafficking. Anti-gang units are tasked with targeting the non-incarcerated MS-13 leadership and restricting the communications capabilities of the leadership in prison.

Opponents and affiliates/allies:
Opponents: The MS-13, Barrio 18, cocaine-transport groups and other smaller criminal groups in El Salvador.
Allies: El Salvador's armed forces, especially under the Bukele administration.

Resources/capabilities: Specialised units combine the use of helicopters, armoured vehicles and assault rifles, partially offsetting the PNC's lack of heavy weapons.

Mara Salvatrucha (MS-13)

Strength: Estimates range from 17,000 to 60,000.[10]

Areas of operation: Estimated to operate in around 93% of the country's municipalities (247 of 262), where each member is part of a network of at least six people.[11]

Leadership and structure: Run by the *ranfla histórica* (national leadership), which sets the overall policies and strategies from prisons throughout El Salvador. Faced with internal fissures, the *ranfla histórica* has devolved some decision-making power to the *ranfla libre* (the gang leadership not in prison). Below them are the *palabreros* (those who delegate orders) and *programas* (groups of highly compartmentalised street-level units, known as *clicas*), with semi-autonomous leadership across multiple neighbourhoods and the clicas.

History: Founded in the 1980s in poor and marginalised neighbourhoods of Los Angeles. In the 1990s, US authorities deported many incarcerated Salvadoran MS-13 members. The MS-13 members arrived in El Salvador with weak community and country ties, at a time when El Salvador was emerging from a bloody civil war with weak institutions, combat veterans and widely available weapons.

Objectives: Control territory in which the gang is free to exercise its own laws and authority (without overthrowing the government at a national level, which would draw unwanted international attention to the MS-13's advances and destabilise the country, impacting the profitability of illicit

Mara Salvatrucha (MS-13)

economies), while displacing traditional, entrenched cocaine-transport groups (such as the Cartel de Texis, Los Perrones and others) for financial gain. As the gang has achieved more official political legitimacy, this strategy may be shifting to embedding members within the state structure to facilitate systemic extortion of entire government agencies rather than targeting individuals.

Opponents and affiliates/allies:
Opponents: Barrio 18.
Allies: The MS-13 structures in Honduras and Guatemala, parts of the Sinaloa Cartel (CPS) and the Cartel Jalisco New Generation (CJNG) in Mexico.
Perception of state security forces fluctuates between being considered the enemy and occasionally a tactical partner.

Resources/capabilities: Financial resources derived from extortion, protecting cocaine loads, kidnapping, human smuggling, murder-for-hire and money laundering. These are not evenly distributed among the gang's clicas. Those groups that control key cocaine-trafficking routes or beach areas for sea-transported loads are better off than those not involved with cocaine routes. Some centralised redistribution exists but inequality among groups on the ground is a constant source of tension. Armoury features a growing number of new weapons, including Dragunov sniper rifles, Uzis, rocket-propelled grenades and a small number of light anti-tank weapons.

Conflict Drivers

Security

Increasing militarisation:
Bukele's push to consolidate power is leading him to cultivate a closer relationship with the military, even at the expense of El Salvador's Peace Accords, which sought to establish a better relationship between the military and other branches of government. In one example of this, Bukele called the military into the National Assembly in February 2020 to physically occupy the building as lawmakers were voting on a crime bill.

The military's ranks are growing; applications for new recruits increased in 2021, with 10,456 Salvadorans applying to enter the armed forces between January and December 2021. This is the highest number of new recruits in the last five years.[12]

The military and other state security forces continued to play an important role in fighting the MS-13, which in part justifies the military's expansion, particularly to regional and international partners. State security forces were deployed in public-security operations, in violation of the 1992 Peace Accords, resulting in a sharp rise in human-rights abuses committed by the state. The most prominent example of this in 2021 was Bukele's deployment of troops to the streets of San Salvador, where they used armoured vehicles to block the exits of poor neighbourhoods and went door to door looking for suspected gang members. The existing truce between the Salvadoran government and the gangs does not seem to be comprehensive or stable enough to completely prevent this type of conflict.

The increase in militarisation comes during a phase of heightened impunity for military abuses, consistent with the authoritarian trend. In September 2021, the Bukele administration removed justice Jorge Guzmán, a prominent judge who was responsible for conducting the investigation into the 1981 El Mozote massacre, during which soldiers killed 978 civilians.

Political

State illegitimacy and entrenched governance flaws:
The government's long-time fragility and lack of effectiveness has translated into a perceived lack of legitimacy, as it has proven itself incapable of controlling territory, delivering essential services and maintaining a monopoly on the use of force. In the most recent comprehensive poll, only 12% of respondents felt the government ran the country, with 42% instead believing power rested with the MS-13.[13]

Economic and social

Socio-economic challenges:
Despite significant economic reforms as part of the 1992 peace agreement, deep economic inequality and high unemployment persist, especially among young people (15–24 years old). With 12% of young people unemployed, 50% underemployed and 24.8% neither studying nor working, there are limited viable alternatives to joining the MS-13, which continues to fuel the conflict.[14]

The economy contracted by 8% in 2020, in one of the worst performances in the region, amid the coronavirus pandemic and two major tropical storms. Although a recovery is under way, with an estimated 10.3% growth in 2021 and a forecast of 3% in 2022, socio-economic conditions remain weak.[15]

Key Events in 2021–22

POLITICAL EVENTS

1 May 2021
Bukele removes five justices from the Supreme Court's Constitutional Chamber and fires the attorney general before naming loyalists to fill the positions, giving him control of all three branches of government.

5 June
El Salvador makes Bitcoin legal tender.

1 July
The United States sanctions seven current and former senior Salvadoran officials for corruption, including Bukele's chief of staff, and security and justice officials.

23 August
El Faro publishes report indicating that the Bukele administration hid evidence of direct negotiations between senior government officials and jailed leaders of the gangs.

27 August
The Bukele-controlled Supreme Court suspends the approved extradition of a senior MS-13 member, Armando Eliú Melgar (also known as Blue), to the US, straining relations.

31 August
The Legislative Assembly, controlled by Bukele's New Ideas party, fires every federal judge over the age of 60, including 61-year-old justice Jorge Guzmán. The move is widely seen as an attempt to stop the investigation into the El Mozote massacre.

MILITARY/VIOLENT EVENTS

21 May 2021
Salvadoran media reveal discovery of a mass grave in the town of Chalchuapa containing over 40 bodies, calling into question the official government statistics about the significant decrease in homicides.

19 July
Bukele issues public statements indicating that he intends to increase the military by 1,000 new recruits every six weeks, doubling its size from 20,000 troops to 40,000 in a little over one year.

9 November
A three-day homicide spike begins, during which gangs kill 46 people. Victims include civilians and individuals with no gang ties and the killings are widely viewed as the result of the breakdown in negotiations between the MS-13 and the government over conjugal visits for gang leaders in prison.

11 November
Bukele deploys El Salvador's military to the streets of San Salvador to blockade poor neighbourhoods and arrest suspected gang members in a government show of force.

8 December
US Department of the Treasury formally sanctions Salvadoran head of prisons and another senior official for negotiating with the MS-13, exchanging improved prison conditions and favours for the gang's electoral support and other actions.

12 January 2022
Technical experts verify that sophisticated Pegasus spyware found on the telephones of dozens of journalists, civil-society leaders and government critics was almost certainly placed by the Salvadoran state, heightening concerns about Bukele's authoritarianism and the lack of legal controls.

31 January
El Salvador rejects IMF recommendation to remove Bitcoin as legal tender.

12 December
Bukele orders police and military units to block major entrances to San Salvador to curb the arrival of buses and trucks carrying thousands of anti-government protesters. This event marks the third anti-Bukele march in just over three months and embarrasses Bukele.

26 January 2022
PNC and Justice Department dismantle an MS-13 criminal structure dedicated to extortion that operated in six departments.

25–27 March
National Assembly approves a 30-day state of emergency following a homicide spike of 87 gang-related killings from 25–27 March. The emergency powers suspend certain constitutional rights, including free assembly, and loosen restrictions on administrative detention.

13 April
Bukele says that authorities have detained more than 10,500 alleged gang members since 25 March.

Conflict Outlook

Political scenarios

There are three likely scenarios for the evolution of the conflict between the MS-13 and the government. The most dangerous would be that Bukele becomes more reliant on and formally allied with the MS-13 as El Salvador's political and economic situation becomes more complicated. Bukele is increasingly alienated from the US, restricted from international lending institutions since introducing Bitcoin as an official currency in September 2021, and is facing rising criticism for his growing authoritarianism. As a result, El Salvador has limited options for paying its ballooning international debt and cutting its massive budget deficit and is facing heightened risks to macroeconomic stability. Against this backdrop, Bukele could decide that his best option for maintaining power is to give the MS-13 greater access to government resources through municipalities and parastate entities (as well as protecting gang leaders from extradition and keeping or expanding the current policy of allowing them to leave prison frequently to conduct business and visit family). Bukele would likely require the gang to keep visible violence and homicides down in return. The second scenario would be that Bukele loses popular support and runs out of

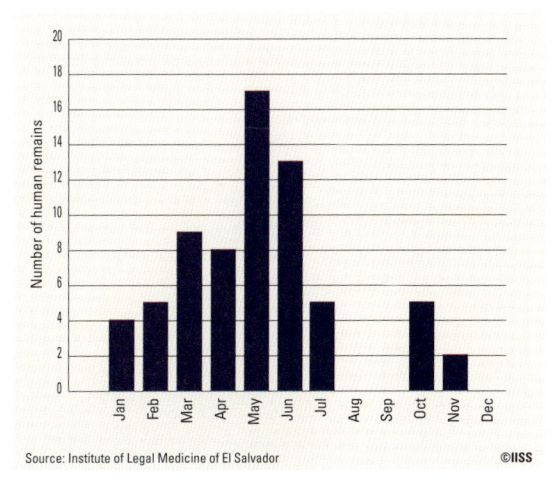

Figure 1: Human remains discovered in 2021 (in addition to recorded homicide cases)

money, making the first option less lucrative for the MS-13 and resulting in a breakdown of the current pact. This would lead to a significant escalation of violence, likely followed by a new pact with new terms. The third scenario would be that the MS-13 expands aggressively into cocaine trafficking, human smuggling, large-scale extortion and other criminal enterprises, and channels its increased income into becoming a more autonomous political actor inside and outside the government. All three scenarios would likely drive increased tensions with the US and further mass migration as the mobility restrictions related to the coronavirus pandemic ease.

Strategic implications and global influences

The Biden administration has partially followed through on its threat to take measures to sanction officials allegedly involved in corruption scandals, imposing sanctions on several members of Bukele's cabinet and inner financial circle. While three rounds of sanctions on individuals have been enacted, the promised anti-corruption task force for El Salvador, Guatemala and Honduras has not yet been established, and other measures to address root causes of migration are still in a nascent stage.[16] The Biden administration's desire to work primarily through non-governmental organisations rather than with the Salvadoran government has led to a sharp reduction in anti-narcotics coordination, intelligence sharing, military and police training, and coordinated anti-gang activities. Bukele's refusal to extradite MS-13 leaders has further restricted judicial, law-enforcement and intelligence collaboration.

Notes

[1] United Nations Office on Drugs and Crime, 'Transnational Organized Crime in Central America and the Caribbean: A Threat Assessment', September 2012, p. 27.

[2] The first evidence of the pacts, including videos of senior officials in Bukele's administration with known close ties to the MS-13 secretly entering prisons to negotiate with gang leaders, was published in El Faro. See Carlos Martínez, Gabriela Cáceres and Oscar Martínez, 'Gobierno de Bukele negoció con las tres pandillas e intent seconder la evidencia' [Bukele's Government Negotiated with the Three Gangs and Tried to Hide the Evidence], 23 August 2021. By issuing sanctions against the head of prisons, Osiris Luna, and the director of the Social Fabric Reconstruction Unit of the Ministry of Justice and Public Security, Carlos Marroquín, the US Treasury alleged that the two negotiated with the MS-13 on behalf of Bukele and as part of the deal agreed to allow jailed MS-13 leaders access to mobile phones and prostitutes. See US Department of the Treasury, 'Treasury Targets Corruption Networks Linked to Transnational Organized Crime', 8 December 2021.

[3] For a high-level overview and analysis of this dynamic, see Seth Robbins, 'Evidence of Gang Negotiations Belie El Salvador President's Claims', InSight Crime, 24 August 2021; and Martínez, Cáceres and Martínez, 'Gobierno de Bukele negoció con las tres pandillas e intent seconder la evidencia'.

[4] In 2021, El Salvador had 1,140 total homicides, approximately 17.6 per 100,000 people, compared to 1,332 in 2020, or approximately 19.7 per 100,000 people. See Parker Asmann and Katie Jones, 'InSight Crime's 2020 Homicide Round-Up', InSight Crime, 29 January 2021; and InSight Crime, 'InSight Crime's 2021 Homicide Round-Up', 1 February 2022.

[5] Lissette Lemus, '2021 cerró con el doble de casos de desapariciones sin resolver, respeto a 2020' [2021 Ended with Double the Number of Cases of Unsolved Disappearances Compared to 2020], elsalvador.com, 9 January 2022.

[6] Karla Arévalo, 'Las cuatro fosas clandestinas encontrados en menos de un año en El Salvador' [The Four Clandestine Graves Found in Less than a Year in El Salvador], elsalvador.com, 7 February 2022.

[7] Human Rights Watch, 'El Salvador: Events of 2021'.

[8] 'Más de 10.000 militares son parte de un plan contra las pandillas en El Salvador' [More Than 10,000 Soldiers Are Part of a Plan Against Gangs in El Salvador], EFE, 20 July 2021.

[9] Jeannette Aguilar, 'Las políticas de seguridad pública en El Salvador 2003–2018' [Public Security Policies in El Salvador 2003–2018], National Civil Police, 10 March 2021, p. 61.

[10] Interviews conducted by IBI Consultants with anti-gang-unit members from the National Civil Police and MS-13 members, January–October 2018. The lower estimates include only hommies (full-fledged members), who constitute less than one-third of the overall gang affiliates. Higher estimates include members who served as paid lookouts, messengers and crack-cocaine and cocaine vendors.

[11] Human Rights Watch, 'World Report 2020', 2020, p. 187.

[12] Claudia Espinoza and David Bernal, '2021 fue el año con más solicitudes para entrar al Ejército' [2021 Was the Year With the Most Applications to Enter the Army], La Prensa Grafica, 13 January 2022.

[13] Parker Asmann, 'El Salvador Citizens Say Gangs, not Government "Rule" the Country', InSight Crime, 8 November 2017.

[14] Organisation for Economic Co-operation and Development, 'Key Issues Affecting Youth in El Salvador'.

[15] IMF, 'World Economic Outlook Database', April 2022.

[16] For an outline of the Biden administration's strategy to address root causes of migration in Central America, see White House, 'Fact Sheet: Strategy to Address the Root Causes of Migration in Central America', 29 July 2021.

HONDURAS

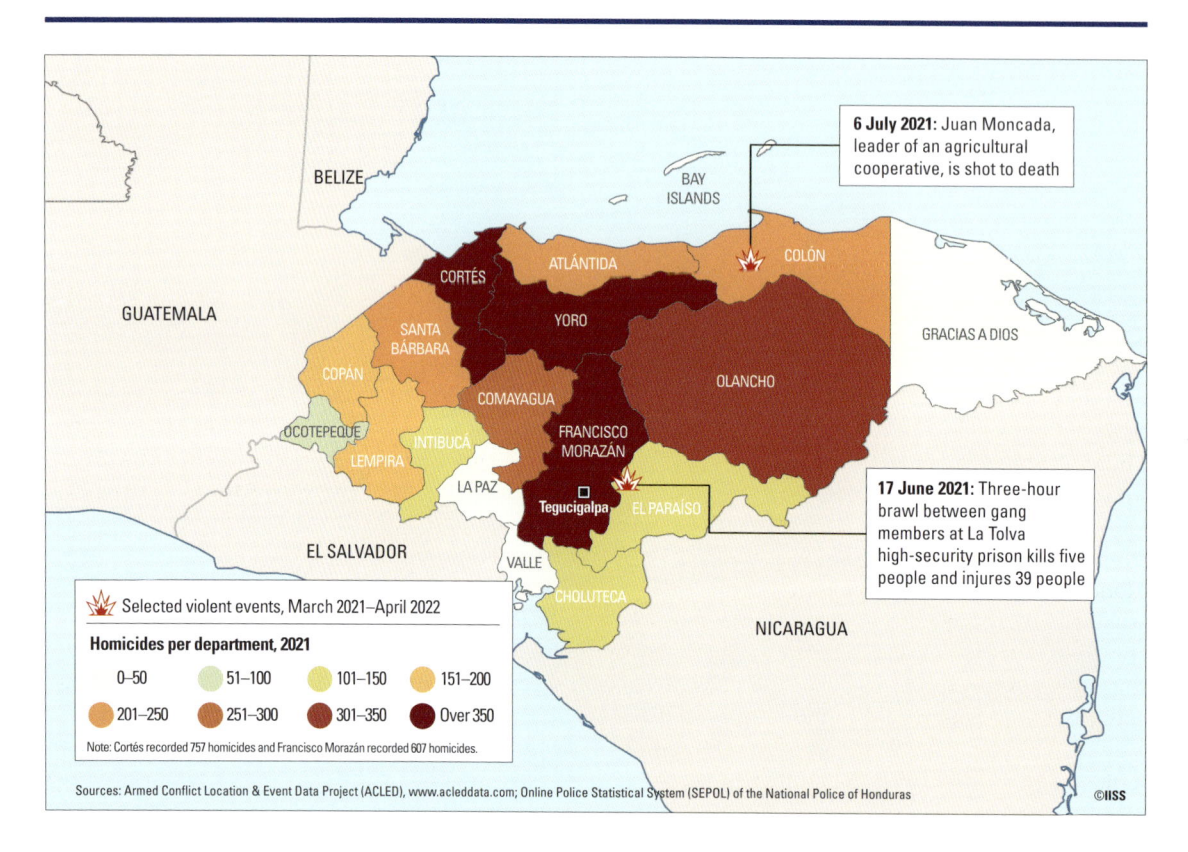

Selected violent events, March 2021–April 2022

6 July 2021: Juan Moncada, leader of an agricultural cooperative, is shot to death

17 June 2021: Three-hour brawl between gang members at La Tolva high-security prison kills five people and injures 39 people

Homicides per department, 2021: 0–50; 51–100; 101–150; 151–200; 201–250; 251–300; 301–350; Over 350

Note: Cortés recorded 757 homicides and Francisco Morazán recorded 607 homicides.

Sources: Armed Conflict Location & Event Data Project (ACLED), www.acleddata.com; Online Police Statistical System (SEPOL) of the National Police of Honduras

Overview

The conflict in Honduras centres on the Mara Salvatrucha (MS-13) gang as it seeks to expand its robust drug-trafficking structure, pitting it against parts of the state and other criminal elements that it seeks to displace. As in El Salvador and Guatemala, the MS-13 in Honduras grew largely from gang members deported from the United States in the late 1990s. In Honduras, the gang established itself as a major player in the cocaine-transportation and production business, before expanding into other drugs, maintaining a near-monopoly on the internal drug market of cocaine, crack cocaine, marijuana and krispy.[1] More recently, its lucrative drug income, particularly from the sale of krispy, allowed the gang to stop extorting local businesses in its areas of control and to gain significant political goodwill from communities, which helped to push out competing criminal groups. The MS-13 also increased its status in the eyes of Mexican drug-trafficking organisations, for whom it became an independent partner instead of an organisation that protected cocaine loads owned by other groups.[2]

The MS-13 continued to expand its criminal, political and economic operations in 2021, collaborating with Mexican transnational criminal organisations such as the Sinaloa Cartel (CPS) and the Cartel Jalisco New Generation (CJNG) to ship cocaine from Colombia and Venezuela to Mexico and increasing its control of cocaine-processing laboratories in Honduras. The group also became increasingly digitally and technologically savvy, using encrypted apps for communications, the dark web and cyber currency for financial transactions, and drones for reconnaissance operations, including for monitoring police forces. As proof of the MS-13's continued expansion, in November 2021 US prosecutors charged the leader of the MS-13 in Honduras, Yulan Andony Archaga Carias, also known as 'Alexander Mendoza'

Armed Conflict Global Relevance Indicator (ACGRI)

- Incidence: 4
- Human impact: 2
- Geopolitical impact: 1

Honduras

Key Conflict Statistics

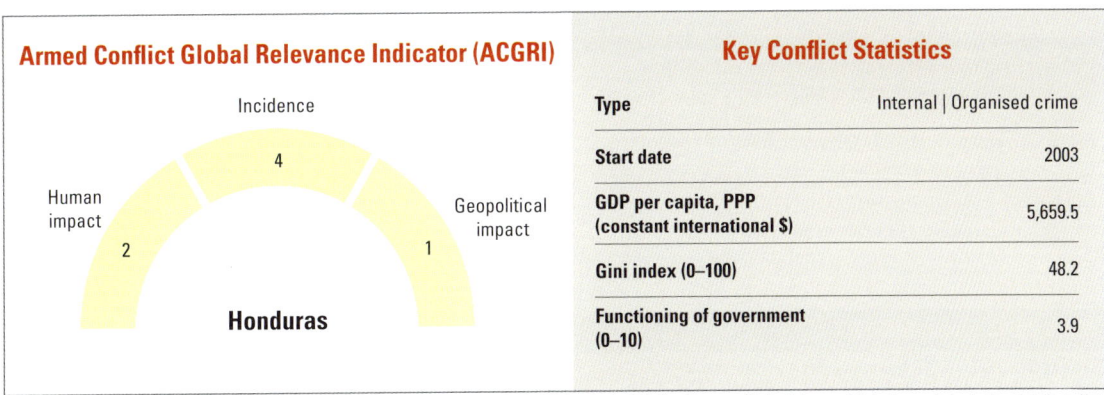

Type	Internal | Organised crime
Start date	2003
GDP per capita, PPP (constant international $)	5,659.5
Gini index (0–100)	48.2
Functioning of government (0–10)	3.9

ACGRI pillars: IISS calculation based on multiple sources for 2021 and January–April 2022 (scale: 0–100). See Notes on Methodology and Data Appendix for further details on Key Conflict Statistics.

or 'Porky', with international cocaine trafficking and related crimes. The charges placed Mendoza on the FBI's most-wanted list, with a US$100,000 reward for information leading to his arrest.[3]

Political developments in 2021 could be relevant for the long-standing governance flaws in Honduras. On 28 November 2021, Xiomara Castro was elected president in an election that was widely considered free and fair. Castro is the wife of Manuel Zelaya, the former democratically elected president who was ousted in the 2009 coup d'état. Her victory is a win for the LIBRE Party, Honduras' leftist party. Castro ran on an anti-corruption platform and promised to address organised crime, poverty, inequality and land reform.

Analysts remain wary of earlier allegations of corruption against Castro's husband and family but her first steps in office signalled her willingness to combat governance flaws.

Immediately following her election, the US Department of Justice unsealed an indictment for drug trafficking and corruption against outgoing president Juan Orlando Hernández, and formally requested his extradition. Hernández is currently under house arrest. On 9 March 2022, the former commander of the National Police, Juan Carlos Bonilla (also known as 'El Tigre'), who directed the National Police from 2012–13, was arrested in a joint US–Honduran operation authorised by Castro and extradited to the US.

An economic recovery began in 2021, with an estimated 12.5% GDP growth.[4] However, this was not sufficient to reverse the massive socio-economic deterioration prompted by the coronavirus pandemic and Hurricane Iota and Tropical Storm Eta. Restrictions on migrant workers and international travel also made it harder for people to leave Honduras and find employment abroad, depriving working-class communities of economic opportunities. Together, these factors resulted in a massive 9% GDP contraction in 2020. GDP per capita at purchasing power parity is not expected to return to its pre-pandemic level until 2022.

In 2021, Honduras registered 3,651 homicide cases, an increase from the 3,599 reported in 2020.[5] Violence remained high in massively overcrowded prisons, with targeted killings, massacres and riots, including a clash between gang members at a high-security prison which killed five people and injured 39.[6]

Conflict Parties

Military Police of Public Order (PMOP) and National Anti-Gang Force (FNAMP)

Strength: The PMOP has around 4,000 members. The FNAMP has 500 members.[7]

Areas of operation: Throughout Honduras, with a focus on areas with high gang and drug-trafficking presences, usually major urban centres or locations with formal or informal border crossings such as Tegucigalpa, San Pedro Sula, Palmerola and the Guatemala–Honduras border centred in Copán.

Leadership and structure: Infantry Col. Rosbel Leonel Hernández Aguilar (PMOP leader). Lt-Col. Amílcar Hernández (FNAMP leader).
The PMOP has eight combat battalions and one canine battalion and reports to the Ministry of Defence. The FNAMP reports to the police but has not publicly defined its operational structure.

Military Police of Public Order (PMOP) and National Anti-Gang Force (FNAMP)

History: The PMOP was created by congress in 2013 to address the increasingly concerning presence of organised criminal groups in Honduras, despite concerns about a militarised police force. FNAMP was formed in July 2018 as a special unit to combat organised crime.

Objectives: Retake territory from the MS-13 and decapitate its operational structures while combatting transnational organised crime and drug trafficking.

Opponents and affiliates/allies:
Opponents: MS-13; other smaller gangs; and local drug-trafficking organisations.
Allies: parts of the Anti-Gang Unit of the National Police; the TIGRES special-forces unit of the police; the military; and US military/police trainers.

Resources/capabilities: Total military budget: US$390 million.[8] Line items of budgets have not been published publicly.

Mara Salvatrucha (MS-13)

Strength: 9,000–15,000 full members and around 40,000 recruits in training, lookouts and messengers waiting to be formally initiated into the gang.

Areas of operation: Throughout Honduras, with concentrated territorial control in the cities of San Pedro Sula, Puerto Cortes and Omoa, and in the department of Copán along the border with Guatemala.

Leadership and structure: Senior MS-13 leadership in Honduras remains largely in prison, though few are identified. The group's national leader, Alexander Mendoza, escaped in February 2020 and remains at large. Carlos Alberto Álvarez (also known as 'Cholo Houston') and Dimas Aguilar (also known as 'Taca el Oso') are considered key leaders. Edgardo Osorio (also known as 'El Cuervo') was a key MS-13 extortionist who was captured by police in 2020 and remains incarcerated.
Compartmentalised leadership structure with numerous *clicas* (highly compartmentalised units at street level), forming *programas* (groups of *clicas*), which in turn report to the *ranfla* (prison-based senior leadership).

History: Founded in the 1980s in poor and marginalised neighbourhoods of Los Angeles. In the 1990s, US authorities deported many incarcerated Honduran MS-13 members. The MS-13 members arrived in Honduras with weak community and country ties and established cells for their own protection.

Objectives: Diversify its criminal portfolio by controlling key cocaine-trafficking nodes, sell krispy and expand into the control of migrant-smuggling routes. Its primary objective is to become a vertically integrated transnational criminal structure allied with Mexican drug-trafficking groups and control multiple criminal revenue streams.

Opponents and affiliates/allies:
Opponents: Sectors of the state security forces not involved in corruption practices; smaller gangs (such as Barrio or Calle 18, the Chirizos and Ponce); extra-judicial paramilitary groups; and rival criminal groups involved in cocaine trafficking.
Allies: The MS-13 structures in El Salvador and Guatemala; the CPS and the CJNG in Mexico; and Venezuelan and Colombian cocaine suppliers.

Resources/capabilities: Proceeds from cocaine trans-shipment and migrant smuggling, as well as controlling local drug markets, provide the group with a yearly income of tens of millions of US dollars. Other localised revenue sources include investments in motels, car lots, private security firms, buses and public transportation. Advanced tunnelling techniques, cocaine-laboratory operation and expanding territorial control have allowed the gang to protect its operations, store products and increase revenues.

Conflict Drivers

Security

Criminal infighting:
In regions where the MS-13 continues to expand, there is constant armed fighting for territorial control between multiple groups, exacerbated by shifting alliances and battle lines in contested areas for drug production and transport. These dynamics reinforce the conflict, drive internal displacement and migration to the Mexico–US border, and undermine state legitimacy. As of December 2019, an estimated 247,000 Hondurans were internally displaced due to violence, at least 55% of whom were women.[9]

Political

Corruption and impunity:
High levels of corruption and impunity allow criminal organisations to expand and grow stronger, ultimately fuelling conflict. The widespread perception of corruption in the ruling

National Party contributed to the turnout for the November 2021 election, in which the National Party experienced major losses while the LIBRE Party conducted successful campaigns.

Economic and social

Poverty and inequality:
According to the 2021 report by the United Nations Economic Commission for Latin America and the Caribbean, 48.3% of Honduras' population lives in poverty and 22.9% in extreme poverty.[10] Whilst incomes have improved since the height of the coronavirus pandemic, they have not fully recovered to their pre-pandemic levels. Hurricane Iota and Tropical Storm Eta both left lasting damage, in particular to smallholders and rural communities, and recovery has been slow. Despite the country's growing industrial base and the government's efforts to diversify exports, unemployment remained high in Honduras and investment low amid widespread violence and corruption.

Natural disasters and the coronavirus pandemic:
The pandemic continues to exacerbate the country's pre-existing environmental, social and political drivers of conflict. Rural and economically disadvantaged communities continue to struggle to access healthcare services. Only 39% of the population had been vaccinated as of December 2021, amid widespread governance flaws and government inefficiency.[11] Natural disasters and the lack of adequate responses continue to present ongoing stability threats. A January 2022 report from the International Rescue Committee named Honduras among the top three countries in Latin America and the Caribbean at highest risk of humanitarian deterioration over the next year.[12] In January 2022, CARE International named Honduras in a list of global humanitarian crises that received insufficient aid in 2021, citing at least 2.8m people in need of humanitarian aid.[13]

Key Events in 2021–22

POLITICAL EVENTS

30 March 2021
US Department of Justice convicts Tony Hernández, former president Juan Orlando Hernández's brother, of drug trafficking and sentences him to life in prison.

1 July
The US releases Section 353 List of Corrupt and Undemocratic Actors for Guatemala, Honduras, and El Salvador, also known as the Engel List.

15 October
The US Department of Justice announces the Task Force to Combat Corruption in Central America.

MILITARY/VIOLENT EVENTS

13 February 2021
MS-13 leader Alexander Mendoza is freed from police custody after 20 gunmen storm a court building in El Progreso and kill three police officers.

13 February
Journalist Henry Fiallos receives death threats after reporting on a homicide investigation that implicated police officers.

17 June
A three-hour brawl between gang members kills five and injures 39 at the La Tolva high-security prison, east of Tegucigalpa.

6 July
Juan Moncada, the leader of a Honduran agricultural cooperative, is shot dead during an ongoing land struggle between large landowners, criminal groups and smallholders.

Timeline

28 November
Xiomara Castro of the LIBRE Party is elected president in a general election that is widely seen as free and fair.

27 January 2022
Castro is sworn in as president of Honduras. She appoints José Manuel Zelaya Rosales, Manuel Zelaya's nephew, as defence minister. Castro expresses her intent to request the assistance of the UN to establish an international anti-corruption commission, and commits to advance legislative reforms to enable the commission to succeed.

15 February
Juan Orlando Hernández is arrested under accusations of cocaine trafficking and corruption in a joint US–Honduras operation.

9 March
Former director of the National Police Juan Carlos 'El Tigre' Bonilla is arrested for drug trafficking and corruption, and extradited to the US.

13 April
The Supreme Court of Honduras signs an extradition order for Juan Orlando Hernández.

21 April
Juan Orlando Hernández is extradited to the US.

3 November
US Department of Justice charges Mendoza with racketeering, narcotics trafficking and firearms offences.

2 February 2022
The Armed Forces of Honduras transfers command of the Army, the Honduran Air Force, and the PMOP, under a decree from Defence Minister José Manuel Zelaya Rosales.

Conflict Outlook

Political scenarios

The electoral victory of Castro and her LIBRE party was largely driven by her promise to tackle the massive cocaine-fuelled corruption of the Hernández era. The MS-13 leadership, seeing the high likelihood of her victory, did not support Hernández's hand-chosen successor. However, the gang has long-standing feuds with Castro and her husband, former president Zelaya.

While the MS-13 may have lost the broad protection and freedom of operations it had under the Hernández administration, it has not lost its firepower, with extensive territorial control and ongoing alliances with Colombian and Mexican drug-trafficking organisations.

There are two likely scenarios for the evolution of the conflict. Firstly, the Castro administration could take advantage of the financial, military and police support offered by the US, European Union, and UN and make a serious effort to retake territorial control and weaken the group's political/military structure. This would likely lead to a spike in violence. Alternatively, the Castro government could quietly negotiate with criminal structures, particularly the MS-13, to allow their operations to continue in exchange for concessions. This could reduce violence in the short term but would likely lead to further consolidation and growth of the MS-13 as a drug-trafficking and alternative governance structure.

Food insecurity and critical-infrastructure damage will remain a high risk as Honduras is very exposed to climate change and regularly affected by tropical storms, floods, droughts and landslides. Ongoing and future disasters will increasingly strain the government's effectiveness to support populations at risk and in need.

Violence, economic hardship and subpar post-hurricane humanitarian assistance will continue to push Hondurans to flee the country, which may empower the MS-13 to further take control of migrant routes and delegitimise the state.

Escalation potential and conflict-related risks

Additional risks are posed by the MS-13's diversified revenue streams from 2021, its expanded transnational operations with Colombian producers and its role as a direct wholesale supplier for Mexican transnational criminal organisations. The ongoing shift in the gang's operations from transit to cultivation and production (with vertically integrated capabilities) has expanded the gang's political power, enhanced its military strength and further undermined anti-corruption efforts. If the Castro administration accommodates the MS-13, these trends will continue to consolidate.

Strategic implications and global influences

The less draconian approach to deterring Central American migration taken by the Biden administration may increase migration flows and create instability in Guatemala and Mexico, as well as along the Mexico–US border. While the Biden administration intends to combat the root causes of migration, its programmes have remained largely in the planning stages with little implementation on the ground. Even the joint task force that was announced as the primary initiative has yet to be created amid the lack of trusted interlocutors under the Hernández administration.

Notes

[1] Krispy is a marijuana derivative sold in blocks and laced with chemicals. In interviews, the drug was described as much more powerful than marijuana. It is favoured by criminal groups because it is more addictive and can be sold at much higher prices than marijuana.

[2] For a broader look at this evolution, see Douglas Farah and Kathryn Babineau, 'The Rapid Evolution of the MS13 in El Salvador and Honduras from Gang to Tier-one Threat to Central America and US Security Interests', Perry Center Occasional Paper, William J. Perry Center for Hemispheric Defense Studies, National Defense University, March 2018.

[3] Department of Justice, 'Leader of MS-13 in Honduras and Drug Supplier for MS-13 Charged in Manhattan Federal Court with Racketeering, Narcotics Trafficking, and Firearms Offenses', 3 November 2021.

[4] IMF, 'World Economic Outlook Database', April 2022

[5] InSight Crime, 'InSight Crime's 2021 Homicide Round-Up', 1 February 2022.

[6] 'At Least 5 Killed, 39 Injured in Gang Brawl in Honduras Prison', Reuters, 18 June 2021.

[7] Washington Office on Latin America, 'El papel de las fuerzas armadas en la seguridad pública en Honduras' [The Role of the Armed Forces in Public Security in Honduras], August 2020; and Iris Amador, 'Honduras Transforms Unit to Counter Maras and Gangs', Diálogo, 20 September 2018.

[8] World Bank, 'Military Expenditure (% of GDP) – Honduras'.

[9] International Committee of the Red Cross, 'Honduras: The Displaced', 15 June 2021.

[10] United Nations Economic Commission for Latin America and the Caribbean, 'Evaluación de los efectos e impactos de la tormenta tropical Eta y el huracán Iota en Honduras' [Evaluation of the Effects and Impacts of Tropical Storm Eta and Hurricane Iota in Honduras], May 2021.

[11] International Rescue Committee, 'Crisis in Honduras: Ongoing Violence and Climate Shocks', 26 January 2022.

[12] International Rescue Committee, 'Press Release: Haiti, Honduras and Venezuela to Face Humanitarian Risks with Regional Impact in 2022 if Unaddressed: IRC Warns', 19 January 2022.

[13] Care International, 'In the Shadow of the Pandemic: 10 Crises That Didn't Make Headlines in 2021', 13 January 2022.

Regional Outlook

The outlook for curbing conflict in the Americas remains bleak amid the intractability of its root causes, the increasing political clout and transnational reach of criminal groups and rising regional and international demand for illicit drugs. However, certain political developments have the potential to lead to some pacification in the region in the medium term, including possible progress on the Venezuela stalemate and steps towards a full implementation (and possible extension) of the peace agreement in Colombia.

Prospects for peace

Substantial progress towards durable peace in the region will remain elusive for the foreseeable future. Nonetheless, there are some glimmers of hope. The modest easing of US sanctions on Venezuela in May 2022 (following a US–Venezuela rapprochement of sorts induced by energy-security concerns) may prompt a revival in negotiations, suspended in October 2021, between the regime of Nicolás Maduro and the opposition. Currently, Venezuela acts as a refuge for Colombia's non-state armed groups and plays a significant role in global criminal networks and economies; any step towards resolving the country's political, economic and institutional crisis would therefore contribute to curbing regional violence trends.

In Colombia, Gustavo Petro's victory in the June 2022 presidential elections may herald some progress towards the country's pacification. His commitment to fully implement the 2016 peace agreement (including its rural and socio-economic development pillars, largely neglected by the outgoing administration) and negotiate with the leftist guerrilla National Liberation Army (ELN) and other conflict parties (including the Gulf Cartel and FARC dissidents) may contribute to easing violence in the medium term, although risks remain. Petro's willingness to re-establish relations with Venezuela may also help to defuse bilateral tensions and improve broader regional and international cooperation against transnational criminal groups.

Escalation potential and regional spillovers

The region remains in a particularly perilous situation following the coronavirus pandemic, which aggravated its many socio-economic, political and institutional fragilities while offering ample opportunities for criminal groups to prosper and entrench themselves in local communities by providing support and job opportunities. Governability challenges will also remain rife amid rising political polarisation and fragmentation; governments facing worsening legitimacy crises will increasingly struggle to deliver basic services.

Rising inflation (boosted by the war in Ukraine that began in February 2022) will be a particular challenge in the short term, curtailing real income, especially that of the poorest, and fuelling, in the absence of major government buffers, food insecurity – already at its highest level in 15 years in late 2020.[1] In fragile countries particularly vulnerable to climate change, such as Haiti or those in Central America's Northern Triangle, increasing inflation and food insecurity will result in heightened domestic instability and drive uncontrolled migration flows, with negative repercussions for regional security and governance.

The constant optimisation and reconfiguration of criminal groups' business according to profit margins and demand will drive contestation and violence around drug-trafficking routes (including ports) and markets. These developments are likely to have impacts in countries that were – until recently – largely spared from drugs-related violence, such as Costa Rica and Panama in Central America (where drugs seizures are on the rise) and Ecuador in South America, where gang rivalries have produced six large-scale prison massacres in Ecuador since the beginning of 2021, leading the government to impose several states of emergency.

Mexican DTOs' push towards fentanyl will continue, driving conflict as these groups reconfigure their business and areas of control accordingly. Although cocaine will remain part of their portfolio in the near term, a shift to mainly fentanyl is a possible scenario in the medium term, with important implications for regional drugs-trafficking dynamics.

Strategic implications and global influences

The transnational character of criminal groups in the Americas has major implications for the rule of law and migration trends, making conflict in the region globally relevant. While the US remains the most consequential external power influencing regional conflict dynamics via its policies on illicit drugs, firearms access and migration, China is increasingly playing a role in these dynamics, notably through its provision of fentanyl precursors and pre-precursors to Mexican DTOs.

Within Latin America, the Venezuela flashpoint is an arena for great-power competition through which – besides China – Iran, Turkey and Russia have gained a foothold in the region. Its migrant outflows and the protection Venezuelan territory affords Colombian criminal groups are also perennial drivers of regional instability. Events in Colombia, the region's cocaine-production powerhouse, are also influencing conflict trends.

Recent political changes in Colombia and Venezuela may herald developments that improve the regional conflict outlook. Petro's electoral victory in Colombia will likely provide further impetus to efforts to reform prevailing – and largely unsuccessful – iron-fist drug policies in the Americas in favour of less repressive approaches that focus on socio-economic development. For Washington, the United States' fentanyl health emergency will likely increase the urgency with which it seeks to tackle drug-demand issues and firearms-trafficking south of the border.

Notes

[1] On inflation, see UN Economic Commission for Latin America and the Caribbean, 'Social Panorama of Latin America', 2021. On food insecurity, see Pan American Health Organization, World Health Organization, 'New UN Report: Hunger in Latin America and the Caribbean Rose by 13.8 Million People in Just One Year', 30 November 2021.

2 Europe and Eurasia

Regional Analysis	102	Nagorno-Karabakh	118
Conflict Reports		**Regional Outlook**	127
Russia–Ukraine	106		

A Ukrainian soldier stands guard over the Odesa National Academic Opera and Ballet Theatre, 14 March 2022

Overview

Russia's large-scale invasion of Ukraine on 24 February 2022 began the largest armed conflict in Europe since the Second World War, with far-reaching implications for Eurasia, Europe and beyond. While Russia's primary goal of imposing a pro-Moscow regime in Ukraine has failed, the outcome of the war remains highly uncertain amid a significant risk that it could escalate to even more intense or destructive forms of conflict.

Elsewhere in the region, relations between Armenia and Azerbaijan remained uneasy. In the absence of a peace settlement to stabilise the ceasefire that ended their war over Nagorno-Karabakh in late 2020, the threat of renewed conflict remains real – especially given developments that suggest Azerbaijan may seek to gain control over further territory.

During the reporting period, Georgia's Russia-occupied breakaway provinces of Abkhazia and South Ossetia remained calm but under tension, while several incidents (including explosions and a rocket attack in April 2022) took place in Moldova's separatist region of Transnistria.

A flare-up of tensions between Tajikistan and Kyrgyzstan in April 2021, which saw approximately 50 people killed, highlighted not only their difficult bilateral relationship but also the larger issue of un-demarcated borders in Central Asia.[1]

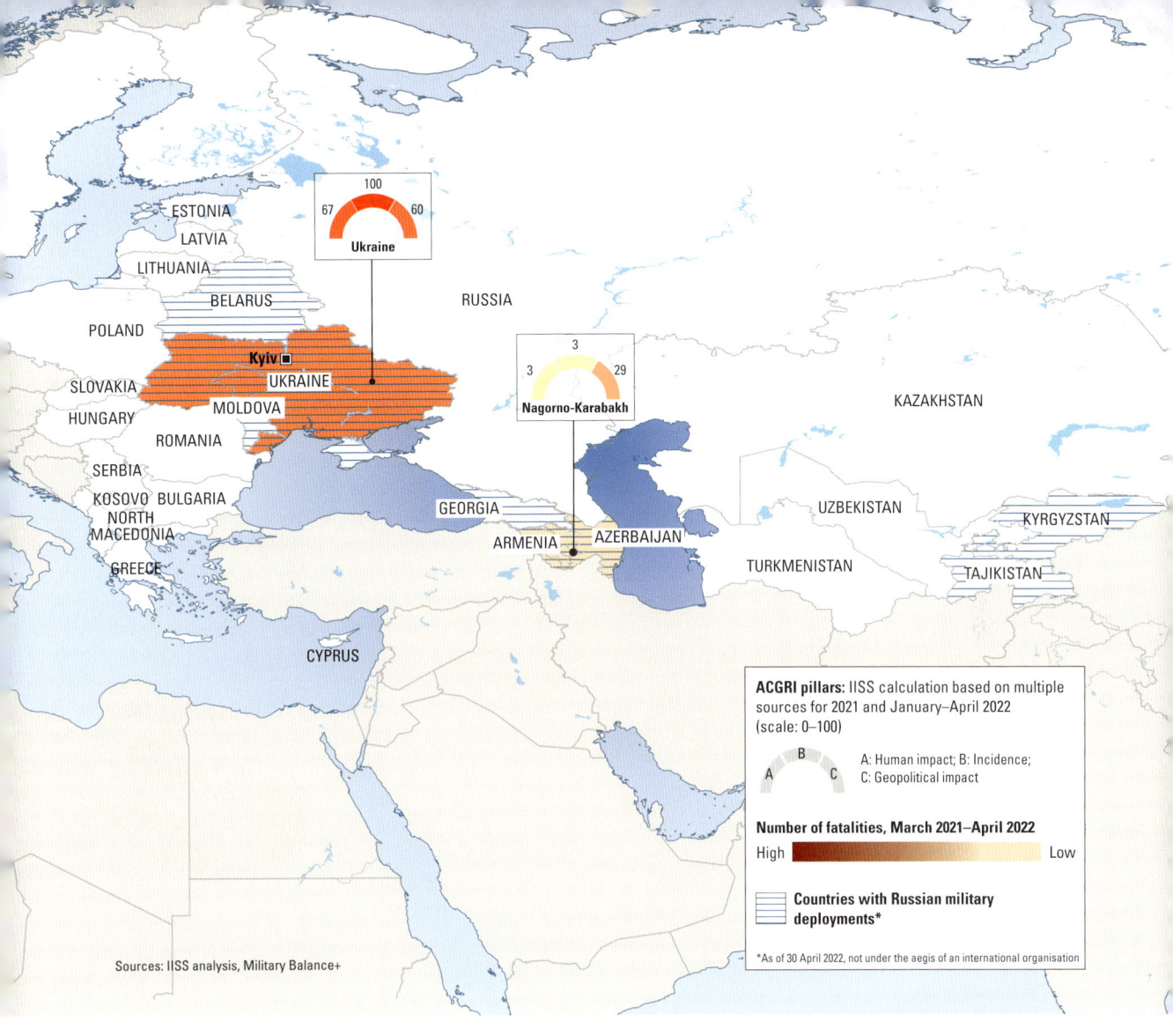

In Focus: Eurasia and the War in Ukraine

Russia's invasion of Ukraine has begun to impact wider security and economic dynamics in Eurasia. In time, the war could influence other recent or incipient regional conflicts and in some cases exacerbate domestic fragility. One already visible consequence of the conflict in Ukraine has been the weakening of Russia's diplomatic influence.

Security effects

In security terms, Russia's invasion of Ukraine is the most potent expression of its broader aspiration to restore Russian influence – and, where possible, dominance – over the former countries of the Soviet Union, a region it continues to describe as the 'near abroad'. While Ukraine plays a uniquely significant role in President Vladimir Putin's conception of Russia's identity and his own historical mission, in most cases Moscow does not aim to occupy and annex territory elsewhere. However, the war demonstrates the cost that Putin is prepared to both inflict and incur to subordinate other territories.

The security risks are most acute for Kazakhstan, which shares with Russia the longest continuous land border in the world. The invasion has intensified the former's concerns – present since independence in 1991 and more pressing since Russia's occupation of Crimea in 2014 – that Moscow might one day try to annex territory in northern Kazakhstan. A social-media post in August 2022 by former president and current deputy head of Russia's Security Council Dmitry Medvedev, which claimed that Kazakhstan was an artificial state that comprised former Russian territories, seemed to confirm these fears. Medvedev later deleted the post and attributed it to hackers.

The war in Ukraine has affected Moldova, which borders Ukraine, more immediately and directly. Since the early 1990s, Russia has dominated and stationed troops in the separatist but unrecognised republic in Transnistria. Tensions between Moldova and Russia have simmered in the past year, ever since the former's President Maia Sandu expressed a determination for her country to join the European Union and gained a supportive parliamentary majority. In April 2022, Transnistria suffered several violent incidents, including explosions and a rocket attack. These events, as well as Russian accusations of Ukrainian 'provocations', raised fears that the former might try to extend the war into Moldova. These concerns intensified when Russian military authorities, notably General Rustam Minnekaev, acting commander of the Central Military District, stated that Russian forces sought to occupy all of southern Ukraine to provide 'another way to Transnistria'.[2] Immediately after the explosions, Sandu convened an urgent meeting of Moldova's Supreme Security Council to discuss their implications.

The war in Ukraine has significant repercussions on Belarusian sovereignty, though in this case a formal Russian attack on the country's territorial integrity appears less likely. Before the invasion, the country's leader, Alexander Lukashenko, had already become more dependent on Russia after the latter supported his suppression of a peaceful nationwide uprising in late 2020. Following joint military exercises in February 2022, Russia kept its troops on Belarusian territory, using the positions to launch both ground and missile attacks against Ukraine once the invasion began. While Lukashenko endorsed the Russian narrative of the war, Belarusian partisans employed physical sabotage and cyber attacks to hinder the movement of troops and materiel by rail. Minsk also resisted pressure from Moscow to send in Belarusian forces to take part in the hostilities in Ukraine, probably calculating that such a move would escalate the risks to Belarus itself and undermine the cohesion of its armed forces, a proportion of which would not wish to aggress Ukraine.

Other implications of the war have demonstrated the limits of Russian power. As Moscow faced growing manpower losses in Ukraine, it began to look for ways to replenish its infantry, including from forces deployed in neighbouring countries. It redeployed some of its forces from the Russian-occupied statelets of Abkhazia and South Ossetia in Georgia to Ukraine. More significantly,

Figure 1: Votes by selected countries in the region on the UN General Assembly resolution 'Aggression against Ukraine', 2 March 2022

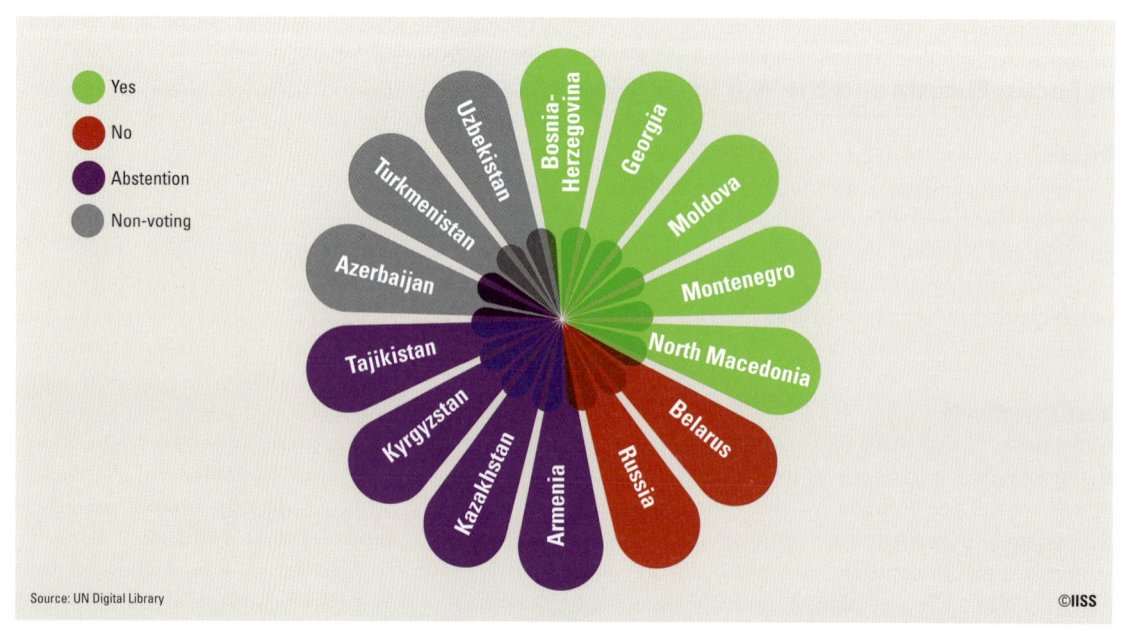

Source: UN Digital Library

Russia redeployed a significant proportion of the 201st Motorised Rifle Division, based in Tajikistan for decades, to fight in the war. In April, Ukraine announced that it had destroyed a battalion tactical group composed of these forces.

A proposal by Anatoly Bibilov, the de facto leader of South Ossetia, to hold a referendum on joining the Russian Federation was dropped after he lost his re-election bid in May 2022. It was a reminder that non-sovereign entities created and sustained in the region by Russia remain sources of uncertainty and, potentially, instability.

Economic effects

Eurasian states that retain close ties to Russia have started to be adversely impacted by the economic fallout of the war and the West's sanctions on Moscow. Russia – as the key regional export market – is shrinking, and its economic travails have caused exchange-rate volatility. Compounding matters, several of Russia's neighbours, notably Kyrgyzstan and Tajikistan, face a significant decline in remittances from migrant labourers in Russia, while the collapse of trade with Ukraine has further weakened economic prospects. On the other hand, hydrocarbon exporters, especially Kazakhstan, received a fiscal windfall from the oil-price spike between February and July 2022. However, a series of disruptions to the flow of oil through the Caspian Pipeline Consortium, a vital export artery (that passes through Russia) for Kazakhstan's three supergiant oilfields, demonstrated the country's economic dependence on its relationship with its northern neighbour.

These economic effects are significant because a decline in living standards is a risk factor for instability. This is especially true in Central Asia, where high inequality, demands for more inclusive growth, and authoritarian rule are already creating conditions for instability and civil conflict.

Diplomatic consequences

Eurasian countries' diplomatic responses to the war in Ukraine reflect how security and economic factors are unsettling the region. Apart from Belarus, no state has sided with Russia in its invasion of Ukraine. Two notable cases stand out. Firstly, Kazakhstan's relationship with Russia became strained due to the former's lack of support for the war and President Kassym-Jomart Tokayev's public refusal to recognise the Donetsk and Luhansk people's republics.

Secondly, although Azerbaijan's President Ilham Aliyev met with Putin two days before Russia invaded Ukraine, Baku continued to supply Kyiv with oil and oil products and to support the principle of territorial integrity with regard to Ukraine. It has also questioned the extension, beyond 2025, of the mandate of Russian peacekeepers deployed in Nagorno-Karabakh following the 2020 war between Armenia and Azerbaijan, in an attempt to also push Armenia to adopt a more conciliatory position in bilateral negotiations.

Russia's war in Ukraine, launched to subjugate one post-Soviet state, has created forces that are undermining its influence elsewhere in Eurasia while also harming the region itself.

Notes

[1] 'Kyrgyzstan, Tajikistan Agree New Ceasefire After Border Clashes', Al-Jazeera, 1 May 2021.

[2] Michael Lipin et al., 'How Russia Tries to Counter Moldova Separatist Region's Westward Drift', Voice of America, 7 May 2022. Original quote in Russian: 'Kontrol nad iuguom Urainii - eto eshche odin vykhod v Pridnyestrov!ye, gde takzhe otmechaiutsia fakty pritesneniia russkoiazichnoguo naseleniia' [Control over the south of Ukraine is another way out to Transnistria, where there are also facts of oppression of the Russian-speaking population]. See 'Voyenniye RF zaiavili o planakh obespechit sukhoputnyi koridor v Krym i vykhod k Pridnestrov!io' [The Military of the Russian Federation Announced Plans to Provide a Land Corridor to the Crimea and Access to Transnistria], Interfax, 22 April 2022.

RUSSIA–UKRAINE

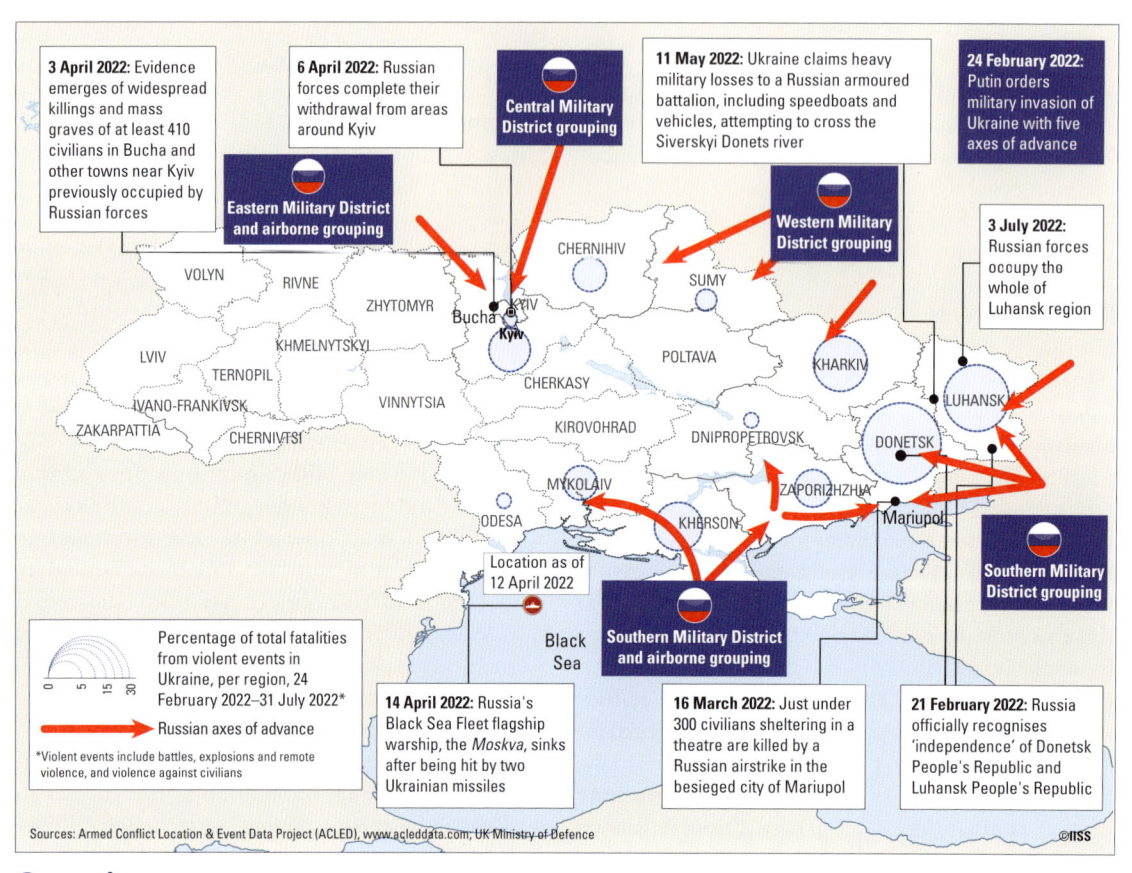

3 April 2022: Evidence emerges of widespread killings and mass graves of at least 410 civilians in Bucha and other towns near Kyiv previously occupied by Russian forces

6 April 2022: Russian forces complete their withdrawal from areas around Kyiv

Central Military District grouping

11 May 2022: Ukraine claims heavy military losses to a Russian armoured battalion, including speedboats and vehicles, attempting to cross the Siverskyi Donets river

24 February 2022: Putin orders military invasion of Ukraine with five axes of advance

Eastern Military District and airborne grouping

Western Military District grouping

3 July 2022: Russian forces occupy the whole of Luhansk region

Percentage of total fatalities from violent events in Ukraine, per region, 24 February 2022–31 July 2022*

→ Russian axes of advance

*Violent events include battles, explosions and remote violence, and violence against civilians

14 April 2022: Russia's Black Sea Fleet flagship warship, the *Moskva*, sinks after being hit by two Ukrainian missiles

Southern Military District and airborne grouping

16 March 2022: Just under 300 civilians sheltering in a theatre are killed by a Russian airstrike in the besieged city of Mariupol

21 February 2022: Russia officially recognises 'independence' of Donetsk People's Republic and Luhansk People's Republic

Southern Military District grouping

Sources: Armed Conflict Location & Event Data Project (ACLED), www.acleddata.com; UK Ministry of Defence

©IISS

Overview

Russia launched a massive and unprovoked invasion of Ukraine on 24 February 2022, having for several months amassed military personnel and equipment close to its border with the country. For the previous eight years, Moscow had waged a limited and mostly low-intensity war in eastern Ukraine's Donbas region through its local proxy forces in the Donetsk and Luhansk people's republics (the DPR and LPR). In 2021, the Organization for Security and Co-operation in Europe Special Monitoring Mission to Ukraine (SMM) reported 91 civilian casualties and 1,133 'explosions attributable to fire from MLRS [multiple-launch rocket systems], artillery, mortars and tanks' from all sides.[1] Developments in early 2022 have transformed this unresolved conflict into the largest inter-state war of aggression in Europe since the Second World War.

The signs of Russia's coming escalation became increasingly visible through 2021. In a rehearsal for its later invasion, between March and April 2021 Russia amassed an estimated 100,000 troops near Ukraine and in the Russian-occupied Crimean peninsula for what the Kremlin called a snap military exercise. September saw the *Zapad* ('West') military exercise held in Russia and Belarus, including in the Russian exclave of Kaliningrad, following a previous *Zapad* exercise in 2017. Russian troops remained in Belarus after the exercise; in the remainder of 2021, Russia amassed its invasion force close to Ukraine's borders.

In July, the Kremlin's website published a 7,000-word essay credited solely to Russian President Vladimir Putin entitled 'On the Historical Unity of Russians and Ukrainians'. It provided a clear

Armed Conflict Global Relevance Indicator (ACGRI)

Ukraine
- Incidence: 100
- Human impact: 67
- Geopolitical impact: 60

Key Conflict Statistics

Type	Inter-state*
Start date	2022
Violent events	12,117
Refugees	5,707,967**
Top three weapons and military-equipment donors to Ukraine	United States (US$6.3bn), Poland (US$1.8bn), and United Kingdom (US$1.1bn)***

ACGRI pillars: IISS calculation based on multiple sources for 2021 and January–April 2022 (scale: 0–100). See Notes on Methodology and Data Appendix for further details on Key Conflict Statistics. *The conflict type was internationalised-internal until 24 February 2022. **As of 4 May 2022. ***Specific commitments, 24 January–1 July 2022. Taken from Arianna Antezza, Andre Frank, Pascal Frank, Lukas Franz, Ekaterina Rebinskaya and Christoph Trebesch, 'The Ukraine Support Tracker: Which countries help Ukraine and how?', Kiel working paper, no. 2218, 2022. For the Russia–Ukraine conflict, the indicator relies mainly on data for Ukraine as this is the theatre of the conflict.

exposition of his personal desire to reimpose Russian imperial control over Ukraine, referencing a distorted historical interpretation of both the Soviet Union's and the Russian Tsarist Empire's control of Ukraine.

On 15 December, the Russian Ministry of Foreign Affairs issued a draft document detailing what it called 'legal security guarantees from the United States and NATO', covering a range of topics and notably calling for a moratorium on the further expansion of NATO – including into Ukraine – despite the fact that neither the Alliance nor Kyiv had any immediate plans in this area. Washington responded by proposing talks on arms control and on the transparency of military deployments in Europe. Putin's claims that Russia was not about to attack Ukraine were exposed as deceitful when the US and United Kingdom released secret intelligence detailing Russia's military build-up around Ukraine in the winter of 2021–22. As a result, some of the initiative was stolen from Russia as its coercive diplomacy was drowned out in global news cycles by evidence-based warnings of imminent invasion. In January, the US government correctly predicted that Russia's invasion of Ukraine would begin sometime the following month.

On 21 February, Putin announced that Russia would recognise the DPR and LPR as independent states. He justified the decision by claiming – without evidence – that the Ukrainian state was perpetrating atrocities against the residents of the DPR and LPR. On 24 February, Putin declared the launch of a 'special military operation' in Ukraine to overthrow its government. He threatened a swift response to any third-party interventions while reminding the world that Russia possessed nuclear weapons. The initial invasion force comprised several disconnected lines of advance that entered Ukraine from western Russia, Crimea and Belarus. By dividing its forces in this way, Russia's early progress was uncoordinated and uneven. The attack on southern Ukraine proved relatively successful, with Russian forces capturing the city of Kherson early in the war. However, those forces targeting Kyiv experienced huge setbacks, floundering in the face of significant Ukrainian resistance and suffering major losses of personnel and equipment in the process. The Kremlin failed to achieve its initial war aim of regime change by advancing into Kyiv[2] and forcefully deposing Ukrainian President Volodymyr Zelenskyy.

In the opening days of the invasion, when Russia's coming defeat around Kyiv was not yet apparent, Zelenskyy refused a US offer to evacuate him. He remained in Ukraine to coordinate the defence against Russian forces and garner international support for Ukraine. To supplement the armed forces, civilians answered government calls to enlist or to engage in civil resistance. The stiff Ukrainian response encountered by the Russian army appeared to take it by surprise, raising questions around the efficacy of Moscow's pre-invasion intelligence assessments. Intercepted personal communications of Russian soldiers indicated that some were suffering from low morale and confusion around the aim of the war. Instances of Russian soldiers asking Ukrainians for food or stealing supplies as they advanced suggested that they had been ordered into Ukraine expecting a campaign that would last days or weeks.

In April, Russia recognised its defeat on Kyiv's outskirts and duly withdrew its forces with the aim of seizing swathes of territory in eastern and southern Ukraine, building on the capture of Kherson and on the foothold provided by DPR and LPR territory. Russia began to withdraw its forces from around Kyiv to redeploy them – alongside fresh forces – to the Donbas. The rest of Ukraine was not spared: Russian missiles continued to intermittently strike cities, including Kyiv, Lviv and Odesa. The Russian Black Sea Fleet flagship, the cruiser *Moskva*, was sunk on 18 April by shore-launched Ukrainian anti-ship missiles, marking a major victory for Ukraine's defensive efforts. In early May, Ukraine secured another victory by relieving the pressure faced by Kharkiv, Ukraine's second-largest city, compelling Russian forces to hasten their realignment of forces towards the Donbas.

Russia's subsequent military progress in the Donbas was slow. After a long siege, on 20 May the defence of the Azovstal steel plant in the southern port city of Mariupol ended as the remaining Ukrainian defenders were told to surrender by their leadership in Kyiv. By capturing Mariupol, which is located at the southern end of Donetsk region, Russia held a contiguous line of captured territory between the DPR, LPR and occupied Crimea. In May and June Moscow switched its focus to Luhansk region. Russian forces encircled the town of Severodonetsk, resulting in protracted street fighting as the Ukrainians fought hard to delay the Russian advance. By June, Severodonetsk was in Russian hands and the nearby city of Lysychansk came under attack. At this point, Russia was close to capturing the entirety of Luhansk region.

Despite their successes, the sluggishness with which Russian forces advanced in the Donbas, their dependence on artillery to devastate Mariupol and Severodonetsk and their inability to mount a larger offensive across several parts of the front line simultaneously indicated continuing problems with morale, logistics and tactical effectiveness. Nevertheless, by the start of June, Zelenskyy confirmed that Russia controlled around 20% of Ukrainian territory and that Ukraine would continue to fight to recapture its occupied lands. At a NATO summit in Madrid in late June, the Alliance pledged continuing support to Ukraine. Countries including the US and the UK were also involved in significant bilateral transfers of military equipment and support. With neither Russia nor Ukraine yet willing to agree to peace talks, the war was set to continue.

Russia's invasion of Ukraine has been deeply consequential for European security, raising fears in Eastern Europe of possible conflict spillovers into its territory. NATO members Hungary, Poland, Romania and Slovakia border Ukraine and have experienced the arrival of refugees fleeing the conflict. NATO's Baltic member states have seen their security situations worsen, with Lithuania notably facing Russian pressure over Moscow's access to its militarised Baltic-coast exclave of Kaliningrad. These countries have benefited from a boost to NATO's deterrence posture in the region post-invasion, including additional measures to defend their airspaces and the deployment of NATO ground forces. Such measures expanded NATO's Enhanced Forward Presence, which first deployed to Poland and the Baltic states in 2016. NATO's Tailored Forward Presence on its southeastern flank has also been boosted, with Romania set to host additional NATO troops. Sweden and Finland, which had previously decided not to seek full membership (instead having the status of NATO Enhanced Opportunity Partners), applied to become NATO member states in 2022.

Moldova, which includes Transnistria, a thin strip of disputed territory under de facto Russian military control since the end of the Cold War, has also been destabilised by the war. Although the Russian forces stationed in Transnistria have not been used to fight in Ukraine, Moldova's territory could come under direct Russian threat if the Ukrainian southwestern coastal town of Odesa is attacked.

In June, both Ukraine and Moldova received a boost from the European Union when their applications to join the organisation were upgraded by Brussels into formal candidacy status, although achieving full membership is contingent on implementing judicial and anti-corruption reforms and therefore likely to take many years.

Conflict Parties

Armed Forces of Ukraine

Strength: 196,600 active military personnel including 125,600 in the army, 35,000 in the air force and 15,000 in the navy prior to Russia's invasion in 2022.

Areas of operation: 500-kilometre contact line in Ukraine's Donbas region between March 2014 and February 2022. Following Russia's invasion in February 2022, Ukraine's armed forces have been active across the entire east of the country in an arc from Kyiv to Mykolaiv.

Leadership: President Volodymyr Zelenskyy (Supreme Commander-in-Chief of the Armed Forces of Ukraine since May 2019); Gen. Valerii Zaluzhnyi (Commander-in-Chief of the Armed Forces of Ukraine, appointed in July 2021).

Structure: The Armed Forces of Ukraine comprise the Ground Troops (or army), Naval Forces, Air Force, Special Operations Forces, Airborne Assault Troops and the recently established Territorial Defence Forces. They are supported by the National Guard of Ukraine, a peacetime gendarmerie that can be mobilised for military operations during wartime.

History: Severely unprepared at the start of the war in 2014, the Armed Forces of Ukraine subsequently underwent a reorganisation and modernisation process, with training and limited equipment support provided by the US and European partner nations. Since February 2022, Ukraine has mobilised its reserve and territorial forces and received substantial donations of military equipment and training support from partner nations.

Objectives: Previous strategies had focused on the control of territory along the Line of Contact in the Donbas. Since February 2022, the objective has been to repel the Russian invasion.

Opponents: Armed Forces of the Russian Federation, DPR, LPR.

Affiliates/allies: NATO member states have provided Ukraine with military supplies. Since 2020, Ukraine has been a NATO Enhanced Opportunities Partner.

Resources/capabilities: In 2021 Ukraine's defence budget was US$4.3 billion, an increase from US$3.97bn in 2019, and more than double its pre-war figure in 2013 when it was US$1.88bn.[3] Prior to the invasion, the Ukrainian air force fielded an estimated 124 combat-capable aircraft, including 70 fourth-generation fighters (Su-27s and MiG-29s). The Ukrainian army fielded 1,818 artillery pieces and 3,309 armoured fighting vehicles, including 858 main battle tanks.

Armed Forces of the Russian Federation

Strength: Around 900,000 active military personnel, including 280,000 in the army, 165,000 in the Aerospace Forces and 150,000 in the navy at the beginning of 2022. Russia's initial invasion force was estimated to comprise around 150,000 personnel from the armed forces and national guard, including around 75% of Russia's total deployable ground-combat power.

Areas of operation: In the first phase of the invasion, Kyiv was the primary Russian target and Kharkiv the secondary target, with parts of southern Ukraine also conquered. In the second phase, Russian forces have primarily focused on southern and eastern Ukraine.

Leadership: President Vladimir Putin (Supreme Commander-in-Chief of the Armed Forces of the Russian Federation); General of the Army Valery Gerasimov (Chief of the General Staff of the Armed Forces of the Russian Federation).

Structure: Russia's invasion force was drawn from across the country and appears to have been organised into multiple axes of attack based on formations' military district of origin. Eastern Military District forces and Assault Troops attacked towards Kyiv from Belarus, Central Military District and Western Military District forces attacked northeastern and eastern Ukraine respectively, while two Southern Military District groupings attacked in the Donbas and from the Crimean peninsula.

History: After a lengthy period of financial and administrative neglect following the collapse of the Soviet Union, the Armed Forces of the Russian Federation have recently undergone a decade of re-equipment and military modernisation, undertaking limited combat operations in eastern Ukraine from early 2014 and in Syria from 2015.

Objectives: In the first phase of the invasion, the objective was regime change and the conquest of Kyiv. Having failed to achieve this, in the second phase objectives switched to the full conquest of the Donbas while occupying large parts of southern Ukraine and launching indiscriminate missile attacks against Ukrainian cities.

Opponents: Armed Forces of Ukraine.

Affiliates/allies: DPR and LPR. Belarus allowed its territory to be used as a launchpad for the invasion.

Resources/capabilities: In 2021 Russia's defence budget was US$48.5bn. Russia's initial invasion force was reported to include 127 battalion tactical groups, with supporting missile and artillery forces, out of a nominal 168 total in the Armed Forces of the Russian Federation.[4] By the second phase of the invasion, this total had increased to around 140. Pre-war Ukrainian intelligence estimates suggest that, excluding the DPR and LPR militias, the invasion force was equipped with at least 1,400 main battle tanks, 4,000 other armoured fighting vehicles and 1,400 large-calibre artillery pieces and multiple rocket launchers.[5] Ukraine also assessed that Russia had 430 combat aircraft and 360 helicopters available for use – although it is unclear how many of these were actually assigned to the operation – and 70 ships and boats in the Black Sea.[6]

Donetsk People's Republic (DPR)

Strength: A 2019 Ukrainian assessment estimated the DPR People's Militia troop strength at around 20,800 personnel.[7]

Areas of operation: Across the Line of Contact in Donetsk region.

Leadership: Led by Denis Pushilin since November 2018. Russian Maj.-Gen. Roman Kutuzov was reportedly assigned to command the 1st Army Corps of the DPR People's Militia and was killed in action in southern Ukraine in early June 2022.

Structure: The primary military formation of the DPR is the 1st Army Corps of the DPR People's Militia. It comprises four motor-rifle brigades and two motor-rifle regiments organised along Russian lines. Ukraine believes that both the DPR 1st Army Corps and the LPR 2nd Army Corps report to the Russian 8th Army and are commanded by serving Russian military officers.

History: Formed by the protesters and volunteers of the 'Revolution of Dignity' protests across Donetsk in 2014, who proclaimed the DPR in June 2014 after seizing government buildings and assets.

Objectives: The DPR has changed its strategy throughout the conflict but hopes to achieve autonomy for Donetsk region by breaking away from Kyiv, becoming either a province of Russia or an independent state.

Opponents: Armed Forces of Ukraine.

Affiliates/allies: LPR, Russia.

Resources/capabilities: In 2019, Ukrainian intelligence assessed the DPR 1st Army Corps as possessing around 280 tanks, 550 other armoured fighting vehicles and 430 large-calibre artillery pieces, mortars and multiple rocket launchers.[8]

Luhansk People's Republic (LPR)

Strength: A 2019 Ukrainian assessment estimated the LPR People's Militia troop strength at around 14,700 personnel.[9]

Areas of operation: Across the Line of Contact, particularly in Luhansk region.

Leadership: Leonid Pasechnik has led the LPR since November 2018. Russian Maj.-Gen. Esedulla Abachev, Deputy Commander of Russia's 8th Army, is reported to also be the commander of the 2nd Army Corps of the LPR People's Militia.

Structure: The primary military formation of the LPR is the 2nd Army Corps of the LPR People's Militia. It comprises three motor-rifle brigades and one motor-rifle regiment organised along Russian lines. Ukraine believes that both the LPR 2nd Army Corps and the DPR 1st Army Corps report to the Russian 8th Army and are commanded by serving Russian military officers.

History: Formed by the protesters and volunteers of the 'Revolution of Dignity' protests across Luhansk in 2014, who proclaimed the LPR in June 2014 after seizing government buildings and assets.

Objectives: Similar to the DPR but aimed at the Luhansk region. In the past it has been harder to ascertain objectives in relation to the LPR since different military sub-groups have had different priorities.

Opponents: Armed Forces of Ukraine.

Affiliates/allies: DPR, Russia.

Resources/capabilities: In 2019, Ukrainian intelligence assessed the LPR 2nd Army Corps as possessing around 200 tanks, 350 other armoured fighting vehicles and 400 large-calibre artillery pieces, mortars and multiple rocket launchers.[10]

Conflict Drivers

Political

Regional divisions:
The prior, limited Donbas war (2014–22) was orchestrated by Russia and its local proxies, building on the sense of alienation that had built up between parts of the Donbas and Kyiv since Ukraine became independent in 1991. There were periodic politicised tensions around the coexistence of the Ukrainian and Russian languages, for instance, while some Donbas residents did not perceive Ukrainian nationalism as being inclusive of their Russian-leaning heritage. There have also been economic tensions around the distribution of wealth by successive governments in Kyiv and the industrial Donbas region. In mounting its full-scale invasion in 2022, Russia sought to exploit these divisions even further.

The Revolution of Dignity:
Russia launched a limited intervention in Ukraine in 2014 in response to the fall of then-president Viktor Yanukovych in February that year. In November 2013, Yanukovych had reversed his plans, under Russian pressure, to sign an association and free-trade agreement with the EU. The move triggered street protests calling for greater integration between Ukraine and the EU, for measures to tackle corruption and for Yanukovych to step down. This event was known as the 'Revolution of Dignity'. It centred around Kyiv and was supported in other parts of Ukraine. However,

there were counter-protests in eastern Donbas region over Yanukovych's ousting; what began with the seizure of government buildings coalesced into a separatist movement supported by Russia. A ceasefire deal – brokered by France and Germany – was signed between Ukraine and Russia in 2015, known as 'Minsk II', to halt the fighting. The agreement set out military and political steps that remain unimplemented.

Russia's geopolitical projection:
Ukraine has become a battleground in Russia's attempts to assert its regional power. Putin's stated motivations for launching the invasion involved the 'denazification' and demilitarisation of Ukraine and denial of the latter's existence as a distinct nation. Putin also articulated a wider set of grievances relating to the role of NATO and the US in the post Cold War security order in Europe, as Russia sought to challenge the diffusion of Western influence in parts of the former Soviet Union, which it saw as threatening its aspirations to retain great-power influence. Russia also seeks control of Ukraine's coastline and to forcibly capture the profits from its substantial grain commodity export market.

Key Events in 2021–22

POLITICAL EVENTS

26 March 2021
Ukraine reports that 45 Ukrainian soldiers have been killed and 317 injured since July 2020.

12 July
Russian President Vladimir Putin publishes the essay 'On the Historical Unity of Russians and Ukrainians'.

9 September
Russia and Belarus announce plans to deepen their economic ties.

Late September
Ukraine and Turkey sign an agreement to establish a joint centre in Ukraine to produce Turkish *Bayraktar* TB2 uninhabited aerial vehicles (UAVs).

15 November
NATO raises alarm over Russia's military build-up on its border with Ukraine.

MILITARY/VIOLENT EVENTS

30 March 2021
Russia amasses an estimated 100,000 troops in proximity to Ukraine.

2–5 April
OSCE monitors report a sharp uptick in ceasefire violations in the Donbas.

22 April
Russia says some of its amassed forces will withdraw following a military exercise.

11 May
Another month of high numbers of ceasefire violations reported by the OSCE.

10–16 September
The *Zapad* 2021 military exercise takes place in Russia and Belarus.

26 October
Ukraine uses Turkish drones against Russia-backed separatists for the first time.

30 October
Russia begins a second build-up of forces on Ukraine's borders.

12 November
Russian officials deny that there are plans for an imminent invasion amid a build-up of Russian troops near the border with Ukraine.

Europe and Eurasia

17 December
Russia issues demands to NATO and the US regarding their European security roles; it also seeks security guarantees.

26 January 2022
The US issues a written response to Russia's 17 December demands relating to European security.

21 February
Russia officially recognises the independence of the DPR and LPR.

16 March
The US rapidly increases its military and humanitarian aid to Ukraine.

6 April
Bilateral Ukraine–Russia peace talks mediated by Turkey stall.

9 May
Putin omits any mention of the Ukraine invasion during an address in Moscow to mark Russia's 'Victory Day'.

23 June
The EU grants Ukraine candidate status.

22 July
Russia and Ukraine agree to restart shipments of blockaded grain in a deal brokered by the United Nations with Turkey's support.

4 December
The US government releases intelligence reporting on Russia's military build-up.

17 January 2022
Russian forces begin deploying to Belarus, ostensibly for joint exercises.

24 February
On Putin's order, Russian forces invade Ukraine, carrying out airstrikes targeting Kyiv.

16 March
Just under 300 civilians sheltering in a theatre in Mariupol are killed by a Russian airstrike.

16 March
The Russian advance on Kyiv stalls in the face of determined Ukrainian defences.

6 April
Russian forces withdraw from Kyiv to focus on operations in the Donbas.

14 April
Ukrainian forces sink the *Moskva*, the flagship of Russia's Black Sea Fleet.

3 April
Evidence emerges of widespread killings and the mass graves of at least 410 civilians in Bucha and other towns near Kyiv previously occupied by Russian forces.

20 May
The siege of the Azovstal steel plant ends, with Russia taking full control of Mariupol.

3 July
Russian forces take control of the entirety of Luhansk region.

29 July
The Ukrainian military reports that over 100 Russian soldiers have been killed in Kherson region.

Responses to the Conflict

Security

Extensive military support has been provided to Ukraine by friendly states, including immediately in advance of the Russian invasion. US and UK deliveries of man-portable anti-armour missile systems, including the US *Javelin* and UK NLAW, played an important role in equipping Ukraine with weapons capable of inflicting devastating losses on advancing Russian forces. NATO has played a leading role in supplying Ukraine with military equipment procured from the Alliance's Eastern European and former Warsaw Pact members that matches Ukraine's existing equipment. Ukraine's partners from across NATO and further afield, including Australia, have also provided weapons, armoured vehicles and artillery pieces. In May, the US and the UK also agreed to supply Ukraine with MLRS.

The US has been the single-largest provider of military support to Ukraine. Total US defence assistance to Ukraine between the start of the invasion and June 2022 amounted to US$4.6bn.[11]

Another foreign-supplied weapons system that provided Ukraine with important capabilities was the Turkish-manufactured *Bayraktar* TB2 medium-altitude UAV. Prior to the invasion, the International Institute for Strategic Studies' *Military Balance 2021* listed six of these UAVs in Ukraine's arsenal. In September 2021, Ukrainian Minister for Foreign Affairs Dmytro Kuleba and his Turkish counterpart Mevlüt Çavuşoğlu signed an agreement to establish a joint centre in Ukraine to produce Turkish *Bayraktar* TB2 UAVs. Since the start of the invasion, Ukraine has procured an unspecified further number of the UAVs and has used them to target Russia's advancing armoured forces.

Economic/development

Russia has incurred massive economic and financial sanctions and seen the withdrawal of numerous international brands in response to its invasion of Ukraine. In the opening months of the invasion, US actions included full blocking sanctions on the Kremlin-controlled VEB and PBS banks. Later the financial sanctions were extended to Sberbank and VTB, which together account for a large percentage of the Russian banking sector. In one of the most hard-hitting measures, the US and its allies froze more than half of the Russian central bank's reserves, making the Kremlin unable to sanctions-proof its economy. The country was also prohibited from selling sovereign bonds on US money markets, while oligarchs with close ties to the Russian president had their US-held assets seized. Since then, major Russian banks have been denied access to SWIFT, the international financial messaging system, preventing their customers from transacting with businesses and individuals in many parts of the world. The US also banned the export to Russia of sensitive technologies (including those produced outside the country using US-origin software, technology or equipment), especially in the aviation, maritime and defence sectors.

The EU has imposed similar sanctions on Russian banks and is looking for ways to phase out Russian energy imports, though Hungary and Bulgaria secured exemptions from an agreed oil-import ban. Germany announced that it was immediately halting the process of certifying the Nord Stream 2 pipeline when Russia recognised the 'independence' of the DPR and LPR just before its invasion of Ukraine. Berlin later decided to axe the project entirely and declared its intent to end the purchase of Russian gas and oil. Countries as far afield as Australia, Japan and Singapore have also imposed sanctions on Russia.

Diplomacy

The Russian invasion was met with widespread international condemnation. On 2 March 2021, the UN General Assembly voted overwhelmingly to call on Russia to cease its offensive in Ukraine, with 141 states voting in favour of the motion. Of the remainder, 35 abstained, including China, India and South Africa, and just five voted against the motion (Belarus, Eritrea, North Korea, Russia and Syria). The vote reflected some splits in the international community, including a desire by China and India to continue benefiting from the purchase of Russian oil and gas, now at a discounted price, and New Delhi's desire to preserve its defence ties with Moscow.

The diplomacy surrounding the Russia–Ukraine conflict itself also evolved significantly following the invasion. It brought about the end of the long-standing Minsk process chaired by the OSCE and the 'Normandy format' talks involving France, Germany, Russia and Ukraine. Reflecting the changed nature of the conflict, a fresh set of diplomatic initiatives began, although none have succeeded in limiting the fighting. Just four days after the invasion started, Russian and Ukrainian negotiators held face-to-face bilateral talks in Belarus. Three rounds of talks were held in Belarus starting on 28 February before they moved online on 14 March. Ukraine and most of its allies have however dismissed the process, saying that there are no signs that Putin is prepared to stop the invasion and de-escalate. Indeed, given Putin's propensity to lie about Moscow's intentions in Ukraine, Russian participation may simply be a façade to allow it to play for time while it seeks further military success.

Several third-party countries have tried mediating between Russia and Ukraine. Turkey hosted talks involving the Ukrainian foreign minister and his Russian counterpart Sergei Lavrov; although proposals for a putative peace deal were exchanged, there has been little progress towards a negotiated settlement. As both sides remain committed to fighting and securing their military objectives, efforts towards a diplomatic solution appear unlikely to succeed for the moment.

Humanitarian aid

A range of donor countries, charities and international organisations have provided humanitarian aid to Ukraine. The US government allocated US$8.9bn in humanitarian aid to Ukraine between 24 January and 1 July 2022. In the same period, the EU earmarked US$1.4bn and the UK provided US$373 million. Other countries and organisations have also provided substantial contributions, with the level of humanitarian support offered to Ukraine continuing to rise as the war escalated during the year.

The Russian invasion brought devastating consequences for Ukrainians. Although estimates vary as to the number of civilians who have died or been injured as a result of the fighting since 24 February, the UN Office of the High Commissioner for Human Rights estimated that by 12 July, there had been 11,544 civilian casualties, including 5,024 killed and 6,520 injured.[12] The number of civilian casualties is likely higher, with these estimates reflecting the difficulties encountered in trying to gather information while the fighting continues.

The invasion also caused a large outflow of Ukrainian refugees. According to the UN High Commissioner for Refugees, as of 7 June, 7.3m border crossings had been recorded from Ukraine, with another 2.3m crossings back into the country and at least 4.8m refugees from Ukraine being recorded across Europe, including people who first entered neighbouring countries before travelling elsewhere.[13] The response of neighbouring countries, such as Poland and Moldova, which host large numbers of Ukrainian refugees, and of international aid agencies and charities to the crisis has been considerable. The EU has advised its member states that their focus should be on offering the refugees access to healthcare, accommodation and employment, although individual EU countries, as well as countries outside the Union, such as the UK and Canada, have enacted their own humanitarian responses to the refugee crisis.

Figure 1: Humanitarian and military aid to Ukraine, 24 January–1 July 2022*

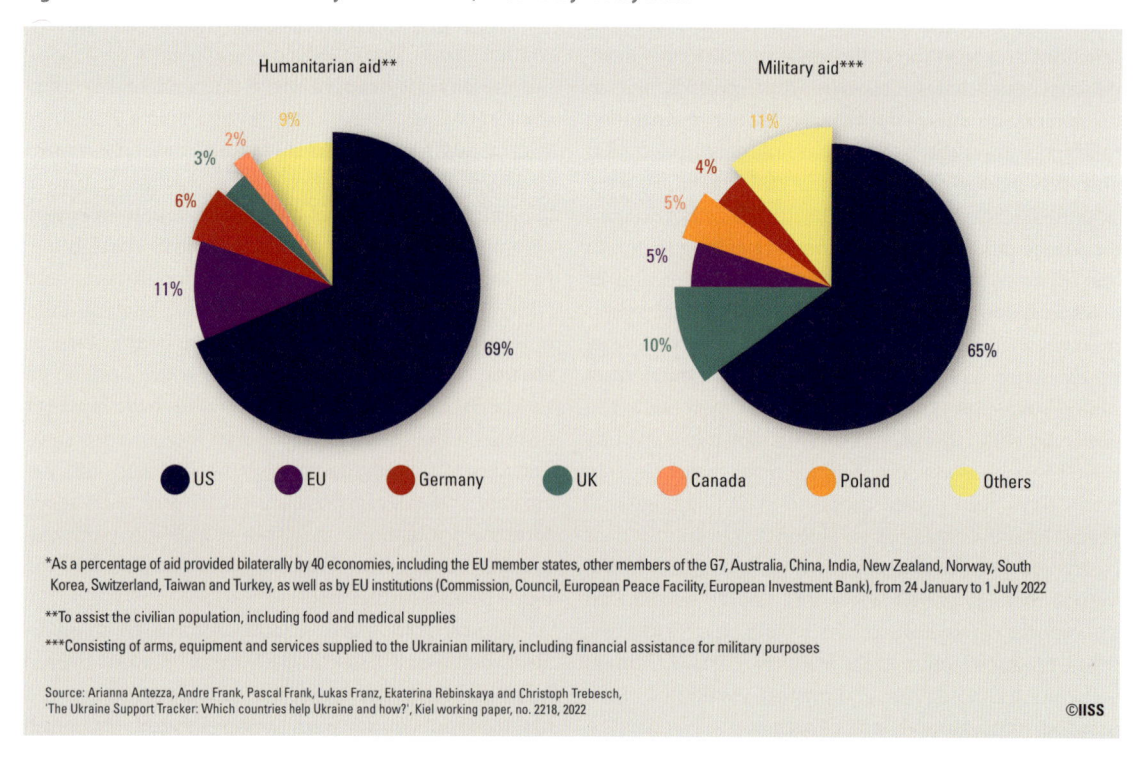

Humanitarian aid**: US 69%, EU 11%, Germany 6%, UK 3%, Canada 2%, Others 9%

Military aid***: US 65%, EU 5%, UK 10%, Canada 5%, Poland 4%, Others 11%

*As a percentage of aid provided bilaterally by 40 economies, including the EU member states, other members of the G7, Australia, China, India, New Zealand, Norway, South Korea, Switzerland, Taiwan and Turkey, as well as by EU institutions (Commission, Council, European Peace Facility, European Investment Bank), from 24 January to 1 July 2022

**To assist the civilian population, including food and medical supplies

***Consisting of arms, equipment and services supplied to the Ukrainian military, including financial assistance for military purposes

Source: Arianna Antezza, Andre Frank, Pascal Frank, Lukas Franz, Ekaterina Rebinskaya and Christoph Trebesch, 'The Ukraine Support Tracker: Which countries help Ukraine and how?', Kiel working paper, no. 2218, 2022

©IISS

Conflict Outlook

Political scenarios

The political leaderships of both sides remain highly motivated to continue the war. This motivation extends to Ukrainian society, driven by the desire to defend sovereign independence, autonomy of political decision-making and the right to practise Ukrainian culture and nationalism. These motivational forces have been bolstered by the considerable support Ukraine has received from its closest international partners, which has included the EU's moves to accelerate Ukraine's candidacy status for full membership in the future.

Russia also remains committed to the invasion. Putin appears to be accepting of the immense costs that his country has already borne, including military casualties and losses of military equipment; its increasing status as a pariah state among much of the international community for waging a war of aggression; and the loss, through sanctions, corporate withdrawals and trade bans, of many of Russia's connections to the global economy.

Escalation potential and conflict-related risks

Escalation in the near term remains likely: as of July 2022, the battlefield situation remained in flux and the ultimate outcome of Russia's invasion was far from being determined. Ukraine remains committed to defending its territory against Russian aggression and to reclaiming territory it has lost. Zelenskyy has also stated that Ukraine is unwilling to trade some of its territory to Russia in exchange for a pause in the fighting.

In July, Ukraine's defence minister indicated that the country's coming counter-offensives would prioritise the south, including recapturing the city of Kherson and occupied portions of Zaporizhzhia region. At the time of writing, Ukrainian forces had already recaptured territory once held by Russia around Kyiv and Kharkiv. However, in both instances, Russian forces had already instigated limited withdrawals as part of their repositioning for the renewed Donbas offensive. Hence, the Ukrainian military was yet to truly challenge embedded Russian forces in large areas that Russia remains determined to continue to occupy.

The battlefield picture inside Ukraine has simplified somewhat in positional terms since the opening week of the invasion and Russia's multi-pronged assault. Having for now given up its aim of capturing cities like Kyiv and Kharkiv, Russian-held territory in July stretched in a broad arc from north to south Ukraine. The focus of Russia's offensives is likely to remain on the Donbas for as long as it takes Russian forces to match its conquest of Luhansk region with a full conquest of Donetsk region. If Russia captures both Donbas regions fully, it remains to be seen whether Putin will offer a cessation of hostilities to Ukraine on terms favourable to Russia, or whether Russian forces will press on with their attempted conquest of further Ukrainian territory. Recent declarations from the Russian foreign minister have suggested that the latter is a more likely scenario.[14]

Foreign-supplied weapons and training are proving crucial in improving Ukraine's prospects for future counter-attacks. However, regardless of how well these progress, Ukraine's prospects for continued military success will likely diminish as the fighting gets closer to Russian territory. From here, as Ukraine found in 2014 when fighting deep in the Donbas, Russia can bombard Ukrainian forces from its own territory and rush in reinforcements quickly.

Assuming Russia's government remains under Putin's control, the near-term prospects for de-escalation and meaningful negotiations to end the war are slim. There remain considerable escalation risks in Ukraine since Russia could still theoretically undertake a general mobilisation to expand the size of its military forces. While Putin has gone to great lengths to avoid doing so to date, likely fearing a domestic political backlash, his risk calculus might change if Russia faces a comprehensive military defeat. At present, without a wider conscription of military personnel Russia will continue to struggle to raise sufficient levels of forces after the losses it suffered at the invasion's start.

Escalation risks in Europe more broadly also remain considerable, especially around the Baltic states and amid tensions between Russia and Lithuania over the former's access to its Kaliningrad territory. Lithuania is a NATO member: any direct aggression against Lithuania by Russia would trigger NATO's Article 5 mutual-defence clause. Other NATO states in Central and Eastern Europe remain alarmed at the prospect of a regional spillover of violence, while in such a febrile environment, miscalculation or inadvertent escalation between

NATO and Russia remains a distinct possibility. While the prospect that Russia uses nuclear weapons in Ukraine – or in response to tensions with other states arising from its invasion – remains low, the risk cannot be written off entirely.

Strategic implications and global influences

NATO's credibility as a defensive alliance has been boosted by its vigorous response to bolstering the defence of its member states in light of Russia's war of aggression and through its expansion to include Sweden and Finland. These two countries will add their considerable military prowess to the organisation's common pool and bring the number of member states to 32.

The Russian blockade of Ukraine's access to the Black Sea and the Azov Sea was used as an additional tool of war. In July, Russia occupied all of Ukraine's access to the Azov Sea and a significant part of its access to the Black Sea. It has also attempted to steal Ukrainian-produced grain and export it illicitly. Rising food (and energy) prices – a partial result of the war – meant that countries in Africa, Asia, Latin America and the Middle East were also feeling its impact. An agreement (under the brokerage of the UN and Turkey) signed by Ukraine and Russia on 22 July to restart shipments of blockaded grain was good news in view of easing mounting global food insecurity.

Notes

[1] OSCE Special Monitoring Mission to Ukraine, '2021 Trends and Observations from the Special Monitoring Mission to Ukraine', 4 February 2022.

[2] A spearhead of Russian advance forces did reach the northern outskirts of Kyiv within two days of the invasion's start. At that time, an audacious bid by Russia's airborne infantry failed to capture Hostomel airport, which is located close to Kyiv and could have been used to fly reinforcements in for an assault on Kyiv if the airstrip had been captured. However, Ukrainian forces successfully defended Hostomel, leaving Russia's assault on Kyiv dependent on land convoys approaching the city along open roads. These convoys were attacked by Ukrainian forces and by March, Russia's advance on Kyiv had stalled.

[3] These figures do not include Foreign Military Financing (FMF) allocations from the US.

[4] US, Department of Defense, 'Senior Defense Official Holds a Background Briefing, March 7, 2022', 7 March 2022.

[5] Permanent Mission of Ukraine to the International Organizations in Vienna, 'Statement by the Delegation of Ukraine at the 1001st FSC Plenary Meeting (16 February 2022): Agenda Item 3, General Statements, on the Subject of "Russia's Ongoing Aggression Against Ukraine and Illegal Occupation of Crimea"', OSCE, 16 February 2022. Quantities are based on figures given in the above source, less the totals assigned to the LPR and DPR in the following Conflict Parties entries.

[6] *Ibid.*

[7] Alexander Isak, 'Мотострелковые корпуса? Что представляют собой "народные милиции" Донбасса' [Motor Rifle Corps? What are the 'People's Militia' of Donbas], Svoboda, 23 February 2020.

[8] *Ibid.*

[9] *Ibid.*

[10] *Ibid.*

[11] US, Department of Defense, 'Fact Sheet on US Security Assistance to Ukraine', 1 June 2022.

[12] UN Office of the High Commissioner for Human Rights, 'Ukraine: Civilian Casualty Update 12 July 2022', 12 July 2022.

[13] UN High Commissioner for Refugees, 'UNHCR Updates Ukraine Refugee Data, Reflecting Recent Movements', 9 June 2022.

[14] Mark Trevelyan, 'Russia Declares Expanded War Goals Beyond Ukraine's Donbas', Reuters, 20 July 2022.

NAGORNO-KARABAKH

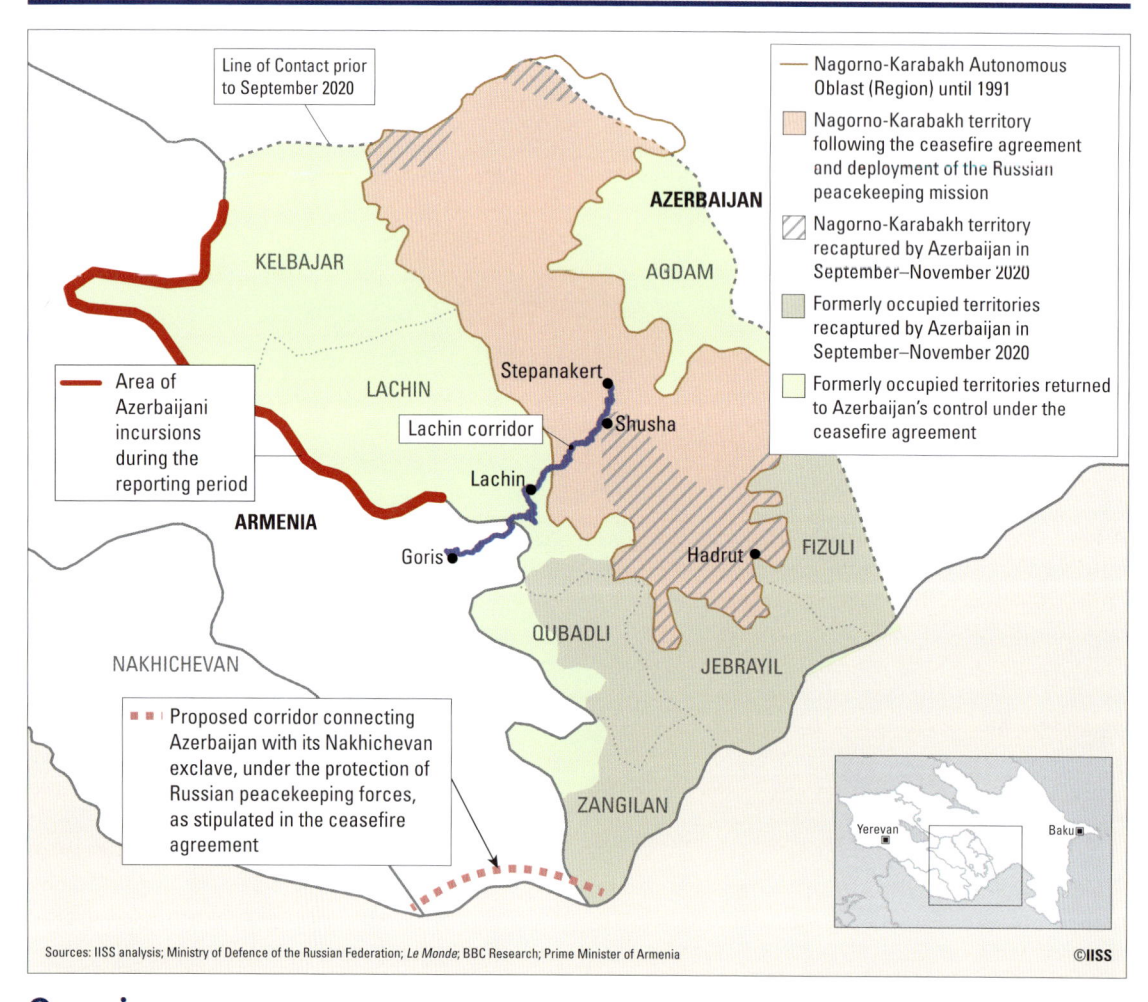

Map legend:
- Line of Contact prior to September 2020
- Area of Azerbaijani incursions during the reporting period
- Nagorno-Karabakh Autonomous Oblast (Region) until 1991
- Nagorno-Karabakh territory following the ceasefire agreement and deployment of the Russian peacekeeping mission
- Nagorno-Karabakh territory recaptured by Azerbaijan in September–November 2020
- Formerly occupied territories recaptured by Azerbaijan in September–November 2020
- Formerly occupied territories returned to Azerbaijan's control under the ceasefire agreement
- Proposed corridor connecting Azerbaijan with its Nakhichevan exclave, under the protection of Russian peacekeeping forces, as stipulated in the ceasefire agreement

Sources: IISS analysis; Ministry of Defence of the Russian Federation; *Le Monde*; BBC Research; Prime Minister of Armenia

Overview

Although one of several 'frozen' conflicts in former Soviet Union territories, the case of Nagorno-Karabakh is unique, having erupted well prior to either Armenia's or Azerbaijan's independence. Timed with the reforms of glasnost and perestroika initiated by Soviet leader Mikhail Gorbachev, in 1987 the local Armenian population in Nagorno-Karabakh launched a civic campaign advocating the territory's legal secession from Azerbaijan and seeking to unify with neighbouring Armenia. That move, which was carefully crafted in legal terms in conformity with the then-Soviet constitution, was bolstered by a referendum marked by overwhelming support for 'independence' from Azerbaijan.[1]

Tensions between the Armenians, who comprised a majority in the territory, and the minority Azerbaijani community quickly escalated and culminated in a series of inter-ethnic clashes. Following the referendum on independence, the parliament of the Nagorno-Karabakh Autonomous Oblast (NKAO) formally voted on 20 February 1988 to unify with Armenia and proclaimed the formation of the (unrecognised) Nagorno-Karabakh Republic (NKR), also known as the Republic of Artsakh.

The implosion of the Soviet Union in 1991 triggered the transformation of the conflict into an all-out military confrontation. The war for Nagorno-Karabakh was driven by Armenia's backing of the

Armed Conflict Global Relevance Indicator (ACGRI)

- Incidence: 3
- Human impact: 3
- Geopolitical impact: 29

Nagorno-Karabakh

Key Conflict Statistics

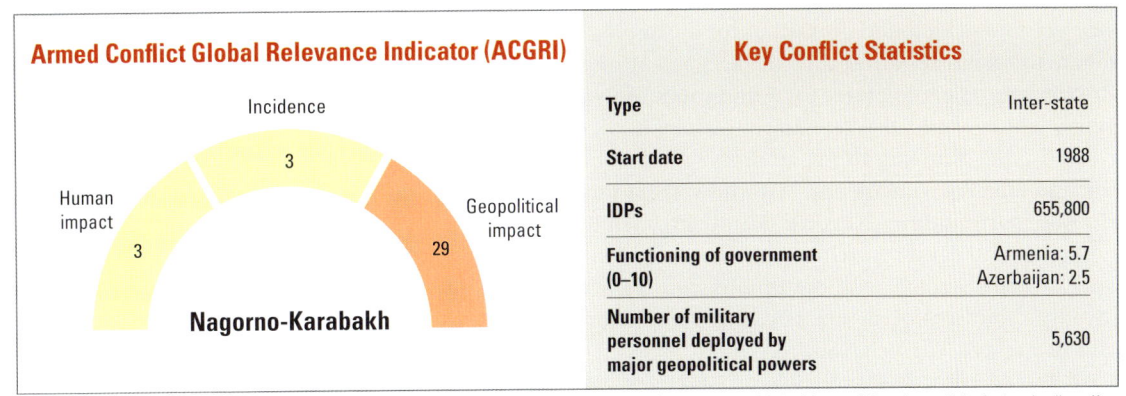

Type	Inter-state
Start date	1988
IDPs	655,800
Functioning of government (0–10)	Armenia: 5.7 Azerbaijan: 2.5
Number of military personnel deployed by major geopolitical powers	5,630

ACGRI pillars: IISS calculation based on multiple sources for 2021 and January–April 2022 (scale: 0–100). See Notes on Methodology and Data Appendix for further details on Key Conflict Statistics.

majority Armenian population against Azerbaijan's attempt to retain the territory by force. The war escalated and by 1993–94, Armenian forces had secured control of most of Nagorno-Karabakh. They went on to seize additional territory beyond its borders. After a forcible population transfer on both sides, hostilities ended with the imposition of a Russian-brokered ceasefire in May 1994. The 1994 ceasefire largely held, despite repeated violations driven by underlying tension. This fragile status quo led to the creation of a roughly 200-kilometre 'Line of Contact' separating the two sides and allowed for the mediation of the Minsk Group – a group of mediating countries under the diplomatic auspices of the Conference on (later the Organization for) Security and Co-operation in Europe (CSCE/OSCE).

At the core of the conflict is the inherent contradiction between the principles of self-determination and territorial integrity: Nagorno-Karabakh is a secessionist de facto state that has never been recognised by any country, including Armenia. Despite that lack of diplomatic recognition, Armenia has provided important military support, even deploying Armenian regular-army conscripts to serve in support of Nagorno-Karabakh.

The two decades that followed the 1994 ceasefire were marked by chronic yet manageable skirmishes. These incidents were limited in terms of intensity and frequency, although sniper fire and occasionally sustained artillery barrages contributed to loss of life on all sides, and took place against the backdrop of a dynamic shift in the regional balance of power. The stalemate changed dramatically in April 2016 when Azerbaijan launched a large-scale military offensive. In what became known as the 'four-day war', brief but intense clashes followed a pre-dawn offensive, as Azerbaijani units launched a well-coordinated, three-front offensive against Armenian positions defending Nagorno-Karabakh. With the deployment and use of heavy weapons and combined arms, the attack triggered the most intense fighting in over two decades. The 2016 offensive was markedly different from previous clashes for two reasons. Firstly, the Azerbaijani campaign had new tactical objectives – to seize and secure territory – for the first time in over two decades. A second key difference was evident in the duration of the combat operations, which only escalated into four days of fighting, as the Armenian and Nagorno-Karabakh forces responded with their own counter-attack, retaking most but not all of the territory initially lost to the Azerbaijani forces. By the fourth day of fighting, Russia moved quickly to broker an informal but immediate cessation of hostilities. In July 2020 another major escalation occurred, with clashes taking place along the Armenia–Azerbaijan border to the north of Nagorno-Karabakh, followed in September by the onset of a full-scale 44-day war along the Line of Contact. The 2020 war saw over 7,000 confirmed fatalities among Armenian and Azerbaijani combatants, in addition to some 170 civilian fatalities.[2] Approximately 130,000 people were displaced, some 90,000 of them Armenians from Nagorno-Karabakh.[3] Azerbaijan had significant support from Turkey and restored control over most of the territories it had lost to Armenian forces in the early 1990s, including approximately one-third of the territory originally under dispute in Nagorno-Karabakh itself. A Russian-mediated ceasefire brought the war to an end on 10 November 2020.

The agreement included provisions for the deployment to Nagorno-Karabakh of a 2,000-strong Russian peacekeeping force for a minimum of five years, which would also safeguard the Lachin corridor linking Armenia to the territory. As part of the agreement, Armenia also withdrew from territories surrounding Nagorno-Karabakh, while both sides pledged to exchange prisoners of war and Armenia agreed to allow unimpeded transit through southern Armenia between Azerbaijan and its exclave Nakhichevan.

Although Russia's invasion of Ukraine in February 2022 has had little to no direct impact on the Russian peacekeeping mission in Nagorno-Karabakh in strictly military terms, Azerbaijan has already taken advantage of the situation by increasing pressure on both Armenia and Nagorno-Karabakh, including by cutting off gas supplies to the latter and launching a successful military operation to seize additional territory. However, Azerbaijan's strategy consists of more than simply taking advantage of the distraction presented by the war in Ukraine to increase pressure on Armenia: Baku's actions are a bold act of defiance vis-à-vis Russia. In this context, Azerbaijan has become emboldened to challenge Russia, bolstered by Turkish support.

Conflict Parties

Azerbaijani armed forces

Strength: 66,950 active service personnel in Azerbaijan's conscript-based armed forces and an estimated 300,000 reservists. Military service lasting 18 months (12 months for university graduates) is mandatory for males aged 18–35.

Areas of operation: Prior to, and during, the 2020 war, the bulk of Azerbaijani forces were deployed along the Line of Contact. Some troops and aviation assets were also deployed to Nakhichevan.

Leadership: President Ilham Aliyev (commander-in-chief); Col-Gen. Zakir Hasanov (minister of defence).

Structure: The majority of troops serve in Azerbaijan's land and air forces. A small navy comprising some 2,200 service personnel is based on the Caspian Sea.

History: Azerbaijan's armed forces were created in 1991–92 from Soviet army units and Azerbaijani militias. The army's slow and disorderly formation was a factor in its defeat by Armenian forces in the First Nagorno-Karabakh War. Substantial military expenditures have significantly upgraded capabilities since that time.

Objectives: The 44-day war of 2020 was a campaign to seize and secure as much territory as possible to restore Azerbaijan's territorial integrity. Although it was successful in retaking several previously Armenian-held districts, the territorial gains in Nagorno-Karabakh itself were more modest, limited to the city of Shusha (spelled Shushi by Armenians) and two separate parts of the border areas.

Opponents: Armenian armed forces; Nagorno-Karabakh Defence Army (NKDA).

Affiliates/allies: Azerbaijan and Turkey have maintained close defence and security ties since the early 1990s and Ankara's support was a significant contributing factor in Azerbaijan's military success in the 2020 war.

Resources/capabilities: Azerbaijan's defence budget for 2021 was US$2.7 billion (4.9% of GDP). Procurement trends have shifted since 2020, with Russia displacing Turkey as the primary source of arms purchases in 2020–22 and declining arms purchases and deliveries from Israel and Pakistan. Azerbaijan retains its military supremacy over Armenia in most areas, particularly in uninhabited aerial vehicles (UAVs) through its inventory of Turkish *Bayraktar* TB2 drones.

Armenian armed forces

Strength: 42,900 service personnel, around half of whom are conscripts. Reservists currently stand at 210,000 members. Military service lasting 24 months is mandatory for males aged 18–27, including dual nationals residing abroad. Although exact figures are unavailable, several units composed of reservists served with the Armenian army during the 2020 war.

Areas of operation: Mainly deployed along the international border with Azerbaijan.

Leadership: Prime Minister Nikol Pashinyan (commander-in-chief); Suren Papikyan (minister of defence).

Structure: Armenia's armed forces – comprising five army corps, air and air-defence forces – have close ties to the NKDA, although a separate command structure is maintained.

History: Officially established in 1991 following the collapse of the Soviet Union. Ex-Soviet army corps and volunteer paramilitary units fighting in Nagorno-Karabakh formed the basis for the Armenian armed forces.

Objectives: Before the 2020 war, to provide extended deterrence to the de facto jurisdiction of the NKR. After the 2020 war, to protect the country's territorial integrity.

Opponents: Azerbaijani armed forces; Turkish armed forces.

Armenian armed forces

Affiliates/allies: Armenia is a founding member of the Russia-led Collective Security Treaty Organisation (CSTO). It is also covered by extended deterrence via bilateral agreements with Russia, which has a military base with an estimated 3,300–5,000 troops in Gyumri near the border with Turkey.

Resources/capabilities: In 2021, Armenia's defence budget was US$622 million. Russia remains Armenia's primary arms supplier; Soviet-era stock in some items was still in use in 2022.

Nagorno-Karabakh Defence Army (NKDA)

Strength: Until 2020, an estimated 18,000–20,000 personnel served in the armed forces of the unrecognised NKR, with over half the troops thought to have been Armenian citizens.[4] By early 2022, however, this number had decreased significantly, to an estimated 11,000 personnel, with an additional depletion of weapons stocks and equipment that has also degraded the order of battle from late 2020–22.[5]

Areas of operation: Prior to the 2020 war, the NKDA was deployed along the heavily fortified Line of Contact. Troops were also deployed to the occupied territories surrounding Nagorno-Karabakh proper. During the 2020 war they were deployed along the Line of Contact and in the main battle areas in Fizuli, Jebrayil, Zangilan, Lachin and Nagorno-Karabakh.

Leadership: Arayik Harutyunyan, Nagorno-Karabakh's de facto president since March 2020 (commander-in-chief); Lt-Gen. Mikael Arzumanyan (defence minister). Decisions on defence and security are taken by the Artsakh Security Council; Vitaly Balasanyan, a 1990s war veteran, general and former presidential candidate, is its secretary.

Structure: The majority of personnel serve in the NKDA's ground forces.

History: Created in 1992 from local paramilitary units engaged in small-scale fighting with Soviet and Azerbaijani forces.

Objectives: The primary objective before the 2020 war was to defend Nagorno-Karabakh and the surrounding occupied territories from Azerbaijani attack. This changed after the war, however, as Armenia no longer provided direct military support to Nagorno-Karabakh.

Opponents: Azerbaijani armed forces and affiliates.

Affiliates/allies: Closely integrated with the Armenian armed forces although they maintain a separate chain of command.

Resources/capabilities: For many years Yerevan provided direct support to the NKR. In the wake of the 2020 war, the Armenian government took decisions that dramatically reduced its patronage of the territory. These included a move to end the long-standing deployment of regular Armenian conscripts to areas in and around the NKR, while also reducing financial support to NKR forces. With the arrival of Russian peacekeepers after the war, Armenian military supplies and equipment donated to the NKR also ended.

Armed Forces of the Russian Federation

Strength: 1,960 peacekeepers.[6] The force is scheduled to rotate every six months and is restricted to one five-year term, to be renewed automatically only if neither Armenia nor Azerbaijan demands its withdrawal. Despite the Russian invasion of Ukraine, the peacekeepers have not been withdrawn or reassigned, mainly because their mission and mandate are more conducive to their current peacekeeping duties than to combat operations.

Areas of operation: The majority of Russian peacekeepers are deployed along the Lachin corridor and in the eastern and southern areas of Nagorno-Karabakh not recaptured by Azerbaijan in 2020. Russia also maintains a military presence including several bases in Armenia. In the aftermath of the 2020 war, Russian border guards established several outposts in southern Armenia near the border with Azerbaijan.

Leadership: President Vladimir Putin (Supreme Commander-in-Chief of the Armed Forces of the Russian Federation); General of the Army Valery Gerasimov (Chief of the General Staff of the Armed Forces of the Russian Federation).

Structure: Most peacekeeping units currently stationed in Nagorno-Karabakh belong to the 15th Separate Motor Rifle Brigade of the Central Military District (Russian Ground Forces). Border guards operating under Federal Security Service (FSB) command are currently deployed in both Armenia and Nagorno-Karabakh.

History: Deployed to Nagorno-Karabakh following the ceasefire signed on 10 November 2020.

Objectives: Ceasefire monitoring in Nagorno-Karabakh for a minimum of five years, subject to renewal. FSB border guards have been instructed to guarantee transport links between Azerbaijan and Nakhichevan, as outlined in the ceasefire agreement.

Opponents: N/A.

Affiliates/allies: Russia and Armenia are founding members of the CSTO. Obligations include mutual assistance and support, although guarantees do not extend to Nagorno-Karabakh.

Resources/capabilities: Russian peacekeepers in Nagorno-Karabakh have light weapons and at least 90 armoured personnel carriers and 380 units of special equipment, including vehicles, at their disposal. Russia's military presence in Armenia is accompanied by advanced-weapons systems; since 2020, this likely includes several *Iskander* short-range ballistic missiles.[7]

Conflict Drivers

Geopolitical and geostrategic influences
External influences:
Russia and Turkey have long used the Nagorno-Karabakh conflict as an instrument of leverage over both Armenia and Azerbaijan. Moscow has ensured that Armenia has remained dependent on Russia for security and military support, while Turkey has bolstered its position as a military patron of Azerbaijan.

Undefined legal status:
Beyond geopolitics, the vague and precarious status of Nagorno-Karabakh itself has also contributed to sustaining the conflict. This has been evident in the virtual diplomatic stalemate over the conflict: due to the exclusion of Nagorno-Karabakh as a direct party to the peace process, the territory has only become more reliant on Armenia to negotiate with Azerbaijan on its behalf. The inherent weakness of the Armenian and Nagorno-Karabakh sides in the peace process has only been exacerbated by the relative diplomatic isolation of the NKR.

Security
Post-war uncertainty and insecurity:
Since Armenia's military defeat in the 2020 war, a new sense of uncertainty and insecurity has prevailed among Armenians in Nagorno-Karabakh. It has been exacerbated by the vague and incomplete terms of the Russian-imposed ceasefire agreement, which effectively consolidated Azerbaijan's significant territorial gains. Although the agreement resulted in a cessation of hostilities, it was not close to resembling a peace accord or a negotiated resolution to the overarching dispute. Furthermore, the agreement deferred the status of Nagorno-Karabakh to a later stage of diplomatic negotiations and did not address several important issues, such as the need for a resumption of diplomatic engagement and the outstanding challenge of post-war border demarcation. Meanwhile, Azerbaijani forces' incursions in Armenia's southern and eastern border areas in mid-2021 added to Nagorno-Karabakh Armenians' sense of uncertainty.

Political
Diverging conflict narratives:
One of the more fundamental challenges arising in diplomatic negotiations over the conflict has been the opposing views of the Azerbaijani and Nagorno-Karabakh Armenian populations. The difference is demonstrated by each side's emphasis on contradictory principles of international law, with the Nagorno-Karabakh Armenians favouring the right of self-determination and the Azerbaijani side stressing the principle of territorial integrity. This difference of views was apparent once again during the 2020 war, where Nagorno-Karabakh's motivations were focused on security and a related emphasis on status, especially given its desire for independence from Azerbaijan, while the Azerbaijani side saw the war as being waged to restore Azerbaijan's territorial integrity.

Key Events in 2021–22

POLITICAL EVENTS

25 March 2021
The Nagorno-Karabakh parliament formally enacts legislation to make Russian an official language in the region, alongside Armenian.

15 June
Azerbaijan and Turkey conclude a new agreement on bilateral military assistance.

MILITARY/VIOLENT EVENTS

12 May 2021
Azerbaijani forces cross the border and advance 3 km into southern Armenia.

12 June
Azerbaijan releases 15 Armenian prisoners of war in exchange for military maps of minefields in an area that came under Azerbaijani control following the 2020 war.

20 June
Incumbent Armenian Prime Minister Nikol Pashinyan secures a mandate of nearly 54% of the vote in early parliamentary elections. Pashinyan's 'Civil Contract' party enters the new Armenian parliament with a decisive majority of 71 seats.[8]

24 September
In their first meeting since the end of the 2020 war, the Armenian and Azerbaijani foreign ministers meet on the sidelines of the United Nations General Assembly in New York.

20 October
The deputy prime ministers of Armenia, Azerbaijan and Russia meet in Moscow to discuss restoring transport communications and agree on a new railway connection.

26 November
A trilateral meeting of the leaders of Armenia, Azerbaijan and Russia takes place in Sochi, Russia.

13 December
The Armenian and Turkish foreign ministers announce the appointment of special envoys empowered to negotiate the 'normalisation' of relations between their countries, as well as plans to resume direct flights between Istanbul and Yerevan.

14 December
European Union officials facilitate a summit in Brussels between Pashinyan and Azerbaijan President Ilham Aliyev, marking the launch of a new EU engagement.

8 March 2022
Azerbaijan cuts the flow of natural gas to Nagorno-Karabakh.

6 April
Pashinyan and Aliyev meet in Brussels and reach an agreement to launch a new peace process.

2–5 August
A skirmish takes place between Azerbaijani and Nagorno-Karabakh forces near the Lachin corridor connecting Nagorno-Karabakh to Armenia, with both sides reporting casualties.

23 November
Pashinyan announces that Armenia has reached an agreement with Azerbaijan to establish a hotline between their defence chiefs to prevent miscalculation and de-escalate border tensions.

24–25 March 2022
Azerbaijani forces seize control of a strategic mountain overlooking Nagorno-Karabakh, defying warnings from nearby Russian peacekeepers.

Responses to the Conflict

Security

When the Russian-imposed ceasefire agreement took effect in November 2020, the security of Nagorno-Karabakh was abruptly altered with the end of the decades-long Armenian security guarantee for the territory's Armenian population. Regular Armenian military units were pushed out from several districts of Azerbaijan beyond the borders of the NKR, while the separate, much smaller NKR armed forces were isolated and cut off from direct support from Armenia proper. As a result, the physical security of the Armenian population of Nagorno-Karabakh became dependent on the presence and performance of the 2,000-strong Russian peacekeeping force.

The unprecedented and unexpected losses incurred during the 2020 war were a shock to Nagorno-Karabakh. After years of complacency and overconfidence, the defeat demonstrated two realities: the end of the 'myth of invincibility' on the Armenian side, and the demise of deterrence, as the weakness of the Nagorno-Karabakh and Armenian armed forces had become clear. Another important outcome in the NKR was the sudden decline in public confidence in the government and institutions. This factor was especially destructive as it overturned years of careful state-building and consistent democratisation, and was most evident in the summer of 2021 when the civilian leadership was challenged by a more hardline faction within the Nagorno-Karabakh security sector. The shock of the war also triggered a first-ever backlash by the Nagorno-Karabakh population against the Armenian government, with a majority expressing feelings of betrayal and abandonment. The result was a shift in the political discourse, as the rising popularity of the Armenian opposition (in Armenia proper) among Nagorno-Karabakh residents forged a deep divide between the territory and Armenia proper. The new discourse also featured discussions of a possible turn towards Russia, rather than Armenia, for security and political patronage.

Economic/development

For Nagorno-Karabakh, the new reality following the 2020 war presented unexpected economic opportunities. These opportunities stemmed from Russian-led efforts to restore regional trade and transport, which would lessen the relative isolation of the territory. The dominance of Russia in the region's post-war economy and overall development has triggered a more assertive and ambitious policy of engagement by the West, the EU and United States in particular. Moreover, the EU's financial support for projects to restore trade and transport were bolstered by the shared challenge of economic recovery following the coronavirus pandemic.

Diplomacy

Amid a new regional geopolitical context characterised by competition between a resurgent Russia and an assertive Turkey jockeying for dominance over Azerbaijan and in the region, the reporting period saw a new diplomatic initiative by the EU in late 2021. By early 2022, as a result of efforts to coordinate talks between the Armenian and Azerbaijani leaders, the EU had displaced Russia as the primary facilitator of such engagements (especially as Moscow was distracted by the war in Ukraine).

Diplomatic negotiations between Armenia and Azerbaijan resumed in New York in September 2021 and quickly intensified, with further talks taking place between the Armenian and Azerbaijani foreign ministers and heads of state in Paris, Sochi and Brussels. Despite notable missteps and misgivings, the overall course of engagement between Yerevan and Baku advanced on a surprisingly consistent trajectory.

The EU's important role as a facilitator – and not as a mediator – of these talks has enabled it to replace the Minsk Group as the primary entity empowered to manage both the Nagorno-Karabakh conflict and the bilateral process of 'normalising' relations between Armenia and Azerbaijan. Brussels's ability to regain its relevance vis-à-vis the conflict and to restore Armenia's and Azerbaijan's faith in its commitment to resolving the dispute is indicative of the strategic significance of the EU's engagement. This aspect also relates to the need – following the 2020 war – for stability and connectivity in the South Caucasus region, as both Armenia and Azerbaijan are now much more interested in deepening ties with Europe. As a result, the EU has a degree of leverage over Azerbaijan, which has never been truly engaged in forging strategic ties with the EU, and also over Nagorno-Karabakh, which seeks to overcome its isolation and offset its overdependence on Russia.

Humanitarian aid

The EU and US engagement mentioned above has been complemented by the humanitarian efforts of the UN and its agencies, including the UN Children's

Figure 1: Refugees from Nagorno-Karabakh in Armenia, October 2020–December 2021

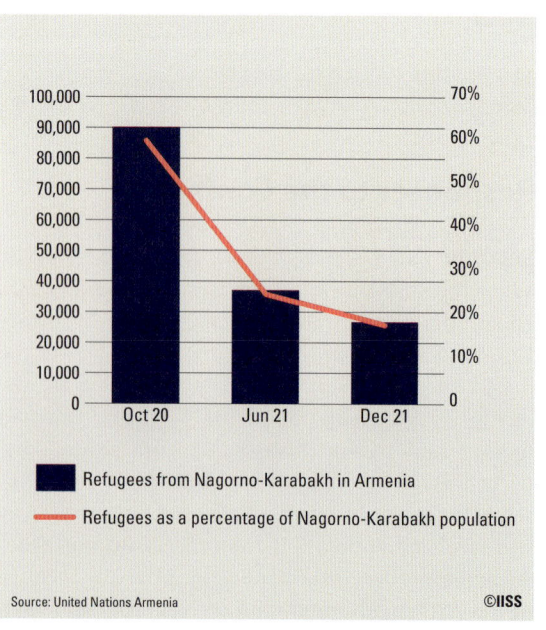

Source: United Nations Armenia ©IISS

Fund and the UN High Commissioner for Refugees, which initiated policies and assistance in early 2021 targeting the most vulnerable Nagorno-Karabakh Armenians. As a result, the majority of refugees who initially fled Nagorno-Karabakh following the war and travelled to southern Armenia had returned to the territory by the end of 2021. The democratic and institutional resilience of the NKR, despite the decline in public confidence in its institutions, meant that it retained sufficient capacity to manage aid distribution and work with the donor community as a reliable partner for inclusive development.

Conflict Outlook

Political scenarios

Given the vulnerability of the Nagorno-Karabakh Armenians following the 2020 war, the political outlook for the territory is precarious and largely dependent on Russian policy. As the only guarantor of its security, the Russian peacekeeping force will be tested as the only deterrence to counter Azerbaijan's attempts to restore its complete subordination of the enclave.

Escalation potential and conflict-related risks

Many aspects of the Nagorno-Karabakh conflict remain dangerously unclear and undefined, raising questions over the territory's 'status', sovereignty and legal standing, among others. And although seemingly deferred in the terms of the ceasefire, the outstanding issues are far from resolved. Beyond the perspective of 'status', there is also justifiable concern over what is not stipulated related to security in the ceasefire agreement, including the issues of demilitarisation and demobilisation of the Nagorno-Karabakh armed forces. Moreover, the ceasefire agreement deferred the status of Nagorno-Karabakh to a later stage of diplomatic negotiations and left several other important issues unaddressed, such as the need for a resumption of diplomatic engagement and the outstanding challenge of post-war border demarcation.

Prospects for peace

For Nagorno-Karabakh's Armenians, the Russian-imposed ceasefire agreement is far from a final peace deal and is seen as deferring the status and security issues to a later but essential period of resumed diplomatic negotiations. For Azerbaijan, however, the war is over and, as victor, it offers no acceptance of the rights or demands of the vanquished. Although any realistic hope for a lasting and durable peace rests on the forging of a consensus and a return to diplomacy, the outlook for such developments appears quite unfavourable.

Strategic implications and global influences

The unilateral deployment of Russian peacekeepers stands out as an important victory for Moscow, which has always sought a military presence in Nagorno-Karabakh. Since the deployment provides a foundation for enhancing Russian power and influence in the region, it seems unlikely that the five-year time limit will be observed. However, Russia's invasion of Ukraine in February 2022 has dramatically altered the already delicate regional geopolitical landscape. As a result of Moscow's efforts to secure greater influence and control in the 'near abroad', Ukraine has become a central – but not the sole – component of a new front line comprising democratic states under threat from stronger authoritarian countries. In fact, Nagorno-Karabakh may emerge as an even more attractive source of leverage to consolidate Russia's power projection in the region, especially given the risk of a resurgent Russia struggling to dominate its neighbours.

Notes

1. The local Azerbaijani population notably boycotted participation in the referendum.
2. See International Crisis Group, 'The Nagorno-Karabakh Conflict: A Visual Explainer', 7 May 2021. The Armed Conflict Location & Event Data Project (ACLED) identifies 6,706 fatalities for Armenia and Azerbaijan in 2020 as a whole. The latest official data as of the time of writing suggests that 2,900 Azerbaijanis were killed in action (including deaths from landmines after the ceasefire). Estimates of Armenians killed in action have been more variable, with 4,000 cited by Armenian officials as a likely approximate total. See 'Azerbaijan Updates Its Death Toll in Nagorno-Karabakh', Caucasian Knot, 3 June 2021.
3. United Nations Office of the High Commissioner for Human Rights, 'Nagorno-Karabakh Conflict: Bachelet Warns of Possible War Crimes as Attacks Continue in Populated Areas', 2 November 2020.
4. Sergey Minasyan, 'Sderzhivanie v Karabakhskom Konflikte' [Deterrence in the Karabakh Conflict] (Yerevan: Caucasus Institute, 2016), pp. 266–9.
5. Based on author's interviews with Armenian defence ministry and Nagorno-Karabakh figures.
6. 'Russia Sends Nearly 2,000 Peacekeepers to Nagorno-Karabakh, Defense Ministry Says', TASS, 10 November 2020. The International Crisis Group subsequently reported a total of 'some 4,000 Russian soldiers and emergency services staff'. See International Crisis Group, 'Post-war Prospects for Nagorno-Karabakh', Report no. 264, 9 June 2021, p. i.
7. In 2019, Russian officials announced plans to double the combat potential of the 102nd Russian military base in Gyumri without increasing the number of personnel.
8. Richard Giragosian, 'Assessing Armenia's Post-war Election', New Europe, 23 June 2021.

Regional Outlook

The conflict outlook in Eurasia will be dominated by the evolution of the war in Ukraine and related possible shifts in Russia's regional role and ambitions. Prospects for durable peace in Nagorno-Karabakh remain dim amid a weakening Russia and an emboldened Azerbaijan, supported by Turkey. More generally, the issue of un-demarcated borders in Central Asia will continue to fuel political risks in the region.

Prospects for peace

Following an initial two months of conflict characterised by rapid changes of fortune among the combatants, the war in Ukraine has entered an attritional phase and appears unlikely to end quickly, either by negotiation or by military victory. Russia's military goals, even in their most minimalist form (occupying the entire Donbas plus two southern oblasts, Kherson and Zaporizhzhia), will not be easy to achieve in light of the Ukrainian determination to continue fighting, Western military aid to Kyiv, widespread insubordination in the occupied regions and inherent flaws in Russia's planning and conduct of the offensive.

Ukraine's success, or at least its ability to decide when to start negotiations for a durable ceasefire on its own terms, will depend on the swift delivery of weapons from the West and on financial and economic support provided by the EU and the United States. Without the latter, the country may be pushed to conclude peace with Russia at the cost of territorial concessions. While there is broad agreement in the West on the need for a Ukrainian military victory, consensus on the form a future relationship with Russia might take appears more difficult to reach.

The prospects for durable peace in Nagorno-Karabakh are also uncertain against the backdrop of a ceasefire agreement that ended hostilities in 2020 but did not define key issues, including the region's legal status, security guarantees and post-war demarcation, among others. The combination of Russia's role as sole security guarantor, an increasingly assertive Azerbaijan and a weakened Armenia will complicate the outlook for a negotiated final peace deal.

Escalation potential and regional spillovers

As long as Russia is preoccupied with the war in Ukraine, the chances of the conflict spilling over into Moldovan territory are slim. Transnistria's separatist forces and the relatively small contingent of Russian forces there cannot launch a major offensive on their own. On the other hand, they could try to provoke destabilisation or fabricate pretexts for Russian intervention if Ukraine is defeated.

The balance of power in Nagorno-Karabakh increasingly favours Azerbaijan. Emboldened by Turkey's support and its success in the 2020 war, Baku appears intent on completely subordinating the enclave. Azerbaijan can also benefit from the EU's need for alternative energy supplies and transit infrastructure: Baku and the EU are seeking to increase deliveries of the former's oil and gas to Europe and are assessing the feasibility of connecting Central Asian and Iranian hydrocarbons to the pipelines that link Baku with Europe.

Belarus has allowed Russian forces to operate and strike from its territory but has not yet used its own forces in combat against Ukraine. As Russia struggles in the war, it may continue to pressure Belarus to do so, thereby expanding the theatre of active military operations.

Strategic implications and global influences

Russia's 'special military operation' in Ukraine has failed to achieve its initial goals of defeating the Ukrainian armed forces, capturing Kyiv and forcing a regime change. The conflict has not only exposed serious shortcomings in the organisation, logistics, armament and intelligence of the Russian military, but also laid bare weaknesses across multiple domains of Russian power. It has also prompted the formation of a countervailing coalition of Western states and major Asian partners that extends across civil society and much of the private sector: their new sense of purpose reverses a recent trend of intervention fatigue and lack of strategic clarity. The war has triggered a Europe-wide reassessment of priorities, enlargement of NATO and rearmament of many European countries. The West is providing significant military aid in equipment, training and intelligence to Ukraine and is imposing sweeping sanctions on Russia.

With virtually no diplomatic support for its war, Russia has tried to break its isolation by engaging with the Global South. Moscow has sought to take advantage of existing tensions between many developing countries and the West while leveraging alliances with other emerging powers, such as China, India and Iran, as part of efforts to attenuate the military, economic and financial pressures imposed by the West and its allies. Such activities may have repercussions on geopolitical alignments, the global balance of power and current international rules and fora.

The conflict in Ukraine has also reinforced drivers of conflict globally, adding to the coronavirus pandemic's disastrous legacy and affecting fragile countries in particular. Disruptions to global supply chains and spikes in energy and food-commodities prices have intensified pre-existing food insecurity and high inflation trends in these states, creating fertile terrain for further instability and conflict. Moreover, the unprecedented humanitarian crisis and reconstruction needs created by the war will limit international humanitarian aid and development funding available for other conflicts and crises for years to come.

3 Middle East and North Africa

Regional Analysis	130	Israel–Palestinian Territories	154	**Conflict Summaries**	
Conflict Reports		Yemen	164	Egypt	186
Syria	134	Libya	174	Turkey	192
Iraq	144			**Regional Outlook**	198

People wave Syrian-opposition flags at a rally marking 11 years since the uprising against the Assad regime began, Afrin, northern Syria, 18 March 2022

Overview

In the Middle East, the decade that followed the Arab Spring was bloody and violent. The hopes of the 2011 protests, which led to the departure of three so-called 'presidents for life' – Zayn al-Abidin Ben Ali in Tunisia, Hosni Mubarak in Egypt and Ali Abdullah Saleh in Yemen – and eventually Muammar Gadhafi in Libya, quickly gave way to infighting and political fragmentation. The following years were marked by the rise of the Islamic State (ISIS), foreign interventions and civil wars.

As of mid-2022, the wars in Libya, Syria and Yemen show no sign of ending. Instead they have evolved, stagnated and become intractable. Only the Israeli–Palestinian conflict, which predates the Arab Spring, saw significant escalation during the reporting period.

In Focus: De-escalation Trends in the Middle East

Current Middle Eastern conflicts can broadly be described as stalemates. Domestic and foreign actors alike are finding themselves unable to achieve their various political goals through military means. This realisation has led to a series of de-escalations. However, for the most part these measures are due to exhaustion and may not be the cause for optimism that they appear at first glance.

Syria and Yemen are the best examples of military stalemates resulting in de-escalation. In the former case, President Bashar al-Assad controls roughly two-thirds of Syrian territory but has little prospect of seizing the rest of the country, which is held by a variety of groups, including the United States-backed Syrian Democratic Forces. Nor is Assad likely to regain the support of many Syrians following a decade of brutal fighting. However, the opposition's prospects for capturing territory held by Assad are even less promising. This context has resulted in a fragmented and fractured state.

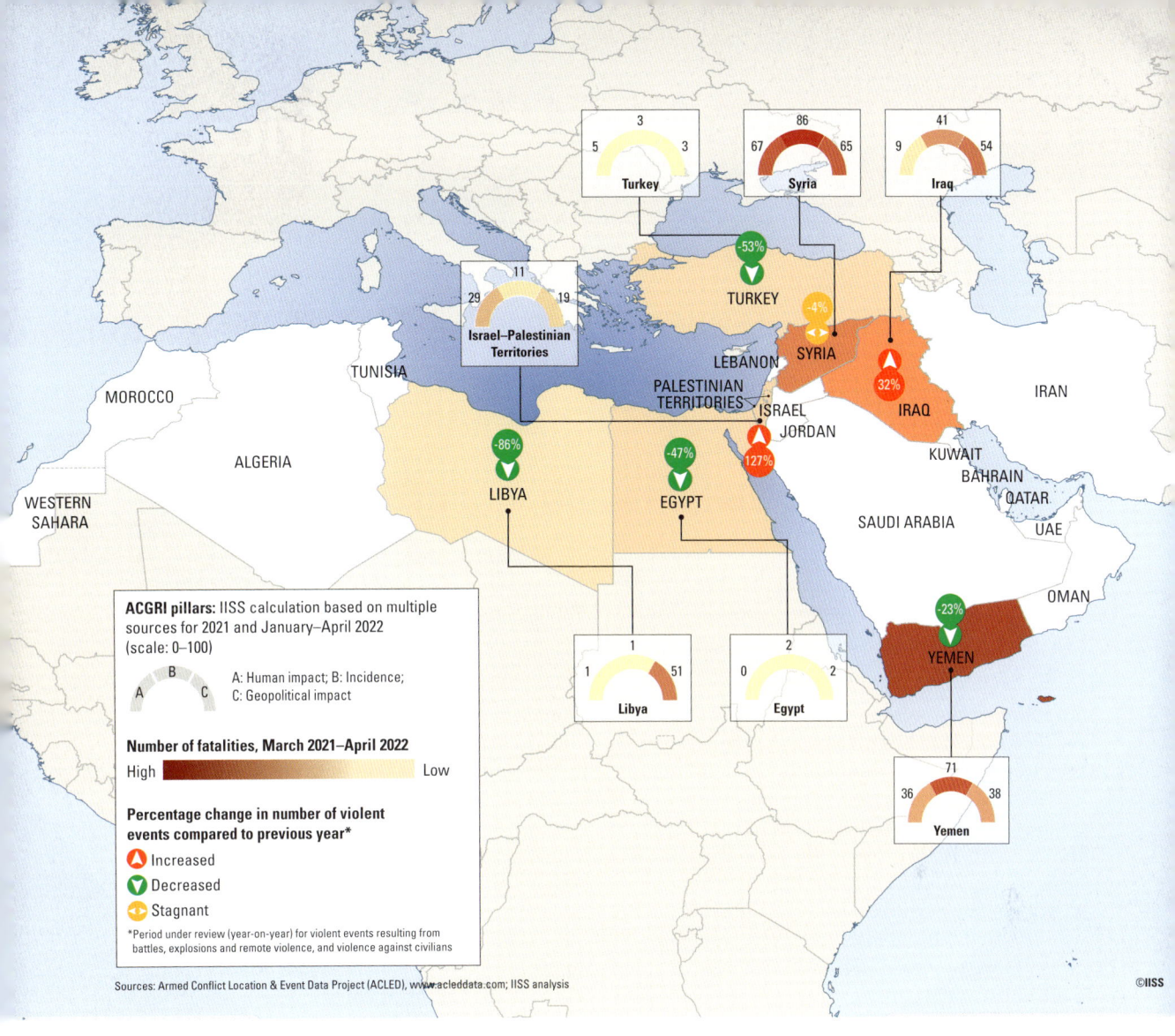

In many respects, Assad has won the war simply by surviving and holding on to power and a portion of Syrian territory. In March 2022, the United Arab Emirates (UAE) recognised this fact by hosting him in Dubai – his first visit to an Arab country since the uprisings began in 2011.[1] Despite US and European pressure, it is likely that more Arab countries will host the Syrian president in the coming months and years.

In Yemen, a military stalemate following years of largely inconclusive fighting has led to de-escalation. In April 2022, the United Nations announced a two-month truce that was subsequently extended for another two months.[2] The truce followed a two-year campaign – still ongoing – by the Houthi movement, also known as Ansarullah ('Partisans of God'), to seize Marib province, which contains oil and gas fields the Houthi leadership believes it must control in order to fulfil its aim of creating a viable independent state.

Shortly after the announcement of the truce, Abd Rabbo Mansour Hadi, who had been in exile in Saudi Arabia for much of the past seven years, announced that he was stepping down as Yemeni president and handing executive authority to an eight-member Presidential Leadership Council (PLC).[3] While the UN and US special envoys for Yemen have prioritised transforming the country's tentative truce into

Figure 1: Food price inflation, 2019–21

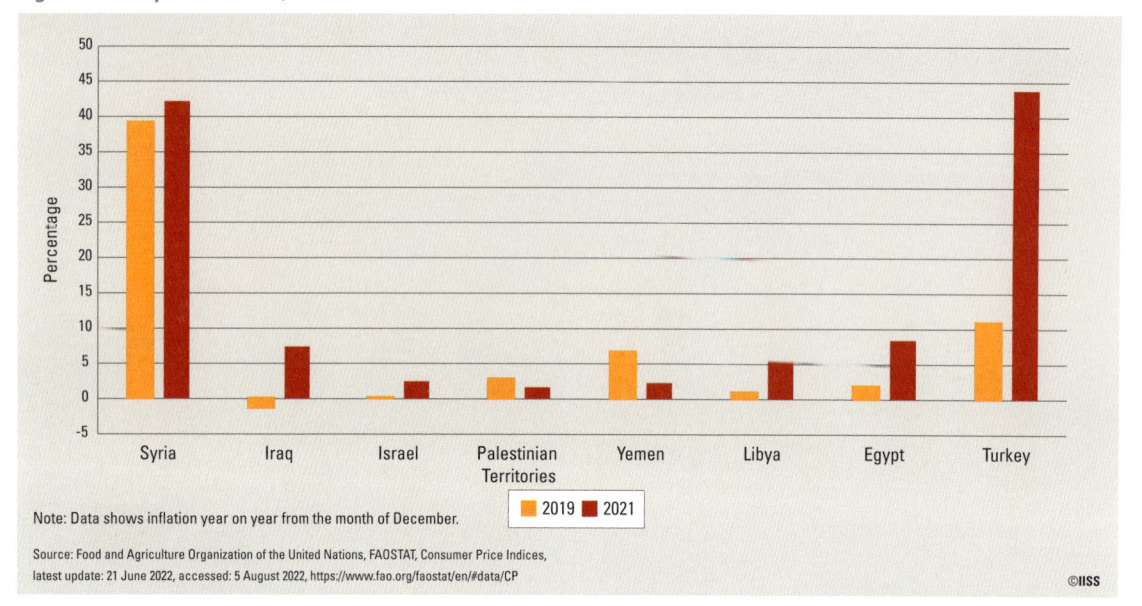

Note: Data shows inflation year on year from the month of December.
Source: Food and Agriculture Organization of the United Nations, FAOSTAT, Consumer Price Indices, latest update: 21 June 2022, accessed: 5 August 2022, https://www.fao.org/faostat/en/#data/CP

a comprehensive peace settlement – capitalising on the new opportunities presented by the creation of the PLC – there is still significant work to be done.[4]

A similar stalemate, although without the political breakthrough, has characterised Turkey's conflict with the Kurdistan Workers' Party (PKK). In Egypt, the conflict between the state and Sinai-based militants is less a stalemate than a fading war. Iraq and Libya remain in tense states of uncertainty. In the former, concerns remain over whether there will be a new nuclear deal with Iran and what this might mean for Iraq, while in Libya presidential elections were postponed and the country remains deeply divided.

Two factors will impede efforts to transform these de-escalations into comprehensive peace settlements. The first is growing sectarianism in the region, which underpins and fuels many of the conflicts. The second is the degree to which several of these conflicts have already resulted in significant political and territorial fragmentation – developments that will be difficult to reverse.

Sectarianism

Three of the region's longest-running and most violent conflicts – in Iraq, Syria and Yemen – have a significant sectarian element. Iranian troops, advisers or militias are present in all these countries, while Tehran is also actively proselytising in each country in the hopes of translating its political and military support into an alliance of co-religionists. In Yemen, where the Houthis are Zaydi Shia, Iran succeeded in convincing the authorities to celebrate Ashura – a Twelver Shia festival – for the first time in the country's history in 2019. In Syria, Iran has been using a combination of financial incentives, aid and scholarships to encourage conversions. In Iraq, where conversion is less of an issue due to the number of Twelver Shiites already in the country, it has continued to exert control over militia groups, which has led to a fracturing of the Shia bloc.[5]

Perceptions of Tehran's gains (particularly those in Yemen and Syria) and concerns over its perceived pursuit of nuclear weapons have driven Iran's regional rivals closer together – most notably Israel and the Gulf states. The Abraham Accords of 2020 have paved the way for further normalisation of ties between Israel and Saudi Arabia and will likely result in a muted response from Gulf states to further developments in the Israeli–Palestinian conflict. Israel continues to carry out strikes on what it says are Iranian positions inside Syria and also appears to be active in the assassination of Iranian scientists and military figures.[6] The increasingly significant sectarian element of Middle Eastern conflicts and growing confrontation between Iran and its regional rivals have opened up divisions that may be impossible to rectify in the near term.

Fragmentation

The political and territorial fragmentation of many Middle Eastern countries is another challenge working against efforts to transform fragile truces and ceasefires into lasting political settlements. Again, the two most obvious cases are Syria and Yemen. However, political fragmentation also plays a role in Libya and Iraq. In Syria, as noted above, Assad controls roughly two-thirds of the country but is unlikely to extend that control over the rest of Syria. This means that the country will continue to be divided and that Assad will be denied the revenues and resources he desperately seeks. Meanwhile, groups in non-government-controlled areas will resist the regime's efforts to regain control for fear of retribution. These circumstances suggest that the conflict will continue for the foreseeable future.

In Yemen, the issue is even starker. The Houthis have control over much of the north, where they have restructured the government, formed a separate economy and implemented their own vision of a state. Indeed, the Houthis do not want to be part of the Yemeni state and see no reason to give up at the bargaining table what has been won on the battlefield.

In Libya and Iraq, political fragmentation and the various armed groups that have emerged over the past decade have also produced a political impasse. In December 2021 presidential elections in Libya were postponed. Iraq, which has an autonomous Kurdish zone in the north, likewise appears to be incapable of piecing the state back together.

Notes

[1] Associated Press, 'Assad Visits UAE in Latest Sign of Re-engagement', *New York Times*, 18 March 2022.

[2] 'Press Statement by UN Special Envoy for Yemen Hans Grundberg on the Renewal of the UN-Mediated Truce', Office of the Special Envoy of the Secretary-General for Yemen, 2 June 2022.

[3] Ben Hubbard, 'Yemeni Leader Hands Power to New Body as His Saudi Backers Seek to End War', *New York Times*, 7 April 2022.

[4] 'Briefing to the United Nations Security Council by the Special Envoy for Yemen Hans Grundberg', ReliefWeb, 14 June 2022.

[5] Jane Arraf, 'Efforts to Form a New Government in Iraq Descend into Chaos', *New York Times*, 13 June 2022.

[6] Farnaz Fassihi and Ronen Bergman, 'Israel Tells US It Killed Iranian Officer', *New York Times*, 27 May 2022.

SYRIA

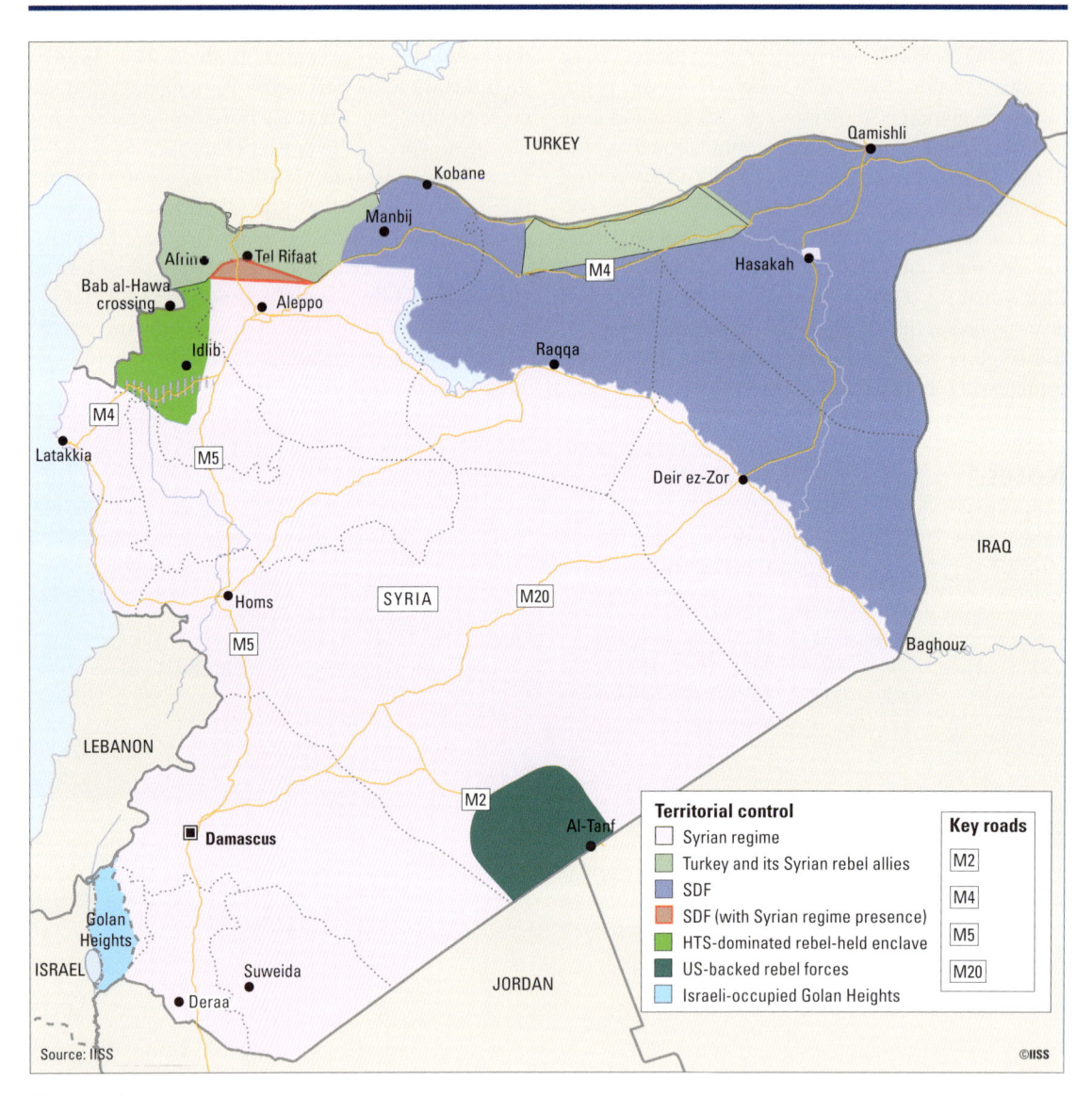

Overview

The Syrian conflict has evolved dramatically since it began in 2011 – in ways that have both reflected and impacted broader regional and geopolitical dynamics. President Bashar al-Assad's regime responded to 2011's peaceful demonstrations with force, inflaming anti-regime sentiment while also blocking non-military paths to change. The uprising evolved into an armed opposition, which drew poorly organised material support from an array of backers but never received the direct Western military intervention hoped for by much of its leadership. Amid territorial losses, the regime held onto power by escalating collective-punishment tactics against civilians in opposition-held areas – firstly with artillery, then from the air, then with sieges and, eventually, by using chemical weapons. When these measures proved insufficient, the regime's backers came to its rescue – firstly Iran and its Shia

Armed Conflict Global Relevance Indicator (ACGRI)

- Incidence: 86
- Human impact: 67
- Geopolitical impact: 65

Syria

Key Conflict Statistics

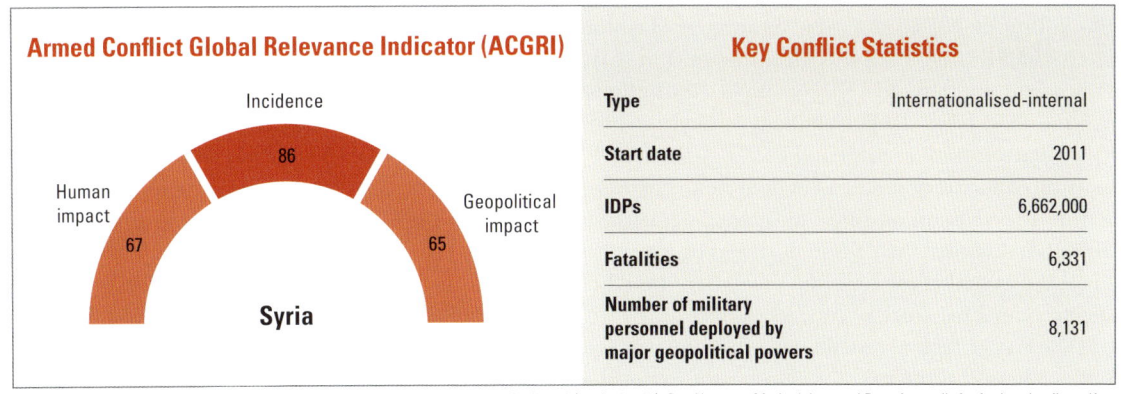

Type	Internationalised-internal
Start date	2011
IDPs	6,662,000
Fatalities	6,331
Number of military personnel deployed by major geopolitical powers	8,131

ACGRI pillars: IISS calculation based on multiple sources for 2021 and January–April 2022 (scale: 0–100). See Notes on Methodology and Data Appendix for further details on Key Conflict Statistics.

militias and then the Russian military. Meanwhile, Sunni jihadists fought alongside and then against Syria's mainstream opposition. The most radical among them – the Islamic State (ISIS) – eventually seized enough territory and resources in Syria and Iraq to push the United States to intervene on both sides of the border. The US partnered with Syrian Kurdish fighters in northeast Syria linked to the Kurdistan Workers' Party (PKK), an organisation that has waged a long insurgency against Turkey. Subsequently, Ankara became more assertive in the conflict and to date has launched four military interventions in northern Syria: one against ISIS, two against Kurdish forces and another to block a Syrian regime offensive towards its border.

During the reporting period, the conflict continued to be a fragile stalemate. Violence was down but political prospects remained bleak and humanitarian needs were higher than ever. External intervention continued to shape the war's trajectory; between March 2020 and April 2022, the net impact of this engagement was to uphold an uneasy freeze of front lines, with each Syrian side reliant on its foreign backers to deter attacks and sustain its economic viability.

As of mid-2022, Assad's regime controlled roughly 65% of Syrian territory, including its three largest cities (Aleppo, Damascus and Homs).[1] However, roughly half of Syrians (including those in northern Syria and refugees outside the country) live outside regime-controlled areas. Most of northeast Syria is controlled by the US-backed and Kurdish-led Syrian Democratic Forces (SDF). Areas north of Aleppo and a small strip of the northeast along the Turkish border are controlled by an array of Turkish-backed armed opposition factions known loosely as the Syrian National Army (SNA). Idlib province in Syria's northwest (and adjacent slivers of neighbouring provinces) is controlled by the Islamist armed faction Hayat Tahrir al-Sham (HTS). Turkey, which intervened militarily in early 2020 to halt a Russian-backed Syrian regime offensive into Idlib, has retained thousands of forces along front lines there in a thus-far successful bid to deter further escalation.

Although the absence of major military offensives since March 2020 has reduced civilian casualty rates, the relative calm is fragile. During the reporting period, insurgent attacks, shelling across lines of control and occasional air and drone strikes continued. The underlying factors that created the conditions for Syria's 2011 popular uprising and fuelled its subsequent civil war remain unaddressed. Syrian actors remain dedicated to mutually irreconcilable objectives and are deeply linked to increasingly volatile geopolitical dynamics. Finally, grim economic conditions, exacerbated by the international impact of the war in Ukraine that began in February 2022, threaten to worsen an already dire humanitarian catastrophe. In May 2022, the United Nations reported that there were 5.6 million refugees outside the country, while 90% of Syrians inside Syria were living below the poverty line, 8.2m needed life-saving aid and 6.9m remained internally displaced.[2]

Events in 2021 and early 2022 illustrated the continued volatility that threatens the current relative calm. A major ISIS attack on an SDF-run prison in northeast Syria, beginning on 20 January 2022, facilitated the escape of an unknown number of ISIS members and led to days of clashes. While the attack showcased the group's ability to generate resources and conduct insurgent operations, the killing of ISIS leader Abu Ibrahim al-Hashimi al-Qurashi during a US special-forces raid in early February highlighted the group's limitations. Yet the SDF faces deeper challenges beyond ISIS: Turkish drone strikes targeting PKK figures in SDF-controlled territory (some of whom held positions within the SDF), in addition to intensified Turkish operations against the PKK in northern Iraq, underlined the potential for renewed escalation linked to the broader PKK–Turkey conflict.

The Assad regime remains in a difficult position politically and economically. During the reporting period, gradual normalisation with the United Arab Emirates (UAE) continued but other Arab states clarified that they would not soon follow, with Western governments signalling that they would continue to apply economic pressure. To stay afloat, the regime is relying increasingly on its illicit narcotics industry and a credit line from Tehran.

Geopolitical dynamics have exacerbated humanitarian need and added further unpredictability. Russia's invasion of Ukraine has reduced wheat availability and increased cost, worsening food insecurity. It also led the US to suspend dialogue with Moscow on Syria. The war's impact on Russia's military posture remains unclear – its forces in Syria seem to be less active but there is no sign of a drawdown. Turkey's military support for Ukraine and closure of its straits to military traffic has fed concerns that Russia may renew escalation in Idlib to (once again) use the threat of refugee flows against Ankara and NATO. Meanwhile, Iran's presence inside Syria continued to prompt occasional Israeli airstrikes – a dynamic that bears close observation if tensions escalate on Iran's nuclear file.

Conflict Parties

Syrian Armed Forces (SAF) / The Syrian Arab Army (SAA)

Strength: Unknown.

Areas of operation: Southern, coastal and central Syria and parts of northern Syria.

Leadership: Bashar al-Assad (commander-in-chief). Key elite units of the SAA, such as the Republican Guard and the 4th Division, fall under the command of Maher al-Assad, the president's brother. Other units are heavily influenced by Russian or Iranian commanders.

Structure: Consists of the army, navy, air force, intelligence services and the National Defence Forces. The SAA adopts a hybrid military structure that compensates for its shrinking military personnel with paramilitary militias and pro-regime fighters, including foreign fighters backed by Iran. Since 2017, with Russian support, efforts have focused on integrating or dissolving these militias and reorganising and equipping the command-and-control structure, with mixed results.

History: Since its establishment in 1945, the SAA has played a key role in Syrian politics. Involved in bringing Hafez al-Assad and the Ba'athist-Alawite dynasty to power in 1970. The high percentage of Alawites in key positions in the SAA exacerbated sectarianism after the 2011 outbreak of war. The disproportionate reliance on Alawite manpower is a key vulnerability, necessitating interventions by Iran's Islamic Revolutionary Guard Corps (IRGC), Hizbullah (beginning in 2013) and Russia (2015) to mitigate the risk of military collapse.

Objectives: Regain military control over the entire Syrian territory.

Opponents: Israeli forces, Turkish forces, US forces, SDF/People's Protection Units (YPG), ISIS and al-Qaeda affiliates, SNA.

Affiliates/allies: Iranian and Iranian-backed forces, Russian and Russian-backed forces, Hizbullah and other Shia militias.

Resources/capabilities: Benefits from significant Russian air, artillery and missile support and intelligence capabilities.

Hayat Tahrir al-Sham (HTS)

Strength: 12,000–15,000 (estimate).[3]

Areas of operation: Idlib province, northwestern Syria.

Leadership: Abu Mohamed al-Golani.

Structure: Maintains a joint military-operations room with other local rebels. The HTS-linked Syrian Salvation Government focuses on territorial control and on the provision of public services via a decentralised governance system and quasi-formal service-provision institutions.

History: Originally known as Jabhat Fatah al-Sham (formerly Jabhat al-Nusra or Al-Nusra Front) and linked to the Islamic State of Iraq, it broke away when the latter declared itself the Islamic State of Iraq and al-Sham (ISIS) in 2013 and later split from al-Qaeda in 2016. In 2017 it merged with several smaller factions and rebranded itself as HTS.

Objectives: Maintain control over Idlib in the short term, including through crushing remaining ISIS and al-Qaeda cells. In the long run, overthrow the Assad regime.

Opponents: SAF, Iranian and Iranian-backed forces, Russian forces, ISIS, al-Qaeda and affiliates.

Affiliates/allies: Turkish forces around the mutual objective of deterring SAA offensives and uprooting radical cells affiliated to ISIS or al-Qaeda.

Hayat Tahrir al-Sham (HTS)

Resources/capabilities: Light weaponry, rocket launchers, anti-tank guided missiles as well as a small number of mechanised vehicles. It has seized weaponry from other rebel groups, including those equipped by Turkey and Western governments. Has used vehicle-borne improvised explosive devices (IEDs) and suicide bombings. Reportedly finances itself primarily through taxation in Idlib province.

(Turkey-sponsored) Syrian National Army (SNA)

Strength: 70,000 (estimate).[4]

Areas of operation: Northern and northwestern Syria.

Leadership: Deployed alongside Turkish military forces and therefore operates under Turkish leadership.

Structure: A conglomerate of dozens of different militias, ranging vastly in size, affiliation and ideology, composed of Syrian militants, who are trained and equipped by Turkey. Divided into seven main legions, each composed of a wide array of divisions and brigades. The National Front for Liberation (NLF), a coalition of more than ten rebel militias, is nominally incorporated within the SNA.

History: Created as a splinter group of the Turkey-backed Free Syrian Army. Trained and equipped by the Turkish government since 2016. In 2019, the Idlib-based and Turkey-sponsored National Front for Liberation was merged into the SNA.

Objectives: Take control of northern Syria.

Opponents: Syrian government forces, Iranian and Iranian-backed forces, SDF/YPG and ISIS.

Affiliates/allies: Turkish forces.

Resources/capabilities: While a handful of formations have received US-sponsored training and equipment, the SNA has been fully reliant on Turkey's support since its creation. Turkey has provided small arms as well as infantry vehicles, and SNA military operations have benefitted from the Turkish army's fire support via artillery and airstrikes.

Syrian Democratic Forces (SDF) / People's Protection Units (YPG)

Strength: 100,000 (estimate).

Areas of operation: Northern Syria.

Leadership: Mazloum Kobani Abdi, also known as Sahin Cilo (military commander). Abdi is a former senior member of the PKK.

Structure: Syrian Kurds lead the YPG and the Women's Protection Units (YPJ), which maintain informal and ideological links to the PKK and provide the SDF's most capable fighters. The broader ranks of the SDF reflect the ethnic diversity of Syria's northeast, are largely non-ideological and in some areas are organised along geographic or tribal lines.

History: Created in 2015 as a direct response to the advance of ISIS into northern Syria, building on various pre-existing alliances. Since then, it has fought against ISIS and the Turkish military.

Objectives: Control northern Syria.

Opponents: Turkish forces, SNA, ISIS, al-Qaeda and affiliates.

Affiliates/allies: PKK, Russia, Syrian regime, US.

Resources/capabilities: While it built upon the experience of its militias, since its formal creation, the SDF has been equipped, trained and advised by the US. SDF units are equipped with small arms and some infantry vehicles.

Islamic State, also known as ISIS or ISIL

Strength: Approximately 6,000–10,000 in Iraq and Syria.[5]

Areas of operation: Across eastern Syria, notably along the Euphrates and the Badiya desert as well as in the governorate of Homs in central Syria and along the M20 highway that runs between Palmyra and Deir ez-Zor.

Leadership: Abu Hasan al-Hashimi al-Qurashi (replaced Abu Ibrahim al-Hashimi al-Qurashi, who was killed by US forces in February 2022).

Structure: The presence of ISIS in Syria has changed considerably since the 2017 loss of Raqqa and its gradual territorial defeat. Its central command remains in place but greater autonomy is granted to local cells across Syria and Iraq to generate resources and facilitate insurgent campaigns.

History: Originated in Iraq around 2003. It fought to establish a caliphate during the Syrian civil war. In the period 2014–17, ISIS controlled many territories in Iraq and Syria and governed more than eight million people. Since 2017 (in Iraq) and 2019 (in Syria), the group has lost control of all the territories it held.

Objectives: Regain territorial hold in Syria and Iraq.

Opponents: SAF, SNA, HTS, Russian, Turkish and US armed forces, Iranian and Iranian-backed and commanded militias and the SDF/YPG.

Affiliates/allies: ISIS fighters in other countries.

Resources/capabilities: Relies on guerrilla warfare, hit-and-run tactics and conventional asymmetrical operations, using light and small weaponry and deploying insurgent tactics including suicide bombings.

Armed Forces of the Russian Federation

Strength: 4,000 (estimate) troops in Syria.

Areas of operation: Across Syria.

Leadership: President Vladimir Putin (Supreme Commander-in-Chief of the Armed Forces of the Russian Federation); General of the Army Valery Gerasimov (Chief of the General Staff of the Armed Forces of the Russian Federation); Sergei Shoigu (defence minister).

Structure: The Russian mission in Syria involves ground forces, special forces, attack aircraft and bombers, an air-defence component and military intelligence. Russian private military contractors operate in front-line roles together with conventional units.

History: Since 2015, Russia has shaped the Syrian battlefield, playing a crucial strategic and operational role to shore up and reorganise Syrian government forces and assist the Assad regime in capturing key areas.

Objectives: Reform the Syrian army, integrate irregular and rebel groups into the SAA and support capacity-building.

Opponents: US forces, SNA, HTS, ISIS, al-Qaeda and affiliates.

Affiliates/allies: SAF, 5th Corps of SAA, Tiger Force.

Resources/capabilities: Has deployed significant air, artillery, missile, missile-defence and intelligence capabilities in Syria, testing new weapons and tactics.

Turkish Armed Forces (TSK)

Strength: 10,000–15,000 in Syria.[6]

Areas of operation: Northwestern and northern Syria.

Leadership: President Recep Tayyip Erdoğan (commander-in-chief); Gen. (retd) Hulusi Akar (minister of national defence); Gen. Yasar Guler (chief of general staff).

Structure: The TSK is present in Syria via ground forces, special forces, military intelligence and reconnaissance.

History: Involved in Syria since the conflict began in 2011. For the first five years, it primarily provided training and equipment to the Syrian armed opposition and humanitarian aid. Military operations increased beginning in 2016 following ISIS terrorist attacks in Turkey and the YPG's territorial gains. Ankara intervened in 2020 to halt a SAF offensive into opposition-controlled Idlib and has maintained thousands of troops in Idlib ever since to deter further offensives.

Objectives: Destroy the PKK, including through eliminating key figures in northern Syria and rolling back territorial gains of its Syrian offshoot (YPG); secure Turkey's border with Syria; limit refugee influx into Turkey; and prevent military defeat of Syrian opposition allies.

Opponents: YPG, ISIS, al-Qaeda and affiliates, SAF, Iranian and Iranian-backed and commanded militias.

Affiliates/allies: Relies extensively on the SNA as a local actor and support force in northern Syria.

Resources/capabilities: Turkey's defence budget for 2021 was US$9.55 billion. Trains, equips and arms the SNA and deploys its own military mechanised infantry battalions on the ground, as well as F-16 fighter jets and ANKA-S uninhabited aerial vehicles (UAVs). Its military capabilities include air attack and intelligence, surveillance and reconnaissance assets such as the F-16 and the *Bayraktar* TB2 UAV, armoured tanks and special-forces units.

Iranian armed forces

Strength: 3,000 in Syria (estimate).

Areas of operation: Southern and eastern Syria, Damascus, Aleppo and some front lines in northwestern Syria.

Leadership: Brig.-Gen. Esmail Ghaani (military leader of the Quds Force, QF).

Structure: Iran operates militarily in the country through a number of military organisations and local and regional Shia militias. Its military operations in Syria are organised by the QF, the ground forces of the IRGC, and a smaller group of units drawn from the regular Iranian army, Artesh, that began to arrive in Syria in early 2016. The QF conducts external military operations in Syria, training and equipping pro-Iranian and regime militias from Afghanistan, Iraq, Lebanon, Pakistan and Syria. Iran maintains substantial influence within certain elements of the SAF, particularly militias nominally incorporated within the Local Defence Forces.

History: Active in Syria since 2011. In the conflict's early stages Tehran provided the Syrian regime with financial aid, arms shipments and communication-jamming equipment. With the gradual intensification of fighting, Iran sent several hundred senior QF and Hizbullah operatives as military advisers and planners, with significant escalation occurring in 2013 amid rebel gains and the weakening of the Assad regime. Iran has sent thousands of fighters from various military organisations to fight in Syria under Iranian leadership and deploys Iranian manpower mainly as battlefield commanders in key positions. Iranian and pro-Iranian forces fought leading battles in Homs (2012–14), Aleppo (2015–16), Deir ez-Zor (2017) and Deraa (2018).

Objectives: Preserve the Assad regime, shore up militia partners, build a military infrastructure inside Syria, contain Russian and Turkish influence, deter Israel.

Opponents: Israeli forces (airstrikes), HTS, ISIS and al-Qaeda affiliates, SNA, SDF/YPG.

Affiliates/allies: Hizbullah and other Shia militias in Afghanistan, Iraq, Lebanon, Pakistan and Syria; SAF, Russian forces.

Resources/capabilities: Operates several military bases and camps inside Syria with entrenched strategic infrastructure throughout the country. Provides an array of weaponry to its allies, including anti-tank guided missiles and UAVs, but its main contributions are command and control along with mobilisation of foreign and militia fighters.

Combined Joint Task Force–*Operation Inherent Resolve* (CJTF–OIR)

Strength: 900 (estimate, including advisers, special forces, etc.).

Areas of operation: Northeastern Syria areas under control of the SDF/YPG, and southern Syria in al-Tanf garrison near the Iraqi and Jordanian borders.

Leadership: Gen. Michael E. Kurilla (US Central Command).

Structure: The US leads the CJTF–OIR, which brings together over 20 coalition partners.

History: Created in October 2014 when the US Department of Defense formalised ongoing military operations against ISIS. In late 2015, the first US ground troops entered Syria to recruit, organise and advise Syrian Kurdish and Arab opposition fighters in the fight against ISIS. The developing partnership between the US and the SDF/YPG became a significant source of tension between the US and Turkey.

In late 2019, under pressure from Ankara and via the unilateral decision of then-president Donald Trump, the US contingency withdrew more than half of its forces (then around 2,000 personnel) and narrowed its military presence to eastern areas of SDF-controlled territory (in addition to al-Tanf).

Objectives: Enable and support SDF counter-insurgency operations against ISIS, while shoring up local stability to deny ISIS opportunities to resurface and expand.

Opponents: ISIS, al-Qaeda and affiliates.

Affiliates/allies: SDF/YPG.

Resources/capabilities: Airstrikes targeting ISIS. Special-forces support to SDF counter-insurgent operations. Armoured vehicles protect CJTF–OIR bases, including adjacent to oilfields in northeastern Syria.

Conflict Drivers

Geopolitical and geostrategic influences

Wrangling over Iran's regional role:
Tehran's fears that the fall of Assad might remove Syria from Iran's regional axis led its IRGC to escalate its role in the war beginning in 2013 and to seek Russia's direct intervention in 2015. Conversely, a sense of geopolitical opportunity helped motivate Gulf states and Turkey to initially back the armed opposition. More recently, as major combat operations wound down, the IRGC shifted focus to consolidating its influence within regime-controlled areas, while Israel has conducted strikes aimed at limiting the military aspects of that entrenchment. Eastern Syria has occasionally witnessed violent exchanges between IRGC-backed forces (which are lead players in areas southwest of the Euphrates, nominally controlled by the Syrian government) and the US (which maintains bases northeast of the Euphrates and at al-Tanf in the southeast).

Competition between Moscow and Washington:
Competition with the US has remained a primary motivating factor for Russia, informing its UN Security Council (UNSC) vetoes and encouraging it to intervene forcefully in 2015. More recently, bipartisan agreement in Washington on the need to prioritise containment of Russian influence amid Moscow's invasion of Ukraine has reinforced the Biden administration's determination to remain in northeast Syria.

The PKK–Turkey conflict:
The 2015 collapse of the Ankara–PKK peace process – negotiations that initially raised hopes of significant Turkish reforms and an end to the PKK's insurgency – catalysed a transborder cycle of violence between Ankara and the group, which continued in northern Syria and northern Iraq during the reporting period.

'Counter-terrorism' and jihadist dynamics:
The arrival of jihadist fighters with experience in Iraq, combined with the Syrian regime's tactical releases of imprisoned Islamist militants, shifted the balance of power within Syria's armed opposition in favour of more hardline forces from late 2011. The rise of ISIS on both sides of the Syria–Iraq border led to the intervention of US-led forces beginning in 2014. The group's capacity for resurgence and the risks associated with leaving a violent vacuum for ISIS and other actors to exploit have convinced Washington to maintain its military role in northeast Syria.

Security

Regime's brutality and dependence on Alawite minority:
Amid the 2011 protests, two key factors within the Syrian security sector provided fuel for conflict. The first was the reliance of the regime's military and security services on brutal tactics and collective punishment to penalise and deter dissent. The second was the structural dependence of those institutions on members of the Alawite minority, who dominate their leadership and provide a disproportionate share of their most reliable fighting forces. Although much has changed in Syria since 2011, these factors have remained relatively consistent and have arguably worsened. Alongside

the significant attrition suffered by regime forces, they help explain why some areas recaptured by the regime remain subject to frequent insurgent attacks.

Economic

Socio-economic inequalities:
While mass protest movements elsewhere in the Arab world helped spark Syria's 2011 uprising, key socio-economic factors rendered the country vulnerable to conflagration. These include the concentration of economic gains among regime-favoured elites (especially in Damascus and Aleppo), while the population in those cities' outskirts and throughout much of the country suffered from under-development and government neglect, compounded by climate change.

Key Events in 2021–22

POLITICAL EVENTS

26 May 2021
President Assad 're-elected' to fourth seven-year term in widely dismissed presidential elections.

9 July
The UNSC renews authorisation for cross-border humanitarian-aid delivery to northwest Syria.

12 January 2022
Jordan seizes 2.7m Captagon pills amid drug-smuggling surge from government-controlled areas of Syria.

MILITARY/VIOLENT EVENTS

21 March 2021
Artillery strikes by regime forces on a hospital in northwest Syria kill six civilians.

26 April
SDF-linked security forces seize a neighbourhood in Qamishli from pro-regime militia, capping days of clashes.

27 June
US airstrikes hit Iran-backed militias in Syria and Iraq in retaliation for strikes on US positions in Iraq.

19–22 August
Turkey initiates a series of drone strikes targeting SDF/YPG personnel allegedly operating on behalf of the PKK.

20 October
An IED attack on a bus carrying soldiers in Damascus kills 14 people; regime forces then strike a rebel-held area in Idlib, killing 13 people.

4 January 2022
Iran-backed forces fire rockets at US positions in Syria on the second anniversary of the killing of former IRGC QF commander Qasem Soleimani.

8 January
Three Turkish soldiers are killed on the Turkish side of the Syrian border in an IED attack claimed by a YPG affiliate.

20 January
ISIS launches a major attack on an SDF-controlled prison, freeing militants and sparking days of clashes.

3 February
ISIS leader Abu Ibrahim al-Hashimi al-Qurashi and his family are killed during a US raid in Idlib.

11 March
Russian President Vladimir Putin approves recruitment of fighters from Syria and other countries for Ukraine deployment.

18 March
Assad visits the UAE, in his first trip to an Arab state since the war began.

7 March
Iran announces the death of two IRGC members killed the previous day by Israeli strikes on Damascus.

Responses to the Conflict

Diplomacy

The UN-facilitated political track has languished for years as a largely uneventful sideshow to the war on the ground. The fundamental challenges it faces have remained relatively consistent: the Assad regime views the process as threatening and has refused to negotiate substantively even on tangential details (much less power-sharing or any form of political transition); Russia and Iran have not pressed Assad to make meaningful concessions; and the leverage which states backing the opposition are willing to apply (i.e., sanctions, withholding support for reconstruction, material backing for armed opposition factions) have been insufficient to fundamentally change the calculus in Damascus, Moscow or Tehran. As a result, UNSC Resolution 2254 (2015), which in principle established the framework for a political process with US and Russian support, is treated as little more than a checkbox on diplomatic talking points.

Shifts in the conflict's military balance and broader geopolitical dynamics have widened the gap between the UN track and the reality on the ground. For example, the regime's regaining of the upper hand, thanks to Moscow's direct military intervention beginning in September 2015, further reduced its incentive to engage meaningfully. Additionally, the margin for US–Russian cooperation was reduced to virtually nil amid the war in Ukraine. Meanwhile, large parts of northern Syria's territory, population and resources are controlled by two groups excluded from the UN political process – the SDF and HTS.

Operating within these constraints, UN Special Envoy for Syria Geir Pedersen has pursued a two-pronged strategy: continuing engagement on an ineffectual constitutional track bequeathed to him by his predecessor while attempting to catalyse more meaningful diplomacy among the key states holding leverage over the conflict's Syrian protagonists. The constitutional track continues because it would be too politically tricky to abort but merits little attention – the Assad regime does not adhere to the current constitution and has made clear that it will not cooperate to draft a new version.

In 2022, the framework the UN is proposing for its inter-state track is 'steps-for-steps', which encourages actors backing the Syrian opposition to leverage their influence to incentivise behavioural change – via specifying conditional steps the backers can take to reduce pressure on the Syrian government – in exchange for definitive, concrete steps by Damascus or its Russian and Iranian backers.

The leverage these Western and regional states hold, while likely insufficient to achieve a change in regime leadership, is nevertheless significant: it includes major US and European sanctions; de facto control over whether significant resources will flow to Syria's reconstruction; the presence and roles of US-led and Turkish military forces in northeast and northwest Syria, respectively; and whether and when Damascus is able to normalise political and economic relations in the region. So far, these states have failed to effectively coordinate and, at times, have burned cards for free (for example, the Trump administration's partial withdrawal from northeast Syria in 2019 and the UAE's gradual, largely unconditional normalisation since 2018). Yet the Biden administration's determination to remain in northeast Syria, combined with growing scepticism among key Arab states regarding the potential utility of improving ties with the Assad regime absent substantive behavioural change, have at least opened the possibility of a joint approach that could eventually lend relevance to UN mediation efforts.

Figure 1: Internal displacements and total number of refugees and IDPs per year, 2011–21

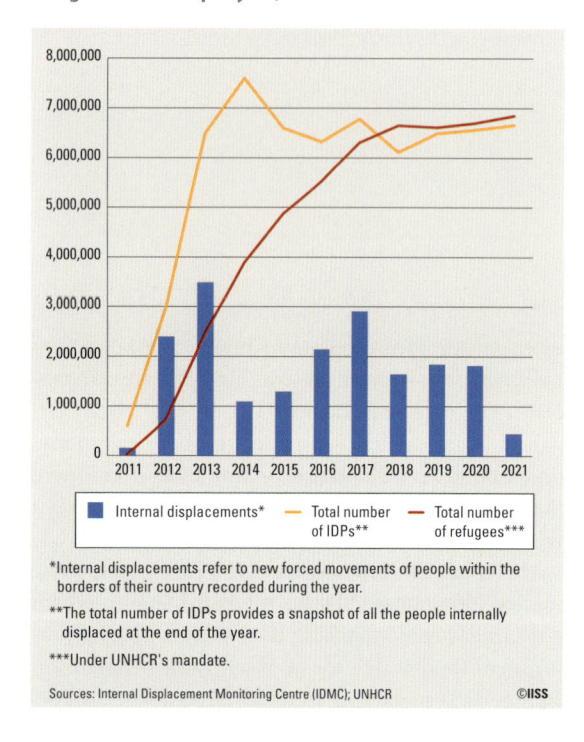

*Internal displacements refer to new forced movements of people within the borders of their country recorded during the year.
**The total number of IDPs provides a snapshot of all the people internally displaced at the end of the year.
***Under UNHCR's mandate.

Sources: Internal Displacement Monitoring Centre (IDMC); UNHCR © IISS

Humanitarian aid

In July 2021, following months of manoeuvring in the UNSC and bilateral negotiations between Russia and the US, Moscow agreed to renew for a year the UN's mandate for cross-border humanitarian operations through the Bab al-Hawa crossing between Turkey and Idlib. Russia had previously blocked renewal of the other three crossings originally authorised by the UNSC in 2014 and has repeatedly signalled its intention to end UN cross-border aid as part of its broader strategy to restore Damascus's leverage – and eventually its control – throughout the country. Moscow agreed to extend the Bab al-Hawa operation as part of a package deal in which the US and its UNSC allies committed to push for more 'cross-line' humanitarian convoys from regime-held areas into Idlib, which are far less efficient than cross-border aid from Turkey and subject to the Syrian government's approval (throughout the conflict, Damascus has often blocked cross-line aid as a means to increase pressure on civilians in opposition-held areas, in some cases to the point of starvation). Also included in the deal was a US pledge to push for more 'early recovery' support to Syrian-government-controlled areas. In effect, this would mean a broadening of humanitarian support beyond immediate, life-saving aid (while stopping short of 'reconstruction' support to government-controlled infrastructure). While this deal was broadly viewed as a net positive, its short duration only delayed the crisis until July 2022, while the complex quid pro quo ensured that negotiations over basic humanitarian access would continue to absorb significant diplomatic bandwidth for another year. In July 2022, acrimonious negotiations in the UNSC led to a further six-month renewal, again briefly delaying the crisis.

Conflict Outlook

Political scenarios

While progress on the UN political track is unlikely and most of the conflict's protagonists remain entrenched in their approaches, one controversial actor stood out for its political dynamism: HTS. The group has been led by Abu Mohamed al-Golani since it appeared in the Syrian theatre in late 2011. Yet the group's external relationships, internal balance of power, strategy, identity and ideology have shifted dramatically over the years.

Three factors help illustrate the substance of HTS's evolution. Firstly, its decisions to split from ISIS (in 2013) and al-Qaeda (2016–17) ultimately proved to be major turning points. The splits fundamentally shifted the balance of power within the group in favour of Golani and his relatively pragmatic inner circle, as more hardline figures defected (to ISIS in the first instance, and later to form and join a new faction – Hurras al-Din – that adopted the al-Qaeda affiliation cast aside by Golani). Secondly, these breaks further hardened through violent confrontation: Golani's group has been at war with ISIS since 2014, forcibly crushed Hurras al-Din in 2020 and continues security crackdowns in Idlib to prevent their re-emergence. Thirdly, HTS has undertaken major strategic shifts that are anathema to the hardliners with whom it once allied, including explicitly banning transnational jihadist activity from Idlib and adhering to the ongoing Turkish–Russian ceasefire in Idlib.

This evolution has its limitations. Governance administered by the HTS-aligned Syrian Salvation Government, while not draconian by regional standards, remains broadly Islamist. Moreover, HTS continues to suppress local dissent. Yet the durability of the March 2020 Turkish–Russian ceasefire, combined with the group's own success in consolidating control there, is leading some actors to expand their imagination as to what might ultimately prove sustainable in Idlib.

Strategic implications and global influences

For most of its duration, the conflict has occupied a space near the centre of the geopolitical arena, with developments inside the country reverberating far outside it. In the coming year, Syria is likely to experience the reverse, with actors adjusting their handling of the conflict in response to dynamics in Ukraine and the nuclear negotiations between Western powers and Iran.

Failure to negotiate a new Iran nuclear deal would heighten tensions, increasing risks of violent exchanges between the IRGC and US forces in eastern Syria, as well as the possibility of broader Israeli military action against Iranian targets in Syria and elsewhere. However, a renewed nuclear deal would also carry risks. Iran is broadly perceived as having invested some of its financial gains from the original agreement into the IRGC's military and militia infrastructure within Syria and elsewhere; this exacerbated instability at the time and could do so again.

Given Russia's prioritisation of the Ukraine invasion, high rates of attrition there and increasingly constrained resources, Moscow could shift manpower and equipment from Syria – or move further towards deploying Syrian fighters on behalf of its Ukraine effort. Alternatively, Russia could attempt to gain leverage over Ukraine's backers by escalating militarily in Idlib, towards NATO's southern flank. Such an attack would be far riskier than the 2019–20 Idlib offensive due to Turkey's deployment along Idlib front lines and capacity to inflict severe damage on advancing regime forces. Moscow would also have to account for other counter-levers Ankara could employ, especially given Russia's reliance on Turkey as an economic and logistical outlet through which to mitigate the impact of Western sanctions. A middle outcome is perhaps most likely, in which Russia maintains its Syrian deployment near current levels but with less proactive military engagement than it undertook in previous phases of the war.

The Russia–Ukraine war could also impact how Turkey approaches its conflict with the PKK and the YPG. The US military presence in eastern Syria and the threat of US sanctions helped convince Ankara to halt its 2019 offensive into northeast Syria. It is possible that Turkey could be sufficiently emboldened by its role in support of Ukraine and its leverage over Finland's and Sweden's NATO accession to challenge that US deterrent – especially in Manbij, the contested western edge of SDF-controlled territory where previous US pledges of YPG withdrawal went largely unimplemented. Ankara may gamble that an offensive on Manbij would not elicit a strong US response; if it miscalculates, it could precipitate further damage to an already reeling Turkish economy, heading into an election year.

Alternatively, Turkey may view Moscow's preoccupation with Ukraine as an opportunity to escalate militarily against the YPG in Tel Rifaat, an area falling within Russia's sphere of influence. Though Tel Rifaat is nominally under regime control and hosts a Russian military presence, the YPG uses it as a staging ground for insurgent attacks against areas held by SNA forces. If Russia steps back from the area, Turkey may see an opportunity to step in. Neither the YPG nor pro-regime forces are in a position to successfully defend the area without Russian backing. However, a Turkish offensive could lead to counter-escalation by the YPG or PKK elsewhere.

Notes

[1] Bashir Nasrollah et al., 'Map of Military Control in Syria End of 2021 and Beginning of 2022', Jusoor for Studies, 24 December 2021.

[2] 'Syria Factsheet', ReliefWeb, 12 May 2022.

[3] United Nations Security Council, 'Twenty-fourth Report of the Analytical Support and Sanctions Monitoring Team Submitted Pursuant to Resolution 2368 (2017) Concerning ISIL (Da'esh), Al-Qaida and Associated Individuals and Entities', S/2019/570, 30 August 2019.

[4] Omer Ozkizilcik, 'Uniting the Syrian Opposition: The Components of the National Army and the Implications of the Unification', SETA, October 2019.

[5] 'Iraq Bombing: IS Says It Was Behind Deadly Suicide Attacks in Baghdad', BBC News, 22 January 2021; and 'Fourteenth report of the Secretary-General on the threat posed by ISIL (Da'esh) to International Peace and Security and the Range of United Nations Efforts in Support of Member States in Countering the Threat', UN Security Council, S/2022/63, 28 January 2022, p. 6.

[6] 'Turkey Has Evacuated Seven Syrian Military Posts', Reuters, 18 December 2020.

IRAQ

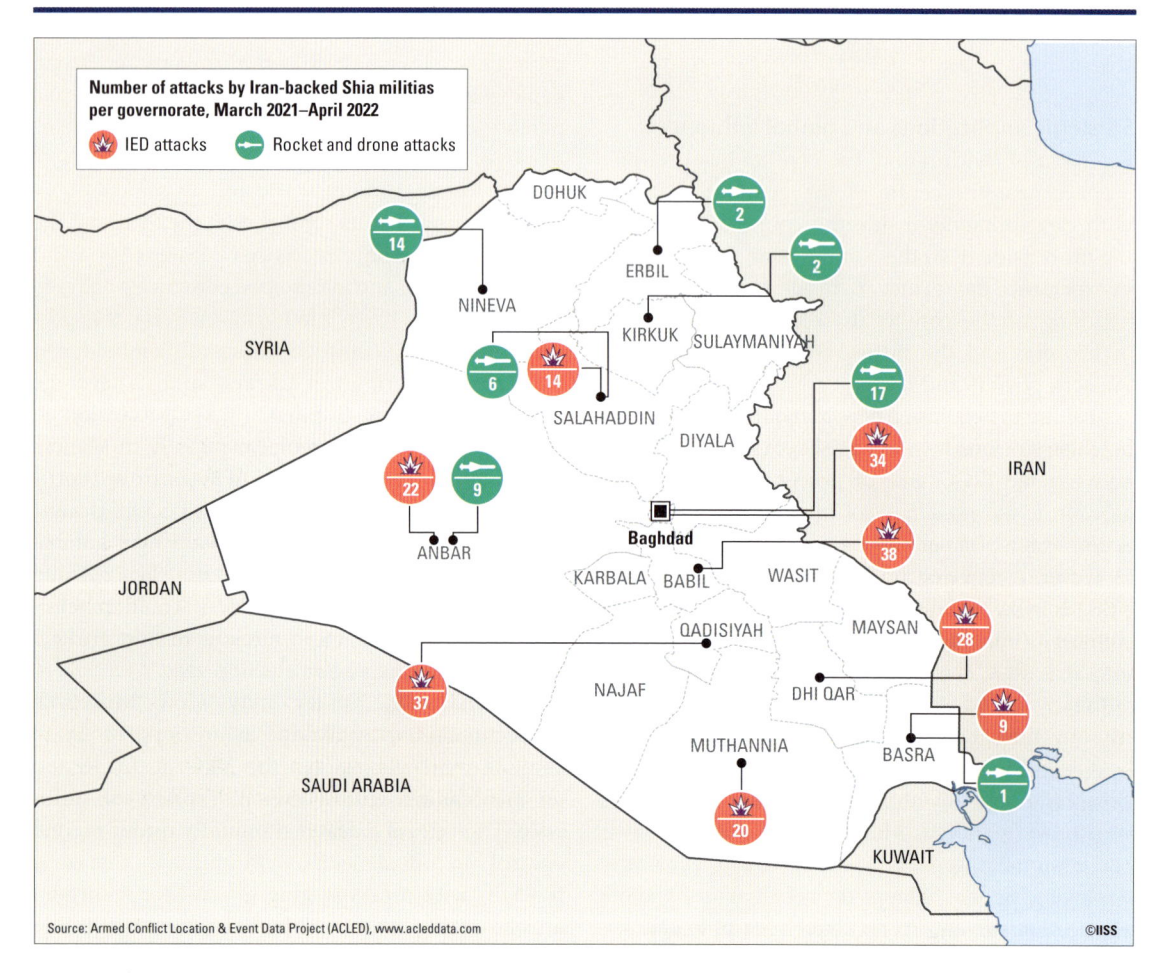

Number of attacks by Iran-backed Shia militias per governorate, March 2021–April 2022
- IED attacks
- Rocket and drone attacks

Nineva: 14 (rocket/drone)
Dohuk: 2 (rocket/drone)
Erbil: 2 (rocket/drone)
Salahaddin: 6 (rocket/drone), 14 (IED)
Sulaymaniyah: 17 (rocket/drone)
Diyala: 34 (IED)
Anbar: 22 (IED), 9 (rocket/drone)
Wasit: 38 (IED)
Maysan: 28 (IED)
Qadisiyah: 37 (IED)
Dhi Qar: 9 (IED)
Muthanna: 20 (IED)
Basra: 1 (rocket/drone)

Source: Armed Conflict Location & Event Data Project (ACLED), www.acleddata.com ©IISS

Overview

Two decades after the US-led invasion overthrew Saddam Hussein's regime, Iraq is still struggling to achieve acceptable levels of internal stability and political cohesion. The main political and security issues remain Sunni–Shia tensions and other ethno-sectarian divides; the lingering presence of the Islamic State (ISIS) in various areas; Turkish military operations against Kurdish militias; and the Kurdistan Regional Government's (KRG) frictions, both internally and vis-à-vis Baghdad.

The social and political fractures caused by Hussein's Ba'ath Party over roughly 20 years of ruthless dictatorship were further exacerbated by the US-sponsored process of 'de-Ba'athification', through which all individuals with previous senior affiliations to the party were banned from government-related jobs soon after the regime fell. This process effectively excluded from power a significant segment of Iraqi society, creating enormous grievances among former Ba'ath members and the broader Sunni minority, which fuelled the creation of armed militias and ultimately pushed many towards al-Qaeda and, later, towards ISIS.

As the country plunged into civil war, Iraq's Shia community saw the rise of cleric Muqtada al-Sadr and his Mahdi Army, a collection of militias that primarily targeted US-led coalition forces, at the same time as Sunni armed militias were emerging from the de-Ba'athification process. The power vacuum provided an opportunity for Iran to expand its

Armed Conflict Global Relevance Indicator (ACGRI)

- Incidence: 41
- Human impact: 9
- Geopolitical impact: 54

Iraq

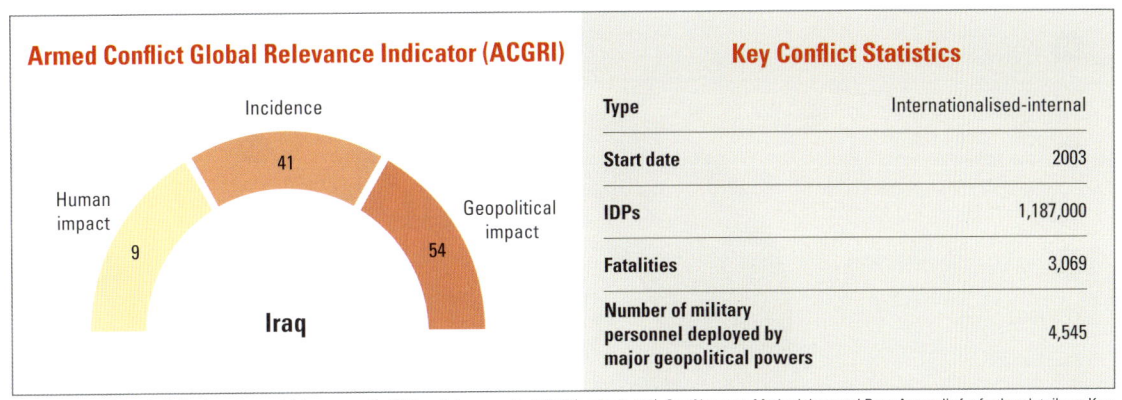

Key Conflict Statistics

Type	Internationalised-internal
Start date	2003
IDPs	1,187,000
Fatalities	3,069
Number of military personnel deployed by major geopolitical powers	4,545

ACGRI pillars: IISS calculation based on multiple sources for 2021 and January–April 2022 (scale: 0–100). See Notes on Methodology and Data Appendix for further details on Key Conflict Statistics.

influence in the country by supporting Sadr's forces as well as the previously Iran-based Badr Brigades and several other militia groups. The emergence of ISIS as a major threat in 2014 raised serious concerns in Tehran, leading it to further expand its role in Iraq. As the religious leadership in Najaf called on the Shia community to take up arms and fight ISIS, Iraq saw a constellation of Iran-backed armed militias – coalesced around the umbrella of Popular Mobilisation Units (PMU) – take root across the country. The presence of multiple, autonomous militias, often more capable than the Iraqi Security Forces (ISF), highlights that the country is still suffering from a governance gap, as deeply rooted ethnic and institutional fractures remain open.

During the reporting period, the potential for internal strife increased amid a persistent and widening cleavage among its main political stakeholders, mostly relating to a stalemate on government formation following the October 2021 elections. Moreover, a weakening yet still potent insurgency, recurring droughts, soaring global food prices and tribal fragmentation added to the volatility of the political transition in Baghdad.

Since Iraq's parliament convened in January 2022, it has been unable to elect a president (who will then be constitutionally required to call on the largest party to form a government). In June, the largest parliamentary bloc – led by Sadr – effectively resigned from the parliament, after having tried and failed to form a government excluding the Shiite Coordination Framework (SCF), which primarily represents parties supported by Iran-backed Shia militia groups (SMGs).[1] By doing so, Sadr has undermined the long-term sustainability of any new government without Sadrist participation.

Following the initial results of the October 2021 elections, Iran-backed SMGs – spearheaded by Kataib Hizbullah (KH) and Asaib Ahl al-Haq (AAH) – and their key rival, the Saraya al-Salam militia (the Sadrist movement's armed wing), engaged in a protracted and violent intimidation campaign against each other. Those three groups, as well as many others, are formally part of the PMU. Their affiliates appear to have conducted assassinations, deployed improvised explosive devices (IEDs) and launched rocket attacks against the residences of political leaders (including an alleged strike using an uninhabited aerial vehicle (UAV) on Prime Minister Mustafa al-Kadhimi's residence in early November 2021) and critical infrastructure, such as financial institutions and oil facilities.

During the reporting period, Iraq faced a weakening but still pervasive ISIS insurgency. The group was responsible for several deadly high-profile attacks, primarily in territories disputed between the central government and the Erbil-based KRG – in Kirkuk and Diyala governorates and in the Hamrin Mountains linking Iraq's central desert with Syria. Major ISIS attacks have been declining since the second half of 2020, with occasional spikes. Quarterly reports released by the United States assessed that there had been a continuous decline in ISIS attacks in Iraq in 2021 and 2022.[2] ISIS attacks in 2022 were increasingly localised and low quality, carried out by small rural cells reliant on hit-and-run and ambushing tactics.

A semi-coordinated counter-insurgency campaign by the US-led Combined Joint Task Force–*Operation Inherent Resolve* (CJTF–OIR), the ISF and the PMU is believed to have caused the decapitation of the ISIS leadership across Iraq and

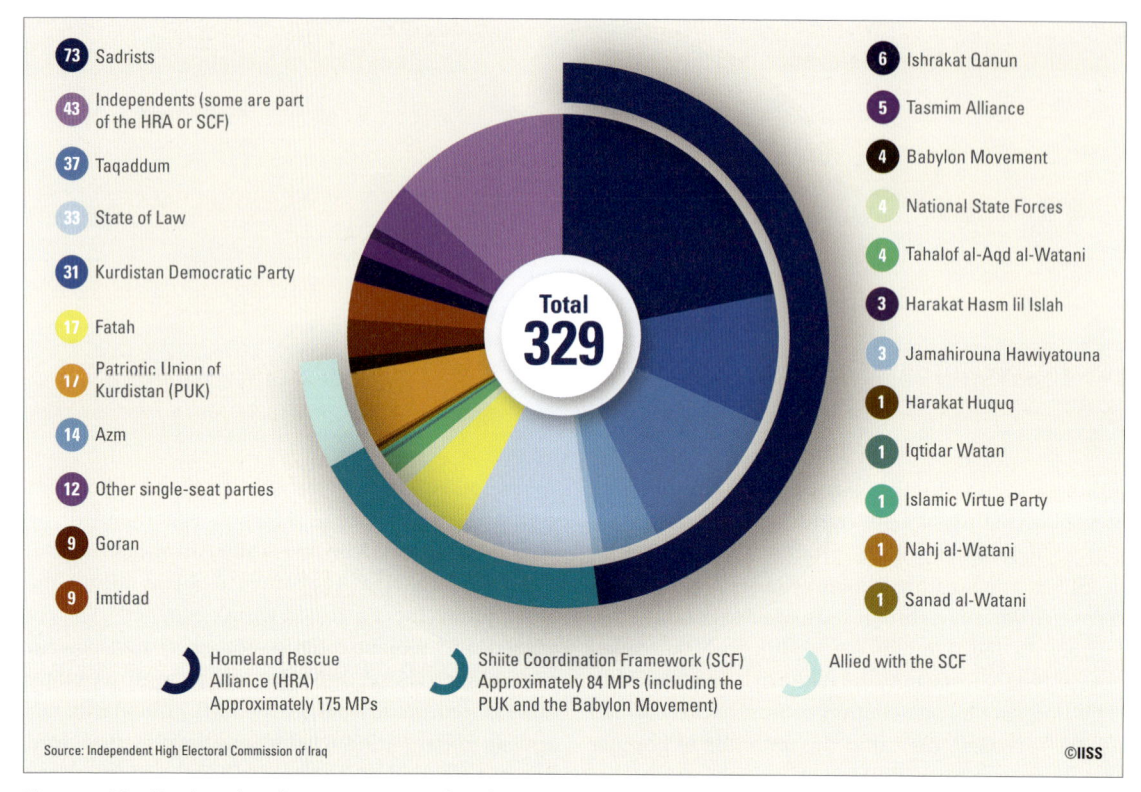

Figure 1: Distribution of parliamentary seats after the October 2021 election

- 73 Sadrists
- 43 Independents (some are part of the HRA or SCF)
- 37 Taqaddum
- 33 State of Law
- 31 Kurdistan Democratic Party
- 17 Fatah
- 17 Patriotic Union of Kurdistan (PUK)
- 14 Azm
- 12 Other single-seat parties
- 9 Goran
- 9 Imtidad
- 6 Ishrakat Qanun
- 5 Tasmim Alliance
- 4 Babylon Movement
- 4 National State Forces
- 4 Tahalof al-Aqd al-Watani
- 3 Harakat Hasm lil Islah
- 3 Jamahirouna Hawiyatouna
- 1 Harakat Huquq
- 1 Iqtidar Watan
- 1 Islamic Virtue Party
- 1 Nahj al-Watani
- 1 Sanad al-Watani

Total **329**

Homeland Rescue Alliance (HRA) Approximately 175 MPs
Shiite Coordination Framework (SCF) Approximately 84 MPs (including the PUK and the Babylon Movement)
Allied with the SCF

Source: Independent High Electoral Commission of Iraq ©IISS

Syria and fragmented the group further. However, persistent political divisions and a limited ability to address grievances in Sunni communities undermine Baghdad's and Erbil's ability to effectively and durably counter the ISIS insurgency.

During the reporting period, Iran-backed SMGs launched regular attacks against the CJTF–OIR and a Turkish military base in northern Iraq. While the attacks aim to force foreign troops out of Iraq and the wider region, they are also leveraged by Iran as a negotiating tool in the country's nuclear talks with the US.

Turkey and Iran both targeted Kurdish insurgents and others on Iraqi soil in 2021 and early 2022. Turkey launched numerous military (ground and aerial) campaigns against Kurdistan Workers' Party (PKK) militants. Ankara's offensive increased in frequency and geographical scope in territories controlled by the Turkey-allied Kurdistan Democratic Party (KDP), extending from Nineva, Erbil and Duhok to Sulaymaniyah, which borders Iran and is controlled by the rival and Tehran-tilted Patriotic Union of Kurdistan (PUK). The ISF also led a military campaign against PKK-affiliated Yezidi militants in Sinjar in Nineva.

Conflict Parties

Iraqi Security Forces (ISF)

Strength: 193,000.

Areas of operation: All areas of Iraq except the Kurdistan Region of Iraq (KRI).

Leadership: Prime Minister Mustafa al-Kadhimi (commander-in-chief); Abdul Amir Rashid Yarallah (army chief of staff); Jummah Enaad al-Jibori (minister of defence); Othman al-Ghanmi (minister of interior).

Structure: The Iraqi armed forces comprise the army, air force and navy. As part of the efforts to combat ISIS, the army has worked with the Federal Police and the Ministry of Interior (MoI) intelligence (the Federal Investigation and Intelligence Agency, Falcons Cell), the Counter-Terrorism Service (CTS), PMU and other intelligence organs. The army reports to the Ministry of Defence, the Federal Police to the MoI and the CTS to the Prime Minister's Office (PMO).

Iraqi Security Forces (ISF)

History: The Islamic State's capture of Tikrit and Mosul in 2014 led to the partial disintegration of the Iraqi armed forces. With aid from the US-led coalition, they have been rebuilt. However, the ISF remains insufficiently equipped for counter-insurgency operations.

Objectives: Defeat ISIS and ensure security across the country. Since the territorial defeat of ISIS, the ISF has prioritised eliminating remaining cells in rural locations. The armed forces also play a role in providing security in the provinces, focusing on tribal conflicts, protest-related violence and criminality.

Opponents: ISIS.

Affiliates/allies: Kurdish Peshmerga, CJTF–OIR, PMU, CTS.

Resources/capabilities: A range of conventional land, air and naval capabilities, including armoured fighting vehicles, anti-tank missile systems, artillery and fixed- and rotary-wing aircraft.

Popular Mobilisation Units (PMU)

Strength: Approximately 160,000.[3]

Areas of operation: Areas previously held by the Islamic State, including Anbar, Diyala, Nineva and Salahaddin provinces, and areas of southern Iraq, particularly Jurf al-Sakhar in Babil province, and shrine cities of Karbala, Najaf, and Samarra (in Salahaddin, north of Baghdad).

Leadership: The PMU has a distinct chain of command from the rest of Iraqi forces. Formally, it is under the PMO and technically directly answerable to the prime minister. However, de facto leadership of the organisation resided with the PMU Commission's chief of staff (formerly Abu Mahdi al-Muhandis) until his assassination in 2020, which led to a leadership struggle. KH commander Abdul-Aziz al-Muhammadawi (also known as Abu Fadak) became leader, although power is thought to reside more with a committee of senior figures. Some PMU brigades loyal to Najaf-based Grand Ayatollah Ali al-Sistani split in practice from the PMU Commission and reorganised as a distinct entity answerable to the PMO, yet are still technically part of the PMU. Some groups within the PMU have a high degree of operational autonomy, including the Sadrists, Saraya al-Salam, the Badr Organisation and Asa'ib Ahl al-Haq.

Structure: Some 40–60 paramilitary units under the umbrella organisation. Formally, the PMU is a branch of the Iraqi security apparatus. However, each unit is organised around an internal leader, influential figures and fighters.

History: Formed in 2014 when Grand Ayatollah Ali al-Sistani called upon Iraqi men to protect their homeland against ISIS, the PMU brought together new and pre-existing groups. In 2016, the units were formally recognised as a branch of the Iraqi security apparatus.

Objectives: At first, to fight ISIS. Some units have evolved into hybrid entities seeking political power. The PMU also functions as an effective counter-protest force and aim to use violence and coercion to intimidate political rivals. At least nominally, all groups are committed to expelling US and foreign forces from Iraq. Tensions between the PMU and Turkey have increased, with a rocket attack on the Turkish military base near Mosul (Zilkan) in April 2021 being attributed to PMU groups.

Opponents: ISIS, US and allied forces, Turkey.

Affiliates/allies: ISF, Iranian Islamic Revolutionary Guard Corps (IRGC).

Resources/capabilities: Units receive state funds but the capabilities of the units differ. Those supported by Iran receive arms and training from the IRGC, including heavy weapons and small arms.

Islamic State, also known as ISIS or ISIL

Strength: Approximately 6,000–10,000 in Iraq and Syria.[4]

Areas of operation: Active primarily in Iraq's northern and central provinces in mountainous and desert areas. Most attacks in 2021–22 occurred in the governorates of Diyala, Kirkuk, and Salahaddin.

Leadership: Abu Hasan al-Hashimi al-Qurashi (replaced Abu Ibrahim al-Hashimi al-Qurashi, who was killed by US forces in February 2022).

Structure: Operates as a covert terrorist network across the country and has a mostly autonomous sleeper-cell structure. ISIS continues to have meticulous bureaucratic structures, high internal discipline, and robust online presence and financial systems.

History: Originated in Iraq around 2003. It fought to establish a caliphate during the Syrian civil war. In the period 2014–17, ISIS controlled many territories in Iraq and Syria and governed more than eight million people. Since 2017 (in Iraq) and 2019 (in Syria), the group has lost control of all the territories it held.

Objectives: ISIS continues to fight and project ideological influence globally. In Iraq it employs decentralised, guerrilla-style insurgent tactics and carries out hit-and-run attacks, kidnappings and killings of civilians and local tribal and political leaders, and targeted assassinations of ISF members.

Opponents: ISF, Kurdish Peshmerga, PMU, CJTF–OIR.

Affiliates/allies: ISIS fighters in other countries.

Resources/capabilities: Small arms, cars, IEDs, suicide-vest IEDs, suicide-vehicle-borne IEDs and mortar bombs.

Kurdish Peshmerga

Strength: Approximately 200,000 personnel.[5]

Areas of operation: KRI.

Leadership: Nechirvan Barzani (commander-in-chief), Shoresh Ismail Abdulla (minister of Peshmerga affairs), Lt-Gen. Jamal Mohammad (Peshmerga chief of staff).

Structure: A Kurdish paramilitary force that acts as the military of the KRG and Iraqi Kurdistan. While remaining independent, it operates officially as part of the Kurdish military system. Peshmerga forces are divided between political factions, the most dominant being the KDP and the Patriotic Union of Kurdistan.

History: Began as a Kurdish nationalist movement in the 1920s and developed into a security organisation. Following the advance of ISIS, the Peshmerga took control of disputed territories in June 2014 – including Kirkuk – which were retaken by the ISF in October 2017.

Objectives: Ensure security in the KRI, including by fighting ISIS.

Opponents: ISIS, PKK, PMU.

Affiliates/allies: CJTF–OIR, ISF.

Resources/capabilities: Poorly equipped, lacking heavy weapons, armed vehicles and facilities. The US has provided some financial assistance and light weapons such as rifles and machine guns.

Kurdistan Workers' Party (PKK)

Strength: 5,000 (estimate) in Iraq.[6]

Areas of operation: Sinjar, northern Iraq.

Leadership: Abdullah Ocalan (ideological leader, despite his imprisonment since 1999); Murat Karayilan (acting leader on the ground since Ocalan's capture); Bahoz Erdal (military commander).

Structure: While operating under the same command and leadership, the PKK's armed wing is divided into the People's Defence Forces (HPG) and the Free Women's Unit (YJA STAR).

History: Founded by Ocalan in 1978. Engaged in an insurgency campaign against the Turkish Armed Forces (TSK) since 1984.

Objectives: Preserve its operational autonomy and capacity with a base of operation in Iraq to support its broader agenda in Turkey.

Opponents: TSK.

Affiliates/allies: Sinjar Alliance in Iraq, PMU.

Resources/capabilities: Depends on money-laundering activities and drug trafficking to raise revenues, as well as donations from the Kurdish community and diaspora and left-wing international supporters. The PKK relies on highly mobile units, employing guerrilla tactics against TSK targets.

Turkish Armed Forces (TSK)

Strength: 5,000–10,000 personnel unilaterally deployed in Iraq (plus 25 under the aegis of NATO Mission Iraq, NMI).[7]

Areas of operation: Northern Iraq, especially Dohuk and Nineva plains. Currently engaged in *Operation Claw-Tiger* against the PKK in Haftanin region. Maintains Zilkan base in Nineva.

Leadership: President Recep Tayyip Erdoğan (commander-in-chief); Gen. (retd) Hulusi Akar (minister of national defence); Gen. Yasar Guler (chief of general staff).

Structure: Turkish Army units operating under the Turkish Land Forces Command and squadrons carrying out airstrikes operating under the Air Force Command are subordinate to the chief of general staff; gendarmerie units reporting to the Gendarmerie Command are subordinate to the Ministry of Interior.

History: Rebuilt following the collapse of the Ottoman Empire in 1922. Significantly restructured after the country joined NATO in 1951, to become NATO's second-largest armed force.

Objectives: Combat the PKK and its allied forces and prevent them from establishing safe havens and mobility corridors in northern Iraq; prevent the PMU from overrunning Sinjar and establishing a land corridor to Syria for Iran.

Opponents: PKK, Sinjar Alliance, PMU.

Affiliates/allies: Miscellaneous local militias, such as those connected to the Iraqi Turkmen Front, which received training from Turkish special forces from 2015.

Resources/capabilities: Turkey's defence budget for 2021 was US$9.55 billion. Its military capabilities include air attack and intelligence, surveillance and reconnaissance assets such as the F-16 and the *Bayraktar* TB2 UAV, armoured tanks and special-forces units.

Combined Joint Task Force–*Operation Inherent Resolve* (CJTF–OIR)

Strength: The exact size of coalition forces (including advisers, special forces, etc.) in Iraq is unclear. Its largest component, provided by the US, comprises 2,500 people. This component has been repositioning its forces and handing over bases to the Iraqi government. The CJTF nominally shifted its role from combatant to advisory by December 2021.

Areas of operation: Working in tandem with the ISF in areas previously held by ISIS, including Anbar, Diyala, Nineva and Salahaddin.

Leadership: Gen. Michael E. Kurilla (US Central Command).

Structure: The US leads the CJTF–OIR, which brings together over 20 coalition partners.

Combined Joint Task Force–Operation Inherent Resolve (CJTF–OIR)

History: Created in October 2014 when the US Department of Defense formalised ongoing military operations against ISIS.

Objectives: Fight ISIS in Iraq and Syria, through airstrikes in support of Iraqi and Kurdish forces. Ground forces are deployed as trainers and advisers.

Opponents: ISIS, PMU.

Affiliates/allies: ISF, Kurdish Peshmerga.

Resources/capabilities: Air support (airstrikes complementing ISF military operations) and artillery.

Conflict Drivers

Geopolitical and geostrategic influences

Geopolitical rivalries:
Iran views Iraq as a critical regional corridor to bolster its offensive capabilities in Syria and those of its ally Hizbullah in Lebanon (against Israel). The tug of war between the two countries also extends to the struggle to form a government in Iraq.

Violence in northern Iraq is mainly driven by the Turkey–PKK conflict and Ankara's intensified counter-PKK operations, which have seen Turkey establish more military bases there and increase its aerial and artillery bombardments and use of UAVs. Iran-backed SMGs collaborate with the PKK, helping the group to target the Turkish military in Bashiqa, Nineva with rockets and UAVs.[8] At the same time, persisting tensions between Iran and Gulf countries over Yemen and normalisation with Israel following the signing of the Abraham Accords drove Iraq's Iran-backed SMGs to attack the United Arab Emirates (UAE) with drones in early February 2022.

Security

State lacking monopoly over the use of force:
The existence of a broad range of armed actors at odds with or hostile to the central government and the ISF remains the primary driver of instability and violence in Iraq. ISIS attacks are mostly focused on fuelling sectarian tensions and delegitimising the Iraqi government. The PMU also acts on the Shia community's grievances, as the Baghdad clashes of November 2021 demonstrated.[9] Capability gaps in the ISF, coupled with broader security-governance deficiencies, mean that militias and other non-state armed actors, both at the local and the national level, can exploit the Iraqi state's inability to claim a monopoly on the use of force within the country.

Tribal violence:
Tribal violence has been persistently high as a result of an increased influx of weaponry into the country, particularly in Basra, Dhi Qar and Maysan governorates. Water scarcity is pushing tribal networks to compete for diminishing resources and revenues from illicit border trade. As poverty grows in the south while oil prices surge, tribal networks coerce oil companies operating in their areas to hire them, a process that also fuels inter-tribal competition over employment. Iraq's post-election political stalemate has also impacted tribal politics. The Iran-backed SMGs and Sadrists have attempted to mobilise allied tribal networks against each other to force the opposite side into a compromise.[10]

Political

Governance gaps:
The power vacuum left by Hussein's overthrow created a major governance gap that, for over two decades, Iraq's various political stakeholders have mostly failed to fill. This situation provided a unique opportunity for Iran to capitalise on Iraq's turmoil, sponsoring and supporting a range of political actors and armed militias to advance the Shia majority's agenda. Moreover, sectarian dynamics and the lack of viable compromise-based political solutions to power-sharing at the national level have contributed extensively to prolonging the ethno-sectarian divisions that characterise Iraqi politics.

Economic

Oil-based patronage and corruption:
The competition between Iraqi elites, political parties and regions to maximise their control of oil revenues is a key driver of conflict and undermines opportunities for economic reform and political cooperation. Sectarianism and patronage prevent Baghdad from effectively exerting authority over the whole country. Government and ministerial positions are hostage to the practice of party-loyalty-based appointments of individuals who then divert resources towards party coffers.

Skyrocketing global oil prices have increased Iraq's foreign-exchange reserves, making reform less of an imperative in 2022 compared to the previous two years. Iraq's increasing unemployment rate,[11] in the context of rising food prices, provides ample opportunities for political stakeholders to draw on growing public funds to build and expand their constituencies.

Key Events in 2021–22

POLITICAL EVENTS

5 March 2021
Pope Francis arrives in Iraq for a four-day visit, meeting with Grand Ayatollah Ali al-Sistani in Najaf.

18 April
Prime Minister Kadhimi mediates talks between Tehran and Riyadh in Baghdad.

4–8 June
Kadhimi holds separate talks with various European leaders on countering terrorism and support for Iraq's October 2021 elections.

26 July
Kadhimi meets with US President Joe Biden in Washington DC; they agree that the US combat mission in Iraq will end by December 2021.

28 August
Iraq hosts a summit in Baghdad aimed at easing regional tensions, attended by the heads of state, heads of government and foreign ministers of regional countries.

10 October
Parliamentary elections take place.

15 November
The UN Security Council (UNSC) issues a statement supporting the results of Iraq's October elections.

MILITARY/VIOLENT EVENTS

3 March 2021
KH launches a rocket attack against Ayn al-Asad air base, killing an American civilian contractor.

14 April
Iran-backed SMGs attack a CJTF–OIR hangar at Erbil International Airport with a fixed-wing drone.

14 April
A Turkish soldier and a child are killed in a rocket attack targeting a Turkish military post in Bashiqa, northern Iraq.

27 June
The US launches an airstrike against three targets – one in Iraq, two in Syria – operated by KH and Kataib Sayyid al-Shuhada. The latter later reports that four of its fighters were killed.

5 September
Ten police officers are killed in an ISIS attack in Kirkuk governorate.

11 October
Kadhimi announces that the Iraqi National Intelligence Service has captured the Islamic State's financial chief.

26 October
Turkey's parliament extends the TSK's mandate to conduct military operations in Iraq and Syria until 30 October 2023.

26 October
ISIS militants carry out an attack in Diyala governorate, killing 15 civilians and wounding dozens.

7 November
Kadhimi's residence in Baghdad is targeted in a drone attack. Iran-backed SMGs are suspected of being responsible.

16 January 2022
The IRGC Quds Force commander arrives in Iraq to mediate between cleric Muqtada al-Sadr and the SCF.

15 February
Iraq's Supreme Federal Court rules that that the energy law adopted by the KRG in 2007 is unconstitutional.

8 March
The Supreme Federal Court summons the finance minister and the governor of Iraq's central bank in relation to a case seeking to reverse a 2020 government decision to devalue the country's currency.

23 April
Iran's foreign ministry announces that Iran and Saudi Arabia have recently held a fifth round of diplomatic talks in Baghdad.

9 May
The White House announces that the US will extend for another year a state of national emergency with respect to stabilisation in Iraq.

17 May
The head of the UN Assistance Mission for Iraq presents an update on Iraq's situation to the UNSC and says Iraqi leaders' determination to find solutions is 'painfully absent'.[12]

2 January 2022
Iran-backed SMGs use two drones to attack the Baghdad Diplomatic Security Center at Baghdad International Airport.

2 February
Alwiyat al-Wa'ad al-Sadiq, a façade group for Iran-backed SMGs, claims responsibility for firing three drones into UAE airspace.

13 March
The IRGC attacks locations in Erbil with ballistic missiles; Iranian state media later claims that a base used by Israel was among the targets.

Responses to the Conflict

Security
During the reporting period, the CJTF–OIR shifted its role from combat to advisory. The restructuring was finalised by December 2021 and involved relocating a logistics headquarters from western Anbar to Kuwait. The change was largely cosmetic, shielding infrastructure from militia rocket and UAV attacks while serving to reduce political pressure on Baghdad (applied primarily by militias) to secure the exit of foreign combat troops from Iraq. The number of US personnel deployed as part of the CJTF–OIR remained unchanged. Moreover, its focus remained training Iraqi forces to tackle the ISIS insurgency and coordinating attacks against the group; facilitating joint counter-insurgency operations between the ISF and the Kurdish Peshmerga; and, unofficially, maintaining a deterrent capability against the SMGs in Iraq and Syria. In an August 2021 meeting facilitated by CJTF–OIR, ISF and Peshmerga military commanders agreed to create two joint brigades to tackle the ISIS insurgency. The development followed plans to establish multiple joint coordination centres for intelligence exchange in Kirkuk, Erbil and Nineva. The establishment of the two brigades was postponed until after the October election; as of mid-2022, they are yet to be created due to reported financial difficulties.

Economic/development
As the second-largest oil producer among the members of the Organization of Petroleum Exporting Countries (OPEC), Iraq's income sources and real GDP growth are dependent on exporting crude oil. Real GDP is forecast to increase from 5.9% in 2021 to

9.5% in 2022, driven by a significant increase in oil prices and related revenues.[13] During the reporting period, this forecasted growth and post-election political conflicts threatened to derail Finance Minister Ali Allawi's economic reforms and plans to diversify the economy away from oil and curtail the bloated public sector. Intensified post-election political polarisation has deprived the incumbent government of a mandate to enact long-term structural reforms. Despite a range of economic issues being hostage to political infighting during the reporting period, in May 2022 the IMF concluded a staff visit to Iraq and discussed macroeconomic and institutional reforms and social policies to sustain growth and mitigate the repercussions of the global rise of food prices on the domestic market. At the same time, the World Bank's policy targets in Iraq are focused on development through the education sector to address what it calls a 'human capital crisis'.[14]

Diplomacy

In 2021 and early 2022, Kadhimi's caretaker government built on the previous government's efforts to develop political and economic ties with Jordan, Egypt and Gulf Cooperation Council (GCC) countries while maintaining strong political communication with Iran. Baghdad has hosted talks between Iran and Saudi Arabia since April 2021 in an effort to extricate Iraq from regional proxy conflicts. Complementing these talks, during the reporting period the government also sought to bolster its regional and international standing by hosting the Baghdad Conference for Cooperation and Partnership in August 2021, which aimed to ease regional tensions. The conference brought together regional leaders and heads of governments in addition to French President Emmanuel Macron.[15]

Humanitarian aid

The number of internally displaced persons (IDPs) in Iraq has been declining following the government's decision in October 2020 to close 13 displacement camps.[16] As of March 2022, there were over 2.5m people in Iraq in need of humanitarian assistance, while 1.2m remained internally displaced. The UN Office for the Coordination of Humanitarian Affairs' Humanitarian Response Plan 2022 – which requires US$400m in funding – will target over 990,000 Iraqis categorised as 'deeply vulnerable' – a figure that includes 180,000 IDPs in formal camps, 234,000 IDPs living outside camps and 577,000 returnees.[17]

Conflict Outlook

Political scenarios

A compromise coalition government, which would be in line with Iran's and the SCF's interests and follow government-formation conventions observed post-2003, is no longer a viable scenario since the Sadrists' withdrawal from the parliament prevents their involvement in a government co-formed with the SCF. Instead, the Sadrists may allow the SCF to form a government on the condition that the prime minister and certain ministerial positions are not held by hostile figures. The current caretaker government led by Kadhimi, who is politically close to the Sadrists, has been able to extend its life in light of the stalemate. However, in doing so it may risk retaliatory violence from the Iran-backed SMGs that constitute the SCF. Political paralysis may persist if the Sadrists fail to prioritise a compromise approach and the opposite side resorts to violence to intimidate them.

The parliament could be dissolved provided the Federal Supreme Court approves a request by the current interim government. The risk of an intra-Shia civil war remains high and episodes of brinkmanship could drag both sides into an armed confrontation. Oil-rich southern Iraq, a stronghold for both camps, is mired with tribal violence that could contribute to and be exacerbated by the current political frictions.

Escalation potential and conflict-related risks

In Iraq, the domestic and external drivers of conflict escalation are often intertwined. There is a high risk associated with the potential breakdown of US–Iran nuclear talks, which could lead to regional frictions and opportunities for the SMGs to escalate against the CJTF–OIR in Iraq and Syria (and possibly Western forces stationed in Jordan and GCC countries).

The Russian invasion of Ukraine in February 2022 boosted the morale of the SMGs, whose social-media outlets have interpreted the conflict as evidence of a weakening US global military footprint. The SMGs had already stepped up anti-CJTF–OIR rocket and drone attacks in the aftermath of the October 2021 elections; a breakdown in nuclear talks, coupled with possible Russian military gains in Ukraine, could bolster the SMGs' confidence and lead them to further expand their high-intensity campaign against the US-led coalition across Iraq and particularly eastern Syria.

Prospects for peace

Ultimately, the conflict in Iraq is a combination of different political and military struggles occurring within the same geographical boundaries. Sectarian clashes occasionally occur in parallel to the fight against ISIS, while Turkish military operations in the KRG take place autonomously. Tensions emanating from corruption and sectarian clientelism add to the sense of abandonment many communities feel after almost two decades of uninterrupted conflict. The prospects for peace are therefore tied to progress being made in all the crises Iraq faces. Much of what the country might be able to achieve in terms of progress towards enhancing stability will likely hinge on Iran's role in the country. For example, the emergence of a 'General Soleimani'-like figure able to corral the various Shia actors and their agendas towards a more unified approach, or a further consolidation of Sadr's political clout over the broader Shia community, could represent first steps towards reducing political fragmentation and violence.

Strategic implications and global influences

A major armed clash between the Sadrist-aligned PMU groups and the Iran-backed SMGs could lead to a resurgence of ISIS, since severe political polarisation is likely to further derail counter-insurgency operations and undermine efforts to consolidate coordination between Baghdad and Erbil. If Iran-backed SMGs launch attacks on oil infrastructure in the Persian Gulf, global oil prices will likely further increase, an outcome that is desirable for Iran but not for the US and its European allies. Another possible outcome of escalating tensions between Iran and the US might be the hindering or collapse of regional talks taking place in Baghdad between Tehran and Riyadh.

Notes

1. Sadr's attempt to exclude other Shia political parties from nominating the prime minister broke with the tradition (in effect since 2003) of having all-inclusive, sect-based parliamentary coalitions nominate a candidate for the position.
2. US, Lead Inspector General for Operation Inherent Resolve, 'Operation Inherent Resolve: Lead Inspector General Report to the United States Congress, April 1, 2021–June 30, 2021', 13 August 2021; Lead Inspector General for Operation Inherent Resolve, 'Operation Inherent Resolve: Lead Inspector General Report to the United States Congress, July 1, 2021–September 30, 2021', 4 November 2021; Lead Inspector General for Operation Inherent Resolve, 'Operation Inherent Resolve: Lead Inspector General Report to the United States Congress, October 1, 2021–December 31, 2021, 15 February 2022; and Lead Inspector General for Operation Inherent Resolve, 'Lead Inspector General Report to the United States Congress, January 1, 2022–March 31, 2022', 3 May 2022.
3. Michael Knights, Hamdi Malik and Aymenn Jawad al-Tamimi, 'Honored, Not Contained: The Future of Iraq's Mobilization Forces', Washington Institute for Near Eastern Policy, 23 March 2020.
4. 'Iraq Bombing: IS Says It Was Behind Deadly Suicide Attacks in Baghdad', BBC News, 22 January 2021; and 'Fourteenth Report of the Secretary-General on the Threat Posed by ISIL (Da'esh) to International Peace and Security and the Range of United Nations Efforts in Support of Member States in Countering the Threat', UN Security Council, S/2022/63, 28 January 2022, p. 6.
5. Erica Gaston and András Derzsi-Horváth, 'Iraq after ISIL: Sub-state Actors, Local Forces, and the Micro-politics of Control', Global Public Policy Institute, March 2018, p. 6.
6. Zhelwan Z. Wali, 'Kurd vs Kurd: Fears of Full-scale War Rise in Northern Iraq', Al-Jazeera, 2 December 2020.
7. Salim Çevik, 'Turkey's Military Operations in Syria and Iraq', German Institute for International and Security Affairs (SWP), 30 May 2022; and Jeyhun Aliyev, 'Turkish Army Consultants to Serve in NATO Mission Iraq', Anadolu Agency, 26 January 2021.
8. Jared Szuba, 'Pentagon: Iran-backed Militias, PKK Coordinated vs. Turkish Troops in Iraq', Al-Monitor, 3 May 2022.
9. Hassan al-Saeed, 'Investigation Finds Militias Involved in Iraqi Post-election Violence', Al-Monitor, 3 December 2021.
10. Tamer Badawi, 'The Growing Tribal Role in Iraq's Post-election Shia Politics', *Sada*, Carnegie Endowment for International Peace, 17 May 2022; and Suadad al-Salhy, 'Iraq: Sadr's Rivals Fear Mass Demonstrations. His Supporters Do Too', Middle East Eye, 13 July 2022.
11. Iraq's unemployment rate was 14.2% in 2021, up from 12.9% in 2019, before the coronavirus pandemic. See World Bank data, 'Overview' for Iraq.
12. 'Iraq's People Still Awaiting Political Class Capable of Addressing Critical Domestic Challenges, Top Official Tells Security Council', UN Meetings Coverage and Press Releases, 17 May 2022.
13. IMF, 'World Economic Outlook: War Sets Back the Global Recovery', April 2022, p. 40.
14. World Bank, 'Iraq Economic Monitor, Spring 2022: Harnessing the Oil Windfall for Sustainable Growth', 16 June 2022.
15. 'Iraq Hosts Summit Aimed at Easing Regional Tensions', Al-Jazeera, 28 August 2021.
16. Firas Al-Khateeb, 'Returning Iraqis Face Dire Conditions Following Camp Closures', UN High Commissioner for Refugees, 27 May 2021.
17. UN Office for the Coordination of Humanitarian Affairs, 'Humanitarian Response Plan: Iraq', 27 March 2022, p. 8.

ISRAEL–PALESTINIAN TERRITORIES

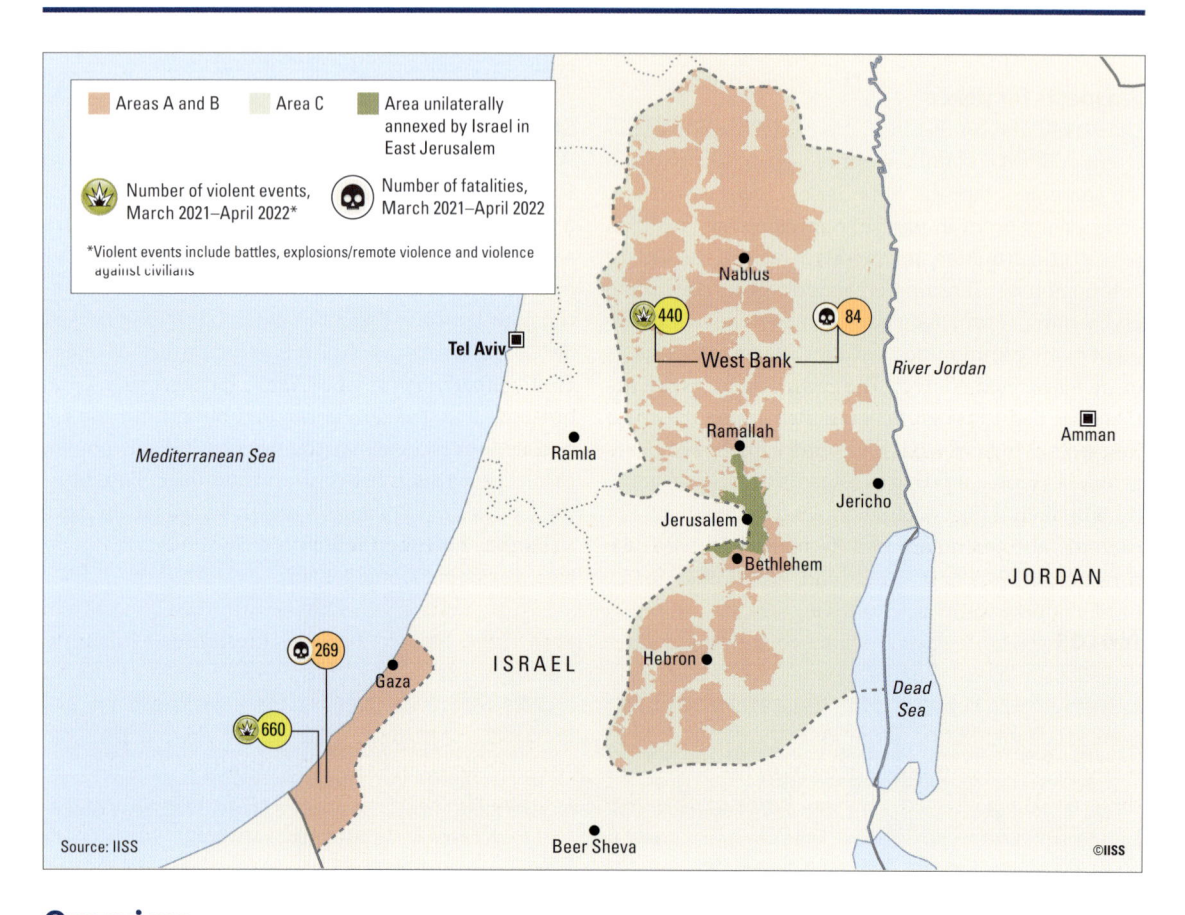

Overview

The Israeli–Palestinian conflict is a national-territorial conflict – with religious components – between Israel and the Palestinian people. Beginning in the late nineteenth century and continuing into the twentieth, rising anti-Semitism and violence in Europe prompted Jewish migration to Palestine spearheaded by the Zionist movement – a national movement calling for Jewish self-determination. The dramatic rise in Jewish immigration impacted the demographic balance and led to tensions with Arab residents, culminating in riots against the Jewish communities in the 1920s and 1930s. On 29 November 1947, the United Nations adopted a partition plan that called for the creation of a Jewish state alongside a Palestinian state (UN Resolution 181), ending the British Mandate of Palestine. The resolution was accepted by the Zionist movement but rejected by the Arab leadership. The following day fighting broke out between local Arab and Jewish communities.

On 14 May 1948, the Zionist leadership declared the establishment of the state of Israel. A day later, the country was attacked by Egypt, Iraq, Syria, Transjordan and contingents from other Arab countries. The 1948 Arab–Israeli War officially ended in July 1949; the armistice agreement between Israel and Egypt, Jordan, Lebanon and Syria drew ceasefire borders (referred to as the Green Line) that exceeded the borders of the Jewish state granted by the UN partition plan. As a result of the 1967 Six-Day War and the 1973 Yom Kippur War, Israel enlarged its territory threefold by capturing East Jerusalem and the West Bank from Jordan, the Gaza Strip and the Sinai Peninsula from Egypt, and the Golan Heights

Armed Conflict Global Relevance Indicator (ACGRI)

- Incidence: 11
- Human impact: 29
- Geopolitical impact: 19

Israel–Palestinian Territories

Key Conflict Statistics

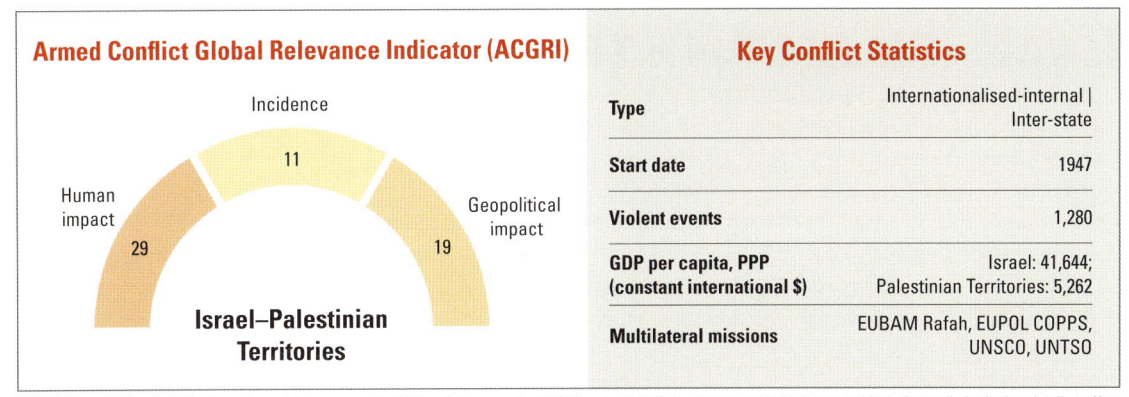

Type	Internationalised-internal | Inter-state
Start date	1947
Violent events	1,280
GDP per capita, PPP (constant international $)	Israel: 41,644; Palestinian Territories: 5,262
Multilateral missions	EUBAM Rafah, EUPOL COPPS, UNSCO, UNTSO

ACGRI pillars: IISS calculation based on multiple sources for 2021 and January–April 2022 (scale: 0–100). See Notes on Methodology and Data Appendix for further details on Key Conflict Statistics.

from Syria. Israel's territorial gains prompted the UN Security Council to issue Resolution 242 and Resolution 338 demanding that Israel withdraw from the occupied territories.

The Palestinian Liberation Organization (PLO), headed by Yasser Arafat, was registered as a terrorist organisation in Israel and the United States until it underwent a formative change starting in 1988, when Arafat declared the establishment of a Palestinian State alongside Israel. This acknowledgement led the way to the Oslo Accords, signed between Israel and the PLO in 1993 and 1995. Designed as an interim agreement to last five years, the accords established the legal basis for the creation of the Palestinian Authority (PA), which would control 40% of the West Bank (Areas A and B; Area C would remain under full Israeli control). The sides were expected to reach a final status agreement within this period; however, the assassination of then Israeli prime minister Yitzhak Rabin by an Israeli who opposed the accords, and terrorist attacks by Palestinians against Israelis, drove the process off track. Attempts to revive the process under the United States' guidance – in 2000, 2007, 2010 and 2014 – were unsuccessful.

In 2007, Hamas violently overthrew the PA in the Gaza Strip and became the de facto ruler there. Israel and Hamas have experienced four rounds of violent escalation in Gaza (in 2008–09, 2012, 2014 and 2021) due to the group's rocket fire targeting civilian communities in the 'Gaza envelope' (the Israeli region surrounding the Gaza Strip to the west and north) and central Israel.

In 2020, Israel signed normalisation agreements with four Arab states: Bahrain, Morocco, Sudan and the United Arab Emirates (UAE). These agreements, also referred to as the Abraham Accords, were brokered by the US and put an end to Israel's declared intention to annex parts of the West Bank. The PA rejected these developments, viewing them as part of the 'Deal of the Century', an American proposal for a political arrangement put forth by then-president Donald Trump.

Parliamentary elections in the Palestinian Territories, called by PA President Mahmoud Abbas in January 2021, were indefinitely postponed in April that year. Abbas blamed Israel for not allowing the vote to go ahead in East Jerusalem.[1] Around the same time, Palestinians protested in Jerusalem's Sheikh Jarrah neighbourhood against a planned eviction of Palestinian families, clashing with right-wing Israelis. These clashes spilled over to the al-Aqsa Mosque compound/Temple Mount, a holy site claimed by both peoples that is effectively under Israeli control and Jordanian custodianship. At this time Israel was also in the midst of an election process, the fourth in two years, and radical players sought to leverage the crisis for political gain. The clashes continued during Ramadan, which coincided with Passover, a context that further fuelled the tensions.

On 10 May, Hamas warned Israel not to allow a national flag march to cross the Damascus Gate of the Old City and demanded that Israeli forces retreat from the compound and release arrested rioters. Israel did not yield to the ultimatum and Hamas fired rockets into Jerusalem and central Israel. This action prompted an 11-day confrontation, culminating in 4,360 rockets and mortar shells fired at Israel, 12 Israeli fatalities and 253 Palestinian fatalities.[2] Unlike during previous rounds of escalation in the Gaza Strip, riots took place in religiously mixed cities in Israel, between Arab citizens of Israel and Jewish Israelis. The PA was not involved in the escalation and only acted in the West Bank to prevent the violence from spilling over, a stance that drew criticism from Palestinians already frustrated by its perceived inability to produce change for the Palestinian people, accusations of corruption and its security cooperation with Israel.

The economic situation in the PA saw a downturn in 2021, with fewer international donations and a high budget deficit. The PA has paid partial salaries to the public sector since the first months of the coronavirus pandemic.[3] As the PA has lost public support, Hamas and the Palestinian Islamic Jihad (PIJ) have become more able to recruit and mobilise.[4] Following a period of relative calm, in March and April 2022 there was an uptick in terrorist attacks in Israel and against Israeli targets in the West Bank. Israel initiated a military campaign in the Jenin region to counter terrorist cells, resulting in Israeli and Palestinian fatalities.

Conflict Parties

Israel Defense Forces (IDF)

Strength: 169,500 active military, 465,000 in reserve.

Areas of operation: Gaza Strip, Iraq, Lebanon, Syria and the West Bank.

Leadership: Aviv Kochavi (chief of staff).

Structure: Divided into a ground force, air force and navy.

History: Founded in 1948 from the paramilitary organisation Haganah, which fought in the 1948 Arab–Israeli War.

Objectives: Homeland defence.

Opponents: Hamas, Hizbullah, Iran and Iran-backed groups.

Affiliates/allies: Maintains close military ties with the US.

Resources/capabilities: The IDF boasts sophisticated equipment and training and receives military aid from the US. It has a highly capable defence industry, including aerospace; intelligence, surveillance and reconnaissance; and counter-rocket systems. It is also believed to have an operational nuclear-weapons capability, although estimates vary as to the size of the IDF's arsenal. The IDF can operate simultaneously in the West Bank, Gaza, Lebanon, Syria and Iraq and often favours a clandestine, incursive nature when conducting operations beyond the Palestinian Territories.

Hamas

Strength: Hamas's military wing, the Izz al-Din al-Qassam Brigades (IDQ), is estimated to comprise around 30,000 fighters, including 400 naval commandos.[5]

Areas of operation: Gaza Strip, Israel and the West Bank.

Leadership: Yahya Sinwar (head of Hamas); Ismail Haniyeh (chief of the central Political Bureau). Their positions were reaffirmed in 2021 following contentious elections.

Structure: Hamas's internal political leadership exercises ultimate authority; other wings and branches, such as the IDQ, observe the strategy and guidelines established by Hamas's Shura Council and Political Bureau, or Politburo.

History: Founded in 1987 by members of the Muslim Brotherhood in the Palestinian Territories, Hamas is the largest Palestinian militant Islamist group. The European Union and the US have designated it a terrorist group. However, many Palestinians view Hamas as a legitimate popular resistance group.

Objectives: The group's original charter called for the obliteration or dissolution of Israel and for the full liberation of Palestine, but Haniyeh announced in 2008 that Hamas would accept a Palestinian state within the borders of the pre-1967 war (the Green Line). This position was confirmed in a new charter in 2017, in which the group agreed to concede to the national consensus regarding a political solution with Israel.

Opponents: Fatah-led PA, Israel, PIJ (periodically) and Salafi jihadi groups.

Affiliates/allies: Iran, Qatar.

Resources/capabilities: The IDQ's capabilities include artillery rockets, mortars, drones, anti-aircraft and anti-tank systems, and an underground tunnel system for defensive and offensive purposes. Before the May 2021 hostilities, the IDF estimated that Hamas and the PIJ had 13,000–15,000 rockets in their combined arsenal.[6] Hamas relies on financial support and arms and technology transfers from Iran. Qatar also transfers US$30 million monthly (on average) into Gaza for civilian purposes, including payment of salaries to Hamas officials.[7]

Palestinian Islamic Jihad (PIJ)

Strength: The PIJ's armed wing, the al-Quds Brigades, is estimated to comprise up to 8,000 combatants.[8]

Areas of operation: Gaza Strip and increasingly inside the West Bank, mainly in Jenin.

Leadership: Ziad al-Nakhaleh.

Structure: Governed by a 15-member leadership council. In 2018, the PIJ council elected nine new members to represent its members in the West Bank, the Gaza Strip, Israeli prisons and abroad.

Palestinian Islamic Jihad (PIJ)

History: Established in 1979 by Fathi Shaqaqi and Abd al-Aziz Awda, who were members of the Egyptian Muslim Brotherhood until the late 1970s. Of the Gaza-based militant groups, PIJ poses the most significant challenge to Hamas's authority in the Strip, having derailed unofficial ceasefire agreements between Hamas and Israel in the past.

Objectives: To establish a sovereign, Islamic Palestinian state within the borders of pre-1948 Palestine.

Opponents: Israel and, periodically, Hamas.

Affiliates/allies: Iran, Syria, Hizbullah.

Resources/capabilities: The PIJ has expanded the size of its weapons cache by building its own rockets. It is estimated to have 6,000 rockets.[9] Iran has provided the group with millions of US dollars of funding in addition to training and weapons. Since the leadership's relocation to Damascus in 1989, the Syrian regime has also offered the group military aid and sanctuary.

Conflict Drivers

Security

Threat of terrorism:

While the threat of terrorism has been a feature of the Israeli–Palestinian conflict since the early twentieth century, the nature of the threat has changed over time. Initially, fedayeen groups – guerrilla militias with a Palestinian-nationalist or Pan-Arab orientation – attacked Israeli civilian and strategic targets, such as water pipelines. After Israel was established, the fedayeen executed cross-border attacks from neighbouring countries. Some groups, such as Black September and the Popular Front for the Liberation of Palestine, adopted international terrorism and operated against Israeli targets abroad. In 1988, Arafat announced that the PLO rejected terrorism. However, Salafi-jihadist groups, such as Hamas and PIJ, which are not under the PLO umbrella, engaged in deadly attacks against Israeli civilians, adopting a method of suicide attacks via explosive vests. Hamas started manufacturing and firing rockets from the Gaza Strip towards Israel in 2001, increasing these activities following the Israeli disengagement from Gaza in 2005, and again after Hamas assumed de facto control in 2007. Israel reacted by sealing the Gaza Strip, referring to the measure as a closure, siege or blockade. Hamas and Israel have since engaged in several rounds of hostilities due to rockets being fired by Hamas into the Gaza envelope.

Political

Israeli settlements:

Israel's occupation of the West Bank following the Six-Day War marked the beginning of its settlement policy. As of January 2022, more than 150 settlements (home to over 490,000 Israelis) have been established across the West Bank (in Area C).[10] The PA and the international community argue that all settlements behind the Green Line are illegal under international law, violating Article 49 of the Fourth Geneva Convention of 1949. The PA views the settlements as proof of Israel's lack of commitment to a two-state solution and an attempt to expand the country's territory while overriding Palestinians' ability to make decisions over the future border. However, Israeli officials claim that the settlements are predominantly adjacent to the 'seam zone' and are needed for natural growth, and that in a final-status agreement they will be replaced by territory of a similar size in land swaps. Some Israeli governments have attempted to restrict or freeze the construction in the settlements: this was the case in the mid-1990s and in 2010 during the tenure of prime minister Benjamin Netanyahu. These periods did not produce significant improvement in bilateral relations and Israel soon resumed construction. As a result of settlement expansion, the territory anticipated by the 1993 Oslo Accords to form a future Palestinian state has shrunk and become increasingly fragmented, making it even more challenging to achieve a two-state solution based on the 4 June 1967 borders.

Key Events in 2021–22

POLITICAL EVENTS

10 March 2021
Hamas concludes a month-long election process in the West Bank, Gaza Strip, Israeli prisons and with Hamas's cadre abroad. Yahya Sinwar is re-elected as Hamas chief in the Gaza Strip following his near defeat by another member.

23 March
Israel holds elections for the fourth time in two years, after a unity government headed by Benjamin Netanyahu and Benny Gantz collapses.

30 April
President Abbas postpones Palestinian elections scheduled for April to an unknown date, blaming Israel for not agreeing to allow Palestinians to place ballots in Jerusalem.

13 June
A new Israeli government is appointed, consisting of a politically diverse coalition containing left-wing, right-wing and Arab parties. The terms of the coalition stipulate a focus on domestic issues and do not mention any plans to make headway on a peace process with the Palestinians.

24 June
Palestinian activist Nizar Banat, a vocal critic of the PA and its security cooperation with Israel, is killed by the Palestinian security apparatus during his arrest, sparking riots across the West Bank against the PA.

MILITARY/VIOLENT EVENTS

April 2021
Protests take place in the Palestinian neighbourhood of Sheikh Jarrah in Jerusalem, ahead of a court ruling on the eviction of four Palestinian families.

15 April
Riots take place in Jerusalem's Old City due to the Israeli police restricting people from sitting on the steps facing the Damascus Gate, a habit of Palestinian youth during Ramadan.

16 April
A TikTok video of a young Palestinian slapping a Haredi man in Jerusalem goes viral, inspiring a trend of attacks recorded on the video-sharing platform.

22 April
Israeli alt-right activists initiate riots across the city of Jerusalem. Dozens of Israelis and Palestinians are injured.

10 May
Israeli police enter the al-Aqsa Mosque compound during Ramadan and arrest Palestinian rioters. Hamas issues an ultimatum demanding that Israel release detained Palestinian rioters, cancel a Jerusalem Day parade and withdraw Israeli forces from Sheikh Jarrah. The ultimatum expires and Hamas fires rockets into Jerusalem and southern Israel.

10–21 May
Israel bombards targets in the Gaza Strip while Hamas fires rockets into Israel; 253 Palestinians and 12 Israelis are killed in the hostilities. During this period, riots take place between Jewish and Arab citizens of Israel in mixed communities inside Israel.

30 August
Abbas meets with Israeli Minister of Defense Benny Gantz in Ramallah – his first meeting with an Israeli official in more than ten years.

24 September
Abbas delivers a speech at the UN General Assembly and gives Israel an ultimatum to withdraw to the pre-1967 lines. He states that the PA will appeal to the International Criminal Court if Israel fails to do so within one year.

November
The PA launches a short military campaign against militant opposition organisations in Jenin.

28 December
Gantz hosts Abbas in Israel. After the meeting, Israel implements a range of confidence-building measures.

29 December
Twelve armed factions in the Gaza Strip hold a joint military exercise.

March 2022
A significant escalation of terrorist attacks takes place in Israel. Attacks in major city centres kill 19 people.

27–28 March 2022
The Negev Summit, the first forum bringing together foreign ministers from Bahrain, Egypt, Israel, Morocco, the UAE and the US, takes place in Israel. The Jordanian Ministry of Foreign Affairs and Expatriates declines to attend.

April
During Ramadan, Israel takes measures in the al-Aqsa Mosque compound to contain Palestinian riots and prevent a recurrence of the events of May 2021.

April
The IDF launches a military campaign to counter terrorist cells in the area of Jenin.

Responses to the Conflict

Economic/development

Since the 1948 war, the international community has been granting assistance to the Palestinians – first mainly to refugees and later also for Palestinian state-building. The 1948 war displaced between 650,000 and 1m Palestinians inside what became Israel's 1948 borders. Palestinians have since called for the right to return to their pre-1948 homes, a key issue in previous negotiations, citing UN Resolution 194. UN Resolution 302 mandated the construction of the UN Relief and Work Agency (UNRWA), an international body created to aid Palestinian refugees until they reach final resettlement. As of 2022, UNRWA's mandate covers education, social-welfare, food-security and health assistance to 5.7m people dispersed in the West Bank, Gaza, Jordan, Lebanon and Syria. UNRWA is funded by the international community; its 2021 pledges stood at US$1.19 billion, with 43% provided by EU member states.[11]

Since the Oslo Accords and the establishment of the PA, the latter has been heavily dependent on foreign aid. Following the signature of the Oslo Accords, the international community constructed the Ad Hoc Liaison Committee, a multilateral forum, chaired by Norway, originally designated to support the financial needs of the peace process and Palestinian statehood. However, with time this forum mainly responded to short-term Palestinian funding needs. After more than two decades of international funding, there is substantial fatigue among the donor community. In 2013, foreign grants and aid was just shy of 35% of the PA's revenue. By 2021, the share had declined drastically to 7%. Between 2020 and 2021, budget support (provided by donors) declined, which could be attributed primarily to the absence of Gulf Cooperation Council aid.[12] Donor fatigue is explained by Israel's continued settlement expansion, the lack of progress towards a peaceful resolution, corruption in the PA leadership and lack of democratic reform, and the need to divert funds

Figure 1: International aid to the Palestinian Authority, 2013–22

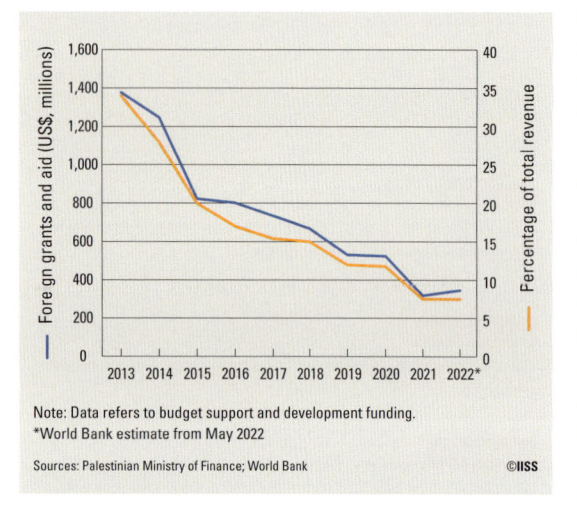

Note: Data refers to budget support and development funding.
*World Bank estimate from May 2022
Sources: Palestinian Ministry of Finance; World Bank   ©IISS

to other pressing causes. The financial downturn caused by the coronavirus pandemic also affected donors' ability to transfer funds towards external purposes, and some donors, such as the US under Trump and the EU Commission, also temporarily froze their assistance due to political disagreements with the PA leadership.

Diplomacy

Foreign actors have attempted to mitigate and mediate the Israeli–Palestinian conflict since its inception. Initially, this was done mainly via resolutions in the UN and the Security Council in reaction to wars and escalations between Israel and the Arab states. The Madrid Conference, in 1991, led by the US, was the first official dialogue between Israel and Palestinians, leading to the Oslo Accords of 1993 and the Peace Accords with Jordan in 1994. The US has been the most dominant player in the arena, with various US presidents continuing to push for progress by continuously drafting new proposals, such as the Clinton Parameters, which inspired the Camp David Summit in 2000, and the Bush Roadmap. In 2007, the US convened a summit in Annapolis that led the way to the most significant process thus far, between Abbas and then-prime minister Ehud Olmert. However, this process concluded prematurely. US president Barack Obama also sent a special envoy to broker peace, and the sides engaged in dialogue again in 2010 and 2014.

In 2020, president Trump presented Peace to Prosperity, a proposal for an agreement, yet the Palestinians rejected it since it diverged from the international consensus. The plan cemented Palestinians' perception of the Trump administration as an unfit mediator. In response they reiterated their commitment to the Arab Peace Initiative from 2002, which was accepted by the Arab League's then-22 members, and conditioned Arab normalisation with Israel upon a set of prerequisites: full withdrawal by Israel from the occupied territories; a 'just settlement' of the Palestinian refugee problem; and the establishment of a Palestinian state, with East Jerusalem as its capital. Nevertheless, in 2020, in an apparent departure from this plan, Bahrain, Morocco, Sudan and the UAE moved to normalise relations with Israel despite a lack of advancement in the peace process. The PA rejected the accords and recalled its ambassadors, referring to the agreements as a 'stab in the back'.[13]

During the reporting period, the main diplomatic developments took place between Israel and its new Arab partners, while the PA refused to partake in any step that could be seen as linked to the umbrella of the Abraham Accords. In late March 2022, the signatories to the accords and Egypt met in Israel for the Negev Summit to discuss regional developments, including the Palestinian issue. Amman and the PA refused to attend the summit, with Jordan's King Abdullah II and Abbas meeting in Ramallah instead.

Conflict Outlook

Political scenarios

Both Israel and the Palestinian Territories are mired in political instability that frustrates prospects for progress towards a resolution of the conflict. In June 2021, Israel managed to form a coalition after four rounds of elections, a process that took two years and paralysed the government. This coalition was enabled by the consent of Ra'am, an Arab-Muslim party, which joined its ranks, along with members of the Israeli left and right. No Arab party has participated in an Israeli coalition before, and the development is even more extraordinary considering the prime minister, Naftali Bennett, is head of a right-wing political party that rejects the notion of Palestinian statehood. Until June 2022, the coalition managed to survive despite setbacks and high volatility but it was ultimately dissolved and a new round of elections was announced. Without a stable political structure, no headway is expected to be made by Israel on the Palestinian issue.

In the Palestinian arena, a major obstacle to the resumption of peace talks is the rivalry between Hamas and Fatah, which also affects the ongoing division between the West Bank and the Gaza Strip. The 2021 PA election process was an attempt to advance reconciliation and a response to international and domestic pressure to promote democracy. However, the ideological and strategic differences between Hamas and Fatah will likely continue to impede progress towards a unified political structure that brings together the West Bank and Gaza and enjoys public legitimacy.

The prospects for inter-Palestinian reconciliation diminished further after the May 2021 hostilities, as Hamas boasted its military achievements and enjoyed increased public support. In June 2021, a poll by the Palestinian Center for Policy and Survey Research, conducted in the West Bank and the Gaza Strip, found that a dominant majority believes that Hamas won the confrontation with Israel (77%) and was acting in defence of Jerusalem and the al-Aqsa Mosque (72%). The same poll also found that if PA presidential elections had been held during the time of the survey, Ismail Haniyyeh would have defeated Abbas 59% to 27%.[14]

Escalation potential and conflict-related risks

Given the political situation in Israel and the Palestinian Territories and the lack of international motivation to push for progress towards a resolution, continued hostility between Israel and the Palestinian leaderships in the West Bank and the Gaza Strip is likely. Another military escalation could occur either in the Gaza Strip, due to rockets fired towards Israel; in the West Bank, due to terrorist activity against Israelis and a harsh IDF response; or in East Jerusalem, due to heightened religious and national confrontations. Moreover, the inter-Palestinian arena is absorbed by the prospect of a post-Abbas landscape and who might replace him. Alliances between potential candidates are emerging, with a possibility of succession battles within Fatah and with Hamas, and these potential inter-Palestinian conflicts run the risk of further worsening Israeli–Palestinian tensions.

Prospects for peace

The decline in international interest in the conflict and in US involvement are also undermining prospects for a resolution. The Trump presidency was seen as detrimental to the Palestinian cause: the US recognised Jerusalem as Israel's capital and relocated its embassy while shutting down the Palestinian consulate; published the Peace to Prosperity plan, which diverged from the internationally recognised norms; and completely cut off aid to the Palestinians. For these reasons, the Palestinian leadership decided to sever ties with the US administration under President Trump. This situation was reversed with the inauguration of Joe Biden, who has presided over a return to the traditional ideas of a two-state solution and adherence to international norms and law. During his presidential campaign, Biden pledged to resume funding, reopen the PLO office in Washington DC and reopen the US consulate to the PA in Jerusalem. While some financial assistance was renewed during the reporting period, the Biden administration did not take significant steps towards the Palestinians and none of these commitments were fulfilled. Furthermore, steps taken by the Biden administration during its first year suggested a US policy of withdrawal from the Middle East.[15]

Notes

1 'Presidential Decree No. (1) of 2021 on the Call for Legislative Presidential and National Elections', Central Elections Commission of Palestine, 15 January 2021; and Nidal al-Mughrabi, Ali Sawafta and Rami Ayyub, 'Palestinian Leader Delays Parliamentary and Presidential Elections, Blaming Israel', Reuters, 30 April 2021.

2 'Escalation from the Gaza Strip – Operation Guardian of the Walls – Summary', Meir Amit Intelligence and Terrorism Information Center, 24 May 2021; and United Nations Office for the Coordination of Humanitarian Affairs, 'Gaza Strip: Escalation of Hostilities as of 25 May 2021', 25 May 2021.

3 Al-Monitor, 'Palestinian Authority to Pay Civil Servants Half Their Monthly Wages amid Cash Crunch', 2 July 2020.

4 Ahmad Melhem, 'Palestinian Islamic Jihad Ramps Up Capabilities in West Bank', Al-Monitor, 1 June 2022.

5 'Senior IDF Commander Says Hamas Has 30,000 Men, 7,000 Rockets, Dozens of Drones', Times of Israel, 11 February 2021.

6 Grant Rumley and Neri Zilber, 'A Military Assessment of the Israel–Hamas Conflict', Washington Institute for Near East Policy, 25 May 2021.

7 Ahmad Abu Amer, 'Egypt, Qatar Agreement with Israel, Hamas Provides Boost for Gaza Economy', Al-Monitor, 23 November 2021.

8 Australian Government, Australian National Security, 'Palestinian Islamic Jihad', 17 January 2022.

9 'Senior IDF Commander Says Hamas Has 30,000 Men, 7,000 Rockets, Dozens of Drones', Times of Israel.

10 This number is based on data provided by the Israeli Central Bureau of Statistics, analysed by the Yesha Council. It does not include Israelis residing in East Jerusalem. See 'דו״ח נתוני אוכלוסייה ביהודה שומרון ובקעת הירדן – נכון לינואר 2022' [Population Data Report in Judea, Samaria and the Jordan Valley – as of January 2022], Yesha Council, 6 March 2022.

11 United Nations Relief and Works Agency for Palestine Refugees in the Near East, 'Government Partners'.

12 World Bank, 'Economic Monitoring Report to the Ad Hoc Liaison Committee', 10 May 2022, pp. 4, 11.

13 Tom O'Connor, 'Palestinians Recall UAE Ambassador, Call Deal with Israel "Betrayal of Jerusalem"', Newsweek, 13 August 2020; and '"Stab in the Back": Palestinians Condemn Israel–Bahrain Deal', Al-Jazeera, 11 September 2020.

14 'Public Opinion Poll No (80)', Palestinian Center for Policy and Survey Research, 4 July 2021.

15 Robert A. Manning and Christopher Preble, 'Reality Check #8: Rethinking US Military Policy in the Greater Middle East', Atlantic Council, 24 June 2021.

YEMEN

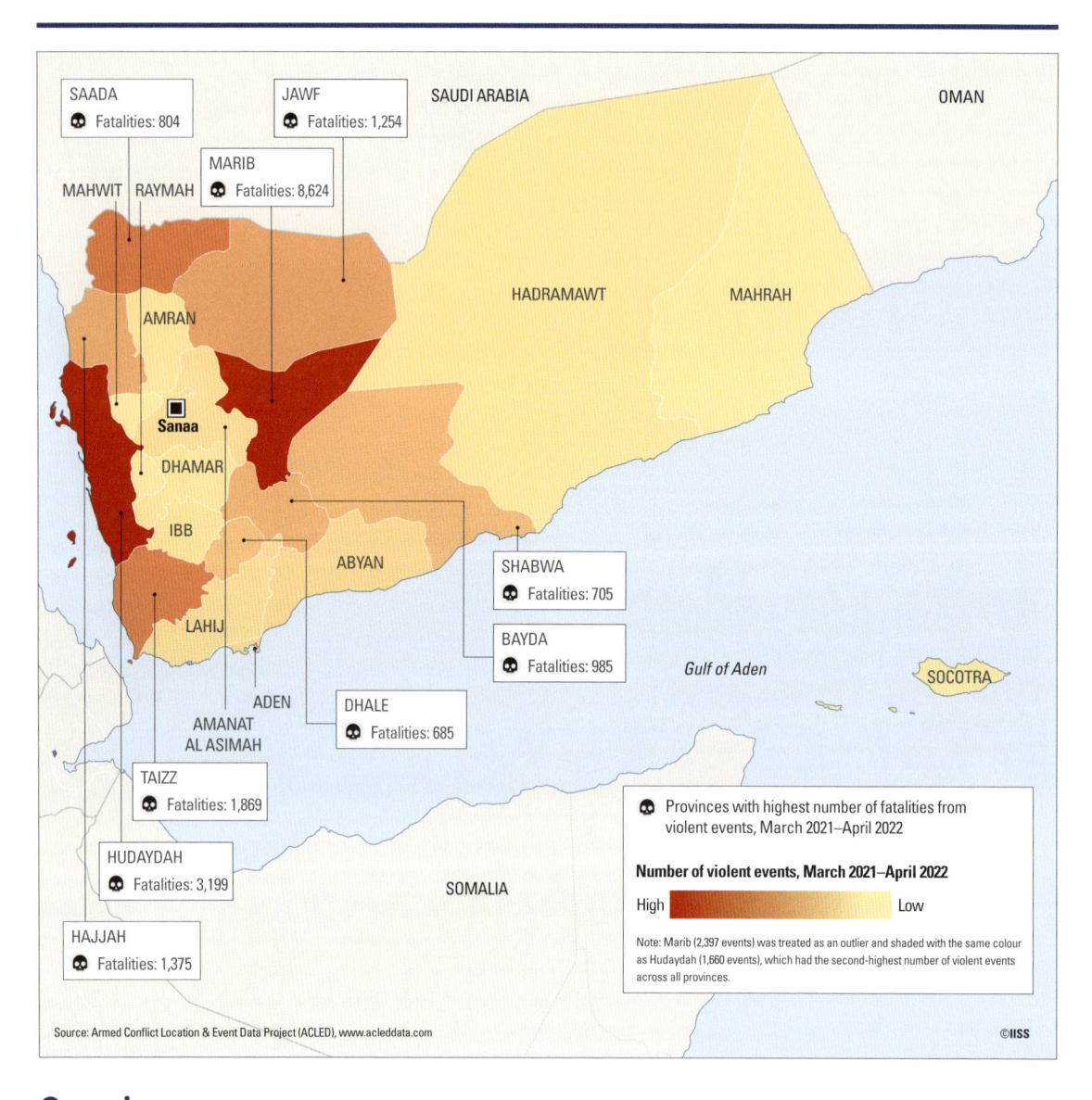

Map labels:
- SAADA — Fatalities: 804
- JAWF — Fatalities: 1,254
- MARIB — Fatalities: 8,624
- TAIZZ — Fatalities: 1,869
- HUDAYDAH — Fatalities: 3,199
- HAJJAH — Fatalities: 1,375
- SHABWA — Fatalities: 705
- BAYDA — Fatalities: 985
- DHALE — Fatalities: 685

Provinces with highest number of fatalities from violent events, March 2021–April 2022

Number of violent events, March 2021–April 2022: High → Low

Note: Marib (2,397 events) was treated as an outlier and shaded with the same colour as Hudaydah (1,660 events), which had the second-highest number of violent events across all provinces.

Source: Armed Conflict Location & Event Data Project (ACLED), www.acleddata.com

©IISS

Overview

The conflict in Yemen began in July 2014 when the Houthi movement, also known as Ansarullah ('Partisans of God'), from Saada province moved into neighbouring Amran province, defeating government forces there and taking control of military installations. Ansarullah then advanced southwards towards Yemen's capital, Sanaa. What began as a civil war in 2014 has since evolved into a regional conflict involving local actors supported by regional powers.

The Houthis took control of Sanaa on 21 September 2014, aided in part by an alliance with their erstwhile enemy, former president Ali Abdullah Saleh, who had been forced to step down two years earlier following the Arab Spring protests. In January 2015, the Houthis placed then-president Abd Rabbo Mansour Hadi under house arrest, leading to his resignation. One month later, he escaped house arrest, fled to the southern port city

Armed Conflict Global Relevance Indicator (ACGRI)

- Incidence: 71
- Human impact: 36
- Geopolitical impact: 38

Yemen

Key Conflict Statistics

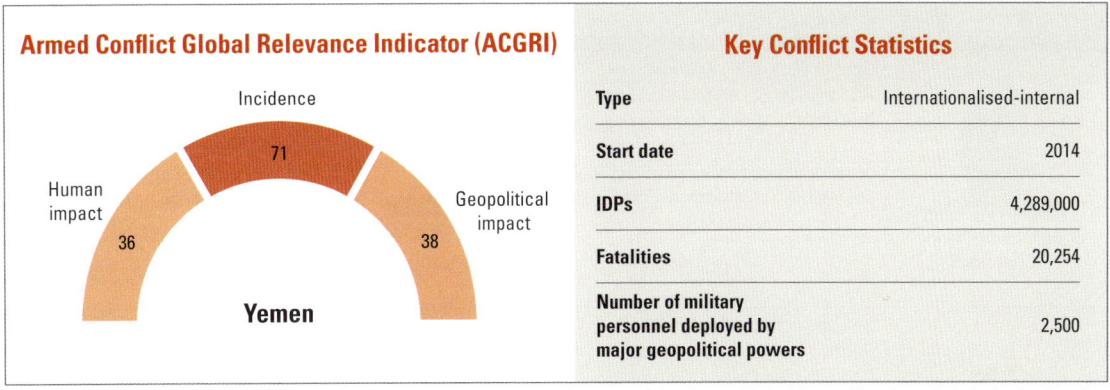

Type	Internationalised-internal
Start date	2014
IDPs	4,289,000
Fatalities	20,254
Number of military personnel deployed by major geopolitical powers	2,500

ACGRI pillars: IISS calculation based on multiple sources for 2021 and January–April 2022 (scale: 0–100). See Notes on Methodology and Data Appendix for further details on Key Conflict Statistics.

of Aden, rescinded his resignation and requested military assistance from Yemen's neighbours in the Gulf Cooperation Council (GCC) to expel the Houthis from Sanaa and restore him to power.

In late March 2015, as Houthi and pro-Saleh forces were advancing on Aden, Saudi Arabia began military operations in Yemen (along with its allies, notably the United Arab Emirates, UAE) to restore Hadi to the presidency. Saudi Arabia was concerned that Ansarullah's alignment with Iran might result in the latter gaining a foothold on the Arabian Peninsula and the former becoming a Hizbullah-like group on the kingdom's southern border. However, over time Saudi Arabia's involvement in Yemen became a self-fulfilling prophecy: the more it attempted to bomb Ansarullah into submission, the more the movement turned to Iran.

UAE troops and local Yemeni forces were able to push Ansarullah and pro-Saleh forces out of Aden in July 2015. However, the counter-offensive quickly stalled. In early 2016, with the war seemingly approaching a stalemate, Hadi dismissed vice president Khaled Bahah, replacing him with Ali Mohsen al-Ahmar, a general with significant experience fighting the Houthis and close ties to the Yemeni Congregation for Reform (al-Islah), an Islamist political party. The decision was likely a hedge against Hadi being replaced by the international community at planned peace talks in Kuwait. It irked the UAE, which was close to Bahah and concerned about al-Islah's ties to the Muslim Brotherhood, which it considers a terrorist group. In response, the UAE began creating, arming and funding local actors throughout southern Yemen, such as the Security Belt Forces (SBF), Hadhrami Elite Forces and Shabwani Elite Forces. Many of these units would later form the military wing of the Southern Transitional Council (STC) following its establishment in 2017.

In December 2017 the Ansarullah–Saleh alliance broke down. During a brief battle in Sanaa, the Houthis killed Saleh. His nephew and top military commander, Tareq Saleh, escaped the fighting and joined the anti-Houthi alliance with backing from the UAE. Throughout 2017, Iran steadily increased its support to Ansarullah, primarily by smuggling ballistic-missile components into Yemen in violation of United Nations Security Council resolutions.[1] The Houthis then assembled the ballistic missiles to strike Riyadh and, later, the UAE.

In mid-2019, following the implementation of the UN-brokered Stockholm Agreement of December 2018, the UAE announced a significant drawdown of troops from Yemen, including from positions in Marib. In January 2020, Ansarullah launched an offensive in Marib in an apparent attempt to seize the province's oil and gas fields.

In January 2021, then United States president Donald Trump designated Ansarullah as a foreign terrorist organisation against the advice of humanitarian organisations, which were concerned that the move would exacerbate Yemen's dire humanitarian situation.[2] The Biden administration eventually rescinded the designation, named its own special envoy for Yemen and pressured Saudi Arabia to end the war.[3] However, in 2021 and early 2022 the Biden administration was not able to exercise any leverage over the Houthis.

In late 2021, the Houthis seized large parts of southern Marib province and three districts in Shabwa province. Alarmed by Ansarullah's southward push, the UAE moved troops from the Giants Brigades (which

Table 1: Members of the Presidential Leadership Council (PLC)

Name	Description	Name	Description
Rashad al-Alimi (Chairman)	Born in Taizz, Alimi was close to Ali Abdullah Saleh, Yemen's former president, and served as the deputy prime minister for defence and security affairs as well as minister of the interior and governor of Saada.	**Abdullah al-Alimi (Bawazeer)**	Alimi is the only member of al-Islah on the Council. He previously served as president Hadi's office director, which afforded him enormous influence over military and political promotions. He is generally distrusted by the UAE.
Faraj al-Bahsani	Bahsani is the governor of Hadramawt, the head of the Hadrami Elite Forces and the overall military commander of Yemen's Second Military Zone, based in Mukalla. Bahsani is close to the UAE.	**Aidarous al-Zubaidi**	Originally from Dhale, Zubaidi is currently the head of the Southern Transitional Council (STC). Although he accepted a spot on the PLC, he has stated that the STC continues to seek an independent southern state. Zubaidi is close to the UAE.
Sultan al-Irada	Irada is a tribesman and the governor of Marib. Previously, he worked with both former presidents Saleh and Hadi. More recently, Irada has been close to al-Islah, which is strong in Marib. Irada's brother, Khalid, was sanctioned by the US in 2017 for alleged links to al-Qaeda.	**Uthman Husayn Mujali**	Perhaps the least well known of the eight members, Mujali is a tribal leader from Saada. His presence on the PLC ensures balance, with four northerners and four southerners, as well as four members backed by the UAE and four backed by Saudi Arabia.
Abdulrahman Abu Zara'a	A Salafi and a commander in the Giants Brigades, Abu Zara'a was instrumental in pushing the Houthis out of Shabwa in late 2021 and early 2022. Although not the most well-known commander in the Giants Brigades, Abu Zara'a now represents them in the PLC. He and the Giants Brigades are backed by the UAE.	**Tareq Saleh**	The nephew of former president Saleh, Tareq has emerged as his uncle's military heir. From 2015–17, Saleh was allied with the Houthis. However, after Ali Abdullah Saleh was killed in 2017, Tareq – along with a core group of former Republican Guard soldiers – escaped to the south and gained UAE support. Saleh and his forces are currently based on the Red Sea coast in Mokha.

Source: IISS

it supports militarily and financially) from bases on the Red Sea coast into Shabwa. The unit quickly pushed the Houthis out of the province and retook territory in southern Marib.[4] In response, Ansarullah launched two separate missile attacks on the UAE in January 2022, signalling that any UAE intervention in Yemen would elicit a direct response.[5] The Giants Brigades stood down and in early April, to coincide with the beginning of Ramadan, a two-month truce – agreed by all parties and brokered by the UN – began.[6]

On 7 April, from exile in Saudi Arabia, Hadi announced his resignation and delegated executive authority to a newly created Presidential Leadership Council (PLC), comprising eight members.[7] Riyadh and Abu Dhabi had pressured Hadi to resign and were responsible for selecting the council members: four from northern Yemen and four from the south. The establishment of the council is an attempt to reconstitute unity within the anti-Houthi alliance, whose members have clashed with one another in the past. It is tasked with negotiating with the Houthis in the first instance and defeating them on the battlefield should negotiations fail.

Conflict Parties

The Houthi movement (Ansarullah)

Strength: 200,000.[8]

Areas of operation: The group holds much of northern Yemen, parts of the Red Sea coast in and around Hudaydah, and is conducting an offensive in Marib province.

Leadership: Abdul Malik al-Houthi.

Structure: Abdul Malik al-Houthi is the supreme commander. However, the organisation has both an official branch of power, the Supreme Political Council, which is headed by President Mahdi al-Mashat, and operates a more informal group of 'supervisors', many of whom are appointed by Mohammad Ali al-Houthi, who heads the Supreme Revolutionary Council.

History: The Houthis began as a Zaydi revivalist movement in the late 1980s, fought six successive wars against the Yemeni government from 2004–10, and took control of Sanaa in 2014.

Objectives: To hold and govern at least northern Yemen, including the oil and gas fields in Marib province.

Opponents: The Saudi-led coalition, including the UAE, the internationally recognised Yemeni government and the anti-Houthi coalition.

Affiliates/allies: Iran and Hizbullah.

Resources/capabilities: Ballistic missiles and uninhabited aerial vehicles (UAV) capable of reaching Riyadh and the UAE.

Southern Transitional Council (STC)

Strength: 55,000.

Areas of operation: Holds Aden, much of Lahij, Socotra and parts of Abyan.

Leadership: Aidarous al-Zubaidi (president of the STC, member of the PLC).

Structure: The STC is led by a president and has a leadership council.

History: The STC was formed in 2017 after Hadi, then Yemen's president, dismissed al-Zubaidi and a number of other influential politicians from their positions.

Objectives: Establish an independent state in southern Yemen.

Opponents: The STC is nominally opposed to the Houthis. Within the anti-Houthi coalition, they are opposed to al-Islah.

Affiliates/allies: The UAE.

Resources/capabilities: Many – although not all – of the local actors that the UAE began establishing in early 2016, including the SBF, form the STC's armed wing.

Joint Forces

Strength: 15,000.

Areas of operation: Red Sea coast, Taizz province.

Leadership: Tareq Saleh, who is also a member of the PLC.

Structure: The group follows a traditional command-and-control military structure, although in 2021 it opened a political office.

History: Following the violent breakup of the Houthi–Saleh alliance in December 2017, Tareq Saleh and a group of former Republican Guard forces moved south and joined UAE troops in Mokha.

Objectives: Ensure a seat at the negotiating table for what remains of Ali Abdullah Saleh's network.

Opponents: The Houthis.

Affiliates/allies: The UAE.

Resources/capabilities: Small arms, light infantry vehicles, and some intelligence, surveillance and reconnaissance (ISR) capabilities. Much of the Joint Forces' resources are provided by the UAE.

Giants Brigades

Strength: Roughly 30,000–35,000.

Areas of operation: Red Sea coast.

Leadership: One of the commanders, Abdulrahman Abu Zara'a, is a member of the PLC.

Structure: Thirteen brigades, backed by the UAE, and led by individual commanders.

History: The UAE established the Giants Brigades in 2016 along the southern Red Sea coast. Much of its initial training took place in and around the Horn of Africa.

Objectives: The Giants Brigades is largely comprised of Salafi fighters. Although largely pro-secession, the leadership does not necessarily support the STC. The Giants Brigades largely supported former president Hadi and it is likely to continue to support the internationally recognised Yemeni government.

Opponents: The Houthis.

Affiliates/allies: The UAE.

Resources/capabilities: Backed and armed by the UAE, which provides small and light arms, infantry vehicles and some ISR capabilities.

Hadhrami Elite Forces

Strength: 7,000.[9]

Areas of operation: Red Sea coast.

Leadership: Faraj al-Bahsani, who is also governor of Hadramawt province and a member of the PLC.

Structure: Recruits from both coastal and Wadi Hadramawt and is organised along traditional military lines, with local commanders in charge of different units.

History: The UAE established the force in 2016 to expel al-Qaeda in the Arabian Peninsula (AQAP) from Mukalla.

Objectives: Ensure a degree of Hadhrami autonomy and security, and revenue capture from Yemen's resources.

Opponents: The Houthis.

Affiliates/allies: The UAE.

Resources/capabilities: Backed and armed by the UAE, which provides small and light arms, light infantry vehicles and some ISR capabilities.

Al-Islah-affiliated forces

Strength: 20,000.

Areas of operation: Red Sea coast, Taizz, Marib and Hadramawt provinces.

Leadership: Muhammad al-Yadumi is the party's chairman, although Abdullah al-Alimi, the former director of president Hadi's office, is a member of the PLC.

Structure: Al-Islah is a political party that has many members serving in prominent positions within the Yemeni armed forces. Al-Islah's affiliated forces do not have their own units or brigades and instead are spread throughout the Yemeni military, although they are concentrated primarily in Taizz, Marib and Wadi Hadramawt.

History: Al-Islah was formed in 1990. Under the Hadi government it cultivated ties with military officers and ensured that its members were promoted through Abdullah al-Alimi.

Objectives: Ensure that Al-Islah has a prominent role in any Yemeni government.

Opponents: The Houthis, the UAE.

Affiliates/allies: Saudi Arabia, some tribal support.

Resources/capabilities: Much of the military in Marib and Taizz provinces and in the 1st Military Region are affiliated with al-Islah and, as such, have light and medium arms, armoured vehicles, missiles and some air capabilities.

Saudi Arabian armed forces

Strength: 15,000 in Yemen.

Areas of operation: Northern border areas, Marib, Aden, Hadramawt, Mahrah provinces and Socotra.

Leadership: Muhammad bin Salman (crown prince and defence minister).

Structure: Units operating in Yemen are part of the kingdom's military and under the command of the Saudi defence ministry.

History: Saudi Arabia entered the war in 2015 as the leader of a ten-country coalition. Following the UAE's drawdown in mid-2019, Saudi Arabia deployed more ground troops and took over the UAE base in Aden.

Objectives: Defeat the Houthis and expel them from Sanaa.

Opponents: The Houthis, Iran.

Affiliates/allies: The UAE, the internationally recognised Yemeni government.

Resources/capabilities: ISR assets (UAVs and satellites), fighter jets, air defences, small arms and light weapons, tanks.

UAE Armed Forces

Strength: 3,000 in Yemen.

Areas of operation: Mokha, Shabwa and throughout southern Yemen via UAE-backed local actors.

Leadership: Sheikh Muhammad bin Zayed Al Nahyan (UAE's de facto ruler).

Structure: Following the UAE drawdown in mid-2019, the remaining forces largely function as advisers.

History: The UAE joined the Saudi-led coalition as its primary partner in 2015. It deployed a number of ground troops and took significant casualties. In mid-2019, as UAE-backed local actors took on greater security responsibilities, the country drew down its forces. However, it retains a small presence in Yemen and is able to influence events through UAE-backed local actors.

Objectives: Gain influence via local actors along Yemen's southern coastline to support the UAE's broader regional strategy, which prioritises shipping lanes and ports.

Opponents: The Houthis and, within the anti-Houthi coalition, al-Islah.

Affiliates/allies: Saudi Arabia and the STC.

Resources/capabilities: ISR assets (UAVs and satellites), fighter jets, air defences, small arms and light weapons.

Other conflict parties

Al-Qaeda in the Arabian Peninsula (AQAP) and the Islamic State in Yemen (ISIS–Y) are also active. AQAP, which numbers roughly 6,000 members, is active in Marib, Bayda and parts of Shabwa. ISIS–Y, which has fewer members than AQAP, is present in southern Yemen.

Conflict Drivers

Geopolitical and geostrategic influences
Saudi Arabia–Iran tensions:
The regional dimension of the conflict is driven by tensions between Riyadh and Tehran. Iran has effectively – and at very limited cost – bogged down Saudi Arabia in Yemen, draining the country's finances and damaging its international reputation. Saudi Arabia, which entered the war out of fears of an Iran-backed Yemeni actor on its southern border, has created the very problem it went to war to avoid.

Security
Territorial fragmentation:
The war in Yemen has effectively fractured the country, enabling armed groups – including, at times, al-Qaeda – to hold and administer territory. More armed groups have appeared as the conflict has endured, with new actors fighting for control of territory and resources to extract revenue. In Yemen, holding territory often ensures a seat at the political table, which is why relatively new armed groups, such as Tareq Saleh's Joint Forces and the STC, have made a concentrated push in recent years to seize and hold territory.

Economic
Competition for control of oil and gas:
The vast majority of Yemen's export revenue (approximately 90% at pre-war levels) is derived from oil and gas. The country's oil and gas fields are located primarily in three provinces (Marib, Shabwa and Hadramawt), which have been described as Yemen's 'triangle of power'.[10] In order for any of Yemen's factions – be it Ansarullah, the STC or the Yemeni government – to survive as an independent state, they must control at least one of these provinces. This reality is partly why the Houthis have been so intent on taking Marib and why the UAE reacted so strongly when the Houthis pushed into Shabwa in late 2021. A Houthi victory in Shabwa could effectively split the south, cutting off Aden from the oilfields in Hadramawt and ending any hope of an independent south led by the STC.

Religious
Growing Shia dominance:
Yemen is largely split between two religious sects: the Zaydi Shia, predominantly in the northern highlands, and the Shafi'i Sunnis in the lowlands. For much of modern Yemen's history these differences existed below the surface, with Zaydis and Shafi'is praying at one another's mosques and inter-marrying. However, the Zaydi ideology of the 1990s and early 2000s, which formed to protect traditional Zaydism from being eroded by the state, reinforced a narrative of traditional Zaydi rule (the last Zaydi imam was overthrown in 1962). As the relationship between the Houthis and Iran has deepened over the course of the conflict, there is now also a growing Twelver Shia community in Yemen. Both Zaydi and Twelver Shia theology stress an intolerance to dissent that makes maintaining a pluralistic society difficult.

Key Events in 2021–22

POLITICAL EVENTS

25 March 2021
Tareq Saleh announces the formation of a political bureau.

12 May
The UN announces that the special envoy for Yemen, Martin Griffiths, is stepping down to take a new position within the organisation.

MILITARY/VIOLENT EVENTS

17 July
The president of the Houthis' Supreme Political Council, Mahdi al-Mashat, has his term extended for one year.

6 August
Swedish diplomat Hans Grundberg is appointed UN special envoy for Yemen.

25 December
President Hadi replaces Mohammed Saleh bin Adyo, the adamantly anti-UAE governor of Shabwa province, with a local tribal sheikh and pro-UAE figure, Awadh al-Awlaki.

28 February 2022
The UN Security Council passes a resolution on Yemen that extends the arms embargo against the Houthi movement and names it a terrorist group.

5 March
The Houthis agree a tentative deal with the UN to transfer oil from a decaying oil tanker off Yemen's coast to another ship.

1 April
The UN announces that a two-month truce will begin on 2 April.

7 April
Hadi resigns as president, handing over all executive authority to a newly created PLC.

14 June 2021
Tareq Saleh says his forces are active on Mayun Island in the Bab el-Mandeb Strait.

23 September
Houthi forces take full control of Bayda province.

September
Houthi forces move into northern districts of Shabwa province.

12 November
The Joint Forces withdraw from positions south of Hudaydah, allowing Houthi fighters to move in.

10 January 2022
Giants Brigades forces push Houthi fighters out of Shabwa province.

17 January
Houthi forces conduct a drone attack targeting Abu Dhabi's international airport, killing three people.

24 January
Houthi forces launch a missile attack against a base in the UAE hosting US forces. The attack is intercepted by air defences.

Responses to the Conflict

Security
Perhaps the most significant military development during the reporting period was the Houthi offensive in northern Shabwa and the UAE's response. In late 2021, as part of a campaign to take control of Marib, Houthi forces seized and held three districts in northern Shabwa. The development was significant for several reasons. Firstly, it constituted a Houthi incursion into southern territory. Secondly, a Houthi takeover of Shabwa would provide the movement with another oil- and gas-producing province and a second outlet to the sea. As a result, Houthi control of the province would effectively end any hopes of an independent southern state by cutting off Aden from Hadramawt's oil and gas fields.

The Houthi incursion into southern Yemen – territory claimed by the UAE's local ally, the STC – crossed one of Abu Dhabi's red lines. The UAE quickly moved forces from the Giants Brigades, which are based in and around the Red Sea coast, to Shabwa to fight the Houthis. The Giants Brigades quickly pushed the Houthis out of Shabwa and back into Marib. The Houthis responded by launching two separate attacks on the UAE in early 2022, one of which saw a response from US personnel in the country. However, the UAE was disappointed with what it believed to be a tepid US response, with some reports that it led Abu Dhabi to abstain from a UN Security Council (UNSC) vote condemning Russia's February 2022 invasion of Ukraine.[11]

Economic/development
Over the course of the conflict Yemen has effectively developed two economies: a Houthi economy based in the north and a government economy based in the south. The Yemeni riyal trades at different rates in the north than in the south and more recently printed government currency is banned in Houthi-controlled areas. This situation is partly the result of former president Hadi's short-sighted decision to split Yemen's central bank in 2016 by moving the government-controlled central bank to Aden and leaving the one in Sanaa under Houthi control.

Following Hadi's abrupt resignation and the formation of the PLC in April 2022, Saudi Arabia announced that it would arrange a US$3 billion aid package for the country.[12] The move helped stabilise the value of the riyal in Aden. However, as with similar deposits in the past, without positive political developments the money is likely to have little long-term impact.

Diplomacy
In April 2022, to coincide with the beginning of Ramadan, the UN announced a scheduled two-month truce. The measure was also intended to allow for some civilian flights out of Sanaa and a reopening of roads into Taizz. The truce held, at least in name, despite multiple violations on fronts in Marib and Taizz. However, civilian flights were not yet departing Sanaa on a regular basis as of late April 2022, despite a number of attempts.

New UN Special Envoy for Yemen Hans Grundberg will likely seek to engage the PLC and make a push for a comprehensive settlement. This will likely require a new UNSC resolution. The most recent UNSC resolution on Yemen, passed in late February 2022, referred to the Houthis as a 'terrorist group'.[13]

Humanitarian aid
Yemen remains one of the world's worst humanitarian crises. Compounding matters, a 'funding crunch' has left the UN unable to provide much needed aid.[14] Ahead of a pledging conference in early 2022, the UN reported that it needed US$4.3bn to address the humanitarian needs of over 17 million people in the country. As of mid-March, it had received pledges amounting to US$1.3bn.[15] More than half of Yemen's population exists in a precarious state and small changes in the value of the riyal have a disproportionate impact on the humanitarian situation.

Conflict Outlook

Political scenarios
The establishment of the PLC in April 2022 was intended to re-impose unity on a deeply divided anti-Houthi alliance and provide momentum for a negotiated settlement with the Houthis or, if that failed, a unified military front. However, several of the eight PLC members hold diametrically opposed views regarding the desired end state in Yemen. The STC seeks an independent southern state, while Tareq Saleh, a northerner, is likely to struggle to find popular support in the south. Al-Islah and the UAE-backed STC have clashed repeatedly in recent years and it is unlikely that their forces will be able to set aside deep differences to unite against a common foe in the Houthis.

Despite its questionable legal basis, the removal of president Hadi and vice president Ahmar may provide opportunities for new negotiations. However, the development is unlikely to bring an end to the conflict. Ansarullah may attend talks but it is unlikely that it will be willing to give up at the negotiating table what it believes it has won on the battlefield.

The course of the conflict over the next year will largely hinge on the battle for Marib. Should the Houthis manage to take Marib and its oil and gas fields, the group will hold much of the north, making Yemen's reunification all but impossible. In such a scenario, the PLC may fracture as the various groups represented scramble to secure their own interests at the expense of internal unity. For example, should the Houthis succeed in capturing Marib, the STC may seek to declare a southern state to prevent Houthi incursions into Shabwa. However, such a move would alienate the PLC's northern members. If the Houthis fail to take Marib, the conflict will likely continue as a war of attrition.

Escalation potential and conflict-related risks
As Houthi missile and drone attacks on the UAE in early 2022 demonstrated, there is a high potential for escalation in the conflict, even beyond Yemen's borders. Should a renewed Joint Comprehensive Plan of Action (JCPOA) with Iran fail to materialise, there may be repercussions in Yemen, as the Houthis have demonstrated a willingness to act on Tehran's behalf in the Arabian Peninsula. Escalation is also likely if the scheduled two-month truce collapses, if the PLC descends into infighting, or if the Houthis renew their offensive on Marib.

AQAP remains a threat in Yemen although the group is fractured by infighting and mistrust and is currently at its weakest point since the group was founded in 2009. However, should Saudi Arabia and the UAE withdraw from Yemen and the conflict revert to a civil war between various local groups, AQAP may be able to stage a comeback and reassert itself as a destination of choice for international recruits.

Prospects for peace
Peace remains a distant prospect in Yemen. As of mid-2022, there are simply too many groups with conflicting aims – and too few resources to satisfy them all. None of Yemen's armed factions have the military strength to force all their opponents to submit to their will. However, nearly all of the armed groups have enough power to act as a spoiler to a political settlement if they perceive that it does not adequately protect their interests.

Strategic implications and global influences
During his first year in office, Biden made ending the war in Yemen a priority. However, he quickly found that without leverage over the Houthis all he could do was pressure US partners, such as Saudi Arabia and the UAE. This approach had the effect of strengthening the Houthis, particularly in Marib. The US is likely to remain nominally involved in encouraging a peaceful solution to the conflict. However, Washington is unlikely to be able to ensure the reunification of Yemen as a single state.

Yemen remains a priority to the international community for three reasons: international shipping lanes, the threat of terrorism and the humanitarian crisis. Absent a political settlement, the humanitarian crisis is likely to deteriorate, particularly if the Yemeni riyal continues to lose value, eroding what little purchasing power most Yemenis still have.

The Houthi presence on the Red Sea coast, sea mines and the decaying floating oil-storage tanker *Safer*, which holds 1.1m barrels of oil and is not being adequately maintained, present potential threats to shipping lanes and global supply lines. To date, the Houthis have used the threat of *Safer* leaking oil or exploding as a way of extracting concessions and money from the international community and may continue to do so in the future.

Notes

1. UN Panel of Experts on Yemen, 'Final Report of the Panel of Experts on Yemen', S/2018/68, 26 January 2018.
2. Press statement by then US secretary of state Mike Pompeo, 'Terrorist Designation of Ansarallah in Yemen', US Department of State, 10 January 2021.
3. Press statement by US Secretary of State Antony Blinken, 'Revocation of the Terrorist Designations of Ansarallah', US Department of State, 12 February 2021.
4. 'Yemen Pro-govt Forces Say They Have Retaken Shabwa from Houthis', Reuters, 10 January 2022.
5. Mona El-Naggar and Eric Schmitt, 'US Helps Thwart Attacks by Yemen Rebels on American Air Base in UAE', *New York Times*, 24 January 2022.
6. 'Press Statement by the UN Special Envoy for Yemen Hans Grundberg on a Two-month Truce', Office of the Special Envoy of the Secretary-General for Yemen, 1 April 2022.
7. Ben Hubbard, 'Yemeni Leader Hands Power to New Body as His Saudi Backers Seek to End War', *New York Times*, 7 April 2022.
8. Naif Al-Qodasi and Adnan Al-Jabrani, 'Parallel Militaries: Anatomy of the Armed Forces Fighting Yemen's War', Almasdar Online, 3 January 2021.
9. Number is an estimate based on author's interviews conducted in Yemen, 2019–22.
10. Ammar al-Aulaqi, 'The Yemeni Government's Triangle of Power', *Yemen Review*, Sana'a Center for Strategic Studies, 9 September 2020.
11. Barak Ravid, 'UAE Abstained from UN Security Council Vote Due to US Response to Houthi attacks', Axios, 2 March 2022.
12. 'Saudi Gives Yemen Money, Urges Peace Talks After Presidential Council Announced', Reuters, 7 April 2022.
13. Colum Lynch, 'Ukraine Crisis Spills into Yemen Diplomacy', *Foreign Policy*, 28 February 2022.
14. '$4.3 Billion Needed to Help Over 17 Million People Across Yemen', UN News, 16 March 2022.
15. 'Yemen Conference 2022: Financial Announcements', ReliefWeb, 16 March 2022.

LIBYA

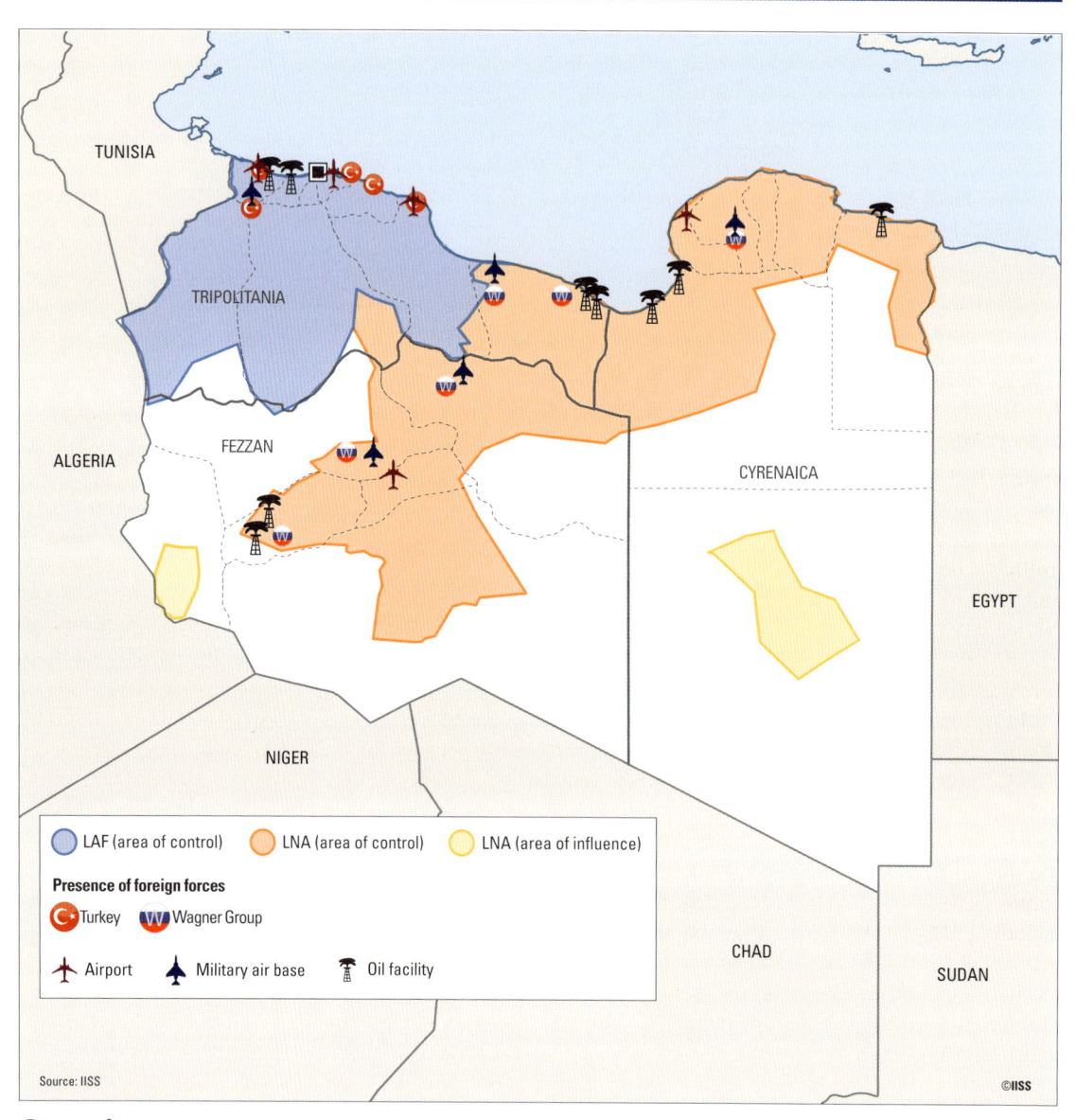

Overview

Mass protests against the rule of Libyan leader Muammar Gadhafi in 2011 ignited a revolution that plunged the country into a civil war between the regime and the rebels. In this first phase of the conflict, the NATO-led intervention informed by the Responsibility to Protect (R2P) principle precipitated a regime change in which revolutionary forces prevailed. However, increasing insecurity and a proliferation of armed groups exposed the weaknesses of transitional institutions. A new rift emerged in 2014, mirroring a regional divide between Islamist and secular forces that had become more evident in Egypt following the country's 2013 military coup. Counter-revolutionary forces that were part of *Operation Dignity* – whose aim was to restore order and fight Islamist and terrorist

Armed Conflict Global Relevance Indicator (ACGRI)

Libya
- Incidence: 1
- Human impact: 1
- Geopolitical impact: 51

Key Conflict Statistics

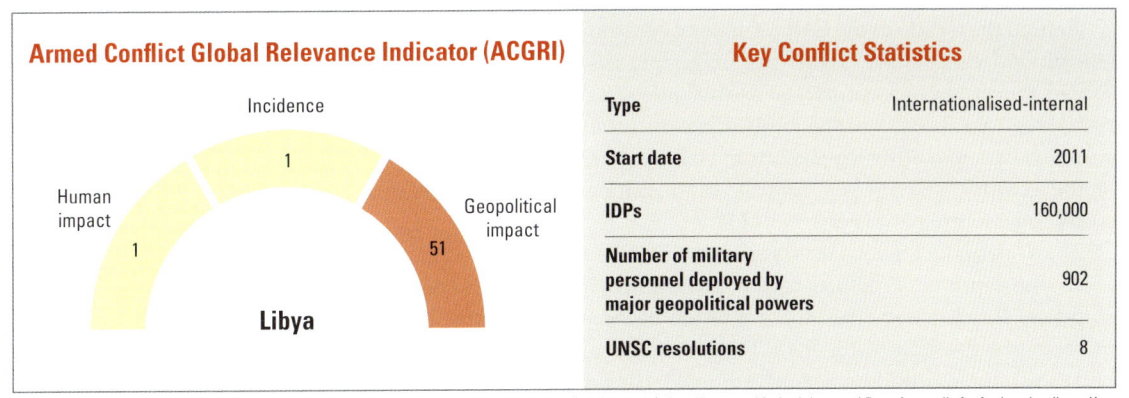

Type	Internationalised-internal
Start date	2011
IDPs	160,000
Number of military personnel deployed by major geopolitical powers	902
UNSC resolutions	8

ACGRI pillars: IISS calculation based on multiple sources for 2021 and January–April 2022 (scale: 0–100). See Notes on Methodology and Data Appendix for further details on Key Conflict Statistics.

groups – clashed with revolutionary and Islamist-leaning forces regrouped under *Operation Libya Dawn*. This second phase of the civil war polarised the country, accelerating its fragmentation and creating a breeding ground for terrorist organisations. Since then, Tripoli and the western region have been under the control of revolutionary groups and militias from the capital and the cities of Misrata and Zintan. In the east and the south, the Libyan National Army (LNA) under the command of Field Marshal Khalifa Haftar has gradually taken control across Cyrenaica and Fezzan.

In April 2019, Haftar launched *Operation Flood of Dignity* against the Government of National Accord (GNA, the internationally recognised national unity government established in 2015) in the capital. The development was a watershed moment, escalating the conflict from low-intensity fighting into a major confrontation. In this period, third-party states, including Russia and Turkey, upped their diplomatic, economic and military support to affiliated local actors, marking the beginning of a third phase of the civil war that revealed the degree of external interference in Libya.

In 2020, the conflict became even more internationalised, developing into yet another theatre of geopolitical confrontation involving regional and global powers. Following the failure of a high-level international conference in Germany that aimed to prevent a military build-up, the LNA lost ground to the Turkey-backed Libyan Armed Forces (LAF, supporting the GNA). The development forced Haftar to pull back the LNA from Tripolitania and abandon his hopes of taking the capital. In the face of a successful LAF counter-offensive – and the prospect of a rapid collapse of Haftar's forces – Cairo (which had backed the LNA's efforts to eradicate Islamist groups in Libya) declared the front line between Sirte and Jufra a 'red line', threatening direct military intervention.

The prospect of Libya transforming from a proxy war into a military confrontation between rival regional and global powers froze the conflict and reinvigorated efforts to move the peace process forward. In October 2020, a landmark ceasefire agreement between rival factions was brokered by the UN Support Mission in Libya (UNSMIL) in Geneva, which served as a prelude to intra-Libyan negotiations conducted by the Libyan Political Dialogue Forum (LPDF) in November. The road map adopted in Tunis by the LPDF was followed by the appointment of a new executive authority in February 2021. Led by a new prime minister, Misrata businessman Abdul Hamid Dbeibah, the newly established Government of National Unity (GNU) had an interim mandate and was tasked with holding elections in December 2021.

The confidence vote granted by the House of Representatives (HoR, the Tobruk-based parliament resulting from elections in 2014) to the GNU on 10 March 2021 represented a remarkable precedent and raised reasonable hopes of an end to Libya's chaotic transition a decade after the revolution. However, unresolved issues threaten the political transition. These include the lack of a comprehensive plan to implement a security-sector reform (SSR) and a disarmament, demobilisation and reintegration (DDR) programme to dissolve the multitude of militias and armed groups present in Libya; and a number of structural factors, including disagreements over the redistribution of oil revenues and the lack of progress on the reunification of the Libyan military.

Behind the façade of the GNU, a state of constant tension between political rivals has frequently disrupted the peace process. Haftar's confrontational stance vis-à-vis the new prime minister has surfaced periodically, preventing Dbeibah from visiting parts of the country under LNA control. More importantly, on multiple occasions the HoR rejected the GNU's draft budget, which was larger than expected given the temporary nature of the government's mandate. In particular, the HoR's attitude became more aggressive following the LPDF's failure to find a common ground on a constitutional basis for future elections. HoR President Agila Saleh's controversial approval of election laws in September and October 2021 coincided with the parliament's decision to challenge the GNU and withdraw its confidence in the prime minister.[1]

As the election deadline approached, the presidential bids of controversial and divisive political figures, such as Dbeibah, Haftar and Saif al-Islam Gadhafi, produced an explosive mix. Amid visible mobilisation of militias and armed groups in and around Tripoli, the High National Elections Commission (HNEC) was forced to call off the elections, a development that undermined the LPDF road map and the UN peace process. The latter also lost credibility following the resignation of the special envoy on Libya and UNSMIL head, Ján Kubiš (announced in November 2021, just a few weeks before the planned elections), and disagreements between the United States and Russia over UNSMIL's mandate and leadership.

The postponement of elections led to unexpected realignments in the Libyan political landscape, as shown by the alliance struck between former foes Haftar and Fathi Bashagha, previously a GNA minister of interior and presidential candidate. The result of this surprising convergence was the establishment of a rival Government of National Stability (GNS) led by Bashagha, appointed by a revived HoR on dubious grounds and rejected by Dbeibah as illegitimate. The resulting institutional split brought back the issue of parallel authorities in a divided Libya, a scenario that had immediate repercussions for the oil industry. The resumption of an oil blockade – by tribesmen and protesters calling for Dbeibah to step down and Bashagha to take office – in areas under LNA control put additional pressure on Dbeibah and his allies and prompted questions about the GNU's resilience in the changed international context following Russia's invasion of Ukraine in February 2022. The blockade also highlighted the malign influence exercised by the Wagner Group, a Russian private military company that, despite recent reports suggesting that it was downsizing its Libya presence due to the ongoing conflict in Ukraine, is still active in the country alongside thousands of other mercenaries, foreign fighters and foreign troops.[2]

Conflict Parties

Libyan Armed Forces (LAF)

Strength: Unclear. Given the undisclosed number of militias fighting on behalf of the LAF and the undefined relationship between these groups and the central command, it is impossible to determine the exact strength.

Areas of operation: After the ceasefire agreement of October 2020, the LAF remained in control of western Libya, including Misrata, Sabratha, Sorman, Tripoli and the Watiya air base.

Leadership: As head of the Presidency Council (PC), Mohammed al-Menfi is supreme commander of the LAF. Maj.-Gen. Mohammed al-Haddad is chief of staff. The PC established seven military zones in Libya. Commanders of the active zones include Maj.-Gen. Abdel Basset Marwan (Tripoli zone), Maj.-Gen. Osama al-Juwaili (Western zone), Maj.-Gen. Mohammed Mousa (Central zone) and Ali Kanna (Southern zone).

Structure: Militias in the capital (including the Abu Salim Brigade, the Bab al-Tajoura Brigade, the Nawasi Brigade and the Tripoli Revolutionaries Brigade) represent the backbone of the LAF. Other militias from Misrata, Zawiya and Zintan are also part of the LAF. Relations between different militias and armed groups are not always easy in light of their different interests and diverging agendas, which re-emerged following Haftar's defeat and the LNA's withdrawal from Tripoli.

History: In the aftermath of Haftar's attack on Tripoli in 2019 the GNA launched a counter-offensive code-named *Operation Volcano of Rage*. Most of the armed groups and militias in Tripoli and western Libya rallied in support of the GNA, which made serious efforts to establish its own army, integrating most of these groups into the LAF.

Libyan Armed Forces (LAF)

Objectives: Initially the LAF's primary objective was to repel the LNA offensive on the capital and thwart Haftar's plan to take control of the country. Since the end of the latest round of fighting in 2020, groups that are part of the LAF have shored up support for the GNA and subsequently the GNU, foiling any attempt to unseat Dbeibah.

Opponents: The LNA, its allies, and terrorist groups such as the Islamic State (also known as ISIS) and al-Qaeda in the Islamic Maghreb (AQIM).

Affiliates/allies: Armed groups opposing the LNA's offensive in western and southern Libya, including Tebu militiamen of the South Protection Force. The GNA has received considerable military support from Turkey, which deployed thousands of mercenaries from the Syrian National Army (SNA) to halt Haftar's offensive on Tripoli. Some of the Chadian rebel forces active in Libya have also backed the LAF in the past.

Resources/capabilities: Following a memorandum of understanding (MoU) signed in 2019, Turkey has sent weapons, advisers and military equipment to shore up support for the GNA. The LAF has received *Bayraktar* TB2 and ANKA S-1 uninhabited aerial vehicles, *Kirpi* armoured vehicles and air-defence systems, including *Hawk* air-defence missile batteries and 3D *Kalakan* radar. Turkey also sent military hardware, including electronic-warfare systems, anti-tank guided missiles, self-propelled air-defence guns and artillery, surface-to-air missile systems, frigates and fighter ground-attack aircraft.

Libyan National Army (LNA) or the Libyan Arab Armed Forces (LAAF)

Strength: Around 25,000 fighters but the regular army is made up of some 7,000 troops. The 106th Brigade is the largest unit, exceeding 5,000 fighters.[3]

Areas of operation: Large swathes of Libya, including Cyrenaica, Fezzan and Sirte.

Leadership: While HoR President Agila Saleh is supreme commander, Haftar, appointed field marshal in 2016, holds the real power. Maj.-Gen. Abdul Razzaq al-Nazhuri is the chief of staff and Oun al-Furjani is chief of staff of Haftar's office. Khaled Haftar, son of Khalifa and leader of the 106th Brigade, is considered a prominent figure and possible successor to his father.

Structure: The LNA includes the Al-Saiqa Special Forces, led by Maj.-Gen. Abdelsalam al-Hassi and comprising 3,500 fighters;[4] the 106th Brigade, led by Khaled Haftar; the 166th Brigade, led by Ayoub Furjani, Haftar's son-in-law; and the 101st Brigade, led by Capt. Mohamed Absayat al-Zway and made up mainly of fighters from Ajdabiya. Other groups include the Awliya al-Dam (Blood Avengers), led by Eyad al-Fessi. The LNA also relies on co-opting local armed groups where the opportunity presents itself.

History: In 2014, in light of a deteriorating security situation, Haftar launched *Operation Dignity*, targeting Islamist factions in Benghazi. In 2015, the HoR gave legitimacy to *Operation Dignity*, prompting the LNA's creation. The LNA is not recognised as the legitimate Libyan military by Haftar's opponents. In the following years the LNA gradually extended its control to Cyrenaica and Fezzan.

Objectives: Initially created to combat Islamist and terrorist groups responsible for attacks, the LNA gradually became key to Haftar's project to seek absolute power and avoid civilian oversight. In light of its anti-Islamist background, the LNA has often been considered a secularist force in the country. However, certain groups inside the LNA have a Salafist orientation, while the influence of the Madkhali doctrine has increased. In its effort to extend its control over Libya, the LNA has been frequently accused of war crimes and violations of international humanitarian law.

Opponents: Islamist groups and terrorist organisations, such as the Muslim Brotherhood, the Benghazi Defence Brigades, AQIM and ISIS–Libya, frequently clash with LNA units. Revolutionary groups, such as the militias in Misrata, Tripoli and Zintan, oppose Haftar's political project and have rallied around the GNA to defend Tripoli. Tebu armed groups and Chadian rebel forces have frequently clashed with the LNA in southern Libya.

Affiliates/allies: About 18,000 fighters are considered auxiliary forces,[5] including tribal militias mainly in eastern Libya (the Awaqir tribe in Cyrenaica) but also in Tripolitania (approximately 2,500 fighters in Zintan) and Fezzan (the al-Ahly and the Awlad Suleiman).[6] In Kufra, the Subol al-Salam Brigade has been affiliated with the LNA since 2015. Madkhalist and Salafist armed groups like the Tariq Ibn Ziyad Brigade (led by Omar Mraje) and the al-Tawhid Brigade also operate under LNA control. Other affiliated armed groups include the eastern and central branches of the Petroleum Facilities Guard (PFG). Sudanese rebel forces and paramilitaries such as the Sudan Liberation Movement/Army–Minni Minnawi, the Sudan Liberation Movement Army–Abdel Wahid al-Nur and the Sudanese Awakening Revolutionary Council have reportedly backed the LNA, as have mercenaries from Chad and private military companies, such as the Wagner Group.

Resources/capabilities: Since the launch of its attack on Tripoli, the LNA's aerial capability has increased, as shown by the use of Chinese-made *Wing Loong* II drones allegedly provided by the United Arab Emirates (UAE) and armed with *Blue Arrow* (BA7) air-to-surface missiles. The UN Security Council (UNSC) Panel of Experts on Libya reported that the UAE has also deployed military personnel and transferred at least five types of military equipment to Libya, including armoured personnel carriers, patrol vehicles and French Dassault *Mirage* 2000-9 fighters.

ISIS–Libya

Strength: Approximately 50 militants.[7]

Areas of operation: Southern areas, such as Murzuq, Sabha and Umm al-Aranib.

Leadership: Counter-terrorism operations have significantly weakened the ISIS leadership in Libya. Former emir Abu Moaz al-Tikrit, also known as Abdul Qader al-Najdi, was killed by the LNA in September 2020 during clashes in Sabha. Another top commander, Mohamed Miloud Ahmed, also known as Abu Omar, was arrested in a raid carried out by the LNA in Obari in March 2021.

Structure: In 2014 the organisation announced the establishment of three *wilayat* (provinces) in the three historical regions of Libya: Wilayah al-Barqa in Cyrenaica, Wilayah al-Fizzan in Fezzan and Wilayah al-Tarablus in Tripolitania. Despite there being some distinction between the three *wilayat*, as indicated by separate claims of responsibility (for example, Wilayah al-Tarablus claimed an attack against the Corinthia hotel in Tripoli in January 2015), ISIS–Libya has maintained a centralised structure.

History: ISIS emerged in Libya in 2014, when it was able to gain a foothold in the eastern city of Derna. Eventually, the local ISIS affiliate was forced to withdraw following clashes with the Abu Salim Martyrs Brigade, an Islamist militia with alleged ties to al-Qaeda and part of the Derna Protection force (DPF), an umbrella group of Islamist and revolutionary militias active in the city. In 2015, ISIS established a presence in Sirte, taking advantage of the marginalisation of the city by Libyan authorities. The group seized neighbouring towns such as Nawfaliya and Harawa, taking control of the Ghardabiya air base and threatening Misrata. Following clashes on the outskirts of Misrata, in May 2016 the GNA launched an offensive against the group in Sirte. Misrata militias comprised the backbone of *Operation Solid Structure*, which took control of the group's stronghold in Sirte in December 2016 with the crucial support of US Africa Command (USAFRICOM), which launched 495 airstrikes during the operation.[8]

Objectives: Despite ISIS being severely weakened by *Operation Solid Structure* and USAFRICOM's frequent airstrikes, the resumption of hostilities in April 2019 provided it with an opportunity to re-establish its presence. Since then, attacks claimed by ISIS have increased, particularly in remote areas of central and southern Libya. Nevertheless, in the short term, it is highly unlikely that the group will be able to take control of territory.

Opponents: The GNU and affiliated militias; the LNA and its local allies; the Muslim Brotherhood and other moderate Islamist groups (including Sufi followers); third parties engaged in the fight against terrorism (the US in particular).

Affiliates/allies: The group has always taken a confrontational stance vis-à-vis other terrorist organisations in Libya. However, since its defeat in Sirte, reports suggest that ISIS is collaborating with other jihadist groups, including AQIM. This limited cooperation has been instrumental in allowing ISIS to regroup and re-establish its presence in central and southern Libya.

Resources/capabilities: ISIS militants have seized trucks carrying fuel and gained revenue from imposing taxes on human traffickers and arms smugglers. The group has also resorted to kidnapping for ransom.

Turkish Armed Forces (TSK)

Strength: Over 700 Turkish military advisers and intelligence officers (on Libyan soil).[9]

Areas of operation: Overlapping with the LAF in southern Tripoli, Sabratha, Sorman and Tarhouna, extending to the outskirts of Jufra and Sirte. Reported presence at the Mitiga airport in Tripoli and the Watiya air base. Turkish troops have also been based at the Tripoli military port, the Khoms naval base, the Zuwara barracks and several bases in Misrata and Tripoli.

Leadership: President Recep Tayyip Erdoğan (commander-in-chief); Gen. (retd) Hulusi Akar (minister of national defence); Gen. Yasar Guler (chief of general staff). The head of the Turkish military mission in Libya is Osman Aytac.

Structure: Turkish army units operating under the Turkish Land Forces Command and squadrons carrying out airstrikes operating under the Air Force Command are subordinate to the chief of general staff.

History: In November 2019 Turkey and the GNA signed an MoU, which provided for Turkish military assistance and training to the LAF. In early 2020, Turkey began to intervene militarily in support of the GNA, contributing significantly to repelling the LNA offensive on Tripoli.

Objectives: At first, to prevent Haftar's forces from taking control of Tripoli. Following the collapse of the LNA offensive, to consolidate the GNA first and then the GNU, while also providing training to the LAF and carrying out demining operations.

Opponents: The LNA and its foreign backers.

Affiliates/allies: The GNU/LAF and Qatar. The TSK has deployed mercenaries and private military contractors in support of the authorities in Tripoli, including from SADAT, a security firm run by Anrar Tanriverdi, a close associate of Erdoğan.

Resources/capabilities: Turkey has sent weapons, advisers and military equipment, including TB-2 *Bayraktar* and ANKA S-1 drones, *Kirpi* armoured vehicles and air-defence systems, such as *Hawk* air-defence missile batteries and 3D *Kalakan* radar to the Libyan theatre. According to the UNSC Panel of Experts, Turkey also sent military hardware, including electronic-warfare systems, anti-tank guided missiles, self-propelled air-defence guns and artillery, surface-to-air missile systems, frigates and fighter ground-attack aircraft. In March 2021, Turkey appeared to have supplied the LAF with US-made M60 tanks for training purposes. Recent images also showed the Turkish-built T-155 *Firtina* self-propelled artillery system and T-122 *Sakaraya* multiple-launch rocket system deployed by Turkish forces in Libya.

Wagner Group

Strength: 1,500–2,000 personnel on the ground in Libya (estimate).[10]

Areas of operation: After having been present along the front line in southern Tripoli, Wagner operatives were spotted at different air bases (Jufra, Brak al-Shati, Ghardabiya, Sabha and Waddan) and oilfields (Sharara and El Feel), having moved to secure facilities and provide support to LNA-affiliated local armed groups. Wagner members were also present at the Es-Sider oil terminal.

Leadership: Dmitry Utkin (commander); Alexander Ermolaev (deputy commander); Andrei Troshev (chief of staff).

Structure: Unknown.

History: The Wagner Group is a Russian security organisation closely linked to the Kremlin and military intelligence. It is used by Russia to carry out a range of officially deniable military and intelligence operations, and commercial activities, abroad, including in the Middle East and Africa. Reports about the presence of the group in Libya first emerged in 2018, when Wagner operatives were spotted in eastern Libya.

Objectives: Initially to provide training, hardware, non-kinetic security services and battlefield advice to the LNA, backing its offensive on Tripoli. Since September 2019, to act as a force multiplier for the LNA, giving it tighter coordination, anti-drone capability, expert snipers and advanced equipment. After the collapse of the LNA offensive, to consolidate Haftar's position and reinforce his grip on critical infrastructures.

Opponents: The GNA, TSK, US.

Affiliates/allies: The LNA and its foreign backers. The Wagner Group reportedly recruited several thousand Syrian mercenaries to back the LNA in 2020. Most of them came from pro-regime militias and paramilitary organisations affiliated with the Syrian Army, including the 5th Corps, the Division 25 (formerly known as Tiger Forces), the Quds Brigade and the so-called ISIS hunters.

Resources/capabilities: Throughout 2020 Russian military cargo aircraft, including Il-76s, supplied the Wagner Group with military armoured vehicles, SA-22 air-defence systems, fuel, ammunition and other supplies. In May 2020, at least 14 MiG-29 and SU-24 jets were deployed from Russia to Libya through Syria, and were reportedly flown by Wagner pilots, who carried out several ground strikes and other missions in support of the LNA. The UAE reportedly provided financial assistance to the Wagner Group to deploy its mercenaries to Libya.

Conflict Drivers

Political

Resuming polarisation:
Divisive politics continues to be a powerful driver of conflict. The power struggle around the presidential elections during the reporting period showed that politics has become the continuation of war by other means. To avoid a relapse into civil war, elections had to be postponed; the immediate consequence of the delay was the bifurcation of the country around two main centres of power, the GNU and the GNS.

The establishment of a parallel executive authority revived the political polarisation between eastern and western Libya, which had partially receded with the initial implementation of the LPDF's road map. Visible cracks also emerged in western Libya, where the establishment of the GNS triggered a realignment of militias that was reinforced by the appointment of the Misratan Bashagha at the helm of the new executive. More importantly, the GNS also certified the political resurrection of Haftar: having been ostracised by internal stakeholders and international partners in the aftermath of the LNA's failed offensive on Tripoli, the field marshal assumed a new role as kingmaker of Libyan politics.

From a structural perspective, these problems were exacerbated by the lack of a cohesive constitutional framework able to join the dots between the 2011 interim Constitutional Declaration, the 2015 Libyan Political Agreement and the LPDF's road map. The result was institutional chaos that derailed plans to hold elections in December 2021.

Economic

The weaponisation of oil:
Converging interests between Haftar and political milieus in Tripolitania had already emerged in September 2020, when an interim agreement between warring factions in Sochi, Russia, had ended the oil blockade imposed by the LNA in Libya. As a result of this agreement, control of oil revenues remained in the hands of the National Oil Corporation (NOC), with funds remaining frozen in the accounts of the Libyan Foreign Bank (LFB), a subsidiary of the Central Bank of Libya (CBL) based in Tripoli.

This temporary mechanism did not outlive the resuming institutional split. Control of oil revenues returned as a point of contention between rival factions, especially in the aftermath of the NOC's decision to disburse US$8 billion to the GNU in April 2022. In response, tribal leaders and protesters in areas under the control of the LNA were responsible for closures of oilfields and oil terminals, with the NOC forced to declare *force majeure* on oil exports. The resuming oil blockade was a clear attempt by Haftar to unseat Dbeibah and favour the entry of the GNS in the capital, just as the previous oil blockade imposed by the LNA in 2020 was intended to choke the GNA, depriving it of the oil revenues. As such, oil, the lifeline of Libya's economy, remains a powerful driver of the conflict, with ramifications extending well beyond the country, where oil markets are suffering from the effects of the ongoing conflict in Ukraine.

Key Events in 2021–22

POLITICAL EVENTS

10 March 2021
An HoR vote grants confidence to the GNU led by Prime Minister Abdul Hamid Dbeibah.

23 June
The Second Berlin Conference on Libya calls for elections to be held on 24 December 2021.

11 August
The LPDF fails to agree on a constitutional basis for elections.

9 September
The HoR approves a law allowing presidential elections to go ahead in December 2021.

21 September
The HoR passes a no-confidence motion against the GNU.

4 October
The HoR approves a law allowing parliamentary elections to go ahead in December 2021.

21 October
The Libya Stabilisation Conference takes place in Tripoli.

12 November
The International Conference on Libya in Paris calls for the withdrawal of mercenaries and foreign fighters from the country.

22 December
The HNEC postpones presidential elections scheduled to take place on 24 December.

MILITARY/VIOLENT EVENTS

14 March 2021
The LNA carries out four airstrikes against ISIS–Libya in Obari.

3 September
Clashes are reported in Tripoli between GNU-affiliated armed groups.

8 October
The Joint Military Commission (JMC) agrees an action plan to remove mercenaries and foreign fighters.

25 November
LNA-affiliated forces attack a court in Sabha, disrupting a session regarding Saif al-Islam's appeal against the rejection of his bid to run in the presidential elections.

16 December
Militias mobilise in Tripoli ahead of planned presidential elections.

17 January 2022
An improvised-explosive-device attack, later claimed by ISIS–Libya, targets the LNA in Umm al-Aranib, killing one person.

10 February 2022
The HoR votes to appoint Fathi Bashagha as Libya's new prime minister.

3 March
Members of the newly formed GNS are sworn in at a ceremony in Tobruk.

Mid-April
Protesters and tribal leaders force the closure of several oilfields and terminals in eastern and southern Libya in LNA-controlled areas.

10 March
Armed groups supporting the GNS withdraw following a confrontation with GNU-affiliated forces near Garabulli.

9 April
The LNA announces that it is suspending its activities in the JMC and boycotting the GNU.

17 May
Clashes erupt between rival militias in Tripoli after Bashagha enters the capital.

Responses to the Conflict

Security

The JMC (also known as 5+5) played a pivotal role in the stabilisation efforts that took place from October 2020 during the post-ceasefire period. Confidence-building measures, such as the exchange of prisoners of war and the reopening of the coastal road between Misrata and Sirte (closed during the third phase of the civil war), greatly contributed to easing tensions, particularly along the Sirte–Jufra axis, which still represents the front line between the rival camps. Furthermore, contact between high-ranking officers of both sides of the conflict never ceased, even when political tensions escalated. For example, the LAF chief of staff, Maj.-Gen. Mohammed al-Haddad, met twice with his counterpart in the LNA, Maj.-Gen. Abdul Razzaq al-Nazhuri, between December 2021 and January 2022 to discuss the reunification of the Libyan military.

In October 2021, the JMC agreed on a seminal action plan for a gradual, balanced and sequenced departure of all mercenaries, foreign fighters and foreign forces from Libya. Nevertheless, these ambitious plans often clashed with the reality of the facts on the ground. Despite the efforts to convince the relevant parties of the need to withdraw mercenaries and foreign fighters, by mid-2022 there was still a considerable lack of buy-in from the main interlocutors, including neighbouring states in the Sahel region. More importantly, recent developments highlighted significant cracks in the JMC framework, which has suffered from the political division resulting from the establishment of the GNS. In particular, the LNA's decision to suspend the activities of its representatives in the 5+5 cast a shadow over reconciliation prospects in the near future.

Diplomacy

The politics that characterised the twilight of the Trump administration in the US – and significantly contributed to escalating the conflict in Libya – has gradually been replaced by a different mindset in the region since US President Joe Biden took office. To a certain extent, Libya has benefitted from the rapprochement between regional foes actively involved in the conflict. Two rounds of high-level talks between Egypt and Turkey touched on the situation in Libya, where the two regional powers have adopted a strategy to diversify their alliances. Both Ankara and Cairo have reached out to former foes in Libya during the reporting period, cultivating relations with internal actors – an approach that indirectly contributed to the stabilisation during 2021.[11]

At the multilateral level, the UN-led peace process lost momentum, particularly following the resignation of UN envoy Ján Kubiš. He was replaced by Stephanie Williams, appointed as UN special adviser on Libya to UN Secretary-General António Guterres. The international community's push for elections (expressed via the international conferences held last year in Berlin, Paris and Tripoli) proved to be short-sighted and risked plunging Libya back into civil war. In general, the progress of the three-track (political, economic and military) Libyan political

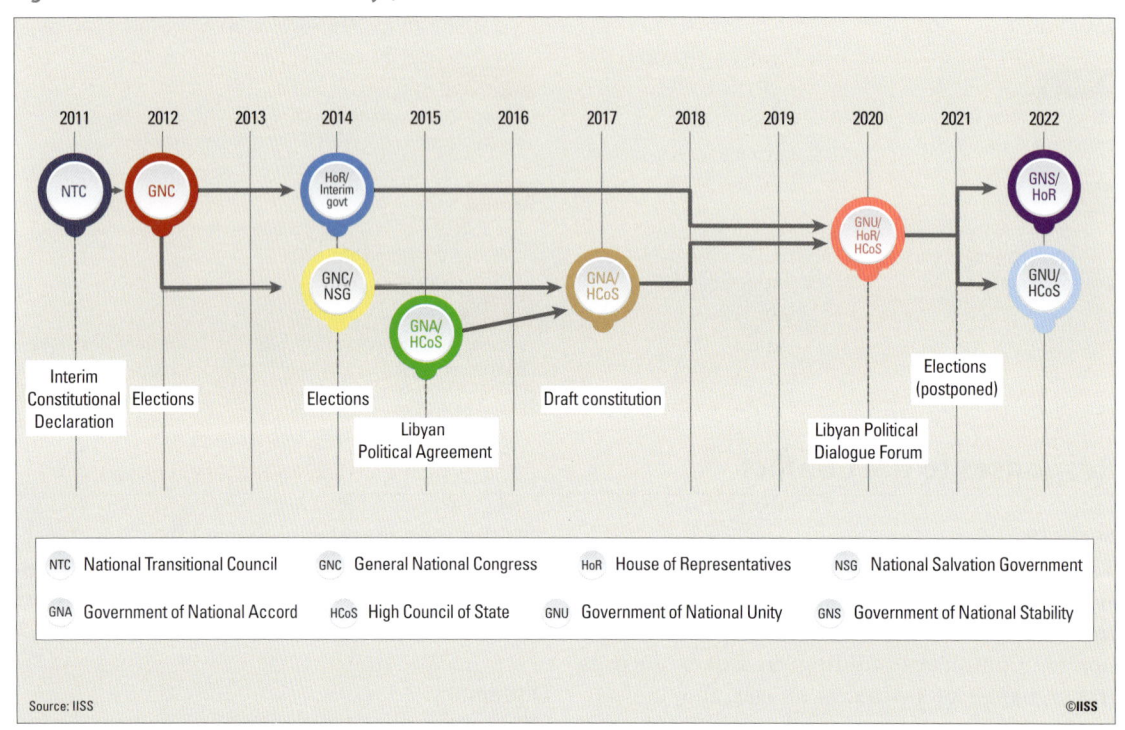

Figure 1: Parallel administrations in Libya, 2011–22

dialogue has been hesitant. The LPDF suffered from internal divisions during the reporting period that pushed the body to the point of irrelevance, making it unable to function as a surrogate to kick-start the political dialogue and overcome the multiple obstacles posed by an assertive and confrontational HoR.

As the peace process began to falter, Libyan actors increasingly took matters into their own hands, creating frictions with the UN-led political dialogue. In particular, the presidency of the HoR became a focal point for controversial political initiatives intended to break the stalemate while monopolising mediation efforts. The elections laws unilaterally adopted by the parliament in Tobruk took out any reference to simultaneous presidential and parliamentary elections, which continued to lack any constitutional basis. Making matters worse, the focus on holding presidential elections contributed to escalating the dormant political polarisation in the country, drawing attention to the hyper-personalisation of Libyan politics and the resulting power struggle.

The delicate constitutional process also became a hostage of increasingly fractured Libyan politics. With the complicity of the Tripoli-based High Council of State (HCoS), in February 2022 the HoR approved the 12th Constitutional Amendment, creating a committee of 24 experts tasked with drafting a new constitution that would replace the 2017 draft approved by the Constitutional Drafting Committee. In a context characterised by the controversial establishment of a new parallel government, the alternative political road map approved by the HoR also called for elections to be held by April 2023, highlighting the dilatory nature of these initiatives, which serve to maintain a status quo of benefit to Libya's political elite.

Conflict Outlook

Political scenarios

The main Libyan parties and involved international actors expect the timeline of the LPDF's road map to run until June 2022, and developments in the lead-up to this deadline will be particularly crucial for Libya's political trajectory. Following the postponement of elections in December 2021, international support to the GNU (in particular from the P3+2)[12] has shielded Dbeibah from the HoR's attempt to unseat him. However, this support has also revived tensions between the eastern camp and the international community. This confrontation also raised legitimate questions about the rhetoric behind the UN-sponsored 'Libyan-led' and 'Libyan-owned' political dialogue, which rings hollow at a time when Libya's main actors effectively present their own, competing road maps.

Facing mounting criticism over his government's spending spree and marred by corruption scandals and bribery allegations, Dbeibah also proposed a plan to hold elections in June 2022. However, the deteriorated security context that has resulted from the resumption of the oil blockade does not bode well for the electoral process. Renewing the legitimacy of discredited institutions that evidently lack a popular mandate is still seen, by international and Libyan actors alike, as the only option to solve the Libyan crisis. However, this approach has already proven counterproductive ahead of the postponed presidential elections,[13] triggering a chain of events that eventually led to parallel authorities. In the absence of a social contract represented by a constitutional framework capable of serving as a guard rail against absolutism and authoritarian tendencies, there remains a risk that powerful figures in Libyan politics will return to centre stage and disrupt the electoral process once more.

Escalation potential and conflict-related risks

A renewed focus on holding presidential elections would likely lead to a new mobilisation of armed groups. These groups hold the effective power on the ground and have shown their ability to navigate Libya's ever-changing political landscape and adapt to new realities. An example of this reconfiguration is the Stability Support Apparatus,[14] which, together with the Sumoud Brigade and the Tripoli Revolutionary Brigade, put significant pressure on Dbeibah, forcing him to overturn a decision to replace the commander of the Tripoli Military Zone just a few days ahead of the planned elections. The episode highlighted Dbeibah's inability to rein in armed groups that, while nominally supportive of the GNU, use it to gain access to political and financial institutions in the capital.

Militias represent a significant obstacle to a fair, free and credible electoral process, as shown by events in Sabha in November 2021, when the LNA-affiliated Tariq Ibn Ziyadh Brigade attacked a court to prevent Saif al-Islam Gadhafi's lawyer from filing an appeal against the rejection of his client's bid to run in the presidential elections. The incident highlighted the rifts in the counter-revolutionary camp between Haftar and Gadhafi.

In the short term, the greatest risk of escalation stems from the confrontation between armed groups supporting the GNS and those backing the GNU, especially in the aftermath of the closure of oilfields and terminals in areas under LNA control. Clashes in Tripoli on 17 May 2022 not only showed Bashagha's inability to enter Tripoli and provide Haftar with further influence and leverage; they also highlighted how the balance of power between armed groups is shifting in Tripolitania.

Strategic implications and global influences

The rapprochement between rival powers in the region has helped to calm domestic tensions, preventing Libya from falling into armed conflict once again. Time will tell whether the regional detente will be a structural re-adjustment or just a temporary realignment between former foes in the age of normalisation following the Abraham Accords. The push for normalisation with Israel had significant ramifications for Libya, especially after reports indicated that a plane belonging to Haftar had landed in Tel Aviv in November 2021 bearing a delegation to discuss military and diplomatic assistance from Israel in exchange for normalisation of ties.

Receding regional tensions have, however, left room for a subtle form of global competition over Libya's resources, especially in the aftermath of Russia's invasion of Ukraine in February 2022. The Wagner Group's presence at oilfields and terminals in Libya was particularly worrying during the reporting period given the informal ties between Wagner and the LNA (and consequently the GNS).[15] Taking advantage of Libya's chronic instability, Moscow could effectively use its presence in Libya as leverage to disrupt energy supplies to Europe, in yet another form of hybrid warfare waged by Russia-affiliated local actors along NATO's southern flank.

Notes

1. The HoR unilaterally passed one law for presidential elections and another for general elections. Critics said that Saleh violated internal proceedings, did not obtain the agreement of the other chamber of the parliament in Tripoli, as required by the law, and passed the law without the required quorum.
2. Umberto Profazio, 'The Bonds That Tie Libya and Ukraine', TRENDS Research & Advisory, 17 May 2022.
3. Jason Pack, 'Kingdom of Militias: Libya's Second War of Post-Qadhafi Succession', Italian Institute for International Political Studies, 31 May 2019; and Jalel Harchaoui and Mohamed-Essaïd Lazib, 'Proxy War Dynamics in Libya', Virginia Tech School of Public and International Affairs in Association with Virginia Tech Publishing, 2019.
4. Ahmed Elumami and Ayman al-Warfalli, 'Battle Rages for Libya's Capital, Airport Bombed', Reuters, 8 April 2019.
5. Pack, 'Kingdom of Militias: Libya's Second War of Post-Qadhafi Succession'.
6. Arnaud Delalande, 'Forces on the Libyan Ground: Who Is Who', Italian Institute for International Political Studies, 28 May 2018.
7. 'Twenty-ninth Report of the Analytical Support and Sanctions Monitoring Team Submitted Pursuant to Resolution 2368 (2017) Concerning ISIL (Da'esh), Al-Qaida and Associated Individuals and Entities', UN Security Council, S/2022/83, 3 February 2022, p. 11.
8. Nate Herring, 'Prime Minister of Libyan Government of National Accord Visits AFRICOM', US Africa Command, 6 April 2017.
9. Fehim Tastekin, 'Three Challenging Scenarios for Turkey in Libya', Al-Monitor, 14 March 2022.
10. Fonti "Nova": almeno 1.500 mercenari russi del gruppo Wagner ancora presenti in Libia' [Sources 'Nova': At Least 1,500 Russian Mercenaries of the Wagner Group Still Present in Libya], Nova News, 12 May 2022.
11. Turkey in particular has started to reach out to relevant political actors in the east. See Fehim Tastekin, 'Turkey Rethinks Its Libya Policy', Al-Monitor, 14 February 2022.
12. France, the United Kingdom and the US, plus Germany and Italy.
13. Tarek Megerisi, 'Libya's Fatally Flawed Elections Are a Catch-22', DAWN, 27 August 2021.
14. See Jalel Harchaoui, 'A Dysfunctional Peace: How Libya's Fault Lines Were Redrawn', War on the Rocks, 24 February 2022.
15. Libya's New Period of Uncertainty', IISS *Strategic Comments*, vol. 28, no. 7, 1 April 2022.

EGYPT

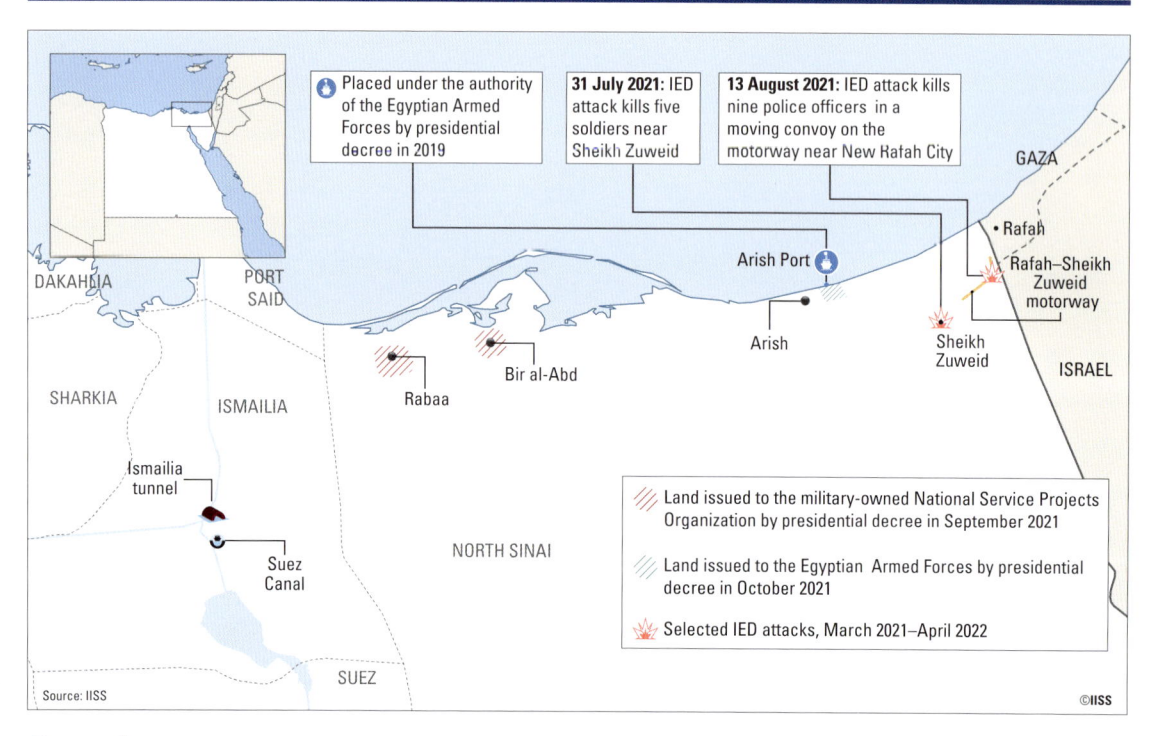

Map of North Sinai region showing:
- *Placed under the authority of the Egyptian Armed Forces by presidential decree in 2019* (Arish Port)
- *31 July 2021: IED attack kills five soldiers near Sheikh Zuweid*
- *13 August 2021: IED attack kills nine police officers in a moving convoy on the motorway near New Rafah City*
- Locations: Dakahlia, Port Said, Sharkia, Ismailia, Suez, Ismailia tunnel, Suez Canal, Rabaa, Bir al-Abd, Arish, Sheikh Zuweid, Rafah–Sheikh Zuweid motorway, Rafah, Gaza, Israel, North Sinai
- Legend: Land issued to the military-owned National Service Projects Organization by presidential decree in September 2021; Land issued to the Egyptian Armed Forces by presidential decree in October 2021; Selected IED attacks, March 2021–April 2022

Source: IISS

Overview

The instability in the Sinai Peninsula has a long history, dating back to 1948 and Egypt–Israel tensions following the latter's founding. The Camp David Accords of 1978, which heralded a period of peace between the two countries, resulted in the peninsula becoming a demilitarised zone. However, it continued to see low-level insurgency by armed groups that had operated in the area for decades. In early 2011, the Arab Spring protests in Egypt and the ensuing regime change resulted in a political vacuum in Cairo and a prolonged period of insecurity. Armed groups capitalised on this context, becoming more active and visible. Since 2014, the most prominent armed group has been Sinai Province, an offshoot of the Islamic State (ISIS) that was formed from the al-Qaeda-allied Ansar Beit Al Maqdis (ABM) after the latter pledged allegiance to ISIS in November that year. The Sinai Peninsula has remained under a state of emergency since the military ousted president Muhammad Morsi in July 2013. Following the formation of Sinai Province, a more proactive and sustained insurgency emerged in the region. While the group has been unable to gain control over most of the peninsula, it has had a continuous presence in North Sinai since 2014 and has conducted regular terror attacks focused on security and military outposts and targets.

The Egyptian Armed Forces (EAF) has sought to remilitarise the area in order to fight the insurgency. In 2018 it launched a year-long campaign, *Operation Sinai*, which saw up to 75,000 troops deployed to the region. At its peak in July 2015, the insurgency battled the EAF for control of Sheikh Zuweid in North Sinai. The presence of ISIS drew in Egypt's allies (namely Israel and the United States, which have provided reconnaissance and intelligence-gathering support), although the number and impact of insurgent attacks have diminished significantly in recent years. In addition, since late 2018 the military has been arming local militia groups that support its fight against the insurgency. Reporting to the Directorate of Military Intelligence (DMI), local Bedouin leaders have long been engaged in providing intelligence to the security forces about suspected militants; increasingly,

Armed Conflict Global Relevance Indicator (ACGRI)

Egypt
- Incidence: 2
- Geopolitical impact: 2
- Human impact: 0

Key Conflict Statistics

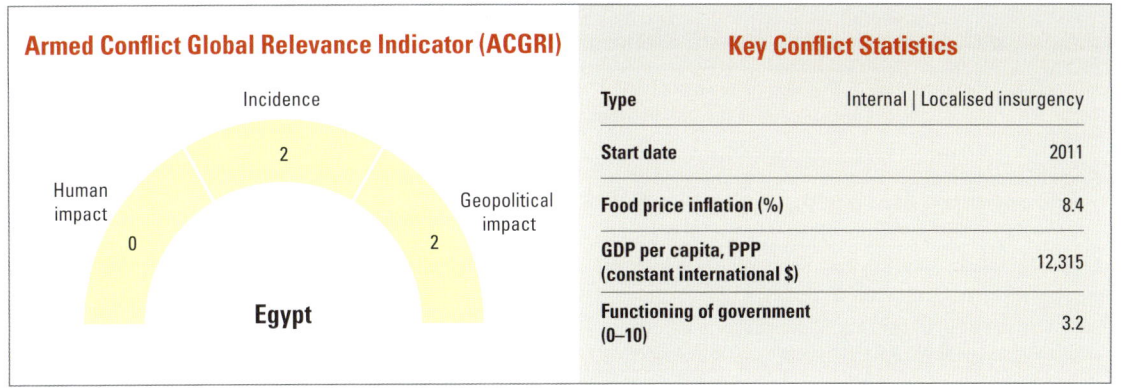

Type	Internal | Localised insurgency
Start date	2011
Food price inflation (%)	8.4
GDP per capita, PPP (constant international $)	12,315
Functioning of government (0–10)	3.2

ACGRI pillars: IISS calculation based on multiple sources for 2021 and January–April 2022 (scale: 0–100). See Notes on Methodology and Data Appendix for further details on Key Conflict Statistics.

armed Bedouin groups form part of the defence against the insurgency.

For the most part the situation in North Sinai was calm in 2021, resulting in a significant return of citizens displaced during the insurgency's peak in earlier years. Much of this trend was localised to Rafah and areas bordering the Gaza Strip, which had seen the most violent fighting since 2015. The westward shift of Sinai Province's activities continued in 2021. As a result, the east saw a revival of sorts, which was further complemented by the intermittent opening of the Rafah border to allow Palestinians to cross. However, US forces' killing of ISIS leader Abu Ibrahim al-Hashimi al-Qurashi in northwestern Syria in February 2022 prompted a spate of ISIS-related violence across the region, with retaliation attacks seen in Egypt, Iraq, Libya and Syria. The result was a steady uptick in violence. A major attack took place close to the Suez Canal in May 2022. Insurgents attacked a water-pumping station, targeting both security personnel and the region's economic infrastructure and killing 11 soldiers.[1] It was the largest attack carried out by ISIS operatives in the Sinai Peninsula in several years. A second attack in northern Sinai several days later killed five soldiers.[2] North Sinai also continued to experience low-level violence affecting civilians (including kidnappings) during the reporting period, notably in the main cities of Arish, Sheikh Zuweid, Bir al-Abd and Rafah, with civilians across the peninsula seeing their freedom of movement significantly curtailed.

Conflict Parties

Egyptian Armed Forces (EAF)

Strength: 438,500 active armed personnel, 479,000 in reserve.

Areas of operation: North Sinai, South Sinai and Red Sea governorates, militarised triangle (Halayeb/Shalateen), Western Desert and Salloum border (Matrouh governorate – the western border with Libya).

Leadership and structure: Supreme Council of the Armed Forces, led by Maj.-Gen. Mohamed Zaki (defence minister) and Maj.-Gen. Osama Askar (chief of staff of armed forces). The EAF consists of the army, air force and navy; paramilitary forces are formed under the Ministry of Interior.

History: The first troop deployments into the Sinai Peninsula to fight the Islamic State began in 2014, triggered by the pledge of allegiance to the Islamic State by militants in the area.

Objectives: Control border security and address all national-security threats originating abroad. Since 2013 it has remilitarised the Sinai Peninsula, notably in North Sinai.

Opponents and affiliates/allies:
Opponents: Sinai Province, ABM and the Muslim Brotherhood.
Allies: France, Germany, Israel, Russia, United Arab Emirates (UAE), United Kingdom, US.

Resources/capabilities: The EAF does not publicise its defence budget. 2021 estimates placed the budget at US$4.84 billion, or 1.2% of GDP. It also receives around US$1.3bn in Foreign Military Assistance annually from the US.

Directorate of Military Intelligence (DMI)

Strength: Unknown, although the ascension of Abdel Fattah al-Sisi to Egypt's presidency in 2014 strengthened the DMI within the armed forces. Sisi was director of the DMI between 2010 and 2012.

Areas of operation: North Sinai governorate (train and assist programme with local Bedouin militias), eastern Libya (train and assist programme with the Libyan National Army).

Leadership and structure: Maj.-Gen. Khaled Megawer (director).

History: The DMI has been the main military actor in the peninsula since December 2018, following the deadly terror attack at the Rawda Mosque in November 2018 that killed over 320 people. The DMI works in conjunction with the EAF to conduct operations in the Sinai against the insurgency.

Objectives: Protect the state, DMI and Sisi from any attack, monitor foreign threats towards Egypt (alongside the General Intelligence Services), lead on local intelligence gathering and community support in the Sinai Peninsula.

Opponents and affiliates/allies:
Opponents: Sinai Province.
Allies: EAF, General Intelligence Services.

Resources/capabilities: Unknown.

Sinai Province

Strength: Estimated 800–1,200 militants.[3] Since 2019 it includes small numbers of Palestinian militants and ISIS foreign fighters displaced from conflict in Iraq and Syria.

Areas of operation: North Sinai.

Leadership and structure: As of June 2019, led by Abu Jafar al-Ansari *(nom de guerre)*. Some evidence suggests that there are training camps in Sinai and the Gaza Strip. Several jihadists are known to have travelled to Syria for training, suggesting that the ISIS leadership structure periodically plays a role in the Sinai insurgency.

History: First established in November 2014 with a pledge of allegiance by ABM fighters to then-ISIS leader Abu Bakr al-Baghdadi. Its activities reached a peak in 2017 with a series of terror attacks in mainland Egypt as well as in the Sinai Peninsula. The group has never been able to seize significant territory in the peninsula but remains an active insurgency.

Objectives: Establish an Islamic state and fight the EAF.

Opponents and affiliates/allies:
Opponents: EAF, wider Egyptian security forces, Israel, non-Sunni Muslims and non-Muslims.

Resources/capabilities: Anecdotal evidence suggests most income is received via economic smuggling between the Sinai Peninsula and Gaza via tunnels. The group also benefits from an active weapons-smuggling war economy bringing weapons from Libya into Sinai.

Conflict Drivers

Geopolitical and geostrategic influences

Regional drivers:
In light of Israel's besiegement of the Gaza Strip, goods and weapons are smuggled into the latter from the Sinai Peninsula via the Rafah border. The Libyan conflict and broader destabilisation across other parts of Africa have led to an increase in weapons smuggling into Egypt and towards the Sinai Peninsula. Funding from Hamas and possibly ISIS supported the creation of localised training camps in North Sinai that, according to Egyptian military intelligence, fuelled the Gaza Strip's militarisation and provided a steady count of militants for Sinai Province.

Among disaffected residents, broad-based Islamists and militants, there is an allegiance to the broader desire for an Islamic state, rooted in the purging of the regime of President Abdel Fattah al-Sisi and the security apparatus that represented it. While international security concerns have prompted informal US and Israeli support to Egypt on intelligence and reconnaissance, fighting the insurgency in Sinai has remained an almost entirely Egyptian undertaking.

Economic and social

Sinai's marginalisation:
The enduring grievances of Sinai's citizens have historically been the primary driver of extremism in the region. Sinai was separated – physically and figuratively – from the Egyptian mainland as a result of the Arab–Israeli wars of the 1960s and 1970s, and remains so in 2022. The peninsula is significantly less developed than mainland Egypt, with subpar access to

basic public services. Cairo has sought to address Sinai's underdevelopment via a large-scale redevelopment plan, touted by the military and launched in 2019, which has seen mainly the building of new cities, such as New Rafah City and New Arish City, and massive development projects along the coast as ports have been developed and mobilised for trade. In 2021, the military escorted displaced residents back to new homes built across North Sinai as part of a broader opening of access that followed a prolonged lull in violent insurgent attacks.

Since Sinai Province was established, support for the insurgency has waned, with an increasing number of communities supporting the military against the jihadists. The military, under the leadership of the DMI, has supported the arming of certain Bedouin groups that have become de facto militias focused on rooting out suspected militants and providing intelligence to the EAF on the ground.

Key Events in 2021–22

POLITICAL EVENTS

5 January 2021
The al-Ula Agreement is signed in Saudi Arabia, beginning a rapprochement between Bahrain, Egypt, Saudi Arabia and the UAE with Qatar.

21 May
Egypt brokers a ceasefire to end an 11-day conflict between Israel and Hamas.

14 September
The US State Department announces that it will withhold US$130 million in annual military aid to Egypt unless Cairo addresses human-rights issues in the country.

23 September
President Sisi issues a decree designating close to 364 square kilometres of land in Sinai to the National Service Projects Organization (NSPO), which is owned and managed by the military and assists with the implementation of economic-development projects.

16 October
Sisi issues a decree that designates approximately 2.3 square kilometres of land in Arish to the armed forces.

MILITARY/VIOLENT EVENTS

31 July 2021
Five soldiers are killed when an improvised explosive device (IED) explodes near Sheikh Zuweid.

1 August
The EAF announces that recent operations in North Sinai resulted in the deaths of 89 Sinai Province militants and the seizure of IEDs, explosive belts, machine guns and vehicles.

12 August
An IED explodes in New Rafah City, killing nine police officers in a moving security convoy. Thirteen militants are killed in subsequent military raids, according to the EAF.

10 September
Senior Sinai Province leader Abu Hamza al-Qadi (also known as Mohamed Saad Kamel) surrenders to an Egyptian tribal union and is handed over to military authorities.

25 October
Sisi announces the end of the nationwide state of emergency in place since 2017. The state of emergency is officially lifted on 5 January 2022.

27 October
Maj.-Gen. Askar is appointed chief of staff of the armed forces.

26 April 2022
Sisi calls for a national dialogue with the political opposition and re-establishes the Presidential Amnesty Committee to address the issue of Egypt's thousands of pre-trial detainees and political prisoners.

7 May 2022
An attack on a water-pumping station close to the Suez Canal kills 11 security personnel and injures ten others.

10 May
An IED explodes near Rafah, killing ten soldiers.

Conflict Outlook

Political scenarios

In April 2022, Sisi announced plans for a national dialogue, which is scheduled to begin in July. He also announced the reformation and new mandate of the Presidential Amnesty Committee, which purports to aid the release of pre-trial detainees and jailed activists. Despite the committee's wide mandate and the apparent opportunity this development presents, people involved in violence – notably those jailed on suspicion of being a member of the Muslim Brotherhood (MB) – or alleged militants from North Sinai are not eligible for consideration for amnesty or release. The dialogue committee has also refused to allow the MB and MB-affiliated political actors to participate in the dialogue process. The situation in North Sinai is also not part of the dialogue mandate.

Escalation potential and conflict-related risks

The insurgency in North Sinai appeared to intensify in mid-2022, with Sinai Province carrying out increasingly bold and deadly attacks against Egyptian security personnel. While attacks in recent years focused on police apparatus in the governorate, over 20 EAF soldiers were killed in attacks in May 2022, the highest combined death toll sustained in two separate attacks since 2018.

The recent uptick in insurgent attacks coincided with rising food insecurity across the global south – an effect of the war in Ukraine. Egypt is in a particularly precarious position given its reliance on Russia and Ukraine for over 55% of its wheat supply.[4] Rising inflation and food insecurity will be felt nationwide: Sinai residents will be no less affected, while the mass military-infrastructure overhaul, which has increased Sisi's popularity (or at least silenced disaffected citizens to an extent), will likely no longer be able to stem the growing dissatisfaction of the domestic population.

The increase in Sinai Province attacks also coincided with a warming of Egypt–Israel relations in early 2022, with Sisi receiving Israeli Prime Minister Naftali Bennett in Sharm el-Sheikh on two occasions. While the central tenet of ISIS ideology is to create a caliphate, also key to ISIS doctrine is the plight of Palestinians and an opposition to the Israeli state. Rising instability in Libya may also spill over into Sinai. While rarely noted as a major conflict driver in the area, shifting regional geopolitics could spark a prolonged period of increased insecurity in the peninsula. Even if Sinai Province activity subsides after the summer months (following a pattern visible in previous years), the group remains live and potent, and the EAF and affiliated armed forces will likely continue to struggle to extinguish the insurgent threat.

Strategic implications and global influences

Instability in North Sinai affects both national and regional strategic objectives – notably in relation to the security of the Suez Canal and broader Red Sea security. The recent escalation of violence in 2022 is a reminder of the insurgency's disruptive and dangerous impact on Egypt's national security and stability as a whole. The country remains on high alert along all its borders, notably as the political and security situations in Libya and Sudan deteriorate.

While Egypt has engaged in active rapprochement efforts with Qatar, it has remained lukewarm in attempts to reach a detente with Turkey amid continued animosity over Ankara's support of the Muslim Brotherhood, including after the military ouster of Morsi. Meanwhile, Egypt has stepped up its relations with Israel, Saudi Arabia and the UAE, building strong economic ties as countries across the region look to address their extreme climate vulnerabilities, which exacerbate domestic tensions and economic pressures. Despite the ongoing security challenges, Egypt has successfully rebranded itself as a major pillar of the Middle East security architecture, highlighted by the role it played in brokering the ceasefire between Hamas and Israel in May 2021.

Notes

[1] 'Egypt: Militant Attack Kills 11 Troops in Sinai, Army Says', DW, 7 May 2022.

[2] 'Five Egyptian Soldiers Killed in Second Deadly Sinai Attack', Reuters, 11 May 2022.

[3] 'Factbox: Pushed into the Shadows, Islamic State Still Has Global Reach', Reuters, 5 February 2022.

[4] Amr Kandil, 'What the Future Holds for Egypt's Wheat Supply amid Global Food Crisis', Ahram Online, 23 May 2022.

TURKEY

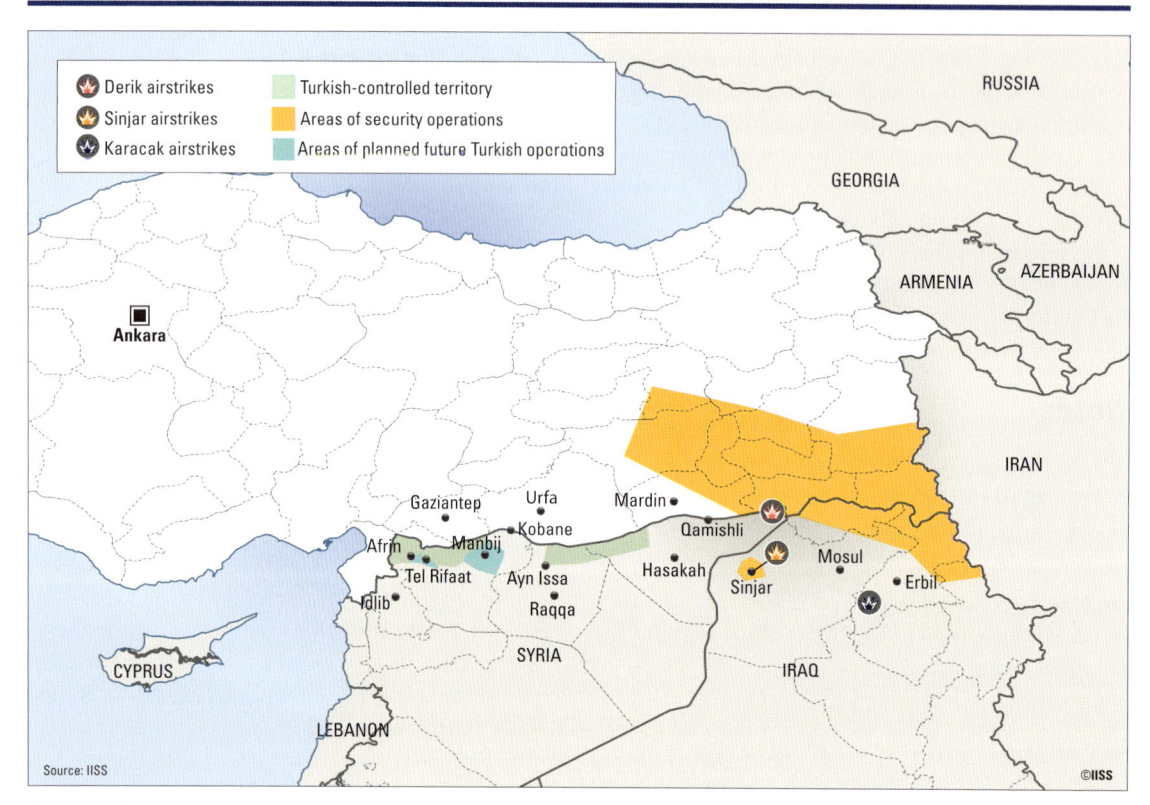

Map legend:
- Derik airstrikes
- Sinjar airstrikes
- Karacak airstrikes
- Turkish-controlled territory
- Areas of security operations
- Areas of planned future Turkish operations

Source: IISS

Overview

Turkey's fight against the Kurdistan Workers' Party (PKK) began in the early 1980s when Abdullah Ocalan created the backbone of the organisation and launched a recruitment campaign for a Kurdish secessionist militia. Since then the fight between Turkish security forces and the PKK has often overshadowed the broader issue at stake: the rights of Turkey's Kurdish minority and its lack of political recognition.

Originally operating between southeastern Turkey and northern Syria, throughout the 1980s and 1990s PKK militias launched insurgent-style attacks against Turkish police, gendarmerie and military forces. They also targeted civilians, especially those cooperating with security forces in areas with a well-established Kurdish presence.

During the first 20 years of conflict, several ceasefires and attempts at peace negotiations were abandoned due to either changing political moods in Ankara or escalations of violence. Ocalan's capture by Turkish forces in 1999 was a turning point for the PKK, which suffered a major organisational setback as a result and struggled to regroup for several years.

The PKK leadership's hawkish wing eventually overcame the organisation's internal strife. It exploited the chaos triggered by the 2003 US-led invasion of Iraq to reorganise its militias in the Qandil Mountains, near the border between Turkey and Iraq's Kurdistan Regional Government (KRG). Between 2004 and 2009, the Turkey–PKK conflict returned to a high level of intensity, particularly following the emergence of a PKK splinter group – the Kurdistan Freedom Falcons (TAK) – which carried out attacks targeting tourist destinations in Turkey.

Partly motivated by a desire to distance itself from TAK, the new PKK leadership declared a new, unilateral ceasefire in 2006. Predictably, uninterrupted skirmishes between Turkish forces and the PKK and the intensification of the former's security operations against the group nullified its impact, with clashes returning to their previous intensity and

Armed Conflict Global Relevance Indicator (ACGRI)

- Incidence: 3
- Human impact: 5
- Geopolitical impact: 3

Turkey

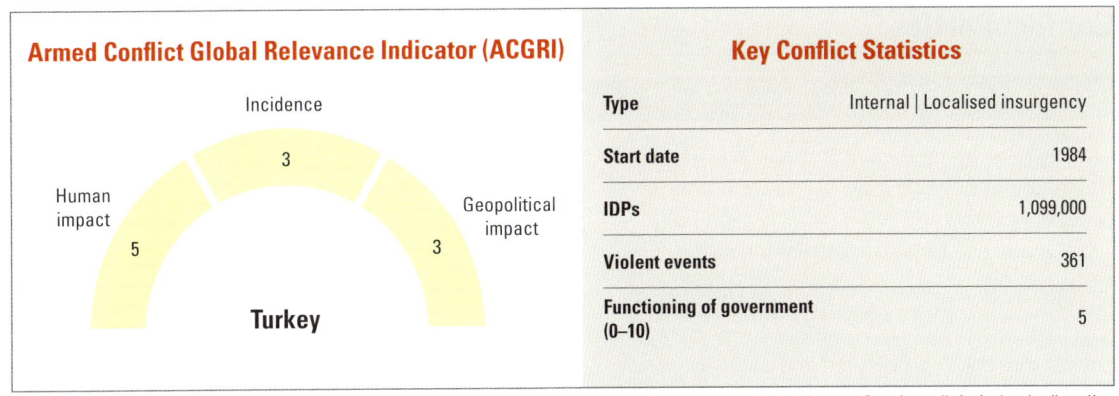

Key Conflict Statistics

Type	Internal | Localised insurgency
Start date	1984
IDPs	1,099,000
Violent events	361
Functioning of government (0–10)	5

ACGRI pillars: IISS calculation based on multiple sources for 2021 and January–April 2022 (scale: 0–100). See Notes on Methodology and Data Appendix for further details on Key Conflict Statistics.

frequency not long after the ceasefire was declared. Since then, Turkey has substantially increased the number and intensity of airstrikes and special-forces operations conducted around the Qandil Mountains to eradicate PKK camps.

The two vectors of Turkish military operations – towards southeastern Turkey and towards northern Iraq – remained unaltered until 2012, when the second-order effects of the Syrian civil war and the consolidation of Kurdish militias' power in northern Syria opened a third front line in the Turkey–PKK conflict. In light of the rapid expansion of the Islamic State (ISIS), the People's Protection Units (YPG) and the Women's Protection Units (YPJ) quickly became of immense geostrategic importance to the international coalition fighting ISIS.[1] Despite having substantive ties to the PKK, which many within the anti-ISIS coalition had listed as a terrorist organisation, the YPG and YPJ received considerable financial and military support as part of the broader Syrian Democratic Forces (SDF) – from France, Germany, the United States and the United Kingdom, among others. This support put the SDF on a collision course with Ankara, which reacted by cracking down on alleged PKK activities inside Turkey (especially in the aftermath of the 2016 failed military coup) and launching a major military campaign into northern Syria. Enlisting the support of a coalition of rebel groups gathered under the so-called Syrian National Army (SNA), the campaign sought to create a buffer zone along the Syria–Turkey border. As is the case with the fight against the PKK within Turkey and northern Iraq, Ankara's efforts in northern Syria seem to have reached a stalemate. Following territorial gains made in 2016–19, various Turkish military offensives have failed to make any major progress.

During the reporting period, low-intensity skirmishes continued to occur within Turkey alongside military operations that sought to disrupt PKK activities. While Turkish forces intensified the campaign against PKK camps in northern Iraq in 2021 and early 2022, the group seemed to further consolidate its presence in northern Syria.

In February 2022, a major airstrike involving some 60 fighter aircraft and uninhabited aerial vehicles (UAVs) targeted the areas surrounding Derik in northern Syria and the Sinjar and Karacak regions of northern Iraq, with Turkish governmental sources reporting that 80 major PKK targets (headquarters, training camps and depots) were destroyed.[2] In mid-2022, Turkish President Recep Tayyip Erdoğan declared that he would authorise a new major offensive in northern Syria to take control of Tel Rifaat and Manbij, two cities of strategic importance firmly held by the SDF.[3]

The Turkey–PKK conflict gained international attention in May 2022 when Finland and Sweden announced their intention to join NATO. Turkey, whose approval would be necessary for their admission, accused the countries of harbouring PKK militants, citing their repeated denials of Turkey's requests to extradite PKK members.

Conflict Parties

Turkish Armed Forces (TSK)

Strength: 512,000 total (355,200 active military, 156,800 active paramilitary). 5,000–10,000 personnel deployed in Iraq, 10,000–15,000 deployed in Syria.[4]

Areas of operation: Southeastern Turkey, northern and northwestern Iraq, northern and northwestern Syria.

Leadership and structure: President Recep Tayyip Erdoğan (commander-in-chief); Gen. (retd) Hulusi Akar (minister of national defence); Gen. Yasar Guler (chief of general staff). Turkish army units operating under the Turkish Land Forces Command and squadrons carrying out airstrikes operating under the Air Force Command are subordinate to the chief of general staff. Gendarmerie units reporting to the Gendarmerie Command are subordinate to the Ministry of Interior.

History: Rebuilt following the collapse of the Ottoman Empire in 1922. Significantly restructured after the country joined NATO in 1951, to become NATO's second-largest armed force.

Objectives: Eradicate the PKK and preserve national unity.

Opponents and affiliates/allies:
Opponents: The PKK and its affiliate organisations, particularly the YPG/SDF in Syria.
Allies: Relies extensively on the SNA as a support force in northern Syria.

Resources/capabilities: Turkey's defence budget for 2021 was US$9.55 billion. Its military capabilities include air attack and intelligence, surveillance and reconnaissance assets, such as the F-16 and the *Bayraktar* TB2 UAV, armoured tanks and special-forces units.

Kurdistan Workers' Party (PKK)

Strength: 30,000 (estimate).

Areas of operation: Southeast Turkey, northern Iraq.

Leadership and structure: Abdullah Ocalan (ideological leader, despite his imprisonment since 1999); Murat Karayilan (acting leader on the ground since Ocalan's capture); Bahoz Erdal (military commander).
While operating under the same command and leadership, the PKK's armed wing is divided into the People's Defence Forces (HPG) and the Free Women's Unit (YJA STAR).

History: Founded by Ocalan in 1978. Engaged in an insurgency campaign against Turkish armed forces since 1984.

Objectives: Political and cultural recognition of the Kurdish minority in Turkey; adoption of a democratic federalist system of governance.

Opponents and affiliates/allies:
Opponents: TSK.
Allies: SDF/YPG in Syria.

Resources/capabilities: Depends on money-laundering activities and drug trafficking to raise revenues, as well as donations from the Kurdish community and diaspora and left-wing international supporters. The PKK relies on highly mobile units, employing guerrilla tactics against TSK targets.

(Turkey-sponsored) Syrian National Army (SNA)

Strength: 70,000 (estimate).[5]

Areas of operation: Northern and northwestern Syria.

Leadership and structure: Deployed alongside Turkish military forces and therefore operates under Turkish leadership. A conglomerate of dozens of different militias, ranging vastly in size, affiliation and ideology, composed of Syrian militants, who are trained and equipped by Turkey. Divided into seven main legions, each composed of a wide array of divisions and brigades. The National Front for Liberation (NLF), a coalition of more than ten rebel militias, is nominally incorporated within the SNA.

History: Created as a splinter group of the Turkey-backed Free Syrian Army. Trained and equipped by the Turkish government since 2016. In 2019, the Idlib-based and Turkey-sponsored National Front for Liberation was merged into the SNA.

Objectives: Take control of northern Syria.

Opponents and affiliates/allies:
Opponents: Syrian government forces, Iranian and Iranian-backed forces, SDF/YPG and ISIS.
Allies: Turkish forces.

Resources/capabilities: While a handful of formations have received US-sponsored training and equipment, the SNA has been fully reliant on Turkey's support since its creation. Turkey has provided small arms as well as infantry vehicles, and SNA military operations have benefitted from the Turkish army's fire support via artillery and airstrikes.

Syrian Democratic Forces (SDF) / People's Protection Units (YPG)

Strength: 100,000 (estimate).[6]

Areas of operation: Northern Syria.

Leadership and structure: Mazloum Kobani Abdi, also known as Sahin Cilo (military commander). Abdi is a former senior PKK member.
Syrian Kurds lead the YPG and the Women's Protection Units (YPJ), which maintain informal and ideological links to the PKK and provide the SDF's most capable fighters. The broader ranks of the SDF reflect the ethnic diversity of Syria's northeast, are largely non-ideological and in some areas are organised along geographic or tribal lines.

History: Created in 2015 as a direct response to the advance of ISIS into northern Syria, building on various pre-existing alliances. Since then, it has fought against ISIS and the Turkish military.

Objectives: Control northern Syria.

Opponents and affiliates/allies:
Opponents: Turkish forces, SNA, ISIS, al-Qaeda and affiliates.
Allies: PKK, Russia, Syrian regime, US.

Resources/capabilities: While it built upon the experience of its militias, since its formal creation, the SDF has been equipped, trained and advised by the US. SDF units are equipped with small arms and some infantry vehicles.

Conflict Drivers

Geopolitical and geostrategic influences

The PKK's transnational front line:
Regional turmoil has often had a significant impact on the Turkey–PKK conflict. Following the capture of Ocalan in 1999, the PKK faced significant organisational challenges. The chaos created by the 2003 invasion of Iraq presented an opportunity for the group to reorganise in northern Iraq. In a similar fashion, the rise and expansion of ISIS in northern Syria and Iraq resulted in the Syrian YPG and YPJ being identified by the international coalition fighting ISIS as the main actors on the ground that could be relied upon. With the creation of the SDF, its PKK/YPG component further solidified its credentials as the coalition's partner of choice.

Security

Turkey's and the PKK's preference for force over dialogue:
With several negotiation attempts having failed spectacularly over the conflict's 40-year course, Ankara and the PKK have preferred to use force to pursue their aims. This approach has contributed to prolonging the conflict despite the evident stalemate. The PKK relies extensively on insurgency-like, hit-and-run attacks that target Turkish military and security forces, while Ankara relentlessly pursues military action against PKK hideouts in the country's southeast and in northern Iraq. The consolidated presence of the YPG and YPJ in northern Syria has further expanded the conflict, as the Turkey–Syria border has become much easier to cross and much more porous than the mountainous border between Turkey and Iraq.

Political

Lack of political recognition for Kurdish minority:
At the core of the conflict is the unresolved issue of Kurdish requests for greater autonomy, rights and recognition from the state. Ankara's unwillingness to recognise the minority rights of the country's largest minority (estimated to number between ten and 15 million, roughly 20% of Turkey's population) is a deeply rooted source of political and social tensions. The PKK is one of the most radical, and yet popular, organisations fighting for change on this front.[7] There is also a transnational element that connects the PKK to parts of the broader Kurdish community in the region. This means the organisation's fight for recognition has found support in northern Iraq and Syria, and that, over decades, the conflict has transcended borders, with the return of a Syrian front line in recent years, after two decades in which the PKK mostly operated from Turkey and northern Iraq.

Key Events in 2021–22

POLITICAL EVENTS

9 April 2021
Turkey accuses Greece of harbouring PKK terrorists.

3 May
Baghdad raises a formal complaint with Ankara over the Turkish defence minister's visit to a Turkish base in Iraq.

21 June
Turkey's Constitutional Court puts the Peoples' Democratic Party (HDP) on trial over alleged ties to the PKK.

26 July
The US offers its condolences to Turkey for two Turkish soldiers killed in a PKK attack in Syria.

4 August
The PKK denies responsibility for starting wildfires in Antalya in late July.

2 September
The Constitutional Court grants the HDP additional time to prepare its defence in the ongoing closure trial.

18 October
Jailed HDP leader Selahattin Demirtas accuses President Erdoğan of exploiting the fight against the PKK for political purposes.

30 November
A KRG official says that the PKK's presence in northern Iraq is a source of instability.

8 December
Turkish Interior Minister Suleyman Soylu claims that there are fewer than 160 PKK members remaining in Turkey.

January 2022
Turkish prosecutors seek a terrorism trial for HDP MP Semra Guzel.

19–20 February
Turkish Minister of National Defence Hulusi Akar meets senior Iraqi officials to discuss Turkey's operations against the PKK.

16 March
SDF commander Sahin Cilo confirms that the SDF held a recent meeting with a US State Department delegation.

MILITARY/VIOLENT EVENTS

4 April 2021
Turkish security services kill two PKK improvised-explosive-device experts in Duhok, northern Iraq.

19 May
The PKK claims responsibility for an attack against a Turkish military base in Diyarbakir.

5 June
A PKK attack kills five Iraqi Peshmerga fighters in Duhok, northern Iraq.

5 August
Turkish security forces kill three PKK militants in Van province.

17 September
Ankara reports that 18,502 PKK militants have been killed since late July 2015.

28 September
Turkey claims a drone strike has killed a member of the PKK central executive committee in Qamishli, northern Syria.

30 October
Turkish forces capture four PKK militants in Avashin, northern Iraq.

22 November
Turkish forces kill six PKK militants in Bitlis province.

9 December
Turkey launches an airstrike in northern Iraq, killing six PKK militants, in retaliation for a PKK attack that killed three Turkish soldiers.

18 January 2022
Turkey launches *Operation Eren* against the PKK in the southeastern province of Bingol.

14 February
Turkish police detains 14 PKK-linked suspects in Adana province.

8 March
Turkish special forces kill 12 PKK militants in northern Syria.

Conflict Outlook

Political scenarios
Turkey's upcoming presidential and general elections, scheduled to take place in June 2023, are likely to lead to the ruling Justice and Development Party (AKP) adopting more nationalist rhetoric and policies since the party's hold on power hinges on its junior coalition partner, the right-wing Nationalist Movement Party (MHP). As a result, Ankara's 'no quarter' approach regarding PKK activities is likely to continue and potentially escalate. The government has often adopted such an approach when faced with other pro-Kurdish activities, conflating them with PKK actions. As such, it is probable that the HDP, which places the Kurdish issue at the forefront of its political agenda and is currently on trial for alleged ties to the PKK, will continue to be targeted by the government. The HDP obtained close to six million votes in the 2018 parliamentary elections.[8] It is Turkey's third-largest political party and the most successful pro-Kurdish party in the country's history; its banning could have massive political and social repercussions, further increasing the PKK's appeal among the most disenfranchised segments of the Kurdish minority.

Escalation potential and conflict-related risks
The anti-PKK narrative has also often played well domestically for incumbent governments, as Erdoğan demonstrated in the 2015 elections. His statements in mid-2022 – declaring that a new wave of major military operations against the SDF in Syria might be imminent – suggest that the president is once again appealing to this narrative. Moreover, these statements are unlikely to be empty words: an all-out escalation against the PKK in Turkey, northern Syria and northern Iraq could provide enough political and electoral momentum to ensure that the AKP is ahead of other parties in the opinion polls by the time of the June 2023 elections.

Prospects for peace
The conflict is likely to continue to be characterised by a lack of opportunities to de-escalate and negotiate a possible resolution. On the ground, military progress by either side is hardly conceivable, while the lack of areas of convergence between the two sides at the political level stymies prospects for dialogue.

Strategic implications and global influences
Divergences between Turkey, its Western allies and other NATO members over how to approach the PKK, the SDF and the broader Kurdish issue will continue to be a source of international tension. Turkey might use any one of the many flashpoints it is currently involved in as a bargaining chip: its position on Finland's and Sweden's bids to join NATO stands as a clear example of how Ankara is willing and able to jeopardise a highly significant diplomatic and geopolitical development to advance its anti-PKK agenda.

Notes

[1] Syria Conflict Report, pp. 134–45.
[2] Daren Butler, 'Turkish Warplanes Attack Kurdish Fighters in Iraq, Syria', Reuters, 2 February 2022.
[3] 'Turkey Says Syria Military Operation to Target Tal Rifaat, Manbij', Al-Jazeera, 1 June 2022.
[4] Salim Çevik, 'Turkey's Military Operations in Syria and Iraq', German Institute for International and Security Affairs (SWP), 30 May 2022; and 'Turkey Has Evacuated Seven Syrian Military Posts', Reuters, 18 December 2020.
[5] Omer Ozkizilcik, 'Uniting the Syrian Opposition: The Components of the National Army and the Implications of the Unification', SETA, October 2019, p. 10.
[6] Lead Inspector General for Operation Inherent Resolve, 'Operation Inherent Resolve: Lead Inspector General Report to the United States Congress April 1 2019 – June 30 2019', US Department of Defense, July 2019, p. 30.
[7] Natasha Turak, 'Conflict, Politics and History: Why Turkey Is Standing in the Way of Sweden and Finland's NATO Bids', CNBC, 8 June 2022.
[8] Dorian Jones, 'Turkey's Opposition HDP Faces Ban', Voice of America, 8 February 2021.

Regional Outlook

Most Middle Eastern conflicts are likely to remain in a state of protracted stalemate in the short to medium term. That said, there are at least two variables that could potentially drive escalation across the region. The first, and most obvious, is Russia's war in Ukraine and the conflict's impact on Ukrainian wheat production and global food prices. A second and related variable is the increasing likelihood of a global recession, which would have a disproportionate impact on the Middle East, leading to more food-insecure people and exacerbating conflicts and current fault lines in ways not immediately predictable.

Political scenarios

The political process is likely to remain gridlocked in many countries as rival powers struggle to impose their visions for a future state. In Iraq, the Sadrist bloc won the parliamentary elections in October 2021, increasing their seat share from 54 to 73 and becoming the largest single bloc in parliament.[1] However, months later, in June 2022, the entire Sadrist bloc resigned and withdrew from parliament after failing to form a government. In Libya, following the postponed presidential elections that had been scheduled to go ahead in December 2021, the United Nations hosted a series of talks between Libya's two largest rival groups, both of which appointed competing prime ministers.[2] However, there appeared to be little agreement on the most contentious issues, as both groups continue to focus on ensuring their survival instead of broader national goals.[3]

Escalation potential and regional spillovers

In both Yemen and Syria prospects for peace remain dim – despite a truce in the former and a military stalemate in the latter – while the potential for escalation remains high. Meanwhile, Turkish President Recep Tayyip Erdoğan continues to suggest that Turkey will launch a new offensive in northern Syria targeting the Syrian Democratic Forces (SDF). Should such a scenario unfold, the SDF has said that it may make common cause with Assad, potentially reshaping and reinvigorating the conflict.[4] Russia, which was frustrated by Ankara's decision to block warships in the Black Sea following its invasion of Ukraine, also urged Turkey not to launch the assault.[5] The Israeli–Palestinian conflict will continue to pose a high risk of escalation, even as Israel's growing relationship with the Arab Gulf states means that it will likely face less regional criticism over its actions in the Palestinian Territories.[6]

Strategic implications and global influences

Russia's war in Ukraine will have a significant impact on conflicts in the Middle East. In Egypt, the government elected to cut more than half a million citizens from ration-card rolls in response to the growing cost of wheat imports.[7] In Yemen, where approximately two-thirds of the population are 'going hungry' according to the UN Office for the Coordination of Humanitarian Affairs, food prices have risen 10% since Russia's invasion of Ukraine and may rise an additional 50% by the end of 2022.[8] Given these worrying developments, the de-escalations of 2021 and early 2022 may give way to renewed conflict in the coming year.

Notes

[1] 'Al-Sadr's Party Wins Most Seats in Iraqi Parliamentary Vote', Voice of America, 11 October 2021.

[2] Thomas M. Hill, 'What's Next for Libya's Protracted Conflict?', US Institute of Peace, 14 June 2022.

[3] Ibid.

[4] 'SDF Will Turn to Assad if Turkey Attacks in Syria', Al-Jazeera, 7 June 2022.

[5] 'Russia Urges Turkey Not to Launch Offensive on Northern Syria', Al-Jazeera, 2 June 2022.

[6] Already one prominent commentator close to the Saudi royal family has re-floated the decades-old idea that Palestinians should be incorporated into Jordan. See Ali Shihabi, 'The Hashemite Kingdom of Palestine', Al Arabiya, 8 June 2022.

[7] 'Egypt Revokes Ration Cards of Half-million Citizens', Al-Monitor, 14 June 2022.

[8] UN Office for the Coordination of Humanitarian Affairs, 'Ghada Eltahir Mudawi, Acting Director, Operations and Advocacy Division, Office for the Coordination of Humanitarian Affairs Remarks on Behalf of the USG for Humanitarian Affairs, Martin Griffiths, at Security Council Meeting on Yemen', ReliefWeb, 14 June 2022.

4 Sub-Saharan Africa

Regional Analysis	200	South Sudan	240	Cameroon	292
Conflict Reports		Ethiopia	252	**Conflict Summaries**	
The Sahel	204	Somalia	262	Mozambique	302
Lake Chad Basin	220	Great Lakes Region	270	Sudan	310
Central African Republic	230	Nigeria	282	**Regional Outlook**	320

UN and Armed Forces of the Democratic Republic of the Congo (FARDC) troops inspect the site of an Allied Democratic Forces (ADF) attack in Ruwenzori, DRC, 9 April 2021

Overview

The scourge of armed conflict in sub-Saharan Africa persisted in 2021 and early 2022. According to the Institute for Economics and Peace's *Global Peace Index 2022*, five of the ten least-peaceful countries globally were in the region: the Central African Republic (CAR), the Democratic Republic of the Congo (DRC), Somalia, South Sudan and Sudan.[1] Additionally, Burkina Faso, Mali, Niger, Nigeria and Somalia ranked among the top ten countries worldwide most impacted by terrorism.[2] During the reporting period, a worsening trend of political instability and authoritarianism was apparent on the continent. A number of coups were staged in 2020–22, including successful military coups in Burkina Faso, Chad, Guinea, Mali (twice) and Sudan, and failed ones in the CAR, Djibouti, Guinea-Bissau, Madagascar and Niger.[3]

Violence and lawlessness further escalated across the Western Sahel and Lake Chad Basin, where radical Islamist groups (both domestic and transnational) expanded their operations and reach to coastal countries. Inter-state tensions reignited in the Great Lakes Region, where ties between the DRC and Rwanda significantly worsened over protracted violence in eastern DRC. In East Africa, Ethiopia registered an uneasy ceasefire between the central government and the Tigray People's Liberation Front (TPLF), a truce that is deemed highly unstable given the multiple regional and identity-based conflicts taking place elsewhere in the country. At the time of writing, the Horn of Africa, particularly Somalia, is suffering from one of its worst droughts in memory, a development that further strains the ability of newly elected President Hassan Sheikh Mohamud to address the country's compounding conflict and humanitarian issues.

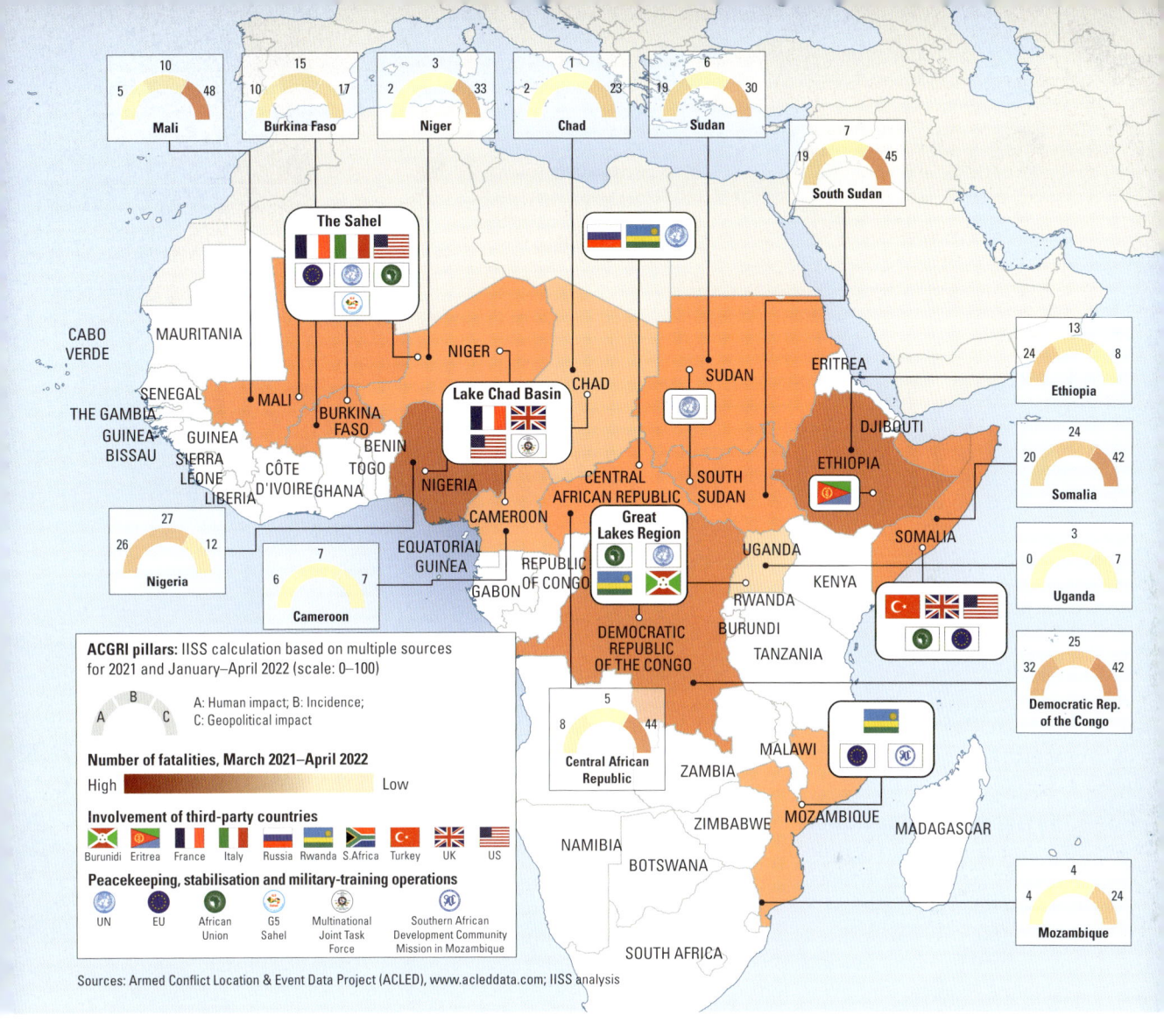

The socio-economic and fiscal fallout of the coronavirus pandemic and the geopolitical and geo-economic ramifications of the war in Ukraine,[4] which threaten food security across the continent, further complicate the regional outlook for peace.

In Focus: the Geopolitical Dimensions of Sub-Saharan Armed Conflicts

A concerning trend in sub-Saharan Africa is the internationalisation of internal armed conflicts, including civil wars. Over the last decade, the region has become fertile terrain for geopolitical competition among great powers and for further penetration by middle powers. This trend has important ramifications for conflict resolution.

Skyrocketing external interventions in civil wars

The global trend of increasing intervention by third-party states in internal conflicts is long-lasting and well documented.[5] In sub-Saharan Africa, this trend is even more pronounced. Twelve so-called internationalised-internal conflicts (i.e., civil wars with external intervention by a state) were recorded in the two decades between 1991 and 2010 (counting each conflict that occurred across multiple years only once). In the following 11-year period (2011–21), 27 such conflicts were recorded. Most of these conflicts were recurring year after year. In 2021, there were 17 internationalised civil wars in sub-Saharan Africa – more than twice the number of internal conflicts without external intervention.[6]

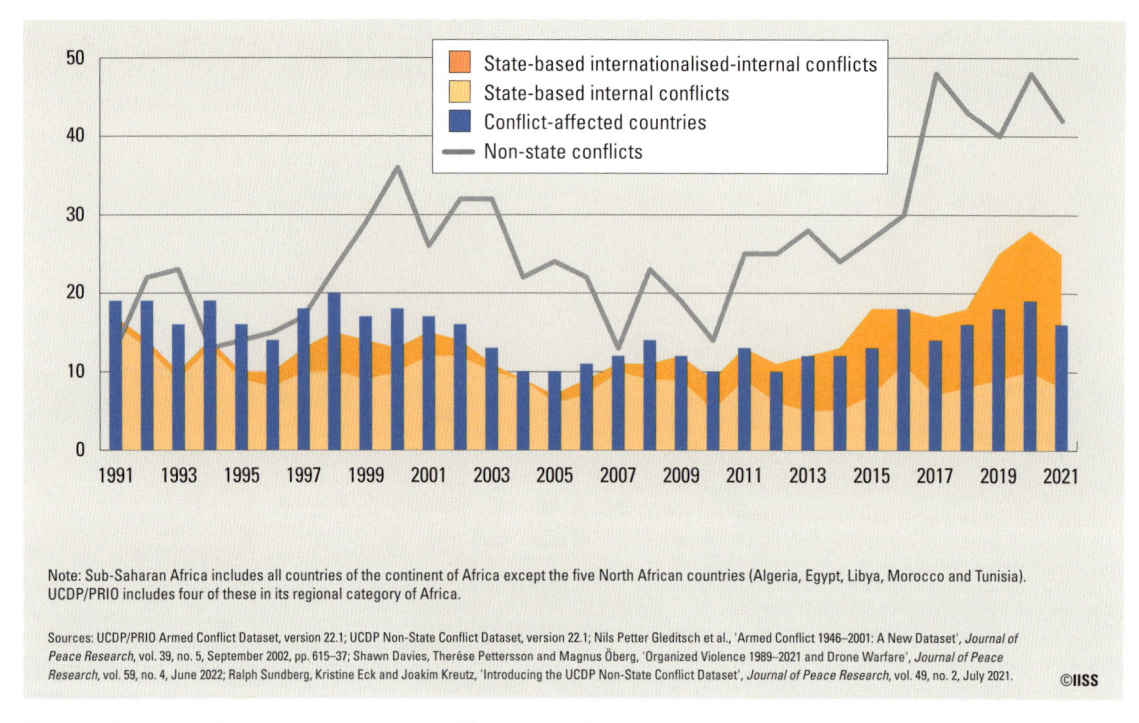

Figure 1: Armed-conflict trends in sub-Saharan Africa, 1991–2021

Note: Sub-Saharan Africa includes all countries of the continent of Africa except the five North African countries (Algeria, Egypt, Libya, Morocco and Tunisia). UCDP/PRIO includes four of these in its regional category of Africa.

Sources: UCDP/PRIO Armed Conflict Dataset, version 22.1; UCDP Non-State Conflict Dataset, version 22.1; Nils Petter Gleditsch et al., 'Armed Conflict 1946–2001: A New Dataset', *Journal of Peace Research*, vol. 39, no. 5, September 2002, pp. 615–37; Shawn Davies, Therése Pettersson and Magnus Öberg, 'Organized Violence 1989–2021 and Drone Warfare', *Journal of Peace Research*, vol. 59, no. 4, June 2022; Ralph Sundberg, Kristine Eck and Joakim Kreutz, 'Introducing the UCDP Non-State Conflict Dataset', *Journal of Peace Research*, vol. 49, no. 2, July 2011.

The rise of emerging powers' interventions

The current proliferation of third-party interventions in sub-Saharan Africa is related to a chaotic global order characterised by rising geopolitical competition. However, this situation is not a new phenomenon. While colonial powers historically exploited endemic conflicts by fomenting divisions among identity-based groups, Cold War era external intervention in African civil wars profoundly altered and complexified the dynamics of internal struggles, often deepening fault lines and escalating violence. After the Cold War, the demise of inter-state wars led to competing sub-Saharan African countries also displaying their rivalries through their support for rival conflict parties in each other's domestic conflicts. This development resulted in an intricate web of alliances between state and non-state actors, with detrimental effects on domestic conflicts.

Today's multipolar (dis)order witnesses both Western powers (the United States and France) and emerging ones (China, Russia and Turkey) intervening in the region in pursuit of diverse and often conflicting interests. Countries like Turkey and the United Arab Emirates (UAE), for example, have political influence and security ties in Somalia and Sudan, respectively. Russia also challenges the established order and during the last decade has renewed its Africa policy. In 2019, President Vladimir Putin hosted the Russia–Africa Summit, which was attended by 43 heads of state from the continent. Moscow aims to cultivate security and economic ties in Africa in order to erode Western influence. Currently, Russia has military agreements with 29 countries in Africa, ranging from arms sales to Russian boots on the ground (primarily via the Wagner Group, a private military company with ties to the Kremlin). Stronger relations with Russia go in parallel with weakened ties to Western countries: in notable examples, the CAR and Mali invited the Wagner Group to operate in their respective countries while entering into a stand-off with France and other Western actors, as recently as early 2022 in the case of Mali.

Adding complexity, inter-state disputes on the continent are on the rise: examples of current tensions include those between the DRC and Rwanda; Ethiopia and Sudan; Kenya and Somalia; and Sudan and South Sudan.

Rising third-party intervention and its effects on multilateral initiatives

Multilateral interventions, including peacekeeping operations and ad hoc coalitions, represent another facet of the internationalisation of current internal conflict in sub-Saharan Africa. Several peacekeeping operations on the continent are protracted, with no end in sight. Further, countries like the DRC, Nigeria, Mali and Burkina Faso constitute the epicentre of complex regional wars engulfing multiple countries in the Great Lakes Region, the Lake Chad Basin and the Western Sahel, respectively. In the Sahel, the decade-long French-led *Operation Barkhane* was reconfigured in 2021, while in 2022 the stand-off between France and Mali led to French troops pulling out of the country.

Generally, Western actors, including France, the United Kingdom and the US, support stabilisation, train local forces and fight violent extremists in several conflict theatres, such as Somalia, the Sahel and the Lake Chad Basin.

Ultimately, the rising trend of interference by states in sovereign countries undergoing internal armed conflict strongly suggests the weakened leverage of multilateral initiatives to address and mitigate conflicts. When external states intervene to support one conflict party over another, they can inadvertently undermine the effectiveness and legitimacy of multilateral norms and initiatives, including peacekeeping operations, mediation offices and the African Union's (AU) peace and security architecture.

Notes

[1] Institute for Economics and Peace (IEP), 'Global Peace Index 2022: Measuring Peace in a Complex World', June 2022.

[2] IEP, 'Global Terrorism Index 2022: Measuring the Impact of Terrorism', March 2022.

[3] Adem Kassie Abebe, 'Africa Is Beset with Coups and Conflicts: How the Trend Can Be Reversed', International Institute for Democracy and Electoral Assistance, 21 February 2022.

[4] Sub-Saharan Africa's GDP is projected to grow by 3.8% in 2022, down 0.7 percentage points from the growth recorded in 2021. See IMF, 'World Economic Outlook Databases'.

[5] 'Interventions in Armed Conflicts: Waning Western Dominance', in IISS, *The Armed Conflict Survey 2021* (Abingdon: Routledge for the International Institute for Strategic Studies, 2021).

[6] Globally, the distribution between internal conflicts with and without external intervention is more balanced than in sub-Saharan Africa: in 2021, there were 25 conflicts of the former type and 27 of the latter. This also means that the overwhelming majority of internationalised-internal conflicts took place in sub-Saharan Africa (17 out of 25), while the ratio for internal conflicts is different: of the 27 internal conflicts without external intervention globally, only eight were on the continent.

THE SAHEL

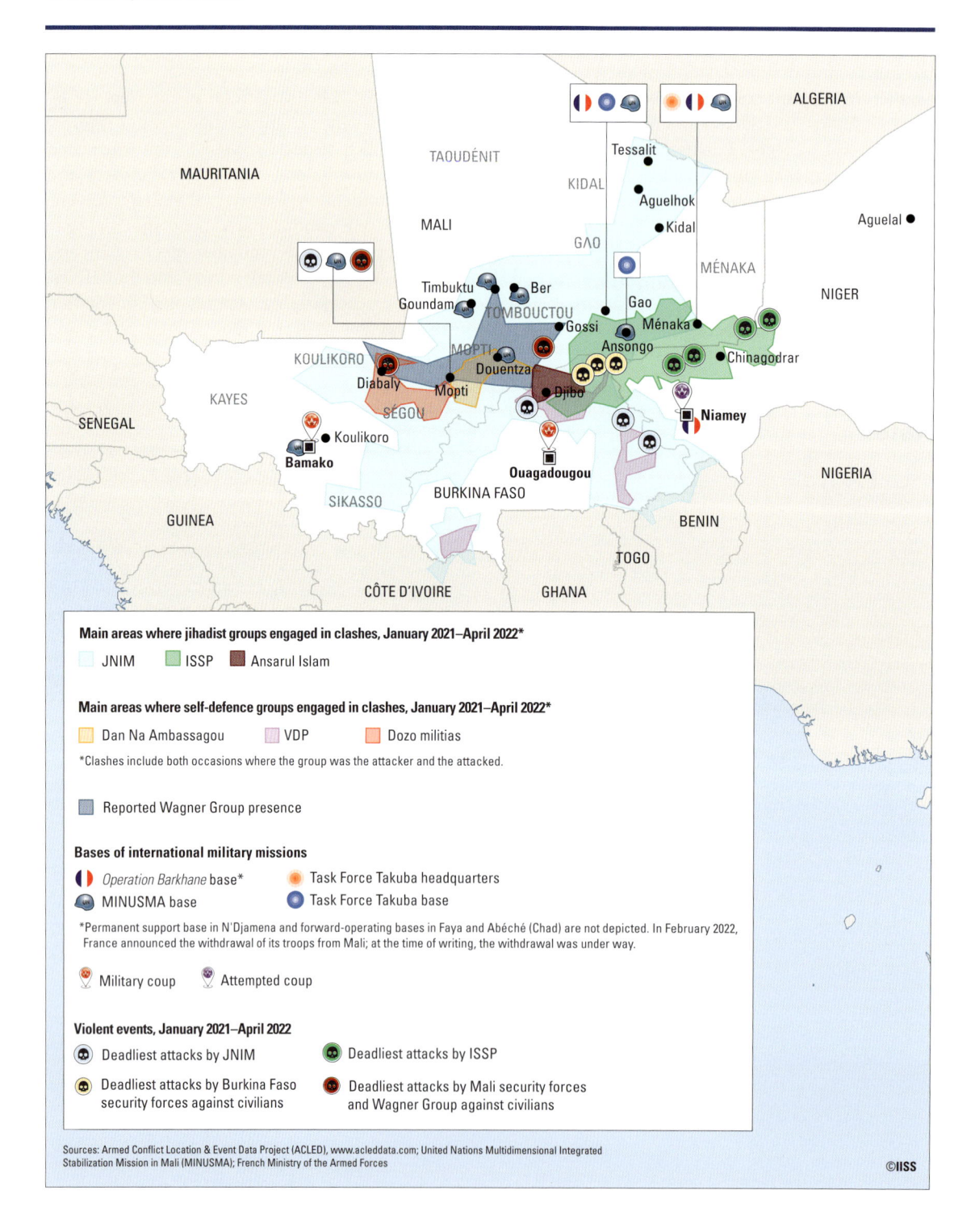

Main areas where jihadist groups engaged in clashes, January 2021–April 2022*
- JNIM
- ISSP
- Ansarul Islam

Main areas where self-defence groups engaged in clashes, January 2021–April 2022*
- Dan Na Ambassagou
- VDP
- Dozo militias

*Clashes include both occasions where the group was the attacker and the attacked.

Reported Wagner Group presence

Bases of international military missions
- Operation Barkhane base*
- Task Force Takuba headquarters
- MINUSMA base
- Task Force Takuba base

*Permanent support base in N'Djamena and forward-operating bases in Faya and Abéché (Chad) are not depicted. In February 2022, France announced the withdrawal of its troops from Mali; at the time of writing, the withdrawal was under way.

- Military coup
- Attempted coup

Violent events, January 2021–April 2022
- Deadliest attacks by JNIM
- Deadliest attacks by ISSP
- Deadliest attacks by Burkina Faso security forces against civilians
- Deadliest attacks by Mali security forces and Wagner Group against civilians

Sources: Armed Conflict Location & Event Data Project (ACLED), www.acleddata.com; United Nations Multidimensional Integrated Stabilization Mission in Mali (MINUSMA); French Ministry of the Armed Forces

©IISS

Armed Conflict Global Relevance Indicator (ACGRI)

Burkina Faso — A: 10; B: 15; C: 17
Mali — A: 5; B: 10; C: 48
Niger — A: 2; B: 3; C: 33

Key Conflict Statistics

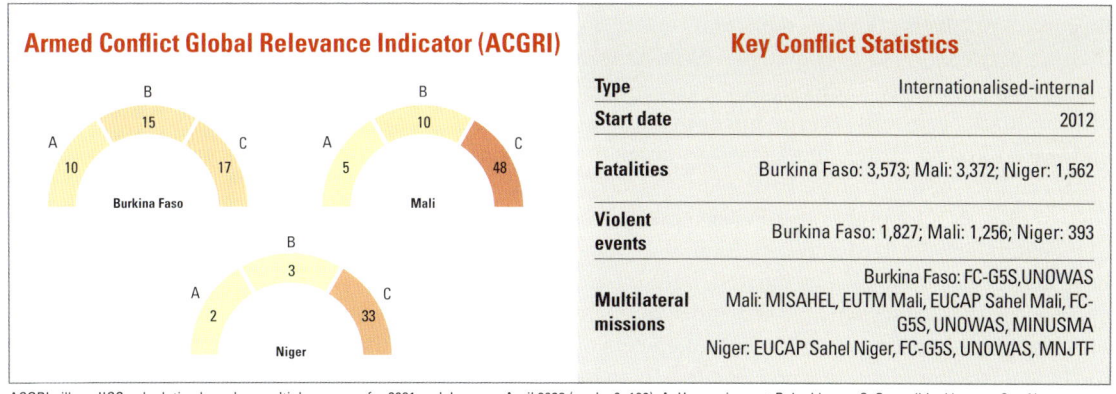

Type	Internationalised-internal
Start date	2012
Fatalities	Burkina Faso: 3,573; Mali: 3,372; Niger: 1,562
Violent events	Burkina Faso: 1,827; Mali: 1,256; Niger: 393
Multilateral missions	Burkina Faso: FC-G5S, UNOWAS Mali: MISAHEL, EUTM Mali, EUCAP Sahel Mali, FC-G5S, UNOWAS, MINUSMA Niger: EUCAP Sahel Niger, FC-G5S, UNOWAS, MNJTF

ACGRI pillars: IISS calculation based on multiple sources for 2021 and January–April 2022 (scale: 0–100). A: Human impact; B: Incidence; C: Geopolitical impact. See Notes on Methodology and Data Appendix for further details on Key Conflict Statistics.

Overview

January 2022 marked the tenth anniversary of the onset of conflict in the Liptako-Gourma region of the Sahel, a tri-border area between Burkina Faso, Mali and Niger. In 2012, a loose coalition of Tuareg and jihadist groups in northern Mali staged a secessionist uprising and drove out an underfunded military and local administration from vast swathes of the country's north and central regions. It was the first act of a deteriorating set of overlapping and interconnected conflicts in the region, featuring myriad non-state armed groups (NSAGs) and fuelled by elected governments' and customary authorities' poor governance records, social and economic grievances, human-rights abuses and political competition.

The secessionist drive in northern Mali and ensuing indiscriminate violence against civilians led France and the United Nations to intervene in 2013, through *Operation Serval* and the UN Multidimensional Integrated Stabilization Mission in Mali (MINUSMA) respectively. The former was replaced in 2014 by *Operation Barkhane*, which also deployed to other regional countries.

For the most part, the international response put rebel and jihadist groups to flight. However, the respite was short-lived. While a 2015 peace agreement – the Algiers accord – between rebel armed groups and the Malian state gradually lowered the intensity and rate of their violent clashes, jihadist violence intensified throughout the region.

In 2014, Burkina Faso's popular uprising ended president Blaise Compaoré's decades-long rule, creating a security vacuum that enabled jihadist groups to spread to the country's north, where they exploited local grievances, and to strike Ouagadougou in 2016. Jihadist violence also spread to Niger, chiefly at its western border with Mali and Burkina Faso.

As the conflict unfolded, two jihadist coalitions emerged as the main perpetrators of violence: the Group to Support Islam and Muslims (JNIM), created in 2017 as a coalition between al-Qaeda-affiliated groups, including al-Qaeda in the Islamic Maghreb–Sahel, Ansar Dine, al-Mourabitoun, Katibat Macina and other smaller groups; and the Islamic State in the Greater Sahara (ISGS) – since rebranded as Islamic State Sahel Province (ISSP) – which emerged from a split within al-Mourabitoun in 2015.

The two jihadist coalitions have put national armies on the backfoot and fuelled a sharp escalation in violence since 2016. While under 1,000 fatalities were recorded in the conflict in 2016, over 5,700 people died in 2021.[1]

Civilians have endured the brunt of the violence. With close to 10,000 killed since 2016, they represent nearly 40% of overall fatalities.[2] The trend significantly worsened in early 2022, with the civilian death toll in the first quarter surpassing the annual totals of previous years.[3] The conflict has also triggered one of the world's fastest-growing internal-displacement crises and exposed millions to food insecurity.

Two factors in particular have fuelled this trend. Firstly, despite continued multilateral efforts to contain jihadist groups in 2021 and early 2022, they expanded into new areas and staged some of their most damaging attacks against both security forces and civilians. Predominantly JNIM-affiliated groups further expanded into western and southwestern

Burkina Faso at the borders with Mali and Côte d'Ivoire and continued to move into West African coastal states. Notably, northern Benin saw its first jihadist attack against its security forces in late 2021 and was rocked by further attacks in early 2022.

Secondly, security forces have played a large role in the rising number of civilian casualties. The governments of Burkina Faso, Mali and Niger have largely favoured a heavy-handed, military-led approach to the conflict that has led to indiscriminate violence against civilians – particularly members of the Fulani Muslim minority, perceived locally to be overrepresented in jihadist groups and stigmatised as a result.

The first months of 2022 marked a stark deterioration as Malian armed forces and allied Russian private military contractors faced mounting accusations of widespread abuses against civilians, notably over the alleged killing of some 300 civilians in the village of Moura in March.[4] Nigerien and Burkinabe troops also continued to face allegations of abuses.

'Self-defence' militias – which have formed chiefly in Mali and Burkina Faso due to armed forces' faltering security responses – have also faced numerous accusations of abuses against civilians. Both militaries and militiamen have generally benefitted from impunity, which has fuelled anti-government resentment and jihadist recruitment.

Against the backdrop of spiralling jihadist violence, several more regional and international security initiatives were established. However, the multiplication of security initiatives has failed to translate into concrete gains on the battlefield and the conflict has largely continued unabated. This security architecture showed signs of deterioration in Mali during the reporting period: forces from *Operation Barkhane* and Task Force Takuba (TFT, a contingent of European special forces under French command focused on counter-terrorism, established in 2020) plan to finish withdrawing from the country in the course of 2022 in a context of rising tensions with Bamako. Moreover, Mali's military junta announced that it would exit the G5 Sahel Joint Force (FC-G5S), a regional counter-terrorism initiative.

In parallel, Burkina Faso, Mali and Niger took steps to bolster their militaries during the reporting period, while also moving tentatively towards dialogue with jihadist groups, a notion which has recently gained traction in the region despite international partners' opposition. However, at the time of writing, these initiatives have failed to alleviate violence or turn the tide in the conflict. Regional governments' inability to stem jihadist violence, largely compounded by their records of poor governance, has contributed to popular discontent and recurring political instability: 2021 saw a military coup in Mali and an attempted coup in Niger, while early 2022 saw a coup in Burkina Faso.

Following a military takeover in 2020, in May 2021 Mali underwent a 'coup within a coup'. The then interim vice president, Colonel Assimi Goïta, concerned that the influence of the 2020 coup leaders was being curtailed by a government reshuffle, seized power and ordered the arrest of the transitional president and the prime minister. The move further strained Mali's relations with its European partners and the Economic Community of West African States (ECOWAS). The military junta backtracked on its promise to hold elections in February 2022 and took steps to adopt a five-year transition timeline, prompting ECOWAS to impose strict political and economic sanctions on Bamako in January 2022, which were lifted in July after the junta adopted a new electoral calendar. Meanwhile, escalating Mali–France tensions led to the expulsion of the French ambassador, also in January. The junta has since cracked down on dissenting voices within the country. In March 2022, it suspended two French media organisations for reporting on allegations of abuse by the armed forces against civilians.

In Burkina Faso, a group of mutineering officers calling themselves the Patriotic Movement for Safeguard and Restoration (MPSR) deposed president Roch Marc Christian Kaboré in January 2022. The coup followed a failed attempt earlier in January and months of mounting discontent, both within the army and among the wider population, over the deteriorating security situation. The November 2021 jihadist attack on Inata, which killed at least 49 gendarmes, marked an important turning point in the lead-up to the coup, exposing the army's lack of resources and prompting popular protests. While the coup was largely welcomed within the country, it drew international criticism and ECOWAS suspended Burkina Faso's membership. The MPSR appointed its leader, Lieutenant-Colonel Paul-Henri Sandaogo Damiba, as interim president in January and convened a transitional legislative assembly in March, setting a three-year transition period (later shortened to two years in July).

In Niger, security forces foiled a reported coup attempt in March 2021 in which mutineering soldiers sought to storm the presidential palace two days before president-elect Mohamed Bazoum's inauguration.

In this context of high political instability, during the reporting period Mali's new military junta triggered a major shift in the conflict's geopolitics. In a bid to cement its grasp on power, it instrumentalised domestic anti-French sentiment to shore up its legitimacy and sought closer ties with Russia and the Wagner Group (a Russian private military company), prompting France (and France's European partners) to prepare their exit from the country and the redeployment of some of their forces to Niger. In parallel, following the coup in Burkina Faso, transitional authorities there announced in early 2022 that they would seek to 'diversify' their security partnerships, potentially signalling a shift away from France and the United States.[5] As alliances are reshaped, increasingly Mali and the wider Sahel have become a battlefield for informational warfare on social media, where France and Russia vie to influence the opinion of local populations. Ten years on from the uprising in northern Mali, the prospects for peace in the region appear more distant than ever.

Conflict Parties

Malian Armed Forces (FAMa)

Strength: 21,000 active military personnel (19,000 army and 2,000 air force) and 20,000 gendarmerie and paramilitary personnel (6,000 gendarmerie, 1,000 national police, 3,000 militia and 10,000 national guard).

Areas of operation: Northern, central and southern Mali, particularly in the tri-border Liptako-Gourma area near Burkina Faso and Niger.

Leadership: Gen. Oumar Diarra (chief of general staff).

Structure: Consists of the army, the National Gendarmerie and the National Guard.

History: Created at independence in 1960. Following years of underinvestment, FAMa has been significantly strengthened over the past decade, including through the European Union's military training mission (EUTM) from 2013–March 2022.

Objectives: Counter-terrorism and territorial security.

Opponents: Ansarul Islam, ISSP, JNIM.

Affiliates/allies: Burkina Faso, ECOWAS, EU, FC-G5S (although Mali announced its withdrawal in May 2022), France (until May 2022), Niger, MINUSMA, US, Russian private military contractors, Russia.

Resources/capabilities: Mali's 2021 defence budget was US$855 million (4.5% of GDP), up from US$787m in 2020.

Niger Armed Forces (FAN)

Strength: 5,300 active military personnel (5,200 army and 100 air force) and 5,400 paramilitary (1,400 gendarmerie, 2,500 republican guard and 1,500 national police).

Areas of operation: Regions of Tahoua and Tillabéri in western Niger, the northern region of Agadez, as well as the southern and southeastern regions of Maradi and Diffa.

Leadership: Brig.-Gen. Salifou Modi.

Structure: Composed of the army, the air force, the gendarmerie, the republican guard and the national police.

History: Founded upon independence in 1961 and officered by French Colonial Forces, it was reorganised following the 1974 military coup. In 2003, it integrated the Nigerien air force.

Objectives: Maintain internal and border security against jihadist groups and protect territorial integrity.

Opponents: Ansarul Islam, ISSP, JNIM, Islamic State West Africa Province (ISWAP).

Affiliates/allies: Burkina Faso, FC-G5S, France, Mali, MINUSMA, US.

Resources/capabilities: Niger's defence budget for 2021 was US$203m (1.4% of GDP), down from US$211m in 2020.

Burkina Faso Armed Forces (FABF)

Strength: 11,200 active military personnel (6,400 army, 600 air force, 4,200 gendarmerie). There are also 45,000 personnel in the People's Militia (reserve military/conscripts) and 250 active paramilitary personnel.

Areas of operation: Active in western, southwestern, northern and eastern Burkina Faso, in particular at border areas with Mali and Niger.

Leadership: Col-Maj. David Kabré (chief of staff).

Burkina Faso Armed Forces (FABF)

Structure: Comprised of the army, the air force, the gendarmerie and paramilitary forces, with the latter notably including the government-sanctioned self-defence group Volunteers for the Defence of the Homeland (VDP).

History: Reached its current form in 1985 with the inauguration of the air force. The government created the VDP via law in January 2020.

Objectives: Maintain national security and territorial integrity and counter jihadist groups.

Opponents: Ansarul Islam, ISSP, JNIM.

Affiliates/allies: Benin, Côte d'Ivoire, FC-G5S, France, Ghana, Mali, MINUSMA, Niger, self-defence groups.

Resources/capabilities: Burkina Faso's defence budget for 2021 was US$459m (2.4% of GDP), up from US$388m in 2020.

Group to Support Islam and Muslims (JNIM)

Strength: Up to 2,000 fighters.[6]

Areas of operation: Most active in northern and central Mali (with an expansion southward towards Bamako), northern and eastern Burkina Faso, and, to a limited extent, western Niger and southern Mali and Burkina Faso. Recent activities reported in northern Benin.

Leadership: Iyad Ag Ghaly, a long-time Tuareg militant who is also the leader of Ansar Dine, one of the main groups constituting JNIM.

Structure: Created as an alliance of equals.

History: JNIM was created in 2017 as a coalition between al-Qaeda-affiliated groups such as Ansar Dine, al-Mourabitoun, al-Qaeda in the Islamic Maghreb–Sahel (AQIM–Sahel), Katibat Macina and other smaller factions. It is known to cooperate with Ansarul Islam although their relationship has been ambiguous.

Objectives: Establish an Islamic state in the Sahel, replacing existing state structures and expelling foreign forces.

Opponents: FAMa, FC-G5S, ISSP, MINUSMA, *Operation Barkhane*, TFT, Russian private military contractors.

Affiliates/allies: Al-Qaeda, al-Qaeda in the Islamic Maghreb–North Africa (AQIM–North Africa), Katibat Macina, Katibat Serma. Cooperates with Ansarul Islam, though their relationship is ambiguous.

Resources/capabilities: Heavy weaponry; improvised explosive devices (IEDs), including vehicle-borne IEDs and suicide-vehicle-borne IEDs.

Islamic State Sahel Province (ISSP)

Strength: Fewer than 500 fighters.[7]

Areas of operation: Mali (Gao, Ménaka, Mopti and Timbuktu), western Niger (Tillabéri, Dosso and Tahoua regions) and Burkina Faso (Sahel, Centre-Nord, Est, Boucle du Mouhoun, Sud-Ouest, Centre-Sud and Cascades).

Leadership: ISSP founder Adnan Abu Walid al-Sahrawi was killed by French forces in August 2021. He was replaced in October 2021 by Abdul Bara al-Sahraoui (also known as al-Ansari).

Structure: Unclear.

History: ISSP emerged from a split within al-Mourabitoun in 2015 and was originally known as ISGS. ISGS pledged allegiance to ISIS in 2015 and in 2019 it became part of ISWAP. ISIS recognised the group as an independent *wilayat* (province) in March 2022 under the name ISSP.

Objectives: Establish an Islamic caliphate based on strict interpretation of the Koran and adherence to ISIS ideology.

Opponents: FABF, FAMa, FAN, JNIM, MINUSMA, *Operation Barkhane*, TFT, Russian private military contractors.

Affiliates/allies: Katibat Salaheddine, ISIS, ISWAP, other smaller militias.

Resources/capabilities: IEDs and light weaponry.

Ansarul Islam

Strength: Estimated to be no more than a few hundred fighters.[8]

Areas of operation: Active chiefly in northern Burkina Faso (Nord and Sahel regions), eastern Burkina Faso and parts of Mali (Mopti region).

Leadership: Jafar Dicko, brother of the founder, Malam Ibrahim Dicko, who passed away in 2017.

Structure: No clear structure. While recruiting mostly among Fulani (Rimaibe in particular) communities, it does not pursue an identity-based insurgency.

History: Formed in 2016 as a local insurgency against provincial authorities and the prevailing social order in Soum, Burkina Faso. The group has become one of the most active groups in northern and eastern Burkina Faso and regularly cooperates with JNIM, with some indications that it has also previously cooperated with ISSP. However, it is not formally affiliated with either of the alliances.

Objectives: The founder was a preacher of radical Islam who vowed to resurrect the ancient kingdom of Djeelgodji. Its main objective now is to challenge the social order in Burkina Faso.

Ansarul Islam

Opponents: FABF, FAMa, FC-G5S, ISSP, *Operation Barkhane*, TFT.

Affiliates/allies: JNIM.

Resources/capabilities: IEDs and light weaponry.

Self-defence groups

Strength: Dozens of groups spread across the region, varying greatly in size and capabilities.

Areas of operation: Central and southern Mali, primarily in Mopti and Ségou; northern, western, eastern and southern Burkina Faso; Tillabéri region in Niger.

Leadership: Most groups are community-led militias and structures may vary greatly. Dan Na Ambassagou, a prominent militia operating in central Mali and northern Burkina Faso, is led by Youssouf Toloba. The government-sanctioned VDP, which operates across Burkina Faso, is led by several coordinators, such as Ali Nana.

Structure: Self-defence groups are usually community-based and organised along ethnic affiliations. These include Bambara, Dogon, Fulani, Fulsé, Mossi and Tuareg Imghad.

History: Self-defence militias proliferated following the 2012 Tuareg rebellion in Mali, with violence increasing and spreading across the region since then. Their presence is symptomatic of governments' inability to impose territorial control. In Burkina Faso, the government created the VDP by law in 2020 on the back of existing self-defence groups, such as the Koglweogo and Dozo.

Objectives: Protect local communities from external threats and maintain law and order on behalf of state authorities.

Opponents: These depend on the ethnic affiliation of individual groups. There is growing antagonism between Fulani groups on one side, and Bambara and Dogon groups on the other, partly due to recruitment by jihadist groups among Fulani communities.

Affiliates/allies: National authorities (FABF, FAMa, FAN).

Resources/capabilities: Light and often old weaponry.

Permanent Strategic Framework (CSP) (a coalition of Coordination of Azawad Movements (CMA) and Platform)

Strength: Prior to the 2015 Algiers accord, the number of CMA fighters was estimated to be between 800 and 4,000.[9] The number of Platform fighters is unknown.

Areas of operation:
CMA: Northern Mali, including the towns of Aguelhok, Dire, Gao, Kidal, Ménaka, Tessalit and Timbuktu.
Platform: Northern Mali, including the towns of Bourem, Gao, Gossi, Gourma, Ménaka, Tilemsi and Timbuktu.

Leadership:
CSP: Bilal Ag Acherif (president), Fahad Ag Almahmoud (vice-president).
CMA: Leadership of the coalition rotates between its members on a regular basis. Then CMA leader Sidi Brahim Ould Sidati was assassinated in April 2021 by unidentified gunmen.
Platform: A loose alliance of autonomous NSAGs and self-defence militias.

Structure:
CSP: The CSP was born out of a merger between the CMA and Platform – the main armed movements in northern Mali and signatories of the Algiers accord.
CMA: A coalition including the National Movement for the Liberation of Azawad (MNLA), the High Council for the Unity of Azawad (HCUA) and a CMA-affiliated faction of the Arab Movement of Azawad (MAA).
Platform: An umbrella organisation that includes the Imghad Tuareg Self-Defence Group and Allies (GATIA), the MAA–Platform faction (MAA–PF), the Coordination for the Movements and Fronts of Patriotic Resistance (CMFPR-1) and Movement for the Salvation of Azawad-Daoussak (MSA-D).

History:
CSP: The CMA and Platform formed the CSP as a new coalition of armed movements in May 2021, under the aegis of the Italian non-governmental organisation (NGO) Ara Pacis, to facilitate the implementation of the Algiers accord.
CMA: Dominated by Tuareg separatist militias fighting for the independence of Azawad, an area in northern Mali. It was created to represent separatist views among combatants, as part of the 2015 Algiers accord.
Platform: Formed in June 2014 during peace negotiations in a bid to better represent the views of NSAGs supporting Malian unity.

Objectives:
CSP: Synergise CMA and Platform efforts for the implementation of the Algiers accord, operationalise joint mechanisms to combat insecurity, and achieve coherence in taking into account the aspirations of the local populations.
CMA: A coalition of Azawad rebel groups originally fighting for self-determination. Independence is no longer an objective but may become so again due to frictions in implementing the Algiers accord.
Platform: Formed in support of Mali's territorial integrity. However, its members have widely differing agendas and interests, with some engaging in local disputes while others support the security forces.

Opponents: ISSP, JNIM.

Affiliates/allies:
CMA: Formally cooperates with FAMa, MINUSMA and Platform but has previously collaborated with jihadist groups.
Platform: FAMa, MINUSMA, *Operation Barkhane*.

Resources/capabilities: Small arms and light weaponry. For CMA, remnants of the Libyan military arsenal left behind after the 2011 ousting of Muammar Gadhafi in Libya.

G5 Sahel Joint Force (FC-G5S)

Strength: Approximately 5,300 troops provided by the five member countries Burkina Faso, Chad, Mali, Mauritania and Niger as of September 2021.

Areas of operation: Border areas of Burkina Faso, Chad, Mali, Mauritania and Niger.

Leadership: Nigerien Gen. Oumarou Namata Gazama (commander).

Structure: A joint counter-terrorism task force, with troops across eight battalions in three sectors across all five countries.

History: While the G5 Sahel as an organisation was established in 2014 (comprising members Burkina Faso, Chad, Mali, Mauritania and Niger), the joint force was created in February 2017 with the support of France and the UN to address threats across the Sahel, such as terrorism and transnational organised crime, including smuggling of goods and human trafficking. Mali announced in May 2022 that it would withdraw from the force.

Objectives: Strengthen security along the borders of member states through intelligence sharing and the deployment of joint patrols.

Opponents: Ansarul Islam, ISSP, JNIM.

Affiliates/allies: Foreign and regional armed forces, MINUSMA.

Resources/capabilities: Suffers from underfunding and unpredictable financing. Troop deployment is slow due to a lack of operating bases, capacity and equipment.

Operation Barkhane and Task Force Takuba (TFT)[10]

Strength:
Operation Barkhane: 4,300 French troops as of mid-2022.[11]
TFT: As of May 2022, 1,000 special forces and soldiers drawn from ten European countries (Belgium, Czech Republic, Denmark, Estonia, France, Hungary, Italy, Netherlands, Portugal, Sweden), though the majority are French.[12] As of July, the TFT had ceased operating in Mali.

Areas of operation:
Operation Barkhane: Burkina Faso, Chad, Mali, Mauritania and Niger, with a particular focus on the Liptako-Gourma tri-border area.
TFT: Mali.

Leadership:
Operation Barkhane: French Gen. Laurent Michon.
TFT: French Col. Vincent took over command in March 2022, replacing Swedish Col. Peter.

Structure:
Operation Barkhane: Three permanent support bases in N'Djamena (Chad), Niamey (Niger) and Gao (Mali), in addition to three forward operating bases in Ménaka (Mali), and Faya and Abéché (Chad). The operation includes ground combat forces and air elements, as well as intelligence capabilities.
TFT: Operates from three military bases of the FAMa, located in Gao, Ansongo and Ménaka.

History:
Operation Barkhane: Replaced *Operation Serval* in August 2014, expanding the French forces' mandate beyond Mali's borders across the Sahel. Following the May 2021 coup in Mali, France announced in June that it would conclude *Operation Barkhane* in 2022 and reconfigure its military presence in the region. Amid increasing tensions with Mali's military junta, France announced in February 2022 that it would fully withdraw *Operation Barkhane* forces from the country within six months.
TFT: A contingent of special forces from individual EU member states, to serve under French command, was announced in March 2020 and became fully operational in April 2021. Amid increasing tensions with Mali's military junta, France and allied European countries announced in February 2022 that they would fully withdraw TFT forces within six months.

Objectives: Enhance the capacities and capabilities of regional host states, support international forces, engage in direct combat against terrorist NSAGs and help improve governance, including through medical aid.

Opponents: Ansarul Islam, ISSP, JNIM.

Affiliates/allies: G5 Sahel countries, MINUSMA, US.

Resources/capabilities: Access to sophisticated military equipment including uninhabited aerial vehicles, infantry-combat vehicles, fighter jets and combat helicopters.

United Nations Multidimensional Integrated Stabilization Mission in Mali (MINUSMA)

Strength: The UN Security Council (UNSC) authorised a total of 13,289 military personnel for MINUSMA, with troops being contributed by 61 member states. As of March 2022, there were 12,266 military personnel deployed in the country.[13]

Areas of operation: Countrywide, with a concentration of forces in the centre and northern regions.

Leadership: Lt-Gen. Cornelis Johannes Matthijssen (force commander).

Structure: As of March 2022, MINUSMA comprised 12,266 military personnel, 1,720 police personnel and 1,180 civilian personnel. In 2019, the three countries contributing the most troops were Bangladesh, Burkina Faso and Chad.

United Nations Multidimensional Integrated Stabilization Mission in Mali (MINUSMA)

History: Established in April 2013 by UNSC Resolution 2100 to support the Malian authorities and stabilise the country following the 2012 Tuareg rebellion. In the same year, the ECOWAS African-led International Support Mission in Mali (AFISMA) was incorporated under MINUSMA's command. Resolution 2584 extended its mandate to June 2022. MINUSMA has seen the largest number of casualties among UN peacekeeping operations. Alongside MINUSMA, there is a series of multilateral organisations and missions, including the EUTM and the African Union Mission to Mali and the Sahel (MISAHEL), which support with capacity-building and peacebuilding activities, including delivering humanitarian aid.

Objectives: Ensure the implementation of the 2015 Algiers accord, including the protection of civilians, the reduction of communal violence and the restoration of state presence in central and northern Mali.

Opponents: Ansarul Islam, ISSP, JNIM.

Affiliates/allies: FAMa, FC-G5S, *Operation Barkhane*, TFT.

Resources/capabilities: A US$1.3 billion budget for 2021, renewed on an annual basis. Military equipment is advanced, including armoured mine-resistant personnel carriers and combat helicopters.

Wagner Group

Strength: Around 1,000.

Areas of operation: Central Mali (Mopti and Ségou), Timbuktu area.

Leadership: Dmitry Utkin (commander); Alexander Ermolaev (deputy commander); Andrei Troshev (chief of staff).

Structure: The company was established by businessman Yevgeny Prigozhin. It has particularly close ties with Russian military intelligence (GRU), the Ministry of Defence and President Vladimir Putin.

History: The Wagner Group is a Russian security organisation closely linked to the Kremlin and military intelligence. It is used by Russia to carry out a range of officially deniable military and intelligence operations, and commercial activities, abroad, including in the Middle East and Africa. News that the government of Mali was negotiating a contract with the Wagner Group first emerged in September 2021. In December 2021, Canada, the United Kingdom and several EU countries announced that Russian contractors had deployed to Mali with Russia's support.[14] While Moscow has denied any ties to the group, Russian Foreign Minister Sergei Lavrov acknowledged in May 2022 that the group was present in the country.[15] However, Mali denies the presence of any mercenaries and insists only Russian military instructors are present on its territory.

Objectives: Reportedly centre around supporting FAMa's security operations against jihadist groups.

Opponents: Ansarul Islam, ISSP, JNIM.

Affiliates/allies: FAMa.

Resources/capabilities: Unclear.

Other conflict parties

Other Russian military contractors are reported to be deployed in the region.

Conflict Drivers

Security

Increasing number and sophistication of jihadist groups:
The proliferation of violent actors in the Sahel is an important driver of violence. The eruption of armed hostilities in northern and central Mali in 2012 and the Burkinabe uprising in 2014 created a security vacuum that enabled NSAGs to establish a durable foothold from which to expand into Niger. By 2022, the number of NSAGs in the region had more than doubled, while the two primary alliances (JNIM and ISSP) have polarised groups along allegiances to either al-Qaeda or ISIS, which has led to intra-jihadist clashes.

These jihadist groups have conducted increasingly ambitious, sophisticated and deadly attacks against state security forces and local communities, competing for influence and territorial control. Their zones of operation have grown too: both ISSP and JNIM have expanded into the northern areas of West African coastal states, such as Benin, Côte d'Ivoire and Togo, as well as westwards towards Senegal.

Fragmentation of security responses:
In response to mounting insecurity, 'self-defence' groups and local militias have proliferated, partly due to the breakdown in state security responses but also in order to respond to alleged mutual targeting of local communities. For instance, JNIM and ISSP have been perceived to be recruiting among the ethnic-minority Fulani communities, prompting predominantly Dogon and Mossi 'self-defence' militias and Tuareg Dhoussahak (MSA-D)

to target these communities in central and eastern Mali and in northern and eastern Burkina Faso.

Reported abuses against civilians by national armed forces (and allied self-defence militias) and Russian private military contractors exacerbate insecurity in the region and play into the hands of jihadist groups by reinforcing existing grievances and ethnic tensions and fuelling recruitment into their ranks.

The proliferation of self-defence groups – a process often implicitly supported by regional governments – is the result of faltering national armed forces and French and multilateral military interventions. Although security budgets in the region grew in recent years, they remained inadequate, undermining the effectiveness of state security strategies. Attempts to pool resources and strengthen capabilities – through initiatives such as the FC-G5S, MINUSMA, *Operation Barkhane* and more recently the TFT – have had little impact. Despite the wide array of actors present in the region, funding issues, limited troop numbers and a narrow focus on counter-terrorism measures by international partners has reduced their efficacy.

Political

Governance crisis:
At the heart of the conflict is a governance crisis characterised by elected officials' and some customary authorities' low levels of legitimacy, lack of state presence in rural areas, government shortcomings in delivering essential public goods and services, unequal resource access and distribution, and deeply hierarchical customary structures influencing societal relations. These factors prompt segments of the population to turn to alternative actors, including jihadist groups. The latter expand by building local alliances and exploiting local communal conflicts. Such conflicts can revolve around intercommunal tensions or relate to intra-community disputes. Ansarul Islam built traction in Burkina Faso's Sahel region by capitalising on local discontent at the prevailing social order in Soum province, taking aim at class hierarchy and corruption among customary authorities. Meanwhile, in Mali, following decades of recurrent conflict between Tuareg populations and central governments, continued delays in the implementation of the 2015 Algiers accord remain a source of discord between signatory armed groups and transitional Malian authorities.

Social

Intercommunal violence and competition over resources:
Particularly in Burkina Faso and Mali, spiralling intercommunal violence has weakened social cohesion and undermined development efforts. This dynamic has been further reinforced by the emergence of self-defence militias often organised along ethnic lines, such as the VDP in Burkina Faso in 2020.

Increasing competition for resources has also played a role in driving violence. Organised criminal activity has flourished amid ineffective government control, providing NSAGs with opportunities to extort, steal and smuggle goods, such as motorbikes, fuel and livestock. Competition for the control of lucrative drug-trade routes has also fuelled significant clashes between NSAGs in northern Mali. Moreover, droughts and land erosion, the development of agro-business activities and demographic expansion have contributed to a diminution of arable lands and further fuelled economic instability and competition over natural resources between herders and farmers, triggering a region-wide food-insecurity crisis.

Key Events in 2021–22

POLITICAL EVENTS

2 April 2021
Niger's President Bazoum takes office, two days after presidential guards repel a reported coup attempt.

6 May
Malian armed groups CMA and Platform form the coalition CSP.

MILITARY/VIOLENT EVENTS

21 March 2021
Suspected jihadists kill at least 141 civilians in several villages in Niger's Tahoua region.

13 April
Unknown gunmen kill CMA president Sidi Brahim Ould Sidati in Bamako.

24 May
A military *coup d'état* takes place in Mali, led by interim vice-president Col. Assimi Goïta.

10 June
President Emmanuel Macron announces that France will phase out *Operation Barkhane* by early 2022 and reconfigure its military presence in the Sahel around the TFT.

21 October
Mali's military junta backtracks on an announcement that it had mandated the country's High Islamic Council to negotiate with JNIM.

Late November
Protesters stop a French military convoy in Kaya (Burkina Faso) and Téra (Niger) amid rising anti-French sentiment in the region.

23 December
Canada and 15 European countries jointly condemn the alleged deployment of the private military company Wagner Group to Mali and accuse Russia of supporting the deployment.

9 January 2022
ECOWAS imposes sweeping economic sanctions on Mali and announces the closure of borders between ECOWAS member states and Mali.

24 January
A military *coup d'état* takes place in Burkina Faso, led by Lt-Col Paul-Henri Sandaogo Damiba.

31 January
Mali's military junta expels the French ambassador.

4–5 June
Suspected jihadists kill over 160 people and displace over 7,000 in Burkina Faso's Solhan village.

17 August
French troops kill ISSP founder Adnan Abu Walid al-Sahrawi in the tri-border area between Burkina Faso, Mali and Niger.

18 August
Jihadist militants kill 80 people near Boukouma in Burkina Faso's Soum province, including 65 civilians.

7 October
French troops kill JNIM-affiliated Ansarul Islam leader Oumarou Mobo Modhi in Mali's Mopti region.

15 October
French forces in Mali kill Nasser al-Tergui, leader of the JNIM-linked jihadist group Katibat Gourma and leading figure of Katiba Serma.

14 November
Suspected JNIM militants kill at least 49 gendarmes and four civilians in Burkina Faso's Inata area.

26 November
1,200 troops from Benin, Burkina Faso, Côte d'Ivoire and Ghana deploy in border areas to counter the threat of jihadist violence.

1–2 December
Suspected jihadist militants attack a military outpost in Benin's northern Porga area, killing two soldiers in the country's first terrorist attack targeting its security forces.

17 February
President Macron and European partners announce the withdrawal of their troops (*Operation Barkhane*/TFT) from Mali, a process expected to take up to six months.

25 February
President Bazoum announces the release of several jihadist leaders as part of ongoing negotiations.

1 April
Burkina Faso creates local dialogue committees to foster talks with militants seeking to demobilise.

12 April
The EU partly suspends EUTM Mali amid increasing tensions with the country's military junta.

2 May
Mali's military junta breaks off from its defence accords with France.

15 May
Mali announces its withdrawal from the G5 Sahel and the FC-G5S.

March 2022
Weeks-long clashes between CSP and ISSP kill hundreds of people in Mali's Gao region.

Late March
Malian forces and suspected Russian private military contractors allegedly execute some 300 civilians in the town of Moura.

Early April
Burkinabe troops allegedly kill over 100 civilians during security operations in Oudalan region.

Responses to the Conflict

Security

France has played a leading role in the Sahel since 2013. However, following Mali's coup in May 2021, Paris temporarily suspended military cooperation and indicated that it would phase out *Operation Barkhane* by early 2022 to reorganise its military presence around the TFT. Amid rising tensions with Mali's junta over the presence of Russian private military contractors, France and its European partners announced in February 2022 that they would withdraw *Operation Barkhane* and TFT forces from Mali within six months.

MINUSMA's mandate is up for renewal in June 2022. Established in 2013 chiefly to assist the country's political process and ensure stabilisation, the protection of civilians, the rebuilding of the security sector and the protection of human rights, over the years it has become the UN's deadliest peacekeeping mission, with over 313 fatalities recorded in its ranks as of mid-2022.[16]

In parallel, the EU has provided military training to Malian forces since 2013, and its civilian capacity-building missions were launched in Niger in 2012 and in Mali in 2015. The EU suspended the EUTM in April 2022 over the presence of Russian private military contractors in Mali. Other key international security partners include the US, which has been present in the region since at least 2012, though it suspended its security assistance to Mali following the August 2020 coup.

Russia's security cooperation with Mali's junta grew stronger during the reporting period. Bamako took delivery of several Russian helicopters and weapons and reportedly contracted the Wagner Group.[17]

At the regional level, the G5 Sahel has coordinated one of the primary security responses to the conflict since 2014. One of its central purposes is to strengthen security cooperation between its members against jihadist organisations in the region. In the wake of the military coups in Mali and Burkina Faso, the G5 Sahel has come under increasing strain. In particular, tensions over the prospect of Mali's junta assuming the organisation's rotating presidency left it in limbo in early 2022 and eventually prompted Bamako to announce in May that it would leave the organisation. In an apparent

Figure 1: Number of people killed in violent events per actor, 2016–April 2022

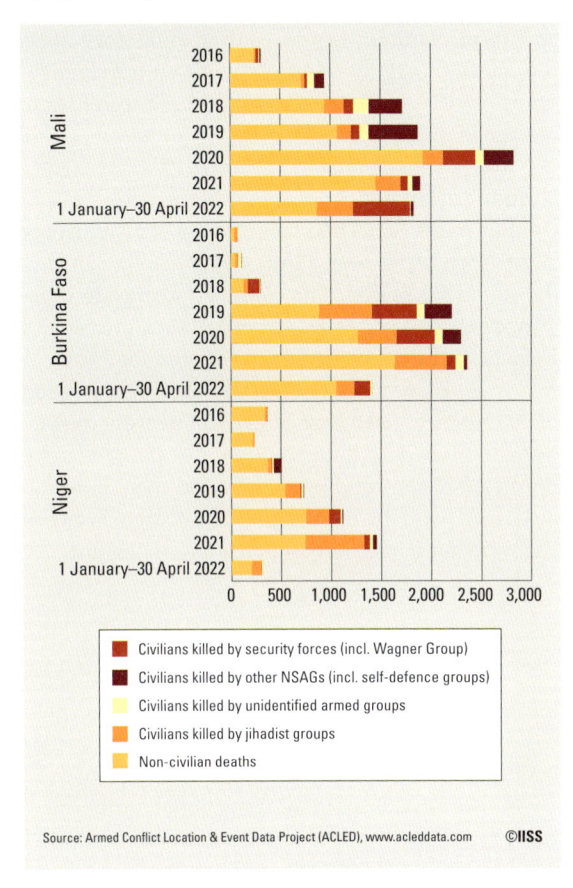

[Stacked bar chart showing annual fatalities for Mali, Burkina Faso, and Niger from 2016 to 1 January–30 April 2022, categorised by: Civilians killed by security forces (incl. Wagner Group); Civilians killed by other NSAGs (incl. self-defence groups); Civilians killed by unidentified armed groups; Civilians killed by jihadist groups; Non-civilian deaths. X-axis ranges from 0 to 3,000.]

Source: Armed Conflict Location & Event Data Project (ACLED), www.acleddata.com ©IISS

search for alternatives, in March Niger's President Bazoum had called on Nigeria to help establish a new regional military task force.

Jihadist spillover into the Gulf of Guinea increased during the reporting period. As a result, the Accra Initiative gained relevance. Launched in 2017 by Benin, Burkina Faso, Côte d'Ivoire, Ghana and Togo (Mali and Niger have observer status), it aims to prevent jihadist violence spilling over from the Sahel and to tackle transnational organised crime and violent extremism in member countries' border areas. In November 2021, the initiative conducted joint operations in border areas involving close to 6,000 soldiers.[18]

At the domestic level, Burkina Faso, Mali and Niger have adopted a heavy-handed, military-led approach to the conflict since its onset. In 2021 and early 2022, they continued to take steps to reinforce their militaries against jihadist groups. In April 2022, Niger increased its recruitment target for the army by over 50% and announced that it would host additional European special forces.[19] In Burkina Faso in March 2022, the junta announced that it would recall all soldiers that had retired in the previous three years. Meanwhile, Mali sought external support from Russian private military contractors to buttress its security forces. Burkina Faso and Mali continued to rely on self-defence groups as army auxiliaries against jihadist groups.

Economic/development

Several international and regional initiatives have taken shape in recent years to support governance and development in the Sahel. Since 2017, the international-donor platform Sahel Alliance has coordinated development assistance chiefly around decentralisation, basic services, agriculture, rural development and food security. By December 2020, the body was financing close to 1,000 projects worth a total of almost US$23bn, with the World Bank leading donations (43.7%), followed by France (12.5%), the EU (12.3%) and the African Development Bank (11.2%).[20] In 2021, the Sahel Alliance and the G5 Sahel launched a new multi-donor financial instrument, the G5 Sahel Facility, to enable rapid and flexible action in crisis situations. Mali's and Burkina Faso's coups negatively impacted development aid: the US restricted its foreign assistance to both, including some US$160m in aid to Burkina Faso in February 2022.[21]

Diplomacy

Conflict parties engaged in several diplomatic initiatives and dialogues in the reporting period. Several actors have taken steps to mediate deteriorated relations between Mali and its European partners and ECOWAS. The latter named former Nigerian president Goodluck Jonathan as a mediator in 2020, but his various initiatives were largely rejected by the junta during the reporting period. In early May 2022, Togolese President Faure Gnassingbé agreed – at the junta's request – to mediate the tensions with Mali's regional and international partners. The situation remained deadlocked in early 2022, until the transitional authorities announced in late June that they would organise a constitutional referendum in March 2023, legislative elections in October and November 2023, and a presidential election in February 2024. ECOWAS agreed to the new transition timeline in early July and lifted the economic and financial sanctions it had imposed on Bamako in January.

In May 2021, the CSP was formed in Rome under the aegis of the Italian NGO Ara Pacis with the objective of fostering the implementation of the Algiers accord. The NGO, which is allegedly close to the Italian intelligence services, then sponsored other meetings, including with the transitional authorities. However, Ara Pacis and CSP have been criticised by the junta and tensions persist.

Faced with mounting attacks by jihadist groups, during the reporting period Niger and Burkina Faso edged closer to a policy of officially supporting dialogue with militants. In Niger, President Bazoum announced in February 2022 that he had freed and spoken with several jihadists – reportedly including ISSP militants – in a bid to foster dialogue. In parallel, in April Burkina Faso officialised a de facto practice ongoing since late 2020 by setting up local dialogue committees with a view to supporting local customary authorities seeking to demobilise young Burkinabe militants.[22] In contrast, while dozens of verbal accords have been struck between jihadists and local communities in central Mali since 2020, they have mostly been agreed without government approval. The military junta continued to refuse to engage in official talks.

Humanitarian aid

Conflict in the Sahel had displaced over 2.5m people as of April 2022, with figures skyrocketing during the reporting period. The conflict – alongside inflation, drought and the effects of Russia's invasion of Ukraine in February – has exacerbated food insecurity. In April, 6.7m people in the Sahel were in need of emergency food assistance.[23] However, despite the situation deteriorating, donor support waned: only 41% of the funding required to meet humanitarian demand in the Sahel was secured between 2020 and 2021 – the lowest percentage since 2015.[24]

Conflict Outlook

Political scenarios

In Mali, the new electoral calendar released by the military junta in late June eased tensions with ECOWAS, which lifted sanctions on Bamako days later. However, the military junta has amended the transition timeline in the past – in early 2022 it postponed elections scheduled for February – and it remains uncertain whether it will keep its latest commitment to return the country to civilian rule by February 2024. Any significant changes to this new timeline would likely trigger a strong response from ECOWAS and renewed sanctions. In the meantime, while Mali's population appeared to have maintained its overwhelming support for the junta in mid-2022, criticism by public figures and political associations increased during the reporting period and could herald further political upheaval.

The Algiers accord came under increasing strain as its implementation continued to stall during the reporting period. Tensions between signatory groups and the military junta have risen and may worsen, potentially leading to renewed clashes. Notably, although the CSP and the junta signed the Rome agreement in February 2022 in a bid to ease tensions and reinvigorate the implementation process, relations soured again in March, with the CMA calling on its members to mobilise and for the junta to 'clarify its position'.[25] A meeting held between the CSP and the transitional authorities later that month failed to yield a consensus.

In Burkina Faso, the transitional authorities' push for a three-year transition time frame threatened to trigger ECOWAS sanctions during the first half of 2022. Both, however, agreed in July 2022 to a two-year transition timeline, staving off the prospect of sanctions. Any extension of the transition period could spark new tensions with ECOWAS and Burkina Faso's international partners. Meanwhile, the junta's failure to deliver on its promise to restore security has begun to erode its popular support. Further deterioration of the security situation could lead to further political destabilisation through mass protests or direct challenges to the junta's rule.

Escalation potential and conflict-related risks

Over 3,500 fatalities were recorded in Burkina Faso, Mali and Niger in the first four months of 2022. Several emerging security dynamics could reinforce this trend and lead to further instability. Firstly, the withdrawal of *Operation Barkhane* and TFT forces from Mali could produce a security vacuum, which Russian private military contractors are unlikely to fill entirely. The withdrawal of French air support to MINUSMA could also limit the UN mission's ability to operate in the country. The mission is also constrained by the junta's increasing restrictions on movement and access, as well as growing tensions between Bamako and several contributing countries. Moreover, Mali's decision in May to withdraw from the G5 Sahel and the FC-G5S could further erode the regional security architecture.

The presence of Russian private military contractors in Mali led to an escalation of violence against civilians in early 2022. Exacerbated levels of indiscriminate violence could aggravate intercommunal conflict and fuel recruitment by jihadist groups.

In Burkina Faso, the military is likely to face increasing pressure from jihadist groups after the latter expanded to previously unaffected areas during the reporting period and inflicted some of the highest death tolls on security forces since the beginning of the conflict.

Following European troops' withdrawal from Mali, jihadist activity is expected to increase in Niger's western border areas – Tillabéri region in particular. With Niger taking steps to bolster its military and host additional foreign troops, higher-intensity clashes are a possibility.

The threat of jihadist spillover into coastal states, and notably Benin, Côte d'Ivoire and Togo, will remain. A further expansion of jihadist violence could prompt a new wave of internal displacement at the national and regional levels and stretch national armed forces already spread thin.

Prospects for peace remain slim. While Burkina Faso and Niger have taken steps towards dialogue with jihadists groups, these initiatives are unlikely to lead to a comprehensive negotiated settlement. Achieving lasting peace would require a coordinated regional approach to negotiations backed by international partners – neither of which is currently likely. In Burkina Faso, transitional authorities have delegated dialogue with jihadists to local customary authorities rather than seeking to engage them directly, limiting prospects for actual negotiations. Meanwhile, as France and its European partners in the Sahel elevate their military presence in Niger, their long-standing opposition to negotiating with jihadists may come to bear on President Bazoum's reported talks with ISSP militants. A full military victory remains unlikely as jihadist groups continued to make gains and spread to new areas in 2021 and early 2022.

Strategic implications and global influences

In early 2022, the Sahel (and Mali in particular) increasingly became a battlefield for informational warfare waged on social media, with France and Russia vying for political influence in the region. In February, reports emerged that a network of Facebook pages in Mali promoting pro-Russian and anti-French narratives had coordinated support for the Wagner Group and the junta's postponement of elections.[26] In April, France accused Russian private military contractors of staging a war crime in Mali in an attempt to frame French forces.[27] These dynamics are likely to persist and possibly escalate in the coming year, including in Niger as the country becomes European actors' primary counter-terrorism partner in the region.

The Sahel is greatly dependent on food imports and will likely be disproportionately affected by the looming global food crisis triggered by Russia's invasion of Ukraine. Heightened food insecurity could prompt further displacement, raise poverty rates and aggravate competition for resources, leading to worsening intercommunal conflict and social unrest and facilitating NSAGs' recruitment.

Notes

1. Armed Conflict Location & Event Data Project (ACLED) www.acleddata.com.
2. *Ibid.*
3. Bakary Sambe (@bakary_sambe), tweet, 9 May 2022.
4. 'Mali: Massacre by Army, Foreign Soldiers', Human Rights Watch, 4 April 2022.
5. Agence France-Presse (AFP), 'Face aux groupes armés, Ouagadougou veut "diversifier" ses partenaires' [Faced with Armed Groups, Ouagadougou Wants to "Diversify" Its Partners], VOA, 4 April 2022.
6. AFP, 'How Qaeda-friendly GSIM Became the Sahel's Leading Jihadists', *Defense Post*, 11 January 2021; and 'Jihadist Competition and Cooperation in West Africa', European Eye on Radicalization, 3 April 2020.
7. US, Office of Inspector General, 'East Africa Counterterrorism Operation North and West Africa Counterterrorism Operation: Lead Inspector General Report to the US Congress, July 1, 2020–September 30, 2020', 24 November 2020, p. 48.
8. Pauline Le Roux, 'Ansaroul Islam: The Rise and Decline of a Militant Islamist Group in the Sahel', African Center for Strategic Studies, 29 July 2019.
9. Baba Ahmed, 'Mali: Le Business du Cantonnement?' [Mali: The Cantonment Business?], *Jeune Afrique*, 26 April 2016; and Baba Ahmed and Christophe Boisbouvier, 'Nord-Mali: Guerre à Huis Clos' [North Mali: War behind Closed Doors], *Jeune Afrique*, 21 February 2012.
10. *Operation Barkhane* and TFT forces are scheduled to fully withdraw from Mali in mid-2022.
11. France, Ministry of the Armed Forces, 'Operation Barkhane'.
12. Ibid. In January 2022, Sweden announced that it would not renew its one-year mandate in March 2022. Mali's military junta demanded in January that Denmark withdraw its troops deployed in the country as part of the TFT. It did so by the end of the month. Norway was due to send a contingent but abandoned the idea in February due to rising tensions with Mali's junta.
13. MINUSMA, 'Personnel', March 2022.
14. France, Ministry for Europe and Foreign Affairs, 'Statement on the Deployment of the Wagner Group in Mali – December 23rd 2021', 23 December 2021.
15. Africa News and AFP, 'Sergei Lavrov: Wagner in Mali and Libya on a "Commercial Basis"', Africa News, 3 May 2022.
16. 'Four UN Peacekeepers Killed, Five Wounded in Attack in Mali', UN, 14 January 2021.
17. News Wire, 'Mali Receives Russian Helicopters and Weapons, Lauds Moscow "Partnership"', France 24, 1 October 2021; and Jaysim Hanspal, 'Mali: More Military Equipment from Russia After Backlash', *Africa Report*, 19 April 2022.
18. 'Afrique de l'Ouest: l'opération anti-terroriste "Koudanlgou 4" a permis l'arrestation de 300 suspects' [West Africa: The 'Koudanlgou 4' Anti-terrorist Operation Led to the Arrest of 300 Suspects], Radio France Internationale (RFI), 1 December 2021.
19. 'Niger: recrutement annoncé de 5000 soldats pour grossir les rangs de l'armée' [Niger: Announced Recruitment of 5,000 Soldiers to Swell the Ranks of the Army], Niamey, 1 April 2022; and 'Niger Approves Hosting More European Forces amid Mali Withdrawal', Al-Jazeera, 22 April 2022.
20. 'Sahel Alliance', Sahel Alliance, 2022.
21. Arshad Mohammed and Humeyra Pamuk, 'Exclusive: US Halts Nearly $160 Million Aid to Burkina Faso after Finding Military Coup Occurred', Reuters, 19 February 2022.
22. 'Burkina: un dialogue avec les groupes armés pour convaincre les jeunes de déposer les armes' [Burkina: A Dialogue with Armed Groups to Convince Young People to Lay Down Their Arms], RFI, 4 March 2022.
23. Marie-France Reveillard, 'En cinq ans, l'Alliance Sahel a triplé ses engagements financiers' [In five years, the Sahel alliance has tripled its financial commitments], *Afrique Tribune*, 8 April 2022.
24. Vince Chadwick, 'Donors Seek "Direction Change" in Africa's Sahel Region', Devex, 7 April 2022.
25. 'Mali: un accord trouvé entre le gouvernement et les groupes armés signataires' [Mali: an Agreement Reached Between the Government and the Signatory Armed Groups], RFI, 2 March 2022; 'Mali: les ex-rebelles contrôlant Kidal haussent le ton' [Mali: Ex-rebels Controlling Kidal Raise their Voices], RFI, 4 March 2022; and 'Au Mali, la CMA veut obtenir des clarifications du gouvernement de transition' [In Mali, the CMA Wants to Obtain Clarifications from the Transitional Government], RFI, 3 June 2022.
26. Jean Le Roux, 'Pro-Russian Facebook Assets in Mali Coordinated Support for Wagner Group, Anti-Democracy Protests', Digital Forensic Research Lab, Atlantic Council, 17 February 2022.
27. Cyril Bensimon and Morgane Le Cam, 'Sahel: in the Information War, the French Army Retaliates and Accuses the Wagner Group', *Le Monde*, 23 April 2022.

LAKE CHAD BASIN

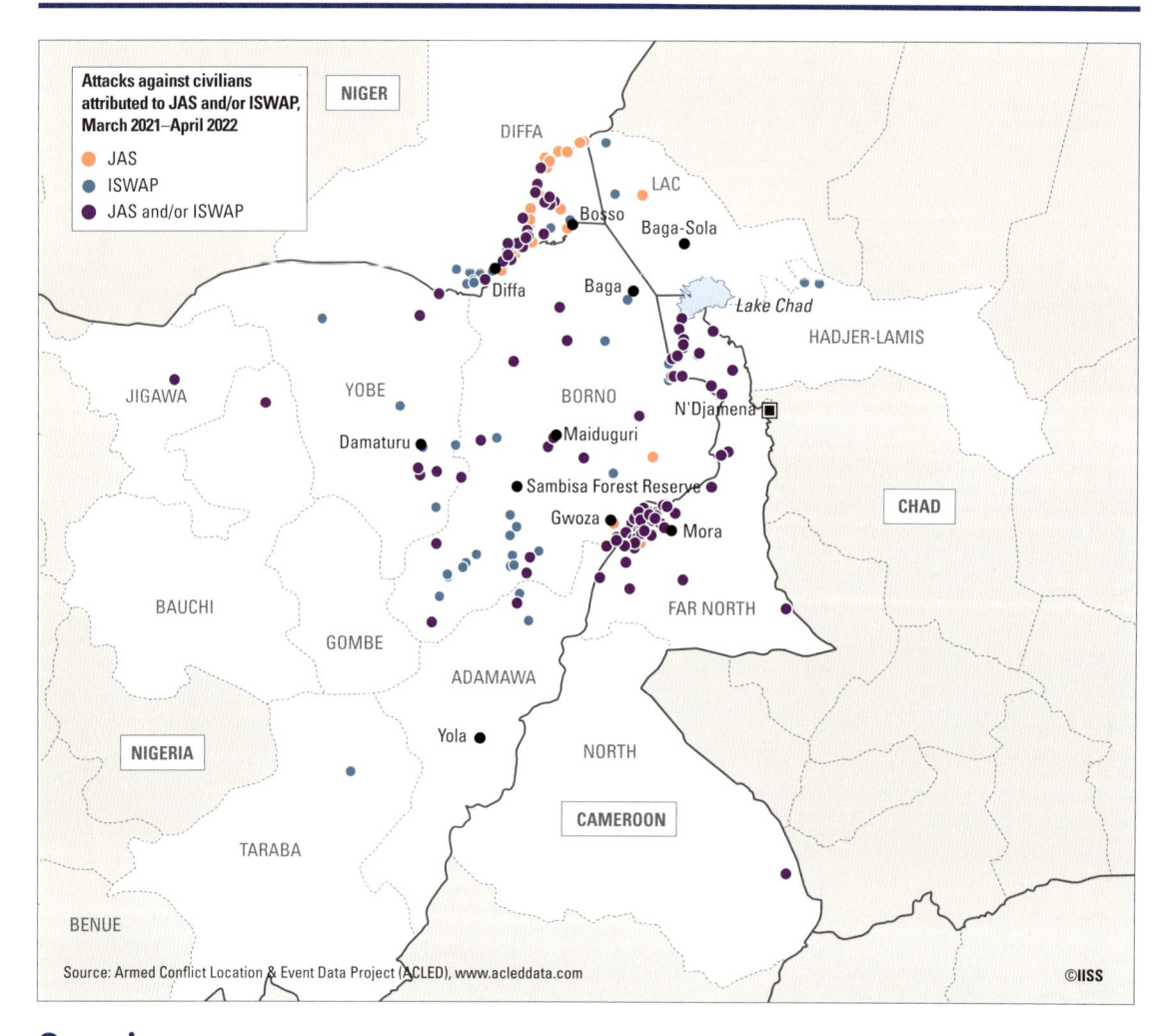

Attacks against civilians attributed to JAS and/or ISWAP, March 2021–April 2022
- JAS
- ISWAP
- JAS and/or ISWAP

Source: Armed Conflict Location & Event Data Project (ACLED), www.acleddata.com

Overview

The Lake Chad Basin has hosted a complex regional conflict for over a decade. Rival factions of the violent Islamist movement known as Boko Haram – Jama'atu Ahlis Sunna Lidda'awati wal-Jihad (JAS) and the Islamic State West Africa Province (ISWAP) – operate in Nigeria's North East and in the border areas of neighbouring Cameroon, Chad and Niger. Authorities have failed to suppress the insurgency, which has claimed thousands of civilian lives and spurred a humanitarian crisis. Boko Haram's presence has affected economic activity and mobility across the region, where an environmental crisis feeds into communal tensions over access to natural resources. Amid serious governance failures, infighting between ISWAP and JAS has occasionally escalated as the groups compete to control territory and resource extraction across the Lake Chad Basin.

Boko Haram was created in Nigeria's North East in 2002 by preacher Mohammed Yusuf. The militant group's aim was to establish sharia law in the country and remove Western-influenced institutions, such as those that underpinned democracy and the education system. Nigerian security forces killed Yusuf in July 2009 and avenging his extrajudicial killing became a key motivation for the group, which reorganised in 2010 under the leadership

Armed Conflict Global Relevance Indicator (ACGRI)

Cameroon — A: 6, B: 7, C: 7
Chad — A: 2, B: 1, C: 23
Niger — A: 2, B: 3, C: 33
Nigeria — A: 26, B: 27, C: 12

Key Conflict Statistics

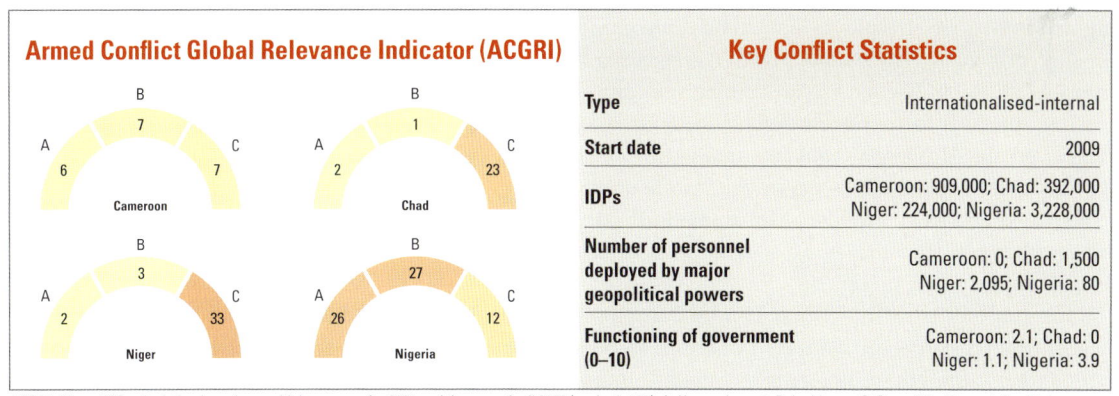

Type	Internationalised-internal
Start date	2009
IDPs	Cameroon: 909,000; Chad: 392,000 Niger: 224,000; Nigeria: 3,228,000
Number of personnel deployed by major geopolitical powers	Cameroon: 0; Chad: 1,500 Niger: 2,095; Nigeria: 80
Functioning of government (0–10)	Cameroon: 2.1; Chad: 0 Niger: 1.1; Nigeria: 3.9

ACGRI pillars: IISS calculation based on multiple sources for 2021 and January–April 2022 (scale: 0–100). A: Human impact; B: Incidence; C: Geopolitical impact. See Notes on Methodology and Data Appendix for further details on Key Conflict Statistics.

of former second-in-command Abubakar Shekau. The group then intensified its violent insurgency, orchestrating high-profile attacks against security forces and civilians while expanding its influence and territorial control. From 2013, Boko Haram's insurgency evolved into a regional crisis, extending into Cameroon, Chad and Niger. Responding to the ensuing large-scale violence, Abuja launched Nigeria's largest military deployment since the 1967–70 Nigerian–Biafran War. Despite the government's repeated claims of victory, the insurgency did not diminish.

In 2015, the group pledged allegiance to the emir of the Islamic State (ISIS) and assumed the name ISWAP. In August 2016, ISIS appointed Yusuf's son Abu Musab al-Barnawi as ISWAP leader in light of rising disagreements between Shekau and senior commander Mamman Nur over the former's intransigent tactics and doctrine. Shekau refused to recognise al-Barnawi and broke away from ISWAP, reverting to the group's original name, JAS. In recent years, internecine fighting between the two groups has turned increasingly violent, with ISWAP becoming the most powerful faction of Boko Haram.

In response to the intensifying crisis and its subsequent regionalisation, in 2015 Benin, Cameroon, Chad, Niger and Nigeria revived the Multinational Joint Task Force (MNJTF), a joint military body supporting counter-terrorism operations. Large-scale MNJTF operations carried out since 2015 have achieved some successes and made inroads into the group's core territory. However, budget limitations and decreasing support from MNJTF contributing countries continues to undermine the task force's efficacy.

While Nigeria confronted an escalating crisis in its North West and in the Middle Belt regions (see Nigeria chapter), conflict in the Lake Chad Basin continued to demonstrate its lethality in 2021 and early 2022. There were 4,423 fatalities resulting from battles, explosions/remote violence and violence against civilians in Chad, Cameroon, Niger and Nigeria between March 2021 and April 2022.[1] Nigeria's North East – which comprises the states of Adamawa, Bauchi, Borno, Gombe, Taraba and Yobe – accounted for approximately three-quarters of total reported fatalities. While fatality numbers decreased in the period under review (4,423 compared to 6,054 between March 2020 and April 2021), the conflict in the Lake Chad Basin remained one of the most violent in Africa.

During the reporting period, ISWAP consolidated its leading role within Boko Haram. The death of JAS leader Shekau, who killed himself by detonating explosives to evade capture by ISWAP militants, in May 2021 was a watershed in the insurgency. Following his death, ISWAP expanded into rural areas in central and southern Borno State, previously a stronghold of JAS. Shekau's death also prompted a wave of defections among JAS recruits and ISWAP absorbed many of them into its ranks, despite suffering the loss of some of its most senior leaders, including al-Barnawi and his designated successor Sani Shuwaram. However, some JAS-aligned fighting groups, including the breakaway Bakura faction, resisted these calls and continued to operate in the northern Lake Chad Basin.

Fear of ISWAP led thousands of JAS fighters and top commanders to surrender en masse to the Nigerian authorities. Demobilisation and de-radicalisation programmes were offered under the revived *Operation Safe Corridor*, a government-sponsored initiative that encourages defections with the aim of reintegrating former fighters into society. Despite its limitations, it succeeded in attracting many fighters to surrender, suggesting a possible shift from Nigeria's long-standing uncompromising approach to counter-insurgency programmes. The overhaul of Nigeria's military establishment in January 2021, when the four service chiefs were unceremoniously sacked by President Muhammadu Buhari, was further indication that Abuja sought a new course in its fight against the group.

Internal shifts within Boko Haram have had wider repercussions for insurgency tactics. In previous years, the Nigerian Army's 'Super Camps' strategy, which prioritised defending large military bases at the expense of protecting villages and rural areas, likely informed the group's increased targeting of civilians. ISWAP's expansion into rural Borno State, where it seeks to consolidate a pretence of governance, resulted in a departure from previous tactics of mass killings and abductions of civilians in favour of small-scale attacks against military installations. Aerial campaigns by the Nigerian Army also forced ISWAP to conduct small-scale yet frequent operations. However, the army's accidental bombings of civilian-populated areas raised questions about the effectiveness of airpower campaigns against ISWAP, which has a history of taking advantage of the military's failure to attract more recruits locally.

Conflict Parties

Nigerian armed forces

Strength: 143,000 military personnel, including 100,000 army personnel. Paramilitary forces number approximately 80,000 troops. An estimated 30,000 troops are deployed in Nigeria's North East.

Areas of operation: Across Nigeria.

Leadership: President Muhammadu Buhari (commander-in-chief of the armed forces), Gen. Leo Irabor (chief of defence staff).

Structure: The Nigerian armed forces comprise the army, the air force and the navy. The army is organised into headquarters, divisions, brigades, battalions, companies, platoons and sections.

History: The military has been fighting Boko Haram since 2009. Strategy has evolved drastically over time, including an expansion from five to eight divisions and the relocation of its headquarters in 2015 to Maiduguri, the capital of Borno State, closer to the epicentre of the insurgency.

Objectives: Secure Nigeria's territorial integrity and end the threat to the populations in the Lake Chad Basin.

Opponents: JAS and ISWAP.

Affiliates/allies: MNJTF, Civilian Joint Task Force (CJTF), Cameroon, Chad, Niger, international partners (France, United Kingdom, United States).

Resources/capabilities: Heavy and light weaponry in land, air, sea and cyber spheres. The Nigerian armed forces have significantly improved the resources and capabilities of the military (including the air force and the Cyber Warfare Command) in recent years. However, poor equipment and training in the army remain areas of concern.

Jama'atu Ahlis Sunna Lidda'awati wal-Jihad (JAS)

Strength: Between 1,500 and 3,000 fighters at its peak.[2]

Areas of operation: Lake Chad Basin, spanning Cameroon, Chad, Niger and Nigeria. Until Shekau's death, core area of control centred around Sambisa Forest and Gwoza Hills, south of Maiduguri (Nigeria).

Leadership: Led by Abubakar Shekau from 2010 until his death in May 2021. Factional leaders include Bakura Shalaba Modu and Bakura Doron.

Structure: Highly decentralised structure with weak command chain, various offshoots and cells that can act independently.

History: Popularly known as Boko Haram, JAS was established in the early 2000s by Mohammad Yusuf. After he was killed in 2009, Shekau escalated the group's violent campaigns and broadened its influence and territorial control. JAS pledged allegiance to ISIS in 2015, operating under the name of ISWAP. In 2016, Shekau split and revived the group's original name, JAS.

Objectives: Establish an Islamic caliphate in the North East of Nigeria and in neighbouring regions.

Opponents: Nigerian armed forces, MNJTF, CJTF, Western states, ISWAP.

Affiliates/allies: ISIS and al-Qaeda.

Resources/capabilities: Stolen weaponry from military bases and acquisitions from the black market, including assault rifles, tanks, rocket-propelled grenades, improvised bombs, mortars and armoured personnel vehicles. It has a limited anti-aircraft capability and reportedly has been using uninhabited aerial vehicles since 2018. The group sustains itself through looting, raiding and kidnapping for ransom.

Islamic State West Africa Province (ISWAP)

Strength: Between 4,000 and 5,000 fighters.[3]

Areas of operation: Lake Chad Basin, spanning Cameroon, Chad, Niger and Nigeria. Core area of territorial control on the islands of Lake Chad and the forests of northern Borno State and eastern Yobe State (Nigeria).

Leadership: Habib Yusuf, also known as Abu Musab al-Barnawi, was named leader for a second time in May 2021 after being ousted in an internal purge in March 2019. Al-Barnawi was reported killed in September 2021. His designated successor Sani Shuwaram, installed as leader in November 2021, was killed in March 2022.

Structure: ISWAP controls parts of northeastern Nigeria, erecting checkpoints and levying taxes on herders, fishermen and farmers.

History: Boko Haram began to be known as ISWAP after Shekau pledged allegiance to ISIS in 2015. Tensions between Shekau and former rival Mamman Nur surfaced in the following months, until ISIS recognised Nur-aligned Abu Musab al-Barnawi, son of Boko Haram founder Mohammad Yusuf, as the new ISWAP leader in August 2016.

Objectives: Establish an Islamic caliphate in Nigeria's North East and in neighbouring regions.

Opponents: Nigerian armed forces, MNJTF, CJTF, Western states, JAS.

Affiliates/allies: ISIS.

Resources/capabilities: ISWAP has acquired much of its weaponry – including assault rifles, rocket-propelled grenades, mortars and armoured personnel vehicles – by raiding military bases and attacking troops. Financial assistance from ISIS was used to acquire looted military equipment from its own fighters.[4] The group also funds itself via taxes collected from local populations.

Civilian Joint Task Force (CJTF)

Strength: Around 26,000 self-defence militants in Borno State (most recent estimate).[5]

Areas of operation: Nigeria's North East (particularly Adamawa, Borno and Yobe states). The CJTF is based in Maiduguri, the capital of Borno State.

Leadership: No overarching leadership. There are local commanders who oversee different sectors.

Structure: The CJTF has a decentralised structure, with local groups and sectors modeled after the Nigerian military.

History: The CJTF was formed in May 2013 as a response to Boko Haram's growing violence in Borno State. It began as a popular youth movement known as *yan gora* ('youth with sticks' in the Hausa language) to protect communities from violence. Its founder Baba Lawan Jafa was a trader from Maiduguri who gained notoriety after confronting a Boko Haram gunman with a stick.

Objectives: Assist the Nigerian armed forces in the fight against Boko Haram and ISWAP; protect local communities from attacks; and free villages and towns from insurgent control. The CJTF patrols the streets, establishes checkpoints and provides intelligence to the security forces.

Opponents: JAS and ISWAP.

Affiliates/allies: Nigerian armed forces and MNJTF.

Resources/capabilities: Bows and arrows, swords, machetes, axes, daggers, cutlasses, handmade muskets and sticks. Most fighters have never received formal military training.

Multinational Joint Task Force (MNJTF)

Strength: Approximately 10,000 troops from the armed forces of Benin, Cameroon, Chad, Niger and Nigeria.[6]

Areas of operation: Lake Chad Basin.

Leadership: Maj.-Gen. Ibrahim Manu Yusuf (MNJTF force commander since November 2019).

Structure: Headquartered in N'Djamena (Chad), the MNJTF comprises four geographical sectors: Baga (Nigeria), Baga Sola (Chad), Diffa (Niger) and Mora (Cameroon). Each sector is led by a commander with wide autonomy while the MNJTF force commander has coordination powers.

History: The MNJTF was first created in 1998 to tackle cross-border crimes and banditry affecting the Basin area. After years of inactivity, the Peace and Security Council of the African Union (AU) agreed to revive the MNJTF in 2015 to counter Boko Haram's growing activity.

Objectives: Coordinate regional counter-insurgency efforts and restore security in areas affected by JAS and ISWAP in the Lake Chad Basin. The force is also involved in supporting stabilisation programmes, humanitarian assistance and the return of those forcibly displaced.

Opponents: JAS and ISWAP.

Affiliates/allies: The national armies of Cameroon, Chad, Niger and Nigeria, as well as international partners (the AU, European Union, US, UK).

Resources/capabilities: The initial operational budget was estimated to be approximately US$700 million. The EU is the main contributor to the force, channelling its funds through the AU. Bureaucratic delays and lack of adequate resources have hampered the MNJTF's ability to fulfil its mandate.

Conflict Drivers

Security
Ineffective government response and regionalisation of the insurgency:
Abuja has persistently failed to restore security and curb a rise in criminality for the populations of northeastern Nigeria. Local communities have been alienated by the government's militarised response to Boko Haram and by human-rights violations perpetrated by state security forces and paramilitaries. Nigeria's violent approach to dealing with Boko Haram fighters – and the killing of Yusuf in police custody – during the first part of the insurgency enabled a more radical leadership to come forward. Subsequently, the Nigerian armed forces and government-sponsored vigilante groups, including the CJTF, have carried out arbitrary detentions, torture, extrajudicial killings and other illegal activities that have elevated civilian insecurity and decreased popular trust in the government.[7] Additionally, porous borders between Nigeria and neighbouring Cameroon, Chad and Niger have enabled Boko Haram to conduct cross-border attacks, recruit fighters among similarly marginalised communities and occasionally establish safe havens across the Lake Chad Basin. A lack of coordination between these countries has often hampered a joint response to the insurgency.

Political
Jihadist ideology and competition:
JAS and ISWAP are Salafi-jihadi groups that aim to create an Islamic caliphate based on sharia law and remove 'Western' influence in the region. Since its creation, Boko Haram has sought to depict its radical version of Salafism as the solution to societal 'evils' represented by Westernised, corrupted elites; inequality and poverty; and Islamic religious leaders who have adopted moderate positions. However, the leadership's mission to create an Islamic caliphate based on sharia law is not fully embraced among the rank and file, who are believed to be motivated less by ideology than by opportunism or pragmatism. Ideological divisions were also at the heart of the split between JAS and ISWAP after the latter disowned Shekau and vowed to end indiscriminate attacks against mosques and markets. This rift has worsened in recent years, with multiple reports of internecine fighting between the two groups.

Economic
Socio-economic grievances:
For many years, communities around the Lake Chad Basin have endured marginalisation, uneven development and environmental degradation. In North East Nigeria and in the Far North region in Cameroon, poverty, illiteracy and youth-unemployment levels are among the highest in their respective countries.[8] Climate change has altered rainfall seasons and growing precipitation unpredictability has undermined livelihoods and aggravated intercommunal conflicts fought over increasingly scarce land and water. As a result of poor economic conditions and long-term neglect on the part of governments, young people from across the Lake Chad Basin are vulnerable to recruitment into criminality or armed groups, such as Boko Haram, which offer spiritual glorification and financial benefits.

Key Events in 2021–22

POLITICAL EVENTS

2 April 2021
Mohamed Bazoum takes office as Niger's new president.

20–21 April
Mahamat Idriss Déby Itno – Idriss Déby Itno's son – is named Chad's interim president and head of a transitional military council.

27 May
President Buhari appoints Maj.-Gen. Farouk Yahaya as Nigeria's chief of army staff.

MILITARY/VIOLENT EVENTS

11 March 2021
ISWAP ambushes a military convoy north of Maiduguri, killing at least 15 Nigerian soldiers and four CJTF troops.

20 April
Chad's President Idriss Déby Itno dies of injuries sustained in clashes with rebels in northern Chad, a day after securing a sixth term in office.

19 May
JAS leader Abubakar Shekau is killed during clashes with ISWAP militants in the Sambisa Forest, Nigeria.

31 May
Buhari appoints Babagana Kingibe as his special envoy to Chad and the Lake Chad Basin.

10 August
The Chadian military junta invites armed groups to take part in an inclusive national dialogue to restore democracy.

25 August
Nigeria announces the signing of a military-cooperation agreement with Russia.

1 September
Buhari reshuffles the Nigerian government, sacking two ministers and redeploying two others.

24 September
President Déby names 93 members of a new interim parliament.

5 October
Chad's interim parliament takes office.

10 January 2022
The leader of Nigeria's All Progressives Congress (APC), Bola Ahmed Tinubu, declares his intention to run for the presidency in 2023.

27 March
Former governor of Nigeria's Nasarawa State Abdullahi Adamu is appointed national chairman of the APC party.

14 April
The US Department of State approves the sale of 12 attack helicopters to Nigeria despite US lawmakers' initial concerns over reported human-rights abuses by the Nigerian government.

Late May
Abu Musab al-Barnawi is reinstated as leader of ISWAP.

5 August
26 Chadian soldiers are killed in clashes with suspected ISWAP fighters near the island of Tchoukou Télia.

15 September
Nigerian airstrikes on suspected militant positions in Yobe State reportedly kill at least ten civilians and wound 19 others.

24 September
ISWAP gunmen kill 30 soldiers in an attack in the Marte area of Borno State, Nigeria.

14 October
The Nigerian Army announces that ISWAP leader al-Barnawi is dead.

5 December
Communal clashes between herders, fishermen and farmers over access to water resources kill dozens in Cameroon's Far North region.

29 January 2022
Nigerien security forces repel an ISWAP attack on Chétima Wangou military camp, killing a dozen militants.

25 February
More than 20 people are killed in ISWAP attacks on three villages in Borno State.

7 March
Suspected militants affiliated with JAS's Bakura faction attack six villages in Diffa region, Niger.

Responses to the Conflict

Security
In early 2022, Boko Haram continued to pose a significant security threat to Nigeria and the other countries across the Lake Chad Basin. The Nigerian military and its allies have failed to counter the group's expansion despite Buhari's repeated pledges to end insecurity. Certain developments in recent years have contributed to increasing the pressure on ISWAP, such as reshuffles within the Nigerian Army's command positions and investment in upgraded weaponry (Nigeria took delivery of 12 US-supplied A-29 *Super Tucano* trainer/light attack aircraft in July and September–October 2021).[9] The 'Super Camps' strategy, which saw Nigerian Army troops regroup in heavily protected garrisons, also improved the military's defence capabilities. However, militants adapted to the changing circumstances, securing control of areas in rural Borno State vacated by the army and mounting small-scale attacks against military positions to escape air raids. Critics also noted that arms sales to Nigeria have often undermined counter-terrorism campaigns and failed to deter violence.

Nigerian authorities have increasingly considered other tactics to defeat Boko Haram. Among these is *Operation Safe Corridor*, an initiative launched in 2016 to encourage defections from jihadist ranks. The programme is intended to de-radicalise former militants and reintegrate them into society. At least 2,000 fighters were reported to have left JAS after its leader, Abubakar Shekau, died in May 2021.[10] Many of these militants feared for their safety under ISWAP and opted to surrender to the Nigerian authorities. During the reporting period, *Operation Safe Corridor* continued to experience significant limitations, including inadequate funding and infrastructure, poor screening, reports of abuses against participants and opposition from local officials and communities. Beyond Nigeria, during the reporting period Cameroonian and Chadian authorities also launched initiatives to counter ISWAP's activity. Among these were the creation of vigilante militias and the provision of services in former Boko Haram strongholds.

Economic/development
The Nigerian economy bounced back in 2021 following the recession caused by the effects of the coronavirus pandemic. Higher private consumption induced by the lifting of coronavirus restrictions and expansionary monetary and fiscal policies led to estimations of real GDP growth of 3.6% year-on-year in 2021, which exceeded initial forecasts and the pre-pandemic pace of growth. Industrial production and growing insecurity moderate the impact of growth, which remains lower than the average rate in sub-Saharan Africa.[11] The outbreak of the war in Ukraine in February 2022 led to an increase in the price of essential commodities, including gasoline, which Nigeria imports despite being an oil-producing country. In April 2022, the Council of the EU reaffirmed its support to the MNJTF and to the AU Lake Chad Regional Stabilisation Strategy, pledging new resources to support 'resilience, stabilisation and economic recovery in the Lake Chad Basin'.[12]

Diplomacy
In 2021 and early 2022, the MNJTF's effectiveness was hampered by contributing countries' security predicaments. Cameroon and Niger faced domestic insurgencies in areas other than the Lake Chad Basin, while Chad's president died in April 2021 after northern rebels launched an offensive towards N'Djamena. Domestic instability curbed the MNJTF's activity, which engaged in fewer large-scale operations during the reporting period. International support to alleviate the humanitarian crisis and for security assistance against Boko Haram

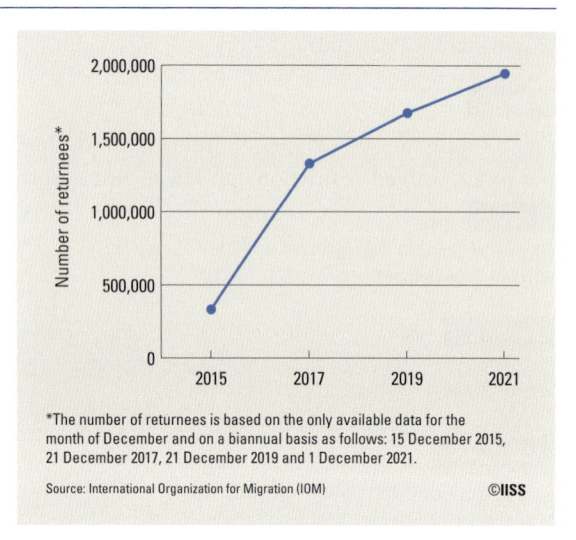

*The number of returnees is based on the only available data for the month of December and on a biannual basis as follows: 15 December 2015, 21 December 2017, 21 December 2019 and 1 December 2021.

Source: International Organization for Migration (IOM) ©IISS

Figure 1: Number of returnees in the Lake Chad Basin, 2015–21

continued in 2021 and early 2022. Nigeria signed a military-cooperation agreement with Russia in August 2021, allegedly due to the reluctance of US Congress to authorise the sale of 12 AH-1 *Cobra* attack helicopters to the country due to the government's human-rights record.[13] After US President Joe Biden waived restrictions on US security assistance to Nigeria, in April 2022 the State Department approved an arms sale worth US$1 billion for the sale of the helicopters and accompanying systems.[14]

Humanitarian aid

The conflict continued to severely affect the humanitarian situation in the Lake Chad Basin in 2021 and early 2022. In January 2022, 11m people were reported to be in need of emergency humanitarian assistance across the region, with 3.3m affected by food insecurity, including 400,000 children who were severely malnourished.[15] In March, there were an estimated 3m internally displaced persons (IDPs), in addition to 2.5m refugees, returnees and third-country nationals hosted in Cameroon, Chad, Niger and Nigeria.[16] Additionally, abductions of aid workers and attacks against humanitarian compounds – including three consecutive raids on the town of Damasak in Borno State in April 2021 – forced some organisations to suspend their operations in the area. At the same time, state authorities' plans to close camps hosting IDPs raised concerns for the safety of the civilian population.[17] Forced resettlements, which involved up to 140,000 people in Maiduguri during the first quarter of 2022, risked endangering civilians who originally resided in ISWAP-controlled areas in Borno State.[18]

Conflict Outlook

Political scenarios

In 2021, Buhari significantly restructured Nigeria's military establishment. Four new service chiefs (of the defence staff, army, navy and air force) were appointed in January to revamp the campaigns against insurgents in the North East and banditry in the North West. In May 2021, Lieutenant-General Farouk Yahaya – then a major-general – was installed as the new chief of army staff to replace Ibrahim Attahiru, who died in a plane crash that month with ten other senior military officers. The plane crash – the fourth deadly incident involving the Nigerian Air Force in 2021 – was mired in controversy and spurred conspiracy theories.[19] These generals, most notably Attahiru and his successor Yahaya, boasted significant combat experience against the insurgents and spearheaded the military's new course in the North East.

Despite these reshuffles, Buhari has failed to meet his promises to fight corruption in the armed forces. While some progress was made during the reporting period, widespread corruption continued to hamper the efficiency of Nigeria's armed and security forces.[20] Arms-procurement scams, impunity and human-rights abuses weakened trust in the military command, including among demoralised rank-and-file soldiers. How to restore security and improve the army's efficiency is likely to be a key issue of the campaigning for the 2023 national elections. Federal and state officials have warned prospective candidates against 'divisive rhetoric' on security, which could widen rifts across the country.[21] Elsewhere across the region, Cameroon, Chad and Niger are preoccupied with other political crises and will seek to continue to contain the spillover of the insurgency in Lake Chad Basin.

Escalation potential and conflict-related risks

The deaths of Shekau, al-Barnawi and other jihadist commanders were major setbacks for JAS and ISWAP. Despite several defections among its ranks, JAS has regrouped around the Bakura faction, retaining an operational, albeit weakened, presence in the islands of the northern Lake Chad Basin. ISWAP has attempted to absorb outgoing fighters from JAS, with mixed success. Factional fighting with JAS is likely to take a toll on ISWAP, which has nonetheless shown its resilience in the face of the death of its historical leader Abu Musab al-Barnawi (himself reportedly wounded in clashes with Bakura fighters). There is a risk that ISWAP might turn to the northwest, building bridges with bandit groups and criminal gangs. However, their fragmented nature and tactical differences means that their co-option by ISWAP is unlikely.[22]

Nigeria's military and its allies are unlikely to roll back ISWAP's gains in the short term. ISWAP has entrenched itself in rural Borno State, taking advantage of the demise of JAS and the military's withdrawal from rural areas into heavily protected super camps. ISWAP's system of governance – consisting of taxation, justice institutions and checkpoints – has ensured its control over large swathes of Nigeria's North East. Moreover, the Nigerian authorities' recent investment in upgraded weaponry and efforts to encourage defections from the jihadist ranks instead suggest that they will focus on containing the insurgents. Increased military pressure, aided by newly acquired *Super Tucano* aircraft, has forced ISWAP to avoid large-scale attacks that would render the group vulnerable to air raids. At the same time, *Operation Safe Corridor* has prevented ISWAP from recruiting Shekau-aligned fighters and further growing in strength. For this strategy to succeed, however, it is essential that the Nigerian military take steps to minimise civilian casualties and that the authorities provide sufficient resources for reintegration and resettlement programmes – to avoid providing ISWAP with opportunities to expand.

Strategic implications and global influences

Economic motivations are at the heart of the security and humanitarian crisis in the Lake Chad Basin.[23] An increase in the price of oil and wheat – Nigeria's largest imports – due to the war in Ukraine could further strain the economic capacity of the Nigerian government and, ultimately, its ability to address the socio-economic roots of the conflict. Notably, in April 2022 the World Food Programme announced that rising fuel and food prices would mean that its operational costs in West Africa would increase by US$136m, while food rations in the region had already been cut before the outbreak of the war in Ukraine.[24] As a result, food insecurity is expected to increase across the region.

Notes

[1] Armed Conflict Location & Event Data Project (ACLED), www.acled.com.

[2] Stig Jarle Hansen, 'The Fractious Future of the Islamic State in West Africa', War on the Rocks, 3 November 2021.

[3] US Congressional Research Service, 'Boko Haram and the Islamic State West Africa Province', *In Focus*, 24 February 2022.

[4] Vincent Foucher, 'The Islamic State Franchises in Africa: Lessons from Lake Chad', International Crisis Group, 29 October 2020.

[5] The figure is difficult to confirm due to the absence of centralised recruitment structures. See International Crisis Group, 'Watchmen of Lake Chad: Vigilante Groups Fighting Boko Haram', Report no. 244, 23 February 2017.

[6] Camillo Casola, 'Multinational Joint Task Force: Security Cooperation in the Lake Chad Basin', Italian Institute for International Political Studies, 19 March 2020.

[7] Chitra Nagarajan, 'To Defend or Harm? Community Militias in Borno State, Nigeria', Center for Civilians in Conflict, 30 April 2020.

[8] United Nations Development Programme, 'Business Case Assessment for Accelerating Development Investments in Famine Response and Prevention: Case Study – North-East Nigeria', 2017; UN Children's Fund (UNICEF), 'Nigeria: Education'; and World Bank, 'Lifting Cameroon's Most Vulnerable Out of Poverty: Building Resilience and Fostering Local Governance to Address the Root Causes of Fragility and Conflict in Northern Regions of Cameroon', 8 November 2019.

[9] International Crisis Group, 'After Shekau: Confronting Jihadists in Nigeria's North East', Briefing no. 180, 29 March 2022.

[10] Malik Samuel, 'Boko Haram Desertions Could Be the Tipping Point', Institute for Security Studies, 18 August 2021.

[11] World Bank, 'Boosting Resilience: The Future of Social Protection in Africa', Africa's Pulse no. 25, 13 April 2022, p. 38.

[12] Council of the EU, 'European Peace Facility: €600 Million for Support to the African Union', 21 April 2022.

[13] US Congressional Research Service, 'Nigeria: Key Issues and U.S. Policy', 25 March 2022; and John Campbell, 'Nigeria and Russia Sign Military Cooperation Agreement', Council on Foreign Relations, 31 August 2021.

[14] Joe Gould and Bryant Harris, 'US State Dept. Approves $1 Billion Sale to Nigeria, Delayed Over Human Rights Concerns', Defense News, 14 April 2022.

[15] UN Office for the Coordination of Humanitarian Affairs, 'Lake Chad Basin: Humanitarian Snapshot', 17 January 2022.

[16] International Organization for Migration, 'Displacement Tracking Matrix: Lake Chad Basin', 28 March 2022.

[17] Amnesty International, 'Nigeria: Plans to Close IDP Camps in Maiduguri Could Endanger Lives', 15 December 2021.

[18] International Crisis Group, 'After Shekau: Confronting Jihadists in Nigeria's North East'.

[19] John Campbell, 'Secrecy and Conspiracy Theories Surround Nigerian Plane Crashes', Council on Foreign Relations, 26 May 2021.

[20] 'Curbing Corruption in the Armed Forces', *Guardian* (Nigeria), 30 March 2021; and 'Nigerian Army Generals Corrupt, Steal Weapons, Sell to Terrorists – the Economist Report', Sahara Reporters, 21 October 2021.

[21] 'Rift on Security Grows Between State Governors and Presidency Amid Claims That Insurgents Threaten the Capital', *Africa Confidential*, vol. 62, no. 9, 3 May 2021.

[22] James Barnett, Murtala Ahmed Rufa'i and Abdulaziz Abdulaziz, 'Northwestern Nigeria: A Jihadization of Banditry, or a "Banditization" of Jihad?', CTC Sentinel, vol. 15, no. 1, January 2022.

[23] William Robert Avis, 'War Economy in North East Nigeria', K4D, 14 January 2020.

[24] UN, 'Daily Press Briefing by the Office of the Spokesperson for the Secretary-General', 14 April 2022.

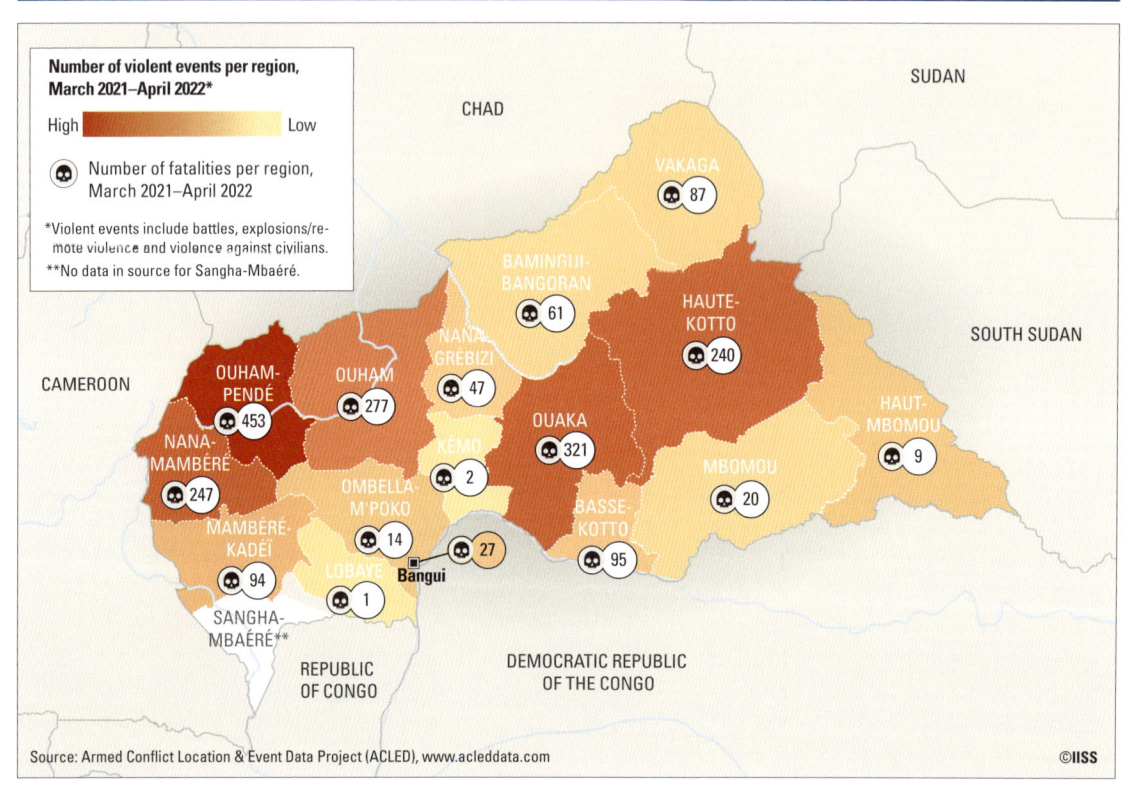

CENTRAL AFRICAN REPUBLIC

Number of violent events per region, March 2021–April 2022

High → Low

Number of fatalities per region, March 2021–April 2022

*Violent events include battles, explosions/remote violence and violence against civilians.
**No data in source for Sangha-Mbaéré.

Regional fatalities:
- VAKAGA: 87
- BAMINGUI-BANGORAN: 61
- HAUTE-KOTTO: 240
- NANA-GRÉBIZI: 47
- OUHAM: 277
- OUHAM-PENDÉ: 453
- NANA-MAMBÉRÉ: 247
- KÉMO: 2
- OUAKA: 321
- HAUT-MBOMOU: 9
- MBOMOU: 20
- OMBELLA-M'POKO: 14
- Bangui: 27
- BASSE-KOTTO: 95
- LOBAYE: 1
- MAMBÉRÉ-KADÉÏ: 94

Source: Armed Conflict Location & Event Data Project (ACLED), www.acleddata.com   ©IISS

Overview

The current conflict in the Central African Republic (CAR) began in 2012 when sustained agitation by several rebel groups threatened to topple the government of then-president François Bozizé. Following the failed implementation of a peace agreement signed in January 2013, the rebel coalition known as Séléka overthrew Bozizé in March that year, plunging the CAR into a war and subsequent protracted conflict and instability. A decade later, the CAR remains unstable and has seen episodic upticks in gruesome violence affecting civilians in several parts of the country.

Years of military regimes, poor governance and a lack of viable state institutions and public services in many parts of the country created a vacuum that armed groups were able to fill. Furthermore, as a result of the length and porosity of the CAR's borders, the country has been exposed to sources of instability originating elsewhere in the region, such as transnational crime, which has spilled over primarily from neighbouring Chad and Sudan (Darfur region).

The United Nations Multidimensional Integrated Stabilization Mission in the CAR (MINUSCA) was deployed in September 2014 to help restore peace and stability in the country. It replaced the African Union (AU)-led International Support Mission in the CAR (MISCA), which had taken over from the Economic Community of Central African States' (ECCAS) Mission for the Consolidation of Peace in Central Africa (MICOPAX). All three organisations – the UN, AU and ECCAS – have been involved in the CAR to various degrees, with the AU leading the negotiations that led to the signing of the 2019 peace agreement (the Khartoum agreement) between the government and 14 armed groups.

At various junctures during the conflict, neighbouring countries and ECCAS member states, such as Angola, Chad, Gabon and the Republic of Congo, have taken leading roles in assisting CAR governments with

Armed Conflict Global Relevance Indicator (ACGRI)

Central African Republic

- Incidence: 5
- Human impact: 8
- Geopolitical impact: 44

Key Conflict Statistics

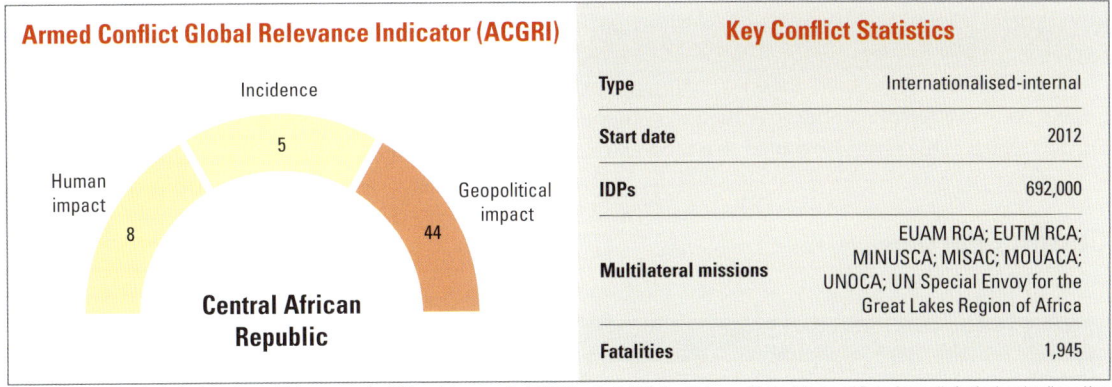

Type	Internationalised-internal
Start date	2012
IDPs	692,000
Multilateral missions	EUAM RCA; EUTM RCA; MINUSCA; MISAC; MOUACA; UNOCA; UN Special Envoy for the Great Lakes Region of Africa
Fatalities	1,945

ACGRI pillars: IISS calculation based on multiple sources for 2021 and January–April 2022 (scale: 0–100). See Notes on Methodology and Data Appendix for further details on Key Conflict Statistics.

the peace process. In particular, Cameroon has provided the main corridor through which vital goods reach the CAR's capital, Bangui, and received regular influxes of refugees from the country.

The primary international and multilateral actors in the CAR have been France, Russia and, more recently, the International Conference on the Great Lakes Region (ICGLR). As the former colonial power, France has been involved in the CAR's internal politics for decades. Russia's influence in the country has invariably strained the relationship between the CAR and France. According to the CAR government, Moscow has provided military support and training to the Central African Armed Forces (FACA), while various reports have indicated the presence of Russian private military company the Wagner Group. As of 2020, Rwanda has provided direct military assistance to the CAR (besides its troops contribution to MINUSCA) to repel rebel attacks and drive them out of the areas they occupy. The CAR's geographical position in sub-Saharan Africa adds a regional dimension to the conflict, while the involvement of regional and international actors further reduces the prospect that there will be a convergence of interests towards brokering durable peace in the country.

Following the havoc wreaked in December 2020 and January 2021 by the Coalition of Patriots for Change (CPC), a group of six major armed-group signatories to the 2019 Khartoum agreement, the situation slowly evolved in the government's favour. On the military front, the FACA – with the support of Russian and Rwandese actors – managed to push back CPC fighters and liberate a number of areas that had been under the control of the armed groups. In spite of these military gains and because of the alleged violations committed by the FACA and Russian operatives – and what Russia stands to gain in the CAR – many observers assess that the CAR government has essentially become subservient to Moscow.

During the reporting period, the FACA (with its Russian and Rwandese allies) fought the rebels (particularly those belonging to the CPC) in the northeast, west and centre of the country. Although the rebels suffered serious setbacks at the hands of the FACA, it remains unlikely that a military resolution of the conflict will prove successful in the medium to long term.

On the political front, incumbent President Faustin-Archange Touadéra was sworn in for a second presidential term on 30 March 2021 amid concerns about the legitimacy of the elections after polls were disrupted by CPC attacks. The finalisation of the electoral cycle (the last bout of legislative elections took place in May 2021) delivered a parliamentary majority for Touadéra's coalition party, United Hearts Movement (MCU).

Preparations for the holding of an inclusive national dialogue between the government and the various CAR stakeholders – including armed groups and the political opposition – culminated in an event held in March 2022 in Bangui. However, the CPC armed groups were excluded from the dialogue, while the opposition also boycotted the gathering at the eleventh hour, meaning important actors did not attend. The political climate in the CAR remained fraught in mid-2022, including within the ruling MCU, where there appeared to be dissenting voices critical of the government's relationship with Russia. Moscow's increasing influence in Bangui also severely strained the government's relationships with its Western partners – especially France.

The idea of yet another national dialogue was largely seen as a remake of the 2015 Bangui National Forum, which at the time was touted as a momentous event that was to set the foundations for a new CAR. Exhuming and implementing recommendations from the Bangui Forum could make a difference in the lives of the hundreds who participated in the grassroots popular consultations that fed into the Forum.

Conflict Parties

Central African Armed Forces (FACA)

Strength: 9,150 active military, 1,000 gendarmerie and paramilitary. 14 territorial battalions.

Areas of operation: Main cities.

Leadership: Claude Rameaux Bireau (defence minister), Gen. Zéphirin Mamadou (chief of the army).

Structure: The army is an infantry force (except for a river unit in charge of patrolling the Ubangi River). The presidential guard is the best trained and equipped unit.

History: Experienced mutinies in 1996 and 1997. Having been involved in many coups since independence, the army evaporated when the Séléka took power in 2013, with many soldiers joining the anti-balaka groups. The army reconstruction process started gradually in 2014, supported by the European Union, Russia and the UN. Since then, the reconstruction process has been slow.

Objectives: Protecting the Touadéra regime and securing CAR territory from external threats and attacks.

Opponents: Armed groups.

Affiliates/allies: MINUSCA, Rwandan soldiers, Wagner Group.

Resources/capabilities: Insufficient budget, limited military equipment and mobility. Wages are often unpaid.

Union for Peace in the Central African Republic (UPC)

Strength: Unknown.

Areas of operation: Central and southeastern CAR (Basse-Kotto, Haute-Kotto, Haut-Mbomou, Kémo, Mbomou and Ouaka provinces), with militiamen deployed in seven out of 16 provinces.

Leadership: Ali Darassa, a long-standing Fulani rebel and bandit, formerly a commander of the Baba Laddé militia. The UPC leadership (*comzones*) is made up of professional bandits and regional mercenaries.

Structure: Unknown.

History: The first group to split from the Séléka coalition in 2014, the UPC has strategically enlarged its territory since then and is widely considered the most powerful armed group currently in the CAR.

Objectives: Officially, the UPC protects Fulani communities but its main objective is to control natural resources and trade routes between the CAR and some of its neighbours.

Opponents: Government forces, some anti-balaka groups.

Affiliates/allies: Return, Reclamation, Rehabilitation (3R) and possibly the Central African Patriotic Movement (MPC). The UPC is a member of the CPC but has kept a low profile within the coalition. In some locations, the UPC has also been cooperating with the Popular Front for the Renaissance in the Central African Republic (FPRC).

Resources/capabilities: Involved in the cattle and gold trade and weapons trafficking between Chad, the Democratic Republic of the Congo (DRC) and South Sudan.

Popular Front for the Renaissance in the Central African Republic (FPRC)

Strength: Unknown.

Areas of operation: Northeastern CAR: Bamingui-Bangoran, Haute-Kotto and Vakaga provinces.

Leadership: Abdoulaye Hissène (military leader) and Noureddine Adam (political leader).

Structure: Originally composed of Rounga, Goula, Chadian and Sudanese fighters; most of the Goula elements left the movement in 2017 and 2018, joining the Patriotic Rally for the Renewal of Central Africa.

History: The FPRC emerged after the fall of the Séléka coalition in 2014. Séléka leaders Hissène and Adam created the FPRC to maintain their hold on northeastern CAR. In 2019, they fought against the Movement of Central African Liberators for Justice (MLCJ) but lost and were pushed out of Birao, the main city in the Vakaga province.

Objectives: The FPRC's political agenda focuses on the protection of Muslim communities and the partition of the country. In 2015, Adam briefly proclaimed the creation of an independent state, the Logone Republic. Since 2015, Adam has tried unsuccessfully to reunite the former Séléka armed groups.

Opponents: MLCJ and government forces.

Affiliates/allies: Member of the CPC.

Popular Front for the Renaissance in the Central African Republic (FPRC)

Resources/capabilities: The FPRC's main sources of revenue are weapons trafficking and the taxation of pastoralists and traders between Sudan, Chad and the CAR. Based in northeastern CAR, it is well connected to the Chadian and Sudanese security services, which send mercenaries and military equipment.

3R (Return, Reclamation, Rehabilitation)

Strength: Unknown.

Areas of operation: Ouham-Pendé and Nana-Mambéré provinces, with headquarters in De Gaulle town.

Leadership: Bi Sidi Souleman, alias Sidiki Abass, a Fulani warlord. Abass was sanctioned by the UN in 2020. His death has been falsely reported several times, including in December 2020.

Structure: Unknown.

History: 3R emerged in late 2015 at the northwest border between the CAR and Cameroon and was mandated by Fulani cattle owners based in Cameroon to protect their cattle during the transhumance. Its recruitment is Fulani-based.

Objectives: Protect Fulani cattle and economic predation.

Opponents: MINUSCA, government forces and anti-balaka groups.

Affiliates/allies: UPC, member of the CPC.

Resources/capabilities: 3R's main sources of revenue are the taxation of Fulani pastoralists and gold and weapons smuggling between Chad and Cameroon. Most of its military equipment comes from Chad.

Central African Patriotic Movement (MPC)

Strength: Unknown.

Areas of operation: Ouham and Nana-Grébizi provinces, with a stronghold in Kaga-Bandoro.

Leadership: Mahamat Al-Khatim, a Chadian whose family has settled in the CAR. He was appointed special adviser to the prime minister after the 2019 Khartoum agreement but resigned in August 2019. The *comzones* are all Chadian fighters.

Structure: Mostly composed of Chadian fighters from the Salamat region. The Salamat traditional leaders have a strong influence over Khatim.

History: The MPC was initially a splinter group of the FPRC, created by Khatim in mid-2015. The MPC is the strongest armed group in Ouham province. In July 2020, Khatim unsuccessfully attempted to form the 'Markounda coalition' under his leadership.

Objectives: Secure the interests of the Salamat communities in the Ouham and Nana-Grebizi provinces (cattle migration, access to land and markets) and economic predation.

Opponents: Anti-balaka groups.

Affiliates/allies: Chadian security forces, member of the CPC.

Resources/capabilities: The main sources of revenue are weapons smuggling between Chad and the CAR, the taxation of pastoralists from Chad and the taxation of trade and artisanal gold mining in the CAR provinces under its control.

Anti-balaka groups

Strength: Unknown.

Areas of operation: Most of the CAR's provinces (except for Bamingui-Bangoran, Haut-Mbomou and Vakaga) but their activity was sporadic in 2021 and early 2022. Some of them have joined the CPC.

Leadership: No central leadership and chain of command but François Bozizé has some political influence over the movement. Two coordination branches (run by Maxime Mokom and by Sébastien Wenezoui and Patrice-Edouard Ngaissona, respectively) present themselves as interlocutors for the movement and have signed the Khartoum agreement. Suspected of war crimes, Ngaissona was arrested in France in 2018 and handed over to the International Criminal Court. Mokom and Wenezoui were both part of the Touadéra government in 2019 but the former was dismissed in January 2021 after joining the CPC.

Structure: No structure.

History: A loose network of anti-Muslim local militias, which initially emerged as a self-defence movement against the Séléka in François Bozizé's ethnic stronghold and spread to western CAR in late 2013. They entered Bangui in December 2013 to drive out the Séléka coalition. In 2014 they became infamous for their retaliations against Muslim communities. In 2017, the movement's territorial reach was extended with the emergence of the so-called 'self-defence' groups in southeastern CAR. At present the active anti-balaka groups focus on banditry and extortion.

Objectives: No clear agenda. The initial goal to drive Muslims out of the CAR quickly morphed into violent economic predation (looting and extortion). Despite their initial anti-Séléka motive, some have allied with Muslim armed groups. In December 2020, two anti-balaka factions close to Bozizé (the Ndomaté and Mokom branches) joined the CPC.

Opponents: Muslim armed groups and other anti-balaka groups.

Anti-balaka groups

Affiliates/allies: Some anti-balaka groups are part of the CPC but not all.

Resources/capabilities: Artisanal weaponry, very few automatic weapons. No organised control of natural resources and trade routes.

Rwanda Defence Force (RDF)

Strength: Deployment in the country estimated to comprise 2,000 infantry troops.

Areas of operation: Throughout the CAR.

Leadership: Rwandan Ministry of Defence.

Structure: Unknown.

History: On 21 December 2020, the Rwandan defence ministry confirmed that it had deployed troops to the CAR under a bilateral security agreement with the CAR government. Rwandan forces participated in the protection of Bangui in December 2020 and in the counter-offensive led by Russian contractors and the FACA against the CPC that started in January 2021.

Objectives: Secure the elections and protect the contingent of Rwandan troops within MINUSCA against targeting by CPC rebels.

Opponents: CPC forces.

Affiliates/allies: MINUSCA, the FACA and Russian contractors (Wagner Group).

Resources/capabilities: Unknown.

Wagner Group

Strength: 2,000–3,000 (estimates).[1]

Areas of operation: Bangui and Lobaye in 2020 and central and eastern provinces in 2021.

Leadership: Dmitry Utkin (commander); Alexander Ermolaev (deputy commander); Andrei Troshev (chief of staff).

Structure: The company was established by businessman Yevgeny Prigozhin. It has particularly close ties with Russian military intelligence (GRU), the Ministry of Defence and President Vladimir Putin.

History: The Wagner Group is a Russian security organisation closely linked to the Kremlin and military intelligence. It is used by Russia to carry out a range of officially deniable military and intelligence operations, and commercial activities, abroad, including in the Middle East and Africa. Reports about the presence of the group in the CAR first emerged in 2018, when Russian instructors were sent to train the CAR army in the Berengo base.

Objectives: Initially, provide close protection for President Touadéra, train the CAR army and set up two bases: Berengo for military training (Lobaye province) and Bria for medical facilities (Haute-Kotto province). Since December 2020 and the CPC attack, protect Bangui and organise a counter-offensive with the FACA and Rwandan troops.

Opponents: CPC forces.

Affiliates/allies: The FACA and Rwandan troops.

Resources/capabilities: In December 2020, cargo aircraft supplied the Wagner Group with ammunition, vehicles and combat helicopters. At the end of January 2021, following discussion about the violation of the UN arms embargo, Russian diplomats announced the withdrawal of these helicopters but there was no confirmation on the ground.

United Nations Multidimensional Integrated Stabilization Mission in the Central African Republic (MINUSCA)

Strength: 15,760 personnel, as of May 2022.[2]

Areas of operation: Throughout the CAR.

Leadership: Valentine Rugwabiza from Rwanda (replaced Mankeur Ndiaye of Senegal as head of MINUSCA in February 2022), Lt-Gen. Daniel Sidiki Traoré (force commander).

Structure: MINUSCA comprises 11,598 military personnel, 2,085 police, 1,236 civilian personnel, 412 chief-of-staff officers, 147 military observers and 281 UN volunteers.[3]

History: MINUSCA was authorised by the UN Security Council on 10 April 2014.

Objectives: MINUSCA's highest priority is the protection of civilians. Other tasks include supporting the transition process, facilitating humanitarian assistance, promoting and protecting human rights, supporting justice and the rule of law, and supporting disarmament, demobilisation, reintegration and repatriation processes.

Opponents: Various armed groups, including 3R.

Affiliates/allies: CAR government.

Resources/capabilities: Approved budget for mid-2021–mid-2022: approximately US$1 billion.[4]

Conflict Drivers

Security

Insecure borders:
The CAR's domestic political, social and economic challenges have been exacerbated – particularly in border areas – by the wider security issues in the region. Historically, the area where the CAR, Chad and Sudan share a border has been replete with insurgents fighting the governments of their respective countries. This area has also become a hotspot of transnational organised crime and illicit activities, which further contribute to insecurity.

Lack of a professional army:
The CAR army, which was structurally weak in the decades following independence and had a history of mutinies, effectively collapsed in 2013. The absence of a capable and professional army to defend the country has encouraged armed banditry and allowed armed groups to take root in and control large parts of the country's territory.

Political

Limited state presence:
Since independence, the effective presence of the state has largely been limited to Bangui and its environs. Moreover, military regimes, poor governance and *coups d'état* have been an integral part of the CAR's political life. François Bozizé himself came to power through a coup in 2003 with the help of mercenaries from Chad and Sudan, a development that created the conditions for the proliferation of mercenary activities and other perpetrators of violence in regions outside the capital city Bangui.

Tensions with non-state armed groups:
Put simply, the conflict is a struggle between the government and dissident or armed groups that seek to grow or conserve their shares of the country's resources. This tension was evident in 2012, when rebel groups demanded that president Bozizé implement various reforms agreed in earlier peace agreements. Since President Touadéra was first elected in 2016, the struggle between the government and rebel groups has constituted the conflict's primary *casus belli*, particularly as rebel groups gained the upper hand militarily in the ensuing years.

Economic

Competition over mineral resources:
The CAR's mineral resources have fuelled conflict and instability in the country. Internal and external actors have been hostile to the prospect of establishing a state order that would prevent the plundering of these resources. Armed groups, as well as militias and mercenaries from neighbouring countries, have financed their activities by controlling areas where minerals are being exploited. Moreover, the UN has reported that some local politicians and international companies may have benefitted from the chaos.

Social

Religious and ethnic divisions:
Although the conflict began as a struggle between Bozizé and armed opposition and other opportunists, it took on religious and ethnic dimensions due to a radical political and war discourse advanced by the belligerents that pitted the Séléka rebels – perceived as foreigners or not Central African enough – against the anti-balaka groups, which were presented as the 'autochthonous' defenders of the nation. As a consequence of this narrative, CAR society is fractured and national cohesion is low, with interreligious, inter-ethnic and intercommunal violence widespread in the country.

Key Events in 2021–22

POLITICAL EVENTS

14 March 2021
The CAR holds a second round of legislative elections (first-round elections are held in areas where the CPC disrupted the process in December 2020).

MILITARY/VIOLENT EVENTS

March–April 2021
The FACA and its allies stage an offensive against the CPC and take control of several towns, including Alindao, Batangafo, Bria, Kabo, Kaga-Bandoro and Markounda.

30 March
President Touadéra is sworn in for a second term.

Late May
The second round of legislative elections takes place in areas which had their first round in March.

8 June
France suspends aid and bilateral military cooperation with the CAR due to Russia's presence and influence in the country.

11 June
Touadéra appoints Henri Marie Dondra as prime minister.

23 June
Touadéra appoints a new 32-member government.

2 July
11 members of the Truth, Justice, Reconciliation and Reparation Commission are sworn in.

16 September
The ICGLR adopts the Joint Roadmap for Peace in the CAR.

15 October
Touadéra declares a unilateral ceasefire.

2–7 February 2022
Different sources report that Dondra either resigns from his post or is dismissed by the president.

7 February
Félix Moloua is appointed prime minister.

21–27 March
The government holds a national dialogue in Bangui. During discussions there, the ruling majority bids for amending the CAR's constitution, which would allow Touadéra to run for a third term.

19 April
The CAR's Special Criminal Court opens its first trial.

12 March
The UN increases MINUSCA's military component by 2,750 soldiers and 940 police officers.

25 March
Sidi Abass, leader of the 3R rebel group, allegedly dies.

31 March
The UN reports on the Wagner Group's and the FACA's connections to human-rights violations and abuses committed in the CAR.

5 April
The UPC announces its withdrawal from the CPC.

30 May
Six Chadian soldiers are killed in skirmishes along the CAR–Chad border. The incident involves rebels groups, the FACA and the Wagner Group.[5]

17 June
The UPC and 3R sign an agreement to form an alliance.

6–7 December
15 civilians are killed in Boyo during clashes between the FACA and rebels.

March 2022
Violent clashes take place between the FACA and the CPC in northern CAR.

Responses to the Conflict

Security
During the reporting period, the government of President Touadéra pursued an outright military confrontation with the CPC. With the help of Russian operatives and Rwandese soldiers, the FACA drove out rebel forces from large swathes of CAR territory. However, Bangui and its allies were not able to establish complete control in these newly liberated areas, leaving room for frequent rebel incursions and resettlement.

The government also continued to push for the operationalisation of mixed security units, which are composed of FACA troops and militiamen from some of the armed groups that signed the Khartoum agreement. The mixed security units have been beset by funding challenges and a lack of equipment.

MINUSCA continued to provide support to the government, particularly in terms of civilian protection. The government's military offensive of early 2021 put MINUSCA in a tight spot given that its mandate exclusively focuses on the protection of civilians, while the FACA and its allies were reportedly perpetrating human-rights abuses against civilians.

Economic/development
The CAR's economy was severely impacted by the coronavirus pandemic in 2020. Predictions of economic growth in 2021 were dampened by the deteriorating security situation brought about by the CPC's attacks and the government's response. Inflation was also on the rise during the reporting period – particularly in Bangui – principally as a result of the CPC cutting supplies via the main corridor between CAR and Cameroon.[6] For these reasons, the government is facing an economic crisis that requires a response that must address both contextual and structural economic challenges if it is to replenish state coffers. The government must also work towards creating the conditions to convince donors, such as the IMF, to give the country access to its extended credit facility.

In April 2022, the CAR adopted a law allowing cryptocurrencies to be used as legal currency in the country,[7] a move that was at odds with sub-regional rules under the monetary union of the Central African region. The development placed the government in a precarious position vis-à-vis other countries of the sub-region, potentially isolating the country even further given Western donors' growing reluctance to continue supporting it in light of Bangui's relationship with Moscow.

All of these challenges will impact the government's ability to keep the economy afloat and finance critical development plans. In 2021, the CAR drew 68% of its budget from external support.[8]

Diplomacy
The flagrant violation of the Khartoum agreement by armed groups during the reporting period did not discourage the government and its partners, who continue to see it as the key to lasting peace in the country. ICGLR initiatives followed the signing of the agreement and culminated in the establishment of the Joint Roadmap for Peace in the CAR in September 2021, which recommended, among other things, that domestic stakeholders to the conflict hold an inclusive national dialogue. As the main guarantor of the agreement, the AU also continued efforts towards its implementation, with the AU Peace and Security Council visiting Bangui in June 2021 to review the progress being made towards this goal.[9]

Amid a growing Russian presence and influence in the CAR, which was allegedly fuelling resentment towards France in the country, Paris froze its budgetary support to Bangui and suspended military cooperation.[10]

On 12 November 2021, the UN Security Council renewed MINUSCA's mandate via Resolution 2065, with 13 votes in favour and two abstentions (China and Russia).[11]

Humanitarian aid
Although most analyses highlight that the conflict's intensity has been decreasing since 2018, in November 2021, the UN Office for the Coordination of Humanitarian Affairs (UNOCHA) indicated that the CAR's humanitarian needs were at their highest since 2015 due to the disruptions triggered by the CPC attacks of December 2020.[12] It reported that 3.1 million people (63% of the population) would be in need of humanitarian assistance in 2022. These numbers included 2.2m people with acute needs and 722,000 internally displaced persons.[13]

Conflict Outlook

Political scenarios

The failure of the March 2022 national dialogue to bring together the CAR's key stakeholders has left the country in a political quagmire. It is likely that the political opposition will continue to contest Touadéra's legitimacy, forcing him into another dialogue or, at the very least, proving a nuisance for his regime. If not pressured internally and by the international community, the president's ruling coalition will likely continue to push for a constitutional amendment to allow Touadéra to run for a third term.

The fate of the Khartoum agreement will depend on which approach the government and its partners take with regards to armed groups, particularly those that belong to the CPC and were excluded from the March 2022 national dialogue. It is likely that renegade armed groups will continue the fight against the FACA and its allies as they seek to regain control of their former strongholds.

Escalation potential and conflict-related risks

The conflict is likely to escalate in the short and medium term, with a strong possibility that the CPC groups will step up attacks against the FACA and its allies, prompting a military response by the state. Moreover, political tensions could worsen as a result of the failed national dialogue in March 2022 and the ruling coalition's efforts to secure a possible third term for Touadéra. The economic downturn and the humanitarian situation are also potential drivers of further escalation.

In order for the conflict to de-escalate, the balance of power will need to continue to shift from armed groups to the government. This should be accompanied by talks towards a negotiated settlement. Bangui will also need to engage in a constructive dialogue with the political opposition, which, in turn, will need to show its willingness to negotiate by first recognising Touadéra's legitimacy. At the time of writing, an escalation of the conflict seems more likely than a de-escalation. The key question will remain how to effectively implement the 2019 Khartoum agreement and the ICGLR Roadmap in the current context.

Figure 1: IDPs and refugees in the Central African Republic as a proportion of the population, December 2021

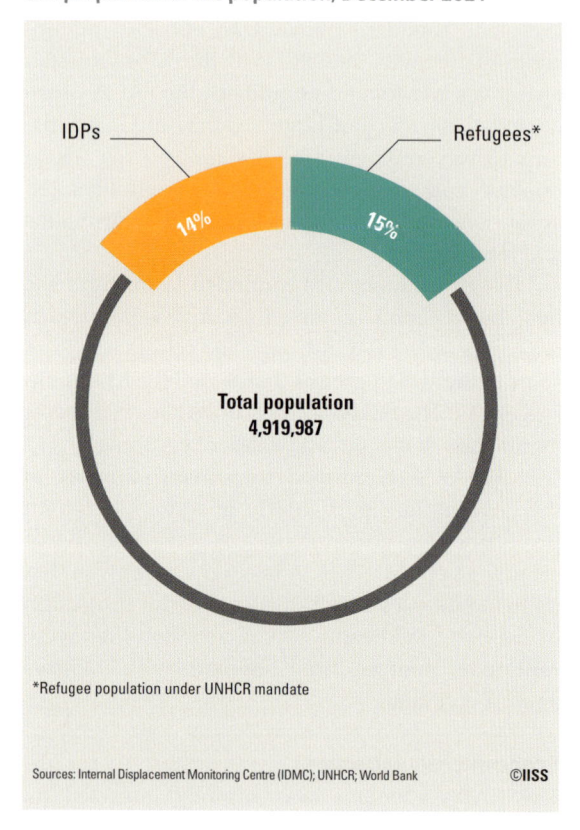

IDPs 14%
Refugees* 15%
Total population 4,919,987

*Refugee population under UNHCR mandate

Sources: Internal Displacement Monitoring Centre (IDMC); UNHCR; World Bank ©IISS

Strategic implications and global influences

Developments in the CAR in 2021 and early 2022 suggest that the country may be witnessing a reversal of gains made in recent years and sliding further into protracted conflict. Ongoing tensions between the CAR's Western partners and Russia – the Touadéra regime's main ally – have been exacerbated by the war in Ukraine and will further undermine Bangui's ability to meet its financial obligations, including the government's most vital expenditures and debt repayments, with potentially serious implications for conflict dynamics in the country. Moreover, the differences between Western countries on the one hand, and Russia and China on the other, seem irreconcilable. As a result, it is likely that these international actors will fail to achieve the consensus required to design and implement a coherent plan for the reconstruction of the CAR that can facilitate the eventual exit of MINUSCA.

Notes

1   Jack Losh, 'In Central Africa, Russia Won the War – But It's Losing the Peace', *Foreign Policy*, 21 August 2021; and Human Rights Watch, 'Central African Republic: Events of 2021'.
2   United Nations Multidimensional Integrated Stabilization Mission in the Central African Republic, 'Facts and Figures', May 2022.
3   *Ibid.*
4   UN Peacekeeping, 'MINUSCA Fact Sheet'.
5   Pacôme Pabandji, 'Tensions entre le Tchad et la Centrafrique sur fond de bras de fer France-Russie' [Tensions between Chad and the Central African Republic against the backdrop of the France–Russia stand-off], *Jeune Afrique*, 1 June 2021.
6   Central African Republic, Ministry of Finance and Budget, 'Rapport d'exécution Budgétaire du Quatrième Trimestre 2021' [Fourth Quarter 2021 Budget Execution Report], 16 February 2022, pp. 2–3.
7   Rodrigue Fénélon Massala, 'La Centrafrique adopte la cryptomonnaie' [The Central African Republic Adopts Cryptocurrency], *Financial Afrik*, 22 April 2022.
8   Central African Republic, Ministry of Finance and Budget, 'Rapport d'exécution Budgétaire du Quatrième Trimestre 2021' [Fourth Quarter 2021 Budget Execution Report]. p. 5.
9   Mohamed M Diatta. 'Will This Week's AU Mission to CAR Deliver a Change in Strategy?', Institute for Security Studies, 30 June 2021.
10 'Centrafrique: la France gèle son aide budgétaire et suspend sa coopération militaire' [Central African Republic: France Freezes Its Budgetary Aid and Suspends Its Military Cooperation], TV5 Monde, 7 June 2021.
11 UN Peacekeeping, 'Résolution 2605 : le nouveau mandate de la MINUSCA est adopté' [Resolution 2605: the New Mandate of MINUSCA Is Adopted], 22 November 2021.
12 UN Office for the Coordination of Humanitarian Affairs 'Central African Republic Humanitarian Needs Overview 2022', 15 December 2021, p. 4.
13 *Ibid.*, p. 2.

SOUTH SUDAN

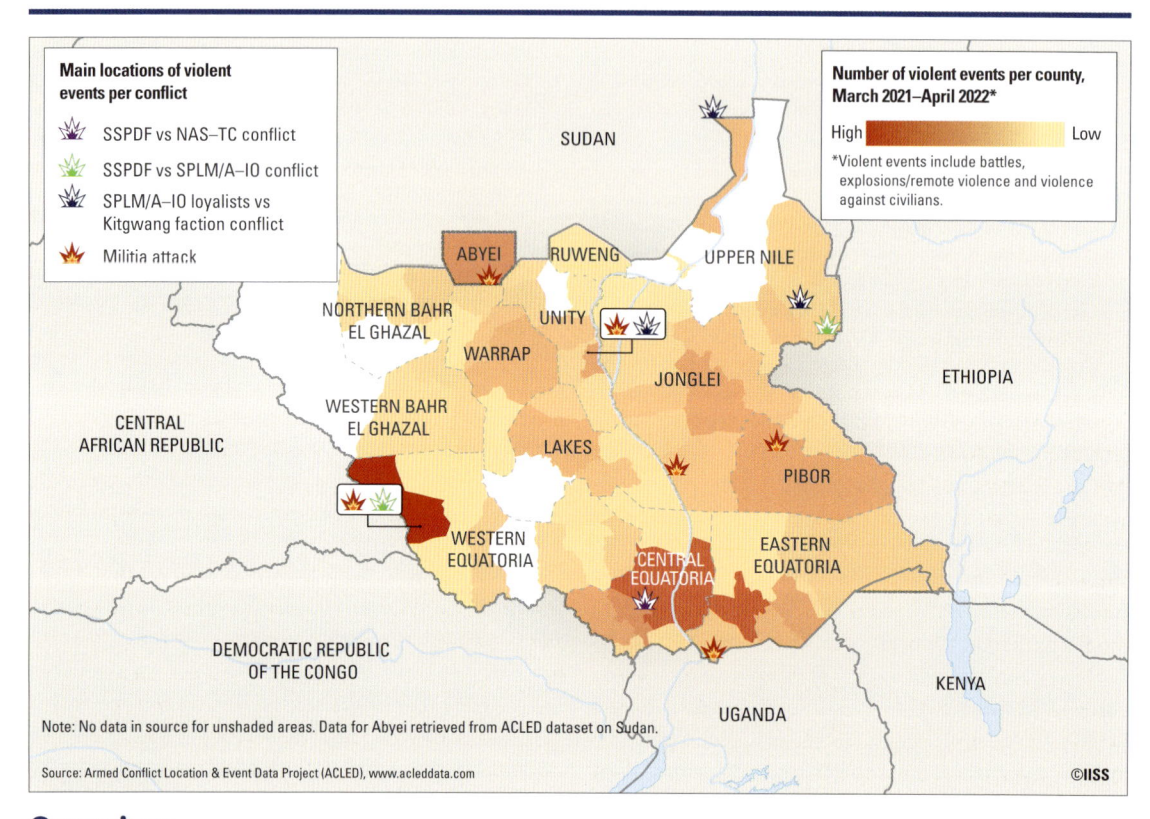

Main locations of violent events per conflict
- SSPDF vs NAS–TC conflict
- SSPDF vs SPLM/A–IO conflict
- SPLM/A–IO loyalists vs Kitgwang faction conflict
- Militia attack

Number of violent events per county, March 2021–April 2022*

High — Low

*Violent events include battles, explosions/remote violence and violence against civilians.

Note: No data in source for unshaded areas. Data for Abyei retrieved from ACLED dataset on Sudan.
Source: Armed Conflict Location & Event Data Project (ACLED), www.acleddata.com
©IISS

Overview

In December 2013, South Sudan descended into a civil war that split the new country's large and unstable security sector in two. The contending forces were largely drawn from the same factions that fought one another in the civil war that led to South Sudan's independence in 2011, including the ruling Sudan People's Liberation Movement/Army (SPLM/A) and a plethora of ex-rebel and paramilitary groups that had been organised along ethnic lines. In the wake of the 2005 Comprehensive Peace Agreement (CPA) reached between the SPLM/A and the Sudanese government, these volatile forces were brought together into a rapidly expanding and unevenly trained army for the South under the command of a notoriously fractious elite.

Throughout 2013, South Sudan's President Salva Kiir struggled to assert authority over the security apparatus and consolidate power within the ruling party amid brewing political threats from then vice-president Riek Machar and elites loyal to Kiir's late predecessor, John Garang. By mid-December, political and military tensions erupted in the capital city of Juba. Fighting broke out between ethnic Dinka and Nuer soldiers serving in the Presidential Guard and a recently formed paramilitary force drawn exclusively from the Dinka engaged in targeted killings of Nuer civilians in Juba, prompting mass defections by Nuer soldiers, who would go on to form the SPLM/A–In Opposition (SPLM/A–IO).[1] Having been dismissed from his post earlier in 2013, Machar manoeuvred himself into the role of SPLM/A–IO leader despite facing opposition from the rebellion's military wing, as ethnicised violence swept across the country's northeast.[2]

The Agreement on the Resolution of the Conflict in the Republic of South Sudan (ARCSS) was signed by the government and the SPLM/A–IO in August 2015 under heavy regional and international pressure. The agreement collapsed in 2016, triggering a second and more complex wave of violence

Armed Conflict Global Relevance Indicator (ACGRI)

- Incidence: 7
- Human impact: 19
- Geopolitical impact: 45

South Sudan

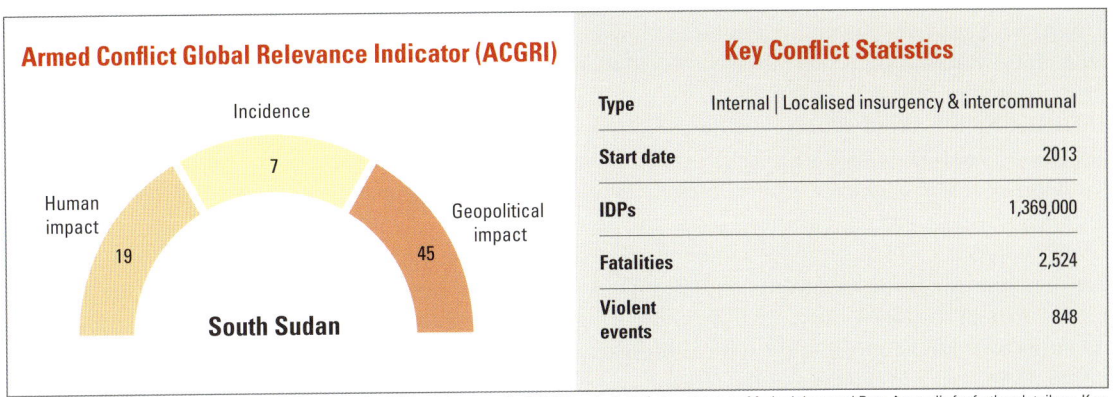

Key Conflict Statistics

Type	Internal | Localised insurgency & intercommunal
Start date	2013
IDPs	1,369,000
Fatalities	2,524
Violent events	848

ACGRI pillars: IISS calculation based on multiple sources for 2021 and January–April 2022 (scale: 0–100). See Notes on Methodology and Data Appendix for further details on Key Conflict Statistics.

that brought war to the country's south and west. Successive negotiations brokered by Uganda and especially Sudan culminated in the Revitalised ARCSS (R-ARCSS) in September 2018, which saw a largely defeated and increasingly fragmented SPLM/A–IO absorbed into a revised power-sharing agreement with the government and coalitions of smaller rebel factions and political parties, including the South Sudan Opposition Alliance (SSOA).

It is uncertain how many people were killed between December 2013 and September 2018.[3] Between 2011 and 2021, there were an estimated 4.8 million internal displacements (out of a population of around 11m–12m), with 1.4m people recorded as being internally displaced at the end of 2021.[4] The war drained South Sudan's oil reserves and dashed hopes that independence would bring relief from the population's suffering in previous decades.

In February 2020, a Transitional Government of National Unity (TGoNU) was formed, though violence has subsequently intensified. Often described as 'intercommunal' violence by South Sudanese politicians and external observers, many of the most serious incidents have been connected to the actions of rival coalitions of elites, sometimes operating from within the security sector.[5] Much of this violence has been of benefit to the Kiir regime and his advisers and enforcers.

Although 2021 was slightly less violent than 2020 – with 2,145 fatalities reported over 762 events, compared to 2,373 fatalities across 799 events in 2020 – in the first quarter of 2022 the number of fatalities was higher than in the previous two years.[6] Several areas witnessed conflicts that reflected the growing schisms within the SPLM/A–IO and between the government and the SPLM/A–IO (of which Juba was often able to take advantage). These conflicts were exacerbated by peace agreements in the country, which have created incentives for commanders and political elites to maximise their interests through organising violent defections. In June–September 2021, a power struggle in Tambura county (bordering the Central African Republic) among the ethnic Zande elite of Western Equatoria set the contours for renewed clashes between government forces (led by a former SPLM/A–IO commander who defected in 2020) and SPLM/A–IO loyalists, with the two sides mobilising militias from their respective Zande and Balanda communities.[7] Hundreds were killed over months of fighting and targeted killings despite there being no recent history of serious conflict between the two communities.

Meanwhile, a new splinter group of the SPLM/A–IO known as the 'Kitgwang faction' emerged in August 2021 and fought with SPLM/A–IO loyalists close to the border with Sudan. The Kitgwang faction gained only modest support from the large numbers of disaffected SPLM/A–IO commanders, in part due to the divisive personalities of the new faction's leaders. However, after prevailing against Machar's forces in a series of battles around their stronghold, the faction negotiated a reasonably generous peace deal with the government in January 2022, prompting larger numbers of commanders to defect to Kitgwang. This expanded the conflict into central Unity and southeastern Upper Nile states, where military tensions intersected with local political agendas to produce mass displacement and human-rights violations.[8]

Elsewhere, raiding and reprisal attacks continued in Jonglei State to the east, pitting several Dinka and Nuer clans against the Murle ethnic group, who are also engaged in sporadic violence with the Anyuak community along both sides of the border with Ethiopia. In the south, the government made a concerted effort to dislodge National Salvation Front–Thomas Cirillo (NAS–TC) rebels from positions in Central Equatoria State, with fighting clustered around mining sites and isolated villages. Concurrently, violence flared between the Madi ethnic group and Bor Dinka pastoralists in Magwi county, igniting simmering disputes over land control and political representation dating back to the time of the CPA.

During the reporting period, the government successfully pursued its regime-survival strategy, which is based on maintaining good relations with neighbouring countries (especially Sudan) and capitalising on discord within the armed opposition by luring disgruntled rebel commanders to its side. There have been no serious efforts by any faction to contain the violent fallout from these disputes for civilians, while the government rarely intervenes in proliferating conflicts involving armed militias and cattle raiders, preferring to allow local elites to exhaust their resources organising or influencing the course of such conflicts.

Conflict Parties

South Sudan People's Defence Force (SSPDF), formerly Sudan People's Liberation Movement/Army (SPLM/A) / Transitional Government of National Unity (TGoNU) / South Sudan armed forces

Strength: The SSPDF's precise size is unknown. Official figures for the army are known to be significantly inflated (with recent budget documents indicating a payroll of over 300,000 for the defence ministry as a whole), though informal figures suggest the SSPDF comprises at most 90,000 soldiers.[9]

Areas of operation: Presence throughout the country, except for small pockets in opposition-controlled areas of Central and Western Equatoria states.

Leadership: Salva Kiir (commander-in-chief).

Structure: 11 divisions, including Presidential Guard (Division 9), Mechanised (Division 10) and a new Division 11 based in Warrap State in breach of the 2018 R-ARCSS. These divisions exist within three geographical sectors, headquartered in Wau, Malakal and Torit. There are three services (ground force, air force and defence, and riverine forces), in addition to military intelligence.

History: The SPLM/A was founded in 1983 by commanders who defected from the Sudanese army to fight for South Sudan's autonomy. The SPLA was the statutory army of the south since 2005, transforming the former rebel group into a large and unevenly trained army, which also functioned as a major employer and de facto welfare provider. Following the outbreak of war, there was a concerted effort to create smaller and more effective units within the army to secure the regime. Such units form a relatively reliable and well-resourced military core. In 2018, the SPLA was renamed the South Sudan People's Defence Forces (SSPDF). Since 2020 it has embarked on a slow integration process with armed groups that signed the R-ARCSS.

Objectives: Defend the sovereignty and territorial integrity of South Sudan.

Opponents: NAS–TC, South Sudan United Front/Army (SSUF/A).

Affiliates/allies: SPLM/A–IO Kitgwang faction (in Upper Nile and Unity states, fighting against SPLM/A–IO loyalists) and assorted SPLM/A–IO defectors awaiting integration. SSPDF elements have links to clan and ethnic militias in several areas on an ad hoc basis. Regionally, the army has close connections to the Uganda People's Defence Force and to the Sudanese Armed Forces and maintains links to several Sudanese rebel groups.

Resources/capabilities: Predominantly an infantry force equipped with heavy artillery, tanks, armoured fighting vehicles and supported by some attack helicopters and amphibious vehicles. The security sector was allocated 15.1% of the total 2021/22 budget,[10] though precise details are unavailable. Significant off-budget security spending is believed to occur, much of which is routed through the Office of the President. In 2022, the UN maintained its arms embargo on South Sudan, despite diplomatic investment made by Juba to relax or end the embargo.

National Security Service (NSS)

Strength: At least 15,000.

Areas of operation: Nationwide, with a strong presence in Juba.

Leadership: Akol Koor (director-general, Internal Security Bureau, ISB), Simon Yien (director-general, General Intelligence Bureau, GIB).

Structure: The ISB is responsible for internal security and surveillance. In addition to operating several detention facilities, it maintains a sizeable Operations Division and Protection Division, which serve as elite military units to secure critical infrastructure and institutions. The GIB is tasked with external affairs and has a presence in several

National Security Service (NSS)

neighbouring countries. Both branches appear to maintain small death squads. The level of institutionalisation is higher in the NSS compared to all other branches of the security sector.

History: The NSS was established in 2011, though several prototype intelligence units emerged within the SPLM/A during the 1990s, which were expanded and trained with assistance from Sudan's notorious National Intelligence and Security Service (NISS) after 2005. These would form the core of the current NSS.[11] Over the course of the war, the NSS became increasingly powerful and militarised and was used by Kiir to counter the growing influence of then-army chief Paul Malong.

Objectives: Regime security, intelligence and counter-intelligence.

Opponents: Though tasked with protecting the regime, concerns about the growing power of Akol Koor led President Kiir to augment SSPDF Military Intelligence as a counterweight to the NSS. This resulted in a proxy war between the two in Warrap State in 2020 that was won by Koor, who has since further consolidated his power.

Affiliates/allies: The NSS has organised pro-government militias during the civil war, though it demonstrates a capacity to subvert the actions of rivals within the government and military through sponsoring militias. Regionally, the NSS had close links with the NISS in Sudan, though the dismantling of the NISS following the 2019 Sudanese coup will have weakened the influence of the NSS in Sudan. Koor recently revived links with Ethiopian security services.

Resources/capabilities: Small arms and light weapons. The NSS is better resourced and equipped than other parts of the security sector, possibly due to its significance to regime security, as well as its connections to business – especially the oil sector.

Sudan People's Liberation Movement/Army–In Opposition (SPLM/A–IO)

Strength: Unknown. At the outset of the civil war, the SPLM/A–IO had around 40,000 fighters. Desertions and military defeats reduced these numbers, though recruitment under the flawed cantonment provisions of the 2015 ARCSS agreement and absorption of new rebel factions replenished some of these losses. Following the 2018 R-ARCSS, SPLM/A–IO forces likely comprised at most 35,000 but recent defections will have reduced this number considerably.

Areas of operation: Following defections beginning mid-2019, the territorial scope of the SPLM/A–IO was reduced to several non-contiguous pockets, with the group possessing uneven levels of control and cohesion within these domains. Current areas occupied include southern Unity State; eastern Upper Nile State; the Greater Wau area of Western Bahr el Ghazal State; several areas of Jonglei and Western Equatoria states; and limited parts of Central and Eastern Equatoria states.

Leadership: Riek Machar.

Structure: SPLM/A–IO administrative and geographical structures mostly mirror those of the SPLA at the time of the onset of the war. These structures have been undermined by Machar's efforts to personalise power and his rivalries with military commanders, as well as the uneasy integration of new factions into the rebellion after 2015.

History: The SPLM/A–IO emerged from mass defections in the security sector in December 2013, though the group's name has been contested due to the unpopularity of the SPLM/A among many members. Initially dominated by ethnic Nuers who were later supplanted by non-Nuer forces in the second half of the conflict. In 2018, the SPLM/A–IO signed the R-ARCSS with the government. Since mid-2019, the group has lost a number of senior commanders and military units, who have defected to or aligned themselves with the government.

Objectives: Prior to the R-ARCSS: remove Kiir from power and govern South Sudan. After the R-ARCSS: secure a favourable position in the new government and the new unified army.

Opponents: SPLM/A–IO Kitgwang faction, NAS–TC.

Affiliates/allies: Nuer militias in parts of Upper Nile, Unity and Jonglei states.

Resources/capabilities: Small arms and light weapons, often taken from government supplies. The SPLM/A–IO has experienced difficulties procuring weapons and ammunition, though it received limited supplies from Sudan during the civil war.[12] The group is likely financed through taxation of trade routes and smuggling.

SPLM/A–IO Kitgwang faction (a.k.a. Kit-Gwang, Kitgweng)

Strength: Unknown.

Areas of operation: Northwestern and southeastern Upper Nile State; central and southern Unity State; small areas of northeastern Jonglei State.

Leadership: Simon Gatwech Dual, Johnson Olonyi.

Structure: Formed out of the relatively cohesive Upper Nile and Jonglei sectors of the SPLM/A–IO, it is unclear whether substantial changes to organisational structures have occurred since the faction's establishment. Reports of disputes between Gatwech and Olonyi, and their signing of separate agreements with the government, indicate that Kitgwang will likely function as a set of loosely aligned components, each organised around ethnic or clan lines, with supporting militias.

History: Existing tensions between SPLM/A–IO leader Machar and heavyweight commanders Gatwech and Olonyi intensified after the TGoNU's formation. Gatwech and Olonyi were concerned about the apparent subordination of the interests of their respective ethnic bases (the Lou Nuer clan,

SPLM/A–IO Kitgwang faction (a.k.a. Kit-Gwang, Kitgweng)

and Shilluk) to Machar's personal ambitions. In August 2021, the commanders signed the Kitgwang Declaration from their stronghold of Meganis along the border with Sudan, announcing the removal of Machar. In January 2022, the Kitgwang leadership signed two separate peace agreements with the government.

Objectives: To reverse the political and military marginalisation of senior commanders and their ethnic groups.

Opponents: SPLM/A–IO.

Affiliates/allies: Has coordinated its activities with the government in parts of Unity and Upper Nile states. Has also received support from Jagei and Haak Nuer militias in Unity and from elements of the Eastern Jikany Nuer in southeastern Upper Nile. Gatwech and Olonyi have connections to Sudan, while Gatwech has close connections to Sudanese military intelligence.[13]

Resources/capabilities: Small arms and light weapons.

National Salvation Front–Thomas Cirillo (NAS–TC)

Strength: Unknown.

Areas of operation: Central and Western Equatoria states.

Leadership: Thomas Cirillo Swaka.

Structure: The NAS–TC mostly appeals to members of the Bari community in the Equatoria region. The group was joined initially by some SPLM/A–IO officials who accused Machar of disenfranchising non-Nuers, though several commanders have since established new splinter factions.

History: Formed in March 2017 by Gen. Thomas Cirillo Swaka, who defected from the SPLA in February 2017. After rejecting the R-ARCSS in 2018, the NAS–TC became the main active armed opposition to the government. Since early 2019, intensive counter-insurgency operations by government forces (sometimes operating alongside SPLM/A–IO rebels) have greatly weakened the group. As a result, its forces are concentrated in mining areas and isolated rural locales close to the Congolese border.

Objectives: Replacement of centralised system of rule under President Kiir with a federal system that allows for greater autonomy of traditionally marginalised groups, particularly in Equatoria.

Opponents: SSPDF, SPLM/A–IO.

Affiliates/allies: Cirillo is chair of the South Sudan Opposition Movements Alliance (SSOMA) and the NAS–TC is the only significant armed group within the alliance. He is based in Addis Ababa, Ethiopia.

Resources/capabilities: The NAS–TC possesses equipment looted from the SSPDF, mainly during ambushes. Weapons include AK-47s and AKM general-purpose machine guns. The group has a small supply of uniforms and ammunition and extracts revenues from mining activities.

United Nations Mission in the Republic of South Sudan (UNMISS)

Strength: 17,982 total personnel, including 13,254 peacekeepers and 1,411 police (as of November 2021).[14]

Areas of operation: Presence across the country.

Leadership: Special Representative of the UN Secretary-General (SRSG) Nicholas Haysom.

Structure: UNMISS comprises a sizeable military, a smaller police contingent and civilian components (including a Political Affairs Division, Civil Affairs Division and Human Rights Division).

History: Established upon South Sudanese independence on 8 July 2011, UNMISS was a successor to the weak UN Mission in Sudan. Under SRSG Hilde Johnson, the mission was tasked with a range of activities, including preventing and resolving violence and supporting the Juba government's state-building efforts. However, UNMISS came under criticism for the perceived closeness of its leadership to leading government figures. During the civil war, the mission oversaw Protection of Civilian (PoC) sites in cities that experienced heavy fighting and ethnic killings, largely abandoning its state-building commitments. The relationship between UNMISS and the government visibly deteriorated as the war progressed.

Objectives: After the war began in 2013, the UNMISS mandate shifted towards civilian protection, human-rights monitoring and supporting humanitarian aid. Recent redeployments of UNMISS forces and the downgrading of several PoC sites to internally displaced persons (IDP) camp status (with security responsibilities transferred to the government) have raised concerns that IDPs in areas such as Malakal will be exposed to renewed violence. Since the 2018 R-ARCSS, UNMISS has reoriented its political activities to focus on implementing the agreement, with a new emphasis on upcoming elections since April 2022.

Opponents: While neutral, UNMISS has experienced numerous violations of its status of forces agreement with the South Sudanese government, including attacks against its personnel and frequent denial-of-access incidents. These incidents have occurred to a lesser extent with SPLM/A–IO rebels.

Affiliates/allies: N/A.

Resources/capabilities: Approved budget (July 2021–June 2022): US$1.202 billion.[15]

Conflict Drivers

Geopolitical and geostrategic influences
Regional geopolitics:
South Sudan has long been one of the primary theatres of regional conflicts in the Horn of Africa. In the run-up to the country's independence, economic ties deepened with Ethiopia, Kenya and Uganda amid fraught relations between Juba and Khartoum. Since mid-2013, South Sudan has aligned its political interests and security structures more closely with Sudan, leading to improved relations. The subsequent civil war unexpectedly led to a rapprochement between Kampala and Khartoum, which removed opportunities for South Sudanese rebel groups to obtain arms or logistical support from neighbouring powers. This regional alignment facilitated integration and mutual dependence between the three authoritarian systems and enabled Juba and Khartoum to coordinate each other's peace processes without causing significant unease in Kampala.[16]

Political
Elite power competition and factionalism:
During the Second Sudanese Civil War (1983–2005), complex realignments of elite coalitions drove conflict between South Sudanese communities. These conflicts often caused more harm to civilians than the overarching war between the SPLM/A and the Sudanese government. These dynamics have continued, and factionalism permeates South Sudan's security systems. Factional disputes are often linked to contests over leadership, resources and ethnic representation, while ruling elites maintain their power through continued vigilance and through coercing or co-opting rivals. The recent civil war closely corresponded with the widening division between President Kiir's Bahr el Ghazal Dinka faction and the largely Nuer ex-South Sudan Defence Forces faction, which tactically aligned with Kiir in 2006. Recent factionalism within the security services drove violence in Warrap and Jonglei states in 2020, while factionalism in the SPLM/A–IO – sometimes manipulated by the government – resulted in elevated insecurity in several regions.

Centre–periphery dynamics:
The South Sudanese leadership has largely replicated the stark centre–periphery inequalities that they supposedly fought to address during the Second Sudanese Civil War. Since 2005, elites have consolidated their wealth and power at the expense of local administration and service provision. Those excluded from these benefits – or on the receiving end of elite impunity – have become embittered, with resentment often directed against the Dinka, from whom many of the elite hail. The increasingly centralised (yet disorganised) system centred on the presidency and a small group of party elites and military commanders has been upheld by the powerful NSS. The regionally brokered ARCSS and R-ARCSS reproduced these dynamics, and most rebel groups have been absorbed back into the system they once contested.

Economic
War economy:
Elite competition for often plentiful resources animated previous rounds of conflict, warping economic structures to facilitate wealth extraction and its movement across international borders. The oil wealth that remains in the country is often unaccounted for or diverted to service debts or finance the military.[17] South Sudan's heavily oil-dependent economy has been in decline since 2012 while instability deters exploration for new reserves which could revive the country's dwindling output. As oil revenues have diminished, gold and timber and proliferating checkpoints (along roads and rivers across the country and along its international borders) have become important sources of wealth.[18] The transition to a decarbonised economy is likely to reinforce the trend towards subnational violence and possibly weaken Juba's grip on elites in the provinces, who previously sought to capture a share of centrally managed oil wealth.

Social
Intercommunal violence:
Violence within and between South Sudan's ethnic groups – particularly involving the numerous clans and sub-sections of the Dinka and Nuer – became increasingly serious in the 1990s and 2000s. Elites often aggravated disputes or undermined judicial mechanisms that could have curbed these conflicts. In the absence of such mechanisms, low-level conflicts and cattle raids can escalate into increasingly indiscriminate reprisal attacks. In multiple cases, political and military elites have been identified as organising or supplying militias engaged in serious clashes or massacres.[19]

Key Events in 2021–22

POLITICAL EVENTS

10 April 2021
President Kiir dismisses the recently appointed head of the SSPDF, the long-serving director of the GIB of the NSS, and the influential minister of presidential affairs, Nhial Deng.

3 August
Senior SPLM/A–IO commanders Gatwech and Olonyi sign the Kitgwang Declaration in Meganis, appointing themselves leader and deputy leader of the SPLM/A–IO, respectively.

30 August
The government suspends peace talks mediated by the Community of Sant'Egidio, claiming the NAS–TC had been attacking vehicles along the strategic Juba–Nimule highway.

16 January 2022
The government signs separate peace agreements with Gatwech (on behalf of the SPLM/A–IO Kitgwang faction) and Olonyi (on behalf of Aguelek forces) in Khartoum.

16 February
The government announces that 50,000 soldiers (comprising existing government forces and rebel signatories to the R-ARCSS) are ready to graduate, despite reports indicating little substantive training occurred.

Early March
A delayed leadership retreat in Uganda to resolve problems affecting peace implementation is postponed indefinitely, amid reports of Khartoum's displeasure with the planned talks.

22 March
Machar suspends SPLM/A–IO participation in the R-ARCSS security mechanisms, in opposition to the government's strategy of encouraging defections from the SPLM/A–IO. Government forces later surround Machar's residence.

12 April
Kiir appoints SPLM/A–IO and SSOA commanders to senior military positions. The government retains 60% of command posts, despite the R-ARCSS stipulating that there should be an equal division between the SSPDF and the SPLM/A–IO. No Kitgwang faction commanders are appointed.

MILITARY/VIOLENT EVENTS

May 2021
Gawaar Nuer and Bor Dinka militias advance on Pibor in Jonglei, clashing with Murle militias. A significant loss of life is reported, in addition to widespread theft and abductions.

19 July
SPLM/A–IO forces and allied Balanda militias clash with SSPDF forces loyal to James Nando supported by Zande militias in Tambura county, Western Equatoria. At least 150 people are killed.

7 August
Heavy fighting between SPLM/A–IO loyalists and the breakaway Kitgwang faction kills dozens of soldiers in northern Manyo county, Upper Nile.

October
Tensions between Rek and Luac-Jang Dinka clans reignite in Tonj East, Warrap, killing dozens.

26 December
A failed SPLM/A–IO loyalist assault on Kitgwang positions in the Meganis area of Upper Nile results in the death of at least 37 loyalists.

5 January 2022
A Misseriya militia kills at least 15 people in Yith Pabol, Northern Bahr el Ghazal.

23 January
A Murle militia raid in Baidit payam near Bor in Jonglei kills dozens of people and raises fears of renewed Dinka and Nuer mobilisation against the Murle.

February
Pro-government militias and the Kitgwang faction clash with SPLM/A–IO loyalists in central Unity and southeastern Upper Nile.

10 February
Twic Dinka and Ngok Dinka clans clash in Agok town, Abyei. The fighting later spreads to other parts of southern Abyei and northern Twic county, killing dozens.

10 May
At least 20 Bor Dinka pastoralists are killed by an unknown group near Nimule town, following violence between local militias and the Bor Dinka in February and March.

Responses to the Conflict

Security
Since the signing of the R-ARCSS, insecurity has shifted downwards to the subnational level. The most serious incidents continued to involve support from or planning by elements of the SSPDF, NSS and SPLM/A–IO, which often advanced their interests or settled contests through mobilising militias or encouraging defections. Although in the reporting period progress was made on military integration – with SPLM/A–IO and SSOA commanders being appointed into the command structures of the army, police and intelligence services – efforts to establish unified security forces were delayed repeatedly and training of joint military forces was reported to have been largely superficial.[20] The January 2022 peace agreement with the SPLM/A–IO Kitgwang faction contained new provisions for the group to be integrated into the army, though no activity was reported to have occurred by the end of the reporting period.

Economic/development
South Sudan's oil production continued to decline in 2021 and early 2022 as existing problems were compounded by flooding damage. Although during the reporting period decreasing production was cushioned by rising global oil prices and the completion of South Sudan's US$3bn payment to Sudan under the 2012 transitional financial arrangements,[21] economic growth has been stagnant since the advent of the coronavirus pandemic.[22] Furthermore, the government is committed to using future oil sales to repay opaque loans taken out with commercial firms, effectively precluding the possibility of stimulus measures.[23] Controversially, in March 2021 the IMF approved an emergency loan of US$174.2m to South Sudan under its Rapid Credit Facility programme. It followed a November 2020 loan of US$52m.[24] A large portion of the loans were used to pay government salary arrears, with only modest conditions for much-needed financial reforms.[25] Since 2020, the World Bank has initiated several large projects relating to infrastructure, local administration, women's empowerment and financial safety nets, signalling a transition following several years in which only emergency food and health projects were implemented.

Growing economic hardship resulted in increased industrial action and youth demonstrations. Non-payment of civil-servant salaries led to nation-wide strikes, notably in Jonglei: in early February 2022, workers attempted to storm the state governor's residence during demonstrations, prompting his evacuation.[26] Strikes continued to affect the oil sector. Demonstrations against oil extraction occurred in Melut county, Upper Nile in June 2021, with local residents denouncing their lack of benefits and environmental damage. Anger at aid agencies' employment conditions and hiring practices led to several violent demonstrations across the country, as legitimate grievances intersected with misplaced anger at a lack of meaningful employment opportunities.[27] Meanwhile, harassment and predation by (typically unpaid) security forces increased in towns and along transport corridors, often targeting commercial vehicles carrying imports.

Diplomacy
Western governments became increasingly reluctant to mediate or finance South Sudan's peace agreements, reflecting both their declining interest in the country amid more visible crises in the region and their wariness of dealing with South Sudan's elite, who have exhausted the patience and commitment of most external interlocutors. Despite reservations, Western actors and UNMISS ultimately offered rhetorical support to the R-ARCSS, while criticising the behaviour of security forces and rebel factions they deemed to be obstructing its implementation – despite increasingly clear signals that the R-ARCSS has reorganised rather than resolved South Sudan's multiple conflicts.[28] In May 2022, the UN Security Council renewed its sanctions (including an arms embargo) for a year, in spite of a significant diplomatic investment by Juba to end the embargo. The government also suspended its participation in peace talks mediated by the Community of Sant'Egidio in August 2021, though it made overtures to NAS–TC rebels to resume talks later in the year, which were rebuffed.

Humanitarian aid
The humanitarian situation continued to deteriorate in 2021 and early 2022. Increasing hunger, insecurity and displacement were reported across much of the country. Between April 2021 and 2022, the number of South Sudanese refugees increased from 2.24m to 2.35m.[29] By the end of 2021, there were 1.4m

people internally displaced.[30] Displacement has long been an objective of war in South Sudan, typically to enable the acquisition of territory and resources or to enhance the power of one community at the expense of another. In the aftermath of the recent civil war, it is unclear whether certain ethnic groups have homes to which they can return, or that they would be welcome in areas from which they were expelled by government forces and affiliated militias.[31]

South Sudanese have continued to bear livelihood distress deriving from conflict legacies and the stuttering transition towards market-based systems of economic distribution. These distresses are aggravated by ongoing violence and flooding. In April 2022, the World Food Programme noted that more than 7.74m people were projected to face severe food insecurity in 2022 (up from 7.2m in 2021), with famine expected in Ayod, Canal/Pigi, Fangak, Pibor counties in Jonglei state; Cueibet and Rumbek North counties of Lakes State; Leer and Mayendit counties of Unity State; and Tonj East in Warrap State.[32] Most of these areas have experienced violence or extensive flooding.

Conflict Outlook

Political scenarios

Since the outbreak of civil war in 2013, the government has pursued a regime-survival strategy in the face of a collapsing economy and an armed insurgency. Kiir has consolidated power relatively effectively in crisis conditions, even if his methods have isolated South Sudan internationally. The president and his inner circle built upon this approach after the R-ARCSS was signed, exploiting opposition divisions and encouraging opponents to expend their energy and resources competing with one another while Kiir conserved oil revenues and remained on good terms with South Sudan's more powerful neighbours. However, as a result the regime is alienated from the general population, which has become more vocal in its discontent.

The long-term sustainability of the current arrangement is unclear, particularly as oil revenues dwindle. In the short term, the greatest threats to South Sudan's political order remain internal to the regime. Much of the subnational violence and the factional clashes pose no serious risk to the regime and often play into its hands. If Kiir is able to deny his opponents opportunities to enhance their power while ensuring that loyalty to his regime is the surest path for elites to advance their interests, then the status quo is likely to endure for the foreseeable future. However, if the regime loses control of the violent forces it has fomented or is

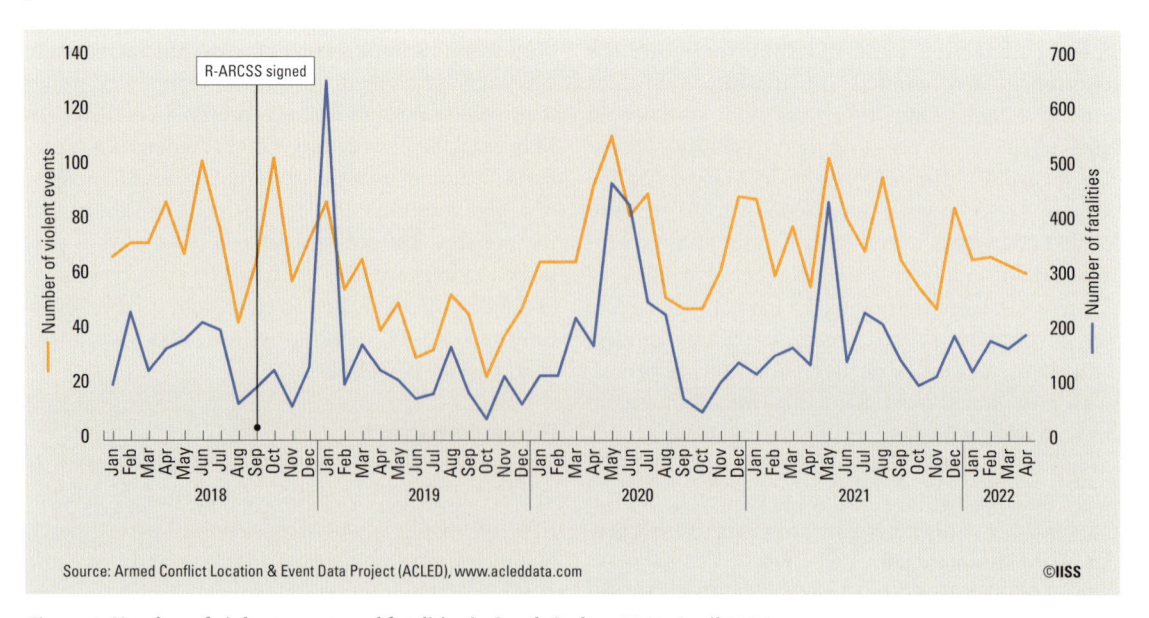

Figure 1: Number of violent events and fatalities in South Sudan, 2018–April 2022

overwhelmed by internally or externally driven crises, then the likelihood of a coup or a dangerous schism developing in the security sector will increase. To that end, the Kiir regime can be expected to further consolidate its power in the short term while encouraging geographically contained conflicts in opposition areas and steering its way through a turbulent regional and strained economic environment.

Escalation potential and conflict-related risks

Recent conflicts in Tambura, Leer and Upper Nile State have resulted in significant loss of life and turned communities against one other. However, such conflicts have rarely been sustained at scale for more than a few months. Meanwhile, increasingly serious clashes have occurred along the borders between Tonj North and Mayom counties and along the disputed border between Twic county and Abyei. Historical grudges between the Bor Dinka and Madi groups have also flared up in Magwi county along the border with Uganda. These areas may become focal points for further violence.

Reports of infighting within the SPLM/A–IO Kitgwang faction have emerged, raising the prospect of a new round of defections as the faction disintegrates into smaller units organised around ethnicity. Amid concerns that elections scheduled for early 2023 would aggravate insecurity, the government has announced that the lifespan of the transitional government established under the R-ARCSS will be extended into February 2025, with elections now scheduled to take place in December 2024.[33] Details on the posts up for election remain unclear and it is unknown whether the enlarged legislature created by the R-ARCSS will be maintained beyond the end of the peace agreement. Fears that elections will trigger a return to full-scale civil war are exaggerated given most rebel groups' limited capacity to embark on a sustained insurgency. However, flare-ups of subnational violence are likely in ethnically polarised areas and in constituencies that are marginal or promise lucrative positions.

Strategic implications and global influences

Although South Sudan is engulfed in seemingly perpetual crises, the internal and external risks posed by instability and disorder have been largely contained as a result of improved relations between Juba, Kampala and Khartoum since 2013. This has limited South Sudanese rebel groups' ability to obtain arms from Sudan and Uganda and has partially stabilised the volatile and contested Sudan–South Sudan border region (though violence resumed in the disputed Abyei area in February 2022). Meanwhile, increased instability in the Horn of Africa – following the advent of the war in northern Ethiopia and clashes between Sudanese and Ethiopian forces in the disputed area of al-Fashaga – threatens to reopen the dormant rift between Khartoum and Addis Ababa. Juba must also contend with the deepening political and economic crisis in Sudan following the October 2021 coup. As a result of these developments, the regime will seek to limit its exposure to regional volatility in 2023 and attempt to mediate or balance its neighbours' competing demands.

Notes

[1] African Union, Commission of Inquiry on South Sudan, 'Final Report of the African Union Commission of Inquiry on South Sudan', 27 October 2015.

[2] John Young, 'A Fractious Rebellion: Inside the SPLM–IO', Small Arms Survey, 2015.

[3] The Armed Conflict Location & Event Data project (ACLED) – which codes fatalities conservatively – provides a total of 22,479 violent deaths during the civil war. A widely used figure of 400,000 has emerged in recent years, which has been rounded up from a 2018 London School of Hygiene & Tropical Medicine study that estimated 383,000 people had died as a direct or indirect result of the conflict (190,000 of whom were estimated to have died a violent death). However, this figure should be treated with caution, given the number of assumptions and extrapolations made from often incomplete data. See Francesco Checchi et al., 'Estimates of Crisis-attributable Mortality in South Sudan, December 2013–April 2018: A Statistical Analysis', London School of Hygiene & Tropical Medicine, September 2018.

[4] Internal Displacement Monitoring Centre (IDMC), 'Country Profile: South Sudan', 2022.

[5] Dan Watson, 'Surface Tension: "Communal" Violence and Elite Ambitions in South Sudan', ACLED, 19 August 2021.

[6] ACLED, www.acleddata.com. 'Events' refers to battles, explosions/remote violence and violence against civilians.

[7] United Nations Mission in South Sudan (UNMISS) and UN High Commissioner for Human Rights, 'Attacks on Civilians in Tambura County, June–September 2021', 1 March 2022.

[8] UNMISS, 'Press Release: Rape, Gang-rape, and Beheadings among Human Right Violations Documented in Leer, South Sudan', 25 April 2022.

9   See Flora McCrone, 'Hollow Promises: The Risks of Military Integration in Western Equatoria', Small Arms Survey, June 2020.
10 Minister of Finance and Planning Agak Achuil Lual, 'Budget Speech for the FY 2021/2022', South Sudan, Revitalized Transitional Government of National Unity, 2 February 2022.
11 Brian Adeba, 'Oversight Mechanisms, Regime Security, and Intelligence Service Autonomy in South Sudan', *Intelligence and National Security*, vol. 35, no. 6, 2020.
12 Conflict Armament Research, 'Weapon Supplies into South Sudan's Civil War: Regional Re-transfers and International Intermediaries', November 2018, pp. 30–3.
13 Small Arms Survey, 'MAAPSS Update 13 September 2021 SPLA–IO Split', Mapping Actors and Alliances Project in South Sudan, update no. 7, 13 September 2021, p. 7.
14 'Facts and Figures', UNMISS website.
15 *Ibid*.
16 Cedric Barnes, 'South Sudan: War, Peace Processes, and Regional Economic Integration', in Jean-Nicolas Bach et al. (eds), *Routledge Handbook of the Horn of Africa* (Abingdon: Routledge, 2022). Juba mediated the 2020 peace agreement in Sudan, while Khartoum mediated the 2018 peace agreement in South Sudan.
17 International Crisis Group, 'Oil or Nothing: Dealing with South Sudan's Bleeding Finances', Report no. 305, 6 October 2021.
18 Peer Schouten, Ken Matthysen and Thomas Muller, 'Checkpoint Economy: The Political Economy of Checkpoints in South Sudan, Ten Years after Independence', Danish Institute for International Studies and the International Peace Information Service, 10 December 2021.
19 'Final Report of the Panel of Experts on South Sudan', UN Security Council (UNSC), 2021, pp. 19–22.
20 See 'Transitional Government Fails to Graduate Unified Forces as Deadline Expires', Radio Tamazuj, 3 June 2022; and 'Final Report of the Panel of Experts on South Sudan Submitted Pursuant to Resolution 2577', UNSC, 28 April 2022, p. 7.
21 'Final Report of the Panel of Experts on South Sudan Submitted Pursuant to Resolution 2577', 28 April 2022.
22 IMF, 'Republic of South Sudan: First Review under the Staff-monitored Program–Press Release; and 'Staff Report', IMF Country Report no. 21/246, 15 November 2021, p. 1.
23 'South Sudan Crude Oil Sold in Advance Till 2027', Radio Tamazuj, 6 May 2022.
24 See IMF, 'IMF Executive Board Approves US$52.3 Million Disbursement to South Sudan to Address the COVID-19 Pandemic', 11 November 2020; and IMF, 'IMF Executive Board Approves US$174.2 Million Emergency Assistance for South Sudan to Address the COVID-19 Pandemic', 30 March 2021.
25 'The IMF Picks Up the Cheque as Officials Grumble', *Africa Confidential*, vol. 62, no. 9, 28 April 2021.
26 Yar Ajak, 'Jonglei Protest: 9 Injured, 2 in Critical Condition', Eye Radio, 9 February 2022.
27 Joshua Craze, 'Don't Apply Here: Why NGO Hiring Practices Are Sparking Protests in South Sudan', *New Humanitarian*, 7 December 2021.
28 Joshua Craze and Ferenc David Marko, 'Death by Peace: How South Sudan's Peace Agreement Ate the Grassroots', *African Arguments*, 6 January 2022.
29 UN High Commissioner for Refugees Operational Data Portal, 'Refugees and Asylum-seekers from South Sudan – Total'.
30 IDMC, 'Country Profile: South Sudan, 2022.
31 See Joshua Craze, 'Why the Return of Displaced People Is Such a Thorny Issue in South Sudan', New Humanitarian, 5 January 2022.
32 World Food Programme South Sudan, 'Situation Report no. 300', 20 April 2022.
33 '18 Killed as Fighting Erupts Between Rival Kitgwang Forces in Panyikang', *Sudan's Post*, 20 July 2022; and Chany Ninrew, '"Extension of Transitional Period Is Not Passion for Power", peace parties', Eye Radio, 4 August 2022.

ETHIOPIA

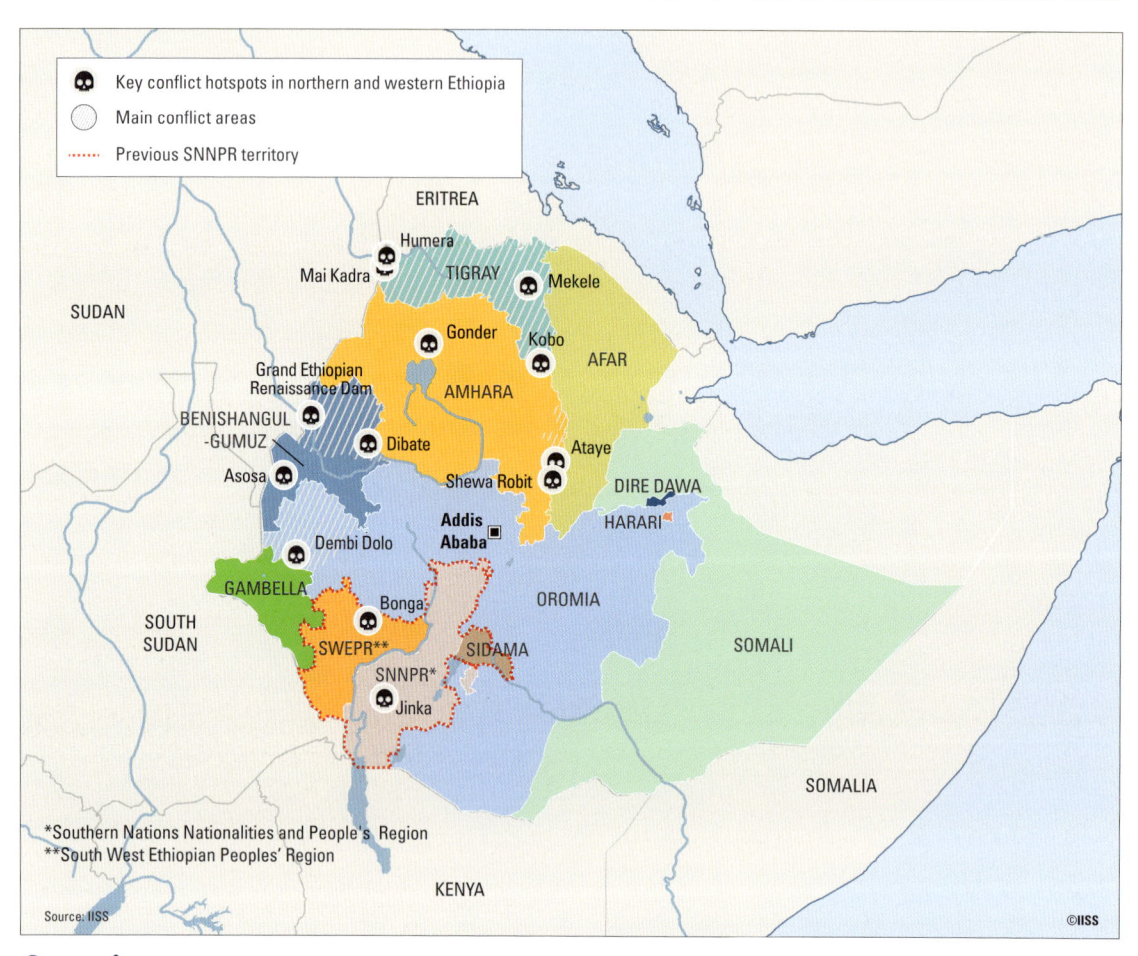

Overview

In November 2020, war broke out between Ethiopia's central government and the Tigray People's Liberation Front (TPLF), which had ruled the country from 1994–2018. Following the socialist regime's military defeat in 1991 by an alliance of ethnic-liberation movements (the Ethiopian People's Revolutionary Democratic Front, EPRDF) led by the TPLF, Ethiopia emerged as a federal democratic republic with significant autonomy for regional states and sustained economic growth at the national level. However, the EPRDF's increasingly autocratic behaviour exacerbated the multiple economic and political fault lines in the country.[1] A series of protests directed at the political establishment (in 2015, mid-2016 and February 2018) and reactive declarations of states of emergency (from October 2016–August 2017 and February–June 2018) led to the resignation of then prime minister Hailemariam Desalegn Boshe in 2018. His successor Abiy Ahmed – then the newly elected chairman of the EPRDF's Oromo party, the Oromo People's Democratic Organisation – authorised sweeping reforms to liberalise the economy and increase political freedoms. Abiy then distanced himself from the TPLF and admitted to various human-rights violations that had occurred under EPRDF rule.

In December 2019, Abiy formed the Prosperity Party by dissolving the EPRDF and amalgamating the ruling parties of the regions. The TPLF refused to join, leaving Tigray as the only region with a

Armed Conflict Global Relevance Indicator (ACGRI)

- Incidence: 13
- Human impact: 24
- Geopolitical impact: 8

Ethiopia

Key Conflict Statistics

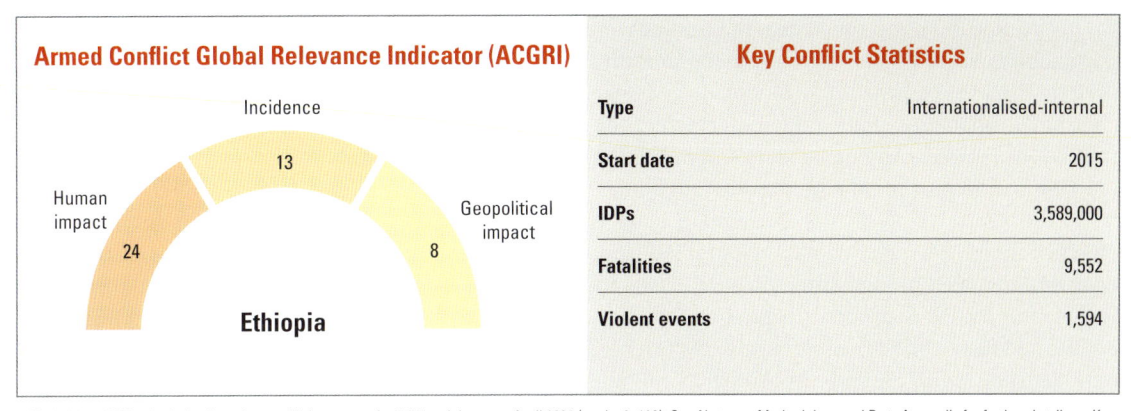

Type	Internationalised-internal
Start date	2015
IDPs	3,589,000
Fatalities	9,552
Violent events	1,594

ACGRI pillars: IISS calculation based on multiple sources for 2021 and January–April 2022 (scale: 0–100). See Notes on Methodology and Data Appendix for further details on Key Conflict Statistics.

ruling party that was not a member of the new national party. Significantly, the new regime struck a peace deal with Eritrea, Ethiopia's long-standing arch-enemy in the Horn of Africa, ending a border dispute and territorial stalemate that had existed between the two countries for more than 20 years.

After national elections were postponed due to the coronavirus pandemic, Tigray held regional elections in 2020 that increased tensions between the federal and regional governments. On 3 November, the TPLF armed forces (Tigray Defence Force, TDF) – under orders from the TPLF – carried out 'a pre-emptive strike' on the headquarters of the Ethiopian National Defence Force (ENDF) Northern Command and on several key units, including air defences. As a result, Ethiopia plunged into a protracted civil war affecting large parts of northern Ethiopia and involving Eritrea. All parties have been accused of committing human-rights violations during the conflict.

Alongside the Tigray war, the Abiy administration faced a variety of inherited conflicts and a fragmented security landscape during the reporting period. Some of these conflicts endured and others erupted between 2018 and early 2022. Ethnic killings of non-Oromo residents across Oromia region – and subsequent killings and counter-attacks by government forces and militias – led to increasing insecurity in Western Oromia and the border areas with Sudan.

2021 and early 2022 saw the expansion of anti-government insurgencies across the country and intensified inter-community violence. In the north, the TPLF and the TDF pushed the front lines from Tigray into neighbouring Afar and Amhara regions. The war in Tigray affected civilians in both regions, amid heavy fighting between the TDF and national and regional security forces. The conflict also increasingly affected Tigrayans living outside the war zones. The government's popular call to arms led to widespread stigmatisation and arbitrary searches and arrests, including among local staff of international and multilateral organisations.[2] The multiple negative consequences of the pandemic, the economic crunch, rising inflation and conflict across Ethiopia led to the forced displacement of over five million people within the country in 2021.[3]

The Prosperity Party's victory in the June 2021 national elections was a critical moment. In the face of multiple active insurgencies, the elections were arguably the most anxiously awaited event in Ethiopia in 2021. Abiy's premiership and popularity suffered from the protracted war in Tigray, which was initially presented to the public as a short law-enforcement campaign against the TPLF leadership. In the lead-up to the elections, the outcome was difficult to predict, and accelerated descent into more conflict seemed a tangible option. Despite those fears, the elections were held in all but three conflict-affected regions (Harari, Somali and SNNPR, delayed due to insecurity) and without significant disruptions across Ethiopia.

In late March 2022, the central government offered the TPLF a unilateral truce, while the opening of humanitarian corridors permitted the delivery of humanitarian aid to Tigray. However, many critics did not trust the truce and predicted that the cold peace would descend into further fighting later in 2022.

In addition to Tigray, other areas of Ethiopia were particularly affected by conflict during the reporting period. The west became prone to violence: Metekel zone in Benishangul-Gumuz region saw violent confrontations between Amhara settlers and militias on one side and Gumuz militias on the other. In January 2021, the central government declared a state of emergency in the area. Government-allied militias were involved in increasing violence across the region and by February 2021 approximately 7,000 people had fled to Sudan.[4] Ethiopia also experienced new tensions with Sudan, as Amhara militants attempting to exploit the Tigray crisis reopened a long-standing border dispute. Further south, in Gambella region bordering South Sudan, the ethnic Nuer-led Gambella Liberation Front (GLF) took up arms in response to what it claimed was a rigged local election.[5] While for some time it appeared that the GLF chairperson had agreed to talks with the government, more recent developments suggested that the GLF had struck a strategic alliance with the Oromo Liberation Army (OLA) to fight the central government in Gambella region.

In April 2022, the Ethiopian Human Rights Council criticised the government for the worsening security situation in southern Ethiopia, where violence continued in Konso and Sidama.[6] In 2022, the renegotiation of zonal boundaries and the creation of the South West Ethiopian Peoples' State, which occurred in 2021, created demands for the Aari people's status to be changed (the Aari comprise a majority in the South Omo zone of Southern Nations, Nationalities and People's Region, SNNPR). These demands led to community violence in Jinka, the zonal administrative centre, in April.[7]

Conflict Parties

Ethiopian National Defence Force (ENDF)

Strength: 138,000 active all-volunteer military personnel (army: 135,000, air force: 3,000).

Areas of operation: Across all regions of Ethiopia.

Leadership: Prime Minister Abiy Ahmed (commander-in-chief), Gen. Berhanu Jula (chief of staff).

Structure: The ENDF is designed to conduct both conventional war (using infantry, armoured vehicles and artillery) and counter-insurgency missions (both inside Ethiopia and across borders). It is organised in commands, each of which have several mechanised and infantry divisions. In October 2020 two new headquarters were formed at Bahir Dar and Addis Ababa, in addition to those at Harar, Hawassa, Mekele and Nekemte, reflecting the increasing internal focus and activities of the ENDF.

History: The ENDF grew out of a coalition of former guerrilla armies, mainly the TPLF and EPRDF. Since the EPRDF took power in 1991, the ENDF has been an all-volunteer force. Over the past two decades it has undergone an ongoing defence-transformation process, making it one of the major military powers in Africa and a major contributor to UN peacekeeping forces. In 2021 and early 2022 several soldiers of Tigrayan ethnic origin participating in peacekeeping missions have refused to return home and instead claimed asylum abroad out of fear of ethnic targeting in the country.

Objectives: Maintain Ethiopia's territorial integrity and fight armed opposition/secessionist movements inside the country.

Opponents: TPLF (TDF), OLA and minor regional separatist movements.

Affiliates/allies: Eritrea, France, Israel, United States.

Resources/capabilities: Before the prolonged conflict in Tigray, the ENDF was the most powerful army in the region. Ethiopia had a defence budget of US$377m in 2021. The effect of the conflict on the strength and equipment of the ENDF is unclear.

TPLF armed forces (also known as the Tigray Defence Force, TDF)

Strength: Likely exceeded 200,000 individuals at the start of the Tigray conflict. Of these, only some 20,000–30,000 were formed in paramilitary units with the remainder composed of village-level militias.[8]

Areas of operation: Tigray, Afar and Amhara regions.

Leadership: The former president of Tigray, Debretsion Gebremichael; Lt-Gen. Tsedkan Gebretensae, the former commander of the ENDF, acted as TDF commander-in-chief until March 2021. He was succeeded by Gen. Tadesse Werede Tesfay.

Structure: The TDF combines all forces in Tigray that came under the command of the Tigrayan government at the outset of the Tigray conflict, including: Special Police/Special Force, organised into paramilitary groupings equivalent to platoons, companies and battalions; regional militia (village-level uniformed and armed defence/security responders), organised into groups of 30–50 at village level under locally elected leadership; and ENDF elements (a few organised elements of the ENDF appeared to have sided with the TPLF at the start of the Tigray conflict).

TPLF armed forces (also known as the Tigray Defence Force, TDF)

History: Following the TPLF's refusal to join the newly created Prosperity Party, it began to form regional forces for the defence of Tigray. In 2021, the TDF operated outside Tigray in Amhara and Afar regions and was accused of violations of human rights in several instances.

Objectives: Defend Tigray's territorial integrity.

Opponents: Ethiopian federal forces (the ENDF and the Federal Police), the Amhara Special Forces, the EDF.

Affiliates/allies: Established an office in Khartoum, Sudan in late February 2021. In mid-2021 the TDF and the OLA signed a military-cooperation deal.

Resources/capabilities: The TDF seized significant amounts of ENDF equipment, including tanks, artillery and long-range rockets. Additional small arms are used by the regional forces and the regional militias.

Regional Special Police – also referred to as 'Special Force'

Strength: Addis Ababa (numbers unknown; formed in late 2019), Afar (2,000–3,000), Amhara (5,000), Benishangul-Gumuz (3,000–4,000), Dire Dawa (2,000–3,000), Gambella (2,000–3,000), Oromia (9,000–10,000), Sidama (numbers unknown), SNNPR (4,000–5,000), Somali (15,000), Tigray (27,000–28,000).[9]

Areas of operation: All regions of Ethiopia.

Leadership: Under regional police commissioners. Under federal system, they are answerable to regional presidents.

Structure: Formed into paramilitary units.

History: Somali became the first region to form a Special Police force in 2008–09. By 2014 all regions had small Special Police forces. From 2016–19 force numbers increased in areas experiencing civil unrest (Amhara, Oromia and SNNPR). In 2019–20 force numbers increased further in areas where neighbouring regions posed a threat (Amhara, Oromia, Tigray).

Objectives: Preserve public order and peace within the region, as constitutionally mandated.

Opponents: Armed political opposition, local *shifta* (armed bandits), neighbouring regional Special Police and militia.

Affiliates/allies: N/A.

Resources/capabilities: Funded from regional police budgets.

Oromo Liberation Army (OLA), previously the Oromo Liberation Front (OLF)

Strength: Over 2,000 estimated OLA fighters in 2020.[10] This number may have increased significantly since, but new estimates are not official.

Areas of operation: Oromia region.

Leadership: The OLA no longer comes under Dawud Ibsa's political leadership and has split into at least four armed factions under local leadership. The OLA–Shane is led by Kumsa Diriba (also known as Jaal Maaro).

Structure: Locally organised into loose groupings of fighters.

History: The OLF was established in 1973 by Oromo nationalists. In mid-2018, the OLF agreed with the central government to lay down its arms and return 1,200 fighters from Eritrea. The OLA officially split from the political OLF party in April 2019 as part of the negotiation process to allow the OLF to become a registered political party. However, various OLA factions have continued to operate under the direction of the Oromo traditional leadership, predominantly in western and southern Oromia.

Objectives: Self-determination for the Oromo people against what they see as Amhara colonial rule.

Opponents: federal government.

Affiliates/allies: Until 2018, Eritrea. Following the rapprochement between Eritrea and Ethiopia this support ceased and the OLA in Oromia survived on local support and resources. In 2020 the TPLF was accused of providing clandestine support, including finance and weapons. The collaboration with the TPLF provided for mutual support and intelligence-sharing.

Resources/capabilities: The OLA acts clandestinely and is weak in military terms.

Fanno

Strength: No official numbers available.

Areas of operation: Amhara, Benishangul-Gumuz, Tigray.

Leadership: Following Abiy's amnesty for previous captives of the TPLF regime, upon his release from prison Gen. Asaminew Tsige engaged in recruiting fighters for the Amhara regional special forces. These fighters were referred to as *fanno*. After the assassination of Asaminew in 2019, Mesfint Tesfa assumed the leadership in 2021.

Structure: Locally organised into loose groupings of fighters with no coherent structure. The *fanno* primarily comprises armed Amhara involved in the territorial defence and/or expansion of Amhara territory. This includes special forces and peasant militias.

History: *Fanno* is a term currently loaded with nationalistic Amhara sentiments that refers to the free peasants who formed the peasant armies of the nineteenth century. The term is also often used to designate the 'patriots' who fought the Italian invasion in the 1930s. The *fanno* emerged as a group parallel to the Oromo *qerroo* movement and – in alliance with the latter – were involved in the protests that brought Abiy to power. With the war in Tigray the groups

Fanno

turned increasingly militant, aiming to protect Amhara settlers in Benishangul-Gumuz and retake perceived Amhara territories in Tigray, such as Welkayt.

Objectives: Territorial expansion of Amhara region and safety of Amhara settlers across Ethiopia.

Opponents: TDF, TPLF, Gumuz militias.

Affiliates/allies: ENDF, Amhara special forces.

Resources/capabilities: Limited.

Gambella Liberation Front (GLF)

Strength: No official numbers available.

Areas of operation: Gambella region.

Leadership: Gatluak Buom Pal. After his GLF lost in the 2021 elections, he began a campaign of armed resistance against the Ethiopian government.

Structure: Recruited mainly from the Nuer community of Gambella with alleged affiliations to Sudanese refugees in the region. Organised into a loose band of young people.

History: The front formed and appeared as an organised group only after the election in 2021. There is limited data apart from self-portrayals on the group.

Objectives: End the Abiy administration's rule over Gambella and restore the region's self-determination in a federal structure.

Opponents: ENDF, regional and federal special forces.

Affiliates/allies: OLA.

Resources/capabilities: Limited.

Eritrean Defence Forces (EDF)

Strength: 201,750 estimated active military personnel (army: 200,000; navy: 1,400; air force: 350).

Areas of operation: The EDF joined the ENDF in military operations in Tigray in November 2020 and was involved in combat until November 2021. Following US sanctions in November 2021, the EDF has withdrawn largely to areas of northern Tigray and remains a threat to TPLF operations.

Leadership: President Isaias Afwerki (commander-in-chief); Maj.-Gen. Filipos Weldeyohanes (chief of staff).

Structure: The EDF comprises mostly conscripts, with only a small cadre of regular troops. National service is universal for Eritrean men and women between the ages of 18 and 40. In 2016, Eritreans between the ages of 40 and 65 were ordered to reservist duty to support the formation of local security militias under the army's intelligence structure. A further call-up of reservists was announced by the president in late November 2020. The army is made up of approximately 41 divisions and divided between five military zones, largely covering the border with Ethiopia. Up to 20 EDF divisions were reported to be in Tigray as of February 2021 (these forces withdrew in November 2021).

History: The EDF was officially formed following Eritrea's separation from Ethiopia in 1993 but it has its roots in the former Eritrean People's Liberation Front (EPLF) armed opposition to the Derg communist regime in Ethiopia. The army has continued to engage in low-level border conflicts with Ethiopia and several other neighbours, including Djibouti, Sudan and Yemen, most notably in the Ethiopian–Eritrean War from 1998 to 2000. From 2000 to 2018, the army was predominantly deployed on the border with Ethiopia.

Objectives: Maintain Eritrea's territorial integrity and fight armed opposition/secessionist movements inside the country.

Opponents: Regional rivals, including Ethiopia until 2018, secessionist movements in Eritrea.

Affiliates/allies: Ethiopia, Saudi Arabia, Somalia, United Arab Emirates (UAE).

Resources/capabilities: The Eritrean defence budget is unknown. Due to prolonged UN sanctions (lifted in November 2018), much of Eritrea's military equipment still comprises outdated Soviet-era systems, which will have resulted in serviceability issues. However, Russia has since agreed to supply Eritrea with light multipurpose helicopters. The navy remains capable of only limited coastal-patrol and interception operations. There is some equipment-maintenance capability but no defence-manufacturing sector.

Conflict Drivers

Geopolitical and geostrategic influences

Reformation of regional alliances:
The current conflict in Tigray has restructured the regional security architecture. Addis Ababa's strategic alliance with Asmara was a dramatic departure from the previous constellation of allies in the Horn of Africa. Eritrea backed Ethiopia militarily while soldiers from neighbouring Somalia received military training in Eritrea – although the alleged involvement of Somali troops in Tigray was often denied. In 2021, Ethiopia–Sudan relations were strained by an influx of Amhara militias in the al-Fashaga Triangle and over the filling of the Grand Ethiopian Renaissance Dam (GERD). The latter issue was a continuing source of tension in the Ethiopia–Egypt relationship too, as Cairo fears

receding upstream irrigation potential. In March 2021, Cairo and Addis Ababa agreed to participate in mediation – led by South Sudan – on the GERD issue. In July 2021, the issue was discussed at the UN Security Council and returned to African Union negotiators without success. Ethiopia's stance and rejection of external pressure as infringing on its sovereignty has strengthened Abiy's position domestically in nationalist camps.

Security
Security fragmentation:
The militarisation of regional Special Police forces in 2020 established rival and competing regional 'armies' within the country. The expanding securitisation of the state – with various new and heavily armed militias – further increased the fragmentation of security. In particular, the use of excessive force by the Special Police across Ethiopia and the lack of accountability between police, regional parliaments and militia groups has led to heightened insecurity nationwide.[11]

Political
Political reform:
Ethiopia has struggled to find a post-TPLF order capable of stabilising domestic politics and clarifying the country's role and relationships in the region. The resulting political instability affects national political orientations and regional alliances alike. Abiy's lack of communication and ideological shift towards a political philosophy based on *medemer* ('synergy') sparked fears that his government harboured centralist aspirations rather than a preference for an inclusive reconciliatory path post-TPLF. Allowing various opposition parties to return from exile without effectively integrating them into the political sphere has stoked ethnic frustrations and led to calls for greater regional autonomy. Members of the Amhara *fanno* movement regrouped and radicalised only after their amnesty granted by the Abiy administration.[12] The OLA entered into a violent campaign only after the OLF was reinvited to the political arena. If the Abiy administration aims to overcome the ethnic divisions that have resulted from 30 years of the ethnic federal political system, its approach must find a way to address and accommodate revived ethno-national sentiments.

Economic
Climate vulnerability and economic volatility:
Environmental change, particularly drought, has driven conflict between pastoralist communities. In March 2022, more than 5m people were displaced as a result of conflict and natural disasters (although 2,848,000 internally displaced persons in Afar, Amhara and Tigray regions returned to their place of origin in the first quarter of 2022).[13] The war in Tigray has also driven inflation, while investors have withdrawn from the country and unemployment is pushing young people towards liberation movements and activist groups.

Key Events in 2021–22

POLITICAL EVENTS

23 March 2021
Largely bowing to international pressure, Abiy admits to the involvement of Eritrean troops in Tigray.

1 May
The Council of Ministers approves a resolution designating the TPLF and OLA–Shane as 'terrorist' organisations.

21 June
National and regional elections go ahead across Ethiopia except in Harari, SNNPR and Somali regions.

19 July
Second phase of filling the GERD is completed.

MILITARY/VIOLENT EVENTS

March–April 2021
Conflict escalates in Oromia and North Shewa zones in Amhara region. OLA splinter groups clash with Amhara special forces.

April
Alleged members of Gumuz militias from Benishangul-Gumuz attack communities in neighbouring Oromia.

29 May
OLA–Shane releases three Chinese mineworkers kidnapped earlier in May in West Wollega zone, Oromia region.

28 June
The government offers a humanitarian ceasefire after TDF forces retake Mekele, the capital of Tigray region.

30 July
The government accuses two international non-governmental organisations working in Tigray region of spreading misinformation and suspends their work for three months.

11 August
The OLA announces that it is allied with the TPLF.

30 September
National and regional elections go ahead in Harari, SNNPR and Somali regions.

4 October
Abiy is sworn in as prime minister for a new five-year term.

5 November
The so-called United Front of Ethiopian Federalist and Confederalist Forces – a newly formed alliance comprising the TPLF, OLA and other anti-government factions – sign a memorandum of understanding in Washington in which they commit to toppling Abiy's government.

12 November
The US enforces sanctions against six actors associated with the Eritrean government, citing their contribution to the conflict in Ethiopia.

17 December
The UN Human Rights Council agrees to establish an independent team of experts to investigate alleged human-rights abuses committed during the conflict.

7 January 2022
The government releases several opposition figures, including Jawar Mohammad, Bekele Gerba and several high-ranking TPLF figures.

6 April
Amnesty International and Human Rights Watch publish a report documenting human-rights abuses committed by Amhara regional security forces and civilian authorities in Ethiopia's Western Tigray in 2020 and 2021.

2 November
The government declares a new nationwide state of emergency in light of the TDF's and OLA's territorial gains.

22 November
State-affiliated media reports that Abiy will travel to the front lines of the conflict to lead Ethiopian forces.

December
The TDF advance reaches a standstill. Its forces retreat into Tigray and the leadership offers the government a ceasefire.

January 2022
30,000 people are reported displaced in North Shewa, Amhara region due to intensified fighting in Western Oromia.

24 February
GLF leader Gatluak Buom Pal surrenders to the government and offers to take part in peace talks.[14]

24 March
The government declares a unilateral truce with TDF and OLA forces.

Responses to the Conflict

Security

From mid-2021, the TDF was able to launch attacks on neighbouring regions to break the humanitarian blockade the government used to cut Tigray off from supplies and aid. The government and Eritrean soldiers were accused of widespread human-rights violations in Tigray region; Addis Ababa responded with a restrictive information policy, jailing and silencing local journalists and expelling international news agencies.[15] The TDF occupied various towns in Amhara and Afar regions, where it was accused of committing human-rights violations similar to those reported to have been committed by the ENDF in Tigray.[16]

In August 2021 the TDF agreed a strategic alliance with the OLA, which was advancing towards Addis Ababa.[17] The government responded by declaring a state of emergency alongside a national call to arms. Self-defence committees were assembled in Addis

Ababa to evoke an image of national resistance against the TPLF. In November 2021, many international agencies, embassies and donor organisations withdrew staff from the capital amid mounting fears of an approaching battle for the city. Ethnic targeting and imprisonment of Tigrayans increased across the country. The advancing TDF came to a standstill in December 2021, retreating into Tigray and offering the government a ceasefire.

Of the two ceasefire offers issued in 2021 – one by the government and one by the TPLF – neither ended hostilities or led to negotiations. Moreover, a complete cessation of hostilities did not follow the government's humanitarian truce of March 2022, with each side accusing the other of planning further attacks while also signalling their availability for negotiations.

Economic/development
The conflict increased investor uncertainty and negatively affected Ethiopia's shrinking GDP and foreign direct investment. Inflation reached 35% in December 2021.[18] US sanctions imposed on Ethiopia in response to reports of human-rights violations were particularly severe. In January 2022, the US also suspended Ethiopia from the Africa Growth and Opportunity Act.[19]

Diplomacy
While the central government sheltered behind its law-enforcement rhetoric and urged concerned onlookers to consider the crisis in northern Ethiopia a domestic issue, the international community focused on the humanitarian crisis in Tigray.[20] This perspective is important but neglects other, equally concerning instabilities across Ethiopia. In February 2022, a US Congress bill referred to as the 'Ethiopia Stabilization, Peace, and Democracy Act' confirmed previous sanctions imposed on the Ethiopian government. The bill aims to further sanction the government for humanitarian misconduct and does not discuss the actions of the other warring parties.[21]

Humanitarian aid
The situation in northern Ethiopia deteriorated dramatically in 2021 and early 2022 due to the government's blocking of humanitarian access in the region and increased hostilities in Afar and northern Amhara regions. The March truce permitted the gradual entry of food aid previously held up on the border of the conflict zones. While there were signs of an improvement in the overall humanitarian situation during the reporting period, weather shocks, political friction, insecurity and a severely weakened economy will continue to exacerbate humanitarian needs for approximately 25.9m people.[22]

Conflict Outlook

Political scenarios
The overlapping conflicts in Ethiopia have resulted from the end of nearly three decades of TPLF rule and the subsequent quest for a new political order between ethno-nationalist/federalist actors and a centralist camp. Although the central government has not attempted to undermine or dissolve federalism, Abiy's leadership style and his government's response to dissenting voices has placed the government in the centralist camp, while its alliance with conservative nationalist groups has not helped this perception. This context created a pretext for opposition groups to fight for regional sovereignty. The war in the north, droughts and inter-ethnic violence have driven up inflation to its highest level in almost a decade.

The March 2022 truce came as a surprise to regional actors and the international community. It was a unilateral declaration by Addis Ababa to allow access to humanitarian aid; as a result, some observers interpreted it as an attempt by the Abiy administration to gain time. US sanctions imposed in November 2021, which brought Abiy's reform plans to a halt, may have been a primary driver for the March declaration. The truce was declared without Eritrea's engagement, which may indicate that the Addis Ababa–Asmara alliance is strained or has been sidetracked to appease Western donors. The war in Tigray led to additional economic travails for an already struggling country; the challenging economic situation may drive the radicalisation of unemployed young people in the short to medium term. Meanwhile, the TPLF and the Amhara stand guard over a renewed confrontation concerning mainly Western Tigray.[23]

Escalation potential and conflict-related risks
Given the scale of the ethnic violence that followed the outbreak of the Tigray war – and the massacres

Figure 1: Number of violent events per region, March 2021–April 2022

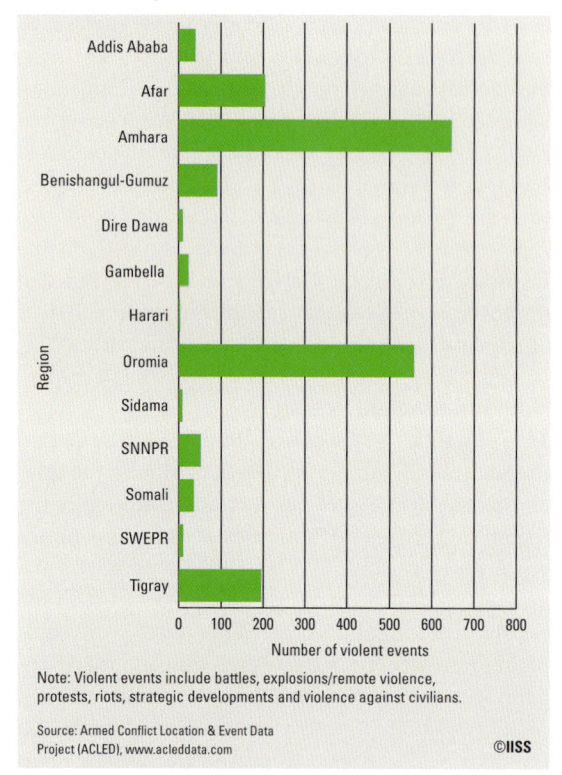

Region	Number of violent events
Addis Ababa	~20
Afar	~200
Amhara	~650
Benishangul-Gumuz	~80
Dire Dawa	~10
Gambella	~30
Harari	0
Oromia	~570
Sidama	~5
SNNPR	~60
Somali	~50
SWEPR	~10
Tigray	~200

Note: Violent events include battles, explosions/remote violence, protests, riots, strategic developments and violence against civilians.

Source: Armed Conflict Location & Event Data Project (ACLED), www.acleddata.com ©IISS

and looting carried out by all parties across Tigray, Amhara and Afar regions – there is a significant risk of conflict escalation. The scale of internal ethnic conflict in Amhara, Benishangul-Gumuz, Gambella and SNNPR regions in 2021 and early 2022 – which drew in local security forces – highlighted the danger posed by simultaneous conflicts waged across the country between multiple ethnic groups. If this situation persists, it may challenge the central government's already overstretched security apparatus. In April 2022, sectarian violence targeting Muslims in Gonder and rising tensions in Aari suggested that the legacies of TPLF-led ethnic federalism will remain a challenge for the country for some time to come.

A national peace dialogue is needed to address violence and conflict in the country. However, it is likely that it would prove difficult for Addis Ababa to reverse several outcomes of the Tigray war through dialogue. The territories claimed and newly occupied by Amhara nationalists, where large-scale displacement has taken place, pose a particular problem. If Abiy were to ask Amhara forces to withdraw from these regions in order to enhance the legitimacy of the Tigray government (loyal to the Abiy administration), his request would inevitably be met with Amhara resistance. In short, there are too many centrifugal forces in Ethiopia that are not balanced by an inclusive force. Compounding this problem, the central government is supported primarily by Ethiopia's more centralist and nationalist factions, while the larger groups in the country are pitted against each other. Furthermore, conflicts are intragroup as well as intergroup: Ethiopia's ethnic groups face constant shifts in intra-ethnic alliances between their larger and smaller sections, as in the case of the Oromo.

Prospects for peace

Ethiopia's multilayered conflicts pose a dilemma: they cannot be dealt with simultaneously but they also require a national solution. The current political crisis is as much about defining a way towards a sustainable future as it is about finding a post-TPLF power arrangement. The different conflicts involve costly anti-guerrilla warfare and ethnic violence in northern Ethiopia, while shifting alliances between and among security forces and militias foster insecurity at the regional level. Efforts to redraw boundaries in volatile southern Ethiopia have produced ethnic alliances and oppositional forces. Developments in the reporting period have shown that instead of bringing about an end to conflict, military intervention often leads to more violence in other parts of the country. The way forward is likely to be found in a series of separate peace talks and a subsequent national dialogue. All parties – dissident groups, separatists, religious leaders, activists and journalists – should be included. However, this process will not be possible without economic growth and measures to control inflation.

To overcome the drivers of conflict in Ethiopia, Addis Ababa will need to secure an inclusive political settlement, address humanitarian needs, promote economic growth and boost employment. The stability of all countries in the Horn of Africa depends, to different degrees, on the success and stability of Ethiopia, as the conflict in Tigray demonstrated. Equally, the country's growth and development could act as a catalyst for similar progress in the region and further afield. If Ethiopia is to return to its 2018 political and economic trajectory, its partners will need to support the country's reforms and refrain from further sanctions.

Strategic implications and global influences

Addis Ababa's growing relationship with Asmara has harmed Ethiopia's international image. US sanctions imposed on the country were just one indicator of the transformation of international relations occurring in the Horn of Africa. Washington's sanctions motivated Ethiopia to strengthen ties with China, Russia, Turkey and the UAE.[24] Domestically, there is a recognisable ideological shift away from Western donors. The European Union and the US are popularly criticised for imposing sanctions on the country and infringing on its sovereignty while favouring the TPLF (despite the fact that the US has also called on the TPLF to refrain from human-rights violations). The government's commitment to destroying the TPLF and its refusal to consider talks to resolve the war in Tigray, its heavy hand on the GERD issue and its rejection of international investigation into human-rights violations have highlighted Ethiopia's powerful position in the Horn of Africa and the limits of Western diplomacy. Ethiopia is on a path of domestic transformation that has taken a heavy toll on the country. Calling on all parties to refrain from violence while simultaneously working towards a swift economic transformation may be an uncomfortable prospect. However, it is likely the only option remaining for international actors.

Notes

[1] See Jonathan Fisher and Meressa Tsehaye Gebrewahd, '"Game Over"? Abiy Ahmed, the Tigrayan People's Liberation Front and Ethiopia's Political Crisis', *African Affairs*, vol. 118, no. 470, January 2019, pp. 194–206.

[2] 'Ethiopia: Mass Arbitrary Arrests Target Tigrayans, Says UN Rights Office', UN News, 16 November 2021.

[3] Jacky Habib, 'Ethiopia Set a World Record for Displacements in a Single Year: 5.1 Million in 2021', National Public Radio (NPR), 28 May 2022.

[4] '7,000 Seek Sudan Asylum After Fleeing Western Ethiopia Violence', Al-Jazeera, 23 February 2021.

[5] Waqo (@waQQN), tweet, 22 July 2021.

[6] 'Ethiopian Human Rights Council Speaks Out Against Violence Along Sidama, Oromia', *Borkena*, 7 April 2022.

[7] Asress Adimi Gikay, 'Security Forces' Attacks on the Aari Threatens South Omo's Harmony', *Ethiopia Insight*, 9 May 2022.

[8] 'Ethiopia's Tigray Crisis: The Long, Medium and Short Story', BBC News, 17 November 2020.

[9] IISS, *The Armed Conflict Survey 2021* (Abingdon: Routledge for IISS), p. 238.

[10] Ibid.

[11] See Emmanuel Akinwotu, 'Video of Armed Men Burning Man Alive in Western Ethiopia Sparks Outrage', *Guardian*, 15 March 2022; and Alemayehu B. Hordofa, 'Ethiopia Must Address Impunity for Human Rights Abuses by Security Forces', *Ethiopia Insight*, 5 April 2022.

[12] See 'News: Gov't "Organizes, Not Disarm" Fano Members Who Fought for Survival of Country: Amhara State', *Addis Standard*, 17 January 2022.

[13] UN High Commissioner for Refugees, 'Response to Internal Displacement in Ethiopia Fact Sheet – January to March 2022', ReliefWeb, 19 May 2022.

[14] This event may have been a political stunt – in June the GLF attacked Gambella town in alliance with the OLA.

[15] See, for example, 'Two Ethiopian Journalists, Held Arbitrarily for Four Months, Due to Appear in Court', Reporters Without Borders, 29 March 2022.

[16] AFP News Agency (@AFP), tweet, 11 March 2022.

[17] Marishet Mohammed Hamza, 'TPLF–OLA Alliance Is a Prelude to Tigray's Secession', *Ethiopia Insight*, 2 September 2021.

[18] David Malingha, 'Ethiopian Inflation Tops 35% in December as Food Costs Surge', Bloomberg, 24 January 2022.

[19] 'US Cuts Off Ethiopia, Mali and Guinea from Trade Programme', Al-Jazeera, 2 January 2022.

[20] See, for example, 'Ethiopia: UN Officials Allege War Crimes in Tigray', DW, 5 March 2021.

[21] Jon Abbink, 'Congress Risks Prolonging the Ethiopian Civil War', *American Conservative*, 30 March 2022.

[22] UN Population Fund, 'UNFPA Ethiopia Humanitarian Response Situation Report – April 2022', ReliefWeb, 17 May 2022.

[23] 'News Analysis: Amhara State Calls Region Security to Ready for Attack by Tigrayan Forces, Respond to Growing Lawlessness, Arms Proliferation in Region', *Addis Standard*, 14 May 2022.

[24] Daniel Munday, 'Ethiopian Diplomacy During the Tigray Conflict: Authoritarian Powers and Abiy's Regime', Democracy in Africa, 6 December 2021.

SOMALIA

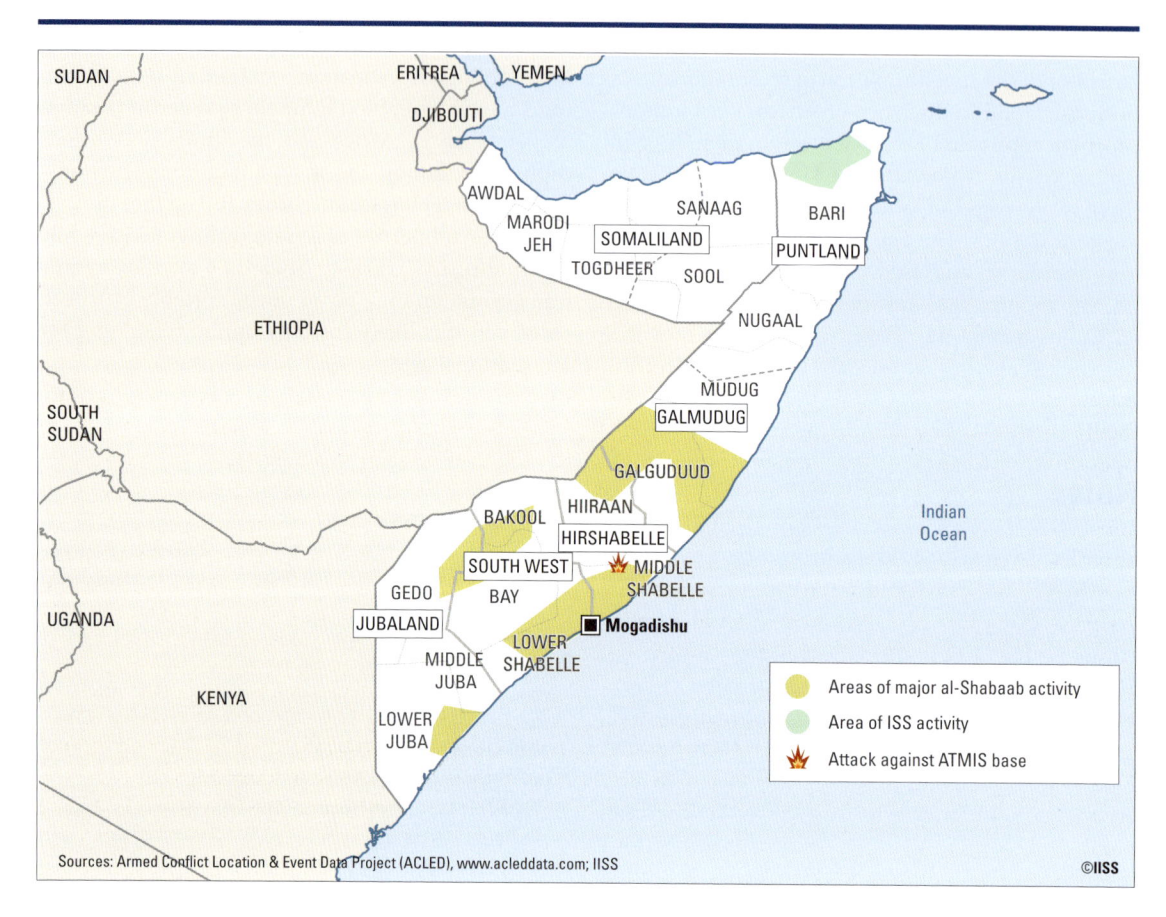

Map of Somalia showing regions including Somaliland, Puntland, Galmudug, Hirshabelle, South West, Jubaland, and areas of al-Shabaab activity, ISS activity, and attacks against ATMIS base.

Sources: Armed Conflict Location & Event Data Project (ACLED), www.acleddata.com; IISS

Overview

Three decades into a crippling civil war, Somalia remained hostage to instability and insecurity in 2021 and early 2022. The conflict began following the collapse of Siad Barre's regime in 1991, which provided an opportunity for existing Islamist militias to expand their presence across the country. The Islamic Courts Union (ICU) dominated the scene by establishing sharia-based courts and controlling territory through its militias. At its peak in 2006 – after expelling the warlords that had controlled Mogadishu since the start of the civil war – the ICU held Somalia's capital, a development that established the organisation as the country's de facto ruling authority, overshadowing the internationally supported Transitional Federal Government (TFG).

Soon after the ICU entered Mogadishu, the TFG's leadership pleaded for Ethiopia's help with a military campaign to support its efforts to retake control of the country. The Ethiopian military campaign made quick progress and swiftly dismantled the ICU but also radicalised large swathes of Somali society, paving the way for the rise of a new insurgent Islamic group, al-Shabaab. Al-Shabaab combined successful military counter-offensives against the Ethiopian–TFG coalition with growing affinities to al-Qaeda's ideology, eventually formalising its allegiance to the terrorist group in 2012.

Since then, international concerns regarding al-Shabaab's expansion have put Somalia under the counter-terrorism and stabilisation spotlight. In March 2007, the African Union (AU) deployed its peacekeeping mission to Somalia (African Union Mission in Somalia, AMISOM) to support the development of the TFG's institutional

Armed Conflict Global Relevance Indicator (ACGRI)

Somalia

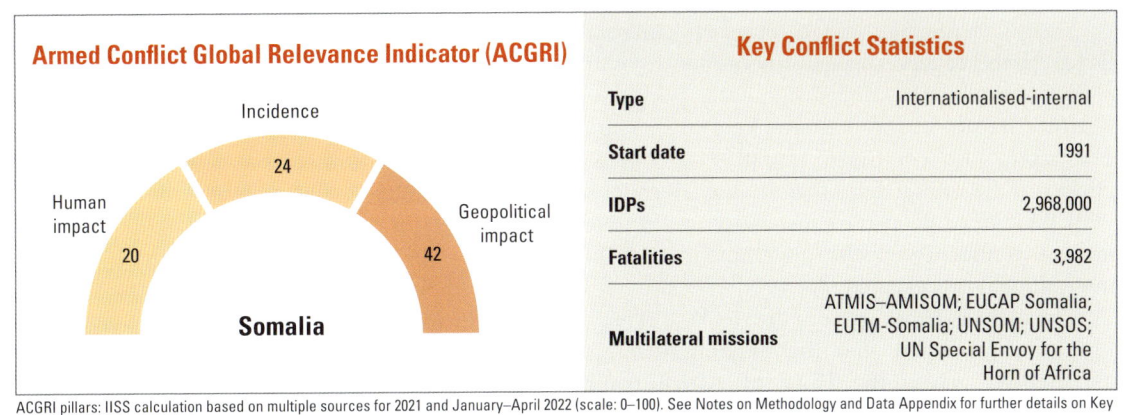

- Incidence: 24
- Human impact: 20
- Geopolitical impact: 42

Key Conflict Statistics

Type	Internationalised-internal
Start date	1991
IDPs	2,968,000
Fatalities	3,982
Multilateral missions	ATMIS–AMISOM; EUCAP Somalia; EUTM-Somalia; UNSOM; UNSOS; UN Special Envoy for the Horn of Africa

ACGRI pillars: IISS calculation based on multiple sources for 2021 and January–April 2022 (scale: 0–100). See Notes on Methodology and Data Appendix for further details on Key Conflict Statistics.

infrastructure, train Somali military forces and facilitate the delivery of humanitarian aid. Initially operating under a six-month mandate, AMISOM was systematically renewed over 15 years until its substitution for a different mission was eventually agreed in March 2022.

The United States is the largest donor to Somalia. As part of the war on terror and in an attempt to support stabilisation efforts within the country, the US has provided in excess of US$1billion to train the Somali National Army (SNA) since 2012, with another US$5bn in foreign aid spent from 2006–20.[1] Financial and humanitarian aid, together with governance support and mentoring, have been running parallel to the United States' own security operations in Somalia. While during the Obama administration these efforts focused mainly on striking al-Shabaab leadership and showcased an extensive use of armed uninhabited aerial vehicles (UAVs), under president Donald Trump US military action against the group's lower levels expanded significantly, despite a reduction in the United States' military presence since late 2020. Still, the return to power of Hassan Sheikh Mohamud encouraged President Joe Biden to authorise the return of a (smaller) US military contingent to Somalia from May 2022.[2]

The geostrategic relevance of Somalia and the fate of the fragile and fragmented Federal Government of Somalia (FGS – which supplanted the TFG in 2012 following the approval of Somalia's constitution) have also garnered the attention and support of other international actors. Soon after the FGS's inauguration, Somalia witnessed, in rapid succession, the establishment of the United Nations Assistance Mission in Somalia and a European Union maritime- and police-focused capacity-building mission, the European Union Capacity Building Mission (EUCAP) Somalia, which runs parallel to the EU's anti-piracy efforts under EU Naval Force Somalia and to the EU Training Mission in Somalia (EUTM–Somalia). The country also saw intensified diplomatic, economic and security-cooperation efforts by other regional actors, such as Turkey and Qatar, as well as Saudi Arabia and the United Arab Emirates (UAE).

From a domestic perspective, Mohamed Abdullahi 'Farmaajo' Mohamed, Somalia's president from 2017 to mid-2022, provided a modicum of continuity to the country's leadership. However, he was not able to address or prevent the downward spiral of political and institutional fragmentation, the instability exacerbated by the presence of al-Shabaab, the proliferation of clan-based militias, and the humanitarian challenges entangling the country. Moreover, al-Shabaab demonstrated its commitment to capitalising on the state apparatus's weaknesses and exploiting the turmoil caused by recurring political crises.

Throughout 2021, Somali politics was dominated by the deadlock over a constitutional crisis on the terms of the next parliamentary elections. Farmaajo committed to staying at the helm as acting president amid growing tensions with the opposition that often led to violent repression and armed clashes. The political crisis substantially hijacked Somalia's political discussion, and the complex electoral process to nominate new MPs contributed to a significant delay in the inauguration of a new parliament. Eventually, in April, seven months after the original deadline, new MPs swore their oaths and subsequently elected President Hassan Sheikh Mohamud.[3]

Meanwhile, Somali armed forces and international peacekeepers clashed intermittently with al-Shabaab, which controlled significant pockets of territory mostly in southern and central Somalia. The group also continued to carry out one-off attacks in the capital and other strategic locations, with the aim of deepening instability and undermining confidence in the government and the international peacekeeping force.[4]

Critically, in February 2022 the UN World Food Programme warned that the ongoing drought experienced across the Horn of Africa could lead to a major humanitarian crisis in Somalia. Altogether, political, security and humanitarian concerns made for a highly challenging year for Somalia's new leadership.

In the reporting period there were changes to the footprint of the international military presence in Somalia, primarily as AMISOM was replaced by the African Union Transition Mission in Somalia (ATMIS) in April 2022, in line with the FGS Somalia Transition Plan (STP). In addition, the expiry of UN Security Council Resolution 2608 in March 2022 had a significant impact on the EU's *Operation Atalanta* counter-piracy mandate. Both decisions were taken in view of the overarching goal to empower the Somali armed forces and ultimately reduce their dependence on external military support. Mohamud's election, however, might bring many of these international endeavours to the status quo ante: contrary to Farmaajo's vision of a Somalia that would take full responsibility for its governance by 2024 regardless of its security sector's overall level of preparedness, Mohamud's has a more pragmatic vision of international support and foreign countries' contribution to Somalia's security, with no hard deadlines for the withdrawal of international forces.

Conflict Parties

Somali National Army (SNA)

Strength: 13,900 active military. 3,000 additional troops under the Puntland government and an unspecified number of militias.

Areas of operation: Galmudug, Hirshabelle, Jubaland, Puntland and southwest (excluding self-declared independent Somaliland).

Leadership: Gen. Odowaa Yusuf Rageh (army chief of staff).

Structure: The SNA is divided into four command divisions and spread across Somalia's operational sectors. It has associated special-forces units such as the US-trained Danaab.

History: Efforts to build the SNA began in 2008. After two decades of state collapse, the SNA had to be built through both new recruitment and the incorporation of existing armed actors, such as clan militias. These efforts were challenged by the lack of coordination among international partners, internecine clan fighting and the ongoing al-Shabaab insurgency. As a result, the SNA continues to suffer from deep-seated internal cleavages and cohesion problems.

Objectives: Secure the territorial authority of the FGS, primarily through the defeat of al-Shabaab.

Opponents: Al-Shabaab, the Islamic State in Somalia (ISS), militias and criminal actors.

Affiliates/allies: AMISOM/ATMIS, the EU, Turkey, the United Kingdom and the US.

Resources/capabilities: The SNA suffers from severe shortages of resources – particularly of small arms – amid widespread internal corruption, including soldiers selling their arms (including to al-Shabaab) to make up for irregular and low salaries.

Harakat al-Shabaab al-Mujahideen ('al-Shabaab')

Strength: Active fighting force of an estimated 7,000 militants.[5]

Areas of operation: Strongest in southern Somalia (Jubaland, Hirshabelle and the southwest). Presence is more limited in Galmudug and Puntland.

Leadership: Ahmad Umar Diriye, better known as Abu Ubaidah, is the current leader, or emir.

Structure: A consultative council (*majlis al-shura*) is the group's central decision-making body, although regional political and military authorities enjoy considerable autonomy. The group's military wing is divided into six regional fighting units. An intelligence wing with transnational reach (*Amniyat*) oversees a large security apparatus through which the group curtails dissent and maintains internal cohesion.

History: Al-Shabaab emerged in December 2006 after breaking away from the ICU, which had offered little resistance against the Ethiopian invasion of Somalia. Over more than a decade, al-Shabaab evolved into a highly effective insurgent group that appeals to nationalist sentiments to boost recruitment and can challenge the authority of the FGS.

Objectives: Defeat the FGS and establish Islamist rule in Somalia.

Opponents: The FGS, SNA and ISS.

Affiliates/allies: Opportunistic alliances with militias and organised-crime syndicates.

Resources/capabilities: Al-Shabaab benefits from access to several sources of income, including checkpoint taxation, extortion, kidnappings, illicit trade, revenues from piracy and funding from transnational Islamist groups.

Islamic State in Somalia (ISS)

Strength: Estimated to have up to 200 fighters in mid-2021.[6]

Areas of operation: Based in the Galgala mountain region of Puntland but periodically conducts targeted attacks in Bosaso and Mogadishu.

Leadership: Led by Abd al-Qadir Mumin, who left al-Shabaab and pledged allegiance to the Islamic State in 2015, taking leadership of ISS.[7]

Structure: Little is known about its internal structure but given the group's small size and the regular targeting of senior figures by both Somali and US forces, it is likely to be relatively decentralised.

History: Mumin broke away from al-Shabaab with a small group of fighters in October 2015 and pledged allegiance to ISIS. Al-Shabaab has vowed to eliminate the rival group.

Objectives: Expand its influence by spreading ISIS ideology within Somalia and neighbouring countries, such as Ethiopia, and to attract broader support.

Opponents: Al-Shabaab, Somali and Puntland security forces.

Affiliates/allies: Believed to have connections with other Islamic State affiliates in Yemen and Central Africa.

Resources/capabilities: Small arms.

African Union Mission in Somalia (AMISOM) – AU Transition Mission to Somalia (ATMIS) since April 2022

Strength: Approximately 20,000 troops.

Areas of operation: The five troop-contributing countries are Burundi, Djibouti, Ethiopia, Kenya and Uganda. Their forces are each responsible for a sector in central and southern Somalia, including Banadir and Lower Shabelle (Uganda), Lower and Middle Juba (Kenya), Bay, Bakool and Gedo (Ethiopia), Hiiraan and Galguduud (Djibouti), and Middle Shabelle (Burundi).

Leadership: Burundian Lt-Gen. Diomede Ndegeya (force commander), appointed in August 2020. Yet there is no centralised command-and-control structure, which makes coordinating operations difficult. Each sector's forces operate under their own command and are ultimately responsible to their own governments.

Structure: AMISOM/ATMIS contingents function as conventional militaries.

History: The UN authorised the AU to deploy a peacekeeping mission in February 2007 to support the TFG. The mission had a six-month mandate and was allowed to use force only in self-defence. In the following years, the situation failed to stabilise and the UN agreed to boost AMISOM troop numbers and extend the mission's mandate and scope. The transition into ATMIS reflected former Somali president Farmaajo's willingness to take full responsibility for the country's security situation as well as a decline in donors' willingness to fund the peacekeeping mission. Mohamud's tenure will need to assuage international donors' concerns about ATMIS's cost–benefit ratio, if he wants to retain the same levels of international military help.

Objectives: Defeat al-Shabaab, retake its territory and protect the FGS.

Opponents: Al-Shabaab.

Affiliates/allies: AMISOM/ATMIS is supported by numerous international governments and periodically by military contingents from allied countries who deliver training, including the EU, Turkey, the UK and the US.

Resources/capabilities: AMISOM/ATMIS draws from the military contingents of contributing countries and is occasionally supported by other international partners.

Conflict Drivers

Security

Al-Shabaab's increasing strength:
Al-Shabaab's allegiance to al-Qaeda has escalated international concerns about its growing presence in the geopolitically sensitive Horn of Africa. The presence of foreign troops on Somali soil has significantly contributed to al-Shabaab's increasing strength and ideological commitment. A trend reversal is not possible, as appeasement of al-Shabaab is out of the question for the FGS and international actors alike. The issue is further exacerbated by the significant organisational and operational weaknesses demonstrated by the SNA and the vast majority of other military and security forces active in the conflict, despite years of financial investments and training initiatives organised by international partners.[8]

Political

Incompatible ideologies:
At the core of the Somali conflict lies al-Shabaab's ideology, which is essentially incompatible with that of the FGS. Despite various factions within the group advocating for differing agendas, the establishment of a sharia-based Islamic state in Somalia is the ultimate, unifying objective across the organisation, alongside a commitment to oppose the 'Western-backed' FGS and the presence of foreign-military troops on Somali land.[9]

From the FGS's perspective, there is no room to negotiate with al-Shabaab. Nor do international actors expect the FGS to try, rendering the conflict a zero-sum game.[10] While Mohamud's approach is yet to be articulated, it is certain to follow the path of his predecessor: since the beginning of his tenure in 2017, Farmaajo had effectively declared an all-out war on al-Shabaab.

Economic
Governance failures:
Somalia's fragile institutional context means that the FGS's economic- and social-governance failures are systematically exploited by al-Shabaab, who aim to recruit in those areas that are most deeply affected by the government's negative performance. Tax revenues and the justice system are two of the governance areas where al-Shabaab has been more effective in supplanting Somalia's central-government authority; grievances emerging from local authorities' abuses and corruption, coupled with a lack of economic opportunities, are leading factors in al-Shabaab's recruitment.[11] Environmental challenges have further exacerbated these trends, as local grievances, together with intra- and intercommunal tensions, have increased in line with the effects of Somalia's persisting drought. Friction at the local level over access to water and other resources, as well as famine- and poverty-dictated migration trends, create opportunities for al-Shabaab to recruit and further destabilise Somalia's governance structure.[12]

Key Events in 2021–22

POLITICAL EVENTS

27 April 2021
Then-prime minister Mohamed Hussein Roble rejects then-president Farmaajo's proposal to extend his term.

1 May
Parliament votes against Farmaajo's decision to extend his presidential term.

29 June
Political leaders agree to hold presidential elections in October.

27 July
The US Agency for International Development earmarks an additional US$200 million for humanitarian assistance to the Somali people.

7 August
Turkey announces a US$30m donation to Somalia to be used for 'budget financing and international capacity building'.[13]

16 September
Farmaajo suspends Roble's executive powers.

22 October
A compromise solution among political leaders produces a new timeline for elections.

19 November
The UN warns that Somalia's drought is rapidly worsening.

7 December
Finland grants US$9m for Somalia's education sector.

MILITARY/VIOLENT EVENTS

28 April 2021
An al-Shabaab suicide-bomb attack kills seven people in Mogadishu.

9 May
An al-Shabaab suicide-bomb attack kills six police officers in Mogadishu.

28 June
An al-Shabaab attack in Galmudug kills 30 people.

10 July
In Mogadishu, the city's chief of police survives a car-bomb assassination attempt carried out by al-Shabaab.

24 August
Somalia and the AU sign an agreement that enables the launch of ATMIS.

25 September
An al-Shabaab car bomb detonated outside the presidential palace kills eight people in Mogadishu.

6 October
Al-Shabaab kills two soldiers in Mogadishu.

25 November
An al-Shabaab car bomb kills eight civilians in Mogadishu.

21 December
The UN Security Council extends AMISOM for three months.

17 January 2022
The UK government announces a US$10m programme to tackle Somalia's drought.

25 February
The deadline to cast votes for parliamentary elections is postponed to 15 March.

11 March
The UN High Commissioner for Refugees announces that it will increase aid to Somali internally displaced persons.

15 April
Parliament swears in 290 lawmakers, marking an important step towards completing the electoral process.

12 January 2022
An al-Shabaab car bomb detonated near Mogadishu's airport kills nine people.

24 February
US forces conduct a drone strike against al-Shabaab after the group attacks Somali forces northwest of Mogadishu.

24 March
A series of al-Shabaab bomb attacks across the country kills 48 people, including a prominent lawmaker.

11 April
Al-Shabaab launches a mortar attack against an Ethiopian military base in southern Somalia.

3 May
Al-Shabaab attacks an ATMIS base in Middle Shabelle region staffed by Burundian peacekeepers.

Responses to the Conflict

Security
In April 2021, the collapse of talks about preparatory work for the next presidential election paved the way for a wave of al-Shabaab attacks across the country.[14] Attempting to exploit the political turmoil, the group launched suicide-bomb, improvised-explosive-device, mortar and small-arms attacks against military, civilian and political targets.

Following a phase of mixed intensity and number of violent incidents between April and August, the offensive regained full pace in September, with several attacks against military and civilian targets in Mogadishu and its surrounding areas and the targeting of political figures across the country. By March 2022, al-Shabaab had killed several prominent political figures and managed to breach the perimeter of Mogadishu's international airport, one of Somalia's most heavily defended facilities.

In response, the FGS launched a string of military operations, either retaking lost territory (often only temporarily), disrupting al-Shabaab's facilities or supporting AMISOM operations. Over the year, FGS–AMISOM tensions grew due to the impending renewal of the latter's mandate. The FGS's preference for a swifter transition of security responsibilities to the SNA and its concerns over civilian deaths during military operations prompted Mogadishu to reject an AU proposal to strengthen AMISOM. As a result, the newly launched ATMIS is supposed to follow a transition timeline that will see its 20,000 personnel – currently deployed across Somalia – complete termination of the mission in 2024.[15]

As much of Somalia's stability hinges on the AU's military presence, ATMIS forces are likely to become al-Shabaab's target of choice. Indeed, a month after the mission's launch, al-Shabaab overran an ATMIS base in Middle Shabelle region staffed by Burundian peacekeepers. While al-Shabaab reported that the attack killed some 200 soldiers, the Burundi army stated that 10–30 soldiers were killed and several others were captured or wounded.[16]

Economic/development
A September 2021 World Bank report on Somalia's economic situation highlighted that the country was recovering from the 'triple shock' of 2020 – a combination of the coronavirus pandemic's effects, extreme flooding and a locust infestation that impacted the farming and livestock sectors.[17] However, the political stalemate over elections prevented the FGS from enacting debt-relief policies that could have reassured external donors and secured further credit lines.[18]

Critically, in March 2022 the IMF also stressed that access to its programme was dependent on Somalia's ability to overcome domestic political turmoil and conclude the electoral process, stating: 'IMF staff would – once a President is elected – confirm the authorities' commitment to the economic program and development partners' plans to resume budget grants.'[19]

Diplomacy

In February 2022, James Swan – the UN Secretary-General's Special Representative for Somalia – briefed the UN Security Council on the FGS's priorities, highlighting that al-Shabaab remains the primary security concern and that a successful transition from AMISOM to ATMIS would be key in countering the group's potential expansion.[20] On 31 March, UN Security Council Resolution 2628 authorised the AU to deploy ATMIS to Somalia 'to reduce the threat posed by Al Shabaab' and 'support the capacity building of the integrated Somali security and police forces', initially under a 12-month mandate.

The EU's security and capacity-building commitments towards Somalia remained in force in the reporting period. The decisions to renew EUTM–Somalia, EUCAP Somalia and *Operation Atalanta* will be taken in late 2022. The UN Security Council's decision not to extend Resolution 2608 (2021), which effectively expired in March 2022 and enabled the presence of international forces in Somali territorial waters, impacted both EUCAP Somalia and *Operation Atalanta*, whose forces must now patrol international waters only.[21]

Competition continued to increase between states with significant foreign-policy capital invested in the country. Somalia–UAE relations saw some progress and Egypt also increased its engagement, launching a series of cooperation and training initiatives in October 2021.[22]

Humanitarian aid

The impact of Ethiopia's conflict and the global-supply disruptions caused by the war in Ukraine heightened the risk of a sharp increase in food scarcity across the Horn of Africa, particularly in Somalia as these impacts are compounded by the effects of severe drought. In early 2022, the UN Food and Agriculture Organization warned that an additional 600,000 people in Somalia could become 'acutely food insecure', bringing the country's overall number of people in this category to 4.1m, with an overall 7.7m Somalis in need of humanitarian assistance.[23]

In February 2022, Swan reported that the UN Office for the Coordination of Humanitarian Affairs' (UNOCHA) 2022 Humanitarian Response Plan for Somalia was severely underfunded, with only 2% of the overall US$1.5bn required for planned activities covered by international donors. As of April, donor pledges to UNOCHA's Somalia fund had reached US$1.39bn.[24]

In April, the US allocated an additional US$200m for humanitarian assistance to Ethiopia, Kenya and Somalia to provide emergency food, medical supplies and access to water. In early 2022, the EU also made available an additional US$63m for humanitarian projects in Somalia, on top of the US$19m allocated in response to the ongoing drought in December 2021.[25]

Conflict Outlook

Political scenarios

The reporting period saw a significant increase in tensions between then president Farmaajo and then-prime minister Roble that highlighted potential fractures within the security sector, since elements of the SNA and the police took sides in the dispute and acted outside their institutional remits. While initial controversies over the electoral process were quickly shelved and Mohamud's assumption of office unfolded smoothly, the political transition heralds a delicate phase for Somali security since al-Shabaab will have additional incentives to conduct violent attacks and destabilise the country. The period will be even more delicate because the transition coincides with the change from AMISOM to ATMIS. Al-Shabaab will likely target ATMIS as it looks to gain ground from a narrative and operational perspective by attacking what it sees as Somalia's invaders.

Escalation potential and conflict-related risks

The emergence of ISS in 2018 and its steady consolidation of power could escalate conflict in Somalia. ISS is a 'third party' in the conflict. Despite pursuing a jihadist agenda with some commonalities to al-Shabaab, the two groups are in competition. However, at present ISS lacks the size, capability and footprint to challenge al-Shabaab.

Table 1: Major military deployments in Somalia, as of April 2022

Mission	Troops
African Union Transition Mission in Somalia (ATMIS)	19,600
European Union Training Mission in Somalia (EUTM)	202
EUNAVFOR Somalia *Operation Atalanta*	150
Turkey (training mission)	200

Source: IISS, Military Balance+, milbalplus.iiss.org

A significant element of Somalia's security hinges on the STP being delivered. Key challenges will likely emerge from the transition of responsibilities from ATMIS to the SNA, which is struggling to reach satisfactory levels of readiness and effectiveness, and from the Somali maritime forces, now in charge of patrolling territorial waters. While piracy-related incidents have drastically reduced since 2013, there are concerns that an international military presence would provide a more effective deterrent.[26]

Strategic implications and global Influences

Influenced by regional conflicts such as the war in Tigray in Ethiopia and the civil war in Yemen, and amid the growing appetite for foreign-military presence in the region, Somalia's geopolitical appeal remains high – the range and scope of foreign military- and economic-assistance programmes is testament to this. Somalia will continue to be of strategic relevance for a wide range of regional and global actors. There remains a risk that the modicum of governance progress achieved in recent years will come undone as Mogadishu contends with al-Shabaab, a fragile political equilibrium, COVID-19-related issues and a looming major humanitarian crisis exacerbated by the second-order effects of the Russia–Ukraine war.

Notes

[1] Paul D. Williams, 'Understanding US Policy in Somalia', Chatham House Research Paper, 14 July 2020.

[2] 'Somalia: President Biden Reverses Trump's Withdrawal of US troops', BBC News, 16 May 2022.

[3] 'Somalia Elects Hassan Sheik Mohamud as New President', Al-Jazeera, 15 May 2022.

[4] Mohammed Dhaysane, 'Somalia Retakes Strategic Town from Al-Shabaab Terrorists', Anadolu Agency, 14 December 2021; and 'Al-Shabaab Take Control of Mataban District in Hiiraan Region', Hiiraan Online, 18 April 2022.

[5] 'IntelBrief: Somalia Continues to Deteriorate as Al-Shabaab Gains Ground', Soufan Center, 18 March 2022.

[6] Australian Government, Australian National Security, 'Islamic State Somalia', 7 May 2021.

[7] International Crisis Group, 'The Islamic State Threat in Somalia's Puntland State', 17 November 2016.

[8] Paul D. Williams, 'Building the Somali National Army: Anatomy of a Failure, 2008–2018', *Journal of Strategic Studies*, vol. 43, no. 3, 2020.

[9] Claire Felter, Jonathan Masters and Mohammed Aly Segie, 'Al-Shabab', Council on Foreign Relations, 19 May 2021.

[10] Abdeta Dribssa Beyene, 'The Security Sector Reform Paradox in Somalia', LSE Conflict Research Programme, 2018.

[11] Jake Harrington and Jared Thompson, 'Examining Extremism: Harakat Al Shabaab al Mujahideen (al Shabaab)', Centre for Strategic and International Studies, 23 September 2021.

[12] Andrew E. Yaw Tchie, 'How Climate Insecurity Could Trigger More Conflict in Somalia', The Conversation, 12 April 2021.

[13] 'Turkey's Latest Donation of $30 Million to Somalia Stirs Debate', *Arab News*, 7 August 2021.

[14] Amanda Sperber, 'Inside Somalia's Impasse: Election Talks Collapse amid Mistrust and Blame', *Guardian*, 8 April 2021.

[15] Aggrey Mutambo, 'Somalia Rejects AU Proposal to Modify Amisom Role', *Somali Times*, 18 July 2021; and 'Al-Shabaab Attacks AU Base in Somalia, Casualties Reported', France 24, 3 May 2022.

[16] Joice Etutu, 'Al-Shabab Attack on African Union Forces in Somalia: What We Know', BBC News, 4 May 2022.

[17] World Bank, 'Somalia Economic Update', June 2021.

[18] Heritage Institute, 'State of Somalia Report', December 2021.

[19] IMF, 'IMF Staff Completes Virtual Mission to Discuss the Second and Third Reviews of the Extended Credit Facility to Somalia', 7 March 2022.

[20] UN Assistance Mission in Somalia, 'UNSOM Newsletter', March 2022.

[21] The most recent iteration of UNSCR 1846 (2008)'s renewal.

[22] Isabel Debre, 'UAE Welcomes Somali Apology for Seized Cash, Easing Dispute', AP News, 2 February 2022; and George Mikhail, 'Egypt Supports Somalia to Counter Turkish Influence', Al-Monitor, 19 January 2022.

[23] UN, 'Somalia, at Critical Juncture, Must Have International Support in Order to Hold Overdue Elections, Restore Stability, Briefers Tell Security Council', 15 February 2022; and Food and Agriculture Organization of the UN, 'Drought in the Horn of Africa: New Analyses Flag Mounting Risks, Need to Support Rural Families' 11 February 2022.

[24] UN Office for the Coordination of Humanitarian Affairs (UNOCHA), 'Humanitarian Response Plan Somalia', December 2021; and UNOCHA, 'Donors Pledge Close to $1.4 Billion for Horn of Africa Drought Response', 26 April 2022.

[25] USAID, 'United States Providing More Than $200 Million in Additional Humanitarian Assistance for the Horn of Africa', 26 April 2022; and European Civil Protection and Humanitarian Aid Operations, 'Somalia Factsheet', 2022.

[26] Paul D. Williams, 'What Went Wrong with the Somali National Army', War on the Rocks, 20 May 2019; and Timothy Walker and Denys Reva, 'Is Somali Piracy Finally Under Control?', ISS Today, 21 April 2022.

GREAT LAKES REGION

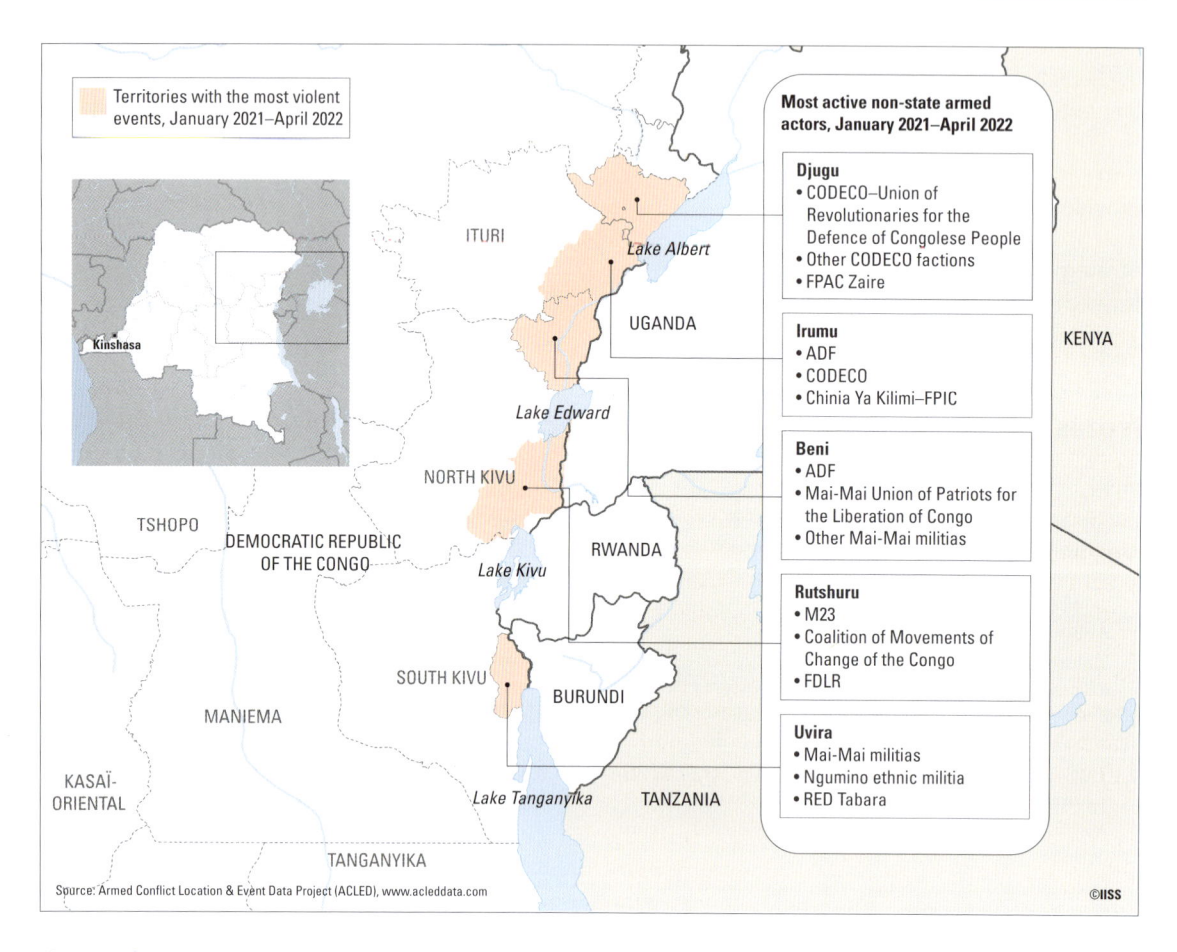

Territories with the most violent events, January 2021–April 2022

Most active non-state armed actors, January 2021–April 2022

Djugu
- CODECO–Union of Revolutionaries for the Defence of Congolese People
- Other CODECO factions
- FPAC Zaire

Irumu
- ADF
- CODECO
- Chinia Ya Kilimi–FPIC

Beni
- ADF
- Mai-Mai Union of Patriots for the Liberation of Congo
- Other Mai-Mai militias

Rutshuru
- M23
- Coalition of Movements of Change of the Congo
- FDLR

Uvira
- Mai-Mai militias
- Ngumino ethnic militia
- RED Tabara

Source: Armed Conflict Location & Event Data Project (ACLED), www.acleddata.com

Overview

The Democratic Republic of the Congo (DRC) has long been the primary theatre of sub-Saharan Africa's armed conflicts, many of which have their roots in the aftermath of the 1994 genocide against the Tutsis in Rwanda. In 1996, the Rwandan Patriotic Front (RPF) invaded Zaire (present-day DRC) to defeat Hutu militants that had fled when the RPF seized power and were aiming to unseat the new government in Kigali. The RPF, under the command of Paul Kagame and with Ugandan support, deposed Mobutu Sese Seko, Zaire's dictatorial leader, and installed Laurent-Désiré Kabila as president. In what became known as the First Congo War (1996–97), an estimated 250,000 combatants and civilians died in a six-month period.[1]

A little over a year after the end of the war, Kabila ordered all Rwandan and Ugandan military forces to leave the DRC, prompting the Second Congo War (1998–2003). Kabila allied with Hutu militants in the east of the country and encouraged them to attack the Banyamulenge and Tutsi populations, who had long suffered from political exclusion and ethnic violence. In turn, the Rwandan government, initially supported by Uganda and to a lesser extent Burundi, formed the Rally for Congolese Democracy (RCD) to fight against Kabila's army. In 1999, tensions escalated between Uganda and Rwanda concerning RCD leadership and strategies. The countries' respective armies clashed in Kisangani, a scenario that would become familiar

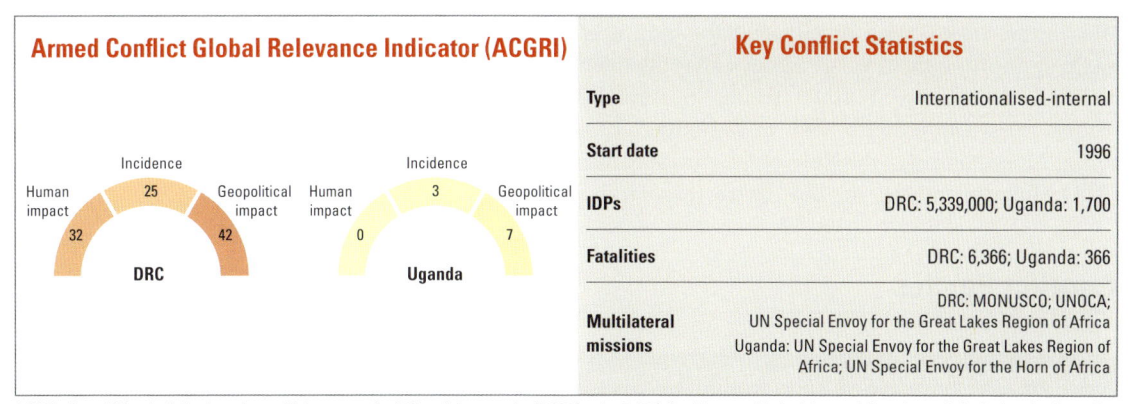

Armed Conflict Global Relevance Indicator (ACGRI)		Key Conflict Statistics	
DRC — Incidence 25; Human impact 32; Geopolitical impact 42	Uganda — Incidence 3; Human impact 0; Geopolitical impact 7	Type	Internationalised-internal
		Start date	1996
		IDPs	DRC: 5,339,000; Uganda: 1,700
		Fatalities	DRC: 6,366; Uganda: 366
		Multilateral missions	DRC: MONUSCO; UNOCA; UN Special Envoy for the Great Lakes Region of Africa. Uganda: UN Special Envoy for the Great Lakes Region of Africa; UN Special Envoy for the Horn of Africa

ACGRI pillars: IISS calculation based on multiple sources for 2021 and January–April 2022 (scale: 0–100). See Notes on Methodology and Data Appendix for further details on Key Conflict Statistics.

in the following years. After the assassination of Kabila in 2001, his son Joseph Kabila took office. Peace talks ensued and in July 2003 the war ended, foreign troops retreated and a transitional government came to power. There is still debate about the Second Congo War's death toll, with estimates ranging from one million to 2.5m.[2]

The DRC's eastern provinces have remained a battleground for rebel groups and regional interests. Hutu militias, such as the Democratic Forces for the Liberation of Rwanda (FDLR), established themselves in the east during the Second Congo War and remain active. In 2012, a Tutsi-led mutiny within the DRC army gave rise to one of the region's most notorious armed groups, the March 23 Movement (M23), which fought against the DRC military and Hutu militias before surrendering in November 2013. A United Nations report alleging that M23 had received significant support from the Rwandan government and military and from the Ugandan government fuelled regional tensions. The region was further destabilised by intensified competition for regional influence between Kigali and Kampala, and between Kigali and Gitega, which saw an uptick in mutual accusations of support for enemy armed groups.

The DRC remained prone to violent conflict in 2021 and early 2022 despite the ongoing 'state of siege' (state of emergency) imposed on 6 May 2021 by President Félix Tshisekedi. During the reporting period there were approximately 130 armed groups operating in the country's eastern provinces. The regional dynamics of the multiple and overlapping conflicts were brought back into the spotlight, with Uganda, Rwanda and Burundi re-emerging as key actors in the hostilities but also as those most capable of leading efforts towards a lasting regional peace.

The state of siege, which saw North Kivu and Ituri provinces placed under martial law, has had little positive effect. Between March 2021 and April 2022, there were 3,182 organised violent events in the DRC (a slight increase in relation to the corresponding period in 2020–21, when there were 2,931), with a death toll of 6,590 (down only slightly, from 6,716).[3] Meanwhile, the Allied Democratic Forces (ADF), formed in Uganda but based in the DRC, strengthened their allegiance to the Islamic State (ISIS) and stepped up their attacks on civilians in both countries, including in Kampala.[4] Although analysts have been cautious in their assessment of the ISIS–ADF relationship – and there is currently no direct chain of command between ISIS leaders and the ADF – the links between the two groups are undeniable. What might have started as an alliance of convenience has given the ADF resources and credibility and greatly facilitated its expansion.

Following ADF attacks in Kampala in November 2021, Tshisekedi authorised the Ugandan army to conduct operations against the ADF on DRC territory alongside the Armed Forces of the DRC (FARDC). As of mid-2022, these have not been successful in stemming the ADF's deadly attacks on civilians but they have gained the attention of Rwanda and Burundi, who perceived Uganda's sudden military involvement as a way to protect its economic interests in the DRC's east. In November 2021, M23 resumed activity in North Kivu, prompting suspicions that Rwanda might be seeking to assert control over the area. The situation deteriorated further in March 2022 as M23 intensified attacks against the FARDC, with the

DRC authorities stating openly that Rwanda was again supporting the rebels, casting a shadow over regional diplomacy. Further south, Burundian troops crossed into South Kivu in December 2021 to fight Resistance for the Rule of Law in Burundi (RED Tabara) rebels in the Uvira highlands.

Meanwhile, the Cooperative for the Development of the Congo (CODECO) and Mai-Mai groups, initially formed as community-based self-defence forces during the Second Congo War, continued to wreak havoc across a huge area stretching from Ituri to Tanganyika provinces.

Conflict Parties

Armed Forces of the Democratic Republic of the Congo (FARDC)

Strength: About 135,000 active personnel, with about 200 generals.

Areas of operation: Countrywide, but deployed mainly to North Kivu and Ituri provinces since the declaration of the state of siege.

Leadership: President Félix Tshisekedi (commander-in-chief), Célestin Mbala (chief of staff), Gilbert Kabanda Kurhenga (defence minister).

Structure: Comprises land forces, the national navy, air forces and a republican guard. Each province has a military governor. The power structure is unclear; many soldiers and factions operate semi-independently and the army is generally considered to be ill-disciplined. The chain of command has been further disrupted by the state of siege.

History: Born out of an international effort to restructure the Congolese army at the end of the Second Congo War through the incorporation of former rebel groups. Since then, it has continuously integrated demobilised combatants from rebel groups and other conflict parties.

Objectives: Formally, to defend the country's borders, protect civilians and neutralise rebel armed groups. In reality, many officers and soldiers form allegiances with rebel groups to pursue their own agendas (whether community defence, wealth accumulation or power grabbing – or often a combination of all three).

Opponents: The other armed groups in the DRC (except those with which the FARDC has an alliance of convenience).

Affiliates/allies: Ugandan People's Defence Force (UPDF), with which it has been carrying out joint operations (*Operation Shujaa*) since November 2021. Also supported by the UN Organization Stabilization Mission in the DRC (MONUSCO).

Resources/capabilities: Despite its size, the Congolese army has been largely unable to exert control over the national territory. It is poorly trained, underfunded and relies mainly on light weapons, although it also has artillery, approximately 400 armoured vehicles, anti-aircraft guns and surface-to-air missiles.

Ugandan People's Defence Force (UPDF)

Strength: 40,000–45,000.

Areas of operation: Countrywide in Uganda (with extensive deployment in Karamoja), DRC (since November 2021), Somalia (as the largest contingent in the African Union Mission in Somalia), other peacekeeping missions.

Leadership: President Yoweri Museveni (commander-in-chief), Wilson Mbadi (chief of defence forces). Muhoozi Kainerugaba, Museveni's son, commands the land forces.

Structure: Comprises land and air forces, as well as the Special Forces Command (SFC), an elite unit responsible for the security of the president.

History: Originated from the National Resistance Army (NRA), a rebel movement led by Museveni that waged a guerrilla war against Milton Obote's regime and took power in 1986 after ousting president Tito Okello.

Objectives: Protect Uganda's interests domestically and abroad, and defend the country's sovereignty and territorial integrity.

Opponents: Domestically, mainly cattle-raiding groups in Karamoja. In Uganda and the DRC, the ADF.

Affiliates/allies: The FARDC, since the beginning of *Operation Shujaa*.

Resources/capabilities: With Uganda long regarded as a Western ally in the region, the UPDF has received support and training from the US and France among others. Possesses mostly light weapons, but also armoured fighting vehicles, artillery and missiles. More effective than the FARDC, as a whole.

Allied Democratic Forces (ADF)

Strength: Estimates range from 1,000–1,500, though those figures may include fighters' family members.[5]

Areas of operation: Ituri and North Kivu provinces; particularly Mambasa, Irumu and Beni territories.

Leadership: Musa Baluku is believed to be the leader of the ADF's biggest faction.

Structure: Split into two factions: a minority faction (no more than 50 fighters) loyal to Jamil Mukulu, the group's original leader (incarcerated in Uganda since 2015), and a much larger faction led by Baluku. The group's leadership and most of its fighters are Ugandan, though they now also include Tanzanians and Burundians, along with smaller numbers of Kenyans, Rwandans, Somalis, South Africans and Mozambicans. It operates from several mobile and semi-mobile camps.

History: Born out of a 1995 merger between Ugandan rebel factions that shared the goal of overthrowing the Museveni government and found a foothold in North Kivu. Following a decade of low-level fighting in the 2000s, it re-emerged in 2013. When Baluku became de facto leader following Mukulu's arrest, he pledged allegiance to ISIS.

Objectives: Current stated objective is to establish an Islamic caliphate in Central Africa. However, analysts believe the ADF's allegiance to ISIS is more opportunistic, as a means of attracting funding and gaining credibility, than ideological. Not currently connected to ISIS leaders by any direct chain of command.

Opponents: The FARDC, UPDF and MONUSCO. Most rebel groups operating in the eastern DRC are also reportedly enemies of the ADF, although it has formed temporary alliances with local armed actors.

Affiliates/allies: The Ugandan diaspora has supported the ADF in the past, especially when it was led by Mukulu. More recently, the group's affiliation with ISIS has revealed some financial support coming from or transiting through South Africa and Kenya. It has also collaborated with Mozambican al-Shabaab insurgents from Cabo Delgado.

Resources/capabilities: Light weapons, along with some more sophisticated weaponry (possibly seized from the FARDC) such as AK-type assault rifles, PKM machine guns, rockets and mortar bombs.[6] It carries out most of its killings using machetes, most often targeting civilians. In 2021 it also stepped up its use of improvised explosive devices and drones.

March 23 Movement (M23)

Strength: Approximately 500.[7]

Areas of operation: North Kivu province, particularly Rutshuru, close to the Ugandan and Rwandan borders.

Leadership: Sultani Makenga is the military commander. An ethnic Tutsi of Congolese nationality, he fought alongside the RPF during the Rwandan civil war and is the target of US sanctions. Bertrand Bisimwa is the group's current president.

Structure: Two factions: an active group led by Makenga, including combatants who found refuge in Uganda in 2013; and a mostly demobilised group under Jean-Marie Runiga Lugerero, including fighters who fled to Rwanda.

History: On 23 March 2009, members of the Rwanda-backed and Tutsi-led National Congress for the Defence of the People signed a peace treaty with the Congolese government and integrated into the FARDC. In 2012, around 300 of them left to create M23, accusing the DRC government of failing to uphold its end of the peace deal. It waged a 19-month rebellion and was eventually defeated by MONUSCO's Force Intervention Brigade in November 2013.

Objectives: Officially, to force the Congolese government to uphold its commitments from the 2013 peace deal and subsequent 2019 road map that followed the 2012–13 M23 rebellion and surrender – particularly the reintegration of ex-combatants into civilian life.

Opponents: FARDC, MONUSCO, FDLR and most other armed groups operating in the eastern DRC, who consider M23 to be 'invaders'.

Affiliates/allies: The group has previously enjoyed Rwandan and Ugandan support, although it is unclear whether it still does. Congolese military authorities accused Rwanda of backing the group in March 2022 but later backtracked.

Resources/capabilities: Unclear. Mostly small arms.

Resistance for the Rule of Law in Burundi (RED Tabara)

Strength: Although probably the strongest of all Burundian rebel groups, it is believed to have no more than 1,000 combatants.

Areas of operation: South Kivu – particularly Uvira and Fizi territories, close to the Burundian border – although sometimes retreats into the highlands. Occasionally also active within Burundi.

Leadership: The alleged leader of the group is Alexis Sinduhije, who lives in exile in Belgium and is the president of opposition party Movement for Solidarity and Development. Its actual military command is unknown.

Structure: Unclear, but designated ranks suggest the group is mimicking a conventional military structure.

History: Founded in 2011 in opposition to the Burundian government led by the National Council for the Defence of Democracy–Forces for the Defence of Democracy (CNDD–FDD). Particularly active since Burundi's 2015 political crisis.[8]

Objectives: The group has called on the CNDD–FDD to organise elections that are 'credible by international standards', release political prisoners and improve the country's political and security environment. It also demands inclusive negotiations with President Ndayishimiye in a neutral third country.[9]

Resistance for the Rule of Law in Burundi (RED Tabara)

Opponents: The FDNB and Imbonerakure, along with their allies in South Kivu (mainly the Twirwaneho and Ngumino militias).

Affiliates/allies: Although their objectives differ, RED Tabara has an alliance of convenience with other Burundian rebel groups such as the National Forces of Liberation (FNL) and the National Council for Renewal and Democracy. It also has local allies in South Kivu, most notably the Mai-Mai Ilunga.

Resources/capabilities: Unclear, but mostly small arms. The group is believed to receive some funding from the Burundian diaspora, as well as support from within Burundi. Burundian authorities have accused Rwanda of supporting the group.

Cooperative for the Development of the Congo (CODECO)

Strength: 2,000–2,500.[10]

Areas of operation: Ituri province in the DRC – mainly Djugu Territory and, to a lesser extent, Mahagi and Irumu territories.

Leadership: Former leader Justin Ngudjolo was assassinated by the FARDC in March 2020; new leadership is unclear.

Structure: Seven different factions (Congo Liberation Army (ALC), Army of Revolutionaries for the Defence of Congolese People (ARDPC), Bon Temple, Force for the Defence against the Balkanisation of Congo (FBDC), Gutsi, Islamic, URDPC), each with its own interests and area of operation.

History: Rooted in the Lendu ethnolinguistic group, which is traditionally agriculturalist and opposed to the pastoralist Hema people. Created as an agricultural cooperative in the 1970s, it became an armed group in 2017, under Ngudjolo.

Objectives: Mainly targets the Hema population but does not have any substantial ideological motivation. Driven by economic considerations, it seeks to exploit the gold mines and other natural resources of mineral-rich Ituri.

Opponents: The FARDC and Hema self-defence groups, especially the FPAC Zaire (Ituri Self-Defense Popular Front). Routinely targets civilians – especially internally displaced persons, on whom they often inflict sexual violence. CODECO factions sometimes also clash with one another.

Affiliates/allies: Fighters often associate with the Patriotic and Integrationist Force of Congo (FPIC), a group composed mainly of ethnic Biras who want to reclaim land occupied by the Hema in Irumu Territory.

Resources/capabilities: Mostly bladed weapons, although in recent years CODECO has increased its use of small arms and light weapons. Its factions are believed to get most of their resources from the pillage and exploitation of gold mines and trading centres, as well as forced taxation.

Mai-Mai (Mayi-Mayi) groups

Strength: Over 60 different Mai-Mai groups have been active in the past year. Some have formed large coalitions of several hundred fighters, but most comprise fewer than 200.

Areas of operation: Most of North and South Kivu, as well as parts of Ituri, Maniema, Haut-Katanga and Tanganyika provinces.

Leadership: Mai-Mai groups operate independently, each having its own leadership structure. Some, such as the Raia Mutomboki, are divided into subgroups that each respond to a particular commander.

Structure: Mai-Mai militias are largely informal and non-hierarchical, though some have notorious commanders.

History: Mai-Mai groups mostly formed as self-defence militias. A majority have anti-Tutsi and anti-Banyamulenge sentiments and see themselves as indigenous defenders against Rwandan foreigners.

Objectives: Ostensibly, community self-defence. In reality, most Mai-Mai militias fight for territorial control and self-enrichment, which they pursue through illegal taxation and looting.

Opponents: Mostly Banyamulenge ethnic militias, such as the Ngumino and Twirwaneho. Mai-Mai groups also regularly clash with the FARDC and with each other, and target civilians.

Affiliates/allies: Mai-Mai groups often form alliances of convenience with each other.

Resources/capabilities: Armed almost exclusively with machetes and other bladed weapons. Some groups, such as the Mai-Mai Yakutumba, control gold mining in their areas.

Burundi National Defence Force (FDNB)

Strength: 30,050.

Areas of operation: Countrywide, with an emphasis on the Kibira forest, where Rwandan armed groups are active, and South Kivu, although the Burundian army denies its operations in the DRC.

Leadership: President Evariste Ndayishimiye (commander-in-chief), Alain Mutabazi (defence minister), Prime Niyongabo (general chief of staff).

Structure: Comprises land and air forces.

History: Origins lie in the colonial-era national guard. In 1972 the Tutsi-led army carried out a series of massacres of the country's Hutus. Some of the army's units supported the failed coup attempt in 2015.

Objectives: Defend Burundi's territorial integrity.

Burundi National Defence Force (FDNB)

Opponents: Domestically, Rwandan rebel groups – mainly the National Liberation Front (FLN) operating in the Kibira forest. In the DRC, Burundian rebel groups – mainly RED Tabara and the FNL – and their local Congolese allies.

Affiliates/allies: In Burundi, the CNDD-FDD ruling party's youth militia, the Imbonerakure. In South Kivu, the FDNB does not cooperate with the FARDC but has forged alliances with local groups such as the Mai-Mai Kijangala, Mai-Mai Kashumba and Gumino to fight against RED Tabara.

Resources/capabilities: Mostly light weapons, along with a small amount of Soviet-era artillery and tanks. Plagued by a lack of discipline: Burundian peacekeepers deployed in UN missions have been accused of human-rights violations.

Rwanda Defence Force (RDF)

Strength: 33,000.

Areas of operation: Deployed in Mozambique's Cabo Delgado and in the Central African Republic (CAR) at the request of Maputo and Bangui. It is also part of UN peacekeeping missions, mainly in South Sudan (UNMIS) and the CAR (MINUSCA). According to accusations by the FARDC, the RDF has also been deployed in North Kivu since June 2022.

Leadership: President Paul Kagame (commander-in-chief), Maj.-Gen. Albert Murasira (minister of defence), Gen. Jean Bosco Kazura (chief of defence staff).

Structure: Includes land forces, a unit of marines and an air force.

History: The RDF's predecessor, the Rwandan Patriotic Army, was made up of Rwandan Tutsis exiled in Uganda who fought alongside the NRA during the Ugandan civil war and went on to overthrow the Hutu regime in Rwanda in 1994.

Objectives: Defend Rwanda's territorial integrity and national sovereignty.

Opponents: Hutu rebel groups operating from Burundi and the DRC, such as the FLN and FDLR, as well as their allies (such as the Nyatura militia in the DRC).

Affiliates/allies: The RDF allegedly provides support to the M23, although MONUSCO and international observers have stated that they do not have evidence to support those allegations.

Resources/capabilities: Although small, the RDF is well trained and effective. It is also well equipped, with armoured fighting vehicles, artillery, missiles, transport aircraft and attack helicopters. As such, it is regarded as one of the best militaries in Africa.

UN Organization Stabilization Mission in the DRC (MONUSCO)

Strength: 14,000 military personnel, as of November 2021. This is the maximum authorised strength in accordance with UN Security Council Resolution 2556 (2020). The resolution also states that the mission will gradually withdraw from the DRC, although a timeline has yet to be determined.

Areas of operation: Although headquartered in Kinshasa, MONUSCO troops are currently operating in the provinces of South Kivu, North Kivu and Ituri. They withdrew from Tanganyika province in June 2022, citing an improved security situation.

Leadership: Bintou Keita is the head of MONUSCO and the Special Representative of the UN Secretary-General in the DRC; Lt-Gen. Affonso Da Costa is MONUSCO's Force Commander.

Structure: In addition to its military personnel, MONUSCO comprises police, military observers and a Force Intervention Brigade (FIB). Unlike the rest of the MONUSCO troops, the FIB is authorised to act offensively against armed actors. MONUSCO's largest military contributors are Pakistan, India and Bangladesh.

History: In 2010, MONUSCO replaced the UN Organization Mission in DRC (MONUC), established in 1999 to supervise the implementation of the Lusaka Ceasefire Agreement.

Objectives: Protect civilians, and support efforts towards stabilisation, the strengthening of public institutions and the reform of governance and security.

Opponents: Non-state armed groups.

Affiliates/allies: Periodically conducts joint operations with the FARDC, but relations are often tense.

Resources/capabilities: With a budget in excess of US$1 billion for 2021–22, MONUSCO is better funded than any of the other conflict parties in the region.[11]

Other conflict parties

The above list contains only the most notorious of the estimated 130 armed groups active in the DRC. The Burundian, Rwandan and Ugandan actors in the conflict almost all operate from the DRC, with the notable exception of ethnic militias in Uganda, among which the Karamojong pastoralists are the most active.

Conflict Drivers

Security

Geographic challenges:
The region's porous borders and the FARDC's inability to respond adequately to the threats it faces are key security drivers of the conflict. The Ruwenzori, Virunga and Uvira mountain ranges are forested and largely inaccessible terrain; they also serve as the borders between the DRC on one side and Uganda, Rwanda and Burundi on the other. Rebel groups have been able to hide and circulate in these areas, evading the countries' respective armies. This issue is particularly salient in the case of M23, which is routinely accused of maintaining bases in Rwanda and Uganda while committing attacks in the DRC.

Ineffective military:
Meanwhile, the FARDC is a poorly trained, disunited and ineffective army, in which many battalions maintain links with rebels. It routinely targets civilians and commits human-rights abuses. Demobilisation programmes, which have integrated former rebels into the army, have failed to reduce the level of violence. Instead, they have often enabled those combatants to access more resources or be rewarded with positions within the military. MONUSCO also suffers from unwilling contingents and bureaucratic processes that limit its efficacy.

Political

Ethnic divisions:
Although the 1994 genocide against the Tutsis in Rwanda was the tipping point for the instability that has since prevailed in the Great Lakes region, its origins lie to a large extent in the region's colonial history, which saw indigenous populations registered according to their ethnicity and set against each other in power struggles.

Domestic politics:
In the DRC, the 2018 election of Félix Tshisekedi as president marked the end of the Kabila era. While Tshisekedi presented stabilisation in the east as one of his priorities, allegations of widespread fraud during the elections weakened his legitimacy, and during his first two years in office he was more concerned with countering Kabila's influence in Kinshasa than with conflict resolution. Furthermore, the distance between Kinshasa and the eastern provinces – about 1,500 kilometres – and the country's deep-rooted institutional weaknesses have rendered the east largely ungovernable. Pervasive links between armed groups and politicians remain, with both local chiefs and provincial elites exploiting conflict dynamics to their own advantage.

Regional politics:
Despite marginal improvements in relations, distrust between Gitega, Kampala, Kigali and Kinshasa still prevails and remains a key driver of regional insecurity. Burundi, Rwanda and Uganda are all accused of seeking to protect their interests in the eastern DRC, backing their favoured rebel groups while opposing others. The problematic relationships between the countries' leaders, marked by personal feuds and long-running grievances, undermine regional diplomacy.

Economic

Competition for natural resources:
Competition over the DRC's valuable natural resources has long been a conflict driver in the region, enticing armed groups and foreign powers to exert control over mineral-rich territories. Both Uganda and Rwanda are export hubs for legally and illegally traded Congolese minerals. The DRC's recent entry into the East African Community (EAC) represents a vast untapped market for its neighbours, who are scrambling to build infrastructure that will facilitate trade. The protection of a road-building project linking Uganda to Beni, Butembo and Goma is understood to be a prime motive for Kampala's deployment of troops in the DRC, fuelling Rwandan discontent. High rates of unemployment also drive the recruitment of young people by armed groups, which often represent their best economic opportunity.

Key Events in 2021–22

POLITICAL EVENTS

6 May 2021
The DRC starts implementing a state of siege, placing Ituri and North Kivu provinces under martial law.

12 May
In Uganda, President Museveni is sworn in for his sixth term.

13 July
Gitega and Kinshasa announce bilateral cooperation against armed groups in the eastern DRC.

30 July
Kigali hands over to Gitega 19 RED Tabara rebels captured in late 2020.

20 September
Regional army chiefs and intelligence directors meet in Kigali to discuss regional security.

19 October
The Burundian authorities hand over 11 FLN rebels to Rwanda.

22 January 2022
In an unforeseen rapprochement between Uganda and Rwanda, Gen. Muhoozi Kainerugaba, Museveni's son, visits Kigali and meets with President Kagame.

8 February
Kagame threatens military intervention in the DRC against armed groups posing a threat to Rwanda.

9 February
The International Court of Justice rules that Uganda must pay the DRC US$325m in reparations for its role in the first and second Congo wars.

MILITARY/VIOLENT EVENTS

12 April 2021
Mai-Mai Raia Mutomboki militants kill at least 73 civilians in South Kivu.

5–29 July
ADF rebels kill at least 76 civilians in Ituri and North Kivu.

19 September
Grenade explosions in Bujumbura, Burundi, kill five people and wound dozens.

7 October
Islamic State Central Africa Province claims its first attack in Uganda.

8 November
DRC army chief Célestin Mbala accuses M23 of attacks in Rutshuru Territory, North Kivu province, the first such allegations since 2017.

16 November
Suicide bombings in Kampala kill three people and wound dozens; ISIS claims responsibility.

30 November
The FARDC and UPDF launch joint operations in the DRC, targeting the ADF.

20 December
RED Tabara claims responsibility for an attack at the DRC–Burundi border, prompting a massive deployment of Burundian troops into South Kivu.

1 February 2022
CODECO rebels kill at least 60 ethnic Hema in a camp for internally displaced persons in Ituri.

7 March
In a step towards normalisation, the Rwanda–Uganda border fully reopens after three years.

21 April
Following the DRC's accession to the EAC on 8 April, EAC heads of government agree to deploy a joint military force to address regional insecurity.

25 April
Nairobi hosts the first round of consultations between armed groups operating in the DRC and the Tshisekedi government.

29 March
A MONUSCO helicopter is shot down; the FARDC accuses M23 and alleges Rwandan support for the militia.

3 April
ADF elements kill 39 civilians and clash with the FARDC in North Kivu.

19 April
The FARDC and MONUSCO take control of key ADF bases around Mount Hoyo, Ituri, after two days of clashes.

Responses to the Conflict

Security

President Tshisekedi declared a state of siege in North Kivu and Ituri provinces in May 2021. Presented as an exceptional and temporary measure that would yield rapid and effective results, it failed to reduce violence during the reporting period. Moreover, human-rights groups have reported that the measure enabled the army and police to commit abuses against civilians with near-total impunity.[12] In July 2021, Tshisekedi launched the fourth national disarmament, demobilisation, community reintegration and stabilisation program (P-DDRCS), but as of mid-2022 it remained largely non-existent on the ground.

Figure 1: Number of fatalities due to political violence in Ituri and North Kivu, May 2020–April 2022

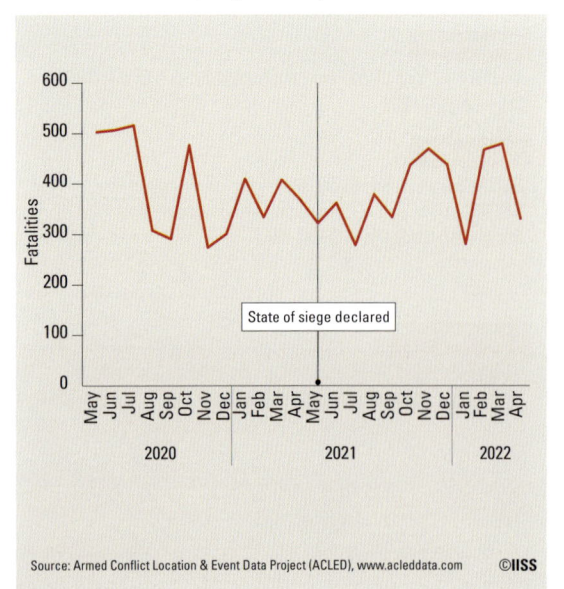

Source: Armed Conflict Location & Event Data Project (ACLED), www.acleddata.com ©IISS

Perhaps the most notable security development was the unexpected deployment of Ugandan troops in the eastern DRC in November 2021, triggered by the October and November ADF attacks (for which ISIS claimed responsibility) in Uganda.[13] The operations targeted key ADF bases and strongholds, with the UPDF claiming to have destroyed the rebels' main camps. However, they did not succeed in curbing the ADF's attacks on civilians; their main impact has been to push the group further west and north. Within Uganda, the security forces targeted the country's Muslim communities (14% of the population), carrying out round-ups, seen by many as indiscriminate, that could further drive ADF recruitment of Ugandan Muslims.

Economic/development

The Great Lakes region suffers from a lack of integrated approaches to development. While the DRC's eastern provinces are connected much more closely to the Great Lakes and the Indian Ocean than to Kinshasa and the western half of the country, international institutions have not been successful in creating cross-border initiatives to address the region's common development challenges. Programmes such as the UN Great Lakes Regional Strategic Framework, renewed in 2021, yielded little in the way of concrete outcomes during the reporting period. Meanwhile, the World Bank's Great Lakes Initiative, launched in 2013 with a budget of more than US$1bn, has not reduced conflict or improved security. The European Union is attempting to develop a Great Lakes strategy but this was yet to be achieved as of mid-2022.

Diplomacy

There were some promising diplomatic developments in 2021 and early 2022. After three years of tensions fuelled by accusations of espionage and support for enemy armed groups, Museveni and Kagame unexpectedly normalised relations between Uganda and Rwanda in January 2022, with their shared border reopening in March. Improved relations could lead to greater military cooperation and intelligence sharing, and cool the two countries' rivalry in the eastern DRC.

Relations between Burundi and Rwanda also improved after President Evariste Ndayishimiye took office in June 2020. The relationship had started to deteriorate in 2013 as Rwanda accused its neighbour of supporting the FDLR. It broke down completely when Kigali granted refugee status to most of the Burundian military and political actors suspected of plotting the 2015 coup attempt. Dialogue resumed in July 2021, though full normalisation remains conditional upon Kigali's handover of the alleged coup plotters.

Tshisekedi's welcoming of Burundian and Ugandan troops into the eastern DRC soured his relationship with Kagame, which deteriorated further in December 2021 when the RDF accused the FARDC of deliberately striking Rwandan territory – accusations subsequently repeated in March, May and June 2022.

In April 2022, as regional leaders met in Nairobi to sign the DRC's accession to the EAC, Kenyan President Uhuru Kenyatta seized the opportunity to organise a mini-summit addressing regional security. The principal outcomes were that Nairobi would host peace consultations between the DRC government and some of the rebel armed groups active in the east of the country, and that the EAC countries would launch a joint military force targeting the rebel groups. Although at first sight a promising development, the exclusion of M23 from the consultations severely limits the initiative's potential, while a joint force might fuel instability.

Humanitarian aid

The DRC has the largest conflict-induced internally displaced population in Africa, and the third highest in the world: approximately 5.6m people in total.[14] In 2021, food insecurity in the country reached its highest level ever recorded, with 27m people going hungry.[15] The UN High Commissioner for Refugees also noted an increase in human-rights abuses in 2021 in Tanganyika, North Kivu, South Kivu and Ituri provinces, with gender-based violence remaining a major concern. Although the eruption of the Nyiragongo volcano in May 2021 attracted international attention, only 44% of the US$2bn in aid required to meet the humanitarian needs of the DRC was provided last year.

Conflict Outlook

Political scenarios

The extension of the state of siege is voted on every two weeks in the DRC parliament. It has been approved by an ever-decreasing margin, without the support of parliamentarians from Ituri and North Kivu who are opposed to the measure. Meanwhile, the laborious launch of the P-DDRCS shows little promise. However, it is in Tshisekedi's best interest to pursue conflict resolution, as he is now concerned with securing a second term in the presidential elections due to be held in 2023 and needs to address his unpopularity in the eastern provinces. The upcoming election cycle will itself be a challenge for the country's stability, as politicians seek to leverage their links to armed groups to advance their agenda, fuelling conflict and further entrenching disunion.

In Uganda, Museveni's age is a cause for concern: Muhoozi has made it clear that when his father is no longer able to govern, he intends to take over. Much less popular than his father, his expected power grab will be met with strong opposition within Uganda, potentially destabilising not only the country but also the entire region. In Burundi there is also much potential for conflict: Ndayishimiye is increasingly isolated within his party, where hardliners such as Prime Minister Alain-Guillaume Bunyoni oppose his moderate stances, especially his diplomatic rapprochement with the country's neighbours. The president is reportedly worried about his personal safety amid frequent rumours about an upcoming coup.

At the regional level, EAC military chiefs of staff met in Goma in June 2022 to put together the regional force agreed upon in Nairobi. It remains to be seen whether this initiative will be implemented, especially given the current Rwanda–DRC stand-off over renewed M23 activity.

Escalation potential and conflict-related risks

The return of the M23 militia in North Kivu since November 2021 threatens the fragile diplomatic rapprochement between the Great Lakes neighbours. Indeed, suspicions of Rwandan support for the group plague the Nairobi consultations, and Kagame has made it clear the RDF is ready to intervene in the DRC, with or without authorisation, if he feels Rwanda is threatened. Furthermore, from May 2022, M23 and FARDC were accusing each other of acts of aggression on an almost daily basis, underscoring that both the rebels and the army are ready to escalate. Further north, the lack of transparency regarding Ugandan operations against the ADF, particularly the apparent lack of an exit plan, raises fears that the UPDF will become a semi-occupying foreign army, staying in the DRC to protect its economic interests and to thwart Rwandan influence.

Prospects for peace

It seems that regional leaders remain committed to diplomacy, offering a sliver of hope. At a bilateral level, President João Lourenço of Angola is mediating between the Congolese and Rwandan presidents in his capacity as president of the International Conference on the Great Lakes Region. In the multilateral arena, the first round of the Nairobi peace talks, held under the aegis of President Kenyatta, ended on 27 April 2022. They have already yielded promising results. The leaders of the participating armed groups have expressed willingness to disarm, and consultations between them and community representatives are under way in Bukavu, Goma and Bunia, facilitated by MONUSCO. Leaders of armed groups operating in Ituri, North Kivu, South Kivu, Tanganyika and Maniema provinces have agreed to participate in the second round of talks in Nairobi, which were set to be held in Nairobi in June 2022.

However, the peace consultations face some hurdles. The Congolese authorities have decided to evict M23 from the talks in light of the resumption of the militia's attacks in North Kivu. Insofar as the return of M23 is one of the biggest threats to the stability of the region, this decision significantly reduces the productive potential of the consultations. It also appears that the ADF, the group responsible for the greatest number of deaths in the region, will not be participating. Reckoning with these limitations and managing expectations will be vital if the Nairobi process is to succeed. Furthermore, the initiative has so far been driven by Kenyatta, who will be replaced by a successor as Kenyan president in September 2022.

Strategic implications and global influences

The return of M23 to eastern DRC has brought back painful memories for the region's civilians and cast a shadow over the previously encouraging rapprochement between the region's leaders. With Rwanda put in a defensive position, the prospects for peace seem to be dwindling. However, regional diplomacy is imperative not solely to defeat M23 but also to achieve long-lasting stability in the Great Lakes. While M23 is currently the major irritant between the neighbours, the ADF remains the greatest threat to civilians. A purely military approach will not be sufficient to meaningfully address the threat the ADF represents. Regardless of the actual motives of its fighters, the group has now evolved to become a transnational jihadist insurgency, with networks extending from South Africa to Somalia via Mozambique, Kenya and the Great Lakes.

Notes

1. Gérard Prunier, *Africa's World War: Congo, the Rwandan Genocide, and the Making of a Continental Catastrophe* (Oxford: Oxford University Press, 2008).
2. International Rescue Committee, 'Mortality in the Democratic Republic of Congo: An Ongoing Crisis', 1 May 2007.
3. Armed Conflict Location & Event Data Project (ACLED), www.acleddata.com.
4. On the ADF's links with ISIS, see Brenda Mugeci Githing'u and Tore Refslund Hamming, '"The Arc of Jihad": The Ecosystem of Militancy in East, Central and Southern Africa', International Centre for the Study of Radicalisation, 2021; Congo Research Group, 'Inside the ADF Rebellion', November 2018; Tara Candland et al., 'The Islamic State in Congo', Program on Extremism, March 2021; and International Crisis Group, 'The Kampala Attacks and Their Regional Implications', 19 November 2021.
5. International Crisis Group, 'A Perilous Free-for-all in the Eastern DR Congo?', *Hold Your Fire!*, 13 May 2022.
6. United Nations Security Council, 'Final Report of the Group of Experts on the Democratic Republic of Congo', 10 June 2021.
7. International Crisis Group, 'A Perilous Free-for-all in the Eastern DR Congo?'.
8. International Crisis Group, 'Averting Proxy Wars in the Eastern DR Congo and Great Lakes', 23 January 2020.
9. RED Tabara (@Red_Tabara), tweet, 23 February 2022, twitter.com/Red_Tabara/status/1496390218051731462.
10. Adolphe Agenonga Chober and Georges Berghezan, 'La CODECO, au cœur de l'insécurité en Ituri' [CODECO, At the Heart of Insecurity in Ituri], Group for Research and Information on Peace and Security, 2 June 2021.
11. UN Peacekeeping, 'MONUSCO Fact Sheet'.
12. Amnesty International, 'DRC: Justice and Freedoms Under Siege in North-Kivu and Ituri', 10 May 2022.
13. 'We're Planning to Attack ADF Terrorists in DR Congo — Museveni', *Daily Monitor*, 28 August 2021.
14. UN High Commissioner for Refugees, 'DR Congo Factsheet - January–March 2022', 23 May 2022.
15. Norwegian Refugee Council, 'The World's Most Neglected Displacement Crises in 2021', 1 June 2022.

NIGERIA

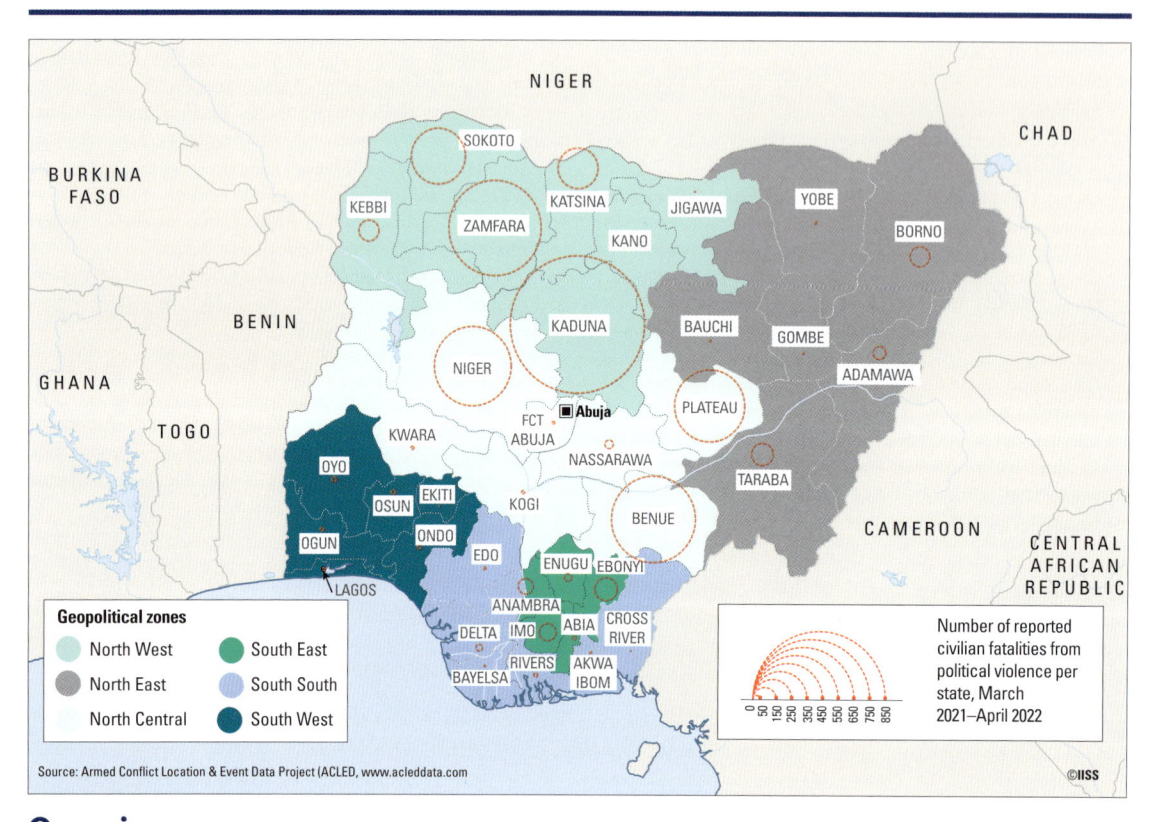

Overview

Nigeria faces a series of distinct yet overlapping security crises that affect almost all of its states. Kidnappings, revenge killings, separatist campaigns and conflicts over livelihood sources are no longer limited to the North East, where a violent Islamist insurgency has been raging for over a decade (see Lake Chad Basin chapter). The Nigerian authorities are increasingly concerned that insurgent and bandit groups could agree tactical alliances to mount an ever-greater challenge to the federal government.

Intermittent violence between Fulani pastoralists from the Sahel region and predominantly Hausa farmers has occurred in the North West and Middle Belt regions since the 1980s. These disputes have escalated for decades due to rising inequalities and corruption; competition over land, water and grazing routes (exacerbated by climate change); the proliferation of small arms; and divisive national and local politics. The disputes have widened social divisions, leading to mobilisation along religious or ethnic lines. The proliferation of vigilante groups recruited to protect farmers has led to the militarisation of local communities.[1] Additionally, the introduction of state laws banning open grazing has bred further tensions between pastoralists and the authorities.

Increasing banditry is a second major source of insecurity. Criminal gangs, commonly referred to as 'bandits', engage in kidnappings, cattle rustling and looting. Many bandits, especially in the North West and Middle Belt regions, are ethnic Fulanis motivated by resentment towards Hausa farmers and vigilante groups. Nigeria's lucrative kidnapping industry has also attracted the interest of violent jihadist organisations, who have attempted to build bridges with bandits in the North West. Groups such as Ansaru (an al-Qaeda-linked group that broke away from Boko Haram), Islamic State in West Africa Province (ISWAP) and Jama'atu Ahlis Sunna Lidda'awati wal-Jihad (JAS) have moved to recruit

Armed Conflict Global Relevance Indicator (ACGRI)

Nigeria
- Incidence: 27
- Human impact: 26
- Geopolitical impact: 12

Key Conflict Statistics

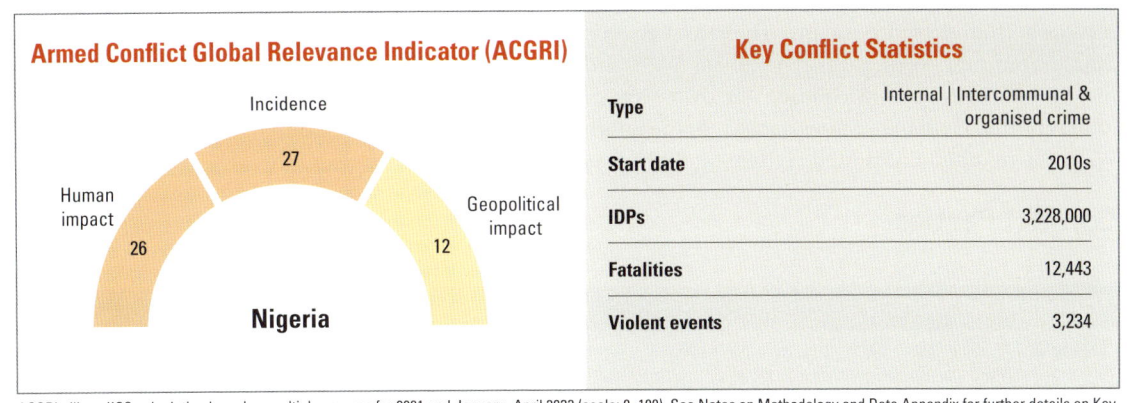

Type	Internal | Intercommunal & organised crime
Start date	2010s
IDPs	3,228,000
Fatalities	12,443
Violent events	3,234

ACGRI pillars: IISS calculation based on multiple sources for 2021 and January–April 2022 (scale: 0–100). See Notes on Methodology and Data Appendix for further details on Key Conflict Statistics.

bandits, expanding their presence beyond their traditional North East strongholds.

A third source of instability lies in the South East, where the separatist Indigenous People of Biafra (IPOB) seeks to form an independent nation for the Igbo ethnic group. In 1967, a civil war broke out when regional leaders declared the independence of Biafra. It lasted nearly three years and left a legacy of Igbo nationalism that has resurfaced in recent years. British-Nigerian activist Nnamdi Kanu established IPOB in 2012 to revive the Biafran independence movement. IPOB's militant wing, the Eastern Security Network (ESN), was formed in 2020 to protect ethnic Igbos from attacks by Fulani pastoralists. Since its inception, the group has engaged in several raids against police stations, checkpoints and other symbols of the federal government. Other armed groups operate in the south, including the Biafran National Guard (BNG), whose members also aspire to achieve secession for the South East, and the Niger Delta People's Volunteer Force, whose members come largely from the Ijaw ethnic group, which has been demanding a greater share of the region's oil wealth. These groups have intermittently cooperated with IPOB against the federal government.

During the reporting period, bandits have abducted and in some cases killed thousands of Nigerians, including 780 schoolchildren kidnapped for ransom.[2] Frequent assaults on transport links have severely impacted the movement of people and goods, potentially disrupting internal food distribution and the country's exports. Criminal gangs have targeted transport infrastructure, particularly in Kaduna State, a major commercial hub and gateway to Nigeria's north. In March 2022, bandits raided Kaduna International Airport and a train carrying 970 passengers on the Abuja–Kaduna railway, abducting 168 passengers and killing eight. The federal government formally designated the country's bandits as terrorists in January 2022.

Violence between farmers and pastoralists continued in Nigeria's Middle Belt during the reporting period. In May 2021, 17 state governors largely from the south of the country banned open grazing in their states, a measure seen as having the potential to escalate existing disputes.[3] The federal government took a different approach, promoting the implementation of the ten-year National Livestock Transformation Plan (NLTP), which aims to promote sustainable development in agropastoral communities by turning grazing reserves into ranches. However, flaws in its implementation, barriers to land use and hostility among semi-nomadic pastoralists towards the prospect of settling into ranches have prevented the NLTP from addressing the drivers of the conflict.

In the South East, the conflict between the government and separatists also escalated in 2021, with multiple attacks on government infrastructure. The security forces launched counter-terrorism operations against the ESN in response. In August 2021, Interpol arrested IPOB leader Nnamdi Kanu in Nairobi, handing him to the Nigerian authorities for trial. Human-rights groups accused the security forces of several abuses, including excessive use of force, torture and extrajudicial killings, in Abia, Anambra, Ebonyi and Imo states – the hotbed of the separatist insurgency.

Overall, the death toll from Nigeria's multiple security crises has been increasing. Nationwide, the Armed Conflict Location & Event Data Project (ACLED) estimated that there were 4,809 fatalities resulting from violence against civilians between March 2021 and April 2022.[4] The North West and the Middle Belt states accounted for over 75% of total reported civilian fatalities in 2021. In the South West, the number of reported civilian fatalities was three times higher than in the previous year. These figures, which are likely to be significant underestimates due to the remote nature of the sites of violence and the limited media reporting, are a testament to the increasing threat.

Conflict Parties

Nigerian armed forces

Strength: 143,000 military personnel, including 100,000 army personnel. Paramilitary forces number approximately 80,000 troops.

Areas of operation: Across Nigeria.

Leadership: President Muhammadu Buhari (commander-in-chief of the armed forces), Gen. Leo Irabor (chief of defence staff).

Structure: The Nigerian armed forces comprise the army, the air force and the navy. The army is organised into headquarters, divisions, brigades, battalions, companies, platoons and sections.

History: Nigeria has the largest army in West Africa. In recent years, reforms have improved its military, counter-terrorism and counter-insurgency capacities.

Objectives: Establish and maintain security across Nigeria.

Opponents: Boko Haram; armed pastoral militias; armed bandits; the ESN.

Affiliates/allies: Vigilante groups; the Multinational Joint Task Force; the Civilian Joint Task Force; Cameroon, Chad and Niger; France, the United Kingdom and the United States.

Resources/capabilities: Heavy and light weaponry in the land, air, sea and cyber spheres. Resources and capabilities (including those of the air force and the Cyber Warfare Command) have significantly improved in recent years, though poor equipment and training in the army remain areas of concern.

Fulani pastoralist militias

Strength: Not known.

Areas of operation: The states in the North West, Middle Belt and South.

Leadership: No formal leadership.

Structure: Fulani groups include both semi-nomadic pastoralists and settled communities in urban and rural areas. Pastoralist communities are highly decentralised, being divided into clans (*lenyi*) and sub-clans. Individuals have significant autonomy over whether to fight or retaliate for perceived wrongs, decisions that may be made without community leaders knowing. For some conflicts, mobilisation occurs along ethnic and kinship lines.

History: Pastoralist–farmer conflicts have a long history in Nigeria. Due to several factors, they have become deadlier in recent years, with the Fulani pastoralist militias acquiring more sophisticated weaponry and cooperating with armed bandits across Nigeria.

Objectives: Protect their traditional 'cattle culture' from banditry and cattle rustling.

Opponents: Sedentary-farmer militias, vigilante groups and the Nigerian armed forces; the ESN in the South East.

Affiliates/allies: Armed bandits.

Resources/capabilities: AK-47s, G3s, Mark-4 rifles, locally made single-barrel shotguns (Dane guns), 'Lebanons' (double-barrel shotguns) and a variety of other locally made guns.

Armed bandits

Strength: Difficult to estimate. There are allegedly more than 120 gangs in the North West.[5] Estimates for the number of bandits range from 10,000–30,000.[6]

Areas of operation: The North West. Most prevalent in Kaduna, Katsina, Niger and Zamfara states.[7]

Leadership: No generally recognised leader.

Structure: No formal structure. The gangs are formed on a local basis.

History: Gangs of cattle rustlers, thieves and other criminals have been active for decades on Nigeria's highways and in both urban and rural areas. Some gangs emerged as ethnic militias or vigilante groups before turning to more lucrative criminal activities.

Objectives: Extract financial resources from illegal activities.

Opponents: Hausa sedentary farmers, vigilante groups, Nigerian armed forces.

Affiliates/allies: Fulani pastoralist militias operating in Nigeria as well as in Niger and Mali.

Resources/capabilities: With the proceeds from cattle rustling, looting and kidnapping, bandits have been able to purchase more sophisticated weaponry, including small arms and light weapons. They often use motorcycles to carry out their attacks.

Farmers, ethnic militias and vigilante groups

Strength: Not known.

Areas of operation: Middle Belt, South West and South East.

Leadership: Within several communities in the conflict areas, active mobilisations are mainly driven by traditional community leaders.

Structure: Farmers' militias mobilise on an ethnic basis, but unlike Fulani combatants, in some cases they also form alliances across ethnic lines, leveraging a Christian religious identity. Militias are recruited predominantly from the Adara, Berom, Tarok, Tiv and other local ethnic groups.

History: Pastoralist–farmer conflicts have a long history in Nigeria. They have become deadlier in recent years, with the farmers often establishing ethnic-based militias and vigilante groups to protect their communities against armed pastoralists.

Objectives: Protect against raids by Fulani pastoralists and bandits.

Opponents: Fulani pastoralists and armed bandits.

Affiliates/allies: Nigerian armed forces; ESN in the South East.

Resources/capabilities: Reliant on locally made weapons.

Eastern Security Network (ESN)

Strength: 50,000 militants, according to estimates by the Nigerian armed forces.[8]

Areas of operation: South East of Nigeria (particularly Imo State).

Leadership: Nnamdi Kanu, founder and leader of the IPOB.

Structure: The ESN is the armed wing of the separatist IPOB.

History: The IPOB established the ESN in December 2020 to protect Igbo communities from armed bandits and Fulani pastoralists. A security crisis escalated in January 2021 after the Nigerian armed forces raided the town of Orlu in Imo State in search of ESN militants.

Objectives: Protect rural communities from armed Fulani pastoralists and achieve the secession of southeastern Nigeria from the rest of the country.

Opponents: Nigerian armed forces and police; Fulani pastoralists.

Affiliates/allies: Ambazonia Governing Council (AGC)

Resources/capabilities: Weaponry includes small arms and locally made weapons. There are reports of arms smuggling from Cameroon.

Conflict Drivers

Security

Insecurity and militarisation:
Widespread insecurity has exacerbated tensions between farmers and pastoralists. In central and northern Nigeria, many Fulani pastoralists seeking new profit sources have turned to 'rural banditry' and theft, targeting farmers, other Fulani pastoralists and the wider civilian population. Cattle rustling, revenge killings and violence resulting from Boko Haram's activities in the Lake Chad Basin have led farmers and pastoralists to arm themselves to protect their livestock. The proliferation of state-sponsored self-defence groups and the subsequent militarisation of local communities have bred animosity along ethnic and religious lines, while increasing demand for weaponry has sustained a transnational criminal economy involved in arms trafficking.

Political

Dispossession and breakdown of farmer–pastoralist arrangements:
Historically, disputes between farmers and pastoralists over access to grazing land, farm destructions and transhumance were resolved through mutually beneficial rules and local mediators. This system of dispute resolution began declining in the 1970s with the active involvement of the police, army and lower courts, which many communities perceived as corrupt and lacking moral authority. In the eyes of many Fulani pastoralists, state institutions turned out to be agents of coercion and exploitation, often criminalising small-scale pastoralists and forcing them to sell their cattle to pay bribes. Restricted access to pastoral land, exacerbated by recent bans on open grazing, have resulted in many pastoralists from Nigeria's North West and Middle Belt becoming destitute and turning to more lucrative criminal activities, including cattle rustling, looting and kidnapping for ransom.[9]

Secessionist sentiments and perceptions of discrimination:
Southeastern Nigeria has a long history of separatism. In 1967, the establishment of the independent Republic of Biafra led to a civil war that resulted in the deaths of over one million people. Since the 1990s, widespread discontent

over political and economic marginalisation, corruption and the management of oil wealth in the Niger Delta has contributed to a revival of nationalism and unrest across Nigeria's South and South East.[10] Secessionist sentiments run high, especially among the Igbo population, which spearheaded the attempted secession of Biafra in 1967. These sentiments culminated in the foundation of the separatist IPOB organisation in 2012. Other ethnic groups in the Niger Delta, including the Ijaw, have become increasingly disaffected with the central government. Over the past two decades, several militant groups operating in southern and southeastern Nigeria have staged attacks against energy infrastructure and Nigerian security forces, demanding a greater share of energy wealth.

Social

Increasing competition over land and water:
Climate change, sustained population growth and increasing urbanisation have driven competition over land and water. High demand for farmland has led to the conversion of land traditionally assigned to grazing into agricultural production. Grazing reserves established in the 1960s have been lost, with land often appropriated by traditional leaders, politicians and other influential elites.[11] The scarcity of pastoral land has pushed semi-nomadic Fulani herders into national parks and forests in central and southern Nigeria. Pastoralists have settled permanently in some cases, igniting tensions with local farmers when livestock have destroyed crops and farmland. Anti-grazing laws passed by several states in recent years are seen as hostile to pastoralists and have failed to contain the escalating violence.

Key Events in 2021–22

POLITICAL EVENTS

6 April 2021
National police chief Muhammed Adamu is sacked after more than 1,800 inmates escape from a prison in Owerri, Imo State.

11 May
The governors of 17 southern states issue a resolution banning open grazing.

27 May
Nigerian President Muhammadu Buhari appoints Maj.-Gen. Farouk Yahaya as the new chief of army staff.

4 June
The government suspends access to Twitter across the country after the platform removes a post by President Buhari for violating its rules.

27 June
Interpol arrests IPOB leader Nnamdi Kanu in Nairobi, Kenya.

25 August
Nigeria announces the signing of a military-cooperation agreement with Russia.

MILTARY/VIOLENT EVENTS

22 March 2021
Gunmen on motorcycles open fire on vigilantes in Mariga district of Niger State, killing 25 people.

29 April
A family of 19 Fulani pastoralists is killed by gunmen in Oyi, Anambra State.

3 June
Suspected cattle rustlers attack villages in the area of Danko/Wasagu, Kebbi State, killing 88 people.

5 July
Armed bandits kidnap 121 students from Bethel Baptist High School in Kaduna State.

3 September
To aid security operations, authorities in Zamfara State order the shutdown of the internet and mobile-phone services.

22 September
The governors of seven northwestern states decide to recruit 3,000 vigilantes to support the actions of the Nigerian armed forces against bandits.

6 November
The All Progressives Grand Alliance candidate, Charles Soludo, is elected governor of Anambra State.

5 January 2022
President Buhari designates the bandit groups operating in the country's northwest as terrorists.

10 January
The leader of Nigeria's All Progressives Congress, Bola Ahmed Tinubu, declares his intention to run for the presidency in 2023.

14 April
The US Department of State approves the sale of 12 attack helicopters to Nigeria despite US lawmakers' initial concerns over reported human-rights abuses by the Nigerian government.

26 September
Suspected Fulani pastoralists kill 40 people from the Madamai and Abun communities in Kaduna State.

14 November
Unidentified gunmen attack the town of Illela in Sokoto State, killing 43 people.

17 December
Fulani pastoralists attack ethnic Tiv farmers in Nasarawa State, killing 45 of them in three days.

5 January 2022
Attacks by suspected bandits, which continue for a week, kill hundreds and displace thousands in Zamfara and Niger states.

11 February
Suspected ESN militants ambush a security patrol near Azia, Anambra State, killing four policemen and a soldier.

26 March
A security guard is killed and air traffic is halted after heavily armed gunmen attack Kaduna International Airport.

28 March
Bandits attack the Abuja–Kaduna train service in Kaduna State, killing eight people and abducting hundreds.

Responses to the Conflict

Security

Some regional authorities have promoted the creation of paramilitary bodies to assist federal security agencies in fighting bandits and armed pastoralists.[12] In January 2020, six southwestern states established the Western Nigeria Security Network, a regional security organisation that seeks to prevent and tackle kidnappings, cattle rustling, violations of anti-grazing laws and other criminal activities. Codenamed *Operation Amotekun*, participants are largely recruited from among ethnic Yorubas and operate under the authority of the states. A similar security network, Ebubeagu, was created in April 2021 in the South East's five ethnic Igbo states. Other vigilante groups, such as the *yan sa kai* (volunteer guards), are active in the North West to protect Hausa farmers from Fulani pastoralists and bandits.

Vigilante groups have been praised by state authorities for assisting the federal security forces and for gaining the acceptance of local populations.[13] However, their status remains unclear and raises concerns over limited accountability, poor training and the potential to stir tensions with federal security forces and between ethnic groups. Additionally, state governors have lamented their powerlessness over policing, calling for greater devolution of security powers to the state level.[14] Human-rights groups have also documented several abuses committed by the Nigerian security forces, especially in the South East.[15]

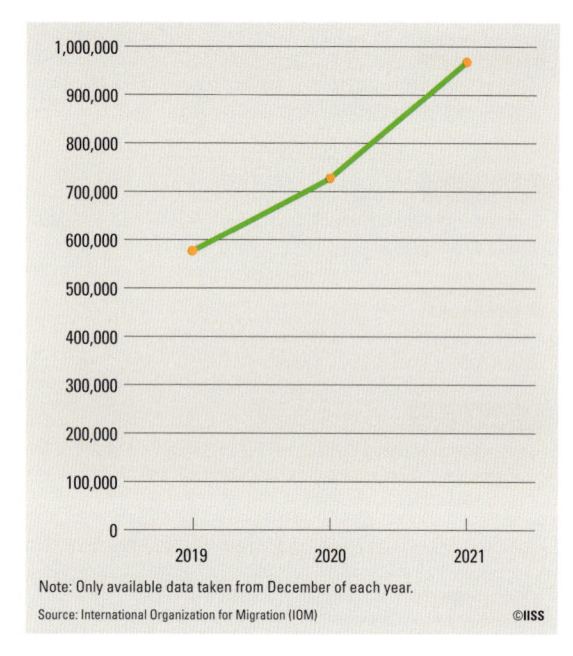

Figure 1: Number of IDPs in North Central and North West Nigeria, 2019–21

Note: Only available data taken from December of each year.
Source: International Organization for Migration (IOM)

Economic/development

Across Nigeria, banditry has major economic implications. The Institute for Economics and Peace estimated that violence negatively affected as much as 8% of the country's GDP.[16] Huge sums were paid in ransom to bandits in North Central and North West Nigeria in 2021.[17] Infrastructure was targeted, with repeated attacks on the Abuja–Kaduna railway forcing the suspension of rail services between the two states.[18] The Abuja–Kaduna highway was also regularly targeted by armed groups, and Kaduna International Airport was attacked in March 2022. In response, the government vowed to improve security along major transport routes.

In May 2021 governors in 17 southern states reacted to farmer–herder violence by banning open grazing in their territories. Similar resolutions were enacted across Nigeria's Middle Belt in previous years. The federal government continued to push for the implementation of the NLTP, which would create new ranches to reduce the demand for open grazing. These measures, coupled with the formation of ethnic-based vigilante militias, were widely perceived among Fulani pastoralists as punitive and threatening their nomadic lifestyle. They viewed the NLTP as protecting the interests of farmers to their detriment.[19]

Diplomacy

Nigeria requested greater security assistance to fight the escalation of violence across the country. The US delivered 12 A-29 *Super Tucano* aircraft in July and September 2021. However, concerns over the Nigerian armed forces' possible human-rights abuses led the US Congress to put off the sale of 12 AH-1 *Cobra* attack helicopters in July 2021.[20] A Nigeria–Russia military-cooperation agreement was announced in August 2021, allegedly after the US had hesitated over a similar deal. US President Joe Biden subsequently waived restrictions on security assistance to Nigeria, and in April 2022 the State Department approved the attack-helicopter sale.

Humanitarian aid

The increasing violence in Nigeria's North West has worsened the humanitarian crisis there. The International Organization for Migration estimated that armed clashes and banditry have displaced close to 1m people across northwestern and north-central Nigeria.[21] An estimated 200,000 refugees from Nigeria's North West are in neighbouring Niger.[22] Additionally, the UN has warned that violence is precipitating an education crisis: over 2,000 schoolchildren were abducted in Nigeria in 2021, while in January 2022 the UN reported that more than 10m children nationwide were not in education – including 900,000 in Katsina State, one of the states most affected by banditry.[23]

Conflict Outlook

Political scenarios

With a presidential election taking place in early 2023, Nigeria's security situation will be a key subject of debate between candidates. Buhari's second term has been characterised by increasing violence across much of the country, with the armed forces unable to prevent the escalation. State governors were initially reluctant to publicly criticise Buhari but the security situation prompted many of them to be more outspoken, including some from the ruling All Progressives Congress. Governors of six southwestern states created a regional security organisation in 2020, while many state governors in the north called for an amnesty and federal support. With many current and former state governors planning to run for office, Buhari's legacy on security is likely to be a controversial issue.

The next president will be expected to oversee implementation of the NLTP, which the federal government has pushed ahead with in an effort to settle farmer–herder disputes. How the presidential candidates plan to implement the NLTP will be a source of contention. Overall, northern presidential candidates are grappling with the fallout of the security crisis, while southern candidates will have to reconcile their divided regional bases while reaching out to the northern wings of their respective parties. However, months of campaigning and coalition-building are likely to divert the attention of senior politicians from the fight against insecurity.

Escalation potential and conflict-related risks

There are growing concerns over the prospect of an alliance between armed bandits of the North West and Boko Haram. High-profile attacks against government infrastructure and escalating violence against civilians have led some observers to suggest a possible 'jihadization of banditry'. However, the fragmented nature of bandit groups, the absence of a unified chain of command and the lack of a coherent political agenda make the 'conversion' of bandits an unlikely prospect.[24] It is still possible, nevertheless, that some jihadist groups will cooperate with bandits, most notably in the northwestern and central states of Kaduna, where the al-Qaeda-linked Ansaru is active, and in Niger, where ISWAP has reportedly established camps.[25] The recent designation of bandits as terrorists, and references by federal and state officials to an 'unholy handshake' behind recent attacks, suggest that Abuja considers the collaboration between violent Islamist groups and bandits a reality.[26]

Further south, the run-up to the 2023 election could exacerbate existing tensions along regional and partisan lines. The government's repression of IPOB and the emergence of ESN have hardened the separatist insurgency in the South East. Other militant leaders in the Niger Delta have expressed solidarity with IPOB and threatened to launch new attacks against oil infrastructure. If militants from the oil-rich region were to join forces with Biafran separatists, this would escalate the security crisis in the south.

Strategic implications and global influences

The implications of Nigeria's security crisis have extended beyond its borders. In the North West, many Nigerians displaced by the conflict have sought refuge in Niger's Maradi region. Armed bandits have also taken advantage of the porous border with Niger to regroup there before launching new raids into Nigeria. Cameroon, Chad and Niger also have large communities of pastoralists and are vulnerable to pastoralist–farmer tensions over land and water access. A botched Nigerian airstrike that killed seven Nigerien children in the border village of Nachadé highlighted the risks of transnational counter-terrorism operations.[27] Nevertheless, concerns over possible human-rights abuses are unlikely to prevent the US from approving arms sales or providing greater security assistance to Nigeria, which – under Buhari – has often turned to Russia or China for weaponry and infrastructure.

Notes

[1] International Crisis Group, 'Violence in Nigeria's North West: Rolling Back the Mayhem', Report no. 288, 18 May 2020.

[2] Amnesty International, 'Nigeria: Escalating Attacks Targeting Children Endanger Right to Education', 2 December 2021.

[3] Alfred Olufemi, 'Horrors on the Plateau: Inside Nigeria's Farmer–Herder Conflict', Al-Jazeera, 8 November 2021.

[4] Armed Conflict Location & Event Data Project (ACLED), www.acleddata.com.

[5] James Barnett and Murtala Rufai, 'The Other Insurgency: Northwest Nigeria's Worsening Bandit Crisis', War on the Rocks, 16 November 2021.

[6] Ibid.; and 'Matawalle: There Are Over 30,000 Bandits in the North', Cable, 2 April 2021.

[7] 'A Splintered Sect', Africa Confidential, vol. 62, no. 21, 21 October 2021.

[8] Sodiq Yusuff, 'Exclusive: Military, Police Set to Launch Major Operations Against "Insurgency" in South-east', Cable, 2 June 2021.

[9] SB Morgen, 'The Economics of the Kidnap Industry in Nigeria', 28 May 2020.

[10] See Nnamdi Obasi, 'Nigeria's Biafran Separatist Upsurge', International Crisis Group, 4 December 2015; and John Campbell and Nolan Quinn, 'What's Behind Growing Separatism in Nigeria?', Council on Foreign Relations, 3 August 2021.

[11] International Crisis Group, 'Herders Against Farmers: Nigeria's Expanding Deadly Conflict', Report no. 252, 19 September 2017.

[12] International Crisis Group, 'Managing Vigilantism in Nigeria: A Near-term Necessity', Report no. 308, 21 April 2022.

[13] See Nigeria, House of Representatives, 'National Security Summit Report', June 2021; 'Insecurity: Makinde Inaugurates Oyo Security Network Board, Amotekun Corps', *Premium Times*, 21 June 2021; Kunle Adebajo, 'Vigilantes Defying the Odds to Protect Lives in Northwest Nigeria', HumAngle, 3 November 2021; and Adeolu Adeyemo, 'Amotekun: So Far, So Good?', *Nigerian Tribune*, 20 December 2021.

[14] 'Rift on Security Grows Between State Governors and Presidency Amid Claims That Insurgents Threaten the Capital', *Africa Confidential*, vol. 62, no. 9, 3 May 2021.

[15] Amnesty International, 'Nigeria: At Least 115 Killed by Security Forces Within Four Months in Country's Southeast – Investigation', 5 August 2021.

[16] Femi Adekoya, 'Nigerians Pay More for Insecurity as Economic Impact Hits N50tr', *Guardian*, 23 March 2021.

[17] Lukman Abolade, 'Tracking the Ransom: How Multi-million Naira Kidnapping Industry Is Growing in Northern Nigeria', International Centre for Investigative Reporting, 25 February 2022.

[18] Oluwole Ojewale, Adewumi Badiora and Freedom Onuoha, 'Kaduna's Train Attacks Add to Nigeria's Deep Security Problems', Institute for Security Studies, 7 April 2022.

[19] Leif Brottem, 'The Growing Complexity of Farmer–Herder Conflict in West and Central Africa', Africa Center for Strategic Studies, Security Brief no. 39, 12 July 2021.

[20] US Congressional Research Service, 'Nigeria: Key Issues and U.S. Policy', 25 March 2022.

[21] Adebowale Oluwaseun, 'Communal Clashes Displace More People in North-central, Northwest Nigeria in 2021 – IOM Report', HumAngle, 10 February 2022.

[22] Boubacar Younoussa Siddo, 'Bandit Attacks Drive Nigerian Villagers to Flee to Niger', United Nations High Commissioner for Refugees, 3 December 2021.

[23] See Emmanuel Akinwotu, 'How Risk of Kidnap Became the Cost of an Education in Nigeria', *Guardian*, 12 November 2021; Adeola Oladipupo, 'Nigeria's Bandit Attacks Continue to Worsen a Humanitarian and Environmental Crisis', *Newlines Magazine*, 4 October 2021; and UN Children's Fund, 'UNICEF Warns of Nigerian Education Crisis as World Celebrates International Day of Education Amid COVID-19 Concerns', 24 January 2022.

[24] James Barnett, Murtala Ahmed Rufa'I and Abdulaziz Abdulaziz, 'Northwestern Nigeria: A Jihadization of Banditry, or a "Banditization" of Jihad?', *CTC Sentinel*, vol. 15, no. 1, January 2022.

[25] Abubakar Ahmadu Maishanu, 'Boko Haram Establishing Camps in Niger State – Official', *Premium Times*, 24 November 2021.

[26] 'Death Toll Hits 154 Following Attack in Central Nigeria', Al-Jazeera, 13 April 2022.

[27] 'Nigerian Forces Kill Children in Airstrike Over Border in Niger, Official Says', Reuters, 20 February 2022.

CAMEROON

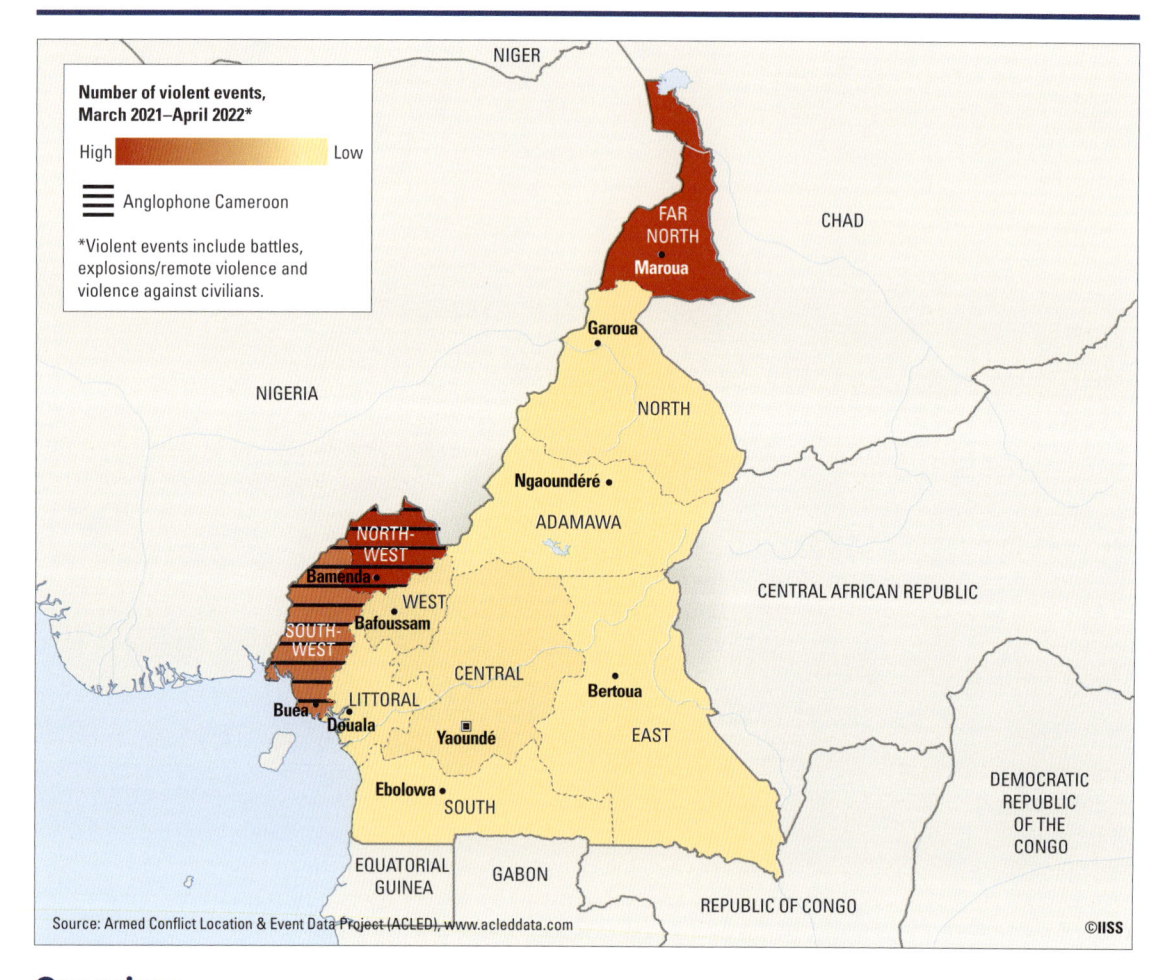

Map: Number of violent events, March 2021–April 2022. Violent events include battles, explosions/remote violence and violence against civilians. Source: Armed Conflict Location & Event Data Project (ACLED), www.acleddata.com

Overview

The intra-state conflict in Cameroon is primarily a crisis with roots in long-lasting grievances – among anglophones – created by the reunification process that followed the end of British and French colonial rule. Prior to independence, Southern Cameroons was under British rule, while East and West Cameroon were under French rule. As a result, the administrations of the regions differed during the colonial period. Following a United Nations-organised referendum in February 1961, these regions became known collectively as the Federal Republic of Cameroon. The 1972 abolishment of the federal system, by which anglophone Cameroon came to be present-day Southwest and Northwest regions, contributed to the centralisation of governance and institutions in francophone Cameroon, which contained 80% of the country's population.[1] Since the 1990s, anglophone Cameroon has challenged the legitimacy of the state, citing an erosion of civil liberties and economic, political and cultural discrimination by the central government.

Protests in 2016 sparked the current phase of the conflict, as teachers, lawyers and civil-society actors in the anglophone region held peaceful rallies to draw attention to the declining quality of life and public services in the region. The central government's violent response escalated regional mobilisation, with protesters rallying around various demands, including for self-determination, autonomy and an independent nation – 'Ambazonia'. Several armed

Armed Conflict Global Relevance Indicator (ACGRI)

- Incidence: 7
- Human impact: 6
- Geopolitical impact: 7

Cameroon

Key Conflict Statistics

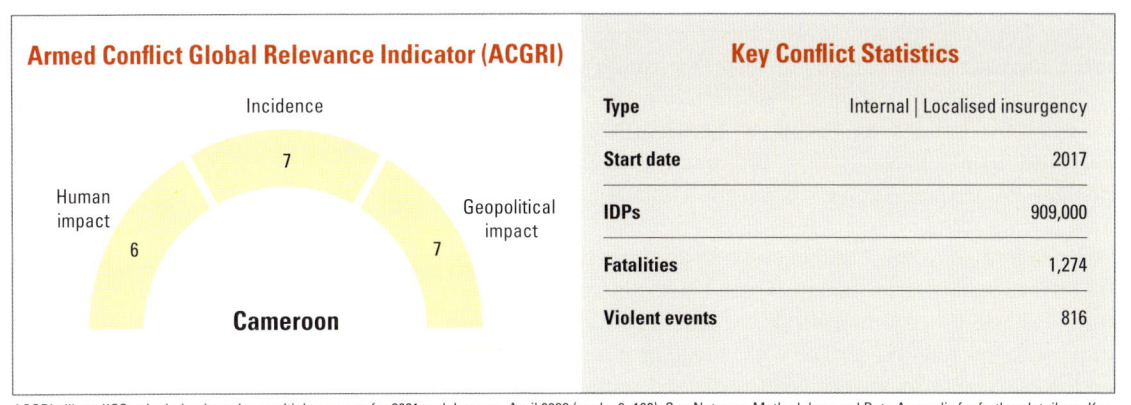

Type	Internal | Localised insurgency
Start date	2017
IDPs	909,000
Fatalities	1,274
Violent events	816

ACGRI pillars: IISS calculation based on multiple sources for 2021 and January–April 2022 (scale: 0–100). See Notes on Methodology and Data Appendix for further details on Key Conflict Statistics.

separatist actors emerged to challenge state forces, launching a secessionist movement in October 2017.

Political organisations within the Ambazonia separatist movement fractured due to disagreements over aims and strategy, leading to the creation of two rival groups, the Interim Government of Ambazonia (IG) and the Ambazonia Governing Council (AGC or AGovC). Both groups united local self-defence groups to create military wings: the IG created the Ambazonia Self-Defence Council (ASDC) and the AGC created the Ambazonia Defence Forces (ADF). Many other militia groups, such as the Southern Cameroons Defence Force (SOCADEF), have chosen to either coalesce or further differentiate themselves from the main political organisations. The continuous fragmentation of political and militia actors has been a notable feature of the conflict, contributing to incoherence and a lack of homogeneity in the Ambazonia movement.

Ambazonian separatist militias have used guerrilla tactics to attack government forces and institutions, intimidated citizens into boycotting commerce and education and kidnapped them for ransom. State forces have responded by deploying the elite Rapid Intervention Battalion (BIR). Claims of the BIR's impunity in conducting reprisal attacks have shadowed Cameroon's human-rights record, as the violence continued to take a significant toll on civilians in urban areas, such as Bamenda, Buea and Limbe, during the reporting period. In late 2021, resistance to Cameroon's re-election to the UN Human Rights Council for another term was based on outstanding claims of crimes against civilians by state forces.[2]

Simultaneously, Cameroon's Far North sees significant spillover from the conflict in the Lake Chad Basin, where Jama'atu Ahlis Sunna Lidda'awati wal-Jihad (JAS, known as Boko Haram) and Islamic State in West Africa Province (ISWAP) are active, among other jihadist militias. As a member of the revived Multinational Joint Task Force (MNJTF) tasked with supporting regional counter-terrorism operations, Cameroonian state forces have been deployed to respond to jihadist attacks in areas of the Lake Chad Basin. So far, the international community has devoted greater attention to the jihadist threat than to the anglophone–francophone crisis. However, both conflicts threaten the resilience of Cameroonian society, revealing significant tensions over the governance of the state.

In 2020, during the first months of the coronavirus pandemic, the central government attempted to engage separatists via peace talks and ceasefires. However, the fracturing of the Ambazonian movement and internal government disagreements over how to approach conflict resolution stalled these efforts. Political infighting and disputes between conflict actors abounded as militias and government forces continued to clash, producing further civilian casualties and disruptions to daily life in affected regions. From the perspective of government forces, following December 2020 elections that saw the ruling Cameroon People's Democratic Movement (RDPC) claim the majority of regions, the future of both conflicts is tied to the figure of President Paul Biya and his potential successors. The slow integration and poor conditions experienced by people enrolled in the government's disarmament, demobilisation and reintegration (DDR) programme – which has led to protests – has reduced public trust in Yaoundé's willingness to end the conflict.

During the reporting period, separatist actors and militias carried out attacks against civilian and state forces, formed new alliances and underwent further fractures, and saw greater diaspora engagement, increasing international focus on the conflict. In April 2021, AGC leaders and the Nigerian separatist group Indigenous People of Biafra (IPOB) announced an alliance, which prompted further pledges of mutual support between Abuja and Yaoundé. Leading up to a self-declared Ambazonia independence day on 1 October, separatists stepped up attacks against government forces. Government forces' killing of two young girls in the region within a span of a few months sparked widespread protests and riots. Attacks by government forces and secessionist militias continued to draw the attention of the Catholic Church and prompted widespread condemnations from humanitarian and civil-society actors. Cameroon's hosting of the African Cup of Nations football tournament was a missed opportunity for a ceasefire, with conflict actors disrupting the flow of the tournament.

In early 2022, fissures in the IG's diasporic leadership further highlighted the fractured nature of the secessionist movement, while AGC–SOCADEF discussions in Ireland in February were an example of secessionist actors' efforts to address their differences internally. The secessionist conflict and the wider jihadist threat in the Lake Chad Basin both worsen intercommunal violence in Cameroon (tensions between herdsmen and agrarian communities exist along ethnic lines) and continue to require multidimensional approaches to resolution. The combined effects of conflicts in Cameroon have led to 816 violent events and 1,274 deaths between March 2021 and April 2022, with 131,000 persons reported forcibly internally displaced in 2021.[3]

Conflict Parties

Cameroonian armed forces

Strength: Approximately 25,400 regular military personnel and 9,000 paramilitaries. The scale of deployment in anglophone Cameroon is unclear but consists of elements of the military police (the gendarmerie) and the elite military force, the BIR.

Areas of operation: Northwest and Southwest regions, in a military region designated RMIA 5.

Leadership: RMIA 5 is led by Gen. Agha Robinson Ndong but the president is commander of the armed forces.

Structure: The BIR has no general staff and is under the authority of the chief of staff of the army. The gendarmerie is under the authority of the secretary of state in the Ministry of Defence.

History: The BIR was created in 2001 to combat banditry along Cameroon's frontiers but has been used since as an elite intervention force. The gendarmerie was created in the early 1960s as a direct descendent of the French colonial-era force.

Objectives: Counter-insurgency against separatist groups in Northwest and Southwest regions and restoration of the regular flow of commerce disrupted by separatist groups.

Opponents: IG, ASDC, AGC, ADF, various smaller militias.

Affiliates/allies: Receives military assistance from France, Israel and the United States.

Resources/capabilities: Much of the equipment inventory is ageing but infantry fighting vehicles and protected patrol vehicles have been acquired from China and South Africa and gifted by the US. The armed forces are improving their intelligence, surveillance and reconnaissance capabilities with fixed-wing aircraft and small uninhabited aerial vehicles.

Interim Government of Ambazonia (IG) / Ambazonia Self-Defence Council (ASDC)

Strength: The ASDC consists of several local self-defence groups including the Ambazonia Restoration Army (ARA), the Manyu Ghost Warriors, the Red Dragons, the Seven Karta Militia, SOCADEF and the Tigers of Ambazonia. Collectively the ASDC can draw on some 1,000–1,500 fighters.[4]

Areas of operation: The ASDC operates throughout Northwest and Southwest regions. The ARA and SOCADEF operate in most divisions in Northwest and Southwest regions. The Seven Karta is primarily present in Mezam division, the Tigers in Manyu and Meme divisions, the Ghost Warriors in Manyu and the Red Dragons in Lebialem.

Leadership: Current elected leader is Iya Marianta Njomia. Before Njomia's appointment, the IG leadership was fractured between Sisiku Julius Ayuk Tabe and Samuel Ikome Sako, following the former's arrest and the latter's election as interim president. The diaspora faction in Maryland, US, is under Sako's leadership, although rifts remain, with an attempted dismissal of Sako taking place in early 2022. The links between the IG and the various groups within the ASDC are often tenuous. Leadership of many of the individual groups is also unknown. The ARA is led by Paxson Agbor, the SOCADEF by Nso Foncha Nkem and the Red Dragons by

Interim Government of Ambazonia (IG) / Ambazonia Self-Defence Council (ASDC)

Lekeaka Oliver. Since May 2019, there have been significant disputes between IG wings loyal to Tabe and those associated with Sako, as well as between the IG and the ASDC.

Structure: Operates a government structure that includes an executive and a legislative body. The ASDC lacks a centralised command structure. The structure of the several localised self-defence organisations that compose it is unclear, yet many leaders are titled 'general'.

History: The IG emerged from the Southern Cameroons Ambazonia Consortium United Front (SCACUF) and declared Ambazonia's independence on 1 October 2017. The ASDC was created in March 2018 as a coordinating mechanism following a call for collective self-defence from the IG.

Objectives: Ambazonia's independence through a strategy of increased international pressure on the Cameroonian government and disruption of commerce.

Opponents: Cameroonian armed forces.

Affiliates/allies: The IG coordinates with other groups through the Southern Cameroons Liberation Council (SCLC), and at times coordinates with the AGC/ADF.

Resources/capabilities: Makeshift weaponry and some imports of small arms from neighbouring Nigeria. Financing of the IG comes primarily from the Cameroonian diaspora. The ASDC reverts to kidnapping for ransom as a means of funding its operations.

Ambazonia Governing Council (AGC) / Ambazonia Defence Forces (ADF)

Strength: Estimated between 200 and 500 fighters.[5]

Areas of operation: Throughout Northwest and Southwest regions, parts of Littoral region.

Leadership: The AGC is led from abroad by Lucas Cho Ayaba, while the chairman of the ADF council is Benedict Kuah.

Structure: The AGC operates a government structure that includes an executive and a legislative branch. Various leaders in the ADF have the title 'general'.

History: The AGC was created in 2013 as a merger of several self-determination movements and remains outside the IG. In September 2017, the AGC declared a war of independence against the Cameroonian government and the ADF was deployed as its official armed wing.

Objectives: Ambazonia's independence through a strategy of insurgency and disruption of commerce. The AGC's goal is to make the anglophone territory ungovernable and thus compel the Cameroonian government to concede.

Opponents: Cameroonian armed forces.

Affiliates/allies: At times interacts with groups in the ASDC and coordinates with SOCADEF. It has a loose relationship with the IG.

Resources/capabilities: Makeshift weaponry and some imports of small arms from neighbouring Nigeria. Financing for the organisation comes primarily from the Cameroonian diaspora as well as ransoms from kidnapping activities.

Southern Cameroons Defence Forces (SOCADEF)

Strength: Approximately 400 members.[6]

Areas of operation: Meme division, Southwest region.

Leadership: Led from abroad by Ebenezer Derek Mbongo Akwanga.

Structure: While SOCADEF is ostensibly the armed wing of the African People's Liberation Movement (APLM), the degree of coordination between the two is unclear. SOCADEF's organisation on the ground is unknown.

History: SOCADEF is an independent armed secessionist group that grew out of the APLM and the Southern Cameroons Youth League.

Objectives: Independence for Ambazonia through a strategy of insurgency and disruption of commerce.

Opponents: Cameroonian armed forces.

Affiliates/allies: Maintains a loose alliance with the AGC/ADF. In March 2019 its parent organisation, the APLM, joined the SCLC.

Resources/capabilities: Makeshift weaponry and some imports of small arms from neighbouring Nigeria.

Various small militias

Strength: Unclear, but approximately 100–150 members in total across nearly a dozen militias, including the Vipers, often going under the generic term 'Amba Boys'.

Areas of operation: Northwest and Southwest regions.

Leadership: Unknown.

Structure: Unknown.

History: Various small militias emerged following the conflict's beginnings in October 2017; their operations blur the line between insurgency and crime.

Objectives: Independence for Ambazonia through insurgency, but many groups also seem to seek short-term material gains from the conflict and are responsible for many of the kidnappings for ransom in the region.

Opponents: Cameroonian armed forces.

Affiliates/allies: The Vipers coordinate with the ADF and SOCADEF on an ad hoc basis.

Resources/capabilities: Makeshift weaponry and small arms imported from Nigeria.

Conflict Drivers

Geopolitical and geostrategic influences
Regional dynamics:
The armed conflict in Cameroon intersects with broader regional dynamics, including widespread insecurity, a counter-insurgency campaign against Boko Haram and conflict spillover in Lake Chad Basin countries. The central government plays an important stabilising role amid insecurity caused by Boko Haram in its Far North region: the lack of international pressure on the Biya government to pursue peace initiatives with separatist groups must be understood in this context. International allies are hesitant to pressure Cameroon given their national interests and the country's strategic role in curbing violent extremism's further expansion.

Political
Long-standing perceptions of discrimination:
The conflict's roots date back to the colonial period. Following Cameroon's independence in the early 1960s, the country operated as a federation, consisting of a larger francophone territory and a smaller anglophone region. In 1972, a referendum abolished federalism and created a unitary state under single-party francophone rule. As a result, anglophone Cameroonians came to perceive the central government as neglectful of their development, culture and political freedoms. These tensions led to widespread anti-government demonstrations in 2016. The heavy-handed government response created a dynamic of mutual escalation. Negotiations collapsed, with separatists coordinating larger-scale strikes and many calling for secession. In response, the government framed the anglophone issue as a direct security threat and made only small concessions.

Patronage, corruption and weak democratic accountability:
Rampant corruption and weak democratic accountability have elevated anglophone Cameroon's sense of alienation. The office of the presidency has distributed patronage to francophone supporters and the ruling RDPC party dominates the political system. Gerrymandering of voting districts and a disproportionate electoral system have increasingly disadvantaged opposition parties, leading to calls for President Biya's resignation. The perception of an entrenched status quo and a powerful elite has pushed anglophone separatists to consider full autonomy as the only solution.

Economic
Limited macroeconomic growth:
Cameroon's economy, which accounts for 44% of the GDP of the Economic and Monetary Community of Central Africa (CEMAC), is highly dependent on natural resources (hydrocarbons, agricultural products and wood).[7] As a result, it is vulnerable to exogenous shocks, especially as it does not process these resources before export. The pace of growth has slowed as a result of ongoing economic problems (decline in public demand, poor clearance of government arrears, deteriorating security conditions and business climate). Youth unemployment was approximately 6.6% in 2021 based on international labour statistics, although there is a high percentage of underemployed university graduates.[8] Cameroon also has a high debt-to-GDP ratio – 47% in 2021.[9]

Social
Complex social environments with high incidences of poverty:
The factors contributing to social vulnerability in Cameroon are multiple and complex. Inequalities in access to resources and basic social services are of concern and affect social cohesion. The significant disparities in living standards between the northern regions and the rest of the country are an additional dimension of fragility. Poverty mapping shows an increase in poverty in the Far North regions (77% in 2019, compared to 74% in 2014).[10] In December 2021, the UN Food and Agriculture Organization estimated that more than 2.4 million people (9% of the population) were extremely food insecure.[11] The vast majority of these people are in the Far North, Northwest, Littoral and Southwest and Adamawa regions.

Key Events in 2021–22

POLITICAL EVENTS

2 March 2021
Cameroon's defence ministry acknowledges an attack by state security forces on Ebam village in Southwest region in March 2020 but refutes allegations of rape.

12 March
Detained IG leader Sisiku Julius Ayuk Tabe restates the group's preconditions for talks with the central government, including state forces returning to barracks, amnesty for separatists and internationally mediated dialogue in a neutral venue.

Early April
The AGC and Nigerian separatist group IPOB announce an alliance.

10 May
Defence Minister Beti Assomo states that secessionist groups are using improvised explosive devices (IEDs) due to their decreasing memberships, reporting that at least 24 troops and civilians were killed in IEDs attacks in the first week of May.

7 June
US Secretary of State Antony Blinken announces visa restrictions on individuals undermining the peaceful resolution of the crisis in anglophone Cameroon.

13 July
Nigerian President Muhammadu Buhari pledges support for Cameroonian institutions, saying Cameroon's stability is in Nigeria's interest.

17 July
During President Biya's visit to Geneva, Switzerland, over 100 protesters attempt to break a police barricade at his hotel, raising tensions in Cameroon.

3 August
Doctors Without Borders withdraws all staff from Northwest region. The organisation's activities were suspended by the government in December 2020 due to accusations of alleged pro-separatist bias.

12 September
Ahead of self-declared Ambazonia Independence Day on 1 October, a faction of the IG announces a three-week lockdown in Northwest and Southwest regions.

21 September
Marches take place in francophone towns calling for a ceasefire between the central government and Ambazonian separatists.

MILITARY/VIOLENT EVENTS

30 March 2021
The military deploys additional forces to the northern border with Nigeria after Boko Haram intensifies attacks in the border area.

11–19 April
Military forces kill several Ambazonian separatist commanders, arresting others.

18 May
Military forces burn over 50 civilian homes near Kumbo, killing two civilians, in a possible revenge attack following an IED attack that reportedly killed two soldiers.

3 June
Ambazonian separatists launch IED attacks targeting military vehicles in Nkum and Kumbo towns in Bui division, Northwest region.

16 July
Military forces clash with Ambazonian separatists in Ngo-Ketunjia division, Northwest region, reportedly killing at least 15.

Timeline

24 July
Boko Haram attacks Sagme village in Logone-et-Chari division, Far North region, at the border with Nigeria, killing eight soldiers. Military forces reportedly kill 20 militants.

5 October
While Prime Minister Dion Ngute is giving a speech in Northwest region, an unidentified assailant fires shots in nearby Matazem village, sparking panic.

14 October
A government soldier opens fire on a car at a checkpoint in Buea, Southwest region, killing a five-year-old child.

12 November
A police officer kills an eight-year-old child while shooting at a car driving away from a checkpoint in Bamenda city, Northwest region.

5 December
The ADF attacks a gendarme post on Alakuma junction and a military post on Mbengwi road near Bamenda city.

12 January 2022
An IED detonation at a police checkpoint near a football stadium wounds three police officers. Three civilians are killed during the military's response.

7 April
In Mbalangi, near Kumba town and Oku subdivision, Ambazonian separatists kidnap at least 12 demonstrators protesting against the separatists' activities.

26 February 2022
The AGC meets representatives of 11 other groups from the Ambazonia Coalition for Talks; they jointly agree to potentially negotiate a settlement with the central government and pursue independence.

11–13 March
Delegates of six Ambazonian groups meet in Germany to discuss refugees, internal displacement and human-rights violations.

Responses to the Conflict

Security

The multiple conflicts in Cameroon have created multidimensional security challenges that put the military under significant pressure. Lake Chad Basin countries have made efforts to coordinate against Boko Haram through the MNJTF. However, their inconsistent commitment to the force, funding problems and disjointed planning have hindered its effectiveness.

In April 2022, Cameroon renewed a military-cooperation agreement with Russia as the latter intensified its offensive in Ukraine. The two countries agreed to exchange information in the fields of international defence and security policy, military training and education, medicine and topography. The terms were vague, making no mention of either the anglophone crisis or the fight against Boko Haram. The agreement came at a time when the Wagner Group, a Russian private military company, has been accused of atrocities and human-rights violations in Africa, notably in the Central African Republic, Libya, Sudan and Mali.

Yaoundé established a national committee for disarmament, demobilisation, and reintegration (DDR) in November 2018 to provide a framework for reintegrating former Boko Haram militants and members of armed groups in Northwest and Southwest regions. DDR programmes often result from a peace agreement or process initiated by conflict parties: as there is no such process in Cameroon, many consider the programme to be premature.

Economic/development

Cameroon has partnerships with key multilateral and bilateral partners to foster economic development. In 2017, the World Bank adopted a new partnership framework with Cameroon for the period 2017–22. This framework is aligned with the objectives of the government's national development strategy for 2020–30 and has three action areas, notably to eliminate poverty in rural areas, strengthen infrastructure and develop the private sector and improve governance.

Corruption is a major issue in Cameroon that impacts sustainable and inclusive economic development. Transparency International's 2021 corruption perception index ranked Cameroon 144 of 180 countries (a higher ranking indicates greater perceived corruption).[12] In June 2021, prominent Cameroonian women came together to urge the IMF to consider making strict anti-corruption controls a condition of a new loan the government announced in May. The advocacy followed an audit report of the Supreme Court of Cameroon that detailed findings of large-scale corruption and mismanagement of funding for a COVID-19 response plan. Cameroonian civil-society actors remained greatly concerned about the perceived complicity of multilateral and bilateral actors. In July 2021, the IMF's executive board approved a three-year arrangement under the Extended Credit Facility (ECF) for approximately US$689.5m, or 175% of Cameroon's quota, to support the country's economic and financial-reform programme.[13] In June 2022, a British subsidiary of mining and trading giant Glencore pleaded guilty to seven counts of bribery in connection with oil operations in Cameroon and other regional countries.

Diplomacy

The dialogue between Yaoundé and Ambazonian separatists has made little progress since initial talks took place in 2020. During the reporting period, the fracturing of separatist groups has meant that some enter peace negotiations while others continue to fight for independence. The central government's efforts to resolve the crisis, which have included the establishment of inter-institutional commissions to promote bilingualism and multiculturalism, disarmament and reintegration, and special status for the English-speaking regions, have not been successful. Rather than holding talks with the separatists, the government implements unilateral initiatives. Any political agreement will need the support of the majority of stakeholders to be sustainable. Meanwhile, in April 2022, the US Department of Homeland Security designated Cameroon for Temporary Protected Status due to the conflict in the country, offering temporary work authorisation and protection from deportation for eligible Cameroonian nationals in the US.

Humanitarian aid

In March 2022, the UN Office for the Coordination of Humanitarian Affairs reported that there were 3.9m people in need of humanitarian assistance and protection in Cameroon, including 936,767 internally displaced people, 485,729 refugees and 518,853 returnees.[14] During the reporting period, nine of the country's ten regions continued to be impacted by three protracted humanitarian crises: one concerning the presence of over 325,000 refugees from the Central African Republic in the eastern region, another caused by continuous violence in the Lake Chad Basin, and another caused by insecurity in Northwest and Southwest regions.[15] Humanitarian needs are compounded by structural-development deficits and chronic vulnerabilities that undermine the long-term recovery of those affected.

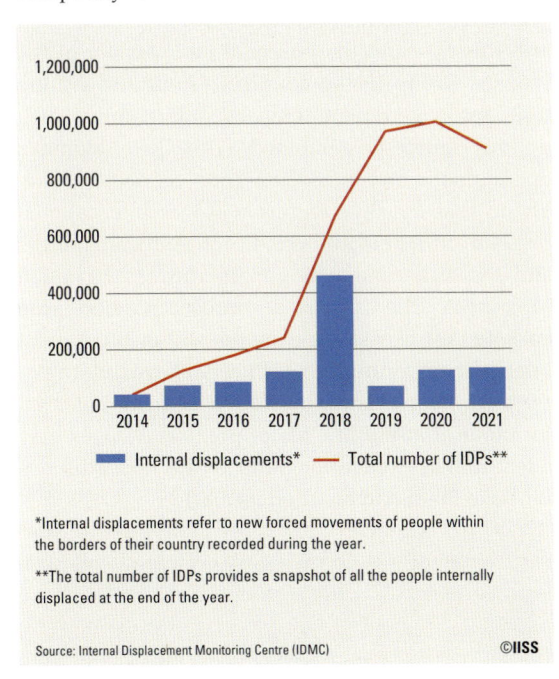

Figure 1: Internal displacements and total number of IDPs per year, 2014–21

*Internal displacements refer to new forced movements of people within the borders of their country recorded during the year.

**The total number of IDPs provides a snapshot of all the people internally displaced at the end of the year.

Source: Internal Displacement Monitoring Centre (IDMC)

The conflict in Ukraine has already had economic repercussions for Cameroon, and food insecurity is likely to worsen. Imports from Russia and Ukraine amounted to US$93.3m and US$2.1m respectively in 2019, consisting mostly of wheat, fertilisers, soybean oil and other products. In addition, disruptions to supply chains and soaring prices negatively impacted humanitarian assistance due to rising costs. Of the US$376m requested for humanitarian assistance by the Cameroon Humanitarian Response Plan in 2022, only 9% was funded as of 30 April.[16]

Conflict Outlook

Political scenarios

As speculation mounts about the health of Cameroon's long-serving President Biya, the country's future also seems to hang in the balance. Cameroon's constitution states that in the case of a presidential vacancy, the president of the senate assumes the role while presidential elections are organised. However, Cameroon has a poor track record of adhering to its constitution. Despite this fact, it is also possible that the country will continue to slowly progress through elite bargains that allow it to withstand economic and political shocks. The implementation of strong enforcement mechanisms by the National Anti-Corruption Commission in Cameroon could bring accountability and reduce corrupt practices in public institutions in the country.

At the same time, discordant voices from opposition parties continue to contest Biya's victory in the 2018 presidential election. The ongoing post-election controversy has heightened the spectre of identity politics in a country noted for its ethnic diversity and rivalries. Meanwhile, social strife, labour strikes by teachers due to non-payment of salaries, public frustration at shrinking political space, gross violations of human rights, corruption scandals, and post-coronavirus economic slowdown and inflation have resulted in growing discontent among the population.

Escalation potential and conflict-related risks

The fractured nature of the Ambazonia separatist movement may result in further violence as competing groups clash, with a risk that civilians will be caught in the crossfire. Targeted violence by separatists against an increasingly disillusioned population (especially local leaders suspected of not supporting separatist causes) may also escalate. Further, worsening intercommunal violence among herdsmen and agrarian communities presents additional challenges. The frequent use of indiscriminate violence in military clearance operations will risk further weakening the legitimacy of the Biya government and encourage anglophone communities to join armed separatist groups. However, the recent attempts of separatist forces to coalesce around shared goals highlights the potential for de-escalation.

Strategic implications and global influences

The April 2022 military deal between Cameroon and Russia – and the potential involvement of the Wagner Group in the country – indicates shifting tides for government interests. International geopolitical interests combined with Boko Haram's operations in northern Cameroon reduce the likelihood that the Biya regime will face international pressure to make any significant political changes and to try harder to negotiate with Ambazonian separatists. The country's strategic position as a backstop for ISWAP's expansion will mean that the international community is likely to have little appetite for regime change and the consequent potential for political instability. Major political changes may affect military operations and create opportunities for Boko Haram to broaden its reach.

Notes

1. International Crisis Group, 'Cameroon's Anglophone Crisis at the Crossroads', Report No. 250, 2 August 2017; Richard Moncrieff, 'Cameroon's Anglophone Crisis Is Escalating. Here's How It Could Be Resolved', African Arguments, 27 September 2017; and Laura-Stella Enonchong, 'The Problem of Systemic Violation of Civil and Political Rights in Cameroon: Towards a Contextualised Conception of Constitutionalism', PhD dissertation, University of Warwick, January 2013.
2. Human Rights Watch, 'UN: Noncompetitive Rights Council Election Aids Abusers', 12 October 2021.
3. Armed Conflict Location & Event Data Project (ACLED), www.acleddata.com. Deaths refers to those resulting from battles, explosions/remote violence and violence against civilians between 1 March 2021 and 30 April 2022. For data on internally displaced persons, see Internal Displacement Monitoring Centre (IDMC), 'Country Profile: Cameroon', 18 May 2022.
4. Institute for Peace and Security Studies, 'Cameroon Conflict Insight', Peace and Security Report, vol. 1, March 2020, p. 8.
5. International Crisis Group, 'Cameroon's Anglophone Crisis: How to Get to Talks?', Report No. 272, 2 May 2019, p. 32.
6. Ibid.
7. IMF, 'Central African Economic and Monetary Community – Common Policies in Support of Member Countries Reform Programs – Staff Report, and Statement by the Executive Director', IMF Country Report No. 21/148, July 2021, p. 21.
8. World Bank data, 'Unemployment, Youth Total (% of Total Labor Force Ages 15–24)', June 2022.
9. IMF, World Economic Outlook Database, April 2022.
10. World Bank, 'Lifting Cameroon's Most Vulnerable Out of Poverty: Building Resilience and Fostering Local Governance to Address the Root Causes of Fragility and Conflict in Northern Regions of Cameroon', Results Briefs, 18 November 2019.
11. 'GIEWS Country Brief: Cameroon 15-December-2021', ReliefWeb, 15 December 2021.
12. Transparency International, 'Corruption Perceptions Index 2021'.
13. IMF, 'Cameroon: 2021 Article IV Consultation and First Reviews Under the Extended Credit Facility and the Extended Fund Facility Arrangements and Requests for Waivers for Performance Criteria Applicability and Nonobservance and Modification of Performance Criterion – Press Release; Staff Report; and Statement by the Executive Director for Cameroon', IMF Staff Country Reports, 11 March 2022.
14. UN Office for the Coordination of Humanitarian Affairs, 'Cameroon', *Humanitarian Bulletin*, no. 31, March–April 2022.
15. Ibid.
16. Ibid.

MOZAMBIQUE

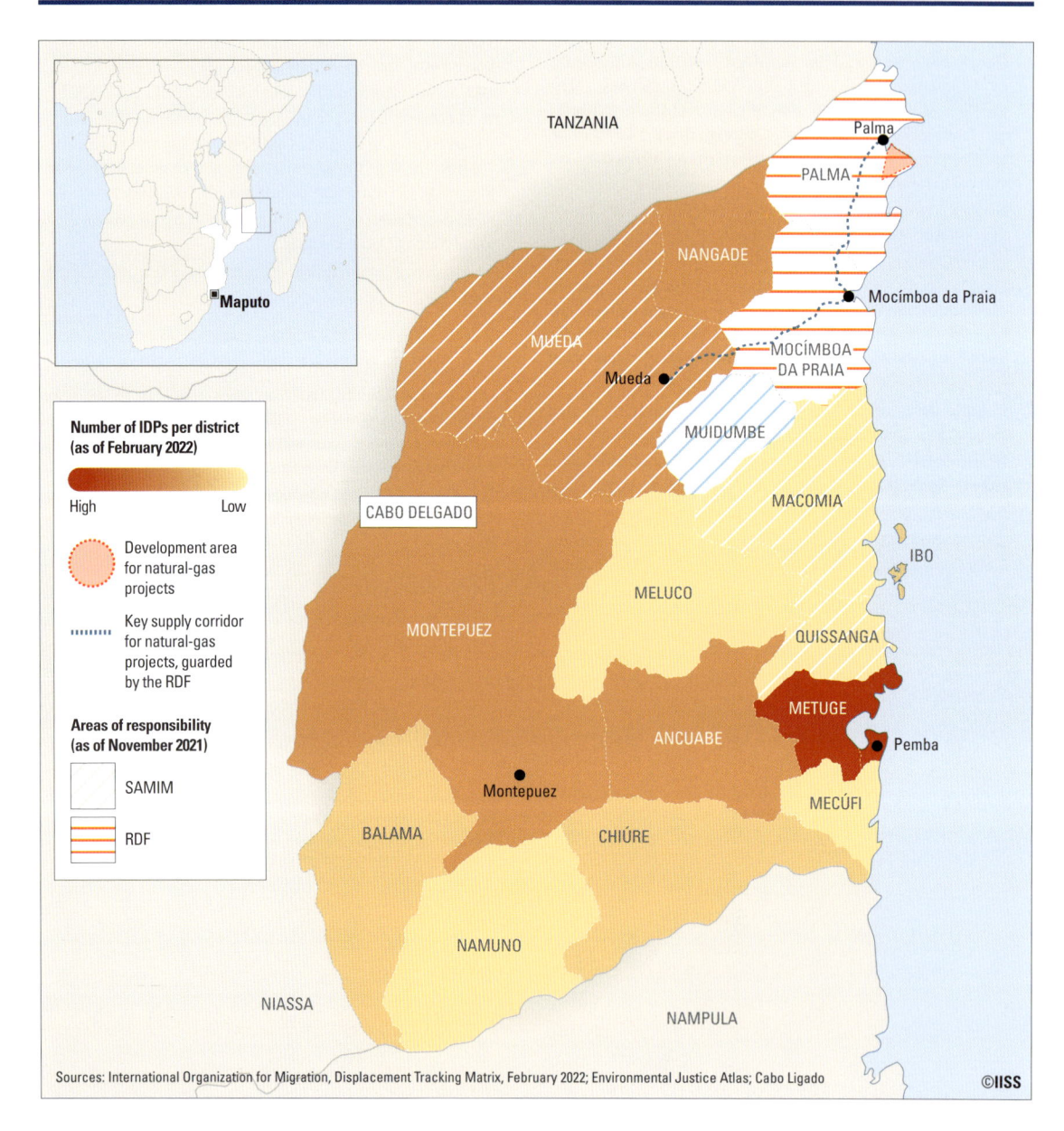

Overview

The insurgency in northern Mozambique arose out of long-standing political and economic grievances held by residents of northeastern Cabo Delgado province against their national government, democratic decline resulting from political elites' attempts to control windfalls from a major natural-gas discovery, and the local insurgency's engagement with other armed groups in the region. Anti-state organising dating back to at least the late 2000s, predominantly among young Muslims in the province's coastal areas, coalesced into the insurgency Ahlu al-Sunnah wal-Jamaah (ASJ, known locally as 'al-Shabaab') in 2017.

Armed Conflict Global Relevance Indicator (ACGRI)

- Incidence: 4
- Human impact: 4
- Geopolitical impact: 24

Mozambique

Key Conflict Statistics

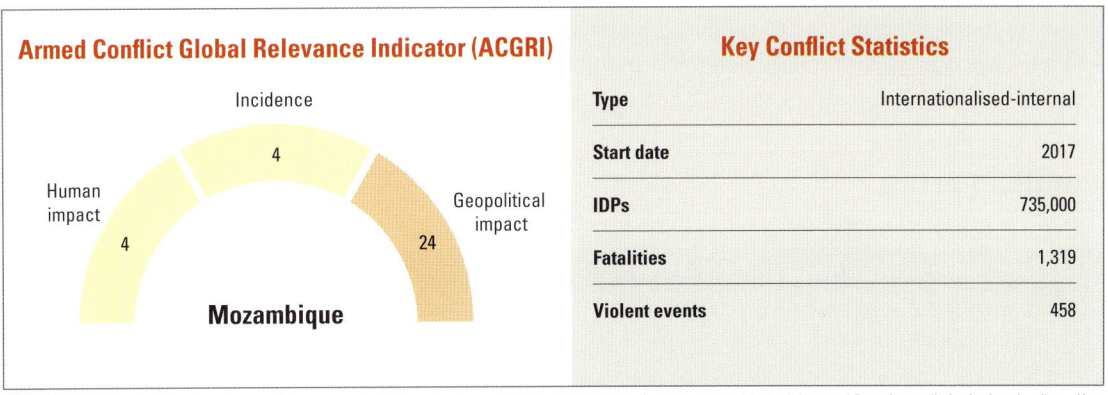

Type	Internationalised-internal
Start date	2017
IDPs	735,000
Fatalities	1,319
Violent events	458

ACGRI pillars: IISS calculation based on multiple sources for 2021 and January–April 2022 (scale: 0–100). See Notes on Methodology and Data Appendix for further details on Key Conflict Statistics.

In October that year, insurgents attacked police stations in Mocímboa da Praia, engaging in a day-long gunfight with local authorities. Using arms gathered from that attack, al-Shabaab slowly expanded, attacking villages and setting up road ambushes mostly in the coastal districts of Mocímboa da Praia, Macomia and Palma. Government security forces proved largely unable to prevent or effectively respond to insurgent attacks and the group developed a modus operandi that emphasised the state's inability to protect civilians. Insurgents frequently arrived in villages unopposed, killed civilians (often those they accused of being involved with the government) and burned houses. This pattern, repeated frequently throughout zones of insurgent influence, led to mass displacement. By December 2021, over 730,000 people were displaced in Mozambique, nearly all as a result of the conflict.[1]

The conflict's first major inflection point came in 2019, when the Islamic State (ISIS) declared the insurgency in Cabo Delgado to be part of the group's Central Africa Province (ISCAP). The shift brought increased international attention to the conflict and a formalisation of the relationship between al-Shabaab and the other wing of ISCAP, the Allied Democratic Forces (ADF) of eastern Democratic Republic of the Congo (DRC). Yet there is little evidence to suggest that the affiliation resulted in either a shift in control to foreign ISIS personnel or a major influx of resources: in the reporting period the group's weaponry continued to be sourced almost exclusively from captured government materiel.[2]

Between 2019 and early 2021, al-Shabaab's range and capabilities steadily increased, reaching high-water marks in April 2020 with an attempt to reach the provincial capital of Pemba[3] and in August 2020 with an offensive that resulted in the capture of Mocímboa da Praia and the sacking of Palma – the town at the heart of the region's liquefied natural gas (LNG) projects – in March 2021. The assault on Palma drew greater international attention, spurring regional actors to consider military intervention and the United States and European Union to offer training assistance to Mozambican security forces. In 2021, however, the insurgency slowed its expansion due to two developments: the arrival of effective foreign intervenors on behalf of the Mozambican government and a decline in the insurgency's ability to acquire resources. Intervention came first from a contingent of Rwandan military and police in July 2021, followed by the Southern African Development Community Standby Force Mission in Mozambique (SAMIM). The former quickly proved its combat effectiveness, retaking Mocímboa da Praia and pushing south to attack insurgent bases in remote parts of the Messalo River valley. SAMIM has been less active offensively but has provided important manpower for an overstretched counter-insurgency effort.

Small groups of insurgents began to surrender in the second half of 2021, reporting severe supply shortages – largely the result of al-Shabaab's widespread displacement strategy.[4] With large swathes of the conflict zone essentially depopulated and most of the insurgents' long-term encampments overrun by August 2021, the group lacked regular access to food and other crucial resources. Yet despite these pressures and increased international support for the Mozambican government, al-Shabaab attacks continued in the reporting period. As the government moves to bring civilians back to their homes in the conflict zone, proximity to civilian commerce and aid will likely alleviate al-Shabaab's supply woes. While in 2021 and early 2022 the insurgency did not expand at a significant pace, the conflict may be far from over. Indeed, in the period under review 411 violent events were registered in Cabo Delgado.[5]

Conflict Parties

The Mozambican Defence Armed Forces (FADM)

Strength: 11,200 active military personnel (air force: 1,000; army: 9,000–10,000; navy: approximately 200).

Areas of operation: Northern (Cabo Delgado and Niassa) and north-central (Manica, Sofala, Tete and Zambezia) Mozambique.

Leadership and structure: Joaquim Rivas Mangrasse (chief of staff) since March 2021. Consists of infantry forces, a navy and an air force. Together with the Police of the Republic of Mozambique (PRM) they form the so-called Defence and Security Forces (FDS).

History: Formed following Mozambique's war of independence in 1975 but reached its current form at the end of the civil war against the Mozambican National Resistance (Renamo) in 1992. The 1992 Rome General Peace Accords provided for the integration of former Renamo fighters into the FADM, a process augmented by a further peace agreement between the government and Renamo signed in 2019.

Objectives: Protect Mozambique's territorial integrity against foreign and domestic enemies. Assist in periods of high civil unrest and insecurity, such as during states of emergency.

Opponents and affiliates/allies:
Opponents: Al-Shabaab, the Renamo Military Junta (RMJ).
Affiliates/allies: PRM, local self-defence militias, SAMIM, Rwanda Defence Force (RDF), Tanzanian armed forces, private military companies, US, Portugal, the EU.

Resources/capabilities: Mozambique's defence budget for 2021 was US$143 million (0.9% of GDP), up from US$131m in 2020.

The Police of the Republic of Mozambique (PRM)

Strength: Unknown.

Areas of operation: Nationwide.

Leadership and structure: Bernardino Rafael (commander-general). Operates under the Ministry of Interior and consists of multi-level police units, including special-operations units that have long been the government's main tool for internal security. In Cabo Delgado, counter-insurgency efforts over the first three years of the conflict were led by the PRM, with support from foreign-owned PMCs to ensure security. Mozambican President Filipe Nyusi turned counter-insurgency leadership over to the FADM in January 2021. Together with the FADM they form the FDS.

History: Replaced the Popular Police force of Mozambique in 1992.

Objectives: Enforce laws and regulations and ensure public security.

Opponents and affiliates/allies:
Opponents: Al-Shabaab, RMJ.
Affiliates/allies: FADM, local self-defence militias, PMCs, SAMIM, RDF.

Resources/capabilities: Unclear.

Ahlu al-Sunnah wal-Jamaah (ASJ), also known as al-Shabaab

Strength: Estimates vary between 350 and 2,000 fighters.[6]

Areas of operation: Cabo Delgado (particularly the districts of Macomia, Meluco, Mocímboa da Praia, Mueda, Muidumbe, Nangade, Palma and Quissanga) and Niassa (particularly the district of Mecula), as well as border areas of Mtwara Region in Tanzania.

Leadership and structure: Abu Yasir Hassan, also known as Abu Qassim; Bonomade Machude Omar. Structure is unclear.

History: Formed between 2015 and 2017; launched its first attack in 2017. In April 2019, ISIS formally recognised it as part of ISCAP.

Objectives: No specific policy programme has been announced. Public statements made by the group indicate its intention to separate Cabo Delgado residents from the Mozambican state, with the ultimate aim of establishing a new state in at least part of Cabo Delgado, drawing on its interpretation of Islamic legal structures.

Opponents and affiliates/allies:
Opponents: FDS, SAMIM, RDF, PMCs, local self-defence militias, Tanzanian armed forces, Mozambican government officials.
Affiliates/allies: ISIS, ADF, ISCAP.

Resources/capabilities: Unclear, but weapons and personnel for the group appear consistently to have been locally sourced.

Rwanda Defence Force (RDF)

Strength: 1,500.

Areas of operation: Palma and Mocímboa da Praia districts, as well as segments of Macomia district, in Cabo Delgado.

Leadership and structure: Innocent Kabandana (maj.-gen.). Structure is unknown, although there are both military and police personnel in the deployment in Mozambique.

History: Deployment began in July 2021.

Objectives: Officially, seeks the defeat of al-Shabaab and the training of Mozambican forces to maintain peace in Cabo Delgado. In practice, it has moved to secure those areas most necessary for work on major natural-gas projects in Cabo Delgado to resume.

Opponents and affiliates/allies:
Opponents: Al-Shabaab.
Affiliates/allies: FDS, local self-defence militias, SAMIM.

Resources/capabilities: Both the Rwandan and Mozambican governments insist that the RDF deployment is funded by the government of Rwanda. The EU is considering backing the Rwandan mission with funding.[7]

Southern African Development Community Standby Force Mission in Mozambique (SAMIM)

Strength: 750.[8]

Areas of operation: Macomia, Muidumbe, Mueda, Nangade and Quissanga districts in Cabo Delgado.

Leadership and structure: Xolani Mankayi (maj.-gen.); Mpho Molomo (civilian chief of mission).
National contingents from Angola, Botswana, DRC, Lesotho, Malawi, South Africa, Tanzania and Zambia operate together in designated areas of operation. Personnel from those countries and other South African Development Community (SADC) members provide logistical support.

History: Established in June 2021 and first deployed the following month.

Objectives: Officially, it has moved from operating under SADC's 'Scenario 6' – intervention to end violent conflict – to working under 'Scenario 5' – a peacekeeping mission.

Opponents and affiliates/allies:
Opponents: Al-Shabaab.
Affiliates/allies: FDS, local self-defence militias, RDF.

Resources/capabilities: SADC has struggled to fund SAMIM and has largely relied on funds and in-kind contributions from member governments. The EU has also appropriated funds to support SAMIM in its shift to Scenario 5.[9]

Conflict Drivers

Geopolitical and geostrategic influences

Armed Islamist organisations in the region:
Between 2012 and 2017, the Tanzanian government tracked and clashed with Islamist organisations that launched attacks against its forces. In the first half of 2017, Tanzanian police undertook operations against these groups, allegedly disappearing over 350 people. Some of those targeted fled south to Mozambique, where they joined with al-Shabaab.[10]

International LNG interests:
While natural-gas investment is primarily driving the conflict through the democratic-decline mechanism, it also incentivises foreign intervention. Since their arrival, Rwandan troops have pursued a strategy seemingly designed to protect LNG developments, first securing the Afungi peninsula where LNG infrastructure is being built and then moving along a crucial supply corridor for projects stretching from Palma to Mueda. This strategy has led many analysts to speculate that Rwanda's intervention has less to do with making Cabo Delgado safe for Mozambicans than with making it safe for energy majors TotalEnergies and ExxonMobil, perhaps in return for financial or political considerations from the French government, which is eager for the TotalEnergies project to go forward.[11]

Political

Democratic decline:
The insurgency arose in the context of democratic decline in the run-up to a natural-gas boom that has yet to materialise. Vast natural-gas reserves were discovered off Cabo Delgado in 2009; ever since, Mozambican politics has revolved around how revenues will be distributed, if and when drilling begins. Attempts to control gas revenues have weakened democratic institutions. Over the 2010s, freedom of the press declined, a massive government fraud went largely unpunished and electoral protections decreased. This trend culminated in the 2019 national elections, which were marred by widespread fraud that was particularly egregious in Cabo Delgado.[12]

Economic and social

Poverty and ethnolinguistic discrimination:
Northern Mozambique faces some of the country's highest poverty rates.[13] However, Cabo Delgado is not unique in that respect – other provinces have similar poverty levels and have not suffered violent conflict. Poverty alone therefore cannot account entirely for the conflict. Another source of grievance is the enduring relationship between politics and ethnolinguistic identity. The ruling Frelimo party is heavily associated in Cabo Delgado with the Makonde ethnic group. Government services are often distributed along ethnolinguistic lines and ethnic minorities, such as the Mwani, often vote with opposition parties. As Frelimo has asserted itself more strongly in the province in the natural-gas era, Kimwani speakers and their political organisations have lost leverage over local government. It is unsurprising, then, that people who have escaped al-Shabaab captivity report that Kimwani speakers are disproportionately represented among the insurgents.[14]

Key Events in 2021–22

POLITICAL EVENTS

12 March 2021
President Nyusi appoints Joaquim Rivas Mangrasse as new chief of staff to succeed Eugénio Mussa, who died of illness in February.

26 March
TotalEnergies evacuates all staff and suspends construction work of LNG facilities at Afungi following al-Shabaab's assault on Palma. Most other companies and public institutions present in the town also evacuate staff to Pemba.

6 April
Dyck Advisory Group (South African private military contractor) contract with Mozambican government expires.

8 April
SADC holds extraordinary summit to discuss coordinated response to the conflict.

27 April
World Bank grants US$100m to Mozambique's Northern Integrated Development Agency for rebuilding Cabo Delgado.

MILITARY/VIOLENT EVENTS

24 March 2021
Al-Shabaab stages a complex assault on Palma, killing many local residents and expatriate workers.

26 March
Al-Shabaab militants ambush a convoy of more than 185 people attempting to flee the Amarula Lodge in Palma.

21–29 June
The Mozambican government claims to have killed 150 insurgents and captured 39 others in the Palma area in a series of operations to reclaim eastern Palma district.

9 July
Rwanda announces a 1,000-troop deployment to Cabo Delgado to support Mozambican counter-insurgency operations.

23 June
SADC announces intention to deploy SAMIM.

26 July–1 August
ISIS claims seven attacks in Cabo Delgado in a week, the first tranche in a string of claims seemingly designed to counter Rwandan and SADC assertions that international deployments are turning the tide of the conflict.

8 August
The RDF and FDS announce that Mocímboa da Praia has been secured by joint Rwandan–Mozambican forces.

12 September
Al-Shabaab deploys its first improvised explosive devices, damaging an RDF vehicle with a modified anti-vehicle landmine.

24–25 September
Rwandan President Paul Kagame visits RDF troops in Mozambique and holds a joint press conference with Nyusi to emphasise their partnership.

15 October
The EU announces it will begin operations on a mission to train a Quick Reaction Force within the Mozambican security services.

25 November
Al-Shabaab launches its first attack outside Cabo Delgado, ambushing a police vehicle in Niassa province.

12 January 2022
SADC leaders agree to extend SAMIM mandate by three months despite funding concerns from member states.

1 January 2022
Al-Shabaab begins raids into Meluco district, a move that threatens to cut off the strategic town of Macomia from the provincial capital.

March
Due to food shortages, al-Shabaab releases over 100 women and children that it had been holding captive.

15–17 March
Al-Shabaab attacks Matemo Island, which had long been a haven for civilians fleeing the conflict.

Conflict Outlook

Political scenarios

The insurgency in Cabo Delgado does not have the capacity to change the political structure of the Mozambican state. However, it has already served as an opportunity for Maputo to increase central-government control over decision-making in the province. The presidentially appointed provincial secretary has explicitly been put in charge of a reconstruction plan released for Cabo Delgado, which aims to spend international-aid money that amounts to several times the pre-conflict government expenditure on the province, sidelining the elected governor.[15] As international donors line up to influence Cabo Delgado's future, the main beneficiaries are likely to be Frelimo leaders in Maputo.

In the meantime, neither al-Shabaab nor the government has shown much interest in negotiating an end to the conflict. This trend is unlikely to change so long as both sides believe they have viable military strategies and the government remains committed to asserting that the insurgency is the work of foreign agitators rather than the result of domestic grievances.

Escalation potential and conflict-related risks

Attacks by al-Shabaab were ongoing in the reporting period but the effectiveness of foreign forces and the resource struggles the group faces have led to predictions that the insurgency will see a sharp decline in the coming year. Such a development is possible but it is much less likely if displaced civilians return to the conflict zone in large numbers, as the Mozambican government is urging them to do. The return of civilians – and the commerce and aid that follow – could serve as a crucial supply base for insurgents, alleviating the self-inflicted pressure from their mass-displacement strategy. If supplies are available for al-Shabaab, the low overall strength of pro-government forces suggests that the insurgents could experience a resurgence rather than a decline.

Strategic implications and global influences

The largest strategic question surrounding the Cabo Delgado conflict concerns the value of the Rwandan and SADC interventions. Rwanda and SADC have both presented their interventions as being fundamentally self-interested, with SADC's goal being to prevent violence from Mozambique spilling over into the rest of southern Africa and Rwanda's aim being to break up the DRC–Mozambique axis of anti-state Islamist violence. If they are successful in bringing the conflict to a close, they will likely become major case studies for African bilateral and multilateral military interventions. If funding or political issues cause them to leave Mozambique before peace can be established, however, it will highlight weaknesses within African regional and continental security structures.

Notes

[1] Internal Displacement Monitoring Center (IDMC), '2021 Internal Displacement', Global Internal Displacement Database.

[2] Calibre Obscura, 'The Weaponry of IS Central Africa (Pt 1): Insurgents in Mozambique', 22 December 2021.

[3] This offensive was turned away largely by airpower provided to the government by Dyck Advisory Group, a South African private military company contracted to support the Mozambican police force's counter-insurgency operations. See 'Cabo Ligado Weekly: 10–17 May 2020', ReliefWeb, 20 May 2020.

[4] Armed Conflict Location & Event Data Project (ACLED), www.acleddata.com.

[5] Ibid.

[6] Eric Morier-Genoud, 'Mozambique's Own Version of Boko Haram Is Tightening Its Deadly Grip', Conversation, 11 June 2018; and Emilia Columbo and Austin C. Doctor, 'Foreign Fighters and the Trajectory of Violence in Northern Mozambique', War on the Rocks, 13 April 2021.

[7] Matthew Hill and Borges Nhammire, 'EU Weighs Funding Rwanda's Fight Against Mozambique Insurgents', Bloomberg, 28 January 2022.

[8] 'Cabo Ligado Weekly: 14–20 February', Cabo Ligado, 23 February 2022.

[9] 'SAMIM to Begin De-escalation to Cabo Delgado', Devdiscourse, 4 April 2022.

[10] Peter Bofin, 'Tanzania and the Political Containment of Terror', Hudson Institute, 26 April 2022.

[11] 'Cabo Ligado Weekly: 7–13 February', Cabo Ligado, 16 February 2022; and Shola Lawal, 'Rwanda Keeps the Peace in Mozambique. Why?', Christian Science Monitor, 20 December 2021.

[12] Mozambique Political Process Bulletin, 'General Elections 15 Oct 2019 Final Report', 26 January 2020.

[13] Baez Ramirez et al., 'Overview – Mozambique Poverty Assessment : Strong But Not Broadly Shared Growth', World Bank, 26 October 2018.

[14] João Feijó, 'Characterization and Social Organization of Machababos from the Discourses of Kidnapped Women', Observatório do Meio Rural, April 2021.

[15] 'Cabo Ligado Monthly: October 2021', Cabo Ligado, 15 November 2021.

SUDAN

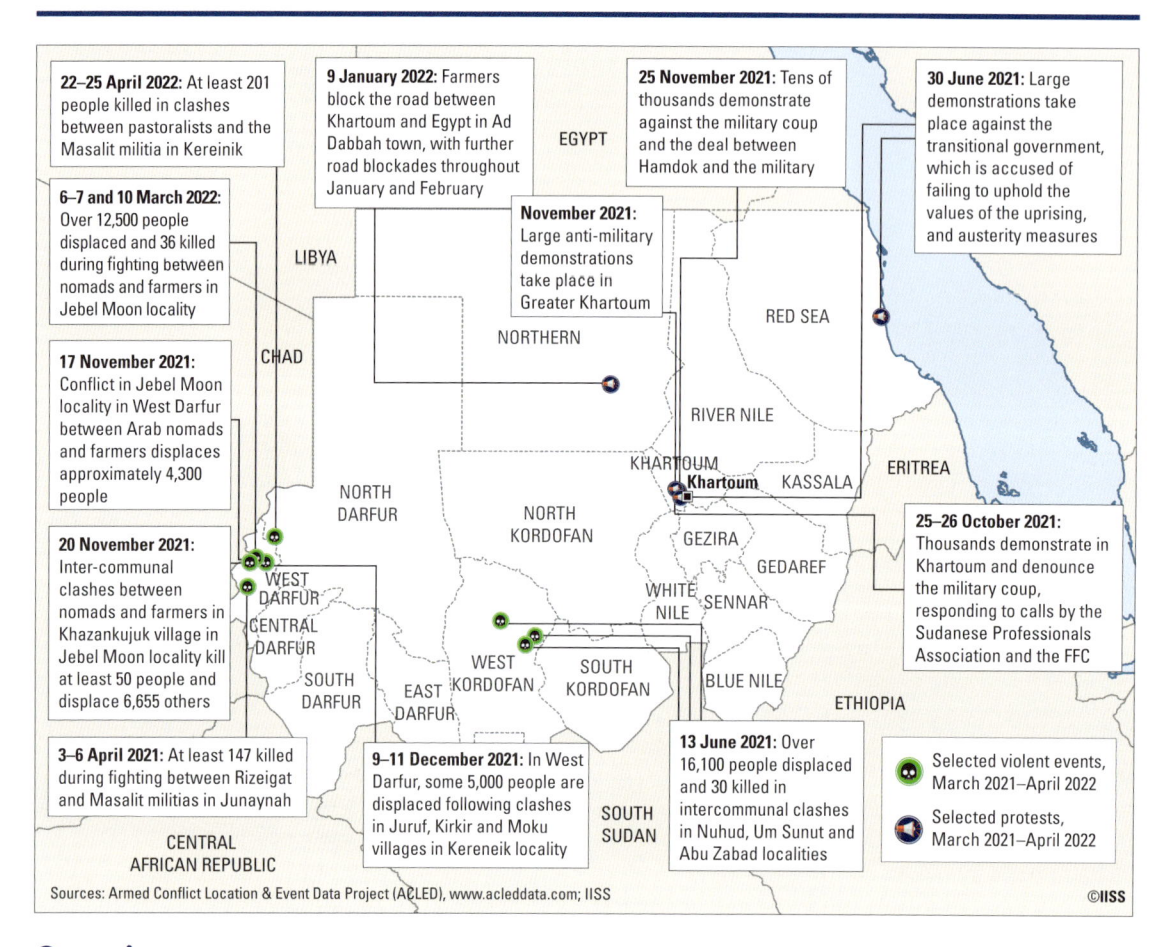

22–25 April 2022: At least 201 people killed in clashes between pastoralists and the Masalit militia in Kereinik

6–7 and 10 March 2022: Over 12,500 people displaced and 36 killed during fighting between nomads and farmers in Jebel Moon locality

17 November 2021: Conflict in Jebel Moon locality in West Darfur between Arab nomads and farmers displaces approximately 4,300 people

20 November 2021: Inter-communal clashes between nomads and farmers in Khazankujuk village in Jebel Moon locality kill at least 50 people and displace 6,655 others

3–6 April 2021: At least 147 killed during fighting between Rizeigat and Masalit militias in Junaynah

9 January 2022: Farmers block the road between Khartoum and Egypt in Ad Dabbah town, with further road blockades throughout January and February

November 2021: Large anti-military demonstrations take place in Greater Khartoum

9–11 December 2021: In West Darfur, some 5,000 people are displaced following clashes in Juruf, Kirkir and Moku villages in Kereneik locality

25 November 2021: Tens of thousands demonstrate against the military coup and the deal between Hamdok and the military

13 June 2021: Over 16,100 people displaced and 30 killed in intercommunal clashes in Nuhud, Um Sunut and Abu Zabad localities

30 June 2021: Large demonstrations take place against the transitional government, which is accused of failing to uphold the values of the uprising, and austerity measures

25–26 October 2021: Thousands demonstrate in Khartoum and denounce the military coup, responding to calls by the Sudanese Professionals Association and the FFC

● Selected violent events, March 2021–April 2022
● Selected protests, March 2021–April 2022

Sources: Armed Conflict Location & Event Data Project (ACLED), www.acleddata.com; IISS

Overview

Darfur and the Two Areas (Blue Nile and South Kordofan states) in Sudan have been affected by conflict since 2003. In Darfur, war broke out that year as armed groups – mainly the Justice and Equality Movement (JEM) and the Sudan Liberation Movement (SLM) – rebelled against the continued marginalisation of the non-Arab population by Omar al-Bashir's government. The conflict, which peaked in 2005, killed and displaced thousands of people as government forces and militias targeted civilians. The conflict in Blue Nile and South Kordofan, fought between government forces and northern affiliates of the Sudan People's Liberation Movement (SPLM), was relatively calm for several years following the signing of the 2005 Comprehensive Peace Agreement. However, it flared up in 2011 when South Sudan achieved independence and Khartoum attempted to disarm combatants that had sided with the south during the civil war. Despite peace efforts and the presence of a joint United Nations–African Union (AU) peacekeeping force (UNAMID), the conflict remained unresolved in 2022.

The persistent violence, coupled with an economic crisis, triggered mass protests across Sudan that ousted Bashir from power in April 2019. Although regime change and the subsequent signing of the Juba Peace Agreement in October 2020 – which involved the transitional government and dominant forces from Darfur and the Two Areas – were seen as promising steps towards finding a durable solution to Sudan's political crisis, tangible benefits failed to materialise.

Armed Conflict Global Relevance Indicator (ACGRI)

Sudan

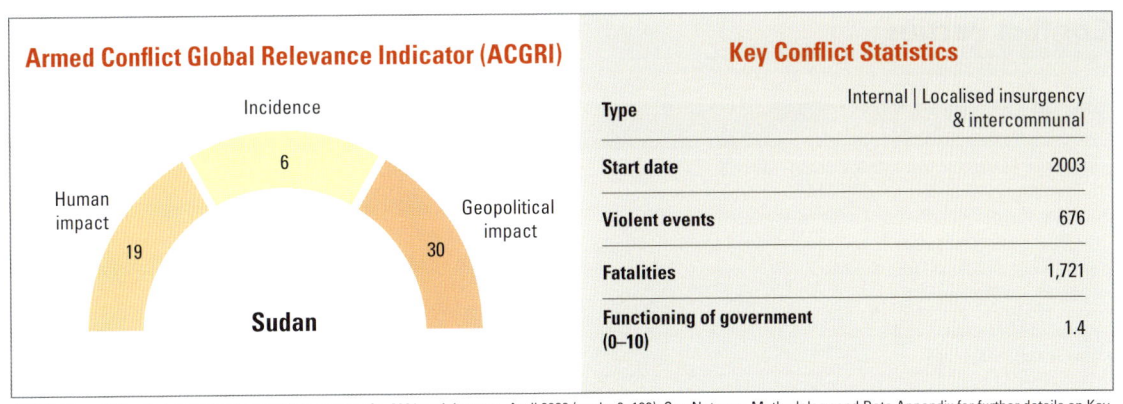

- Incidence: 6
- Human impact: 19
- Geopolitical impact: 30

Key Conflict Statistics

Type	Internal | Localised insurgency & intercommunal
Start date	2003
Violent events	676
Fatalities	1,721
Functioning of government (0–10)	1.4

ACGRI pillars: IISS calculation based on multiple sources for 2021 and January–April 2022 (scale: 0–100). See Notes on Methodology and Data Appendix for further details on Key Conflict Statistics.

In 2021 and early 2022, increased political instability, intercommunal violence, high inflation and surging commodity prices shocked Sudan. In the first half of 2021 the transitional government implemented major economic reforms, lifting fuel subsidies and unifying multiple exchange rates.[1] The transitional government also attempted to implement key elements of the Juba Peace Agreement, including the establishment of the Joint High Military Committee for Security Arrangements and the Permanent Ceasefire Committee, and the appointment of state governors for North Darfur, West Darfur and Blue Nile. Efforts to bring non-signatories to the table continued, as talks resumed with the SPLM–North (SPLM–N) faction led by Abdelaziz al-Hilu in May 2021.

Disagreements between the military and civilian components of the transitional government intensified in the second half of 2021 and on 25 October the Sudanese army took power, arresting then-prime minister Abdalla Hamdok and other officials, mainly from the Forces for Freedom and Change (FFC).[2] Accordingly, Lieutenant-General Abdel Fattah al-Burhan – chairperson of the Sovereign Council and commander of the Sudanese Armed Forces (SAF) – declared a state of emergency, dissolved civilian political institutions and pledged to hold an election in mid-2023. The move prompted mass demonstrations, initially in Khartoum but later nationwide.

International actors, including the AU and UN, condemned the coup; their continued pressure on the military forced Hamdok's release from detention on 21 November 2021 and his reinstatement. However, despite Hamdok's and the international community's efforts to find a political solution to the crisis, political divisions and protests intensified in the following months, leading to the prime minister's resignation on 2 January 2022.

The coup was accompanied by intercommunal conflict. Clashes between armed groups intensified in several parts of the country, particularly in Darfur, South Kordofan and Blue Nile. In Darfur, recurrent intercommunal clashes were reported in various localities (South, North and Central), most of which arose from disputes over land ownership and access to resources. Intermittent fighting between government forces and non-state groups also continued.[3]

From March 2021–April 2022, there were 378 reported violent incidents in Darfur, which resulted in 1,087 fatalities,[4] a 27.7% increase in incidents but a 1.4% decrease in fatalities compared to March 2020–April 2021.[5] Intercommunal clashes in the region spiked in the second half of 2021, particularly following the October coup.[6] As a result, the number of fatalities resulting from violence against civilians increased in the period under review, showing a 30% rise compared to the same period in 2020.[7] In South Kordofan and Blue Nile, the second half of 2021 was also marked by increased intercommunal clashes among local militias, with 52 violent incidents recorded in July–December 2021, an 18% increase from the first half of the year.[8]

These conflicts led to the displacement of hundreds of thousands of people across the country, with more than 430,000 new displacements recorded between January and October 2021.[9] From October 2021–February 2022, over 89,000 people were displaced from their homes in Darfur alone.[10]

The security situation in the eastern part of the country remained volatile during the reporting period, with clashes and continued protests reported in Port Sudan and the Red Sea states as resistance to the Juba Peace Agreement's eastern Sudan track grew.[11]

Conflict Parties

Sudanese Armed Forces (SAF)

Strength: 104,300 active military personnel (100,000 army, 1,300 navy, 3,000 air force), with 40,000 active gendarmerie and paramilitary. These numbers are expected to grow over the next three years as fighters from various non-state armed groups are integrated into the national army as part of the Juba Peace Agreement.

Areas of operation: Across Sudan, including the restive Darfur and Two Areas.

Leadership and structure: Lt-Gen. Abdel Fattah al-Burhan (commander-in-chief and chairman of the governing Sovereignty Council).

History: The SAF is the military apparatus of the country, consisting of the army, navy and air force, as well as the Popular Defence Forces (now changed to Reserve Department) and paramilitary forces, including the Rapid Support Forces (RSF). Under the new government, the SAF is under the command of the Sovereignty Council.

Objectives: Suppress rebel insurgencies and their supporters in Darfur and the Two Areas.

Opponents and affiliates/allies:
Opponents: Several armed groups based in Darfur and the Two Areas.
Affiliates/allies: Allied with other elements of the state security apparatus, including the National Intelligence and Security Service and other paramilitary forces, such as the Reserve Department, the Border Guards and the RSF.

Resources/capabilities: Acquires its military equipment – including ammunition, small arms and armoured vehicles – from a mix of domestic and international manufacturers, financed by the state. Allegedly controls a vast number of commercial companies in several sectors, including gold mining and agricultural production, which provides an additional resource base.

Rapid Support Forces (RSF)

Strength: 30,000–40,000 (estimate).[12]

Areas of operation: Deployed throughout Sudan to stop violence and tribal clashes.

Leadership and structure: Gen. Mohamed Hamdan Dagalo, commonly known as 'Hemeti' (currently deputy chairman of the Sovereignty Council).
The RSF was to integrate into the SAF under the Constitutional Document signed in August 2019.

History: Established in 2013, the RSF is a paramilitary force made up of former militias, mainly the Janjaweed. The force was deployed by Bashir's government in Darfur, South Kordofan and Blue Nile to repress dissent. It has also quelled various protests across the country. Although the RSF was to integrate into the SAF under the Constitutional Document signed in August 2019, the force remains effectively under Dagalo's command. Accused of committing atrocities in Sudan over the years, particularly in Darfur, and during recent violent crackdowns on protesters, including on 3 June 2019 in Khartoum.

Objectives: Provide support and assistance to the SAF and other regular forces in defending the country from internal and external threats. During the Bashir era, the force was deployed in Darfur and the Two Areas to repress dissent.

Opponents and affiliates/allies:
Opponents: Various armed groups across the country.
Affiliates/allies: SAF and local militias; its leader also maintains a strong relationship with the leaders of the United Arab Emirates and Saudi Arabia.

Resources/capabilities: Primarily funded by the state as part of the state security apparatus. Also mobilises resources from its participation in mercenary activities in Libya and Yemen.

Sudan Liberation Movement/Army–Abdel Wahid al-Nur (SLM/A–AW)

Strength: 100–150 fighters, moving between Darfur and Libya.[13]

Areas of operation: Maintains presence in Darfur, controlling pockets of the Jebel Marra Mountains and South Darfur.

Leadership and structure: Abdel Wahid al-Nur (founder and current leader).

History: The SLM/A–AW is an important Darfuri-based rebel movement that has the primary goal of overthrowing the regime in Khartoum. The force emerged from a split within the SLM, drawing support from among the Fur tribe, including internally displaced persons (IDPs) in the Darfur camps. Over the years, the SLM/A–AW's strength has been limited due to strong government offensives, internal splits and fragmentation. The continued clashes between the factions have resulted in tensions and violent incidents in South and Central Darfur areas, including IDP camps. The SLM/A–AW is one of the few groups that did not sign the October 2020 peace agreement. Al-Nur refused support to the Sudan transitional government. Although efforts are under way to bring the movement into the peace process, SLM/A–AW has yet to reach a deal with the government.

Objectives: Previously to overthrow Bashir's regime and address the root causes of conflict (including issues around land rights) in the Darfur region. Following Sudan's political transition, the group remained outside the negotiation process, calling for the prioritisation of security and disarmament of Janjaweed militias as a precondition for peace deals. Al-Nur denounced the October 2021 coup and called for a popular revolution to overthrow the military and restore Hamdok.[14]

Sudan Liberation Movement/Army–Abdel Wahid al-Nur (SLM/A–AW)

Opponents and affiliates/allies:
Opponents: As one of the non-signatories to the Juba Peace Agreement, SLM/A–AW forces engaged in intermittent clashes with government forces throughout the reporting period. Infighting between various factions of the SLM/A–AW also took place in 2021 and early 2022 over issues related to leadership and control of areas.

Resources/capabilities: Bolstered its military capability by acquiring weapons and ammunition using income generated from gold-mining operations and taxation of controlled territories in the Jebel Marra area and IDP camps.

Sudan Liberation Movement/Army–Minni Minnawi (SLM/A–MM)

Strength: Over 1,000 combatants in Libya.[15]

Areas of operation: Active in Libya (and South Sudan) since it lost its foothold in Darfur in 2014.

Leadership and structure: Minni Minnawi (leader).

History: The SLM/A–MM is one of the Darfur-based armed movements that emerged from a split within the SLA in 2006, fighting the Janjaweed militias alleged to have committed atrocities in Darfur. Although the force joined the Sudan Revolutionary Front (SRF) in 2011, it withdrew from the coalition in May 2020.

Objectives: Before 2019, the main objective of the SLM/A–MM was to fight the Janjaweed militias. Following the formation of the transitional government, the group was one of the first to sign the Juba agreement. However, Minnawi was very vocal about the lack of progress in the implementation of the peace deal – mainly the delays in finalising the transitional governance structures and implementation of the security arrangements, as well as appointment of state governors. On 29 April 2021, Minnawi was appointed governor of the Darfur region.

Opponents and affiliates/allies:
Opponents: The SAF, the RSF and the SLM/A–AW.
Affiliates/allies: Affiliated with the SRF (although later broke away from it). Fights alongside the Libyan National Army in Libya.

Resources/capabilities: Generates income from its mercenary activities in Libya.

Justice and Equality Movement (JEM)

Strength: Between 100 and 200 combatants and an additional 100 combatants in South Sudan.[16]

Areas of operation: The JEM is a Darfur-based rebel movement (primarily West Darfur). However, its operations in Darfur have been defunct for years, with its remaining small contingent having relocated to South Sudan. That said, in the reporting period, JEM elements were reported to be involved in clashes with the RSF in North Darfur. The group also maintains a small presence in Blue Nile and South Kordofan.

Leadership and structure: Gibril Ibrahim (chairman since 2012).

History: Established in 2003, the JEM is an Islamist group that used to pursue armed struggle to obtain regime change and reform the political and security dynamics in Darfur. The group is comprised of non-Arab rebels with an Islamist background. Although the group's main operational area is Darfur, it also recruits individuals from other parts of the country (including South Kordofan and Abyei), making it a rebel force with a broad national agenda. The JEM is part of the SRF. The group declared a unilateral cessation of hostilities in February 2019 and took part in peace talks with the transitional government.

Objectives: Until it declared a cessation of hostilities in 2019, JEM aimed to fight marginalisation and bring about regime change and national reform in Sudan (by establishing a federal and democratic government of national unity). The group signed the Juba agreement following the formation of the transitional government and joined the new regime.[17]

Opponents and affiliates/allies:
Affiliates/allies: Joined the SRF in November 2011. It also has close links with the Libyan National Army. JEM has established an alliance with Sudan's military transitional government.[18]

Resources/capabilities: Said to receive financial support for its activities from the South Sudanese and Ugandan governments and its Islamist diaspora supporters. Previously gathered support primarily from the Chadian and Libyan governments.

Sudan People's Liberation Movement/Army–North (SPLM/A–N)

Strength: Unknown.

Areas of operation: The faction led by Abdelaziz al-Hilu is present in parts of Blue Nile and South Kordofan, while the forces of Malik Agar are present in parts of Blue Nile.

Leadership and structure: Malik Agar (SPLM/A–N Agar) and Abdelaziz al-Hilu (SPLM/A–N al-Hilu).

History: The SPLM/A–N is the main rebel force in the Two Areas. It was formed in 2011, originating from the Sudan People's Liberation Movement/Army (SPLM/A). Its main aim was fighting the multilayered marginalisation in South Kordofan and Blue Nile. The group experienced a split in 2017 due to differences in the movement's orientation and ultimate goal. While one group (led by Agar) was more committed to

Sudan People's Liberation Movement/Army–North (SPLM/A–N)

comprehensive reform and peace, the other faction (led by al-Hilu) held demands for self-determination. Clashes between the two factions have been the cause of tension and violence in Blue Nile and South Kordofan, including in IDP camps, resulting in the loss of several lives.

Objectives: The Agar faction is more committed to comprehensive reform and peace and signed the Juba Peace Agreement in October 2020, becoming a member of the Sovereignty Council. The al-Hilu faction demands self-determination and the secularisation of Sudan. The al-Hilu faction signed a joint agreement with Hamdok on 3 September 2020, paving the way for a final peace agreement. The group denounced the October coup and called for the restoration of the transitional government.

Opponents and affiliates/allies:
Opponents: The two factions fight each other, as well as government forces.
Affiliates/allies: Member of the SRF coalition and supported by South Sudan. The al-Hilu faction signed a political declaration with the SLM/A–AW on 29 July.

Resources/capabilities: SPLM/A–N-al-Hilu is said to have heavy weapons, such as tanks and long-range artillery, and armoured vehicles.

Conflict Drivers

Geopolitical and geostrategic influences

Regional disputes:
With the dispute between Ethiopia and Sudan over the al-Fashaga Triangle continuing to simmer, the worsening relationship between Khartoum and Addis Ababa has been a concern for regional security. The two states' border conflict stretches back over a century and escalated into a military confrontation in November 2020. Continued disagreement between the two governments over the Grand Ethiopian Renaissance Dam (GERD) and the civil war in Ethiopia, which has resulted in the flow of refugees into Sudan, further aggravated the al-Fashaga dispute. The relationship deteriorated after Ethiopia rejected Sudan's offer to mediate the conflict in Tigray region, leading Sudan to recall its ambassador.[19] However, the situation is expected to improve as the two nations have agreed to resume talks to resolve the disputed issues.[20]

Political

Marginalisation of the periphery:
In Sudan, the marginalisation of the periphery has been an important source of discontent that has allowed armed movements to proliferate, mainly in Darfur and the Two States. The government's highly militarised approach to addressing community grievances and growing resistance further polarised communities and created much distrust of the government and its security forces, resulting in persistent intercommunal disputes and clashes between government forces and armed groups. While the transitional government was established based on a military–civilian power-sharing agreement, the union was marked by mutual distrust that culminated in a military takeover in October 2021, triggering mass protests across the country by pro-democracy groups.

Economic and social

Worsening economic situation:
Sudan's economy has been on a downward spiral since the significant loss of its main source of national income – oil – following South Sudan's secession in 2011.[21] The resulting high inflation and spike in commodity prices led to popular unrest that unseated Bashir's government. Despite the introduction of some reforms that allowed Sudan to access financial support, the economic crisis deepened following the October coup, which resulted in the suspension of international funding assistance. Erratic rainfall contributed to the worsening economic situation and exacerbated intercommunal clashes and instability – including in the eastern part of the country – resulting in the closure of the main road into Port Sudan in October 2021.

Key Events in 2021–22

POLITICAL EVENTS

29 April 2021
Minni Minnawi is appointed governor of the Darfur region.

9 June
Fuel subsidies are fully lifted.

14 June
Prime minister Hamdok appoints new state governors for North Darfur, West Darfur and Blue Nile.

22 June
Hamdok launches a national initiative called 'The National Crisis and Issues of the Transition – The Way Forward'.

22 June
The customs exchange rate is abolished.

29 June
The IMF and the World Bank approve initial debt relief for Sudan.

30 June
Sovereignty Council Chairperson Burhan establishes the Joint High Military Committee for Security Arrangements, the Permanent Ceasefire Committee and sectoral and area committees.

MILITARY/VIOLENT EVENTS

18 May 2021
A clash between the RSF and SLM/A–AW in Fanga Suk, North Jebel Marra, Central Darfur displaces over 1,000 people.

24 May
Authorities in Port Sudan declare a state of emergency and impose a curfew following violence between the Beja and Nuba tribes that killed five and wounded 13 people.

5 June
Conflict in South Darfur between the Fallata and Ta'isha tribes in Umm Dafog locality kills at least 36 people.

9 June
Attack by Nuba Logan, Kenana and Kawahla tribesmen in South Kordofan leaves 39 people dead and displaces 5,700 others in Kalogi locality.

13 June
Intercommunal clashes in West Kordofan result in 30 fatalities and the displacement of over 16,100 people in Nuhud, Um Sunut and Abu Zabad localities.

3–4 July
Clashes between Tama and Gimr tribes in West Darfur result in the deaths of five people.

11 July
The South Kordofan governor declares a state of emergency across six localities (Abu Kershola, Abu Jibeha, Aleri, Gedir, Habila and Talodi) in response to rising intercommunal violence in the area.

11–18 July
SLM/A–AW elements and the SAF clash in Sortony, North Darfur.

21 September
A coup fails in Khartoum. Sudanese authorities accuse soldiers loyal to former president Bashir of being responsible for the attempt.

25 October
The Sudanese army takes power, detaining Hamdok and other prominent officials.

25 October
The United States announces the suspension of US$700 million in emergency assistance to Sudan.

26 October
Hamdok is released from detention.

27 October
As a result of the coup, World Bank Group pauses all disbursements to Sudan, the AU Peace and Security Council suspends the country's participation in all its activities until the effective restoration of the civilian-led transition and Germany suspends aid to the country.

28 October
The UN Security Council issues a statement calling on Sudanese military authorities to restore the civilian-led transitional government.

11 November
Burhan announces the formation of a reconstituted Sovereign Council.

21 November
Burhan and Hamdok sign an agreement to work together to resolve the constitutional and political crisis in Sudan.

16 December
The deputy chairman of the Sovereign Council and the commander of the RSF announce the suspension of the eastern track of the Juba Peace Agreement.

2 January 2022
Hamdok resigns as prime minister.

3 October
Demonstrators protesting eastern Sudan's marginalisation and poor economic conditions force the closure of Port Sudan.

17 November
Conflict in Jebel Moon locality in West Darfur between Arab nomads and farmers displaces approximately 4,300 people.

20 November
Intercommunal clashes between nomads and farmers in Khazankujuk village in Jebel Moon locality kill at least 50 people and displace 6,655 others.

30 November
Conflict in Abu Jibeha locality displaces approximately 13,600 people.

9–11 December
In West Darfur, some 5,000 people are displaced following clashes in Juruf, Kirkir and Moku villages in Kereneik locality.

10 December
An attack on farmers from Nuba tribe displaces 2,000 people from Kadbar in South Kordofan.

12 December
Over 3,000 people are displaced from Amar Jadeed in South Darfur due to attacks by armed pastoralists.

6–7 and 10 March 2022
Over 12,500 people displaced and 36 killed during fighting between nomads and farmers in Jebel Moon locality.

22–25 April
At least 201 people killed in clashes between pastoralists and the Masalit militia in Kereinik.

Conflict Outlook

Political scenarios
Sudan's security forces play a crucial role in the country's politics; this role became increasingly apparent during the reporting period. While the Burhan-led SAF is in power and the RSF dominates in rural areas,[22] it is important to note that these forces are not coherent entities: as developments in June 2021 and April 2022 highlighted, SAF–RSF tensions carry a high risk of breaking out into violent confrontation.[23] Should that happen again and factional conflicts worsen, the scramble for power could see the country descend into a devastating civil war.[24] For this reason, the relationship between the security and paramilitary forces will have the most impact on Sudan's political and security trajectory in the coming years. Moreover, fragmentation between civilian components of the transitional government and among opposition parties[25] will likely continue in 2022, further complicating Sudan's political challenges.

Escalation potential and conflict-related risks
Sudan has been without a functioning government since the October 2021 coup. Increased intercommunal violence in Darfur and the Two Areas and the continued targeting of civilians have highlighted the government's failure to protect the latter. In the absence of a political solution, the tensions within the various security forces are likely to fuel further intercommunal conflict, pitting communities against each other for political gains. In this regard, the consultation led by the UN Integrated Transition Assistance Mission in Sudan (UNITMAS) on a political process is a promising step forward towards finding an amicable solution to the political deadlock.[26]

Further factors increasing instability include the suspension of international financial assistance, which will significantly affect economic prospects and the humanitarian situation. Increased violence and a prolonged dry season will impact Darfur and the Two Areas in particular. Accordingly, the number of people in Sudan likely to face acute food insecurity by September 2022 will rise to 18m (40% of the total population and double the number from 2021).[27] Sudan's humanitarian challenges are exacerbated by ongoing conflicts in neighbouring countries: in 2021, over 105,511 new refugees entered Sudan, primarily from South Sudan and Ethiopia.[28]

Strategic implications and global influences
The number of international and regional actors involved in Sudan's political and economic affairs has expanded in recent years. Moreover, while the United States' influence has appeared to wane, China's and Russia's influence has increased. Turkey and Egypt strengthened their ties with the military component of the transitional government in the post-Bashir era. These actors, however, often have competing interests that are further complicated by the intricacies of regional and geopolitical dynamics.[29] As such, the ways in which these opposing interests affect the situation in Sudan will have a substantial impact on its future trajectory, especially in the absence of a dominant player with overwhelming influence.

Notes

1. United Nations Security Council (UNSC), 'Situation in the Sudan and the Activities of the United Nations Integrated Transition Assistance Mission in the Sudan – Report of the Secretary-General', 1 September 2021.
2. The Forces for Freedom and Change (FFC) is a political coalition of civilian and rebel groups, including the Sudanese Professionals Association. The FFC drafted a 'Declaration of Freedom and Change', coordinated protests against Bashir and participated in the power-sharing negotiation that led to the establishment of the transitional government.
3. 'State of Emergency Declared in North Darfur Localities to Secure Harvest', ReliefWeb, 20 October 2021.
4. Armed Conflict Location & Event Data Project (ACLED), www.acleddata.com.
5. Ibid.
6. Ibid.
7. Ibid. Between March 2020 and April 2021 there were 205 violent incidents against civilians, which resulted in the deaths of 319 people.
8. Ibid. Between January and June 2021, 44 fatalities were recorded, resulting from 42 incidents of violence against civilians in Blue Nile and South Kordofan.
9. Norwegian Refugee Council, 'Sudan: Continued Conflict in Darfur Causes Massive Displacements', 8 December 2021.
10. UNSC, 'Situation in the Sudan and the Activities of the United Nations Integrated Transition Assistance Mission in the Sudan', 2 March 2022.
11. See, for example, 'Tribal Protesters Block Port Sudan for Fifth Day', Middle East Monitor, 22 September 2021; and 'Sudan: Beja Council to Resume Protests against Eastern Sudan Peace Protocol', All Africa, 16 December 2021.
12. Central Intelligence Agency, 'The World Factbook: Sudan', 4 May 2022.
13. European Asylum Support Office, 'Country of Origin Information: Sudan', 13 October 2020.
14. 'Sudan Rebel Leader Abdelwahid El Nur Calls for "Comprehensive Popular Revolution to Overthrow Coup"', Dabanga, 4 November 2021.
15. European Asylum Support Office, 'Country of Origin Information: Sudan', 13 October 2020.
16. Ibid.
17. 'Girbil Ibrahim Denies Participating in Sudan's Military Coup', Sudan Tribune, 20 February 2022.
18. 'What Next for the Juba Peace Agreement? Evolving Political and Security Dynamics in Darfur: Sudan Rapid Response Update 2', Rift Valley Institute Briefing Paper, XCEPT, January/February 2022.
19. 'Sudan Recalls Ambassador to Ethiopia amid Frayed Ties', Al-Jazeera, 8 August 2021.
20. 'Ethiopia Says Ready for Talks with Sudan over Disputed Issues', Sudan Tribune, 9 February 2022.
21. World Bank, 'Sudan Country Economic Brief', Issue no. 2012-02, December 2012.
22. '10 Conflicts to Worry About in 2022 – Sudan', ACLED, 2022.
23. 'A General, a Warlord and an Economist Vie to Run Sudan', The Economist, 15 July 2021; and 'A Praetorian Transition', Africa Confidential, vol. 63, no. 1, 7 January 2022. See also 'Sudan's PM Calls for Unified Military after Tensions Surface', Reuters, 22 June 2021; and 'Sudanese Army, RSF Clash in West Darfur Capital', Sudan Tribune, 22 April 2022.
24. 'Appetite for Destruction: The Military Counter-revolution in Sudan', ACLED, 2021.
25. On 8 September 2021 the FFC coalition signed a new political declaration of unity, while later that month a parallel, additional faction of the FFC emerged comprising eight signatories to the Juba Peace Agreement, including the JEM and the SLM/A–MM. See 'Situation in the Sudan and the Activities of the United Nations Integrated Transition Assistance Mission in the Sudan – Report of the Secretary-General (S/2021/1008)', ReliefWeb, 8 December 2021.
26. UNSC, 'Report of the Secretary-General on the Situation in Sudan and the Activities of the United Nations Integrated Transition Assistance Mission in the Sudan (S/2022/172)', 28 March 2022.
27. World Food Programme, 'WFP Sudan Country Brief March 2022', March 2022.
28. UNSC, 'Situation in the Sudan and the Activities of the United Nations Integrated Transition Assistance Mission in the Sudan – Report of the Secretary-General', 2 March 2022.
29. Ismail Numan Telci, 'Is Sudan's Crisis the Result of Power Competition in Africa?', Daily Sabah, 5 November 2021.

Regional Outlook

Prospects for peace

After two decades of sustained growth, sub-Saharan Africa's regional outlook has been complicated by the double shock of the coronavirus pandemic and the war in Ukraine (the latter impacting the cost of key commodities, including wheat and gasoline). The outlook is especially concerning for fragile and conflict-affected countries that exhibit more social, economic and environmental vulnerabilities.

Despite this challenging context, some progress on peace and security is possible as a result of the ceasefire and upcoming negotiations between Ethiopia and the Tigray People's Liberation Front (TPLF). Neighbouring Somalia is also in a period of transition. Under newly elected President Hassan Sheikh Mohamud, it is hoped that the country will repair some of its internal fractures. A new phase in the struggle against al-Shabaab is opening with the transition from the African Union Mission in Somalia (AMISOM) – active for 15 years – to the newly established AU Transition Mission in Somalia (ATMIS). It is expected that ATMIS will transfer responsibilities to the Somali National Army by 2024.

Escalation potential and regional spillovers

Most conflict-affected countries experience a chronic deficit of governance in their peripheries (e.g., the CAR and Sudan), suffer from multiple conflicts (e.g., Ethiopia and Nigeria) or from overlapping local insurgencies and transnational jihadism (e.g., Mozambique and Somalia), and feature non-state armed groups (NSAGs) engaged in the exploitation of natural resources and illicit trafficking (e.g., South Sudan). In most conflicts in the region, insurgencies are seemingly content with the status quo, do not seek to take over central power and lack a cohesive agenda. Such features reinforce the protractedness and intractability of armed conflicts on the continent.

The conflicts in the Sahel, the Lake Chad Basin and the Great Lakes Region are fuelled by transnational dynamics: the existence of porous borders among sub-Saharan African countries amplifies the potential for escalation. Radical Islamist groups affiliated to either the Islamic State (ISIS) or al-Qaeda aim to progressively expand violence and their reach. In 2021 and early 2022, violence in the Sahel spread to a number of West Africa's coastal countries. Benin, Côte d'Ivoire and Togo together experienced 19 attacks in 2021 – from none in 2019 – and could see an uptick in attacks and NSAG expansion in the future.

The growing number of inter-state disputes in sub-Saharan Africa is another factor that could contribute to increasing regional instability. Ethiopia and Sudan engaged in deadly border clashes in the al-Fashaga Triangle as late as June 2022 in a dispute that intersects with tensions over the Grand Ethiopian Renaissance Dam – a dynamic that also involves Egypt. In the eastern DRC, tensions between Kinshasa and Kigali have also risen due to the presence of NSAGs in border regions.

Strategic implications and global influences

The war in Ukraine represents a critical inflection point for the sub-Saharan African countries that strengthened relations with Russia in the last decade. The war exacerbates the geopolitical divisions on the continent, with a 'with Russia' versus 'against Russia' dynamic becoming increasingly prominent in relationships among regional countries and in the continent's international relations.

Such divisions were on full display at the UN General Assembly on 2 March 2022, during the vote on Resolution ES–11/1 condemning the war. Globally, 141 countries voted against Russia's actions. African countries' votes were highly polarised when compared with other regions. Of the 47 countries that abstained or did not vote, 23 were from sub-Saharan Africa, while 24 countries in the region voted in favour of the resolution and only one (Eritrea) against it.[1] Of the countries analysed in *The Armed Conflict Survey 2022*, Chad, the DRC, Niger, Nigeria, Rwanda and Somalia voted against Russia. Burkina Faso, Burundi, the CAR, Ethiopia, Mali, Mozambique, South Sudan, Sudan and Uganda decided not to condemn Russia due to their standing relations with Moscow.

The reversal of the rule-based order operated by Russia may exacerbate the trend of external interference in civil wars by fuelling a quest for foreign patrons by sub-Saharan African countries. However, it also gives the continent an opportunity to further strengthen the AU's architecture on peace and security, devise a continental approach to security promotion and increase the organisation's strategic independence on the global scene. Marking the 20th anniversary since its creation, the AU was active on the global scene in early 2022. On the eve of Russia's invasion of Ukraine, the sixth European Union–AU Summit in Brussels reinforced the partnership on peace and development between the two organisations. Furthermore, the visit of Senegal President and AU Chairperson Macky Sall to Moscow in June 2022 to unlock the blockade of Russian and Ukrainian grain exports suggests that African countries have the political will to act multilaterally and aim for strategic independence.

At the time of writing several conflict hotspots in sub-Saharan Africa were in the midst of a humanitarian crisis, including the Horn of Africa, which was experiencing its worst drought in four decades. The situation was compounded by food-price rises and a reduction in exports driven by the war in Ukraine. The Food and Agricultural Organization of the UN reported in June 2022 that more than ten African countries rely on Russia and Ukraine for at least half of their wheat imports.[2] A cohesive multilateral stand by African countries will be necessary to face the food-security emergency in the short term, in addition to armed conflict.

Notes

[1] Emily Ferguson, 'Which Countries Abstained from UN Vote on Ukraine? Result of General Assembly's Resolution on Russia Explained', inews, 3 March 2022.

[2] Food and Agriculture Organization of the UN, 'The Importance of Ukraine and the Russian Federation for Global Agricultural Markets and the Risks Associated with the War in Ukraine', 10 June 2022, p. 11.

5 Asia

Regional Analysis	322	Myanmar	350	Thailand	382
Conflict Reports		**Conflict Summaries**		Philippines	390
Afghanistan	326	Pakistan	362	**Regional Outlook**	399
Kashmir	338	India	372		

Taliban members attend a ceremony to raise the Taliban flag in Kabul, 31 March 2022

Overview

Across the sub-regions of South, Southeast and East Asia, protracted armed conflicts show little sign of ending. Notably, regime changes in 2021 in Afghanistan and Myanmar impacted the trajectories of two of the region's most intractable armed conflicts.

In August 2021, the Afghan Taliban seized power in Kabul following a military victory over the NATO-backed Afghan National Defence and Security Forces (ANDSF), marking the end of a 20-year US-led foreign intervention and leaving the country's future stability deeply uncertain. In Myanmar, the junta took power via a coup in Naypyidaw in February 2021. An ensuing violent crackdown targeted pro-democracy protesters, with the latter evolving into an anti-junta insurgency, adding further complex layers of violence to Myanmar's existing internal armed conflicts. Asia's other internal armed conflicts have also continued unabated with no prospects for durable resolutions.

India–Pakistan tensions remain acute over Kashmir, where violence has persisted. Moreover, inter-state tensions that threaten to escalate into full-blown wars are a growing security concern in Asia, notably in relation to US–China tensions over Taiwan, as well as the persistent state of instability on the Korean Peninsula resulting from North Korean missile-testing activities.

In Focus: China's Role in Asia's Armed Conflicts

Although China is not a direct combatant in Asia's active armed conflicts, its influence is felt through the stature of its economy and its regional presence. Beijing prefers to deal bilaterally with conflict-affected countries through diplomatic and economic engagements to further its national objectives – rather than to decisively influence the course of the conflicts – while offering only limited support to the international conflict responses of multilateral organisations, such as the United Nations.

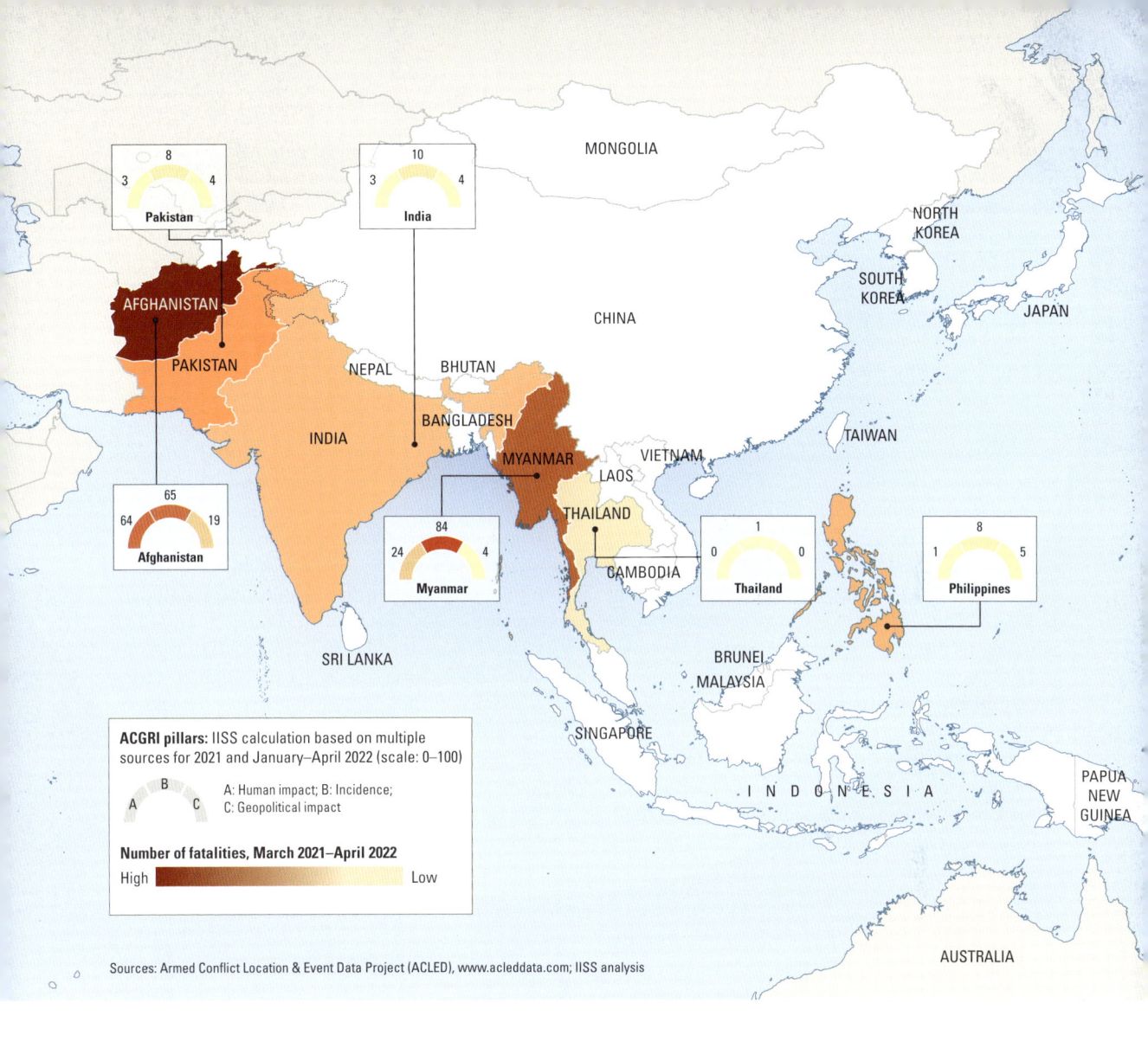

Countering terrorism in Afghanistan, Pakistan and Central Asia

China's primary security concern is to counter terrorism threats emanating from the region's conflicts, which feature Islamist armed groups that could inspire or enable separatist terrorism in China's restive Xinjiang province. The Taliban's victory in Afghanistan was especially concerning for China because it involved the overthrow of a government following decades of struggle – a message that could inspire Xinjiang's would-be Uighur separatists, whose activities Beijing has sought to suppress. China shares borders with Afghanistan and Pakistan and has tried to monitor and influence the security situations in both countries to avoid terrorism spillover into its territory.

In Afghanistan, Beijing reached out to the Taliban soon after the group came to power to foster direct relations. However, it did not recognise the Taliban as the country's legitimate government. Following its first high-level public meeting with the group in July 2021, Beijing appointed experienced diplomat Yue Xiaoyong as China's special envoy to Afghanistan to work with Pakistan and the Taliban to ensure stability in the country.

China conducts counter-terrorism exercises with Shanghai Cooperation Organisation member states. In September 2021 it participated in *Peace Mission 2021* in Donguz, Russia, which involved 4,000 personnel drawn from China, India, Kazakhstan, Kyrgyzstan, Pakistan, Russia, Tajikistan and Uzbekistan.[1] Also in September, China and Pakistan held a bilateral exercise, the *Joint Anti-Terrorist Exercise* (JATE), in Khyber Pakhtunkhwa (KP), Pakistan.

Central Asia is also of interest to China's regional counter-terrorism efforts given the proximity of Central Asian states to Afghanistan and the activities of local Islamist armed groups. In Tajikistan, China has a military outpost in Shaymak, near the Wakhan Corridor in Afghanistan, and is reportedly funding a new paramilitary base in Ishkashim. However, Beijing and Dushanbe have not acknowledged the existence of either location.[2] China is vigilant of the activities of the East Turkestan Islamic Movement and has requested that the Taliban clamp down on the group in Afghanistan.

BRI and arms-sales priorities in Myanmar and Pakistan

China's involvement in the region's conflicts tends to be greater where Belt and Road Initiative (BRI) projects – and the Chinese nationals working on them – are endangered, such as in Pakistan and Myanmar. Another motivation for China's involvement is its arms sales to selected conflict-affected countries in the region, which Beijing uses to enhance its bilateral influence.

China engages with Pakistan to reduce security threats to the China–Pakistan Economic Corridor, which is a key BRI project. While it tends to rely on Pakistan's security forces to guard Chinese nationals and infrastructure projects in the country, on some occasions China has intervened directly. After nine Chinese nationals were killed in a Tehrik-e-Taliban Pakistan (TTP) attack at the Dasu hydropower project in KP in July 2021, Beijing condemned the attack and dispatched an investigation team.[3] Another attack on Chinese nationals took place in Gwadar Port in August 2021, which was claimed by the Balochistan Liberation Army (BLA).[4] The BLA has declared its intent to target local Chinese-funded projects; further attacks by the group and TTP on Chinese interests in Pakistan could prompt a direct Chinese intervention in support of Pakistani forces.

China has further enhanced its security relationship with Pakistan via arms sales. Between

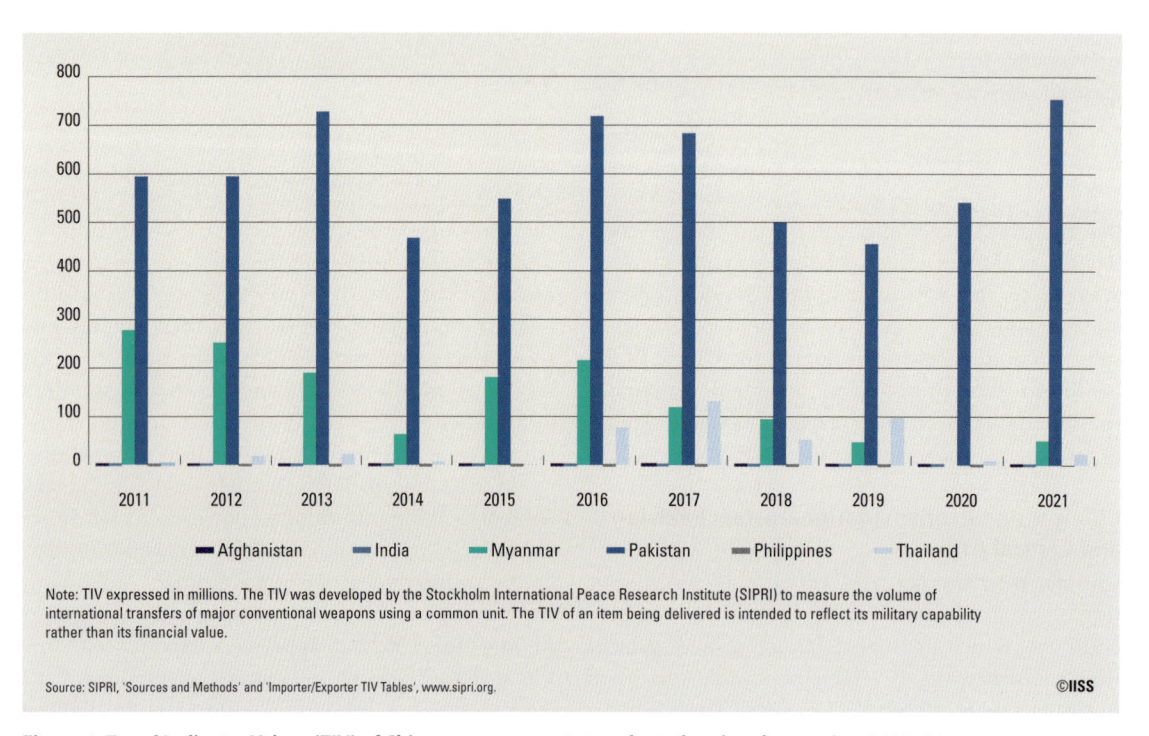

Figure 1: Trend Indicator Values (TIV) of Chinese arms exports to selected regional countries, 2011–21

2016 and 2020, 38% of China's arms exports went to Pakistan.[5] The Kashmir conflict provides another point of influence for Beijing; China's diplomatic backing of Pakistan's position has become more steadfast since August 2019, when the Indian government revoked the special autonomous status of Jammu and Kashmir. However, China and Pakistan failed to bring the matter to the UN Security Council and instead issued a joint statement opposing 'any unilateral actions that complicate the situation' in Kashmir.[6] The combination of Chinese investments, arms sales and diplomatic cooperation has ensured that Beijing's link with Islamabad remains one of its most strategically important relationships in Asia.

China has been accepting of Myanmar's military junta, backing it internationally, providing aid and increasing its economic investments in BRI projects, while other states and businesses withdrew their support. Arms imports from China accounted for approximately 50% of Myanmar's total arms imports from 2014–19.[7] Since the coup, additional Chinese troops have been deployed at Jiegao, a Chinese town near Myanmar, to guard the Kyaukpyu pipeline, which runs from China's Yunnan province via Myanmar to the Bay of Bengal.[8] In August 2021, China donated over US$6 million to the junta under the Lancang–Mekong Cooperation framework to fund development projects.[9] In December, China transferred a former People's Liberation Army Navy (PLAN) diesel-electric attack submarine to Myanmar.

China as an armed-conflict combatant

In recent years, the closest China has come to becoming a warring party in an armed conflict was in May 2020 when Chinese and Indian soldiers clashed in Galwan Valley. Since then, the foreign ministers of China and India have issued a Five-Point Consensus for disengagement and dialogue and there have been talks between the PLA and the Indian Army to calm the situation. Going forward, China may find that its own regional antagonisms, including the border dispute with India, flare up and transform it into an active-combatant country – a role that China has not played in an Asian armed conflict since its war with Vietnam in 1979. The likelihood of China launching new military interventions in Asia would increase if conflict in Myanmar or Afghanistan intensified such that the security of China's border was seriously threatened. Moreover, an increase in terrorist and insurgent attacks in Pakistan against Chinese nationals and infrastructure projects could prompt Beijing to consider direct intervention alongside Pakistan's security forces.

Notes

[1] China sent 550 troops. See 'Peace Mission-2021: CSO Countries Involved in Joint Drills', Warsaw Institute, 20 September 2021; and 'Russian Federation Announces Peace Mission-2021', Joint Forces, 19 July 2021.

[2] Catherine Putz, 'China's Security Infrastructure Continues to Grow in Tajikistan', *Diplomat*, 27 October 2021.

[3] 'Pakistan Releases Findings of Dasu Terrorist Attack', ARY News, 12 August 2021.

[4] Embassy of the People's Republic of China in the Islamic Republic of Pakistan, 'Statement by the Chinese Embassy in Pakistan on the Suicide Attack on the Gwadar Eastbay Expressway Project', 20 August 2021.

[5] Maryann Xue, 'China's Arms Trade: Which Countries Does It Buy From and Sell To?', *South China Morning Post*, 4 July 2021.

[6] State Council of the People's Republic of China, 'Full Text of China–Pakistan Joint Statement', 18 March 2020.

[7] Data from the Stockholm International Peace Research Institute (SIPRI), quoted in Marwaan Macan-Markar, 'Myanmar Embraces Russian Arms to Offset China's Influence', Nikkei Asia, 9 February 2021.

[8] 'Chinese Troops Gather on Myanmar's Border to "Protect Pipelines"', *Irrawaddy*, 1 April 2021.

[9] Sebastian Strangio, 'China Announces Aid Dispersal to Myanmar's Military Junta', *Diplomat*, 11 August 2021.

AFGHANISTAN

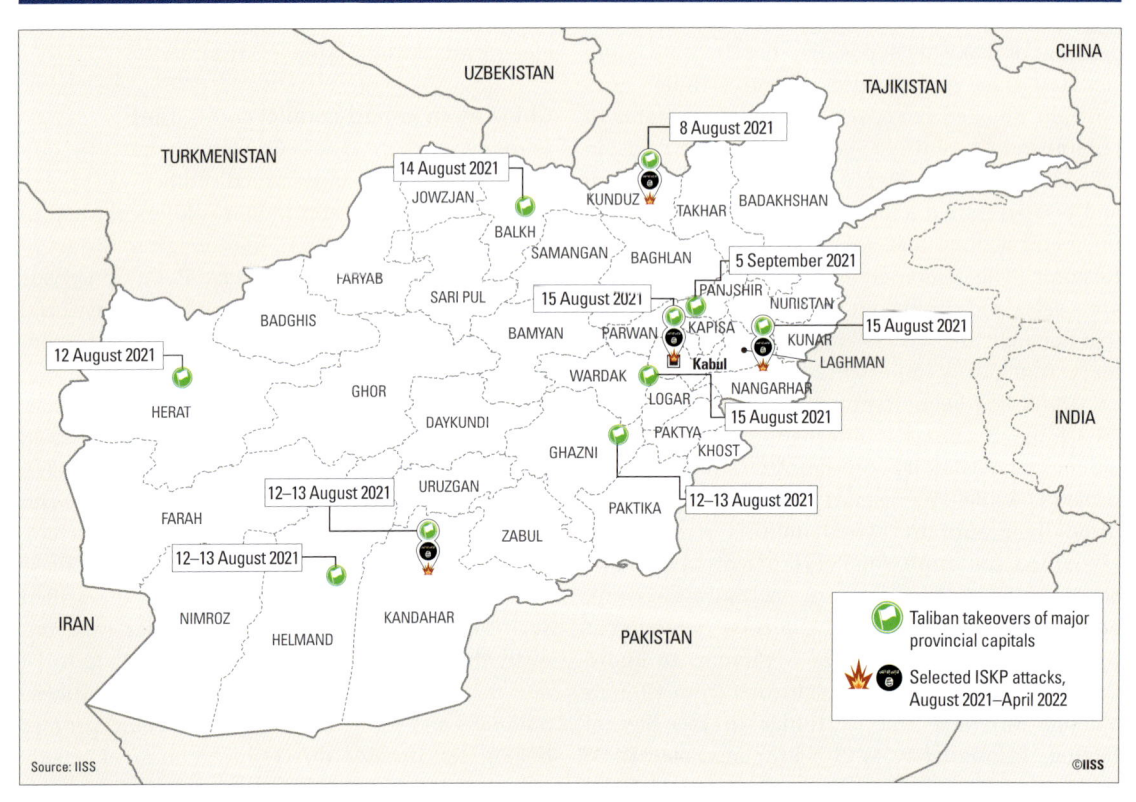

Overview

The conflict in Afghanistan has endured for over four decades and seen multiple phases, including the 1979–89 Soviet–Afghan War, the 1992–96 Afghan civil war (during which the Taliban consolidated its power) and the United States' invasion of Afghanistan in October 2001, followed by nearly 20 years of fighting between the Taliban, Afghan security forces and a US-led international coalition.

The US invasion initially aimed to destroy al-Qaeda. The objective later grew to include the overthrow of the Taliban regime once its then-leader Mullah Omar refused to hand over al-Qaeda founder Osama bin Laden to the US. In November 2001, the US-led operation removed the Taliban from power via a combination of special forces, conventional units and a strategic partnership with the Northern Alliance (an anti-Taliban group formed in 1996). Consequently, the Taliban's structure and leadership rapidly dissipated. In December 2001, the Bonn Conference laid the groundwork for a new Afghan government led by Hamid Karzai and prompted the United Nations Security Council to establish the International Security Assistance Force (ISAF) to train and aid the newly formed Afghan National Defence and Security Forces (ANDSF).

While the first three years post-invasion were relatively stable, the low US security presence – which comprised most of the ISAF – and the minimally capable ANDSF created a situation where local strongmen (sometimes backed by US forces) were able to fill the power vacuum. This context also enabled the Taliban to reorganise in Pakistan and Afghanistan. By 2005, Taliban fighters had started to conduct more significant operations in Afghanistan, which intensified year-on-year up to 2010. In response, coalition forces increased troop numbers and expanded their presence throughout the country.

The number of US security personnel deployed in Afghanistan peaked at more than 100,000 in 2010–11 as part of then-president Barack Obama's surge strategy. It fell to approximately 9,000 in 2016.[1]

Armed Conflict Global Relevance Indicator (ACGRI)

- Incidence: 65
- Human impact: 64
- Geopolitical impact: 19

Afghanistan

Key Conflict Statistics

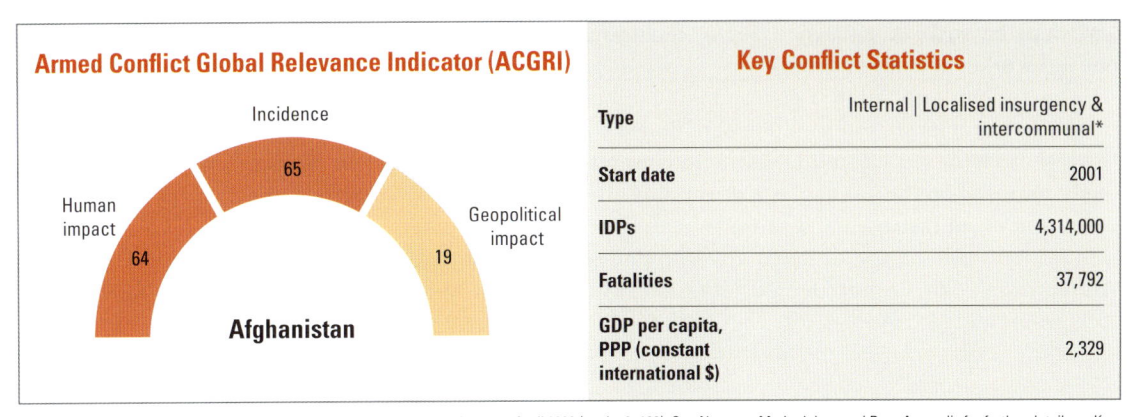

Type	Internal | Localised insurgency & intercommunal*
Start date	2001
IDPs	4,314,000
Fatalities	37,792
GDP per capita, PPP (constant international $)	2,329

ACGRI pillars: IISS calculation based on multiple sources for 2021 and January–April 2022 (scale: 0–100). See Notes on Methodology and Data Appendix for further details on Key Conflict Statistics. *The conflict type was internationalised-internal until 1 September 2021.

In 2014, foreign forces' offensive combat operations ostensibly concluded. The ANDSF took the lead in operations against the Taliban but was still heavily reliant on US air support, while US ground troops occasionally re-entered combat to support ANDSF units. The Taliban gradually contested more districts as the ANDSF lost ground. After several years of Taliban territorial gains and amid US intervention fatigue, president Donald Trump appointed Ambassador Zalmay Khalilzad as the US Special Representative for Afghanistan Reconciliation in September 2018 to negotiate an agreement with the Taliban. The primary goal of the negotiations was to enable an acceptable US military withdrawal.

On 29 February 2020, the Taliban and the US signed the Agreement for Bringing Peace to Afghanistan ('US–Taliban agreement'). It called for the release of up to 5,000 Taliban prisoners by the Afghan government, the eventual removal of US and UN sanctions on the Taliban and the gradual reduction of US forces towards a full withdrawal by May 2021. In exchange, the Taliban would participate in intra-Afghan negotiations with the Kabul government, work towards a ceasefire and a political settlement and prevent any group (including al-Qaeda) from using Afghan soil to threaten the security of the US and its allies. Intra-Afghan negotiations began six months late and produced no results. US President Joe Biden inherited the agreement. Announcing in April 2021 that the US military would begin its final withdrawal in May,[2] Biden claimed that the military strategy had failed and that it was long past time for US troops to return home, in spite of the Taliban failing to fulfil most of its obligations.

The Taliban made rapid gains throughout July in northern Afghanistan, taking dozens of districts. Some poorly supplied ANDSF outposts fell with little to no resistance and elite units became increasingly overstretched. The Taliban engaged in information operations to demoralise the ANDSF rank and file, spreading images of surrendering units.[3] It also used local elders and power brokers to facilitate surrenders. In August, the Taliban rapidly seized border posts and provincial capitals, eventually capturing major cities, including Herat, which also led to the arrest of prominent militia leader Ismail Khan.

On 15 August, the Taliban entered Kabul without a fight and then-president Ashraf Ghani and other senior Afghan officials fled. Prominent militia leaders Ata Noor and Abdul Rashid Dostum also fled the country following fighting in the north.[4] A potential meeting between remaining Afghan leaders and the Taliban to establish an interim government never occurred and the Taliban declared an emirate. Throughout August, the US deployed approximately 6,000 troops to Kabul's Hamid Karzai International Airport (along with troops from other NATO countries) to facilitate the mass evacuation of remaining US citizens, former interpreters and Afghan citizens admitted on humanitarian grounds.[5] On 26 August, an Islamic State Khorasan Province (ISKP) suicide bomber killed 13 US service members and at least 170 Afghans. It was the first loss of US troops since the US–Taliban agreement was signed. On 29 August, fearing another ISKP attack, the US launched a drone strike on a car that it claimed was filled with explosives headed for Kabul's airport. Further investigations revealed no such explosives existed and that the strike killed ten civilians, including one aid worker and seven children.

The Taliban appointed a government cabinet that included at least 15 individuals sanctioned by the UN as terrorists. US and UN sanctions previously imposed on the Taliban as a terrorist group operating as an insurgency followed the Taliban into its new role as the de facto government of Afghanistan – an unprecedented situation. The foreign-exchange reserves of Da Afghanistan Bank (Afghanistan's central bank) were also frozen in the US and Europe. Afghanistan's pre-existing economic troubles were compounded by the chilling effect of sanctions, the flight of US dollars, frozen foreign-exchange reserves, drought in some parts of the country and a reduction in outside investment. Moreover, following the Taliban takeover Afghanistan still faced ISKP attacks and fighting between the Taliban and resistance groups.

Conflict Parties

Afghan National Defence and Security Forces (ANDSF) (defunct as of 15 August 2021)

Strength: In April 2021, Combined Security Transition Command–Afghanistan reported that there were 300,699 ANDSF personnel (182,071 with the Ministry of Defense, 118,628 with the Ministry of Interior) biometrically enrolled and eligible for pay in the Afghan Personnel and Pay System.[6]

Areas of operation: Operated in all 34 provinces but with more limited freedom of movement in areas then controlled or contested by the Taliban.

Leadership: Under the command of the then Islamic Republic of Afghanistan. President Ashraf Ghani (commander-in-chief), Asadullah Khalid (defence minister) and Gen. Mohammad Yasin Zia (chief of general staff).

Structure: Organised under the defence minister and chief of general staff with five regional commands (or corps) – the 201st in Kabul, the 203rd in Gardez, the 205th in Kandahar, the 207th in Herat and the 209th in Mazar-e-Sharif. Separate commands existed for the Kabul military training centre, the military academy and the general staff college.

History: Established in 2002 following the collapse of the Taliban regime. Initial growth was slow, with only 27,000 troops by 2005, but increased after the Taliban resurgence. New commandos began training and entered service in 2007. Took full responsibility for security in Afghanistan in 2015 after the official end of combat operations by coalition forces in 2014. In practice, the ANDSF was still highly dependent on foreign aid, training and direct and indirect operational support until its demise.

Objectives: (Aspired to) control all districts within Afghanistan without any challenge from non-state actors.

Opponents: Taliban, ISKP and other anti-government forces.

Affiliates/allies: Relied on US support through the 2014 Bilateral Security Agreement.

Resources/capabilities: The US spent an estimated US$3.1 billion directly on Afghan security forces in 2021 and requested US$3.3bn for 2022 prior to their collapse.[7] The ANDSF had 174 aircraft (including fixed-wing platforms and helicopters), artillery, mortars, armoured vehicles and drones. However, it lacked the human resources needed to maintain and operate the aircraft and was therefore reliant upon support from foreign advisers.[8]

The Taliban (insurgency from October 2001–August 2021; Islamic Emirate of Afghanistan or de facto government of Afghanistan post-August 2021)

Strength: 165,000 (75,000 full-time fighters and 90,000 local militia). 110,000 fighters claimed by Acting Minister of Defense Muhammad Yaqoob in April 2022 but it is unclear if this number is in addition to the core 60,000 Taliban fighters estimated to have existed during the insurgency.[9]

Areas of operation: Deployed throughout Afghanistan with kinetic activity concentrated in Baghlan, Kabul, Nangarhar, Panjshir and along the border with Pakistan.

Leadership: Mullah Haibatullah Akhundzada (emir); Mohammad Yaqoob (acting defence minister); Mullah Fazal Mazloom (deputy defence minister);[10] Haji Mali Khan (deputy chief of army staff);[11] Amanuddin Mansour (commander of the air force);[12] Abdul Haq Wasiq (intelligence director). Sirajuddin Haqqani (interior minister) maintains significant influence over security matters and effectively controls security in Kabul. During the insurgency era, it maintained 'shadow governments' in the districts it controlled throughout the country and named shadow provincial governors in all 34 provinces. Since the Taliban takeover, these offices have been re-staffed and held in the open.

Structure: A mix of formal ministries and informal insurgency-era units in the process of shifting towards a formal military structure. The organisation is historically polycentric but power is increasingly concentrated in the hands of Mullah Haibatullah Akhundzada. During the insurgency era, the Taliban consisted of the leader (emir) and deputy leaders,

The Taliban (insurgency from October 2001–August 2021; Islamic Emirate of Afghanistan or de facto government of Afghanistan post-August 2021)

executive offices, a shura (leadership council) and 12 commissions covering military affairs, political affairs, economic affairs, education, prisoners, martyrs and disabled members, as well as the Council of Ulema (Council of Senior Religious Scholars).

History: The Taliban (translated as 'the students') movement began in the Afghan refugee camps of Pakistan following the 1979 Soviet invasion and occupation of Afghanistan. Under Mullah Mohammad Omar, the group entered the Afghan civil war in 1994 and captured Kandahar city. Taliban fighters quickly conquered other areas of Afghanistan and the group officially ruled as an Islamic emirate from 1996–2001, though it never controlled the whole country. The Taliban seized control over the entire country in August 2021 following a 20-year insurgency.

Objectives: After achieving its primary goals of expelling foreign troops and overthrowing the previous Afghan government (considered a foreign puppet), the Taliban has focused on maintaining territorial control and security, disarming all non-Taliban citizens and fighting ISKP. Some evidence also suggests that the Taliban is prioritising arrests and executions of former members of the ANDSF and National Directorate of Security.

Opponents: During the insurgency era, its primary opponents were US- and NATO-led forces, the Afghan government and ISKP. Since August 2021, the Taliban has targeted ISKP, coalescing resistance groups throughout Afghanistan and, in some isolated cases, the Pakistan Armed Forces along the shared border with Pakistan.

Affiliates/allies: Has connections of varying formality with non-state armed groups in South Asia, including al-Qaeda, the Islamic Movement of Uzbekistan and the Tehrik-e-Taliban Pakistan (TTP).

Resources/capabilities: Estimates of the Taliban's annual revenue before it took control of the country range from US$300 million to US$1.6bn.[13] Much of this revenue comes from the group's involvement in the drug trade, extortion practices or from taxes collected in the territory it controls. However, projected figures for the group's revenue vary, especially that which is gained from the drug trade.[14] The Taliban has local and expeditionary units that use small arms, mortars, improvised explosive devices (IEDs), vehicle-borne improvised explosive devices (VBIEDs) and unencrypted communications equipment. It also benefits from equipment seized from the ANDSF, including night-vision goggles, armoured vehicles and rotary-wing aircraft. The Taliban now collects revenue as the de facto government of Afghanistan through cross-border trade.

Islamic State Khorasan Province (ISKP)

Strength: 1,500–4,000 in Afghanistan (estimate).[15]

Areas of operation: Primarily confined to Nangarhar province in eastern Afghanistan but able to carry out complex attacks in Kabul and present in nearly all provinces.[16]

Leadership: Led by Sanaullah Ghafari (alias 'Shahab al-Muhajir'). The original leader, Hafiz Saeed Khan (previously head of the TTP Orakzai faction), was killed in a US drone strike in July 2016. Successive leaders were also either killed in US strikes or arrested.[17]

Structure: An Islamist militant organisation, formally affiliated with the larger Islamic State (ISIS), of which it is the Central and South Asia branch.

History: Formed and pledged loyalty to then-ISIS leader Abu Bakr al-Baghdadi in October 2014. The initial membership primarily comprised disgruntled and estranged TTP members.

Objectives: Similar to ISIS, ISKP maintains both local and global ambitions to establish a caliphate in Central and South Asia to be governed under a strict Islamic system, modelled after the group's own interpretation of a caliphate.

Opponents: Mainly focuses on fighting the de facto Taliban government and attacking the Hazara community.

Affiliates/allies: ISIS.

Resources/capabilities: Since its founding in 2014, ISIS has invested in improving ISKP's organisation and capabilities. However, with the decline of its territory in Iraq and Syria, ISIS has fewer resources to invest in foreign networks and therefore its investment in the group has declined. ISKP relies on small arms, IEDs and VBIEDs.

Al-Qaeda

Strength: Several dozen to 500 fighters in Afghanistan.[18]

Areas of operation: The mountainous region between Afghanistan and Pakistan. Al-Qaeda is resident in at least 15 Afghan provinces, primarily in the eastern, southern and southeastern regions.[19]

Leadership: Led by Ayman al-Zawahiri since 2011.

Structure: Below Zawahiri and his immediate advisers, maintains a Shura Council and committees for communications, finance and military operations.

History: Created as a broad alliance structure by Arab fighters who travelled to Afghanistan and Pakistan to fight against the Soviet invasion in the 1980s. The organisation (officially formed in 1988) was initially led by Osama bin Laden, who envisioned it as a base for a global jihadist movement to train operatives and to support other jihadist organisations. The group was responsible for several high-profile terrorist attacks against the US, including the 9/11 attacks. Bin Laden was killed in a US special-operations raid in Abbottabad, Pakistan in 2011.

Al-Qaeda

Objectives: Focus has always been to fight the 'far enemy' (the West) and particularly the US, which supports current Middle Eastern regimes, and bring about Islamist governance in the Muslim world. Its affiliate groups often pursue local objectives independent of the goals and strategy of the central organisation.

Opponents: US and other Western countries supporting non-Islamic regimes.

Affiliates/allies: Currently maintains an affiliation with five groups: al-Qaeda in the Islamic Maghreb (AQIM) in North Africa, al-Qaeda in the Arabian Peninsula (AQAP) in Yemen, al-Qaeda in the Indian Subcontinent (AQIS) in South Asia, Jabhat al-Nusra in Syria and al-Shabaab in Somalia. As of early 2022, it maintains a strong relationship with the Taliban.

Resources/capabilities: Capable of engaging in complex terrorist attacks on hard and soft targets. It has also provided military advice to the Afghan Taliban.

Anti-Taliban resistance groups

Strength: Unknown.

Areas of operation: Primarily in Panjshir province and Andarab district, Baghlan province.

Leadership: Ahmad Massoud, Amrullah Saleh, others.

Structure: Militia, including former ANDSF soldiers.

History: After the collapse of the ANDSF in August 2021 and the flight of most prominent anti-Taliban warlords, a group of former Afghan commandos retreated to Panjshir to continue fighting. The Taliban ultimately took control of Panjshir but resistance groups began to coalesce and reorganise inside Afghanistan and abroad, such as the National Resistance Front organised by Ahmad Massoud and Amrullah Saleh, the Afghanistan Freedom Front, the Afghanistan Islamist National and Liberation Movement, and Unknown Soldiers of Hazaristan.

Objectives: Liberate key areas of Afghanistan and ultimately remove the Taliban from power in Afghanistan.

Opponents: The Taliban.

Affiliates/allies: Unclear but seeking support from the US, European countries and some regional countries.

Resources/capabilities: Unknown.

Resolute Support Mission (RSM), including *Operation Freedom's Sentinel* (formerly International Security Assistance Force (ISAF) and *Operation Enduring Freedom*) (RSM terminated September 2021)

Strength: NATO countries and partners contributed 9,592 personnel to the RSM, including 2,500 US troops as part of *Operation Freedom's Sentinel*. After the US, the four countries that contributed the most troops were Germany (1,300), Italy (895), Georgia (860) and the United Kingdom (750).[20]

Areas of operation: *Operation Freedom's Sentinel* conducted counter-terrorism missions throughout the country and the RSM maintained a central command in Kabul, with supporting commands in Mazar-e-Sharif, Herat, Kandahar and Laghman.

Leadership: Gen. Austin Scott Miller (commanded both US forces and the NATO mission in Afghanistan from September 2018 until July 2021 when authority was transferred to US Central Command led by Gen. Frank McKenzie).

Structure: Coalition forces in Afghanistan were divided into two missions: US forces focusing on counter-terrorism operations under *Operation Freedom's Sentinel* and NATO forces focusing on training and advising under the RSM.

History: Coalition forces entered Afghanistan in 2001 and the ISAF was created at the 2001 Bonn Conference. With the official conclusion of offensive combat operations by foreign forces in 2014, the ISAF became the RSM and US forces transitioned from *Operation Enduring Freedom* to *Operation Freedom's Sentinel*.

Objectives: Supported the Kabul government in democratisation and development. Prevented the rise of transnational terrorist organisations that might have used Afghanistan as a base to plan and coordinate international attacks.

Opponents: The Taliban insurgency (although the ANDSF were the primary actors engaging the Taliban) and terrorist groups, including al-Qaeda and ISKP.

Affiliates/allies: As many as 36 countries participated in various missions in Afghanistan through the RSM. The UN also maintained a mission in the country to promote peace and stability, the UN Assistance Mission in Afghanistan (UNAMA).

Resources/capabilities: The US has spent nearly US$2 trillion on the conflict in Afghanistan. The estimated annual budget for all US operations, including reconstruction efforts, was approximately US$50bn. The NATO-led mission had sophisticated aircraft, artillery, mortars, High Mobility Artillery Rocket Systems (HIMARS), surveillance drones, armoured vehicles and advanced communications technology.

Pakistan Armed Forces (PAF)

Strength: 651,800 active military; 291,000 active paramilitary.

Areas of operation: Deployed throughout Pakistan (particularly along the Line of Control with India) and against insurgent groups in Balochistan and Khyber Pakhtunkhwa, including the former Federally Administered Tribal Areas.

Leadership: Gen. Qamar Javed Bajwa (chief of army staff); Adm. Muhammad Amjad Khan Niazi (chief of naval staff); Air Chief Marshal Zaheer Ahmed Baber Sidhu (chief of air staff); Lt-Gen. Nadeem Anjum (director-general, Inter-Services Intelligence, ISI). ISI falls outside the military command structure but its leaders are drawn from the military and have significant oversight over some operations.

Pakistan Armed Forces (PAF)

Structure: The PAF consists of nine 'Corps' commands, an Air Defence Command, and a Strategic Forces Command. *Operation Radd-ul-Fasaad* involves an array of PAF units that support the police and the Pakistani Civil Armed Forces (PCAF) in counter-terrorism operations.

History: The ongoing *Operation Radd-ul-Fasaad* succeeded the 2014–17 *Operation Zarb-e-Azb*. It was launched in response to a resurgence in attacks by TTP splinter group Jamaat-ul-Ahrar. *Operation Khyber-4* was launched in 2017 under *Operation Radd-ul-Fasaad* with the goal of eliminating terrorists in what is now Rajgal valley, Khyber district.

Objectives: Eliminate insurgent groups that threaten the Pakistani state, control or eliminate the TTP, ensure border security with Afghanistan.

Opponents: TTP, Balochistan Liberation Army and other Baloch separatist groups, ISKP.

Affiliates/allies: PCAF, Pakistani police. The PAF enjoys a cordial but increasingly strained relationship with the Afghan Taliban due to the group's support of the TTP.

Resources/capabilities: Well resourced with an array of weapons systems and equipment. The defence budget for 2021 was US$10.3bn.

Conflict Drivers

Geopolitical and geostrategic influences

Third parties' involvement:
Third parties played an enormous role in the war in Afghanistan from 2001–21. The Afghan government and security forces were propped up economically, logistically and militarily by the US-led international coalition. The Taliban was enabled by a diverse group of foreign donors and sponsors that at various times included China, private Gulf donors, Iran and, most importantly, Pakistan. The Taliban also relied on safe havens in Pakistan. The withdrawal of foreign troops from Afghanistan, worsening relations between the Taliban and Pakistan, European and US preoccupation with the conflict in Ukraine and rising concerns over China in Washington and Asian capitals have greatly diminished third parties' interest in and relevance to the ongoing conflict in Afghanistan.

Political

Democratic legitimacy and governance flaws:
Weak governance and widespread corruption plagued the Karzai and Ghani administrations and the Afghan republic writ large. Between May 2009 and 31 December 2019, the US Special Inspector General for Afghanistan Reconstruction (SIGAR) found US$19bn in waste, fraud and abuse.[21] The SIGAR also found that the US Department of Defense and its Combined Security Transition Command–Afghanistan failed to monitor funds from the NATO Afghan National Army Trust Fund routed through the Afghan Security Forces Fund account, nor did it track performance.[22] SIGAR audits found millions of US dollars in 'questioned costs' from US-based contractors operating in Afghanistan.[23] This context – together with the highly contested Afghan elections in 2014 and 2019, low electoral participation and cronyism – contributed to a legitimacy crisis for the Kabul government and particularly the Ghani administration. As an insurgency, the Taliban capitalised on this crisis to take control of districts alienated by the central government or international coalition, touting its self-proclaimed adherence to Islam, removal of foreign forces and claimed ability to provide security.

Social

Ideological and subnational divisions:
Ideological and ethnic divisions are a major driver of violence and have contributed to conflict in the country for four decades. Afghanistan has at least 14 ethnic groups and is divided along urban–rural and sectarian lines. Ethnic tensions have hardened since the Pashtun-dominated Taliban became the de facto government of Afghanistan. Of the 33 senior positions in the Taliban's 'caretaker government', 30 belonged to Pashtuns when it was first announced.[24] During the reporting period, there were reports of ethnic-based violence by the Taliban, particularly in Panjshir, which was home to Ahmad Shah Massoud, the anti-Taliban leader of the Northern Alliance. In 2021 and early 2022, the Hazara minority continued to be disproportionately targeted by groups like ISKP. Budding resistance groups to the Taliban have organised along ethnic lines.

Key Events in 2021–22

POLITICAL EVENTS

MILITARY/VIOLENT EVENTS

2 March 2021
Three women working in the media are shot dead in Jalalabad. ISKP later claims responsibility for the attack.

14 April
President Biden announces that US troops will withdraw from Afghanistan.

1 May
The Taliban launches a 'summer offensive' beginning in Helmand province.

8 May
A car bombing likely perpetrated by ISKP at a girls' school in the Hazara neighbourhood of Dasht-e-Barchi in Kabul kills at least 90 people. The majority of casualties are between 11 and 15 years old.

16 June
The Taliban executes 22 Afghan commandos in Dawlat Abad, Faryab province as they try to surrender.

22 June
The Taliban captures Shir Khan Bandar, Afghanistan's main border crossing with Tajikistan.

25 June
Media reports suggest the US intends to keep 650 troops in Afghanistan after the withdrawal.

29 June
The Taliban gains control of 157 of Afghanistan's 407 districts, entering the cities of Kunduz and Pul-i-Khumri.

29–30 June
Germany and Italy withdraw their troops from Afghanistan.

2 July
The US military leaves Bagram Airfield, which is strategically located north of Kabul.

5–9 July
In one week, the Taliban captures the northern province of Badakhshan and the main border crossings with China, Iran, Pakistan, Tajikistan and Turkmenistan.

6 August
The Taliban captures Zaranj, the capital of Nimroz province.

7 August
The Taliban captures Sheberghan, the capital of the Jowzjan province.

8 August
The Taliban takes control of Sar-e-Pul province, captures the northern city of Kunduz and Taluqan, the capital of Takhar province.

9 August
The Taliban captures Aybak, the capital of Samangan province.

10 August
The Taliban captures Farah, the capital of Farah province and Faizabad, the capital of Badakhshan province.

12–13 August
The Taliban captures the southeastern province of Ghazni, Afghanistan's third-largest city, Herat, and its second-largest city, Kandahar. Taliban seizes Lashkar Gah (capital of Helmand province), Pul-e-Alam (capital of Logar province), Tarin Kot (capital of Uruzgan province), Chaghcharan (capital of Ghor province), Qala-e-Naw (capital of Badghis province) and Qalat (capital of Zabul province).

14 August
The Taliban captures Mazar-i-Sharif (capital of Balkh province), Nili (capital of Daykundi province), Maimana (capital of Faryab province), Mehtar Lam (capital of Laghman province), Asadabad (capital of Kunar province) and Sharan (capital of Paktika province). President Biden authorises a deployment of 5,000 US troops to Afghanistan.

15 August
The Taliban captures Jalalabad (capital of Nangarhar province) and Maidan Shahr (capital of Wardak province). Taliban also captures Khost. Kabul falls and then-president Ghani flees the country. The Pentagon announces an additional deployment of 1,000 US troops to assist with the evacuation of Kabul.

26 August
An ISKP bomb attack at Kabul's airport kills 13 US service members and at least 170 Afghan civilians.

29 August
A US drone strike targets a car in Kabul that the US claimed was loaded with explosives headed for Kabul's airport. Further investigations reveal the strike killed ten civilians, including an aid worker and seven children.

30 August
Last US service member departs Afghanistan.

5 September
The Taliban captures Bazarak, capital of Panjshir province.

8 October
An ISKP bomb attack targeting a Shia mosque in Kunduz kills 72 people and injures 140 others.

18 August 2021
The US freezes nearly US$9.5bn in assets belonging to the Afghan central bank, followed by a halt in operations by the IMF and the World Bank.

31 August 2021
The US embassy in Kabul suspends operations. The diplomatic missions of China, Iran, Pakistan and Russia continue to operate in Afghanistan despite the Taliban takeover.

7 September
The Taliban forms a self-proclaimed 'interim government', naming Mullah Muhammad Hassan Akhund interim prime minister.

8 September
The Taliban bans protests that do not have its approval.

19 September
Via the acting mayor of Kabul, Hamdullah Nohmani, the Taliban tells women employees of the Kabul city government to remain at home, specifically banning them from government work.

23 September
China urges G20 foreign ministers to end 'unilateral' sanctions on Taliban.

29 September
The Taliban's Ministry of Rural Rehabilitation and Development orders men to return to work but postpones the return to work of women.

11 February 2022
The Biden administration issues an executive order to block the frozen foreign-exchange reserves belonging to Afghanistan's central bank, Da Afghanistan Bank, from being transferred, setting aside US$3.5bn 'to benefit the Afghan people' while retaining the other US$3.5bn subject to ongoing litigation by 9/11 victims and their families.[25]

23 March
The Taliban reopens girls' high schools and then reverses the decision on the same day, announcing that girls' education from the sixth grade has been suspended until further notice. Following the decision, US Special Representative for Afghanistan Thomas West cancels meetings with the Taliban at the Doha Forum.

15 October
Two ISKP members detonate explosives inside Kandahar's Bibi Fatima mosque, killing 63 people and injuring 83 others.

16 April 2022
Pakistan conducts pre-dawn airstrikes in Afghanistan's Khost and Kunar provinces, killing at least 47 people, including many civilians.

Responses to the Conflict

Security
The US, NATO and regional countries viewed the Taliban's takeover of Afghanistan as a security risk. The group's refusal to break with al-Qaeda was documented by US intelligence and UN assessments, while its refusal to break with the TTP as the group targeted Pakistan's security forces prompted Pakistan to conduct airstrikes inside Afghanistan in mid-April 2021. China is concerned by the Taliban's continued connections with separatist groups, such as the East Turkestan Islamic Movement. Cross-border clashes have occurred with Iran and Pakistan since the Taliban assumed power.

The Taliban is aligned with Western countries and its neighbours in the fight against ISKP but it is unclear whether any coordination has occurred. In early 2022, US Special Representative for Afghanistan Thomas West indicated that the Taliban did not want the help of the US in combating ISKP.[26] He added that the Taliban's intent to defeat ISKP appeared genuine but noted that it may lack the capacity.

Economic/development
Afghanistan's economy was in crisis even before the Taliban takeover and ensuing flight of Western aid. In 2019, the World Bank reported that foreign grants accounted for 75% of the government's public spending.[27] Afghanistan was also dependent on a 'war economy' in which construction and provision of goods and services revolved around the war effort and the presence of foreign troops. Reliable information on Afghanistan's economy is severely limited and during the reporting period the IMF could not provide figures for Afghanistan's annual GDP beyond 2020. However, market prices were closely

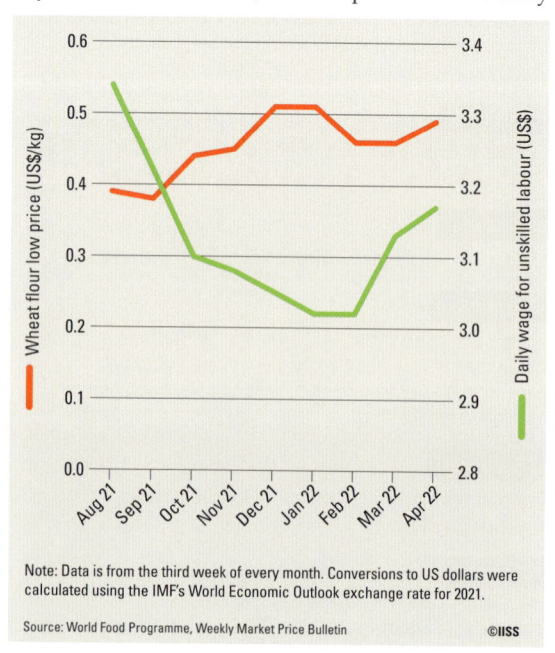

Note: Data is from the third week of every month. Conversions to US dollars were calculated using the IMF's World Economic Outlook exchange rate for 2021.

Source: World Food Programme, Weekly Market Price Bulletin ©IISS

Figure 1: Changes in wheat prices and wages for unskilled labour, August 2021–April 2022

tracked through the UN World Food Programme. As of the end of March 2022, the price of wheat, cooking oil and bread increased by 35.4%, 32.3% and 13.3% respectively compared to June 2021.[28] These figures were worrisome in isolation but became especially concerning when compared to the cost of skilled and unskilled labour, which decreased by 11.5% and 8.6% respectively in the same period.[29]

The flight of US dollars and freezing of the Afghanistan central bank's foreign-exchange reserves in the US and Europe led to a liquidity crisis. Formal cross-border trade was disrupted by a lack of US dollars for transactions, as well as US and UN sanctions on the Taliban as a non-state actor transitioning to sanctions on the Taliban as the de facto government. On 25 February 2022, the US Treasury Department's Office of Foreign Asset Control (OFAC) issued General License No. 20, which exempted US sanctions on certain aspects of commercial trade with the Taliban by permitting incidental payments, such as customs duties and licensing fees related to commercial transactions and cross-border trade with Afghanistan. It is unlikely these measures will overcome the overall effect of US sanctions. In early 2022, much of Afghanistan's cross-border trade continued to be financed through informal Hawala networks.[30]

Diplomacy

The majority of diplomatic missions in Afghanistan shuttered their physical operations following the Taliban takeover. However, those of China, Iran, Pakistan and Russia continued to operate in Afghanistan with little or no interruption and the United Arab Emirates quickly reopened its embassy. Following the closure of its embassy, US diplomacy with the Taliban was conducted in Doha, Qatar through Special Representative for Afghanistan West but public outreach came to a halt after the Taliban once again closed secondary schools for Afghan girls in March 2022. A senior Taliban delegation travelled to Oslo, Norway in late January 2022 to meet with Western officials and Afghan human-rights activists. Various European Union and UN officials travelled to Kabul to meet with Taliban leaders. In the reporting period, no country recognised the Taliban as Afghanistan's legitimate government. However, Taliban members were drafted to staff the country's diplomatic missions in Pakistan and Russia.

Humanitarian aid

According to the UN, 24.4m people are in humanitarian need and there is serious risk of widespread famine. The effects of the sanctions and asset freezing have contributed to the near collapse of the state, which is highly dependent on the aid economy to provide essential services and pay government salaries. The US has pledged or delivered more than US$720m in humanitarian aid to Afghanistan since August 2021.[31] The EU allocated over US$235m in humanitarian funding in 2021 and another US$120m in early–mid 2022 to Afghanistan and the region.[32] OFAC also issued six general licences carving out sanction exceptions for humanitarian and development activities, followed by a seventh related to commercial activities.

Conflict Outlook

Political scenarios

Prior to the collapse of the Afghan government and security forces, the US was the most consequential foreign actor affecting Afghanistan's short-term trajectory, given its position as the primary supporter of the ANDSF and the Taliban's explicit objective to see the withdrawal of US troops. Following the Taliban takeover, the US still wields significant influence through its sanctions regime on the Taliban and its continued role as a major international-aid donor to Afghanistan. Donor countries and the UN hope that economic and political leverage through international aid, potential sanctions relief and the prospect of global recognition could influence the Taliban's behaviour. The success of this strategy will depend on how much the group values its international legitimacy and ability to keep the economy afloat.

The Taliban's leadership has demonstrated a willingness to prioritise ideology and cohesion over pragmatism. Since taking power, its positions on women's rights, education, civil liberties (such as the right to protest), criminal-justice methods and relations with terrorist organisations have regressed towards the hardline policies of the Taliban Emirate of the 1990s. Policy divisions exist within the Taliban, particularly between the hardline figures close to Mullah Akhundzada and those who led negotiations with the US in Doha, sometimes nicknamed the 'Doha Taliban'. Figures in the Ministry of Foreign Affairs and Taliban spokespeople sometimes contradict official Taliban edicts. Significant divisions also existed during the era of the Taliban insurgency and should not be mistaken for disunity or factionalism. The Taliban is likely to remain a cohesive and insular government for the foreseeable future.

Weak governance and failure to provide basic services present serious challenges for the Taliban as Afghanistan's de facto government. Furthermore, the group's ability to provide security is in question as groups like ISKP target civilians, which is likely to undermine the Taliban's legitimacy.

Escalation potential and conflict-related risks
A collapse of the Taliban-led government in the short term is improbable. However, resistance groups have begun to coalesce and contest Taliban control in parts of Panjshir and Baghlan provinces. These groups have largely organised along ethnic lines and are unlikely to be able to recruit across ethnic groups in large numbers. They will also require significant state-sponsored support, which they are unlikely to receive, to adequately challenge the Taliban. ISKP will continue to engage in mass civilian-casualty attacks to undermine the Taliban's self-proclaimed credentials as a security provider.

Prospects for peace
The withdrawal of foreign troops from Afghanistan in 2021, ensuing collapse of the Afghan government and security forces and Taliban takeover brought a cessation to the Taliban insurgency's war with the ANDSF and US-led coalition. Overall violence in Afghanistan has reduced significantly since August 2021. However, revenge killings by the Taliban, ISKP violence and clashes between the Taliban and resistance groups continue. Worsening relations between Pakistan and the Afghan Taliban over the latter's continued support for the TTP may lead to future cross-border clashes. Prospects for total peace in 2022 are limited but it is unlikely that Afghanistan will descend into a civil war.

Strategic implications and global influences
The Taliban's rigid style of governance, disregard for human rights and refusal to break fully from terrorist organisations like al-Qaeda has made it a pariah government. Structural problems in Afghanistan's landlocked economy, a liquidity crisis and the chilling effect of US sanctions add to the country's economic isolation and troubles. A halt to the war economy of the last 20 years is also responsible for Afghanistan's economic downturn. Significant foreign direct investment outside of humanitarian aid is unlikely due to security concerns and lack of infrastructure. ISKP and al-Qaeda continue to operate in Afghanistan and the latter maintains relations with the Taliban. This situation presents a moderate but growing threat to countries and soft Western targets in the region. According to the UN High Commissioner for Refugees, in April 2022 there were over 2m registered refugees in Afghanistan's neighbouring countries, including over 177,000 new refugees since 1 January 2022.[33]

As of mid-2022, no country has recognised the Taliban as Afghanistan's legitimate government. The EU, Norway, the UK and the US continue to engage in diplomatic outreach to the Taliban as Afghanistan's de facto government. Before Russia's invasion of Ukraine in February 2022, Moscow played a significant role in regional dialogue with the Taliban. Taliban relations with Pakistan and Iran are strained and skirmishes have occurred on Afghanistan's borders with both countries. Beginning in May 2022, the Taliban hosted talks in Kabul between Pakistan's military and the TTP in an attempt to restrain the latter and smooth its relations with Islamabad. China retained its ambassador and diplomatic staff in Afghanistan after the Taliban's takeover and is engaged in small development projects. However, Beijing has yet to engage in large-scale development or aid, viewing Afghanistan as too high risk.

Notes

1 Special Inspector General for Afghanistan Reconstruction (SIGAR), 'Quarterly Report to the United States Congress', 30 April 2018, Figure 3.32, p. 90.
2 White House, 'Remarks by President Biden on the Way Forward in Afghanistan', 14 April 2021.
3 Benjamin Jenson, 'How the Taliban Did It: Inside the "Operational Art" of Its Military Victory', Atlantic Council, 15 August 2021.
4 'Afghan Militia Leaders Atta Noor, Dostum Escape "Conspiracy"', Reuters, 14 August 2021; and Ata Mohammad Noor (@Atamohammadnoor), tweet, 14 August 2021.
5 Dan Lamothe and Alex Horton, 'Documents Reveal US Military's Frustration with White House, Diplomats Over Afghanistan Evacuation', *Washington Post*, 8 February 2022.
6 SIGAR, 'Quarterly Report to the United States Congress', 30 July 2021, p. 63. Although these were official figures, they are widely believed to be significant overestimates.
7 Office of the Under Secretary of Defense (Comptroller)/Chief Financial Officer, US Department of Defense, 'Defense Budget Overview: United States Department of Defense Fiscal Year 2022 Budget Request', May 2021, p. 80.
8 Jonathan Schroden, 'Afghanistan's Security Forces versus the Taliban: A Net Assessment', *CTC Sentinel*, vol. 14, no. 1, January 2021, pp. 20–9.
9 See Muhammad Jalal (@MJalal313), tweet, 27 April 2022; Akmal Dawi, 'Taliban Seeking 110,000-Strong Army After 6 Months in Power', VOA, 15 February 2022; and Schroden, 'Afghanistan's Security Forces versus the Taliban: A Net Assessment'.
10 'House-to-House Searches Enter 6th Day Despite Intl Criticism', TOLO News, 2 March 2022.
11 See Abd. Sayed (@abdsayedd), tweet, 17 April 2022; and Muhammad Jalal (@MJalal313), tweet, 18 April 2022.
12 'Islamic Emirate Air Force Performs Exercises in Balkh Province', TOLO News, 29 November 2021.
13 Antonio Giustozzi, *The Taliban at War, 2001–2018* (London: Hurst, 2019).
14 David Mansfield, 'Understanding Control and Influence: What Opium Poppy and Tax Reveal about the Writ of the Afghan State', Afghanistan Research and Evaluation Unit, August 2017.
15 UN Security Council (UNSC), 'Fourteenth Report of the Secretary-General on the Threat Posed by ISIL (Da'esh) to International Peace and Security and the Range of United Nations Efforts in Support of Member States in Countering the Threat', S/2022/63, 28 January 2022, p. 7; and UNSC, 'Letter dated 25 May 2022 from the Chair of the Security Council Committee established pursuant to resolution 1988 (2011) addressed to the President of the Security Council', S/2022/419, 26 May 2022, p. 18.
16 UN Assistance Mission in Afghanistan, 'SRSG Lyons Briefing to the UNSC on the Situation in Afghanistan', 17 November 2021.
17 Andrew Mines and Amira Jadoon, 'Can the Islamic State's Afghan Province Survive Its Leadership Losses?', Lawfare, 17 May 2020. See also Amira Jadoon and Andrew Mines, 'Broken, but Not Defeated: An Examination of State-Led Operations Against Islamic State Khorasan in Afghanistan and Pakistan (2015–2018)', Combating Terrorism Center, March 2020.
18 UNSC, 'Letter dated 20 May 2021 from the Chair of the Security Council Committee established pursuant to resolution 1988 (2011) addressed to the President of the Security Council', S/2021/486, 1 June 2021, p. 13; and UNSC, 'Letter dated 25 May 2022 from the Chair of the Security Council Committee established pursuant to resolution 1988 (2011) addressed to the President of the Security Council', p. 13.
19 UNSC, 'Letter dated 20 May 2021 from the Chair of the Security Council Committee established pursuant to resolution 1988 (2011) addressed to the President of the Security Council', p. 12.
20 North Atlantic Treaty Organisation, 'Resolute Support Mission (RSM): Key Facts and Figures', February 2021.
21 Special Inspector General for Afghanistan Reconstruction (SIGAR), 'Quarterly Report to the United States Congress', 30 October 2020, p. 25.
22 SIGAR, 'NATO Afghan National Army Trust Fund: DOD Did Not Fulfil Monitoring and Oversight Requirements, Evaluate Project Outcomes, or Align Projects with the Former Afghan Army's Requirement Plans', October 2021.
23 See SIGAR, 'Department of State's Office of Antiterrorism Assistance Program in Afghanistan: Audit of Costs Incurred by Miracle Systems LLC Identified Almost $8 Million in Questioned Costs', September 2021.
24 Andrew Watkins, 'Five Questions on the Taliban's Caretaker Government', United States Institute of Peace, 9 September 2021.
25 White House, 'FACT SHEET: Executive Order to Preserve Certain Afghanistan Central Bank Assets for the People of Afghanistan', 11 February 2022.
26 United States Institute of Peace, 'US Engagement with Afghanistan After Six Months of Taliban Rule: A Discussion with U.S. Special Representative Tom West', 15 February 2022. See 27:32–30:00.
27 World Bank, 'Afghanistan: Public Expenditure Update', 29 July 2019.
28 World Food Programme (Vulnerability Analysis and Mapping), 'Afghanistan: Countrywide Monthly Market Price Bulletin', no. 22, ReliefWeb, 13 April 2022.
29 *Ibid.*
30 *Hawala* networks are informal money-transfer services that typically deliver foreign remittances into jurisdictions without formal financial institutions. They are susceptible to money laundering and criminal and terrorist financing like any financial transfer service but are sometimes deemed higher risk due to lack of regulation.
31 Afghanistan Humanitarian Response Plan 2022', ReliefWeb, 11 January 2022; and US Department of State, 'United States Announces Additional Humanitarian Assistance for the People of Afghanistan' 31 March 2022.
32 European Commission, Directorate-General for European Civil Protection and Humanitarian Aid Operations 'ECHO Factsheet – Afghanistan (Last updated 31/03/2022)', Reliefweb, 31 March 2022.
33 Operational Data Portal, UN High Commissioner for Refugees, 'Registered Refugees from Afghanistan (in Iran, Pakistan, Tajikistan, Uzbekistan, Turkmenistan)', April 2022.

KASHMIR

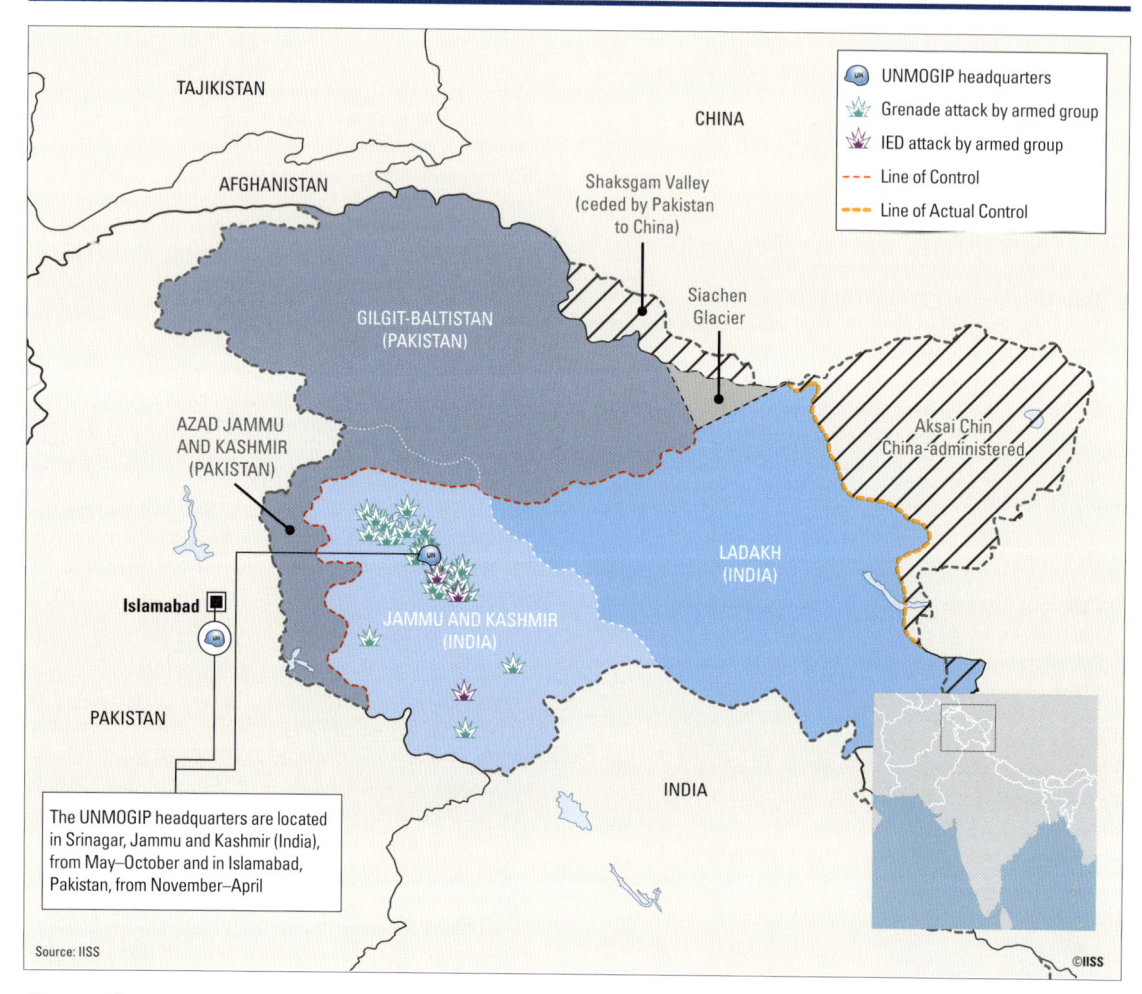

Map legend:
- UNMOGIP headquarters
- Grenade attack by armed group
- IED attack by armed group
- Line of Control
- Line of Actual Control

Map labels: TAJIKISTAN, AFGHANISTAN, CHINA, Shaksgam Valley (ceded by Pakistan to China), Siachen Glacier, GILGIT-BALTISTAN (PAKISTAN), AZAD JAMMU AND KASHMIR (PAKISTAN), Aksai Chin China-administered, LADAKH (INDIA), Islamabad, JAMMU AND KASHMIR (INDIA), PAKISTAN, INDIA

The UNMOGIP headquarters are located in Srinagar, Jammu and Kashmir (India), from May–October and in Islamabad, Pakistan, from November–April.

Source: IISS

Overview

The Kashmir conflict is a long-lasting militarised dispute between India and Pakistan over sovereignty in the Muslim-majority region of Jammu and Kashmir (India). The conflict emerged in 1947 following the end of the British Raj. In August that year, Muslim rebels in Jammu province of Jammu and Kashmir (J&K) gained control of the border district of Poonch; in October, they proclaimed a provisional 'Azad' (free) government. Several thousand armed fighters from Pakistan then entered the region to remove its Hindu Maharaja, who was being indecisive about accession to Pakistan. Faced with an external threat and internal rebellion, the ruler provisionally acceded to the Indian Union in order to receive military assistance. Indian troops landed at Srinagar airport later that year, resulting in the First Kashmir War between India and Pakistan. The issue was referred to the United Nations, where India claimed the territory based on the accession deed signed by the Maharaja, while Pakistan contested the accession and argued that the region's final status should be determined through a plebiscite. The UN Commission for India and Pakistan (UNCIP) brokered a ceasefire that came into effect in January 1949, dividing the formerly independent kingdom, comprising an area of 220,000 square kilometres, into India-administered and Pakistan-administered regions.

Armed Conflict Global Relevance Indicator (ACGRI)

India — Incidence: 10; Human impact: 3; Geopolitical impact: 4

Pakistan — Incidence: 8; Human impact: 3; Geopolitical impact: 4

Key Conflict Statistics

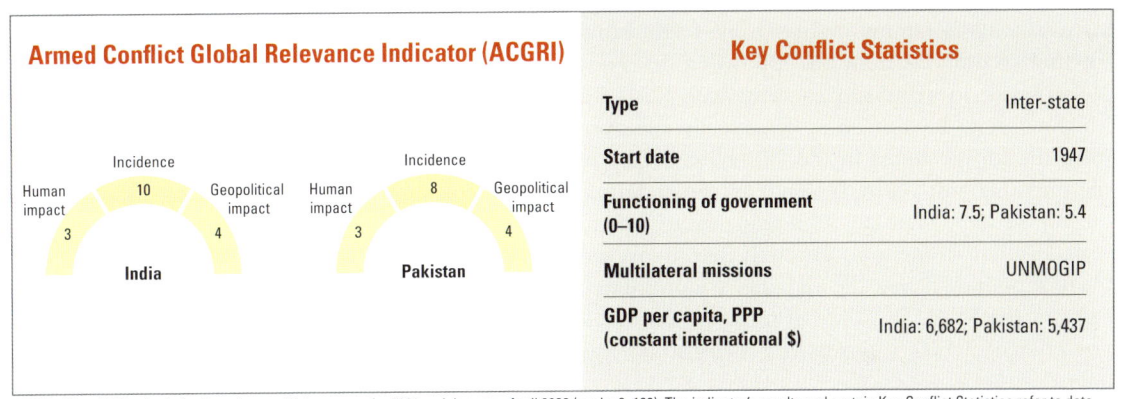

Type	Inter-state
Start date	1947
Functioning of government (0–10)	India: 7.5; Pakistan: 5.4
Multilateral missions	UNMOGIP
GDP per capita, PPP (constant international $)	India: 6,682; Pakistan: 5,437

ACGRI pillars: IISS calculation based on multiple sources for 2021 and January–April 2022 (scale: 0–100). The indicator's results and certain Key Conflict Statistics refer to data for the whole of either India or Pakistan, rather than the specific conflict covered in this chapter. See Notes on Methodology and Data Appendix for further details on Key Conflict Statistics.

Both countries agreed to a plebiscite but no agreement was ever reached on the issue of demilitarisation, with the UNCIP and neutral mediators failing to secure the parties' agreement to implement the UN plan. A tense status quo persisted for more than a decade. Following failed negotiations between Pakistan and India in 1962–63, a war broke out in 1965 that resulted in a stalemate.

In the late 1980s, Kashmiri dissidents launched an armed struggle with Pakistan's support. In response, New Delhi took direct control of the region and conducted a series of brutal counter-insurgency campaigns. In July 1990, the Indian government declared Kashmir a 'disturbed area' and in September it was brought under the Armed Forces Special Powers Act (AFSPA). The conflict saw severe human-rights abuses by the Indian armed forces and non-state armed groups alike, with thousands of people killed and hundreds of families displaced, particularly among minorities.

Peace negotiations between Pakistan and India took place from 1997–2008 alongside talks between the latter and Kashmiri separatist leaders. The situation improved within Kashmir, with yearly fatalities gradually decreasing from over 3,000 in 2002 to approximately 500 in 2008.[1] However, the impasse on the core issue of Kashmir continued.

Between 2008 and 2016, three mass anti-India uprisings erupted in the region, catalysing a 'new-age militancy' that was further boosted by social media. The new-age militancy was largely concentrated in the Kashmir Valley and sought either independence or a merger with Pakistan.

In August 2019, India's Bharatiya Janata Party (BJP) government revoked J&K's special autonomous status by abrogating Article 370 of the Indian constitution and split the region into centrally controlled 'Union Territories' – Jammu and Kashmir, and Ladakh.[2] In 2020, New Delhi introduced new land and domicile laws in J&K with far-reaching implications for residents. Local political leaders, including former chief ministers, were released from detention. In October, local parties founded the People's Alliance for Gupkar Declaration (PAGD), which challenged the revocation of Article 370 in the Supreme Court of India and opposed the new laws, claiming that they aimed to alter J&K's demographic composition, as desired by the BJP's parent organisation, the Hindu-nationalist Rashtriya Swayamsevak Sangh, which exerts considerable influence on Prime Minister Narendra Modi's domestic policies. The PAGD agenda and rhetoric alienated some of its members, who switched loyalties to parties outside the alliance. In the first District Development Council elections held in late 2020, the PAGD won the largest number of seats. In February 2021, India and Pakistan agreed to halt exchanges of fire across the Line of Control (LoC). Both sides adhered to the agreement during the reporting period.

In March 2022, Indian Home Minister Amit Shah said that elections to the J&K Legislative Assembly, which was dissolved in November 2018, would be held after the completion of a delimitation of the constituencies, promising the restoration of J&K's statehood after the elections. In the meantime, New Delhi has floated new political parties and actors to reconfigure J&K's political landscape and undercut the influence of the Jammu and Kashmir National Conference (JKNC) and the People's Democratic Party (PDP), the two major regional parties. The Jammu and Kashmir Delimitation Commission, established in March 2020, has proposed allotting six new seats to Jammu and only one to Kashmir, inviting accusations from the opposition that New Delhi seeks to politically disempower Kashmiri Muslims, who have been systematically removed from the top positions in the J&K bureaucracy in the previous four years. Through gerrymandering, the BJP seeks to maintain its dominance in Jammu – its election stronghold. Through defections and via new political actors, the BJP aims to gain enough seats in the Kashmir Valley to form the next J&K government, where it wants its policies to operate unopposed in order to achieve its long-term objectives. In early 2022, the J&K administration signed several memoranda of understanding (MoUs) with foreign companies but investment has been limited amid concerns about investing in a conflict zone. The unemployment rate in J&K in 2021–22 remained relatively high. The security situation was also volatile during the reporting period despite Indian security forces killing the armed groups' top leadership. Targeted killings, grenade attacks and gunfights were frequent in 2021 and early 2022.

Conflict Parties

Indian Armed Forces

Strength: Approximately 500,000 Indian security personnel, including over 200,000 army soldiers; 58,000 infantry troops within the Rashtriya Rifles (RR), the special counter-insurgency unit; 158,000 paramilitary personnel of the Central Reserve Police Force (CRPF), Border Security Force (BSF), Indo-Tibetan Border Police (ITBP), Sashastra Seema Bal (SSB) and Central Industrial Security Force (CISF);[3] around 100,000 personnel of the J&K Police (JKP); 30,000 Special Police Officers (SPOs); and personnel within various intelligence wings.

Areas of operation: All districts of J&K (India) and along the LoC. The CRPF's Jammu and Kashmir Zone Srinagar Sector covers Budgam, Ganderbal and Srinagar districts, its Kashmir Operations Sector covers Anantnag, Awantipora and Baramulla districts and its Jammu Sector covers the Jammu region.

Leadership: Indian troops in the region are under the Northern Command based in Udhampur (Jammu and Kashmir Union Territory) and led by Lt-Gen. Upendra Dwivedi. The CRPF, the primary paramilitary force, is under the Ministry of Home Affairs. A special director general has overall command of the CRPF in J&K, while inspectors general command the respective sectors.

Structure: The Northern Command is composed of seven divisions, three corps and one brigade. The RR has 65 battalions, each comprising six infantry companies, and five headquarters. Srinagar-based 15th Corps has operational command of the Kashmir Valley.

History: A heavy troop presence has been maintained along the LoC since 1949. Thousands of troops were used to crush an anti-India armed rebellion in the late 1980s. Initially, paramilitary and regular army troops fought the Pakistan-backed insurgents. In 1994 the RR was introduced, which coordinates with other security agencies, including the Special Operations Group (SOG), a JKP counter-insurgency unit.

Objectives: Guard the LoC and defeat armed opposition.

Opponents: Armed groups (Hizbul Mujahideen, HM; Lashkar-e-Taiba, LeT; Jaysh-e-Mohammad, JeM; The Resistance Front, TRF; Ansar Ghazwat-ul-Hind; Al-Badr) and Pakistan Armed Forces.

Affiliates/allies: Village Defence Committees, volunteer state-armed groups concentrated in hilly and border areas with sizeable Hindu populations (Doda, Kathua, Kishtwar, Poonch, Rajouri, Ramban and Reasi districts).

Resources/capabilities: Ministry of Defence and Ministry of Home Affairs budgetary funds, voluntary donations through the National Defence Fund, the Army Central Welfare Fund, the Armed Forces Battle Casualties Welfare Fund, web-based public donations through portals like 'Bharat Ke Veer' (India's Bravehearts), and government contracts under *Operation Sadhbhavana*.[4]

Pakistan Armed Forces (PAF)

Strength: In total, Pakistan has some 651,800 active military personnel and 291,000 active paramilitary personnel across the country. Two Pakistan Army strike corps are deployed in Azad Jammu and Kashmir (Pakistan); their strength is believed to be approximately 125,000.

Areas of operation: All districts of Azad Jammu and Kashmir and along the LoC.

Leadership: Pakistani troops in the region are under I and X Corps of the Pakistan Army. I Corps is based in Mangla (Azad Jammu and Kashmir) and led by Lt-Gen. Shaheen Mazhar Mehmood. X Corps is based in Rawalpindi (Pakistan) and led by Lt-Gen. Sahir Shamshad Mirza. The Mujahid Force, a paramilitary unit, is headquartered in Bhimber (Azad Jammu and Kashmir) and works under the National Guard of Pakistan, which is controlled and commanded by the chief of army staff based in General Headquarters in Rawalpindi.

Structure: X corps consists of three infantry divisions and also division-sized Force Command Northern Areas, which

Pakistan Armed Forces (PAF)

operates in the Gilgit-Baltistan area. I corps is composed of two infantry divisions and an armoured division. I corps may have an independent armoured brigade and an air-defence brigade.[5]

History: Pakistan has maintained a heavy troop presence along the LoC since 1949. The Azad Army, an anti-Maharaja militia composed of ex-servicemen of the British Indian Army, captured the main districts of Muzaffarabad and Mirpur before the Pakistan Army officially entered Jammu and Kashmir in May 1948 to take control and consolidate the territorial gains. The Pakistan Army has not faced any insurgency within Azad Jammu and Kashmir; its operations are directed at Indian forces and the LoC.

Objectives: Guard the LoC and China-Pakistan Economic Corridor (CPEC).

Opponents: Indian Armed Forces.

Affiliates/allies: Anti-India armed groups based in Azad Jammu and Kashmir (Pakistan).

Resources/capabilities: Ministry of Defence budgetary funds, arms exports, government contracts and commercial ventures under army-controlled charitable foundations, such as Fauji Foundation, Army Welfare Trust, Shaheen Foundation and Bahria Foundation.

Hizbul Mujahideen (HM)

Strength: Fewer than 100 members active in Jammu and Kashmir (India) and over 1,000 members based in Azad Jammu and Kashmir (Pakistan). Additional overground workers – a term used by Indian security forces for people supporting insurgents and insurgent sympathisers – provide logistical support and information.

Areas of operation: Concentrated in Anantnag, Kulgam, Pulwama and Shopian districts, with marginal presence in northern Kashmir districts.

Leadership: Headed by Mohammad Yusuf Shah (alias Syed Salahuddin). Farooq Ahmad Bhat (alias Farooq Nali) is the chief commander in the Kashmir Valley – the epicentre of the low-intensity armed conflict-overseeing area commanders for each district.

Structure: Headquarters in Muzaffarabad, Azad Jammu and Kashmir (Pakistan). Cadres comprise mostly local Kashmiris who receive rudimentary arms training from senior members. Divisional commanders work under a semi-autonomous structure but also receive instructions from across the LoC via satellite communication and encrypted messaging apps.

History: Indigenous armed group with a pro-Pakistan ideology, founded in September 1989 by Mohammad Ahsan Dar, a former member of the pro-independence organisation Jammu Kashmir Liberation Front (JKLF) and Jamaat-e-Islami affiliate, a pro-Pakistan religio-political organisation in J&K. Many JKLF members joined HM after 1994, when the former suffered heavy losses and voluntarily quit the armed conflict to pursue non-violent means. HM recruitment of local Kashmiri youth also surged after the death of its young commander Burhan Muzaffar Wani in July 2016. Despite suffering heavy losses between 2017 and 2020, HM survived by procuring funds and weapons locally.

Objectives: Dislodge Indian rule in Kashmir and merge the region with Pakistan through a war of attrition. The group has stated that it would support negotiated settlement through dialogue under certain circumstances.[6]

Opponents: Indian government.

Affiliates/allies: LeT, JeM and TRF.

Resources/capabilities: Resources (including weapons and improvised explosive devices) procured locally by associates and sympathisers. Funding channels from charities, mosque-based donations across Pakistan and the Pakistani military establishment.

Lashkar-e-Taiba (LeT)

Strength: Largest armed group in Kashmir in early 2022.[7]

Areas of operation: Across the Kashmir Valley, but mostly active in the northern districts of Baramulla, Bandipora and Kupwara.

Leadership: Hafiz Muhammad Saeed. Overall command is in the hands of a divisional commander, who is often a non-Kashmiri. Mohammad Yusuf Dar (alias Yusuf Kantroo) was the last 'operational head' of the group in the Kashmir Valley.

Structure: Headquarters in Muridke, Punjab province, Pakistan. Valley-based cadres are mostly Pakistani nationals working under district commanders and trained in camps.

History: Founded in the late 1980s by Pakistan-based cleric Hafiz Muhammad Saeed, who also heads the missionary organisation Jamaat-ud-Dawa (JuD). Since LeT entered Kashmir in the early 1990s, it has carried out several deadly attacks against Indian Armed Forces and political workers. Despite losing its commanders in quick succession since the launch of the Indian army's *Operation All Out*, the group has survived and has recruited increasing numbers of local youth, particularly in the last three years.

Objectives: Merge Kashmir with Pakistan. The group has supported efforts to achieve a peaceful resolution to the conflict.

Opponents: Indian government.

Affiliates/allies: HM, JeM, TRF, Al-Badr. Though banned by the Pakistani government in 2002, LeT is believed to maintain connections to Pakistani intelligence agencies.

Resources/capabilities: Fundraising through charities in Pakistan (e.g., JuD and Falah-e-Insaniyat), which receive government and public contributions, and social networks in Pakistan and Afghanistan. Funds also raised through collection and selling of sacrificial-animal skins on Eid.

Jaysh-e-Mohammad (JeM)

Strength: Second-largest armed group in Kashmir in 2022.

Areas of operation: Conducts attacks mainly in southern Kashmir.

Leadership: Local resident Wakeel Ahmad Shah, who was killed in August 2021, was the last top commander of the group in the Valley.

Structure: Headquartered in Bahawalpur, Punjab province, Pakistan. JeM is Pakistan-based and its members are mostly Pakistanis. Divisional commanders work under the chief operational commander based in Kashmir.

History: Founded by Pakistani Masood Azhar in 2000. JeM entered Kashmir in the early 2000s and introduced suicide attacks. The Pakistani government banned the group in 2002. After a period of dormancy, JeM re-emerged in 2017 with an attack on a paramilitary camp in Pulwama.

Objectives: Merge Kashmir with Pakistan.

Opponents: Indian government.

Affiliates/allies: HM and LeT. Believed to have ties to the Taliban in Afghanistan.

Resources/capabilities: The most powerful insurgent group in Kashmir, with highly trained cadres and better resources than other groups. Fundraising through seminaries, mosques (e.g., Binori Town Mosque) and charities in Pakistan (e.g., Al Rashid Trust) and donation appeals published in magazines and pamphlets. Money also raised through legal businesses operating in Pakistan and funds allegedly received from political (e.g., Jamiat-e-Ulema-e-Islam) and other militant organisations in Pakistan.

The Resistance Front (TRF)

Strength: The TRF was the largest recruiter in 2020 after HM, LeT and JeM.

Areas of operation: Has carried out attacks in northern, central and southern districts of Kashmir Valley.

Leadership: No central leadership. Mohammad Abbas Sheikh, who was killed in August 2021, was the last leader of the group.

Structure: Composite organisation without defined structure. JKP claims that the TRF is a hybrid militant outfit composed of cadres from existing armed groups such as LeT and HM. TRF militants killed by Indian security forces and arrested TRF sympathisers have been identified as native Kashmiris.

History: Founded after the abrogation of Article 370 in August 2019, the TRF started by lobbing grenades in Srinagar in late 2019. The group has used social media to publish statements and claim attacks.

Objectives: Dislodge Indian rule in Kashmir and deter (through violence) potential settlers from mainland India.

Opponents: Indian government.

Affiliates/allies: Believed to have ties with LeT.

Resources/capabilities: JKP claims that the TRF uses 'overground workers' who are not formally part of the group – and do not feature in police records – to carry out some targeted killings.

United Nations Military Observer Group in India and Pakistan (UNMOGIP)

Strength: Forty-three observers from Croatia, South Korea, the Philippines, Thailand, Sweden, Switzerland, Uruguay, Argentina, Italy and Romania (in descending order of troop numbers). Sixty-eight civilian staff, including Pakistanis, Indians and international members.[8]

Areas of operation: UN field stations: six based in Azad Jammu and Kashmir (Pakistan) and four based in J&K (India). The Sialkot field station in Pakistan monitors the working boundary, which is the international border between Punjab province, Pakistan and the disputed territory of Jammu and Kashmir.

Leadership: Maj.-Gen. José Alcaín from Uruguay (chief military observer and head of mission); Nester Odaga-Jalomayo from Uganda (chief of mission support).

Structure: UNMOGIP is mandated by UN Security Council (UNSC) Resolution 91. Headquarters alternates between Islamabad in November–April and Srinagar in May–October.

History: In January 1948, UNCIP was created under UNSC Resolution 39. In January 1949, the first team of unarmed military observers arrived to supervise the ceasefire between India and Pakistan. Under UNSC Resolution 91 of March 1951, UNCIP was replaced by UNMOGIP. After UNSC Resolution 307 (1971), India and Pakistan made minor adjustments to the ceasefire line and in 1972 established the LoC to be supervised by UN military observers.

Objectives: As a neutral observer, monitor, investigate and report ceasefire violations along the 770km LoC and working boundary between India and Pakistan. Receive petitions from political groups within Kashmir on the situation at the LoC and submit findings to both India and Pakistan and the UN Secretary-General.

Opponents: N/A.

Affiliates/allies: UN departments of Peace Operations and Operational Support.

Resources/capabilities: UN approved budget: US$10,519,800 for 2021.[9]

Conflict Drivers

Geopolitical and geostrategic influences

Regional geopolitics:
Since 1947, Pakistan has employed various tactics to militarily gain control of J&K or at least the Kashmir Valley. Conventional wars – in 1948, 1965 and 1999 – resulted in stalemate, while Pakistan's use of sub-conventional tactics (including funding Kashmiri insurgent groups) has been moderately successful in sustaining pressure on India. The enduring India–Pakistan rivalry over Kashmir has led to an arms race and nuclear brinkmanship and affected economic development, particularly Pakistan's – its defence budget has been consistently over 2% of GDP since 2008. In 2021, India had a defence budget of over US$64 billion, double the overall troop strength of Pakistan, and its GDP was over eight times larger. However, its numerical superiority in arms and relative power has not produced strategic dominance over Pakistan. Undeterred, Islamabad has maintained pressure on India, providing operational space to anti-India armed groups as part of its sub-conventional campaign. Pakistan's military balance against India relies on its formal alliance with China, development of deployable tactical nuclear weapons and robust defences in Kashmir, where the difficult mountainous terrain favours the defender over ground offensives. J&K's abundant water resources are vital to the food, water and energy security of both India and Pakistan: they feed vast agricultural lands in Pakistan and generate more than 2,000 megawatts of electricity for India's government-owned National Hydroelectric Power Corporation.[10]

Political

Centralising policies and Kashmiri resistance:
The origins of the Kashmir conflict lie in competing sovereignty claims over the former princely state of J&K, which Pakistan insisted formed part of its territory and India claimed based on the 1947 accession. Both countries accepted the principle of plebiscite to ascertain the wishes of the people. Many Kashmiris favoured either independence or merger with Muslim-majority Pakistan. Leading Kashmiri nationalist organisation JKNC negotiated a special autonomous status for J&K within the Indian Union. Despite New Delhi formally recognising the special status under Article 370 of the Indian constitution (which exempted the full applicability of the Indian constitution to Kashmir), successive governments gradually brought the state under most central laws.

New Delhi's refusal to recognise the demands of Kashmiri self-determination outside the framework of the Indian constitution and its centralising tendencies have created a sense of betrayal among Kashmiris and the conditions for intensified political resistance against India. Forcible integration through removal of constitutionally guaranteed autonomy has vindicated perceptions that India's Hindu-nationalist government aims to disempower Kashmiri Muslims and alter the region's demographic composition by settling outsiders there.

Rise of the Hindutva movement:
The Hindu nationalist movement, of which the BJP is the leading political face, is based on the ideology of Hindutva (Hindu ethno-nationalism), which seeks dissolution of the distinct cultural identity of Indian Muslims (some 14% of India's population).[11] The BJP opposed and abrogated Article 370 because it extended autonomy to Muslim-majority J&K, allowing the state to preserve its distinct identity through a separate constitution and flag. Another strand of the Hindu nationalist movement aims to establish Akhand Bharat (a supposed undivided India that includes much of South Asia) by incorporating areas bordering India, including Azad Jammu and Kashmir (Pakistan).

In becoming a centrally ruled Union Territory, J&K came under greater control of the Modi government. J&K's domicile law and land laws were changed in March and October 2020 respectively. As a result, 'non-permanent' residents were able to secure domiciles in the disputed region, acquire lands and apply for public-sector jobs previously reserved for local J&K residents under Articles 370 and 35A of the Indian constitution. Other enacted laws have empowered authorities to evict residents of populated areas for the purpose of establishing industrial centres and 'strategic areas' for the military. These changes are viewed with increased suspicion and concern by the local population, as many fear that there is a larger conspiracy to alter the region's demography and, in the long term, dispossess them of their land and resources.

Key Events in 2021–22

POLITICAL EVENTS

5 May 2021
Jailed Tehreek-e-Hurriyat chairman Muhammad Ashraf Sehrai dies in a Jammu hospital aged 78.

10 July
The J&K government dismisses 11 employees under Article 311 of the Indian constitution for alleged separatist links or ideology.

18 August
The JKP arrests four separatist leaders for allegedly selling access to medical courses in Pakistan to Kashmiri students in order to fund separatist activities.

1 September
Syed Ali Shah Geelani, the foremost Kashmiri separatist leader and former chairperson of the All Parties Hurriyat Conference (APHC), dies aged 92 at his Srinagar residence. Indian security forces put heavy restrictions on civilian movement to thwart protests.

1 November
The J&K government establishes the State Investigation Agency (SIA) as a nodal agency to coordinate with the federal anti-terrorism National Investigation Agency (NIA) and other central agencies.

22 November
Khurram Pervez, prominent Kashmiri human-rights defender and the chairperson of the Asian Federation against Involuntary Disappearances, is arrested by the NIA at his home under an anti-terrorism law.

27 December
The J&K government and the Ministry of Housing and Urban Affairs organise the first-ever 'Jammu and Kashmir Real Estate Summit' in Jammu. Kashmiri regional parties, the JKNC, the PDP and the separatist alliance APHC criticise the event as a looting of local resources and a step towards altering the region's demographic composition.

31 December
The JKP places Kashmiri political leaders, including former chief ministers, under house arrest to thwart proposed protests against the delimitation commission's recommendations.

4 February 2022
The JKP arrests Fahad Shah, editor-in-chief of *Kashmir Walla* newspaper, a month after his colleague Sajad Gul is booked for posting a video about a protest after a militant's killing.

MILITARY/VIOLENT EVENTS

2 August 2021
On Twitter, the JKP releases a list of its top-ten most-wanted militants.

21 August
Three JeM militants, including the group's commander Wakeel Ahmad Shah, are killed in a gunfight with Indian security forces in Pulwama district.

23 August
The JKP kills TRF leader Mohammad Abbas Sheikh and deputy leader Saqib Manzoor in Srinagar.

13 December
Militants attack a police vehicle in Srinagar district. Three police officers are killed and at least ten others are injured.

3 January 2022
Two LeT militants, including top commander Salim Parray, are killed in gunfights with Indian security forces in Srinagar.

30 January
Five militants, including Zahid Ahmad Wani, a top JeM commander, are killed in separate gunfights with Indian security forces in Pulwama and Budgam districts. The JKP inspector general later claims that Indian security forces killed 21 militants in 11 gunfights in January 2022, including 13 local and eight foreign (Pakistani) militants.

16 February
SIA conducts multiple raids in the Kashmir Valley and claims to have arrested alleged militant supporters of JeM.

Conflict Report: Kashmir

26 February
The PAGD issues a 'white paper' titled 'The Betrayal' critiquing the BJP government's Kashmir policy and calling the delimitation commission's proposals illegitimate.

14 March
The delimitation commission makes its draft report public. Most regional parties oppose the report's findings.

22 March
A 36-member delegation from the United Arab Emirates (UAE) visits Kashmir on the invitation of the J&K government to explore investment opportunities.

7 April
The Enforcement Directorate, a federal financial-investigation agency, questions former J&K chief minister Omar Abdullah in connection with a decade-old case of alleged irregularities in state-owned Jammu and Kashmir Bank.

7 April
A court in Pakistan sentences Hafiz Muhammad Saeed, the founder of LeT, to over 30 years in prison in connection with terrorism-financing cases.

9 April
The JKP arrests 13 young men for secessionist sloganeering inside Jama Mosque in Srinagar under sedition laws.

13 April
The JKP arrests 11 people under the Public Safety Act (PSA) for alleged subversive activities in Bandipora district.

17 April
New Prime Minister of Pakistan Shehbaz Sharif makes a peace overture to Prime Minister Modi, expressing a desire for meaningful engagement on J&K.

19 February
Two Indian army soldiers of the Rashtriya Rifles and a militant are killed in a gunfight in Zainpora area, Shopian district.

9 March
A cruise missile launched from India lands near Mian Channu, Pakistan.

17 March
The JKP claims to have arrested 150 overground workers of different anti-India armed groups in 2022.

31 March
The JKP claims to have arrested a woman who threw a petrol bomb at a CRPF picket in Sopore town, Baramulla district, on 29 March. The JKP claims more women are assisting armed groups.

21 April
Two LeT militants, including its operational chief Mohammad Yusuf Dar (alias Yusuf Kantroo), are killed in a gunfight with Indian security forces in Malwah village, Baramulla district. Four soldiers and a policeman are injured in the fighting.

22 April
Militants attack a CISF bus in Sunjwan garrison town in southern Jammu province, killing a CISF official and injuring several others, two days before Prime Minister Modi's scheduled visit to Jammu's Samba district. Two JeM militants are killed in an ensuing gunfight with Indian security forces.

Responses to the Conflict

Security

During the 2020 China–India military clashes along the Line of Actual Control (LAC) – a poorly demarcated line that separates Chinese- and Indian-held territories in J&K – the People's Liberation Army occupied territories long controlled by Indian forces. India increased the number of China-facing army divisions from 12 to 14, while reducing the number of Pakistan-facing army divisions from 25 to 22. The Indian Army's Uttar Pradesh-based I Corps was re-tasked to become a mountain strike corps geared for the Ladakh theatre. This major rearrangement of one of the four strike corps normally deployed on the India–Pakistan border (versus seven of Pakistan's nine army corps) reduced India's quantitative advantage over Pakistan. The hostile northern front along the LAC has exhausted India's Northern Command and Army Headquarters' reserves, since these forces were deployed to check Chinese ingress. It is in these circumstances that India's and Pakistan's directors-general of military operations made a

Table 1: Proposed investment and approved investment in Jammu and Kashmir (India) from April 2021–April 2022

Division	Investment (US$bn)	Land (acres)
Proposed investment		
Jammu	3.6	2,390
Kashmir	3.1	2,498
Total	6.7	4,877
Approved investment		
Jammu	2.8	1,544
Kashmir	1.9	702
Total	4.7	2,246

Source: *Times of India*. Note: Conversions to US dollars were calculated using the IMF's World Economic Outlook exchange rate for 2021.

joint statement on 25 February 2021 recommitting themselves to the 2003 ceasefire agreement and calling 'for strict observance of all agreements, understandings and cease firing' along the LoC and 'all other sectors'.[12] In March 2022, Indian Minister of State for Defence Ajay Bhatt told the Indian parliament that the situation along the LoC had remained stable following the February 2021 agreement.[13] Pakistan's army chief also reported that the situation at the LoC was 'satisfactory and fairly peaceful'.[14]

Economic/development

The Modi government attributed continuing political unrest and secessionism in J&K to lack of development and youth unemployment, justifying the abrogation of Article 370 as necessary for bringing in foreign investment and creating jobs. However, the J&K government's planned flagship business event, the J&K Global Investors Summit, was repeatedly delayed, while the MoUs signed by the government with large Indian corporates in 2020 remained largely on paper. Amid these failures to attract private investment, the J&K youth unemployment rate soared to 46% in April–June 2021.[15]

Following the controversial real-estate summit in December 2021, the J&K government hosted a delegation of 36 UAE businessmen in March 2022 in Srinagar, which resulted in the signing of several MoUs pledging investment in J&K between the J&K government and Gulf-based private companies. Total investment from the UAE is expected to be approximately US$400 million, while estimated total foreign investment in J&K is projected to be almost US$9bn.[16]

Despite a US$3.6bn 'Industrial Development Package' announced by the J&K government in January 2021 that promised 450,000 new jobs, unemployment rates have remained very high.[17] Against an all India unemployment rate of 7%, J&K's reached 25% in March 2022.[18]

Diplomacy

The timing of the Gulf Investors Summit was seemingly strategic as it coincided with the Council of Foreign Ministers meeting convened by the Organisation of Islamic Corporation (OIC) in Islamabad on 22–23 March. The OIC session issued the 'Islamabad Declaration', which was highly critical of New Delhi's Kashmir policy, stating and reiterating its rejection of what it labelled India's illegal and unilateral actions since 5 August 2019. India rejected the OIC's stance, in line with its long-held position of rejecting any third-party involvement in the Kashmir dispute. In July 2021, the 57-member OIC's proposal to assist India–Pakistan talks on Kashmir was similarly rejected by New Delhi.

The UAE's involvement in the normalisation process in J&K post-Article 370 is a diplomatic achievement for India, which has seen deepening bilateral relations with influential OIC members, such as the UAE and Saudi Arabia. The March 2022 Islamabad Declaration, however, has highlighted the limitations of such cooperation. Saudi Arabia, the kingpin of the OIC, has a strategic and security partnership with Pakistan and must remain sensitive to Pakistan's interests while pursuing its growing relationship with India.

Continuing curbs on political and civil rights in J&K invited criticism globally, including from UN High Commissioner for Human Rights Michelle Bachelet in September 2021. EU Special Representative for Human Rights Eamon Gilmore also raised the situation in J&K with the Indian government in April 2022. Also in 2022, Freedom House designated Kashmir as 'Not Free' for a second year.

Conflict Outlook

Political scenarios
The BJP government will retain control over J&K through the unelected office of the lieutenant governor and outside bureaucrats whose postings and promotions are controlled by the Ministry of Home Affairs. State crackdowns against separatist organisations and civil society has shrunk the opposition's ability to organise. The death of separatist leader Syed Ali Geelani has left the separatist alliance without effective leadership. As of mid-2022, organised separatist opposition – coordinated via the Joint Resistance Leadership – has ceased to exist and the BJP will continue to apply pressure to prevent its resurgence. Formal censorship under 'Media Policy 2020' and informal pressures applied by the authorities are coordinated to ensure the central government's narrative prevails. Large-scale military presence on roads, draconian laws such as the Unlawful Activities Prevention Act and the PSA, and enhanced surveillance infrastructure and crowd-control tactics will limit mass street protests in the future.

The J&K government is constructing a high-security prison in Kathua district, Jammu region 'to lodge treasonous and insurgent criminals', suggesting that the Modi government intends to prolong the incarceration of J&K political detainees and expects more arrests in coming years.[19]

Escalation potential and conflict-related risks
Militant violence is unlikely to decrease in the foreseeable future. Greater state repression has intensified the local population's resentment, creating conditions for militant recruitment and activity. Despite measures to curb recruitment, the trend from the previous decade showed that in any year there were 150–200 active militants in J&K. Insurgent groups will likely continue pursuing civilian targets, particularly BJP-affiliated members and politicians and Indian settlers. Possibly through links to Afghanistan, militants have acquired advanced technology, such as Iridium satellite phones (banned under India's Telegraph Act) and Wi-Fi-enabled thermal-imagery devices that can help militants flee their hideouts during security forces' search operations.[20] Evidence of foreign war equipment in the hands of J&K-based armed groups indicated that such groups have arms-supply channels as yet uncracked by Indian intelligence.

Prospects for peace
Prime Minister Sharif has indicated a willingness to engage with India. Modi has also expressed a desire for 'peace and stability in the region'. However, unlike the previous BJP government under Atal Bihari Vajpayee (1999–2004), the current Indian government is relatively hardline and would not include Kashmir in an India–Pakistan dialogue.

The Sharif government will be wary of opposing the Pakistan Army, which is widely believed to control the country's defence and foreign policy. In April 2022, Pakistan's Chief of Army Staff Qamar Javed Bajwa indicated that the Pakistan Army was willing 'to move on' on the Kashmir issue and would rather focus on geo-economics.[21]

The February 2021 ceasefire will likely be preserved as it benefits both countries. India can strengthen defences on its northern border with China, which has reportedly amassed some 60,000 troops in Ladakh.[22] For Pakistan, peace along the LoC will enable a focus on the security challenges posed by Tehrik-e-Taliban Pakistan and the resurgent Balochistan insurgency.

Sharif's tone towards Modi will matter if bilateral relations are to move forward. Unlike the previous Pakistani government, Sharif's has not made future India–Pakistan dialogue conditional on an Indian pledge to re-establish J&K's statehood, which New Delhi has promised only at an 'appropriate time'.[23]

Strategic implications and global influences
Since June 2018, Pakistan has been on the Financial Action Task Force's (FATF) grey list. Securing its removal from the list is Islamabad's foremost priority. Pakistan's cumulative real GDP losses due to the listing are estimated at $US38bn.[24] In convicting LeT chief Hafiz Saeed, Pakistan expects to be removed.

It is unclear whether state crackdowns against anti-India armed groups in Pakistan will affect the groups' operations within J&K. Pakistan has used non-state actors as part of its sub-conventional campaign against India to pressurise the latter on the Kashmir issue. If there is a paradigm shift in Pakistan Army thinking, this may result in a decline in the intensity of the Kashmir insurgency in the long term.

While the United States Commission on International Religious Freedom (USCIRF) designated India a 'country of particular concern' citing deteriorating religious freedoms,[25] such criticism is unlikely to affect the United States' India policy: New Delhi is an important ally for the Quadrilateral Security Dialogue (or Quad) comprising Australia, India, Japan and the US. Beijing sees the Quad as 'essentially a tool for containing and besieging China'.[26] By continuing to apply military pressure at the LAC, Beijing will seek to discourage New Delhi from pursuing the Quad, and also aim to secure Gilgit-Baltistan (Pakistan) as the route of CPEC.

During the 2022 Raisina Dialogue, a foreign-policy conference in New Delhi, European Commission President Ursula von der Leyen cautioned that the Russia and China nexus could harm India given the two countries' avowed commitment to 'no forbidden areas of cooperation'.[27] However, despite the European Union and United States pressuring India to condemn Moscow for its February 2022 invasion of Ukraine, the Modi government did not oblige, partly because much of India's arms inventory is of Russian origin, including MiG-21 and Sukhoi Su-30MKI fighter aircraft, the front-line combat fighters of the Indian Air Force. While New Delhi's Russia policy will frustrate the EU and the US, India's economic and strategic value is too great for Washington and its allies to push the issue. The US aims to minimise India's dependence on Russian arms by developing India's domestic defence production through cooperation with US companies. China will bolster Pakistan's military capabilities by providing advanced J-10C fighter jets, Type 054A frigates and Type 041 submarines.[28] The shifting geopolitical situation in Asia suggests a renewed arms race between India and Pakistan, as both countries seek to modernise their armed forces in collaboration with two major powers and global competitors.

Notes

[1] See 'Yearly Fatalities', Datasheet – Jammu & Kashmir, South Asia Terrorism Portal.

[2] When referring to developments before 15 August 2019, the acronym 'J&K' refers to the state of Jammu and Kashmir (including Kashmir, Jammu and Ladakh regions, which India controls). For developments after the abrogation of Article 370 and the bifurcation of J&K in 2019, J&K refers to the Union Territory of Jammu and Kashmir (including Jammu and Kashmir regions, which India controls).

[3] An additional 300 companies of paramilitary forces will be deployed for the security of the annual Hindu pilgrimage in the Kashmir Valley. Some of these paramilitary companies had already arrived in Kashmir in April 2022. See 'J&K: 300 additional companies security forces to be deployed for Amarnath Yatra', All India Radio News, 21 April 2022.

[4] The Indian Army's Northern Command launched *Operation Sadhbhavna* in 1998 as a public-outreach programme that built civilian infrastructure and provided some public services. According to official estimates, Northern Command has spent over US$70m on the operation since 1998. See Indian Army website, 'Operation Sadbhavana'.

[5] CLAWS Research Team, 'Strategic Reserves of Pakistan', *Scholar Warrior*, Centre for Land Warfare Studies, Autumn 2011, p. 83.

[6] Shujaat Bukhari, 'We Are Not Against Dialogue: Hizb Chief', *Hindu*, 15 December 2016.

[7] Data on the number of active militants in Kashmir is provided by the J&K Police. Membership estimates for individual groups are not officially available. However, based on the pattern of fatalities suffered by each armed group in previous years, LeT appears to be the largest armed group followed by JeM and HM. In 2022, the three major armed groups suffered 39, 15 and six fatalities, respectively. The remaining fatalities are attributed to smaller groups, such as Al-Badr, the TRF and Ansar Ghazwat-ul-Hind.

[8] 'UNMOGIP Fact Sheet', UN Peacekeeping, November 2021.

[9] 'UNMOGIP Fact Sheet', UN Peacekeeping, 17 June 2022.

[10] See 'Power Stations' on NHPC website. See also 'Kashmir and the Politics of Water', Al-Jazeera, 1 August 2011.

[11] See Audrey Truschke, 'Hindutva's Dangerous Rewriting of History', *South Asia Multidisciplinary Academic Journal*, no. 24/25, 2020; and 'Religion Census 2011'; and Ziya US Salam, 'Christophe Jaffrelot: "At Stake Is Survival of Indo-Islamic Civilisation"', *Frontline*, 17 December 2021.

[12] India, Ministry of Defence, 'Joint Statement', 25 February 2021.

[13] Press Trust of India (PTI), 'Situation Along LoC Stable: Govt in Rajya Sabha', *Times of India*, 21 March 2022.

[14] PTI, 'Pakistan Army Chief Bajwa Says All Disputes with India Should Be Settled Peacefully Through Dialogue', *Indian Express*, 2 April 2022.

[15] India, Ministry of Statistics and Programme Implementation, 'Periodic Labour Force Survey', April–June 2021, p. A-35.

[16] Peerzada Ashiq, 'Huge Potential for Investments in Jammu & Kashmir: Gulf Delegation', *Hindu*, 22 March 2022.

[17] Safwat Zargar, 'Despite Investments, Why Has Unemployment Soared in Jammu and Kashmir?', ScrolL.in, 26 April 2022.

[18] Mukeet Akmali, 'Unemployment Rate Touches 25% in J&K', *Greater Kashmir*, 15 April 2022.

[19] Mukeet Akmali, 'High-security Prison to Be Built in Kathua', *Greater Kashmir*, 6 March 2022.

[20] PTI, 'Iridium Sat Phones, Wi-Fi-enabled Thermal Imagery Tools Find Way to Terror Groups in Kashmir', *Economic Times*, 17 April 2022.
[21] Pravin Sawhney, 'Why Pakistan Wants Peace with India', *TheWeek*, 17 April 2022.
[22] Esha Roy and Shubhakit Roy, 'Keen on Good Ties with Pak But It Must End Terror, Bids to Draw Global Attention to J&K: General Naravane', *Indian Express*, 30 April 2022.
[23] PTI, '"Centre Will Grant Jammu and Kashmir Statehood at an Appropriate Time": Amit Shah', *Wire*, 14 February 2021.
[24] Naafey Sardar, 'Bearing the Cost of Global Politics: The Impact of FATF Grey-listing on Pakistan's Economy', Working Paper 07, Tabadlab, 2021.
[25] G. Sampath, 'India's Designation by the USCIRF', *Hindu*, 27 April 2022.
[26] China, Ministry of Foreign Affairs, 'Foreign Ministry Spokesperson Zhao Lijian's Regular Press Conference on February 11, 2022', 11 February 2022.
[27] 'India Defends Its Russia Position, Criticizes West at Raisina Dialogue', DW, 29 April 2022.
[28] 'China Moves to Counter India with Arms Sales to Pakistan', *Financial Times*, 18 February 2022.

MYANMAR

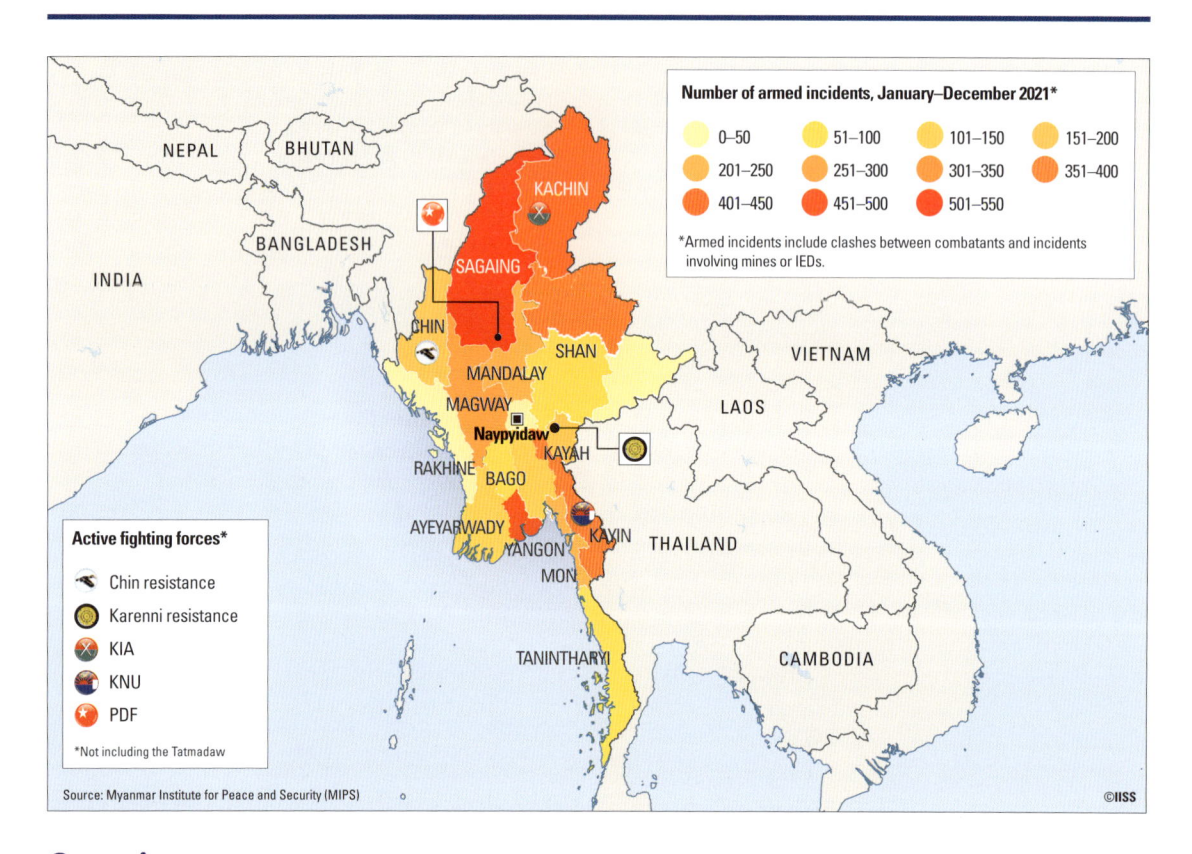

Number of armed incidents, January–December 2021*

- 0–50
- 51–100
- 101–150
- 151–200
- 201–250
- 251–300
- 301–350
- 351–400
- 401–450
- 451–500
- 501–550

*Armed incidents include clashes between combatants and incidents involving mines or IEDs.

Active fighting forces*
- Chin resistance
- Karenni resistance
- KIA
- KNU
- PDF

*Not including the Tatmadaw

Source: Myanmar Institute for Peace and Security (MIPS)

© IISS

Overview

The Myanmar military, or the Tatmadaw, has waged multiple continuous wars against a wide array of armed actors since the country became independent in 1948. The experience of an existential struggle against the China-backed Communist Party of Burma, which lasted until 1989, made the military deeply suspicious of its neighbours, prompting the Tatmadaw to characterise itself as protector of the nation. Driven by a distorted sense of duty, the military has entrenched itself at the heart of Myanmar politics and undertaken a decades-long struggle to crush the country's democratic movement. Over the last three decades, it has continued its attempt to forge a Bamar-centric nation and worked to quell ethnic armed organisations (EAOs) fighting for greater autonomy. The military has long responded to threats with brute force, gaining international notoriety for crackdowns on protesters and scorched-earth campaigns against the Karen, Kachin and – more recently – Rohingya communities.

Myanmar's conflicts are further stoked by China, which despite its occasional role as a mediator continues to supply all sides with weapons and shield the Tatmadaw from international backlash. The result is a perennial state of violence, humanitarian catastrophe and severe underdevelopment.

After a long period as an international pariah, in 2003 the military junta formulated a new approach to managing ethnic armed insurgency and democratic opposition by endorsing a seven-point road map to democracy. A new constitution in 2008 placed the country on a path towards a semi-democratic transition. The military also launched a new peace process under the framework of the Nationwide Ceasefire Agreement (NCA) and invited prominent EAOs to join talks to discuss a federal democratic union. The NCA was signed in October 2015 and the National League for Democracy (NLD) under Aung San Suu Kyi's leadership swept the first free and

Armed Conflict Global Relevance Indicator (ACGRI)

Myanmar
- Incidence: 84
- Human impact: 24
- Geopolitical impact: 4

Key Conflict Statistics

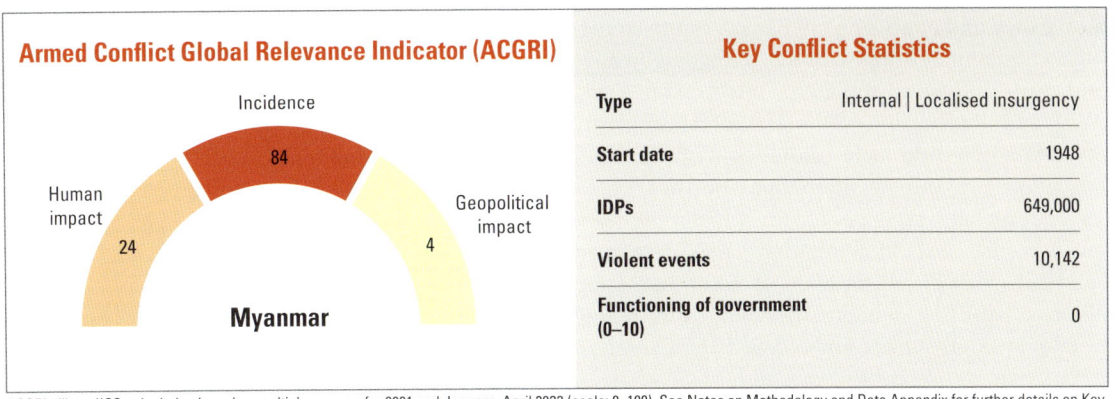

Type	Internal | Localised insurgency
Start date	1948
IDPs	649,000
Violent events	10,142
Functioning of government (0–10)	0

ACGRI pillars: IISS calculation based on multiple sources for 2021 and January–April 2022 (scale: 0–100). See Notes on Methodology and Data Appendix for further details on Key Conflict Statistics.

open general elections a month later. Myanmar entered an era of optimism with renewed hopes for democracy and peace.

The democratic transition and NCA-driven peace process quickly became strained. In protest against the military's refusal to include all active EAOs in the peace process, seven of the nine key EAOs invited declined to sign the peace deal. The partial ceasefire and non-inclusive dialogue that followed failed to prevent the situation from deteriorating; between 2015 and 2020, several conflicts expanded and intensified.[1] Meanwhile, tensions between the military, which retained one-quarter of parliamentary seats, and the ruling NLD escalated as the two sides vied for control of the nation's instruments of power. Dismayed by Aung San Suu Kyi's second electoral victory in November 2020, the military lobbed accusations of voter fraud against the Union Election Commission and the NLD and threatened a coup. Last-minute efforts to mediate a compromise failed and on the morning of 1 February 2021 the military seized all levers of judicial, legislative and executive power.

Public opposition to the coup was near universal, with urban protests spreading to rural areas. The regime unleashed a brutal crackdown on civilians in late February, killing hundreds in the streets. Ousted members of the elected civilian government formed the Committee Representing Pyidaungsu Hluttaw (CRPH) and later the National Unity Government (NUG), a 'parallel' government that claims legitimate rule over Myanmar. As the regime's violence intensified, elements of the traditionally non-violent democratic movement began to consider armed struggle. In March 2021, the CRPH announced that citizens had 'the right to self-defense', prompting thousands of young protesters to flee the cities and seek military training in areas controlled by EAOs.[2]

The NUG abandoned non-violent struggle, announced the formation of a People's Defence Force (PDF) in May 2021 and called for a nationwide 'defensive war' against the junta.[3] Hundreds of localised resistance groups, urban guerrilla outfits and PDF units proliferated across the country. Resistance groups began to target civil servants, junta administrators and alleged regime informants. Later, anti-regime fighters built homemade weapons and launched ambush attacks on security forces. By 2022, a full-scale insurgency was under way in Myanmar's central plains, an area inhabited mainly by the ethnic Bamar majority where violence had been absent for decades. In response, the military began arming militias formed by supporters of the extreme Buddhist nationalist group Ma Ba Tha and launched a ferocious scorched-earth campaign to destroy the PDF.

Responses to the junta's crackdown among Myanmar's most influential EAOs were more mixed and ambiguous, tempered by complex political and military considerations. The Karen National Union (KNU), the most influential EAO signatory of the NCA, wavered between upholding the ceasefire and responding more forcefully to the regime's crimes, leading to limited but intense bouts of renewed fighting. After years of calm in the north, the Kachin Independence Army (KIA) took newly formed PDF units under its command and launched a limited campaign to retake lost territory. Smaller groups like the Chin National Front (CNF) and the Karenni National Progressive Party (KNPP) joined forces with nascent resistance outfits to fight the military, which responded with air barrage and attacks on civilians. Despite engaging in frequent fighting with the Tatmadaw in 2019 and 2020, following the coup, the Arakan Army (AA) and the Ta'ang National Liberation Army (TNLA) entered de facto ceasefires with the military in order to pursue alternative priorities.

The global response to Myanmar's worsening violence and humanitarian crisis remained subdued, with the Association of Southeast Asian Nations (ASEAN) notably hesitating and failing to take a tough stance. Emboldened by a sense of impunity, the military continued to disregard a five-point consensus agreed by ASEAN in April 2021, mounting continued attacks on the opposition and civilians. A firmer stance by some ASEAN members and a renewed diplomatic push led by Cambodia in early 2022 suggested the organisation's increasing concern. However, most observers doubt the viability of ASEAN's proposed road map towards a solution. There seems to be little chance of talks between the junta and the NUG or PDF as both sides continue to seek one another's destruction.

Conflict Parties

State Administrative Council (SAC) (Myanmar armed forces or Tatmadaw)

Strength: Estimates range from 100,000–356,000 active military, 107,000 active paramilitary, with increasing deployment of auxiliary and non-combat forces to fight the growing resistance movement.

Areas of operation: Operates nationwide. Headquarters in Naypyidaw.

Leadership: Senior-General Min Aung Hlaing (commander-in-chief), who assumed the role of SAC chairperson following the 1 February 2021 coup and later declared himself prime minister.

Structure: Six Bureaus of Special Operations with 14 regional military commands. It also fields ten light infantry divisions – elite units tasked with spearheading offensives.

History: Seized power in 1962 and ruled via several successive regimes until 2011 when it began a process of democratisation. However, it continued to reserve one-quarter of parliamentary seats, as enshrined in the 2008 constitution.

Objectives: Preserve the union, quell ethnic and political dissent, maintain political power, conduct Bamar-centric state building, modernise the military and secure international credibility.

Opponents: More than 20 EAOs, the NUG/PDF, localised resistance groups and the general population.

Affiliates/allies: Has integrated various armed organisations into its command under the People's Militia Force and Border Guard Force (BGF) schemes. Currently arming groups collectively referred to as 'Pyusawhti' – localised militias formed by veterans, pro-military civilians and Buddhist extremists at the village level.

Resources/capabilities: Likely self-sufficient in the production of small arms and munitions. Increasingly reliant on airpower, it possesses MiG-29 and Yak-130 aircraft and Mi-17 and Mi-24 helicopters from Russia and China. It has demonstrated joint naval, air and land operations and is capable of mounting major operations on multiple fronts. However, new challenges posed by the PDF mean that its forces have been overstretched.

Arakan Army/United League of Arakan (AA/ULA)

Strength: Up to 10,000 fighters, the majority deployed in Rakhine State.[4]

Areas of operation: Most active in northern and central Rakhine State as well as southern Chin State. Limited operations in Kachin State, northern Shan State and possibly Bangladesh.

Leadership: Twan Mrat Naing (founder and commander-in-chief); Nyo Twan Awng (vice deputy commander); Oo Hlaw Saw (political chief).

Structure: Top commanders direct operations from headquarters in either Kachin State or Shan State. Regular fighters operate from villages, jungle hideouts and fixed positions.

History: Founded in 2009 in Kachin State under the tutelage of the KIA, the group started to build a presence in Rakhine State as early as 2013.

Objectives: Establish autonomous control over Rakhine State and liberate the Rakhine people.

Opponents: The Tatmadaw and the former NLD-led civilian government.

Affiliates/allies: Member of the Federal Political Negotiation Consultative Committee (FPNCC), a 'political' alliance of EAOs outside the NCA. It is also a member of two military alliances, the Northern Alliance and the Brotherhood Alliance.

Resources/capabilities: Capable of mobilising large contingents of fighters to stage frontal assaults on military and police positions. Fields small arms, mortars, improvised explosive devices (IEDs), 107 millimetre surface-to-surface rockets and satellite-communications equipment. Wields significant administrative control in Rakhine State and has strong support from the local population.

Kachin Independence Army/Kachin Independence Organisation (KIA/KIO)

Strength: Up to 10,000 regulars.

Areas of operation: Historically controlled large static swaths of Kachin State and maintained mobile units in northern Shan State, where its presence is not recognised by the Tatmadaw. Following the 2021 coup, the KIA expanded in northern Sagaing Region and was reportedly operating in parts of Mandalay Region.

Leadership: Gen. N'Ban La heads the KIO and is the senior commander of the KIA.

Structure: Divided into ten brigades, with control over multiple subordinate PDF units.

History: Formed in 1961. Signed a ceasefire agreement in 1994 that broke down in 2011. The KIA founded the Northern Alliance in 2016 before launching a major joint offensive against the Tatmadaw.

Objectives: Seek Kachin autonomy within a federal democratic union and dismantle the Tatmadaw military-political institution.

Opponents: The Tatmadaw.

Affiliates/allies: Member of the FPNCC and leader of the Northern Alliance. Participant in the National Unity Consultative Council (NUCC) and the Central Command and Coordination Committee (C3C) organised by the NUG.

Resources/capabilities: Generates income through formal and informal activities. Enjoys large and active diaspora support. Likely manufactures or assembles small arms and ammunition in its area of control. Possesses 107 mm unguided rockets. Demonstrated ability to capture territory, down helicopters and raise proxy forces.

Karen National Liberation Army/Karen National Union (KNLA/KNU)

Strength: Between 4,000 and 5,000 regulars, up to 2,000 home-guard fighters organised as the Karen National Defence Organisation (KNDO), and control over multiple PDF units.[5] Its size is likely growing.

Areas of operation: Military operations in Bago Region, Kayin State, Mon State and Tanintharyi Region. Political elements active in Thailand.

Leadership: Gen. Saw Mutu Sae Poe (chairperson); Padoh Saw Kwe Htoo Win (vice chairperson); Padoh Saw Tadoh Moo (general secretary).

Structure: The KNLA is formed of seven brigades and a special force.

History: The KNU was established in 1947. That same year, it formed the KNDO, a collection of local armed units that later evolved into the KNLA. The KNLA/KNU signed a ceasefire with the Tatmadaw in 2012 and signed the NCA in 2015. It served as the leader of the Peace Process Steering Team (PPST) until 2018. The KNDO re-emerged as a relevant fighting element following the 2021 coup.

Objectives: Seek Karen self-determination within a federal democratic union, oppose military rule through either peaceful or revolutionary means.

Opponents: The Tatmadaw and some elements of the BGF.

Affiliates/allies: Though it once led the PPST as an NCA signatory, the KNU signalled its intent to withdraw from the bloc in April 2022. It participates in the NUCC.

Resources/capabilities: Primarily fields small arms including leftover US-made Vietnam War-era M-16s and guns sold in Thailand's civilian weapons market. Also has rocket-propelled grenades (RPGs) and landmines.

Karenni Nationalities Defense Force (KNDF)

Strength: 1,000 regulars from the KNPP and 3,000–6,000 fighters under the KNDF.[6]

Areas of operation: Kayah State and the area around Pekon, southern Shan State.

Leadership: The KNDF is an umbrella group of various Karenni resistance outfits organised under the command of the KNPP. The KNPP is led by Khu Oo Reh (chairperson); Abel Tweed (vice chairperson); Khu Plureh (general secretary).[7]

Structure: Organised into as many as 18 volunteer battalions.[8]

History: The KNPP was founded in Kayah State in 1957. It signed a state- and union-level ceasefire in 2012 but never signed the NCA despite encouragement from the military and fellow EAOs. The KNDF was formed on 31 May 2021 to consolidate and coordinate various ethnic-Karenni resistance outfits that sprang up in opposition to the military coup of February 2021. KNDF forces besieged Loikaw, Kayah State's capital, in January 2022.

Objectives: Reversal of the coup, overthrow of the Tatmadaw, ethnic and national liberation.

Opponents: The Tatmadaw.

Affiliates/allies: KNPP and KNDF forces fight alongside PDF units under the NUG's command. Karenni resistance likely coordinates on some level with elements from the KNU. The KNPP is active in the NUCC.

Resources/capabilities: The KNDF quickly emerged as a potent fighting force capable of staging major assaults on urban areas, supported by the KNPP's arms and training. It fights with automatic rifles, launchers, mines and homemade weapons, including commercial drones armed with IEDs.

Myanmar National Democratic Alliance Army/ Myanmar National Truth and Justice Party (MNDAA/MNTJP)

Strength: Between 3,000 and 4,000 fighters.

Areas of operation: Kokang self-administered zone, northern Shan State.

Leadership: Peng Deren (commander-in-chief); Yang Wenzhou (deputy commander).

Structure: Three brigades: 211st, 311th and 511th.

History: Formed in 1989 by Peng Jiasheng as a breakaway of the Communist Party of Burma. Suffered an internal split in 2009 after Peng refused to transform the group into a border guard. A subsequent Tatmadaw offensive expelled Peng from Laukkai; an MNDAA bid to retake it in 2015 ultimately failed.

Objectives: Liberate the Kokang people, oppose authoritarianism.

Opponents: The Tatmadaw.

Affiliates/allies: Member of the FPNCC, the Northern Alliance and the Brotherhood Alliance.

Resources/capabilities: Fields small arms including AK pattern rifles, RPGs, mortars and landmines. Often operates in combined units with the TNLA.

Shan State Army–North/Shan State Progress Party (SSA–N/SSPP)

Strength: Between 3,000 and 4,000 fighters.

Areas of operation: Primary operational area in northern Shan State with some possible unarmed activities in neighbouring Mandalay Region. The SSPP now operates in parts of southern Shan State following a series of victories over the Restoration Council of Shan State (RCSS) in late 2021.

Leadership: Lt-Gen. Pang Fa (commander of the SSA–N and chairperson of the SSPP).

Structure: Three brigades split into nine battalions.[9]

History: The SSPP signed a ceasefire with the government in 1989. It maintains an intense rivalry with the RCSS.

Objectives: Seek Shan unity and self-determination within the multi-ethnic Shan State.

Opponents: The Tatmadaw and RCSS.

Affiliates/allies: Member of the FPNCC and military partner to the TNLA in its fight against the RCSS.

Resources/capabilities: Relies heavily on the United Wa State Army (UWSA) for small arms and support.

Shan State Army–South/Restoration Council of Shan State (SSA–S/RCSS)

Strength: Between 8,000 and 10,000 fighters.

Areas of operation: Headquartered at Loi Tai Leng in southern Shan State. Began operations in northern Shan State as early as 2011, with further expansion there after 2015. Retreated from parts of northern Shan State in late 2021.

Leadership: Yawd Serk (founder and chairperson).

Structure: Ten brigades.

History: The SSA–S was formed by a breakaway faction of the Mong Tai Army in 1996 after refusing to surrender to the government. The RCSS, the group's political wing, was then established in 1999. The SSA–S/RCSS signed an initial ceasefire with the government in 2011 and joined the NCA in 2015.

Objectives: Shan self-determination within a federal democratic union.

Opponents: The Tatmadaw, TNLA and SSPP.

Affiliates/allies: Member of the PPST as a signatory to the NCA.

Resources/capabilities: Fields small arms, landmines, RPGs and mortars.

Ta'ang National Liberation Army/Palaung State Liberation Front (TNLA/PSLF)

Strength: Between 8,000 and 10,000 fighters, including irregulars.

Areas of operation: Strongest presence in the Palaung self-administered zone but operates in nearly every Palaung area in northern Shan State. May be increasing presence in parts of southern Shan State.

Leadership: Tar Aik Bong (chairperson); Tar Ho Plan (commander-in-chief); Tar Bone Kyaw (first secretary-general).

Structure: Mobile command structure drawing on both regular and irregular fighters.

History: Its predecessor, the Palaung State Liberation Army (PSLA), signed a ceasefire in 1991 before disarming in 2005. Former PSLA cadres rearmed and formed the TNLA/PSLF in 2009. The TNLA leads the Brotherhood Alliance together with the AA and MNDAA. In 2019, it spearheaded a major offensive along the primary overland trade corridor linking Myanmar with China.

Objectives: Liberate ethnic Palaung people and form an autonomous Palaung state within a federal union.

Opponents: The Tatmadaw, RCSS and Pan Say Militia.

Affiliates/allies: Member of the FPNCC, the Northern Alliance and leader of the Brotherhood Alliance.

Resources/capabilities: Capable of conducting large-scale offensive operations in areas under government control. Demonstrated coordinated military action with alliance partners. Fields small arms, mortars, landmines and 107 mm surface-to-surface rockets. Relies heavily on 'taxation' for income generation.

National Unity Government/People's Defence Force (NUG/PDF) and Pa Kha Pha

Strength: The NUG claims there are 50,000–100,000 fighters organised under either the PDF or the Pa Kha Pha (localised resistance groups). It has not specified how many are under its command.

Areas of operation: Active nationwide, with strongest presence in Magway, Mandalay, Sagaing and Yangon regions and Kayin State. De facto headquarters located within KNU-controlled territory, likely in Kayin State. Political and bureaucratic elements are active in Thailand.

Leadership: Aung San Suu Kyi (state counsellor); U Win Myint (president); Duwa Lashi La (acting president); Mahn Winn Khaing Thann (prime minister); U Yee Mon (defence minister).

Structure: The NUG functions as the executive while the CRPH serves as an interim legislature comprised mostly of NLD parliamentarians ousted by the military. The NUG operates 17 ministries. The Ministry of Defense commands the PDF and, in theory, the Pa Kha Pha or Local People's Defence Forces (LPDF). However, the NUG's command and control is weak and most LPDFs operate autonomously at the village or ward level. LPDFs vary greatly in structure and form, ranging from small groups of vigilante justice seekers to dogged urban guerrilla cells. Within the PDF scheme, the Ministry of Defense plans to raise one division for each of the five regional commands.

History: In March 2021, anti-coup protesters organised into teams of street defenders to ward off the crackdown by security forces. The idea of 'people's defence' grew from these teams after the ousted civilian government said citizens had a right to self-defence. The NUG formed the PDF under its command in May 2021 and localised groups proliferated rapidly after the NUG called for a nationwide uprising in September that year.

Objectives: National liberation via the overthrow and dismantling of the Tatmadaw (to be replaced by a federal army) and the creation of a democratic federal union.

Opponents: The Tatmadaw and 'Pyusawhti' militias.

Affiliates/allies: Officially allied with the CNF. Cooperates with multiple EAOs including the KIA, KNU and KNPP, as well as various strike councils, civil-society organisations and political parties. Political and military coordination undertaken via the NUCC and C3C respectively.

Resources/capabilities: The NUG, PDF and LPDFs are comparatively impoverished, lacking sufficient access to finances and weaponry. The NUG raises funds through taxes and donations from the grassroots and diaspora. It also issues bonds denoted in the cryptocurrency 'Tether'. PDFs operating alongside EAOs are usually better equipped with automatic rifles and RPGs. LPDFs fight primarily with IEDs and a wide assortment of improvised weapons, such as single-shot rifles, pipe mortars, clones and shotguns.

Other conflict parties

Arakan Liberation Party (ALP), Chin National Front (CNF), Democratic Karen Benevolent Army (DKBA), Karen National Union–Peace Council (KNU–PC), National Democratic Alliance Army (NDAA), New Mon State Party (NMSP), Pa-Oh National Liberation Army (PNLO), United Wa State Army (UWSA).

Conflict Drivers

Security

Transient ceasefires and group recognition:
Since 1989, the military has sought ceasefires with some groups while it has escalated attacks on others. Most of the fighting in the last decade has taken place between the military and the four Northern Alliance groups not party to any ceasefire. Prior to 2019, the military refused to even recognise three of the groups as potential dialogue partners. A lack of recognition fuelled conflict by precluding avenues for dialogue and, in the absence of territorial demarcation, rendering entire geographical spaces as contested. Similarly, the SAC and the NUG/PDF label one another as terrorist groups, leaving no potential avenue for dialogue or humanitarian coordination. Overstretched by a growing insurrection in the central plains, the military hopes to avoid any full-scale confrontation with the EAOs and maintains its recognition of agreed ceasefires. However, the junta's crusade against the PDF, many units of which operate in EAO-controlled territory, has led to increased fighting with the EAOs.

Political

Military rule and ethnic marginalisation:
Myanmar's armed conflicts are driven by a resistance to military rule and ethnic struggles for greater autonomy. Though in 1947 the national father, General Aung San, promised ethnic self-determination and the right to secede, since Myanmar's independence Bamar-centric regimes have dominated national politics and pulled wealth and resources from the peripheries at the expense of minority populations. To crush enduring ethnic ambitions, the military has

long deployed collective punishment and discriminatory policies, leading to a sense of trauma that drives protracted support for armed resistance.

Although the military periodically has managed to co-opt the Bamar majority into supporting its wars against ethnic resistance fighters, the general population has never accepted military rule. Since the junta's crackdown on protesters in 1988, Aung San Suu Kyi, revered locally as 'Mother Suu', has led a non-violent movement to unseat the military from power and restore democracy.

Economic
Illicit economies, land access and development:
Illicit economies sustain armed actors on all sides. During the Cold War, the military junta sought assistance from the United States to combat its opponents under the pretence of efforts to eradicate the illegal-drugs trade, as some rebel groups became immensely rich from opium production. More recently, Myanmar has transitioned into the world's largest producer of methamphetamine. Though state-backed militias are likely the primary culprits behind the illicit industry, some EAOs profit from the trade by taxing smugglers, leasing land to producers and providing security to transnational crime syndicates. Myanmar is also the world's largest producer of jade, a billion-dollar industry based primarily on grey- and black-market export to China. Valuable resources like jade, amber, timber and gold are concentrated in areas contested by the military and EAOs. The Tatmadaw has also profited from offshore gas production and by awarding mining licences for rare gems and other minerals. The struggle for control over resource-rich lands prolongs armed conflict while poorly regulated, China-backed investments like dams, a gas pipeline and banana plantations harm the environment and disaffect local communities.

Key Events in 2021–22

POLITICAL EVENTS

16 April 2021
CRPH forms the NUG, a 'parallel' government in opposition to the military junta.

21 May
Myanmar's junta-backed election commission announces that it will dissolve Aung San Suu Kyi's NLD for alleged electoral fraud committed during November 2020 elections.

14 June
Regime prosecutors put Aung San Suu Kyi on trial.

12 July
Citizens queue for hours for oxygen cylinders as a devastating third COVID-19 wave sweeps Myanmar.

1 August
SAC chairperson Min Aung Hlaing declares himself prime minister of a caretaker government and pledges elections by 2023.

MILITARY/VIOLENT EVENTS

27 March 2021
On Myanmar's Armed Forces Day, the Tatmadaw kills over 100 protesters across the country.

27 March
The KNLA's Brigade 5 overruns the Tatmadaw's border base at Thee Mu Hta in Hpapun district, Kayin State.

9 April
Regime forces kill more than 80 people in Bago, an industrial city near Yangon.

5 May
The NUG announces the formation of the PDF under its command.

3 August
The MNDAA launches an offensive to retake territory around Mongko, a strategic town on the border with China.

Timeline

15 October
ASEAN countries decide to exclude Min Aung Hlaing from its upcoming regional summit in Brunei.

15 November
Junta authorities release US journalist Danny Fenster shortly after sentencing him to 11 years in prison.

7 January 2022
Cambodian Prime Minister Hun Sen arrives in Myanmar in the first visit by a foreign leader since the military's February 2021 coup.

27 January
The NUCC convenes its first People's Congress.

31 January
Myanmar's population stages a nationwide 'silent strike' to mark the anniversary of the coup.

21 March
The ASEAN special envoy to Myanmar, Prak Sokhonn, meets with junta leaders in his first visit to the country.

3 April
EAO signatories to the NCA conclude the 4th PPST conference in Chiang Mai, Thailand.

7 September
The NUG calls for a national revolt against the military junta, labelling the moment as 'D-Day'.

October
The RCSS withdraws from its northern stronghold at Hu Hsun in northern Shan State following a series of defeats inflicted by the TNLA and SSPP.

15 December
Heavy fighting between the KNLA and the Tatmadaw breaks out in the flashpoint village of Lay Kay Kaw, Kayin State.

24 December
Tatmadaw soldiers kill more than 30 people in Hpruso, Kayah State, galvanising Karenni resistance forces.

January 2022
Local media and human-rights groups estimate that more than half the population of Kayah State has fled as clashes worsen between the Tatmadaw and Karenni fighters.

1 February
Conflict between the KIA and Tatmadaw intensifies after the former launches an offensive in Puta-O, Kachin State.

February
The Tatmadaw escalates its scorched-earth campaign against the growing resistance movement in the central plains.

Responses to the Conflict

Security

In response to the 2021 coup and the military's killing of civilians, the general population supported the proliferation of the PDF, urban guerrilla cells and localised resistance groups through grassroots fundraising. Nascent resistance outfits initiated a campaign targeting junta administrators, military-linked businesses and alleged regime collaborators. According to the Myanmar Institute for Peace and Security, at least 698 civilians were killed in this campaign between March and December 2021 as violence spread to more than half of Myanmar's 358 townships. By early 2022, there was a full-blown insurgency in Magway, Mandalay and Sagaing regions.

In Kachin State, the KIA launched a limited offensive to recapture territory in strategic areas, such as Tanai and Hpakant. The KIA's partner, the MNDAA, attempted to retake territory around the town of Mongko. Angered by the military's crackdown on civilians, smaller groups, such as the CNF and KNPP, led ethnic resistance groups in renewed insurgencies in Chin and Kayah states, respectively. In southern Myanmar, KNU leaders debated whether to uphold the troubled ceasefire or take the fight to the regime. Some units launched attacks on the military, which responded with airstrikes on KNU and civilian targets.

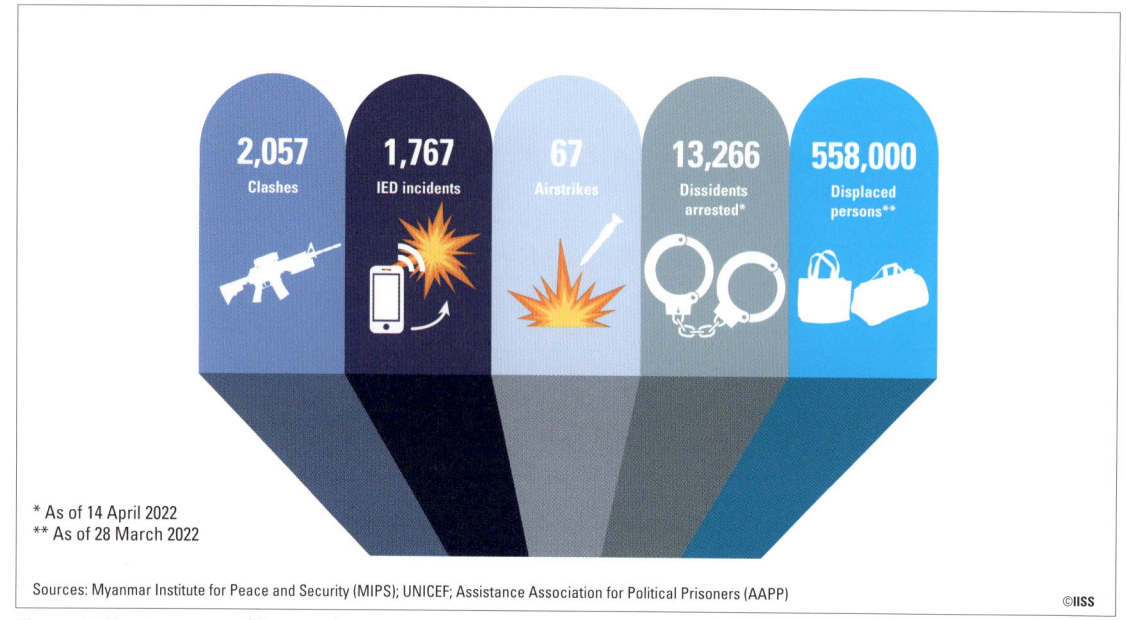

Figure 1: Post-coup conflict trends, 2021

- 2,057 Clashes
- 1,767 IED incidents
- 67 Airstrikes
- 13,266 Dissidents arrested*
- 558,000 Displaced persons**

* As of 14 April 2022
** As of 28 March 2022

Sources: Myanmar Institute for Peace and Security (MIPS); UNICEF; Assistance Association for Political Prisoners (AAPP)

©IISS

Despite heavy fighting between 2018 and 2020, the AA and TNLA de-escalated tensions with the military and upheld de facto ceasefires. For the AA, the Tatmadaw's preoccupation with anti-coup resistance offered a window of respite, which it used to consolidate administrative control in Rakhine State. Likewise, a combined force of TNLA and SSPP fighters renewed efforts to expel the RCSS from northern Shan State, achieving significant success by late 2021.

For the Tatmadaw, the rise of new armed groups in formerly pacified areas posed a significant challenge. With few exceptions, it kept the bulk of its strike divisions deployed against the EAOs and directed local and auxiliary units against the PDF. It likely aims to avoid full-scale confrontation against powerful EAOs by offering peace talks and limiting retaliatory strikes. In contrast, it views the PDF and urban guerrilla groups as 'terrorists', vowing to destroy them.

Economic/development

Myanmar's economy contracted by 17.9% in 2021 and is forecasted to grow by only 1.6% in 2022.[10] By September 2021, the kyat had lost 60% of its value and Myanmar's central bank began requiring exporters to sell excess foreign exchange within 30 days.[11] By April 2022, the bank had sold off US$553.8 million and issued an order demanding that foreign-exchange earnings be converted into local currency within one working day.[12] It also outlined plans to accept Thai baht, Chinese renminbi and Indian rupees for cross-border transactions to reduce dependency on the US dollar. Following the coup, major donors – including the European Union, the United Kingdom and Japan – suspended development assistance to the military government, while worsening violence and economic woes prompted an exodus of international firms. Energy giants Total and Chevron announced their withdrawal in January 2022, citing human-rights concerns.[13]

Diplomacy

In April 2021, ASEAN reached a 'five-point consensus' that called for a cessation of hostilities, dialogue, an ASEAN-led mediation process, humanitarian assistance and an ASEAN special envoy's visit to Myanmar. The first envoy, Brunei's second minister of foreign affairs, was appointed in August but enjoyed little success as the military escalated attacks on the opposition. In January 2022, Cambodia launched a renewed diplomatic push, with the prime minister meeting with SAC chairperson Min Aung Hlaing. Cambodian Foreign Minister Prak Sokhonn was appointed ASEAN envoy in early 2022. In March, Nippon Foundation chairperson Yōhei Sasakawa met separately with Sokhonn and the ethnic signatories to the NCA, suggesting that the two parties cooperate. Though the United Nations General Assembly formally condemned the military's coup in a June

2021 resolution,[14] a UN Security Council resolution was precluded by Russia and China's support for the regime. UN Secretary-General António Guterres appointed Singapore's Noeleen Heyzer as his Special Envoy on Myanmar in October 2021.

Humanitarian aid
In February–March 2022, up to 558,000 people were displaced by violence, with 308,600 displaced in Chin State and Magway and Sagaing regions where the military launched a scorched-earth campaign against resistance groups and their supporters.[15] According to the open-source monitoring organisation Data for Myanmar, the military razed 7,973 civilian houses across 222 locations between February 2021 and March 2022.[16] In January 2022, the UN Office for the Coordination of Humanitarian Affairs (UNOCHA) estimated that 14.4m people would need humanitarian assistance in 2022, with 6.2m requiring urgent support.[17] UNOCHA's Myanmar Humanitarian Response Plan requested US$826m; only 10.4% was secured by 31 May 2022.[18]

Conflict Outlook

Political scenarios
The Tatmadaw's 2021 coup is far from a fait accompli. The military was surprised by the public's reaction and poorly equipped to combat a massive armed uprising in Bamar-majority areas. The resistance bombing campaign targeting government offices and employees crippled the regime's administration. Though it maintained tenuous control over cities and major towns in the reporting period, its authority in rural areas, where 70% of the population resides, is severely limited. The SAC's economic policies and handling of the coronavirus pandemic have invited disaster. Major cities like Yangon and Mandalay have faced severe power shortages and essential-commodity prices continue to rise as a consequence of worsening instability.

Most of the population recognises the NUG as the legitimate government and readily offers financial support. Though they face significant challenges, the NUG and PDF continued to strengthen and expand in the reporting period. The NUG has also achieved limited international recognition, being considered by ASEAN as a key actor to include in any dialogue. However, the rigid formality of the international system means that it will continue to be difficult for embassies to deal with the NUG as the SAC retains control of most state functions.

Though the SAC promised to hold elections, it warned that it would not be possible to do so if the security situation remained unstable. Given the PDF's ascendancy and the SAC's vow to destroy it, the conflict is expected to intensify in the coming year. The military will likely make every effort to further entrench itself at the core of Myanmar politics; any future election it holds will be viewed by the population as a sham, prolonging the conflict. Though it is attempting to restart the peace process, most EAOs have indicated that they are reluctant to join talks given the military's ongoing widespread attacks on the population. The most likely scenario for the near future is a continued violent contest between the SAC and the NUG/PDF accompanied by social and economic turmoil.

Escalation potential and conflict-related risks
The new insurgency in the central plains poses a high risk for escalation and spiralling violence at the communal level. Due to competing commitments and unfamiliarity with the terrain, the Tatmadaw armed local militias ('Pyusawhti'). Alongside its scorched-earth campaign, the military's arming of sympathetic villages ignited a cycle of retributive killings, wherein PDF units and Pyusawhti militias attacked one another and the opposing side's families.

Confronted with the military's detention of protesters and activists, the public quickly grew wary of 'dalans' – neighbourhood residents accused of being spies. To combat the regime's intelligence network, nascent underground groups began targeting suspected regime collaborators. Targets were often chosen in a highly decentralised process, doxed online and killed. Though the resistance justified the murder of collaborators as necessary, such vigilante justice is not systematic and there have been cases of mistaken identity. Moreover, the tactic of using social-media hitlists also risks sparking reprisal. Similar pro-regime social-media accounts outed regular citizens for supporting the NUG/PDF and offered rewards for their killing.

The future of the conflict between the Tatmadaw and EAOs is uncertain. Though the KIA and KNU escalated their operations against the military in the reporting period, neither group desired renewed displacement and devastation in their communities. Moreover, both China and Thailand pressured the EAOs to maintain border stability. In 2021 and early 2022, the Tatmadaw remained preoccupied with the nationwide uprising and lacked the resources to wage full-scale offensive operations against the KNU or KIA. Instead, it responded to attacks by targeting implicated units and punishing civilians, leading to episodes of limited or controlled escalation. However, the SAC also vowed to 'annihilate' the PDF: since the PDF operates in EAO areas, attacking it risks confrontation with the EAOs. An unintended escalatory spiral is a real possibility.

Strategic implications and global influences

Most Western actors were relatively uninterested in the situation in Myanmar while the UN Security Council had little power to change the conflict's course given China and Russia's protection of the junta. China appeared to accept the military's rule, adopting a 'business as usual' approach to the situation. Though on occasion China and Thailand may have pressured EAOs to avoid fighting along their borders, both countries remain key weapons markets. While ASEAN represents the greatest prospect for international mediation, it is unlikely that its five-point consensus will be implemented. Regardless, negotiation among conflict parties is politically inconceivable since the general population demands the military's overthrow. Myanmar's conflicts will likely continue to play out in near isolation.

Notes

[1] Stein Tønnesson, Min Zaw Oo and Maung Ne Lynn Aung, 'Non-inclusive Ceasefires Do Not Bring Peace: Findings from Myanmar', *Small Wars & Insurgencies*, vol. 33, no. 3, 2022, pp. 313–49.

[2] CRPH Myanmar (@CPRHMyanmar), tweet, 14 March 2021.

[3] 'Myanmar Shadow Government Calls for Uprising Against Military', Al-Jazeera, 7 September 2021.

[4] Estimates of strength numbers for the AA, KIA, KNLA, MNDAA, RCSS, SSPP and TNLA are taken from Stein Tønnesson, Min Zaw Oo and Ne Lynn Aung, 'Pretending to Be States: The Use of Facebook by Armed Groups in Myanmar', *Journal of Contemporary Asia*, vol. 52, no. 2, May 2021.

[5] Author's interview with Myanmar-based journalist, April 2022.

[6] Free Burma Rangers, 'A Popular Uprising in Karenni State, Burma', 21 February 2022.

[7] *Kantarawaddy Times*, 'KNPP Prioritizes Exposing Regime's Human Rights Violations', BNI Online, 6 January 2022.

[8] Free Burma Rangers, 'A Popular Uprising in Karenni State, Burma'.

[9] Author's interview with Francesco Buscemi, Researcher, Sant'Anna School of Advanced Studies, 27 May 2021.

[10] IMF, World Economic Outlook database, April 2022.

[11] 'Myanmar Central Bank Sees Currency Stabilising on New Measures', Reuters, 7 October 2021.

[12] Sebastian Strangio, 'Myanmar's Military Junta Tightens Control Over Foreign Currency Flows', *Diplomat*, 5 April 2022.

[13] Rebecca Ratcliffe, 'Chevron and Total Withdraw from Myanmar Gas Project', *Guardian*, 21 January 2021.

[14] Cameron Peters, 'The UN Condemned Myanmar's Coup. Will That Matter?', Vox, 20 June 2021.

[15] UN Children's Fund, 'UNICEF Myanmar Humanitarian Situation Report No. 2: 31 March 2022', Reliefweb, 1 April 2022.

[16] See Data for Myanmar, 'Reported Number of Houses Burned Down by Myanmar's Military', Datawrapper.

[17] UN Office for the Coordination of Humanitarian Affairs, 'Myanmar Humanitarian Response Plan 2022', 30 January 2022.

[18] Myanmar Humanitarian Response Plan, Financial Tracking Service.

PAKISTAN

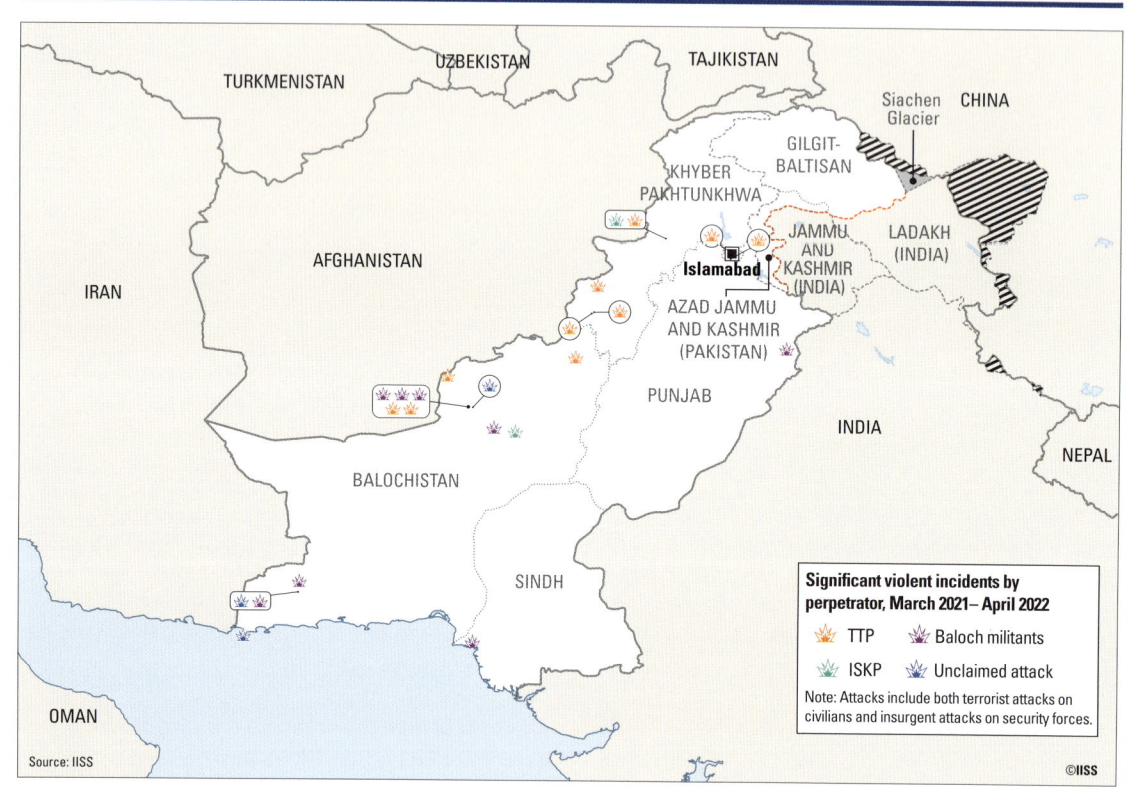

Significant violent incidents by perpetrator, March 2021– April 2022
- TTP
- Baloch militants
- ISKP
- Unclaimed attack

Note: Attacks include both terrorist attacks on civilians and insurgent attacks on security forces.

Source: IISS

Overview

Since gaining independence in 1947, Pakistan has experienced ethnic and centre–province tensions resulting from the perceived marginalisation of the Baloch, Pashtuns and Sindhis by the Punjabi majority. The 1971 secession of East Pakistan to form Bangladesh made Punjab the country's majority province in terms of population, escalating this dynamic.[1] The mass migrations that followed British India's partition also enflamed ethnic tensions, as Urdu-speaking migrants, or Mohajirs, emigrated from contemporary northern India to Sindh province in Pakistan. This history means that the conflict landscape in Pakistan sometimes conflates demands for increased civil liberties and provincial autonomy with violent separatist insurgent movements, primarily in Balochistan and Khyber Pakhtunkhwa (KP). Terrorist groups and violent separatist insurgent movements capitalise on the dynamic of underlying ethnic and economic agitation (and the repressive state crackdowns that follow terrorist attacks) to stoke tensions even further.

In several periods since Pakistan's formation, the Baloch insurgency has fought against the state seeking greater autonomy or the secession of Balochistan, waging campaigns in 1948, 1958, 1962 and 1973. The return to violence in 2003 launched the phase of the insurgency that continues today. Baloch armed groups have fragmented on several occasions and some splinter organisations have demobilised. However, since 2018, these groups have set aside some of their differences to form a coalition with the Baloch Republican Army (BRA) under the banner of the Baloch Raaji Ajoi Sangar (BRAS). The Balochistan Liberation Army (BLA) continues to be the most significant threat to the Pakistani state in Balochistan and Karachi, which is in Sindh province and is Pakistan's financial capital and most populous city.

Armed Conflict Global Relevance Indicator (ACGRI)

Pakistan

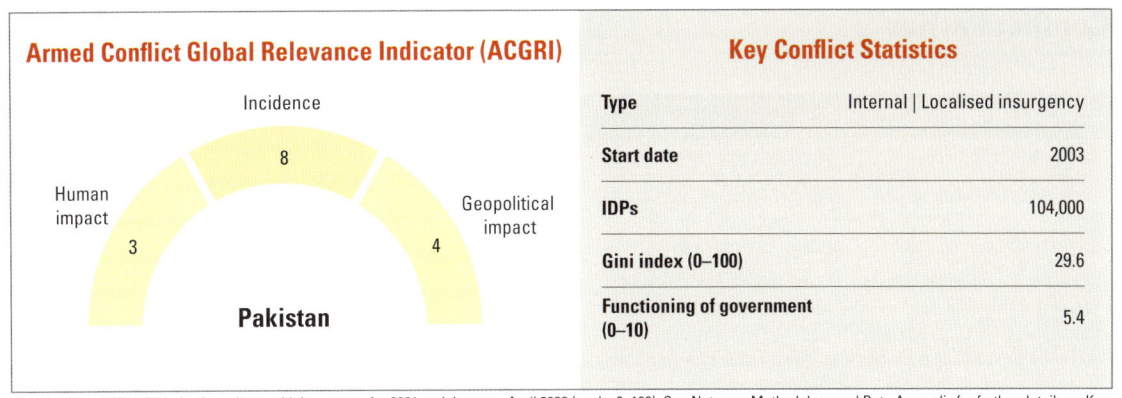

- Incidence: 8
- Human impact: 3
- Geopolitical impact: 4

Key Conflict Statistics

Type	Internal | Localised insurgency
Start date	2003
IDPs	104,000
Gini index (0–100)	29.6
Functioning of government (0–10)	5.4

ACGRI pillars: IISS calculation based on multiple sources for 2021 and January–April 2022 (scale: 0–100). See Notes on Methodology and Data Appendix for further details on Key Conflict Statistics.

Groups originating in KP and Pashtun tribal areas (formerly known as the Federally Administered Tribal Areas, FATA) have also fought against the state and the Shia religious minority. Following the 9/11 terrorist attacks, increased Pakistani incursions into the then FATA targeting al-Qaeda members raised tensions, with militant groups coalescing to form what is often referred to as the Pakistani Taliban, which eventually became the Tehrik-e-Taliban Pakistan (TTP). In 2009, Islamabad launched a counter-insurgency campaign against the TTP that at first lacked a coherent strategy. The TTP's attack on the Army Public School in Peshawar in December 2014 marked an inflection point and led the government to formulate its first counter-terrorism policy, the National Action Plan. *Operation Zarb-e-Azb* and *Operation Radd-ul-Fasaad*, launched in 2014 and 2017 respectively, led to a significant reduction in insurgent attacks.

Pakistan's security situation worsened over 2021 and deteriorated significantly in early 2022 even as tensions along the Line of Control with India remained relatively calm. The Afghan Taliban's victory over the internationally backed government in Afghanistan in August 2021 galvanised the TTP, which reaffirmed its loyalty to the Afghan Taliban's leadership and escalated attacks against Pakistani security forces. The TTP grew in strength in the former FATA, particularly Waziristan, as it found an even greater sanctuary across the border in Afghanistan under the protection of the Taliban-led government. In the reporting period, relations between Pashtun tribes and state authorities continued to be strained by the slow progress of reforms following the 2018 merger of the former FATA into KP, heavy-handed responses to the Pashtun Tahaffuz Movement's political and civil-rights activism and arrests of elected officials from the former FATA. Islamic State Khorasan Province (ISKP) also intensified terrorist attacks on civilian targets in the country. An uptick in Baloch separatist attacks targeting Pakistani security forces and Chinese citizens occurred throughout 2021 and continued in early 2022. Pakistan's Inter-Services Public Relations office announced that 97 Pakistani officers and soldiers were killed in the first three months of 2022 alone.

Conflict Parties

Pakistan Armed Forces (PAF)

Strength: 651,800 active military; 291,000 active paramilitary.

Areas of operation: Deployed throughout Pakistan (particularly along the Line of Control with India) and against insurgent groups in Balochistan and KP (including the former FATA).

Leadership and structure: Gen. Qamar Javed Bajwa (chief of army staff); Adm. Muhammad Amjad Khan Niazi (chief of naval staff); Air Chief Marshal Zaheer Ahmed Baber Sidhu (chief of air staff); Lt-Gen. Nadeem Anjum (director-general, Inter-Services Intelligence, ISI). ISI falls outside the military command structure but its leaders are drawn from the military and have significant oversight over some operations.
The PAF consists of nine 'Corps' commands, an Air Defence Command and a Strategic Forces Command. *Operation Radd-ul-Fasaad* involves an array of PAF units that support the police and the Pakistani Civil Armed Forces (PCAF) in counter-terrorism operations.

History: The ongoing *Operation Radd-ul-Fasaad* succeeded the 2014–17 *Operation Zarb-e-Azb*. It was launched in response to a resurgence in attacks by TTP splinter group Jamaat-ul-Ahrar. *Operation Khyber-4* was launched in 2017 under *Operation Radd-ul-Fasaad* with the goal of eliminating terrorists in what is now Rajgal valley, Khyber district.

Objectives: Eliminate insurgent groups that threaten the Pakistani state.

Opponents and affiliates/allies:
Opponents: TTP, BLA and other Baloch separatist groups, ISKP.
Affiliates/allies: PCAF, Pakistani police.

Resources/capabilities: Well resourced with an array of weapons systems and equipment. The defence budget for 2021 was US$10.3 billion.

Pakistani Civil Armed Forces (PCAF)

Strength: Unknown.

Areas of operation: Throughout Pakistan but most active fighting is against insurgent groups in Balochistan and KP.

Leadership and structure: Founded by the Interior Ministry, although most divisions are commanded by officers seconded from the PAF.
The main divisions of the PCAF involved in conflict with insurgent groups and participating in the PAF-led *Operation Radd-ul-Fasaad* are the Frontier Corps (Frontier Corps KP and Frontier Corps Balochistan), the Frontier Constabulary, the Sindh Rangers and the Punjab Rangers. Each group's authority is limited to its respective geographic area.

History: Contributed to *Operation Radd-ul-Fasaad* since its establishment in 2017 and to the Special Security Division since 2016.

Objectives: Eliminate insurgent groups that threaten the Pakistani state.

Opponents and affiliates/allies:
Opponents: TTP, BLA and other Baloch separatist groups, ISKP.
Affiliates/allies: PAF, Pakistani police.

Resources/capabilities: Primarily equipped with small arms and light weapons, with some shorter-range artillery and mortars.

Tehrik-e-Taliban Pakistan (TTP)

Strength: Circa 6,000 in Afghanistan, where the majority of TTP fighters are currently based.[2] Strength in Pakistan unknown, although recent analysis suggests there may be several thousand fighters in the country.

Areas of operation: Balochistan, KP.

Leadership and structure: Mufti Noor Wali Mehsud (emir and overarching leader), supported by a central shura council. Divided by locality into factions, or constituencies, each of which is led by a local emir and supported by a local shura council, which report to the central shura council. Each faction has a *qazi* (judge) to adjudicate local disputes.

History: Following the 2001 NATO invasion of Afghanistan, al-Qaeda and Taliban militants sought haven in the tribal areas of Pakistan. Operations by Pakistani (and later US) forces against al-Qaeda led several groups to form a loose coalition known as the Pakistan Taliban. In 2007, some of these factions unified as the TTP under the leadership of Baitullah Mehsud, who was killed in a US airstrike in 2009. A TTP shura elected Hakimullah Mehsud as the organisation's second emir, but internal divisions grew under his leadership over legitimate targets for attacks and peace talks with the government and worsened under Fazal Hayat (Mullah Fazlullah) between 2013 and 2018, causing several factions to break away, including leaders that formed ISKP in 2014. The 2014 TTP attack on the Army Public School in Peshawar triggered a major PAF counter-offensive that further weakened the group. Following Hayat's death in 2018, the leadership reverted to the Mehsud clan under Mufti Noor Wali, who sought to reunite and rebuild the group. In 2020, this process culminated with the reintegration of the Hizb-ul-Ahrar, Jamaat-ul-Ahrar and Amjad Farouqi groups and the Hakimullah Mehsud faction into the TTP fold. TPP leader Noor Wali Mehsud reiterated his allegiance to the Afghan Taliban's leadership following the latter's takeover of Afghanistan and likened the group to an extension of the Taliban in Pakistan.[3] On 2 April 2022, the TTP launched its al-Badr spring offensive and began to target Pakistani soldiers and police.

Tehrik-e-Taliban Pakistan (TTP)

Objectives: To defend and promote a rigid Islamist ideology in KP, including in the former FATA.

Opponents and affiliates/allies:
Opponents: PAF, PCAF.

Affiliates/allies: Afghan Taliban, al-Qaeda.

Resources/capabilities: Has access to small arms and improvised explosive devices (IEDs).

Baloch Raaji Ajoi Sangar (BRAS, an alliance that includes the Balochistan Liberation Army, BLA; the Baloch Republican Army, BRA; and the Baloch Liberation Front, BLF)[4]

Strength: Unknown.

Areas of operation: Balochistan.

Leadership and structure: BLA: Leadership contested between Hyrbyair Marri and Bashar Zaib; BRA: Brahumdagh Bugti; BLF: Dr Allah Nazar Baloch.
The BRAS is an alliance of the BLA, BRA and BLF. The BLA is divided into different factions. Pakistan's government alleges that several factions of the BLA exist and are led by different individuals. The insurgency is deeply divided, with different groups, infighting and fragmentation.

History: The alliance was formed in 2018. The BLA is the largest group and was formed in 2000 under the leadership of Afghanistan-based Balach Marri, who was subsequently killed in an airstrike in Helmand in 2007. Its leadership since then has been subject to additional deaths and significant internal contestation. In July 2019, the US State Department listed the BLA as a Specially Designated Global Terrorist organisation.

Objectives: Seeks independence for the region of Balochistan as a solution to perceived discrimination against the Baloch people. Opposes the extraction of natural resources in Balochistan by Pakistani and foreign actors, especially China, due to the implications of the China-Pakistan Economic Corridor (CPEC) for Baloch aspirations.

Opponents and affiliates/allies:
Opponents: PAF, PCAF.
Affiliates/allies: None.

Resources/capabilities: Attacks by BRAS members have involved small arms and IEDs, including suicide vests and car bombs.

Islamic State Khorasan Province (ISKP)[5]

Strength: Unclear. 1,500–4,000 in Afghanistan (estimate).[6]

Areas of operation: Balochistan, KP, Afghanistan.

Leadership and structure: Led by Sanaullah Ghafari (alias 'Shahab al-Muhajir'). The original leader, Hafiz Saeed Khan (previously head of the TTP Orakzai faction), was killed in a US drone strike in July 2016. Successive leaders were also either killed in US strikes or arrested.[7]
An Islamist militant organisation, formally affiliated with the larger Islamic State (ISIS), of which it is the Central and South Asia branch.

History: The Islamic State (ISIS) announced the establishment of the ISKP in 2014 by former TTP members to conduct operations in Afghanistan and Pakistan. Its first four emirs were killed in US airstrikes in Afghanistan.

Objectives: Similar to ISIS, ISKP maintains both local and global ambitions to establish a caliphate in Central and South Asia to be governed under a strict Islamic system, modelled after the group's own interpretation of a caliphate. To this end, it seeks to delegitimise the Pakistani state and expel religious minorities from Pakistan.

Opponents and affiliates/allies:
Opponents: PAF, PCAF.
Affiliates/allies: ISIS.

Resources/capabilities: Since its founding in 2014, ISIS has invested in improving ISKP's organisation and capabilities. However, with the decline of its territory in Iraq and Syria, ISIS has fewer resources to invest in foreign networks and therefore its investment in the group has declined. ISKP relies on small arms, IEDs and VBIEDs.

Conflict Drivers

Geopolitical and geostrategic influences

Afghan Taliban's victory galvanises the TTP:
For 20 years, insurgent and terrorist groups have utilised the mountainous areas on both sides of Pakistan's border with Afghanistan to conduct cross-border operations. Following a series of major operations by the PAF in the late 2000s and mid-2010s, the TTP had to retreat into Afghanistan and the majority of TTP fighters are currently based there. This trend was magnified in 2021 following the Afghan Taliban's takeover of Afghanistan. Islamabad identified the safe haven for terrorist groups in Afghanistan during the era of the Afghan republic as a primary driver of terrorist violence against Pakistan. However, this situation was more the

result of Kabul's lack of control in the country's southeastern provinces than any sponsor–proxy relationship. A genuine relationship does exist between the Afghan Taliban and the TTP: the latter has pledged allegiance to the former and views itself as an extension of the group.

Economic and social

Economic grievances:
Baloch groups allege that the government violates their civil, political and human rights and also object to Islamabad's distribution of economic benefits gained from the extraction of Balochistan's natural resources. CPEC, part of China's Belt and Road Initiative, is often referred to as the latter's pilot project and includes the construction of power plants, mines, highways, railways and improvements to a warm deep-water port in Gwadar. Baloch groups question whether the Baloch people will profit from CPEC or if benefits will instead go to China and its partners in the Pakistani government. Baloch insurgents' strategy of attacking Chinese targets threatens CPEC's progress and Pakistan's most important bilateral relationship.

While economic investment is not a core demand of groups like the TTP or ISKP, underdevelopment in the former FATA and the failure to fully integrate it with KP may partially explain their appeal to new recruits. Furthermore, an economically isolated Afghanistan with a weak government may provide an ideal environment for groups that engage in cross-border attacks, such as the ISKP.

Religious divisions:
Pakistan's population is 96.28% Muslim according to the country's Bureau of Statistics, but it does not delineate by sect.[8] Estimates suggest that the Sunni population comprises 85–90% and the Shia 10–15%.[9] Pakistan's Sunni Muslims are primarily divided among the Barelvi and Deobandi subsects, with a growing Ahl-e-Hadith community. Groups like the TTP and ISKP take advantage of Pakistan's sectarian landscape and exert their strength by targeting minority religious sects. Shia mosques are notably targeted by groups like ISKP.

Key Events in 2021–22

POLITICAL EVENTS

MILITARY/VIOLENT EVENTS

7 March 2021
Two Pakistan Navy personnel are killed in an attack by unidentified assailants while travelling from Jiwani to Ganz in Balochistan.

8 March
TTP militants kill a police officer in Rawalpindi, Punjab province.

23 March
A TTP bomb blast kills three people and injures 13 others in Chaman, Balochistan.

21 April
A bomb explosion at a hotel in Quetta, Balochistan, later claimed by the TPP, kills five people.

Conflict Summary: Pakistan

30 August 2021
Taliban takes control of the entirety of Afghanistan as the last US soldiers depart the country.

4 September
Pakistan's then-ISI chief Lt-Gen. Faiz Hamid visits Kabul following the Taliban takeover and tells the press, 'don't worry, everything will be ok'.[10]

6 October
Lt-Gen. Nadeem Ahmed Anjum replaces Lt-Gen. Faiz Hamid as ISI chief. Hamid becomes Commander of the Peshawar-based XI Corps.

5 May
Four Pakistani soldiers are killed in Zhob, Balochistan, by suspected TTP fighters.

28 May
The BLA attacks a Pakistan Army supply vehicle and kills four army personnel in Kohlu, Balochistan.

31 May
The BLA kills four Frontier Corps soldiers and injures eight others in two attacks in Turbat and Quetta, Balochistan.

3 June
The TTP kills two police officers in Islamabad.

8 June
The BLA attacks a Pakistan Army camp in the Karakdan area of the Bolan Pass, Balochistan, killing two army personnel.

14 June
Four Pakistani soldiers are killed in an IED attack near Marget Mines east of Quetta.

17 June
A Pakistan Army soldier is killed near Turbat airport, likely by a separatist group(s).

1 July
A bomb targeting Frontier Corps forces injures six people near Quetta airport.

11–12 August
A Pakistan Army soldier is killed in a suspected TTP attack in Sararogha in South Waziristan, KP.

18 August
A Pakistan Army soldier is killed in a suspected TTP attack in the Kanniguram area of South Waziristan, KP.

20 August
A suicide bombing claimed by the BLA kills two children while targeting Chinese nationals in Quetta.

5 September
A suicide bombing attributed to the TTP kills three people in Quetta.

26 September
The BRA uses a bomb to destroy a statue of Pakistan's founder, Mohammad Ali Jinnah, in Gwadar, Balochistan.

10 October
The BLA kills Pakistani journalist Shahid Zehri in a targeted bomb attack in Hub, Balochistan.

20 January 2022
A bomb blast in Anarkali market in Lahore, Punjab province kills three people and injures 33 others. The Baloch Nationalist Army claims responsibility for the attack.

Timeline

3 April 2022
Then-prime minister Imran Khan instructs Pakistan's president to dissolve the National Assembly to prevent a no-confidence vote.

7 April
The Supreme Court of Pakistan reinstates the National Assembly.

10 April
Imran Khan is removed from office via a vote of no confidence. He blames a US-backed plot seeking regime change.

11 April
The National Assembly elects Pakistan Muslim League–Nawaz political-party president Shehbaz Sharif as Pakistan's prime minister.

14 April
Pakistan's Inter-Services Public Relations office states that the chief of army staff, Gen. Qamar Javed Bajwa, will retire in November 2022.

April
Imran Khan stages large political rallies across the country and continues to blame a US-backed conspiracy – involving Pakistan's opposition parties – to remove him from office for his downfall.

25 January
Ten Pakistani soldiers are killed in Kech district, southwestern Balochistan by reported terrorists.

2 March
A roadside bomb potentially placed by the BLA kills three people, including a senior police officer, in Quetta.

4 March
ISKP detonates a bomb in a Shiite Mosque in Peshawar, killing at least 56 people.

8 March
An attack claimed by the ISKP kills six Pakistani paramilitary personnel in Sibi district, Balochistan.

23 March
Militants kill four Pakistan Army soldiers in North Waziristan, KP.

2 April
The TTP launches its al-Badr spring offensive on the Pakistani state.

14 April
A shoot-out between Pakistani forces and the TTP takes place in North Waziristan. Seven soldiers and four TTP fighters are killed.

26 April
A BLA suicide bombing at Karachi University kills four people, including three Chinese nationals.

Conflict Outlook

Political scenarios

Pakistan's political system is stable but domestic politics are likely to remain turbulent over the next year. Prime Minister Sharif was elected with a small margin – 172 votes in the National Assembly were required to ensure his election, and he received 174 – and his coalition appears to agree on little more than their opposition to Imran Khan. It is unclear when a general election will be held. However, Pakistan's military leadership is likely to shift, as Chief of Army Staff Qamar Bajwa confirmed he will not seek an extension beyond November 2022. The military plays a prominent role in crafting foreign policy, particularly in relation to national security.

While Pakistan was largely able to contain the coronavirus and its impacts in the reporting period, rising macroeconomic challenges will negatively impact political stability: in the reporting period, inflation (forecasted to rise to 11.2% in 2022 from 8.9% in 2021)[11] continued to drive up the price of food staples, exports remained relatively low by regional standards and the value of the Pakistani rupee depreciated – trends that will likely continue. In April 2022, the Pakistani government requested that the IMF extend its programme in Pakistan to June 2023 and increase its loan by US$2bn.[12]

In 2018, the Financial Action Task Force placed Pakistan on its 'grey list' of states with structural deficiencies in anti-money laundering and countering the financing of terrorism. It issued a 27-point improvement plan for Pakistan. The country has completed 26 of these points but remains on the list due to a final item related to anti-terror prosecutions. On 8 April 2022, founder of Lashkar-e-Taiba Hafiz Saeed was sentenced to 31 years in prison. This action may improve Pakistan's chances of being removed from the list.

Escalation potential and conflict-related risks

There were 424 terrorism-related incidents in Pakistan in 2021, up from 319 in 2020.[13] Terrorism-related deaths (excluding attackers) numbered 440 in 2021, a 21% increase from 2020.[14] Such deaths in 2022 are on track to surpass 2021 by a significant margin unless trends change. Although these figures are low compared to those registered in 2006–15, they suggest a concerning upward trajectory. Citizens in Balochistan and KP (including the former FATA) continued to suffer from insurgent violence, terrorist attacks, military checkpoints, forced disappearances, arbitrary detentions, arrests on dubious charges and restriction of movement during the reporting period. The Shia and the Hazara ethnic minority, which is also predominantly Shia, particularly faced high levels of violence perpetrated by groups such as ISKP.

Terrorist violence in Pakistan is unlikely to return to the peaks of 2007–15, which coincided with the siege of Lal Masjid and the TTP's formation, followed by reduced terrorism in the wake of *Operation Zarb-e-Azb*. However, the underlying political and economic drivers of violence in Balochistan persist and Baloch separatists appear intent on escalating violence with a particular focus on Pakistan's security forces and Chinese nationals. The TTP is emboldened by the Afghan Taliban's victory and seeks to replicate some form of it in KP province. ISKP is also ascendant and has proved able to conduct high-casualty attacks on civilian targets.

Strategic implications and global influences

Western governments, including the United States, have shifted their focus to the war in Ukraine and the rise of China. Pakistan's war with terrorist organisations is likely to be viewed as a Pakistani problem in the short term. However, if groups like the TTP, ISKP, al-Qaeda and anti-India terrorist groups increase their activity or lethality, then the US–Pakistan security relationship may be prioritised once again.

The uptick in insurgent violence in Balochistan is unlikely to significantly alter bilateral ties between China and Pakistan, which are based on security ties. Chinese investment in the region is also likely to continue despite targeted killings of Chinese nationals.

Notes

1. Michael Kugelman and Adam Weinstein, 'In Pakistan, a Tale of Two Very Different Political Movements', *Lawfare*, 4 January 2021.
2. Asfandyar Mir, 'Afghanistan's Terrorism Challenge: The Political Trajectories of Al-Qaeda, the Afghan Taliban, and the Islamic State', Middle East Institute, 20 October 2020; US Department of Defense Office of Inspector General, 'Operation Freedom's Sentinel: Lead Inspector General Report to the United States Congress', 21 May 2019, p. 25; and Daud Khattak, 'The Pakistan Taliban Is Back', *Diplomat*, 9 March 2021.
3. Asfandyar Mir, 'After the Taliban's Takeover: Pakistan's TTP Problem', United States Institute of Peace, 19 January 2022.
4. A new Baloch separatist group known as the Baloch Nationalist Army also emerged and claimed a bombing attack in Lahore in January 2022.
5. The Islamic State–Pakistan Province (IS–PP) is a less relevant splinter of ISKP that is sometimes referenced in the media or used interchangeably with ISKP.
6. UN Security Council (UNSC), 'Fourteenth Report of the Secretary-General on the Threat Posed by ISIL (Da'esh) to International Peace and Security and the Range of United Nations Efforts in Support of Member States in Countering the Threat', S/2022/63, 28 January 2022, p. 7; and UNSC, 'Letter dated 25 May 2022 from the Chair of the Security Council Committee established pursuant to resolution 1988 (2011) addressed to the President of the Security Council', S/2022/419, 26 May 2022, p. 18.
7. Andrew Mines and Amira Jadoon, 'Can the Islamic State's Afghan Province Survive Its Leadership Losses?', Lawfare, 17 May 2020. See also Amira Jadoon and Andrew Mines, 'Broken, but Not Defeated: An Examination of State-Led Operations Against Islamic State Khorasan in Afghanistan and Pakistan (2015–2018)', Combating Terrorism Center, March 2020.
8. See Pakistan Bureau of Statistics, 'Population by Religion', 2020. It records the Ahmadi sect separately since the group is not recognised as Muslim by the government.
9. US Commission on International Religious Freedom, 'Pakistan: USCIRF-recommended for Countries of Particular Concern (CPC)', Annual Report, April 2020, p. 33.
10. Naveed Siddiqui, '"Don't Worry, Everything Will Be Okay": ISI Chief During Kabul Visit', *Dawn*, 4 September 2021.
11. IMF, 'World Economic Outlook Database', April 2022.
12. 'Stocks Post Second Weekly Loss as IMF Euphoria Subsides', *Dawn*, 30 April 2022.
13. See 'Number of Terrorism Related Incidents Year Wise' for Pakistan, South Asia Terrorism Portal (SATP), Institute for Conflict Management, accessed 17 April 2022.
14. See 'Yearly Fatalities' for Pakistan, SATP, Institute for Conflict Management, accessed 17 April 2022.

INDIA

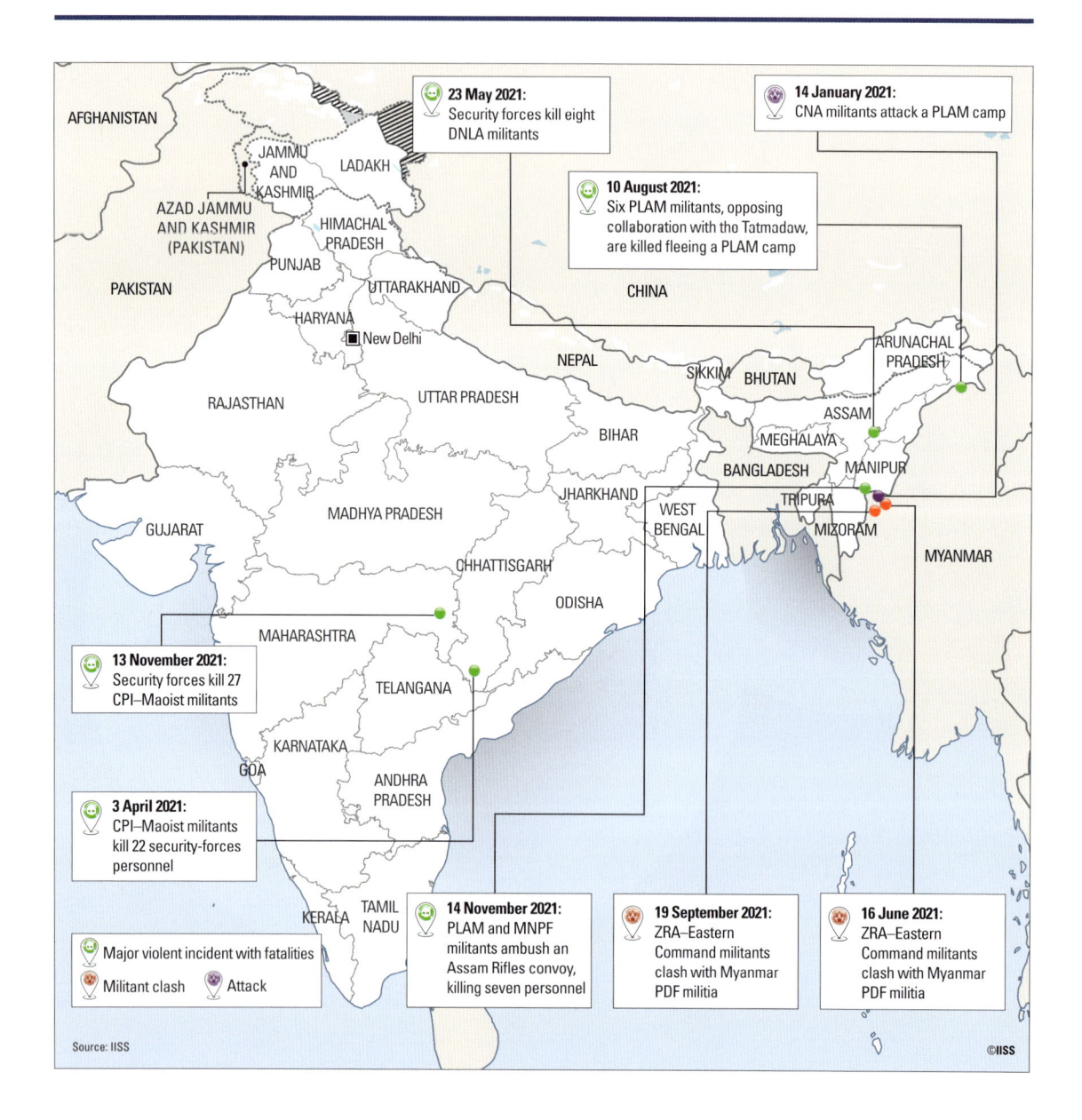

Overview

The protracted conflicts in India's central heartland and northeastern borderlands have long been considered peripheral conflicts to be contained or managed, as opposed to the politically more important Kashmir conflict. The conflicts in Northeast and Central India are better described as disparate clusters of overlapping insurgencies, which all emerged as a result of perceived neglect and fear of exploitation or assimilation either by the 'mainland' or by a class-based or ethnic 'other'.

The Naga conflict is the longest and most politically significant of northeast India's conflicts,

Armed Conflict Global Relevance Indicator (ACGRI)

- Incidence: 10
- Human impact: 3
- Geopolitical impact: 4

India

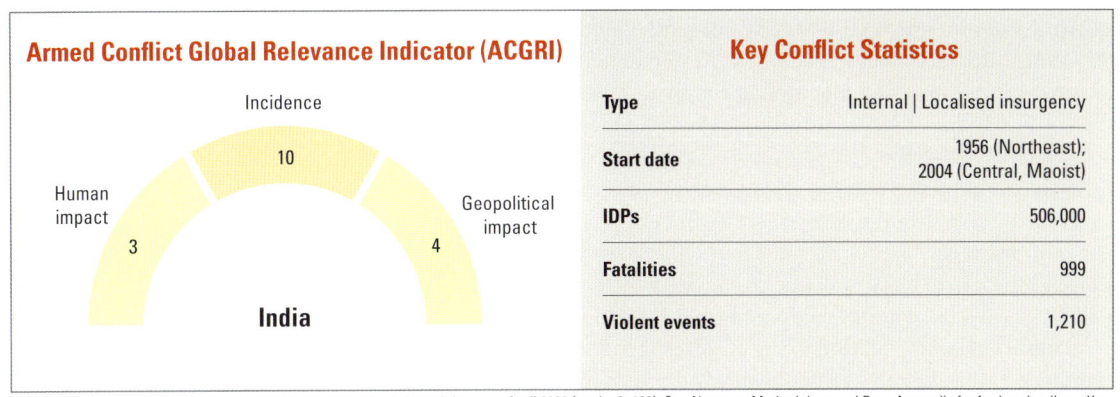

Key Conflict Statistics

Type	Internal | Localised insurgency
Start date	1956 (Northeast); 2004 (Central, Maoist)
IDPs	506,000
Fatalities	999
Violent events	1,210

ACGRI pillars: IISS calculation based on multiple sources for 2021 and January–April 2022 (scale: 0–100). See Notes on Methodology and Data Appendix for further details on Key Conflict Statistics.

beginning during the 1950s when the Naga National Council (NNC) mobilised for insurgency amid fears that the Naga people would be forcibly assimilated into India. Far from resolving the conflict, several rounds of negotiations, including those leading to the creation of the State of Nagaland in 1962, the 1975 Shillong Accord and a series of ceasefires concluded since 1997, have only deepened divisions within the movement. While the main factions – the National Socialist Council of Nagalim–Isak Muivah (NSCN–IM) and the National Socialist Council of Nagaland–Khaplang (NSCN–K) – signed ceasefires with the Indian government in 1997 and 2001 respectively, the NSCN–K rescinded its ceasefire in 2015. Despite signing a 2015 Framework Agreement, the NSCN–IM's own peace process with New Delhi has been gridlocked because of unresolved issues. The replacement in September 2021 of the government's interlocutor for talks with the group, R.N. Ravi, did not appear to resolve these tensions, and a mistaken army ambush that killed 15 civilians in December 2021 undermined the Naga civil society's confidence in the Indian government.[1] Whilst a number of key demobilisations occurred in Assam during 2021, including one coronavirus-induced unilateral ceasefire by the anti-talks United Liberation Front of Asom–Independent (ULFA–I), conflict-related fatalities rose across northeast India for the first time since 2012. A number of factors contributed to this, including tensions in the Naga peace process, intensified militant and counter-insurgent activities in Karbi Anglong, and the run-up to the Manipur Legislative Assembly elections in February–March 2022.

While the Maoist insurgency in Central India has remained comparatively insulated from geopolitical dynamics, northeast India's borders are international, which has historically allowed insurgent groups to benefit from cross-border support and sanctuary. Significantly, the military coup in Myanmar in February 2021 reduced pressure from the Myanmar military (Tatmadaw) on anti-talks groups encamped along the India–Myanmar border; groups from Manipur secured sanctuary by collaborating with the Tatmadaw against People's Defence Forces (PDF) militias (the armed wing of the anti-coup movement in Myanmar) in northern Chin State, Myanmar. A lethal ambush led by the People's Liberation Army of Manipur (PLAM) against an Assam Rifles convoy in Manipur on 13 November 2021 took place near the India–Myanmar border in Churachandpur district, likely indicating that reduced Tatmadaw pressure played a key role in reviving cross-border insurgent operations during 2021.

Although communist insurgencies seeking to overthrow feudal structures and impose a new socialist economic order in Central India date back to the early post-Independence years, the peasant revolt at Naxalbari in 1967 gave rise to the first major 'Naxalite' movement. The movement has ebbed and flowed in the face of state repression, with its most recent manifestation emerging in 2004 under the banner of the Communist Party of India-Maoist (CPI–Maoist) to consolidate a large belt of territory known as the 'Red Corridor'. At its peak during 2009–10, this Maoist-affected belt spanned much of Bihar, Chhattisgarh, Jharkhand, Maharashtra and West Bengal. Particularly lethal Maoist attacks on security forces, such as an attack in April 2010 in which CPI–Maoist militants killed 76 Central Reserve Police Force (CRPF) personnel, led then-prime minister Manmohan Singh to label the conflict India's biggest security challenge. Since 2014, successes by the security forces have eroded CPI–Maoist influence and the group is now concentrated around a few core hotspot areas; in February 2021, Minister of State for Home Affairs Nityanand Rai said that there were now just 46 Maoist-affected districts across the country compared to 91 in 2019.[2]

Conflict-related fatalities in Central India remained at a largely static level compared to 2020, with 237 during 2021, following 239 in 2020, indicating a fairly steady overall pattern of successful containment of the CPI–Maoist at a national level. Most of these fatalities were concentrated across three states: Chhattisgarh, Maharashtra and Jharkhand. Security forces in Gadchiroli, Maharashtra, conducted a series of ambushes and operations against the CPI–Maoist, leading to a significant rise in district-level fatalities from 16 in 2020 to 53 in 2021 (49 CPI–Maoist fatalities and zero security-forces fatalities).[3] In Chhattisgarh's Bastar region – the historical headquarters of the CPI–Maoist insurgency and where 94.91% of Chhattisgarh's conflict-related fatalities took place in 2021 – security forces incurred 44 fatalities and the CPI–Maoist incurred 45 fatalities.[4] Kill–death ratios usually heavily favour state forces in counter-insurgency campaigns, reflecting the region's continued status as a key battleground of the conflict. The fact that 41 of the 44 security-forces fatalities in Chhattisgarh occurred between January and June reflects the intensity of the annual Maoist Tactical Counter-Offensive Campaign, which is launched before the monsoon.

Conflict Parties

Indian Armed Forces

Strength: 1,460,350.

Areas of operation: Northeast (III and IV Corps). The army does not play a direct role in anti-CPI–Maoist operations in Central India.

Leadership and structure: Zonal command structure subdivided into corps commands.

History: The Indian Army was formed as a direct successor to the British Indian Army after Independence in 1947. The army, navy and air force are primarily responsible for external defence, but the army and air force have played a pivotal role in Indian counter-insurgency operations since the 1950s.

Objectives: Counter-insurgency, border defence.

Opponents and affiliates/allies:
Opponents: Non-state armed groups.
Affiliates/allies: Other state forces, although coordination challenges exist.

Resources/capabilities: Most suitably equipped and trained to operate in the difficult, rugged terrain of northeast India, drawing upon logistics and air power to supply distant outposts. Heavy weaponry is rarely deployed to counter-insurgency operations, though there have been exceptions.

Assam Rifles

Strength: 65,150.

Areas of operation: Within the operational jurisdiction of the Indian Army.

Leadership and structure: Led by a director general, typically a military officer of lt-gen. rank.
Organised into 46 battalions officered by army personnel. It is under the jurisdiction of the Ministry of Defence, but as a central paramilitary force is answerable to the Ministry of Home Affairs.

History: Originally formed as the Cachar Levy in 1835, the

Assam Rifles plays a central role in counter-insurgency operations in northeast India.

Objectives: Counter-insurgency, border defence.

Opponents and affiliates/allies:
Opponents: Non-state armed groups.
Affiliates/allies: Cooperates with other state forces, although challenges exist around intelligence sharing, overlapping jurisdictions and operational coordination.

Resources/capabilities: Battalions are typically equipped to the same standard as an Indian Army infantry battalion, with small arms and mortar capabilities.

Central Reserve Police Force (CRPF)

Strength: 324,800.

Areas of operation: Northeast and Central/Eastern India. Takes a leading role in Central India, in states such as Chhattisgarh, Maharashtra, Bihar, Andhra Pradesh, Jharkhand and Odisha.

Leadership and structure: CRPF battalions are central government forces but are deployed to state governments to assist in law-and-order activities. CRPF forces are designed to augment existing state police forces to combat CPI–Maoist insurgents across the Red Corridor. The central government is responsible for deploying CRPF forces and for coordinating with individual state governments.

Central Reserve Police Force (CRPF)

History: Originally founded as the Crown Representative Police Force in 1939 before being rechristened after Independence. The force has evolved into one of the largest of the central police forces with the broadest remit of supporting state governments in law-and-order duties, as well as a limited counter-insurgency remit.

Objectives: Support state-level law enforcement in counter-insurgency duties.

Opponents and affiliates/allies:
Opponents: Non-state armed groups.
Affiliates/allies: Other Indian security forces, though coordination challenges exist.

Resources/capabilities: CRPF battalions vary in degrees of modernisation. While special units such as the CRPF's 'Commando Battalions for Resolute Action' are equipped with modern INSAS and AK-series rifles, this varies across units. Some units have anti-mine vehicles; however, these are rare and CRPF units are thus often vulnerable to improvised explosive device (IED) attacks.

State Police Forces

Strength: 450,000.

Areas of operation: Varied.

Leadership and structure: Led by the director general of the police, answerable to state government political leadership.

History: Varied according to the formation of individual states.

Objectives: Law and order, counter-insurgency duties.

Opponents and affiliates/allies:
Opponents: Non-state armed groups.
Affiliates/allies: Cooperates with other state forces, although challenges exist around intelligence sharing, overlapping jurisdictions and operational coordination.

Resources/capabilities: While special armed police units are better equipped and have undergone modernisation, the bulk of state police forces face logistical challenges in navigating treacherous terrain and fair-weather roads, as well as deficiencies in firearms, including reliance on old, colonial-era rifles.

Main armed groups in talks with the Indian government

National Socialist Council of Nagalim–Isak Muivah (NSCN–IM)

Strength: 5,000.

Areas of operation: Naga-inhabited northeast India: Nagaland, Arunachal Pradesh, Assam, Manipur.

Leadership and structure: Led by its 'general secretary', Thuingaleng Muivah. The group is organised centrally but is demographically dominated by the Tangkhul tribe of Manipur.

History: After splitting from the original NSCN in 1988, the NSCN–IM has since emerged as one of the most powerful non-state armed groups in northeast India. Observing a ceasefire limited to the territorial jurisdiction of Nagaland with the Indian government since 1997, the group continues to recruit, clashes with rivals and occasionally Indian security forces in non-ceasefire areas, and runs its own parallel government from its 'capital' in Camp Hebron, on the outskirts of Dimapur. In 2015 it signed a Framework Agreement with the government of India, with the view to concluding a comprehensive settlement, but the group's ethnic composition remains a bone of contention.

Objectives: Gain hybrid 'sovereignty' over Nagaland, incorporating Nagas under one territorial entity with a separate flag and constitution.

Opponents and affiliates/allies:
Opponents: State forces, the NSCN–K, Zeliangrong United Front (ZUF), Kuki armed groups.
Affiliates/allies: Limited, tacit cooperation with security forces, as well as allied civil-society bodies (e.g., Naga People's Movement for Human Rights, United Naga Council Manipur)

Resources/capabilities: The best equipped of northeast India-based insurgents with connections to the Southeast Asia regional arms market.

Working Committee (WC)

Strength: Umbrella organisation of seven armed groups.[5]

Areas of operation: Nagaland, Arunachal Pradesh, Manipur.

Leadership and structure: A conglomerate of smaller armed groups.

History: Formed as the Working Group in 2016, the WC is an umbrella organisation now consisting of seven separate armed groups, often referred to as 'Naga political groups', which joined together to increase their political clout in the peace process. The WC signed its own Framework Agreement with the central government on 17 November 2017, forming a basis for future negotiations.

Objectives: Secure a peace deal granting Naga autonomy within the Indian constitution.

Opponents and affiliates/allies:
Opponents: The NSCN–IM and smaller Naga pro-talks groups outside the umbrella structure.
Affiliates/allies: Alliances between constituent groups.

Resources/capabilities: Varied across membership. The NSCN–Reformation (NSCN–R) is the most operationally competent faction, followed by the NSCN–Kitovi-Neokpao/Unification (NSCN–KN/U).

United Liberation Front of Asom–Independent (ULFA–I)

Strength: 250.[6]

Areas of operation: Upper Assam, areas adjacent to India–Myanmar border.

Leadership and structure: The group has long concentrated power in its military wing, headed by Commander-in-Chief Paresh Baruah. In 2021, the group's 'constitutional infrastructure' was paused with a view to being reconstituted; however, the 'defence department' remained untouched.

History: Once the most powerful armed group in Assam, ULFA was formed in 1979 as a radical wing of the Assam Movement. At its peak (1985–91), the undivided ULFA extended its influence across Assam. ULFA's militant wing has been significantly weakened by counter-insurgency and diplomacy offensives, internal splits and defections to ULFA's pro-talks faction (formed in 2012) and declining popular support. In 2021, the group declared a unilateral ceasefire in response to the COVID-19 pandemic.

Objectives: Gain sovereignty over Assam.

Opponents and affiliates/allies:
Opponents: State forces. Coronavirus-related ceasefire most likely tactical in nature.
Affiliates/allies: PLAM, NSCN–K/YA.

Resources/capabilities: IEDs, grenades, rocket-propelled grenades, rifles including HK-33s, AK-56s, INSAS, MQ-81s and M-22s.

Main armed groups not in talks with the Indian government

Communist Party of India-Maoist (CPI–Maoist)

Strength: Police estimate the CPI–Maoist strength at around 2,500 in the Chhattisgarh–Maharashtra region, with up to 40% of members being women.[7]

Areas of operation: Andhra Pradesh, Bihar, Chhattisgarh, Jharkhand, Kerala, Madhya Pradesh, Maharashtra, Odisha, Telangana, West Bengal. Hotspot of CPI–Maoist activity in the Bastar region of Chhattisgarh.

Leadership and structure: Comprised of a central committee made up of representatives from the various states. Local command structures include 'zonal' commanders (zones roughly correspond to Indian districts) and local 'area' commanders under sub-committees.

History: Formed in 2004 following the merger of the Communist Party of India (Marxist–Leninist), People's War (People's War Group) and the Maoist Communist Centre of India. The organisation peaked in its control of territory in approximately 2009, leading then-prime minister Singh to label the insurgency the country's single-largest security challenge. Since 2014, counter-insurgency operations and organisational splits have led to the group's gradual decline.

Objectives: Overthrow Indian parliamentary democracy in favour of a communist regime through rural insurgency. Mobilise a power base by tapping into marginalised communities in India's hinterlands. Deploys hit-and-run attacks against Indian security forces.

Opponents and affiliates/allies:
Opponents: Indian federal and state security forces, as well as civilians suspected of collaborating with security forces; smaller splinter factions such as the Peoples' Liberation Front of India (PLFI).
Affiliates/allies: Seeks to cultivate alliances with disempowered local civilians.

Resources/capabilities: Primarily arms itself with home-made firearms, although its elite fighting units wield AK-47s and semi-automatic weapons seized from police. The group also makes frequent use of IEDs.

National Socialist Council of Nagaland–Khaplang/Yung Aung (NSCN–K/YA)

Strength: Unknown.

Areas of operation: Myanmar (Sagaing); Nagaland, Arunachal Pradesh, Manipur.

Leadership and structure: Led by Burmese Naga Yung Aung after death of S.S. Khaplang in 2017. Various factions have split from the NSCN–K, including the pro-talks NSCN–R in 2016, the pro-talks NSCN–Khango-Konyak (NSCN–KK) in 2018 and the now pro-talks NSCN–Nyemlang Konyak (which has since been renamed as the NSCN–K/Niki Sumi) in 2020.

History: Formed as a splinter group of the original NSCN in 1988, the NSCN–K drew particular recruitment strength from the Konyaks of eastern Nagaland and Myanmar. Although it signed a ceasefire with the government in 2001, it rescinded this in April 2015 and began conducting operations against security forces in cooperation with other non-state armed groups in Manipur and Assam.

Objectives: Gain sovereignty over an independent Nagaland through armed struggle; cross-border strikes.

Opponents and affiliates/allies:
Opponents: State forces, the NSCN–IM, other rival NSCN factions.
Affiliates/allies: Leading member of the United National Liberation Front of Western South East Asia (UNLFWESEA), allied with Coordination Committee (CorCom).

Resources/capabilities: Unknown.

Coordination Committee (CorCom)

Strength: Umbrella organisation of six armed groups.[8]

Areas of operation: Arunachal Pradesh, Manipur, Myanmar.

Leadership and structure: Umbrella organisation incorporating numerous anti-talks armed groups.

History: When formed in 2011, CorCom included a seventh armed group, the United People's Party of Kangleipak (UPPK); however, the UPPK was expelled from the group in 2013 after it began responding to peace overtures from the Indian government.

Objectives: Gain sovereignty over Manipur.

Opponents and affiliates/allies:
Opponents: State forces, rival anti- and pro-talks Manipuri armed groups.
Affiliates/allies: Some of its constituent organisations have aligned with the Myanmar military as of 2021.

Resources/capabilities: Significant variation in capabilities. Whereas the PLAM and United National Liberation Front (UNLF) are well-trained, disciplined and cohesive outfits, the Kangleipak Communist Party (KCP) is a series of small, fragmented factions.

Manipur Naga People's Front (MNPF)

Strength: Unknown.

Areas of operation: Manipur, Myanmar.

Leadership and structure: Small armed group coordinating with key anti-talks groups such as the PLAM.

History: Formed in 2013 following the merger of the Manipur Naga Revolutionary Front and the United Naga People's Council, the MNPF has long cooperated with Manipur plains-based armed groups and opposed its local rival, the NSCN–IM.

Objectives: Gain sovereignty for Naga people.

Opponents and affiliates/allies:
Opponents: State forces, the NSCN–IM.
Affiliates/allies: Forms a tactical alliance with the PLAM due to its opposition to the NSCN–IM.

Resources/capabilities: Unknown.

Other conflict parties

The above is a non-exhaustive summary of the main state and insurgent conflict parties relevant to developments in 2021. The Zomi Revolutionary Army (ZRA) of Manipur, which signed a ceasefire with the Indian government in 2005, has entered into cooperation with the Myanmar military alongside other Manipur-based armed groups (see Conflict Drivers below).

Conflict Drivers

Geopolitical and geostrategic influences

Impact of Myanmar coup on insurgencies in northeast India:
In recent years, a string of camps within Myanmar has been key to sustaining northeast India's insurgencies, providing armed groups with sanctuary from Indian Army pressure, as well as access to regional arms markets. During 2019, there was a major blow to these sanctuaries when the Tatmadaw launched operations to disrupt the network of camps adjacent to the Indian border and support the Indian government. The popular resistance and mobilisation against the 2021 military coup forced the Tatmadaw to shift priorities away from dealing with Indian rebel groups towards fighting the PDF militias. As a result, reports have emerged that up to 3,000 militants from Indian insurgent groups such as the PLAM, Kanglei Yawol Kanna Lup (KYKL), the People's Revolutionary Party of Kangleipak (PREPAK), the NSCN–K/YA and the Zomi Revolutionary Army–Eastern Command (ZRA–Eastern Command) had regrouped on the Myanmar side of the border, with some relocating to the Naga areas of Sagaing and others redeploying to northern Chin State.[9] Reports suggested that most groups had re-established the arrangement of paying local Tatmadaw commanders in return for non-interference.[10] Some, such as the PLAM and ZRA–Eastern Command, however, entered into deeper tactical arrangements

with the Tatmadaw and carried out attacks on the PDF in return for continued sanctuary.[11] These new developments have had a bearing on insurgent violence across the border in India.

Economic and social

Remedying grievances and alienation:
Insurgents in both central and northeast India have long exploited deep patterns of socio-economic inequality and perceived exploitation, whether by 'class' enemies as in the case of the CPI–Maoist or by ethnic 'others' as in the case of insurgent groups in northeast India. CPI–Maoist influence has reduced significantly as a result of government development projects and security-forces operations. However, state governments, such as that of Jharkhand, have expressed concern that reductions in the coverage of Special Central Assistance (extra funding provided to states to fill gaps in public services and infrastructure), infrastructural security expenditure and budgets for the deployment of paramilitary forces were premature and would prevent the Indian government from consolidating the advances made in recent years. In northeast India, the peace accord struck between the government and six Karbi armed factions on 4 September 2021 contained provisions to protect local economic development and culture in a clear bid to address the underlying causes of insurgency.

Key Events in 2021–22

POLITICAL EVENTS

4 March 2021
The NSCN–IM says that government interlocutor R.N. Ravi's statement that peace talks have been concluded is 'reckless'.

12 April
The central government extends its ceasefires with the NSCN–R, NSCN–KN/U and NSCN–KK for another year until April 2022.

15 May
As the Assam state government led by the Bharatiya Janata Party retains power after winning the state assembly elections, the ULFA–I declares a three-month unilateral ceasefire on account of the coronavirus pandemic, renewing the ceasefire later in August.

22–23 June
Ravi declares that 'tax' can only be collected by the Indian government. The NSCN–IM accuses him of violating the Framework Agreement, declaring tax a sovereign matter of the Naga people.

4 July
The WC of seven Naga armed groups accuses the NSCN–K/Niki Sumi faction of acting aggressively in Dimapur town. The Niki Sumi faction turned down an offer to join the WC in late 2020.

MILITARY/VIOLENT EVENTS

23 March 2021
CPI–Maoist militants kill five District Reserve Guard personnel in an ambush in Narayanpur, Chhattisgarh.

3 April
CPI–Maoist militants ambush security forces near Jonaguda, Sukma district of Chhattisgarh, killing 22 in the worst Maoist attack on security forces since 2017.

23 May
Security forces kill eight DNLA militants in Karbi Anglong district.

16 June
ZRA–Eastern Command militants clash with PDF militias in northern Chin State, Myanmar.

15 July
Security forces shoot and kill a CPI–Maoist 'zonal commander' and member of the Bihar–Jharkhand CPI–Maoist regional committee in Gumla, Jharkhand.

15 August
The NSCN–IM says that the Nagas cannot forgo the demand for a separate flag and constitution in the peace talks with the Indian government, while the Nagaland government unites with the opposition to present a united front to expedite the peace process.

8 September
The NSCN–K/Niki Sumi, which split from the NSCN–K/YA in 2020, signs a ceasefire agreement with the government.

9 September
Ravi is repositioned as governor of Tamil Nadu. He then resigns as interlocutor for peace talks, amid tensions with the NSCN–IM, on 22 September.

28 October
The central and Assam state governments sign a six-month ceasefire with the Dimasa National Liberation Army (DNLA).

19 November
The NSCN–R, a member of the WC, expels former vice president Akato Chophy, who forms a new faction, the NSCN–R/Akato Chophy, which is no longer aligned with the WC.

2 December
The Kamtapur Liberation Organisation, an armed group operating in Western Assam, expresses its willingness to enter peace talks with the government.

21 January 2022
CPI–Maoist 'zonal commander' and Central Committee member Maharaj Pramanik surrenders to police in Jharkhand state.

28 February–5 March
Polling begins in Manipur for the state assembly elections. Key issues include the Armed Forces Special Powers Act and a proposed bill for hill-district autonomy in the state. In Central India, the CPI–Maoist calls for a boycott of the state assembly elections taking place across India.

18 April
The government's new interlocutor for peace talks, A.K. Mishra, arrives in Nagaland to initiate talks with the various Naga armed groups.

23 April
Mishra holds a historic meeting at Camp Hebron for talks. Mishra says that a peace agreement will be based on the premises of the Framework Agreement.

10 August
Following a desertion attempt resulting in factional clashes, six PLAM militants are killed in Sagaing region of Myanmar, opposite the Pangsau Pass in Changlang district, Arunachal Pradesh. The defectors had reportedly tried to flee to avoid fighting alongside the Myanmar military.

19 September
ZRA–Eastern Command militants clash with PDF resistance forces in Tedim and Tonzang, northern Chin State.

10 October
Assam Rifles clash with Kuki National Liberation Army (KNLA) militants in Hingojang, Kangpokpi district of Manipur. Four militants are killed.

13 November
Security forces kill 27 CPI–Maoist militants in Gadchiroli, Maharashtra.

14 November
PLAM and MNPF militants ambush an Assam Rifles convoy in Churachandpur, Manipur, killing seven. Five soldiers are killed, including one commanding officer, and his wife and five-year-old son.

5 December
Army soldiers in Nagaland kill 15 civilians during a botched counter-insurgency operation.

14 January 2022
Chin National Army (CNA) militants in Myanmar attack a camp housing PLAM and other Manipur-based militants in Sagaing Region.

27 February
Security forces kill two female CPI–Maoist cadres during a clash in Bijapur, Chhattisgarh.

6 March
Assam Rifles clash with NSCN–IM militants in Tirap, Arunachal Pradesh.

1 April
The Armed Forces Special Powers Act is lifted from 15 police station areas across seven districts of Nagaland, 15 police station areas across six districts of Manipur, and 23 full districts and one partial district in Assam.

Conflict Outlook

Political scenarios

While the prospect of a new interlocutor for the Naga peace talks has raised hopes that issues can be quickly resolved, this is unlikely to be the case. Lingering questions over the status of the Naga flag and constitution, unresolved tensions over granting autonomy to the Nagas of Manipur's hills, the continued stand-offs and clashes between the state and Naga ceasefire signatory groups, factionalism within the Naga movement and deep societal distrust towards Delhi in the aftermath of the December 2021 Mon district ambush mean that confidence will need to be slowly rebuilt with the new interlocutor in 2022. The April 2022 decision to lift the Armed Forces Special Powers Act from a significant number of districts across the Northeast region is likely to provide an early boost to this process.

Escalation potential and conflict-related risks

In addition to ongoing difficulties in northeast India, continued violence in and around the Bastar region is likely in 2022. Security forces were able to significantly curb the CPI–Maoist's nascent efforts to build a Maharashtra–Madhya Pradesh–Chhattisgarh area of influence (MMC) by inflicting heavy casualties on the organisation in the area, including on Milind Teltumbde, the Central Committee member tasked with control of this new zone. During 2022, it is likely that the CPI–Maoist will use the January–June Tactical Counter-Offensive Campaign season to defend its base areas in Bastar (Chhattisgarh), but also seek to renew its efforts to establish the MMC. Given that the CPI–Maoist has historically struggled to establish base areas in the MMC region, it will likely struggle in these efforts as opposed to in Bastar, where it is likely to again inflict large numbers of casualties on security forces.

Strategic implications and global influences

As a new phase of cross-border insurgency emerges, power dynamics within the anti-talks groups camped in Myanmar will likely shift. While the ULFA–I and the NSCN–K/YA have traditionally headed the UNLFWESEA, the NSCN–K/YA appears to be avoiding embroiling itself in the conflict in Myanmar. The ULFA–I's unilateral coronavirus ceasefire, moreover, is likely a tactical decision in light of the group's recent losses, which suggests that both groups may be focusing on consolidating and recuperating in the immediate term. Manipuri armed groups such as the PLAM, MNPF and ZRA–Eastern Command have more directly involved themselves in attacks both in Myanmar and India, indicating that they have been in a stronger position to operate, at least during the first half of 2022. With the relocation of a number of Manipur-based militants to Chin State, it is likely that Manipur's Churachandpur district will witness an increase in cross-border insurgent activity.

Notes

1. Rahul Karmakar and Dinakar Peri, 'Army Operation in Nagaland Goes Awry, 15 Civilians Dead', *Hindu*, 5 December 2021.
2. 'Maoist Influence Down to Just 46 Districts in 2021 from 96 in 2010: Centre', *Outlook India*, 9 February 2022; and IISS, *Armed Conflict Survey 2021* (Abingdon: Routledge for the IISS, 2021), p. 358.
3. Deepak Kumar Nayak, 'Maharashtra: Cementing Gains', *South Asia Intelligence Review*, 2022.
4. Deepak Kumar Nayak, 'Chhattisgarh: Maoists Contained', *South Asia Intelligence Review*, 2022.
5. Including the NSCN–Kitovi-Neokpao/Unification (NSCN–KN/U), NSCN–R, NNC/Federal Government of Nagaland (NNC/FGN), NNC–Parent, National People's Government of Nagaland/Naga National Council–Non-Accord (NPGN/NNC–NA), Government of the Democratic Republic of Nagaland/Naga National Council–Non-Accord (GDRN/NNC–NA) and the NSCN–Khango-Konyak (NSCN–KK).
6. Satyendra Garg, 'Ministry of Home Affairs Notification S.O.3187(E)', 2020, p. 67.
7. '"40% of Armed Maoists in Chhattisgarh, Maharashtra Region Are Women"', *Hindustan Times*, 15 August 2021.
8. Including the People's Liberation Army of Manipur (PLAM), People's Revolutionary Party of Kangleipak (PREPAK), PREPAK–Progressive (PREPAK–Pro), United National Liberation Front (UNLF), Kanglei Yawol Kanna Lup (KYKL), and the Kangleipak Communist Party (KCP).
9. Rajeev Bhattacharyya, 'Indian Rebel Outfits Regrouping in Myanmar Again', *Diplomat*, 3 January 2022; and Anthony Davis, 'India's Ties With Myanmar Junta in Focus After Chin Group's Attack on Manipur Rebels', *Irrawaddy*, 26 January 2022.
10. Davis, 'India's Ties With Myanmar Junta in Focus After Chin Group's Attack on Manipur Rebels'.
11. 'Revealed: How Zomi Revolutionary Army–Eastern Command Becomes the Puppet Fighters of Myanmar's Military Council', *Chindwin*, 6 October 2021; and Rahul Karmakar, 'Myanmar Army Stint Beefed Up Manipur PLA: Intelligence Report', *Hindu*, 23 November 2021.

THAILAND

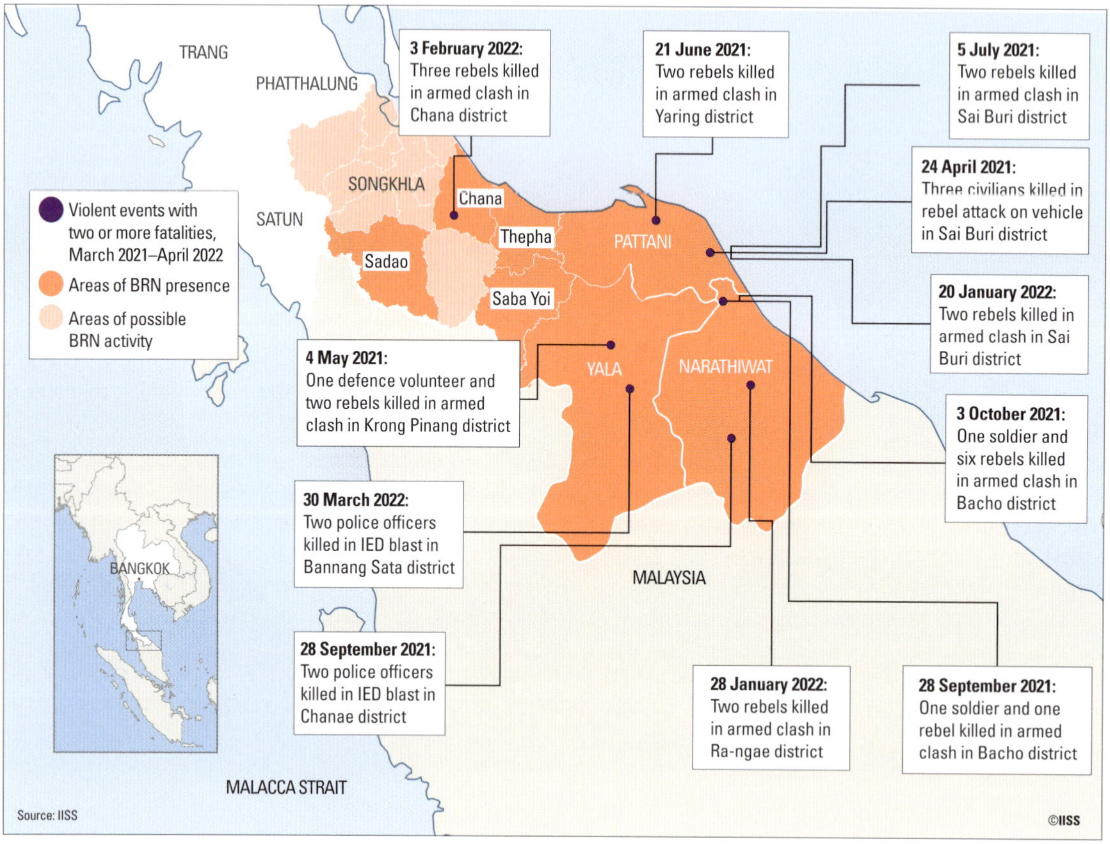
TRANG
PHATTHALUNG
SONGKHLA
SATUN
Chana
Thepha
Sadao
Saba Yoi
PATTANI
YALA
NARATHIWAT
MALAYSIA
BANGKOK
MALACCA STRAIT
Violent events with two or more fatalities, March 2021–April 2022
Areas of BRN presence
Areas of possible BRN activity
3 February 2022: Three rebels killed in armed clash in Chana district
21 June 2021: Two rebels killed in armed clash in Yaring district
5 July 2021: Two rebels killed in armed clash in Sai Buri district
24 April 2021: Three civilians killed in rebel attack on vehicle in Sai Buri district
20 January 2022: Two rebels killed in armed clash in Sai Buri district
4 May 2021: One defence volunteer and two rebels killed in armed clash in Krong Pinang district
3 October 2021: One soldier and six rebels killed in armed clash in Bacho district
30 March 2022: Two police officers killed in IED blast in Bannang Sata district
28 September 2021: Two police officers killed in IED blast in Chanae district
28 January 2022: Two rebels killed in armed clash in Ra-ngae district
28 September 2021: One soldier and one rebel killed in armed clash in Bacho district
Source: IISS
©IISS

Overview

For decades, Malay Muslim separatists have battled the Thai state for independence or autonomy in three southern provinces – Narathiwat, Pattani and Yala – and four districts of Songkhla province. The conflict has its roots in the early twentieth century, when the 1909 Anglo-Siamese Treaty divided the territory of the defunct historical Islamic sultanate of Patani and split the region from Muslim-majority Malaysia, which was then under British colonial control. Formally subsumed within what was then the kingdom of Siam, the area has remained under Thai rule as the treaty effectively demarcated the modern-day border.

The region failed to assimilate with Buddhist-majority Thailand and most Muslim residents rejected Bangkok's authority, with political grievances escalating into an armed insurgency by the late 1950s. This campaign of guerrilla warfare was led by the Patani United Liberation Organisation (PULO), before the violence receded in the 1990s following counter-insurgency operations. The conflict reignited in 2001 with sporadic rebel attacks and intensified in 2004 when then prime minister Thaksin Shinawatra ordered a military crackdown. In April and October of that year, the storming of the Krue Se Mosque by security forces and the Tak Bai massacre became powerful rallying points for the separatist cause.

The Patani Malay National Revolutionary Front (or Barisan Revolusi Nasional, BRN) emerged as the predominant actor, launching ambushes and bomb attacks targeting the Royal Thai Army and police in rural districts. Village Defence Volunteers also

Armed Conflict Global Relevance Indicator (ACGRI)

- Incidence: 1
- Human impact: 0
- Geopolitical impact: 0

Thailand

Key Conflict Statistics

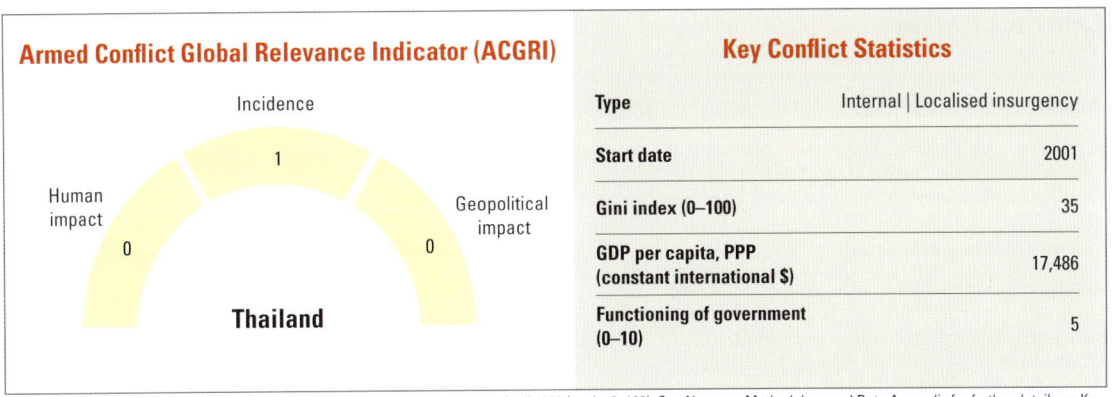

Type	Internal | Localised insurgency
Start date	2001
Gini index (0–100)	35
GDP per capita, PPP (constant international $)	17,486
Functioning of government (0–10)	5

ACGRI pillars: IISS calculation based on multiple sources for 2021 and January–April 2022 (scale: 0–100). See Notes on Methodology and Data Appendix for further details on Key Conflict Statistics.

became targets, as did Muslim civilians seen by the rebels as collaborating with the state, while infrequent but high-profile bombings targeted Bangkok and beach resorts popular with tourists. Violence peaked in the late 2000s and has steadily declined since then, though an attack on a checkpoint in Muang district of Yala province in November 2019 killed 15 security personnel, serving as a deadly reminder of the BRN's capabilities.[1]

Peace initiatives have made little progress. After the May 2014 coup, the then-ruling military junta, known as the National Council for Peace and Order (NCPO), held on-and-off negotiations until 2019 with Mara Patani, an umbrella grouping representing southern rebels. The process was scuppered by the fact that the BRN, the most powerful insurgent group, was excluded from talks, leaving Mara Patani powerless to halt violence on the ground. After the election of a nominal civilian government in March 2019, with coup chief Gen. Prayuth Chan-ocha installed as prime minister, the BRN came to the negotiating table. Two rounds of formal talks were held in January and March 2020, mediated by Malaysia. Yet a humanitarian ceasefire declared at the beginning of the coronavirus pandemic failed to hold, and violence rebounded.

Rebel attacks continued unabated in 2021 in the absence of a peace dialogue, albeit at a lower level than at the height of hostilities. Narathiwat, Pattani, Songkhla and Yala all saw clashes between the BRN and the Royal Thai Army. Rebel tactics remained in line with historical precedent, with the BRN using firearms and explosives to attack security checkpoints and ambush military patrols on rural roads. On several occasions, cargo and passenger trains were attacked, disrupting trade and injuring railway workers. Rebel bombings also targeted infrastructure such as electricity pylons and ATMs, aiming to have a disruptive effect rather than inflict civilian casualties.

The Royal Thai Army, aided by the police and paramilitaries, continued to impose pressure on rebel forces by conducting armed raids and manning a network of security checkpoints. The region remains heavily militarised, with a rolling three-month Emergency Decree continually extended since it was first imposed in 2005. Local violence has often been retaliatory and cyclical, with the BRN avenging the killing of its members by attacking security forces nearby, and vice versa. Violence intensified for several months after a statement by the BRN on 6 September 2021 urging rebels to 'resume self-defence operations' in response to alleged 'raids and summary executions' by Thai troops.[2]

In early 2022, direct peace talks between the BRN and the Thai government's Peace Dialogue Panel (PDP) resumed for the first time in two years. Two rounds of talks, brokered by Malaysian facilitator Abdul Rahim Noor, took place in January and March in Kuala Lumpur. After the first round on 11–12 January, the two sides agreed to establish a joint working group to discuss violence reduction, public participation and political solutions. The second round, from 31 March–1 April, resulted in a 40-day truce, with both sides committing to halt violence over Ramadan and the army permitting unarmed rebels to visit their families. The head of the BRN delegation, Anas Abdulrahman, voiced satisfaction with the outcome, while Rahim Noor said the halt to violence was intended to build trust and confidence ahead of future talks. The government delegation made clear that the army would respond if attacked.

Conflict Parties

Royal Thai Army

Strength: 245,000 personnel.

Areas of operation: The Fourth Area Army of the Royal Thai Army, headquartered in Nakhon Si Thammarat, operates across the four insurgency-affected provinces of Narathiwat, Pattani, Songkhla and Yala.

Leadership and structure: Lt-Gen. Kriangkrai Srirak commands the Fourth Area Army, operating under Royal Thai Army commander Gen. Narongpan Jitkaewthae. Coordinates operations with the Internal Security Operations Command (ISOC). Soldiers serve in infantry, cavalry and armoured divisions, as well as in special-forces units.

History: Formed in 1874 and shaped by nationwide counter-insurgency campaigns starting in the 1960s. Since 1932, the armed forces have carried out 13 successful coups, the most recent in 2014.[3]

Objectives: Preserve the current political order, centred on the monarchy, and ensure the stability of the government led by former army chief Prayuth Chan-ocha. In southern Thailand the army aims to pacify the Malay Muslim population and prevent the insurgency spreading to provinces further north.

Opponents and affiliates/allies:
Opponents: The BRN and other separatist groups.
Affiliates/allies: The Thai monarchy and the ruling Palang Pracharath party. Supported in operations against rebels by the police and paramilitary forces, including Village Defence Volunteers.

Resources/capabilities: Equipped with small arms, including pistols, rifles and machine guns. Also possesses tanks, armoured vehicles and attack helicopters. Equipment is purchased primarily from the United States and other Western allies.

Thai paramilitary forces

Strength: 79,000 (estimate) across the southern provinces of Narathiwat, Pattani, Songkhla and Yala.[4]

Areas of operation: Paramilitary forces provide security along the border with Malaysia, while local recruits serve in their communities and at road checkpoints across the four southern provinces.

Leadership and structure: Paramilitary forces active across the south include the Rangers, Border Patrol Police (BPP) and Volunteer Defence Corps (VDC). At the local level, Village Defence Volunteers (*Chor ror bor*) and Village Protection Volunteers (*Or ror bor*) defend communities. These forces are coordinated by the Royal Thai Army and ISOC, while the BPP is under the jurisdiction of the national police.

History: Paramilitary forces were created to aid the Royal Thai Army in counter-insurgency operations and border protection. The BPP was formed in 1951, the VDC in 1954 and the Rangers in 1978, initially to fight communist rebels. Village-level volunteer units were formed in 2004 as the southern conflict intensified.

Objectives: The Rangers, BPP and VDC have a more conventional security role, serving alongside the Royal Thai Army and police to limit the activity of insurgents, through manning security posts and conducting regular patrols. Village volunteers serve to protect Buddhist communities in the south and provide local surveillance and intelligence support to the military.

Opponents and affiliates/allies:
Opponents: The BRN and other separatist groups in the south.
Affiliates/allies: Formally allied to the Royal Thai Army and the national police.

Resources/capabilities: Paramilitary forces are typically more lightly armed than the military. Village forces are provided with rifles and shotguns, receive a monthly stipend and undergo 10–15 days' training.[5]

Patani Malay National Revolutionary Front (BRN)

Strength: Approximately 3,000.[6]

Areas of operation: Narathiwat, Pattani and Yala provinces. Also operates in four southeastern districts of Songkhla province (Chana, Saba Yoi, Sadao and Thepha). Infrequent bomb attacks have targeted tourist islands and Bangkok, though the BRN has no presence there.

Leadership and structure: Led by an executive council, the Dewan Pimpinan Parti, under secretary-general Sama-ae Kho Zari. Anas Abdulrahman serves as the lead negotiator in peace talks with the Thai government. Five organisational units cover politics, economic and financial affairs, women's affairs, youth and armed forces. BRN fighters operate in a loose, cell-like structure. Religious teachers play a central role in recruitment to the BRN from Islamic schools.

History: Founded in 1960 by religious teacher Haji Abdul Karim Hassan. By 1984 it had split into three factions: BRN-Coordinate (BRN-C), BRN-Congress and BRN-Ulama. BRN-C became dominant and constitutes the BRN today. A separate, 500-strong armed wing, the Runda Kumpulan Kecil (RKK), emerged in 2000 but is now integrated within the main organisation.

Objectives: Initially established to fight for independence in the territory of the historical Patani sultanate, which was conquered by the kingdom of Siam in 1786. Now appears open to negotiating with Thailand for autonomy or self-determination, while continuing attacks aimed at making the region ungovernable in the short term.

Patani Malay National Revolutionary Front (Barisan Revolusi Nasional, BRN)

Opponents and affiliates/allies:
Opponents: The Royal Thai Army and Thai paramilitary forces in the south. The BRN also opposes local civilians whom it perceives to be collaborating with the Thai state, including village headmen and teachers.
Affiliates/allies: PULO remnants and other active Malay separatist groups.

Resources/capabilities: Firearms including M-16 and AK-47 assault rifles. Reported to have obtained AK-102 rifles stolen from a military base in May 2021.[7] Uses pipe bombs and retains the capability to construct low-grade improvised explosive devices (IEDs).

Conflict Drivers

Security

Militarisation of the south:
The pervasive influence of military and paramilitary forces in the south reinforces the grievances of Muslims. Since 2005, the region has been governed under an Emergency Decree, facilitating a network of security checkpoints and lending authorities the power to arbitrarily detain suspected rebels for up to 30 days without charge. Allegations of torture and mistreatment of detainees at the hands of the military have regularly triggered waves of rebel attacks, while raising inter-communal tensions and leaving Muslim civilians fearful of suspicion by association. A 2019 law requiring residents of rebel-affected provinces to register mobile-phone SIM cards with fingerprints and facial images is increasingly being enforced, fuelling concerns of enhanced digital surveillance.

Political

Contrasting identity politics:
For decades, Thai government policy – particularly the promotion of Buddhism as the state religion – has further hardened the grievances of Malays, who account for 85% of the southern population and reject forced assimilation.[8] Even after a fruitful start to peace talks in 2022, the two sides remain far apart on their vision for the region: the BRN wants a 'Patani Darussalam' autonomous region, with classes taught in Malay in an Islamic education system, while Thai hardliners, unwilling to offer autonomy or devolution, would view this as eroding territorial integrity and Buddhist traditions.[9]

Economic and social

Economic marginalisation:
Pattani and Narathiwat, which historically have seen the highest levels of violence, are the country's poorest provinces, with poverty rates around 34%.[10] Other border regions fare much better, while Thailand as a whole has achieved higher-middle-income status, with a national poverty rate of 6.2%.[11] Malay-speaking households are poorer, with those unable to speak Thai or English struggling to access higher education or employment. As a result, Malay youths, especially men, risk social exclusion and indoctrination by rebel groups. While the service sector in Bangkok has expanded and other coastal areas have benefited from the tourism boom, the south has been left behind, with agriculture, fishing and construction remaining the main industries.

Key Events in 2021–22

POLITICAL EVENTS

3 March 2021
Facebook takes down 185 accounts allegedly linked to the Thai military over information-influencing posts related to the southern insurgency.

15 July
A group of lawyers and civil-society activists calls on the Thai government to lift the Emergency Decree in place in southern Thailand since 2005.

6 September
The BRN issues an online statement urging rebels to 'resume self-defence operations' in response to alleged Thai military 'raids' and 'executions'.

16 September
The Thai parliament approves the first reading of the Prevention and Suppression of Torture and Enforced Disappearance Bill.

11 December
PDP chief Gen. Wanlop Rugsanaoh says that 'with the COVID-19 situation improving', face-to-face talks with the BRN will resume in January 2022.

MILITARY/VIOLENT EVENTS

24 April 2021
Suspected insurgents open fire on a vehicle before setting it ablaze in Sai Buri district, Pattani province, killing its three civilian occupants.

4 May
Two suspected rebels are killed in a stand-off with soldiers after shooting dead a territorial-defence volunteer in Krong Pinang district, Yala province.

20 June
Government troops kill two suspected rebels during a stand-off at a beach resort in Yaring district, Pattani province.

5 July
Insurgents besiege an Islamic school in Sai Buri district, Pattani province. Two rebels are killed after a 17-hour stand-off, while five others escape.

3 August
Rebels attack the operations base of the 45th Ranger Task Force in Tak Bai district, Narathiwat province, killing one soldier and injuring another four.

28 September
Rebels engage the Thai military in a shoot-out in Bacho district, Narathiwat province, leaving one insurgent and one soldier dead.

28 September
An IED detonates next to a road in Chanae district, Narathiwat province, targeting a police convoy. Two officers are killed and four are injured.

3 October
Six rebels and one soldier are killed in a gun battle after Thai government forces surround rebels in a swamp in Bacho district, Narathiwat province.

28 November
Rebels bomb a convoy of eight vehicles carrying ballot boxes after a local election in Bannang Sata district, Yala province, injuring a polling agent.

15 December
The Thai government approves a draft five-year development plan for the southern provinces, which aims to end the insurgency by 2027.

13 December
Suspected insurgents bomb a passenger train in Khok Pho district, Pattani province, wounding a passenger and two railway employees.

31 December
Bombs explode in six locations in Yala province, targeting a mobile-phone signal tower and electricity pylons. The blasts cause local power outages.

11–12 January 2022
Negotiating panels from the Thai government and BRN hold formal peace talks in Kuala Lumpur and agree to establish a joint working group.

20 January 2022
Government forces clash with rebels in Sai Buri district, Pattani province, leaving two insurgents dead and one soldier wounded.

15 January
The Thai government says it has agreed a three-point framework with the BRN as the basis for future peace talks. It covers violence reduction, public participation and political solutions.

28 January
A joint force of soldiers and police officers raids a house in Ra-ngae district, Narathiwat province, killing two suspected insurgents.

24 January
Rachada Dhnadirek is appointed by the Thai government as special envoy to talks with the BRN, with the role of promoting women's inclusion.

28–29 January
Thirteen explosions occur across two days in Yala province, wounding one civilian. Convenience stores and a car-repair garage are among the targets.

3 February
Abdul Rahim Noor, Malaysian facilitator of the peace process, says clashes between the Thai military and BRN 'will not affect the peace talks'.

3 February
Government troops clash with insurgents near a mosque in Chana district, Songkhla province, leaving three rebels dead.

13 March
Banners declaring 'Free Patani – Patani is not Siam' are displayed across the southern provinces to mark the 62nd anniversary of the founding of the BRN.

31 March–1 April
Negotiating panels from the Thai government and BRN hold formal peace talks in Kuala Lumpur, agreeing a 40-day truce covering Ramadan.

30 March
A roadside IED explodes in Bannang Sata district, Yala province, killing two police officers in a passing pick-up truck. Another two officers are injured.

Conflict Outlook

Political scenarios

The resumption of dialogue in early 2022 between the PDP and the BRN, which culminated in a set of 'general principles' being agreed on 1 April, provides an initial basis for further rounds of talks to take place. Yet for concrete progress to be made in the political arena, compromise will be required on both sides. In response to youth-led pro-democracy street protests, the government has reinforced its commitment to the 2017 military-drafted constitution that enshrines Thailand as a 'one and indivisible kingdom' with the monarch as head of state. This rules out full independence for the south but leaves open the possibility of devolution of powers. It is likely that any concessions would be merely symbolic at first, such as recognising Malay culture and Islamic traditions, but this could promote goodwill and pave the way for discussions on the final political status of the disputed territory. Yet without a clear public commitment from the Thai side that it would offer self-governance, progress is likely to be slow.

Escalation potential and conflict-related risks

Whether the rebooted political process can achieve a reduction in violence depends on the extent to which the BRN negotiation panel is able to influence fighters on the ground. Mara Patani, the rebel umbrella group engaged in peace negotiations from 2015–19, ultimately proved unable to do so. On 3 February 2022, Malaysian facilitator Abdul Rahim Noor said that ongoing violence would 'not affect the peace talks'. However, a future spate of rebel attacks or heavy-handed tactics by the military would inevitably raise tensions at the negotiating table. The loose, cell-like structure of the BRN and a lack of accountability and discipline among paramilitaries make it probable that cyclical violence at the local level will continue, regardless of any ceasefire or progress in talks. Attacks by remnants of other groups, such as the PULO, may also prove disruptive to the peace dialogue.[12] However, given the embedded security infrastructure in the south, a major surge in rebel violence is unlikely. Rebel attacks further north remain a rarity.

Strategic implications and global influences

Malaysia retains a strategic interest in the conflict being resolved, as demonstrated by its role as facilitator in the peace process. Sharing close diplomatic ties with Thailand, while having sympathy for the plight of Malay Muslims living in the far south, Malaysia is viewed as impartial by both parties, and retaining this position of neutrality will be key to the prospects of resolution. The inclusion of foreign observers from more countries would strengthen existing peace efforts. Malaysia is also motivated by the need to maintain stability along its northern frontier. Following an ambush in the border district of Tak Bai, in Narathiwat, on 3 August 2021, in which rebel forces attacked a Rangers base before fleeing across the Kolok River to Malaysia, the state police chief in Kelantan vowed to tighten security on the Malaysian side. While Salafist ideology has become more prevalent since the early 2000s, coinciding with the BRN's rise, the conflict remains firmly grounded in local grievances, with no evidence that the Islamic State (ISIS) or other jihadists are influencing events.

Notes

[1] Teeranai Charuvastra, 'BRN Blamed for Checkpoint Attack That Killed 15', *Khaosod*, 7 November 2019.

[2] Matahari Ismail and Mariyam Ahmad, 'Violent Day in Thai Deep South Claims Highest Toll in September', Benar News, 28 September 2021.

[3] 'Grading Thailand's 13 Successful Coups', *Thai Enquirer*, 22 May 2020.

[4] The estimated 79,000 paramilitary personnel in southern Thailand comprise 8,000 VDC members, 59,000 Village Defence Volunteers, 4,000 Village Protection Volunteers and an estimated 8,000 Rangers. It is unknown how many BPP officers are in the south. See Paul Chambers, 'Irregular and Inappropriate: Thailand's Paramilitaries and Pro-government Militias', Fulcrum, ISEAS – Yusof Ishak Institute, 12 April 2021.

[5] Pro-Government Militias Guidebook, 'Village Protection Volunteers (Or Ror Bor) (Thailand)', undated.

[6] Srisompob Jitpiromsri, Napisa Waitoolkiat and Paul Chambers, 'Special Issue: Quagmire of Violence in Thailand's Southern Borderlands Chapter 1: Introduction', *Asian Affairs: An American Review*, vol. 45, no. 2, 28 April 2019.

[7] 'Thai Police Announce Missing Firearms Were Stolen, Sold', *Borneo Bulletin*, 31 May 2021.

[8] Matthew Wheeler, 'Behind the Insurgent Attack in Southern Thailand', International Crisis Group, 8 November 2019.

[9] Tara Abhasakun, 'Thai Government, Patani Malay Southern Rebels Still Disagree on Key Issues', Thaiger, 19 January 2022.

[10] Judy Yang, 'Reducing Poverty and Improving Equity in Thailand: Why It Still Matters', World Bank, 17 October 2019.

[11] 'Poverty & Equity Brief: East Asia & Pacific: Thailand', World Bank, April 2021.

[12] Mariyam Ahmad, 'Sidelined in Peace Talks, PULO Rebels Claim Responsibility for Deep South Bombing', Benar News, 15 April 2022.

PHILIPPINES

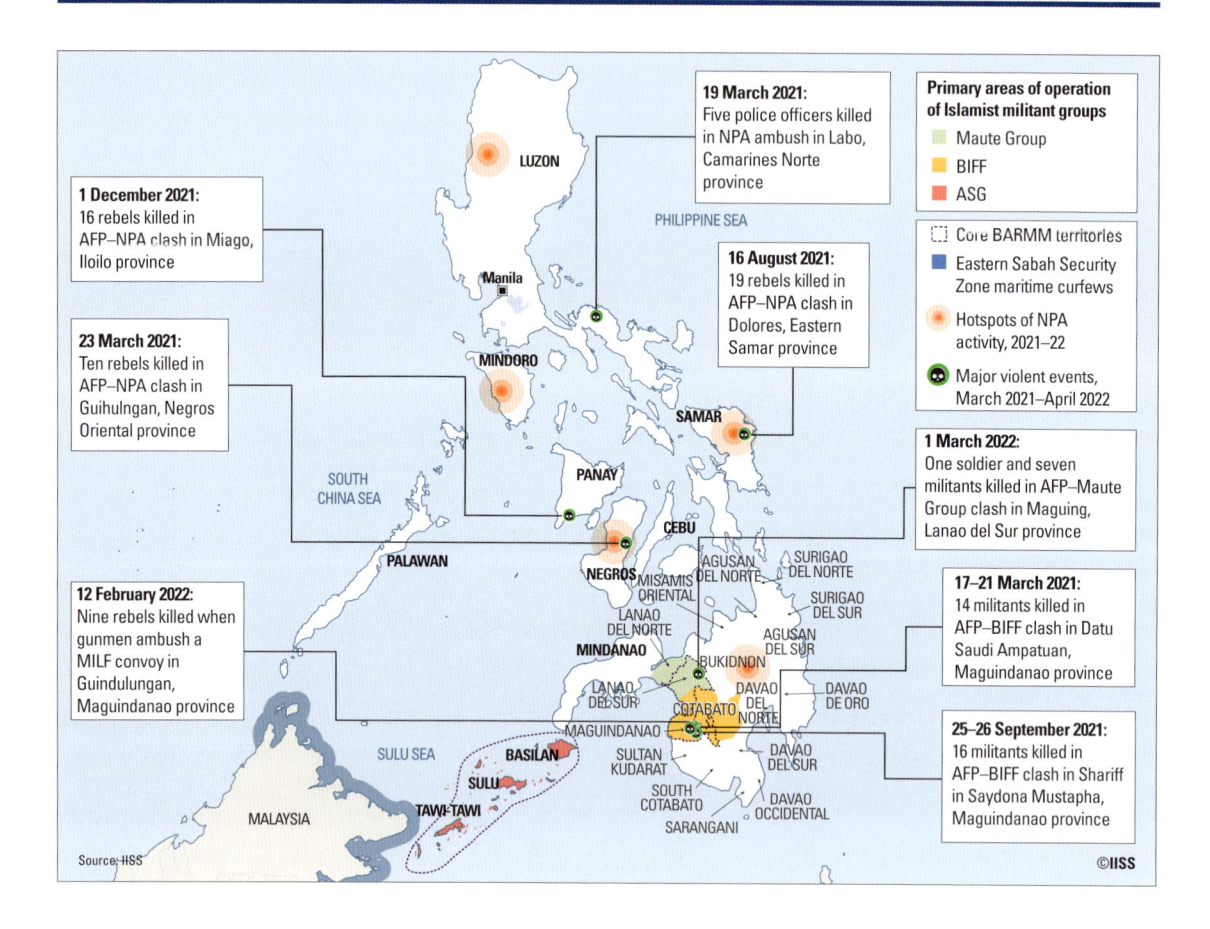

Overview

The Philippine government has been battling Moro-separatist insurgencies in the country's southwest and communist New People's Army (NPA) rebels nationwide since the early 1970s. Following earlier uprisings by Muslim rebels against colonisers from Spain and the United States, the March 1968 Jabidah massacre of Moro army recruits by the Philippine military sparked revived secessionist activities. From 1972, the Moro National Liberation Front (MNLF) waged an armed campaign for independence fuelled by alleged political, cultural and religious oppression of Muslims in western Mindanao. After signing peace accords with the government in 1976 and 1996, the MNLF was displaced as the main conflict actor by a powerful splinter group, the Moro Islamic Liberation Front (MILF). In the 1990s, the MILF engaged in large-scale clashes with the national armed forces in remote parts of western Mindanao, while simultaneously engaging in peace talks with Manila. These talks eventually led to the signing of the Bangsamoro Organic Law (BOL) in 2018, which legislated for self-governance in exchange for disarmament. The BOL was ratified via a referendum in early 2019, creating the new Bangsamoro Autonomous Region in Muslim Mindanao (BARMM), led by MILF chairman Al Haj Murad Ebrahim.

With the MNLF largely inactive and the MILF's 40,000 members disarming, several radical Islamist militant groups continued to fight government forces for full independence, including the Abu Sayyaf Group (ASG) in the island

Armed Conflict Global Relevance Indicator (ACGRI)

- Incidence: 8
- Human impact: 1
- Geopolitical impact: 5

Philippines

Key Conflict Statistics

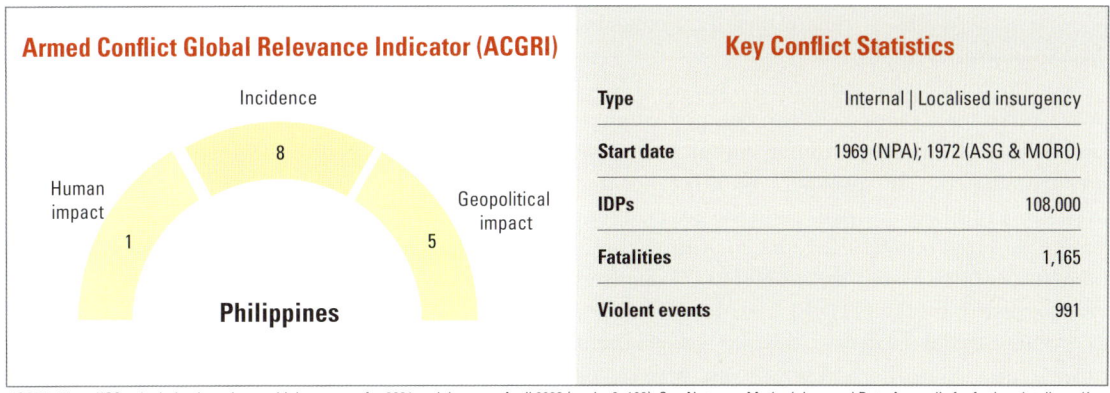

Type	Internal | Localised insurgency
Start date	1969 (NPA); 1972 (ASG & MORO)
IDPs	108,000
Fatalities	1,165
Violent events	991

ACGRI pillars: IISS calculation based on multiple sources for 2021 and January–April 2022 (scale: 0–100). See Notes on Methodology and Data Appendix for further details on Key Conflict Statistics.

provinces of Basilan, Sulu and Tawi-Tawi, and the Bangsamoro Islamic Freedom Fighters (BIFF) and Maute Group on mainland western Mindanao. These three groups joined forces under the banner of the Islamic State (ISIS) in 2017 to lay siege to the city of Marawi for five months, displacing 350,000 people before being defeated by the Armed Forces of the Philippines (AFP).[1]

The post-independence Maoist rebellion in the Philippines began in 1969 with the founding of the NPA as the armed wing of the Communist Party of the Philippines (CPP). Since then, the NPA has waged a guerrilla war in rural areas across the Philippines with the aim of replacing the government in Manila with a socialist political system. The insurgency peaked in intensity in the early 1980s, when the NPA had 26,000 fighters. In the post-1986 democratic era the conflict receded, though the NPA continued to ambush government forces and police officers in its remote strongholds in eastern Mindanao, the Visayas and northern Luzon.

Intermittent talks between Manila and the CPP–NPA's negotiating arm, the National Democratic Front of the Philippines (NDFP), have failed to negotiate an end to the insurgency under six successive administrations since the 1980s. A ceasefire and several rounds of dialogue in Oslo, Rome and Amsterdam followed the election of President Rodrigo Duterte in 2016. However, talks collapsed and Duterte terminated national-level negotiations in November 2017. Despite localised peace talks and efforts to encourage rebels to surrender in exchange for livelihood aid through a National Task Force to End Local Communist Armed Conflict (NTF–ELCAC), violence has rebounded in rural areas.

Progress made by the BARMM transitional government – originally set to rule for three years from 2019 until parliamentary elections in May 2022 – slowed during 2021. Only three of six priority laws were passed, while the disarmament of MILF insurgents halted amid the coronavirus pandemic. Regional leaders continued to call for a three-year extension of the Bangsamoro Transition Authority's (BTA) mandate to allow democratic governance structures to take root. In September, the Philippine Senate and House of Representatives passed bills to extend the transition period. The extension was ratified by Duterte in October, postponing the first BARMM parliamentary elections to 2025. MILF chairman Ebrahim said the extension was 'never about power' and would enable a 'strong regional bureaucracy' to develop.[2] The MILF-led United Bangsamoro Justice Party (UBJP) is expected to be a leading candidate in the 2025 polls.

The MNLF remained broadly supportive of the peace process in 2020–21. Militant groups aligned to the Islamic State came under increasing pressure from government forces: BIFF leader Salahuddin Hassan (alias 'Orak') and ASG sub-leader Majan Sahidjuan (alias 'Apo Mike') were killed in AFP operations. While the ASG's main faction in Sulu – led by Mundi Sawadjaan – remains a threat, factions in Basilan and Tawi-Tawi are smaller and more splintered, having suffered significant losses. The AFP continued to launch aerial attacks targeting BIFF positions in central Maguindanao and Maute Group camps in Lanao del Norte and Lanao del Sur, denting their capabilities. In the time period under review no major attacks on civilians were carried out by Islamist groups, which now operate as networks of cells rather than coherent organisations.

For the fourth year running, no national-level peace talks took place between the government and the NDFP in 2021, leaving violence in rural areas unabated. The prospect of talks became even more unlikely in April when the government designated 19 senior CPP leaders, including chairman Jose Maria Sison, as 'terrorists'. Localised talks overseen by the NTF–ELCAC largely failed to prevent rebel violence, despite government propaganda that the strategy was proving a success. The NPA remained strongest in its traditional rural strongholds in eastern Mindanao and across the Visayas, with hotspots on Negros Island and Samar. Rebels continued to launch ambushes targeting AFP and Philippine National Police (PNP) vehicles on rural roads, with civilian bystanders and health workers sometimes caught in the crossfire. AFP troops, supported by the PNP, carried out anti-NPA raids based on intelligence reports, destroying rebel camps in airstrikes and targeting its leaders. The NPA's top-ranking commander, Jorge Madlos (alias 'Ka Oris'), was shot dead in Bukidnon in October, while senior Mindanao commanders Menandro Villanueva (alias 'Bok') and Pedro Codaste (alias 'Gonyong') were killed in January 2022.

Conflict Parties

Armed Forces of the Philippines (AFP)

Strength: 145,300 regular combatants across the army, navy and air force. Reserve force of 131,000, including 50,000 reservists serving in Citizen Armed Forces Geographical Units.

Areas of operation: Operates nationwide. Headquarters, Camp Aguinaldo, is in Quezon city, Metro Manila.

Leadership and structure: Led by Chief of Staff Lt-Gen. Andres Centino, appointed in November 2021.
Divided into six area unified commands (with the Western Mindanao Command tasked with tackling Islamist groups and the Eastern Mindanao Command primarily tasked with fighting the NPA). AFP battalions are comprised of 500 soldiers.

History: Established by the 1935 National Defense Act under US colonial rule. Passed to Philippine control upon independence in 1946.

Objectives: Defeat the NPA nationwide by June 2022 and defeat Islamist militant groups active in western Mindanao. To this effect, launches targeted raids and air/ground offensives and conducts routine patrols in areas of militant activity, often over difficult terrain.

Opponents and affiliates/allies:
Opponents: The ASG, the BIFF, the Maute Group and the NPA.
Affiliates/allies: The MILF and the MNLF, which provide intelligence support. Supported by the PNP in gun battles and law-enforcement raids.

Resources/capabilities: Access to combat tanks and armoured trucks. The army uses rifles and artillery in operations against rebels and is assisted by air-force rapid-attack aircraft and helicopters. Naval assets are deployed in the Sulu Sea to prevent transit of militants.

Abu Sayyaf Group (ASG)

Strength: 300 active members (estimate), including 132 fighters in Sulu (AFP estimate).[3]

Areas of operation: Active presence in the maritime provinces of Basilan, Sulu and Tawi-Tawi. Limited presence along the coast of the Zamboanga peninsula and in Malaysia's Sabah State, which it has used as a hideout and a base for maritime kidnap-for-ransom operations. Presence in Sulu and Celebes seas is restricted by naval patrols.

Leadership and structure: Mundi Sawadjaan and Radullan Sahiron command ASG factions in Sulu province. Leaders in Basilan and Tawi-Tawi unknown, as the ASG has no centralised command structure there.
Operates as a loose network of cells arranged along clan and family lines.

History: Formed in 1991 by radical Islamist preacher Abdurajak Abubakar Janjalani. In the 2000s, the group became notorious for hostage-taking in the Sulu Sea. The ASG temporarily joined forces with the BIFF and the Maute Group in 2017 to lay siege to the city of Marawi. It has since retreated to outlying islands.

Objectives: Re-establish an Islamic sultanate in the Sulu archipelago. In 2014, then-leader Isnilon Hapilon (now deceased) declared allegiance to the Islamic State and sought the creation of a regional caliphate in Southeast Asia.

Opponents and affiliates/allies:
Opponents: The AFP, the MILF and an MNLF faction led by Muslimin Sema. A smaller faction of the MNLF based in Sulu, led by Nur Misuari, is tolerant of the ASG but not openly supportive. Affiliates/allies: Allied ideologically with the Islamic State, the BIFF and the Maute Group but has limited operational ties.

Resources and capabilities: Uses high-powered firearms and improvised explosive devices (IEDs) to attack AFP troops. Deploys speedboats in maritime kidnappings and has used firearms and knives to kill hostages. Since 2018, the group has carried out suicide bombings and retains bomb-making skills.

Bangsamoro Islamic Freedom Fighters (BIFF)

Strength: 300 active fighters (estimate).

Areas of operation: Most active in an area typified by marshy terrain known as the 'SPMS box' (encompassing the towns of Shariff Aguak, Pagatin, Mamasapano and Datu Salibo) in central Maguindanao. BIFF is also known to operate in North Cotabato and Sultan Kudarat provinces.

Leadership and structure: Divided into three factions, led by Esmael Abdulmalik (alias 'Abu Toraife'), Ismael Abubakar (alias 'Imam Bongos') and Ustadz Karialan (alias 'Imam Minimbang'). Though it has no centralised leadership, BIFF factions cooperate in a tactical alliance against the AFP.

History: Formed as a splinter of the MILF in 2010 when its founder, Ameril Umbra Kato, grew frustrated with the MILF's decision to drop demands for independence in favour of autonomy and self-governance. Fought in the 2017 siege of Marawi and has since clashed with the AFP in central Maguindanao province.

Objectives: Establish an independent homeland for the Moro people. The BIFF pledged allegiance to the Islamic State in 2014 and fought to establish a regional caliphate. Only the most extreme BIFF faction, commanded by Abu Turaife, still holds this ambition.

Opponents and affiliates/allies:
Opponents: The AFP and the MNLF. The MILF, despite being its parent group, is opposed to the BIFF and has cooperated with the AFP in recent years in attacks against BIFF militants.
Affiliates/allies: Nominally allied to the ASG and the Maute Group.

Resources/capabilities: Uses high-powered rifles in battles with AFP troops and retains the ability to construct IEDs. The BIFF occasionally launches IED attacks or ambushes on military and civilian targets but is now mostly on the defensive, engaging AFP troops when attacked.

Maute Group

Strength: 60–70 active fighters (AFP estimate).[4] The Maute Group previously comprised up to 1,000 members but most were killed by AFP troops during the 2017 siege of Marawi.

Areas of operation: Active on the northern side of Lake Lanao in Lanao del Norte and Lanao del Sur provinces. Operates primarily in rural and mountainous areas.

Leadership and structure: Faharudin Hadji Satar (aliases 'Abu Bakar' and 'Abu Zacaria'). According to the AFP, the Maute Group leader is also the 'emir' of the Islamic State in Southeast Asia.
Since founders Abdullah and Omar Maute were killed during the 2017 Marawi siege, the group lacks a defined structure.

History: Founded in 2010–11 and espouses an extreme form of Salafi-Wahhabi ideology more often associated with jihadist groups in the Middle East. The Maute Group led the siege of Marawi, in which its senior leaders were killed and its capabilities damaged. It has since retreated to mountainous hideouts.

Objectives: Through seizing and holding territory, the Maute Group aimed to forge a regional Islamic caliphate in Southeast Asia, centred on Mindanao. It is unclear whether the group retains this aim.

Opponents and affiliates/allies:
Opponents: The AFP, the MILF and the MNLF.
Affiliates/allies: Pledged firm allegiance to the Islamic State, though any operational ties are uncertain. Ideologically allied to the ASG and the BIFF.

Resources/capabilities: Possesses a limited cache of rifles. The AFP seized improvised rocket components after raiding a Maute Group camp in March 2022, indicating the group is looking to further its capabilities.

Moro Islamic Liberation Front (MILF)

Strength: 20,655 active fighters serving in its Bangsamoro Islamic Armed Forces (BIAF), down from 40,000 in 2019 as 19,345 have since been demobilised.[5] The remainder of the BIAF force is set to be decommissioned under the terms of the Comprehensive Agreement on the Bangsamoro (CAB), signed in 2014.

Areas of operation: Western Mindanao. Most fighters remain encamped in a network of MILF bases and no longer fight AFP forces. Several hundred demobilised MILF rebels now serve alongside the AFP and PNP in Joint Peace and Security Teams (JPSTs). The MILF's headquarters, Camp Darapanan, is in Maguindanao province.

Leadership and structure: Led by chairman Al Haj Murad Ebrahim, who serves as Chief Minister of the BARMM. Operates similarly to a regular army, with battalions and a centralised leadership body. The MILF is in the process of decommissioning and has formed a political party – the UBJP – to contest future BARMM elections.

History: Founded in 1997 by Hashim Salamat after breaking away from the MNLF. Fought the AFP for decades to secure independence for Moro Muslims in western Mindanao.

Objectives: Initially advocated for an independent Moro state and targeted the AFP in ambushes and bomb attacks. In the late 1990s the MILF began peace talks with Manila, seeking autonomy. After signing the CAB in 2014, the MILF committed to peace and now aims to become the leading political force in the BARMM.

Opponents and affiliates/allies:
Opponents: The ASG, the BIFF and the Maute Group. MILF members still clash intermittently with rival MNLF factions but fighting is short-lived and localised.
Affiliates/allies: Formally allied to the AFP.

Resources/capabilities: Access to high-powered rifles, grenade launchers and other conventional weapons. These will be decommissioned under the CAB, with the process expected to be complete in 2024.

Moro National Liberation Front (MNLF)

Strength: Fewer than 10,000 active fighters. The MNLF's strength has declined since the 1970s, when it had around 30,000 members.

Areas of operation: Western Mindanao and the Sulu archipelago. Most fighters are encamped and rarely engage in combat, aside from local inter-factional and clan disputes with the MILF or other MNLF members.

Leadership and structure: Led by chairman Muslimin Sema. MNLF founder Nur Misuari remains an influential figure and leads a 3,000-strong faction in Sulu.
Initially a centralised organisation, the MNLF splintered after signing a peace agreement with the government in 1996.

History: Formed as a splinter of the now-defunct Muslim Independence Movement (MIM) in 1972 and fought the AFP with the aim of forging an independent Moro state in western Mindanao.

Objectives: No longer advocates for full Moro independence and has been broadly supportive of the government–MILF peace process that established the BARMM. Nur Misuari has at times criticised the peace deal with the MILF but has so far not proved disruptive.

Opponents and affiliates/allies:
Opponents: the BIFF and the Maute Group. The main MNLF group led by Muslimin Sema is opposed to the ASG, although the Nur Misuari faction retains kinship ties. The MILF is a major rival of the MNLF but the two sides rarely resort to violence. Affiliates/allies: the AFP since a 1996 peace deal but violence has occasionally broken out – most notoriously in the 2013 siege of Zamboanga.

Resources/capabilities: The group no longer fights the AFP but retains access to a wide network of bases and high-powered rifles. The Nur Misuari-led faction remains a powerful but dormant actor in the conflict.

New People's Army (NPA)

Strength: 3,500 fighters (AFP estimate) spread across at least 43 guerrilla fronts nationwide.[6] Includes 1,000 fighters in eastern Mindanao.[7] Despite significant annual losses, the NPA's estimated strength has remained between 3,000 and 4,000 over the past decade.

Areas of operation: Most active in its traditional strongholds of eastern Mindanao and the Visayas. NPA presence also continues to be reported in northern Luzon and other rural communities nationwide.

Leadership and structure: Led by founder and CPP chairman Jose Maria Sison from self-imposed exile in the Netherlands. Sison has little influence over day-to-day conflict, which is overseen by a network of ground commanders. Rebels operate in small, closely knit units in the countryside, while hit squads operate in Special Partisan Units in urban areas. The NPA is the armed wing of the CPP, which is represented in peace talks by the NDFP. Julie de Lima serves as interim chairperson of the NDFP peace-negotiation panel.

History: The NPA was formed in 1969, shortly after the founding of the CPP. It has battled government troops for more than 50 years, with fighting centred on rural areas. NDFP-led peace talks have failed under six presidents in the post-1986 democratic era.

Objectives: Ideology has remained unchanged since the 1960s. The NPA is fighting what it labels a 'protracted people's war' to overthrow the Manila government and replace it with a socialist system. It does not seize and hold territory but exercises de facto control in its rural strongholds via extortion and intimidation. Launches ambushes targeting AFP troops, aimed at diminishing morale.

Opponents and affiliates/allies:
Opponents: Opposes the AFP and the PNP. The NPA does not engage in conflict with Moro or Islamist rebel groups in Mindanao.
Affiliates/allies: Has no known affiliates, though in its early years received funds and weapons from China and like-minded Maoist rebel groups based abroad.

Resources/capabilities: High-powered rifles looted from AFP and PNP bases, and other firearms seized from private security guards during armed raids on businesses. Also deploys IEDs and rudimentary explosives.

Other conflict parties

The Revolutionary Proletarian Army–Alex Boncayao Brigade (RPA–ABB) did not engage in any clashes with the NPA in 2021 or early 2022. While RPA–ABB remnants had engaged in small-scale gun battles with NPA insurgents in recent years to defend their communities from attack, the group can now be considered defunct. Having emerged from the NPA as a splinter group in 1997, its rebels were demobilised after signing a peace deal with the government in 2000. Any remnants active since then were operating autonomously without a centralised leadership and can now be considered inactive. Ansar Khalifah Philippines (AKP), also known as the Maguid Group, was active in recent years in the southern provinces of Sarangani and South Cotabato. AKP remnants, estimated to number fewer than 50, have been subsumed into the BIFF and primarily operate further north in Maguindanao and North Cotabato, while retaining a limited presence further south in their past strongholds. Philippine authorities increasingly use the looser term 'Dawlah Islamiyah', meaning Islamic State, to refer to all Islamist militants active on mainland Mindanao, whether affiliated to the AKP, the BIFF or the Maute Group.

Conflict Drivers

Political

Opposition to the Philippine state:
Both Islamist militant groups and the communist NPA view the Philippine state as illegitimate. The roots of Moro separatism lie in the oppression of Muslims, who account for one-quarter of the residents on the Catholic-majority island of Mindanao. Despite being present since the arrival of Arab traders in Sulu in the fourteenth century, the Moros were denied an independent homeland by Spanish and US colonisers and later by the post-1946 Philippine state. Christian migration southward stoked grievances and although the two main Moro fronts have committed to peace, militants reject Manila's rule and still harbour ambitions to revive a past Muslim sultanate or forge an Islamic State-inspired caliphate. The NPA views Philippine rule as imperialist; having retained an anti-capitalist ideology since its founding, the group refuses to compromise on its demand to replace the government with a socialist system.

Economic and social

Poverty and economic exclusion:
Economic marginalisation in western Mindanao has long driven recruitment to Moro separatist and Islamist militant groups. In 2021, the BARMM remained the poorest region of the Philippines, with a poverty rate of 39.4% compared to the national average of 23.7%.[8] The maritime province of Sulu, plagued by the ASG since the early 1990s, is the most impoverished province nationally, with 71.9% of families living in poverty. Despite having fertile soils and being rich in natural resources, infrastructure and public services have remained underdeveloped in the five BARMM provinces while the national government and multinational firms have profited. NPA recruitment has also been aided by rural poverty, which stands at 24.5% compared to 9.3% in urban centres. Job opportunities in remote regions are limited, with farmers and fisherfolk poorer than any other occupation.[9] This leaves disenfranchised youths vulnerable to NPA recruitment, inspired by a narrative that rural areas have been left behind by market forces.

Geographical and social advantages:
Islamist and NPA rebels are firmly embedded within the communities and natural environments in which they operate, complicating the AFP's efforts to track and defeat these groups via conventional means. The ASG's strongest faction is based in Jolo's mountainous interior, while its members have lifelong familiarity with the coastlines of the Sulu archipelago and extensive family ties in the Tausug communities that populate the islands. The Maute Group operates in mountains north of Lake Lanao while the BIFF is able to hide out in the marshlands of Maguindanao's interior. The NPA, with fronts spread across the Philippines' 7,000 islands, operates on densely forested and inaccessible terrain as a strategic choice – its fighters working in small groups and moving between temporary camps.

Key Events in 2021–22

POLITICAL EVENTS

5 March 2021
At a meeting of the NTF–ELCAC, President Duterte orders the AFP and PNP to 'forget about human rights' and 'finish off' NPA rebels.[10]

21 April
The Anti-Terrorism Council (ATC) designates 19 CPP–NPA leaders, including CPP chairman and founder Jose Maria Sison, as terrorists.

7 June
Duterte says 'no peace talks can ever succeed' while the NPA continues to attack government and civilian targets.

23 June
The ATC formally designates the NDFP as a terrorist organisation.

6–15 September
The Philippine Senate and House of Representatives pass legislation to extend the mandate of the BARMM transitional government until 2025.

28 October
Duterte signs Republic Act No. 11593, pushing back the first scheduled BARMM elections from 2022 to 2025.

12 November
AFP Chief-of-Staff Lt-Gen. Andres Centino sets a target to defeat the NPA by the end of Duterte's term in June 2022.

14 December
The Philippine Senate and House of Representatives set the NTF–ELCAC's budget for 2022 at PHP17.1 billion (US$327 million), down from PHP19bn (US$364m) in 2021.

MILITARY/VIOLENT EVENTS

17–21 March 2021
AFP troops clash with the BIFF in Datu Saudi Ampatuan, Maguindanao province, leaving 14 militants dead.

19 March
NPA rebels ambush police guarding a road-construction project in Labo, Camarines Norte province, killing five PNP officers.

20 March
ASG sub-leader Majan Sahidjuan is killed by AFP troops in Languyan, Tawi-Tawi province.

23 March
AFP troops clash with the NPA in Guihulngan, Negros Oriental province, killing ten insurgents.

23 April
Mujafal Sawadjaan, brother of ASG leader Mundi Sawadjaan, is killed in a clash with AFP troops in Patikul, Sulu province.

17 May
Malaysian police kill five ASG militants during a clash in Beaufort in northern Sabah state, Malaysia.

28 May
Two NDFP peace consultants are killed: Reynaldo Bocala is killed by the PNP in Iloilo province and Rustico Tan is shot dead by unidentified gunmen in Cebu province.

3 June
Three civilians are killed and five wounded after BIFF militants set fire to a public bus in M'lang, North Cotabato province.

16 August
AFP troops attack an NPA encampment and explosives factory in Dolores, Eastern Samar province, killing 19 NPA rebels.

25–26 September
AFP troops clash with the BIFF in Shariff Saydona Mustapha, Maguindanao province, leaving one soldier and 16 militants dead.

29 October
AFP troops kill senior BIFF leader Salahuddin Hassan during a raid in Talayan, Maguindanao province.

30 October
Jorge Madlos, chief of the 'National Operations Command' of the NPA, is killed by AFP troops in Impasugong, Bukidnon province.

8 November
Phase 3 of the MILF decommissioning process begins, during which 14,000 rebels are set to be disarmed and 2,500 weapons turned in.

28 December
The BARMM's annual budget for 2022 of PHP79.8bn (US$1.5bn) is approved by the BTA, an increase of 6% on the 2021 budget.

8 January 2022
The MNLF launches its first political party, the Bangsamoro Party (BAPA), and vows to 'engage in a peaceful and participatory politics'.

24 January
The Philippine Senate adopts a resolution granting amnesty to MILF, MNLF and RPA–ABB rebels for 'crimes in furtherance of their political beliefs'.

21 February
Duterte approves retaining the 80-member BTA to serve a second three-year term as the transitional BARMM government.

23 February
The ATC designates 16 social and labour organisations as 'terrorist' entities, citing alleged links to the CPP–NPA.

23 April
BARMM Chief Minister Ebrahim endorses Leni Robredo as the MILF's preferred candidate to be the next Philippine president.

9 May
Ferdinand Marcos Jr wins the presidential election.

1 December
AFP troops clash with the NPA in Miagao, Iloilo province, killing 16 rebels.

5 January 2022
Menandro Villanueva, the most senior NPA commander in Mindanao, is killed by AFP troops in Mabini, Davao de Oro province.

12 February
Unidentified gunmen ambush a convoy of MILF vehicles in Guindulungan, Maguindanao province, killing nine insurgents.

1 March
The AFP launches an offensive targeting a Maute Group camp in Maguing, Lanao del Sur province, leaving seven militants and one soldier dead.

Conflict Outlook

Political scenarios
With the BTA's mandate extended until 2025, the political climate in the BARMM is likely to remain stable. The interim regional administration will continue to be led by the MILF, which retains 41 of the 80 BTA seats. In a particularly promising sign, the MILF's historical rival, the MNLF, launched the BAPA in January 2022, with chair Muslimin Sema committing to a 'peaceful and participatory politics' and vowing support for the MILF-led interim regime. However, the hardline Nur Misuari-led faction of the MNLF in Sulu, which is waiting to judge the results of self-governance under the MILF, could yet take on a spoiler role. In the coming year, the BTA will look to pass delayed legislation on elections, revenue and local government to strengthen institutional capacity in the BARMM. The reconstruction of Marawi city by a government-led task force, which as of September 2021 was 85% complete, is set to be finished in 2022 and will reinforce good relations between the BTA and the central government.[11]

While Duterte has ruled out national-level dialogue with the CPP–NPA for the remainder of his term, the election of a new president in May 2022 could reopen a path to peace talks.

Escalation potential and conflict-related risks
Islamist militant groups are on the back foot in western Mindanao and the coming year is likely to see intensified AFP crackdowns. In 2022, the AFP plans to deploy a newly created 4,500-strong army division of experienced recruits, which will be based in Jolo and assume operational responsibility for the anti-ASG campaign in the island provinces of Basilan, Sulu and Tawi-Tawi.[12] As the ASG comes under increasing pressure, there is a chance it could turn to more proactive terrorist tactics and look to make use of explosives before they are seized and before militant

camps are overrun. On mainland Mindanao, BIFF and Maute Group militants are likely to lay low as they look to regroup and replenish their ranks following sustained AFP aerial bombardment. Presidential Adviser on the Peace Process Carlito G. Galvez has warned that the economic impacts of the coronavirus pandemic have created conditions for renewed BIFF recruitment. As the MILF continues to disarm, the two Moro fronts once central to the insurgency now pose little threat, while former MILF–BIAF rebels integrated into JPSTs alongside AFP and PNP personnel will adopt a stabilising role in the BARMM.

The NPA conflict will likely continue unabated. Numerous past deadlines set by the military to defeat the group have gone unmet. Under Duterte's watch the AFP has made little distinction between rebels and alleged supporters of the Maoist movement; indigenous groups residing in rural areas and left-leaning political figures at the community level will increasingly be in the firing line in Duterte's final months as president.

Strategic implications and global influences

While the Philippines' conflicts are internal in nature, neighbouring Malaysia seeks to minimise the spillover risk associated with the Islamist insurgency in the south. In 2021, there was more evidence of ASG infiltration into Malaysia's eastern Sabah state, where soldiers killed ASG members and discovered a makeshift militant base in a mangrove swamp. Malaysia will police a 1,457 kilometre-long Eastern Sabah Security Zone (ESSZ) and enforce a dusk-to-dawn curfew for civilian vessels along the coastline to ward off further infiltration. In September 2021, Malaysia announced plans to install new control posts in Kuala Meruap and Siguntur and a forward-operations base on Tambisan island. Trilateral naval patrols by Indonesia, Malaysia and the Philippines will serve as a further deterrent, as will US counter-terrorism support to the AFP in Mindanao, which includes use of reconnaissance drones.

Notes

[1] Amnesty International, 'Philippines: "Battle of Marawi" Leaves Trail of Death and Destruction', 17 November 2017.

[2] Rommel Rebollido, 'Murad Hails Signing of Law Postponing BARMM Elections', Rappler, 29 October 2021.

[3] Noel Punzalan, 'BARMM Lauds Military Report on Declining ASG Threat in BaSulTa', Philippine News Agency, 5 May 2021.

[4] Froilan Gallardo, 'Seized Rocket Components Indicate Planned Terror Attacks in Mindanao – Military', Rappler, 4 March 2022.

[5] Lade Jean Kabagani, 'Close to 2K MILF Combatants Decommissioned in Q1 2022', Philippine News Agency, 7 March 2022.

[6] Jamaine Punzalan, '43 Guerrilla Fronts Still Active, Says AFP Chief 7 Mos. Before Target Date to End Communist Insurgency', ABS-CBN News, 29 November 2021.

[7] Jauhn Etienne Villaruel, '"Fake Clash": Communist Party Says NPA's Ka Oris Was "Ambushed"', ABS-CBN, 1 November 2021.

[8] Philippine Statistics Authority, 'Highlights of the First Semester 2021 Official Poverty Statistics', 17 December 2021.

[9] Philippine Statistics Authority, 'Farmers, Fisherfolks, Individuals Residing in Rural Areas and Children Posted the Highest Poverty Incidences Among the Basic Sectors in 2018', 3 June 2020.

[10] '"Kill Them": Duterte Wants To "Finish Off" Communist Rebels', Al-Jazeera, 6 March 2021.

[11] Froilan Gallardo, 'Marawi Rehab "85 Percent" Completed – del Rosario', Minda News, 22 September 2021.

[12] Rio N. Araja, 'DND Plans to Spend P1b to Deploy 4,500 Men in Sulu', *Manila Standard*, 5 September 2021.

Regional Outlook

Asia plays host to several active intra-state conflicts, none of which show signs of definitive resolution in the immediate future. These conflicts tend to be long-standing and have seen various phases. There is also a possibility that new inter-state conflicts will erupt in the future as China increasingly asserts its power in the region and other countries seek to counter Beijing's actions.

Prospects for peace

None of Asia's intra-state armed conflicts offer firm prospects for peace in the short term. However, in certain cases there is room for cautious optimism: although peace talks may not bring conflicts to an end, they may provide an avenue for dialogue that ensures violence remains at a low level. This is the case in Thailand, where an agreement between the Thai government's Peace Dialogue Panel and the Patani Malay National Revolutionary Front in April 2022 provided a basis for further talks. In the Philippines, security forces have placed Islamist militant groups under pressure in western Mindanao; although this development may not lead to a stable peace, a reduction in violence may be possible. It remains to be seen how the new government in Manila will approach the country's armed conflicts.

Escalation potential and regional spillovers

The conflict in Myanmar presents a high risk of escalation amid the insurgency in the central plains and clashes between the People's Defence Force and the junta. It is unclear how the Taliban's rule in Afghanistan will influence regional security. Although it has not seen a relapse into outright war, violence has involved armed groups such as Islamic State Khorasan Province (ISKP), the National Resistance Front, the Afghanistan Freedom Front and the High Council of National Resistance. The country remains conflict-prone with bleak economic and humanitarian outlooks. The Taliban faces challenges in providing healthcare, education and financial services amid a deepening humanitarian crisis caused by food insecurity. Local grievances could inspire anti-Taliban violence, leading to further deterioration of the security environment.

If the security situation in Afghanistan were to deteriorate, the spillover of instability to Pakistan would be considerable. For some years, the level of insurgent and terrorist violence there has been considerably lower than the peak of 2007–15. However, emboldened by the Taliban's victory in Afghanistan, the Tehrik-e-Taliban Pakistan is increasingly challenging the Pakistani state in Khyber Pakhtunkhwa. In addition, Baloch separatists are likely to continue targeting Chinese infrastructure projects and ISKP remains active, meaning that Pakistan's security challenges will persist for the foreseeable future.

The India–Pakistan relationship remains a potential threat to Asia's stability. In Kashmir, militant violence is unlikely to subside in the short term, while it is doubtful that Pakistani Prime Minister Shehbaz Sharif will be able to engage productively with Indian Prime Minister Narendra Modi on the issue given the latter's hardline stance. Since a meaningful resolution of tensions is unlikely, the best possible scenario is an avoidance of further escalation.

Strategic implications and global influences

Inter-state tensions are on the rise in Asia. Worsening US–China tensions over Taiwan remain the region's most acute flashpoint for new inter-state armed conflict. On multiple occasions in 2022 the US has declared a more strident willingness to defend Taiwan in the event of a Chinese invasion, partly motivated by a desire to avoid an armed conflict breaking out in Asia comparable to Russia's invasion of Ukraine. On the Korean Peninsula, enduring inter-Korean tensions and Pyongyang's unpredictability and ballistic-missile tests remain a cause for concern.

Other bilateral relationships important to security in the Asia-Pacific came under additional stress in 2021 and early 2022. The Australia–China relationship was strained by the latter's signing of a security deal with Solomon Islands, which will see Beijing provide security assistance to a state traditionally viewed as within Australia's regional orbit. Elsewhere, alongside the other members of the G7, Japan has stepped up its economic statecraft against Russia following the latter's invasion of Ukraine, which has led to a freezing of Japan–Russia ties. The development has raised concerns that Russia may now heighten its naval cooperation with China in northern Asia, which will in turn have implications for Japan's national-security policies. As a result, Tokyo is likely to seek greater security collaboration with Washington.

Data Appendix

Number of fatalities due to violent events, by country, 1 March 2021–30 April 2022

Number of reported fatalities due to violent events (defined by the Armed Conflict Location & Event Data Project (ACLED) as battles, explosion/remote violence or violence against civilians) from 1 March 2021 to 30 April 2022. Data collected on 11 May 2022. **Source:** IISS calculation based on ACLED data, www.acleddata.com.

	Number of fatalities
Afghanistan	37,792
Yemen	20,254
Myanmar	17,865
Nigeria	12,443
Ethiopia	9,552
Mexico	9,271
Ukraine	6,729
Brazil	6,456
Democratic Republic of the Congo	6,366
Syria	6,331
Somalia	3,982
Burkina Faso	3,573
Mali	3,372
Iraq	3,069
South Sudan	2,524
Central African Republic	1,945
Pakistan	1,744
Sudan	1,721
Colombia	1,630

	Number of fatalities
Niger	1,562
Mozambique	1,319
Cameroon	1,274
Philippines	1,165
India	999
Chad	846
Haiti	676
Honduras	646
El Salvador	432
Israel–Palestinian Territories*	394
Uganda	366
Egypt	323
Turkey	308
Libya	158
Thailand	71
Nagorno-Karabakh*	57

*The figure represents the sum of fatalities for the two parties involved in the conflict. For the Nagorno-Karabakh conflict it represents the sum of fatalities for Armenia and Azerbaijan.

Number of refugees (total), counted by country of origin, as of 31 December 2021

Total number of refugees, specifically those in a refugee-like situation under the mandate of the United Nations High Commissioner for Refugeees (UNHCR), and Palestinian refugees recorded by the UN Relief and Works Agency for Palestine Refugees in the Near East (UNRWA).

A refugee is someone who is unable or unwilling to return to their country of origin owing to a well-founded fear of being persecuted for reasons of race, religion, nationality, membership of a particular social group or political opinion (as per the UNHCR 1951 Refugee Convention). In the case of Palestinian refugees, these are persons whose normal place of residence was Palestine during the period 1 June 1946 to 15 May 1948, and who lost both home and means of livelihood as a result of the 1948 conflict.

Data from UNHCR and UNRWA is updated to 31 December 2021 and was collected on 22 June 2022. Data on Ukraine is updated to 4 May 2022 and was collected on 4 July 2022.

Sources: UNHCR, www.unhcr.org/refugee-statistics/download; UNHCR 'Ukraine Situation Flash Update #11', data.unhcr.org/en/documents/details/92542; and UNRWA 'Refugee Data Finder', www.unhcr.org/refugee-statistics/download/?url=p7aBkY.

	Number of refugees
Syria	6,848,845
Israel–Palestinian Territories*	5,793,360
Ukraine	5,707,967
Afghanistan	2,712,858
South Sudan	2,362,759
Myanmar	1,177,029
Democratic Republic of the Congo	908,401
Sudan	825,290
Somalia	776,678
Central African Republic	737,658
Nigeria	383,660
Iraq	343,897
Mali	183,392
Ethiopia	149,125
Pakistan	132,817
Cameroon	125,475
Colombia	115,793
Turkey	105,019
El Salvador	52,041

	Number of refugees
Nagorno-Karabakh*	51,733
Honduras	51,687
Yemen	37,611
Haiti	29,454
Egypt	27,498
Niger	21,901
Burkina Faso	20,209
Libya	19,090
Mexico	16,403
India	14,230
Chad	11,771
Uganda	7,886
Brazil	1,954
Philippines	521
Thailand	181
Mozambique	90

*The figure represents the sum of refugees for the two parties involved in the conflict. For the Nagorno-Karabakh conflict it represents the sum of refugees for Armenia and Azerbaijan.

Number of internally displaced persons (total), by country, as of 31 December 2021

Total number of internally displaced persons (IDPs) due to conflict and violence recorded by the Internal Displacement Monitoring Centre (IDMC), or most recent available data by UNHCR or the International Organization for Migration (IOM).

IDPs are persons or groups of persons who have been forced or obliged to flee or to leave their homes or places of habitual residence, in particular as a result of or in order to avoid the effects of armed conflict, situations of generalised violence, violations of human rights or natural or human-made disasters, and who have not crossed an internationally recognised state border (as per 1998 UN Guiding Principles on Internal Displacement).

Data from the IDMC is as of 31 December 2021 for all countries except Egypt, for which the data is as of 31 December 2018, collected on 22 June 2022. Data for El Salvador is as of 31 December 2020, from UNHCR, collected on 4 July 2022. Data for Ukraine is as of 3 May 2022, collected from IOM on 4 July 2022.

Sources: IDMC, www.internal-displacement.org/database/displacement-data; UNHCR, www.unhcr.org/refugee-statistics/; IOM, 'El Salvador: Factsheet - April 2022', data.unhcr.org/en/documents/details/93179; and IOM, 'Ukraine — Internal Displacement Report — General Population Survey Round 4 (29 April – 3 May 2022)', displacement.iom.int/reports/ukraine-internal-displacement-report-general-population-survey-round-4-29-april-3-may-2022

	Number of IDPs (conflict and violence)
Ukraine	8,029,000
Syria	6,662,000
Democratic Republic of the Congo	5,339,000
Colombia	5,235,000
Afghanistan	4,314,000
Yemen	4,289,000
Ethiopia	3,589,000
Nigeria	3,228,000
Sudan	3,175,000
Somalia	2,968,000
Burkina Faso	1,580,000
South Sudan	1,369,000
Iraq	1,187,000
Turkey	1,099,000
Cameroon	909,000
Mozambique	735,000
Central African Republic	692,000
Nagorno-Karabakh*	655,800
Myanmar	649,000

	Number of IDPs (conflict and violence)
India	506,000
Chad	392,000
Mexico	379,000
Mali	326,000
Honduras	247,000
Niger	224,000
Libya	160,000
Philippines	108,000
Pakistan	104,000
El Salvador**	71,500
Thailand	41,000
Brazil	21,000
Haiti	17,000
Israel–Palestinian Territories*	12,000
Egypt**	3,200
Uganda	1,700

*The figure represents the sum of IDPs for the two parties involved in the conflict. For the conflict in Israel–Palestinian Territories, it only includes Palestinian IDPs since there is no data available for Israel.

**Most recent available data

Number of violent events, by country, 1 March 2021–30 April 2022

Number of violent events (defined by ACLED as battles, explosion/remote violence or violence against civilians) from 1 March 2021 to 30 April 2022. Data collected on 11 May 2022.

Source: IISS calculation based on ACLED data, www.acleddata.com

	Number of violent events
Ukraine	12,117
Syria	10,391
Myanmar	10,142
Yemen	8,550
Brazil	7,977
Mexico	7,923
Afghanistan	7,889
Iraq	4,957
Nigeria	3,234
Democratic Republic of the Congo	3,026
Somalia	2,946
Burkina Faso	1,827
Ethiopia	1,594
Colombia	1,589
Israel–Palestinian Territories*	1,280
Mali	1,256
India	1,210
Philippines	991
Pakistan	969

	Number of violent events
South Sudan	848
Cameroon	816
Sudan	676
Central African Republic	633
Haiti	567
Honduras	538
Mozambique	458
El Salvador	444
Nagorno-Karabakh*	394
Niger	393
Turkey	361
Uganda	356
Egypt	280
Thailand	141
Libya	140
Chad	137

*The figure represents the sum of events for the two parties involved in the conflict.

Number of foreign countries 'involved' in the conflict, by country, as of 30 April 2022

Number of foreign countries deemed to be involved in the conflict.

For *internal conflicts:* foreign countries are considered 'involved' if they are either present through the deployment of military capabilities (outside of a multilateral mission as defined in the Armed Conflict Global Relevance Indicator (ACGRI)) or they meet all the following criteria: presence of intelligence assets; provision of military financial support; role in an advisory or operational command-and-control capacity; and sale or transfer of military equipment.

For *inter-state conflicts:* third-party countries are considered 'involved' if they are either present through the deployment of military capabilities (outside of a multilateral mission as defined in the ACGRI) or they meet two or more of the following criteria: presence of intelligence assets; provision of military financial support; role in an advisory or operational command-and-control capacity; and sale or transfer of military equipment. Data collected on 30 April 2022 from the Military Balance+. Military-aid data for Ukraine is from 28 June 2022, collected on 5 July 2022 from the Ukraine Support Tracker by the Kiel Institute for the World Economy, and covers the time period from 24 January to 1 July 2022.

Sources: IISS calculation based on the Military Balance+, milbalplus.iiss.org; and Arianna Antezza, Andre Frank, Pascal Frank, Lukas Franz, Ekaterina Rebinskaya and Christoph Trebesch, 'The Ukraine Support Tracker: Which countries help Ukraine and how?', Kiel working paper, no. 2218, 2022.

	Foreign countries 'involved' in the conflict	Number of foreign countries 'involved' in the conflict
Ukraine	Germany New Zealand Norway Sweden UK US	6
Syria	Iran Israel Russia Turkey US	5
Iraq	Iran *Operation Inherent Resolve* (US)* Turkey	4
Yemen	Iran *Operation Restoring Hope* (Saudi Arabia)* UAE	4
Democratic Republic of the Congo	Burundi Rwanda Uganda	3
Libya	Italy Russia Turkey	3
Mozambique	Rwanda Southern African Development Community Mission in Mozambique (SAMIM) (South Africa)*	3
Niger	France Italy US	3
Nagorno-Karabakh	Russia Turkey	2
Burkina Faso	France US	2

	Foreign countries 'involved' in the conflict	Number of foreign countries 'involved' in the conflict
Central African Republic	Russia Rwanda	2
Mali	*Operation Barkhane* (France)*	2
Chad	France	1
Ethiopia	Eritrea	1
Israel–Palestinian Territories	Iran	1
Nigeria	UK	1
Afghanistan	None	0
Brazil	None	0
Cameroon	None	0
Colombia	None	0
Egypt	None	0
El Salvador	None	0
Honduras	None	0
India	None	0
Mexico	None	0
Myanmar	None	0
Pakistan	None	0
Philippines	None	0
Somalia	None	0
South Sudan	None	0
Sudan	None	0
Thailand	None	0
Turkey	None	0
Haiti	None	0
Uganda	None	0

*In the case of involvement of coalitions of countries, the name of the coalition and the country leading it are displayed. Each coalition is assigned a score of two for the purposes of the ACGRI's calculation.

Number of military personnel deployed by major geopolitical powers in conflict-affected countries, by country, as of 30 April 2022*

Total number of military personnel deployed into conflict-affected countries by geopolitical powers within the G20 group (including unilaterally, as part of a combat coalition or a mission under the aegis of an international organisation and excluding deployments which are not conflict related). Data collected on 30 April 2022.

Source: IISS calculation based on Military Balance+, milbalplus.iiss.org

	Number of personnel deployed
Ukraine	120,000
Syria	8,131
Nagorno-Karabakh**	5,630
Iraq	4,545
Democratic Republic of the Congo	4,113
Mali	3,994
South Sudan	3,756
Yemen	2,500
Niger	2,095
Chad	1,500
Libya	902
Egypt	645
Somalia	432
Burkina Faso	400
Honduras	400
Central African Republic	376
Philippines	309
Mozambique	272
El Salvador	100
Israel–Palestinian Territories**	100
Nigeria	80
Colombia	70
Sudan	12

	Number of personnel deployed
India***	11
Pakistan***	11
Afghanistan	0
Brazil	0
Cameroon	0
Ethiopia	0
Haiti	0
Mexico	0
Myanmar	0
Thailand	0
Turkey	0
Uganda	0

*The variable covers only deployments related to the specific conflict. This means that either the deployed military forces are conflict parties or the deployment has an explicit mandate to assist the conflict parties with training and capability building. The US deployments in Thailand and Turkey are not considered conflict related and are not included in the variable calculation for either country.

**The figure represents the sum of deployments in the two parties involved in the conflict.

*** The personnel deployed as part of the UN Military Observer Group in India and Pakistan (UNMOGIP) are attributed to both India and Pakistan.

Number of UNSC resolutions concerning conflicts under review, by country, 1 March 2021–30 April 2022

Number of resolutions announced by the UN Security Council (UNSC) between 1 March 2021 and 30 April 2022 concerning the country and conflict under review. Countries for which no resolution was announced receive a value of 0.

Source: IISS calculation based on UNSC, www.un.org/securitycouncil/content/resolutions-0

	Number of resolutions
Libya	8
Somalia	6
South Sudan	6
Afghanistan	5
Syria	5
Sudan	5
Iraq	4
Central African Republic	3
Colombia	2
Democratic Republic of the Congo	2
Mali	2
Yemen	2
Turkey	1
Ukraine	1
Haiti	1
Brazil	0
Burkina Faso	0
Cameroon	0

	Number of resolutions
Egypt	0
El Salvador	0
Ethiopia	0
Honduras	0
India	0
Mexico	0
Mozambique	0
Myanmar	0
Nagorno-Karabakh	0
Nigeria	0
Pakistan	0
Philippines	0
Thailand	0
Chad	0
Niger	0
Israel–Palestinian Territories	0
Uganda	0

Number of operational peacekeeping, special political and military missions, and other multilateral missions concerning conflicts in countries under review as of 30 April 2022

Number of multilateral peacekeeping operations, special political and military missions, and other multilateral presences under the aegis of international organisations present in a country. These include missions undertaken by the UN, regional organisations or ad hoc groups related to UN sanctions/UNSC resolutions or endorsed by the UN and other international organisations. Data refers to active missions as of 30 April 2022 that fulfil the two following criteria: 1) objective (relating to multidimensional peace and conflict resolution) and 2) geographical scope (relating to the analysed conflicts in the countries under review). Data collected on 30 April 2022 from the Military Balance+, the Stockholm International Peace Research Institute's (SIPRI) Map of Multilateral Peace Operations 2022 published in May 2022 and the UN Geospatial map of Special Political Missions and Other Political Presences 2022, published in March 2022.

Source: IISS calculations based on Military Balance+, milbalplus.iiss.org; SIPRI, www.sipri.org/publications/2022/sipri-map-multilateral-peace-operations-2022; UN Geospatial, www.un.org/geospatial/content/united-nations-special-political-missions-and-other-political-presences-2022; and the official websites of the UN, European Union, regional organisations and ad hoc coalitions.

	Number of missions	Names of missions
Central African Republic	7	AU Observer Mission to the Central African Republic (MOUACA) AU Mission for the CAR and Central Africa (MISAC) EU Advisory Mission in the Central African Republic (EUAM RCA) EU Training Mission in the Central African Republic (EUTM RCA) Special Envoy of the Secretary-General for the Great Lakes Region of Africa UN Multidimensional Integrated Stabilization Mission in the Central African Republic (MINUSCA) UN Regional Office for Central Africa (UNOCA)
Mali	6	AU Mission for Mali and the Sahel (MISAHEL) EU Capacity Building Mission Sahel Mali (EUCAP Sahel Mali) EU Training Mission Mali (EUTM Mali) G5 Sahel Joint Force (FC-G5S) UN Office for West Africa and the Sahel (UNOWAS) UN Multidimensional Integrated Stabilization Mission in Mali (MINUSMA)
Somalia	6	AU Transition Mission in Somalia (ATMIS) – AU Mission in Somalia (AMISOM) EU Capacity Building Mission in Somalia (EUCAP Somalia) EU Training Mission Somalia (EUTM Somalia) Special Envoy of the Secretary-General for the Horn of Africa UN Assistance Mission in Somalia (UNSOM) UN Support Office in Somalia (UNSOS)
Chad	4	G5 Sahel Joint Force (FC-G5S) Multinational Joint Task Force (MNJTF) UN Office for West Africa and the Sahel (UNOWAS) UN Regional Office for Central Africa (UNOCA)
Israel–Palestinian Territories	4	EU Border Assistance Mission for the Rafah Crossing Point (EUBAM Rafah) EU Police and Rule of Law Mission for the Palestinian Territory, EU Coordinating Office for Palestinian Police Support (EUPOL COPPS) UN Special Coordinator for the Middle East Peace Process (UNSCO) UN Truce Supervision Organization (UNTSO)
Niger	4	EU Capacity Building Mission Sahel Niger (EUCAP Sahel Niger) G5 Sahel Joint Force (FC-G5S) Multinational Joint Task Force (MNJTF) UN Office for West Africa and the Sahel (UNOWAS)
South Sudan	4	Intergovernmental Authority on Development (IGAD) Ceasefire & Transitional Security Arrangements Monitoring & Verification Mechanism (CTSAMVM) Special Envoy of the Secretary-General for the Great Lakes Region of Africa Special Envoy of the Secretary-General for the Horn of Africa UN Mission in the Republic of South Sudan (UNMISS)
Sudan	4	Special Envoy of the Secretary-General for the Great Lakes Region of Africa Special Envoy of the Secretary-General for the Horn of Africa UN Integrated Transitional Assistance Mission in Sudan (UNITAMS) UN Interim Security Force for Abyei (UNISFA)
Democratic Republic of the Congo	3	Special Envoy of the Secretary-General for the Great Lakes Region of Africa UN Organization Stabilization Mission in the Democratic Republic of the Congo (MONUSCO) UN Regional Office for Central Africa (UNOCA)

	Number of missions	Names of missions
Iraq	3	EU Advisory Mission in support of Security Sector Reform in Iraq (EUAM Iraq) NATO Mission Iraq (NMI) UN Assistance Mission for Iraq (UNAMI)
Libya	3	AU Mission in Libya EU Border Assistance Mission in Libya (EUBAM Libya) UN Support Mission in Libya (UNSMIL)
Mozambique	3	EU Training Mission in Mozambique (EUTM Mozambique) Personal Envoy of the Secretary-General for Mozambique Southern African Development Community Mission in Mozambique (SAMIM)
Burkina Faso	2	G5 Sahel Joint Force (FC-G5S) UN Office for West Africa and the Sahel (UNOWAS)
Cameroon	2	Multinational Joint Task Force (MNJTF) UN Regional Office for Central Africa (UNOCA)
Colombia	2	OAS Mission to Support the Peace Process in Colombia (MAPP/OEA) UN Verification Mission in Colombia (UNVMC)
Nigeria	2	Multinational Joint Task Force (MNJTF) UN Office for West Africa and the Sahel (UNOWAS)
Ukraine	2	EU Advisory Mission Ukraine (EUAM Ukraine) Organization for Security and Co-operation in Europe (OSCE) Project Co-ordinator in Ukraine
Yemen	2	Special Envoy of the Secretary-General for Yemen UN Mission to Support the Hudaydah Agreement (UNMHA)
Uganda	2	Special Envoy of the Secretary-General for the Great Lakes Region of Africa Special Envoy of the Secretary-General for the Horn of Africa
Afghanistan	1	UN Assistance Mission in Afghanistan (UNAMA)
Nagorno-Karabakh	1	Personal Representative of the Chairperson-in-Office on the conflict dealt with by the OSCE Minsk Conference
Ethiopia	1	Special Envoy of the Secretary-General for the Horn of Africa
India	1	UN Military Observer Group in India and Pakistan (UNMOGIP)
Myanmar	1	Special Envoy of the Secretary-General on Myanmar
Pakistan	1	UN Military Observer Group in India and Pakistan (UNMOGIP)
Philippines	1	International Monitoring Team (IMT)
Syria	1	Special Envoy of the Secretary-General for Syria
Haiti	1	UN Integrated Office in Haiti (BINUH)
Brazil	0	N/A
Egypt	0	N/A
El Salvador	0	N/A
Honduras	0	N/A
Mexico	0	N/A
Thailand	0	N/A
Turkey	0	N/A

Gini index, by country, latest available data

The Gini index measures the extent to which the distribution of income (or, in some cases, consumption expenditure) among individuals or households within an economy deviates from a perfectly equal distribution. A Lorenz curve plots the cumulative percentages of total income received against the cumulative number of recipients, starting with the poorest individual or household. The Gini index measures the area between the Lorenz curve and a hypothetical line of absolute equality, expressed as a percentage of the maximum area under the line. Thus a Gini index of 0 represents perfect equality, whilst an index of 100 implies perfect inequality.

Source: World Bank, data.worldbank.org/indicator/SI.POV.GINI?most_recent_year_desc=true

	Gini index
Central African Republic	56.2 (2008)
Colombia	54.2 (2020)
Mozambique	54 (2014)
Brazil	48.9 (2020)
Honduras	48.2 (2019)
Burkina Faso	47.3 (2018)
Cameroon	46.6 (2014)
Mexico	45.4 (2020)
South Sudan	44.1 (2016)
Uganda	42.7 (2019)
Philippines	42.3 (2018)
Democratic Republic of the Congo	42.1 (2012)
Turkey	41.9 (2019)
Haiti	41.1 (2012)
El Salvador	38.8 (2019)
Israel	38.6 (2018)
Chad	37.5 (2018)
Syria	37.5 (2003)
Niger	37.3 (2018)
Somalia	36.8 (2017)

	Gini index
Yemen	36.7 (2014)
Mali	36.1 (2018)
India	35.7 (2011)
Nigeria	35.1 (2018)
Ethiopia	35 (2015)
Thailand	35 (2020)
Sudan	34.2 (2014)
Palestinian Territories*	33.7 (2016)
Egypt	31.5 (2017)
Myanmar	30.7 (2017)
Pakistan	29.6 (2018)
Iraq	29.5 (2012)
Azerbaijan	26.6 (2005)
Ukraine	25.6 (2020)
Armenia	25.2 (2020)
Afghanistan	N/A
Libya	N/A

*Refers to the West Bank and Gaza

GDP per capita, constant prices, purchasing power parity (international dollars), per country, 2021

GDP per capita represents the constant price purchasing-power-parity (PPP) terms of final goods and services produced within a country during a specified time period divided by the total population. The variable is expressed in 2017 international dollars. Data collected on 5 July 2022 from the World Economic Outlook (April 2022) by the IMF.

Source: IMF, www.imf.org/en/Publications/WEO/weo-database/2022/April

	GDP per capita
Israel	41,644.1
Turkey	31,635.9
Mexico	18,820.1
Thailand	17,485.5
Libya	15,335.7
Colombia	14,916.0
Brazil	14,710.2
Azerbaijan	14,456.7
Armenia	13,345.4
Ukraine	13,039.5
Egypt	12,315.6
Iraq	9,741.6
El Salvador	8,842.3
Philippines	8,351.7
India	6,682.1
Honduras	5,659.5
Pakistan	5,437.0
Palestinian Territories**	5,262.8
Nigeria	4,969.2
Myanmar	4,050.7
Sudan	3,891.4
Cameroon	3,704.3
Ethiopia	2,855.4
Haiti	2,759.7
Uganda	2,490.5
Afghanistan*	2,328.8
Burkina Faso	2,241.7
Mali	2,227.2
Yemen	1,799.8
Chad	1,454.8
Mozambique	1,221.0
Niger	1,192.7
Somalia	1,130.1
Democratic Republic of the Congo	1,093.5
Central African Republic	929.4
South Sudan	767.8
Syria	N/A

*As of 2020
**Refers to the West Bank and Gaza

Functioning of government, by country, 2021

The functioning of government, a pillar of the Economist Intelligence Unit (EIU) Democracy Index, assesses the effectiveness of the system of checks and balances on the exercise of government authority as well as elements such as openness and transparency of government, public access to information, government accountability, pervasiveness of corruption, public confidence in government and political parties. The functioning of government is scored on a 0–10 scale. Data collected on 12 May 2022 from the EIU Democracy Index 2021.

Source: EIU, www.eiu.com/n/democracy-index-2021-less-than-half-the-world-lives-in-a-democracy/

	Functioning of government
India	7.5
Israel	7.5
Armenia	5.7
Colombia	5.7
Pakistan	5.3
Brazil	5.4
Mexico	5
Philippines	5
Thailand	5
Turkey	5
El Salvador	3.9
Honduras	3.9
Nigeria	3.9
Egypt	3.2
Ethiopia	3.2
Uganda	3.2
Azerbaijan	2.5
Burkina Faso	2.4
Ukraine	2.4
Cameroon	2.1
Mozambique	1.4
Sudan	1.4
Niger	1.1
Afghanistan	0.1
Palestinian Territories	0.1
Central African Republic	0
Chad	0
Democratic Republic of the Congo	0
Haiti	0
Iraq	0
Libya	0
Mali	0
Myanmar	0
Syria	0
Yemen	0
Somalia	N/A
South Sudan	N/A

Food-risk score, per country, 2021

The food-risk indicator is proxied by the prevalence of stunting in children under five, which is measured by the proportion of children with a height-for-age z-score that is more than two standard deviations below the World Health Organization's median growth reference standards for a healthy population. The estimate is the average prevalence of stunting at the ADMIN1 sub-national level. Where data were not available, values were imputed based on the average of a country's ADMIN1 prevalence of stunting. If these values were unavailable, the World Bank country estimates were used. The prevalence of stunting was then normalised on a 1–5 scale to determine the overall food-risk indicator. Data published in October 2021 in the Ecological Threat Report 2021 by the Institute for Economics and Peace (IEP). Data collected on 25 July 2022.

Source: IEP, www.visionofhumanity.org/maps/ecological-threat-register-2021/#/

	Food-risk score
Afghanistan	5
Burkina Faso	5
Cameroon	5
Central African Republic	5
Chad	5
Democratic Republic of the Congo	5
Ethiopia	5
Honduras	5
India	5
Israel	5
Mali	5
Mozambique	5
Myanmar	5
Niger	5
Nigeria	5
Pakistan	5
Philippines	5
South Sudan	5
Sudan	5

	Food-risk score
Uganda	5
Yemen	5
Armenia	4
Haiti	4
Somalia	4
Syria	4
Turkey	4
El Salvador	3
Iraq	3
Libya	3
Ukraine	3
Colombia	2
Egypt	2
Russia	2
Thailand	2
Azerbaijan	1
Brazil	1
Mexico	1
Palestinian Territories	1

Climate-change vulnerability and readiness score, per country, 2020

The Notre Dame Global Adaptation Initiative (ND-GAIN) Country Index summarises a country's vulnerability to climate change and other global challenges in combination with its readiness to improve resilience. It is scored on a 0–100 scale (higher is better). Data collected on 22 July 2022.
Source: ND-GAIN, gain.nd.edu/our-work/country-index/

	ND-GAIN Country Index score
Israel	61
Russia	60
Turkey	57
Armenia	56
Thailand	52
Ukraine	52
Azerbaijan	50
Brazil	48
Colombia	48
Mexico	47
Egypt	45
El Salvador	45
India	44
Philippines	44
Iraq	43
Libya	42
Honduras	40
Cameroon	39
Pakistan	39
Mozambique	38
Myanmar	38
Nigeria	38
Syria	38
Burkina Faso	37
Ethiopia	37
Haiti	35
Mali	35
Uganda	35
Somalia	34
Yemen	34
Afghanistan	33
Niger	33
Sudan	32
Democratic Republic of the Congo	31
Central African Republic	27
Chad	27
Palestinian Territories	N/A
South Sudan	N/A

Food-price inflation (%), per country, as of December 2021

Food-price inflation measures inflation rates of food and general consumer price indices (CPI). The figures represent annual year-on-year inflation, which is the percentage change related to the same month in the previous year. Data collected on 5 August 2022 from the FAOSTAT statistical database by the Food and Agriculture Organization of the United Nations (FAO).
Source: Food and Agriculture Organization of the United Nations, FAOSTAT, Consumer Price Indices for December 2021, latest update: 21 June 2022, www.fao.org/faostat/en/#data/CP

	Food-price inflation
Sudan	191.6
Turkey	43.8
Syria	42.1
Ethiopia	41.6
South Sudan	32.0
Haiti	26.3
Afghanistan	17.7
Nigeria	17.3
Colombia	17.2
Azerbaijan	16.2
Burkina Faso	13.8
Armenia	12.9
Ukraine	12.7
Myanmar	12.4
Russia	12.2
Mexico	11.6
Mali	11.3
Pakistan	10.3
Niger	10.2
Mozambique	9.8
Egypt	8.4
Brazil	8.0
El Salvador	8.0
Cameroon	7.6
Iraq	7.3
Honduras	6.8
Libya	5.4
Uganda	5.2
India	4.5
Philippines	3.1
Chad	3.0
Israel	2.4
Yemen	2.3
Palestinian Territories	1.6
Democratic Republic of the Congo	1.5
Thailand	0.8
Central African Republic	N/A
Somalia	N/A

Index

A

Abbas, Mahmoud 155, 158–161
Abdulrahman, Anas 383, 384
Abkhazia (Georgia) 8, 102, 104
Abraham Accords 132, 149, 155, 160, 183
Abu Sayyaf Group (Philippines) 390–398
Afghanistan 6, 9, 20–21, 27, 51, 322–337, 341, 342, 347, 363–367, 370, 399
    Afghan National Defence and Security Forces 322, 326–330, 335, 336
African Development Bank 215
African Union 203, 211, 223, 226, 228, 230, 237, 239, 249, 257, 262, 264–269, 272, 310, 311, 316, 320, 321
    Lake Chad Regional Stabilisation Strategy 226
    Mission in Somalia 262–269, 272, 320
    Peace and Security Council 223, 237, 316
    Transition Mission to Somalia 264–269, 320
Agreement for Bringing Peace to Afghanistan 327
Agreement on the Resolution of the Conflict in the Republic of South Sudan 240–249
Ahlu al-Sunnah wal-Jamaah / al-Shabaab (Mozambique) 273, 303–308
Ahmed 218, 225, 228, 252, 254, 261, 287, 290
Ahmed, Abiy 252, 254, 261
Akhundzada, Mullah Haibatullah 328
al-Assad, Bashar 9, 130–131, 133–136, 138–141, 198
al-Barnawi, Abu Musab 221, 223, 225, 227
al-Bashir, Omar 28, 310
al-Burhan, Abdel Fattah 311, 312
al-Fashaga Triangle 256, 314, 320
Algiers accord 205, 209, 211, 212, 216
Aliyev, Ilham 105, 120, 123
al-Kadhimi, Mustafa 145, 146, 150, 152
Allied Democratic Forces 200, 271–273, 277, 278, 280, 281, 293–295, 298, 303, 304
al-Qaeda 9, 136, 137–139, 142, 144, 166, 168, 169, 177, 178, 186, 195, 205, 208, 211, 222, 262, 265, 282, 289, 320, 326, 327, 329, 330, 334, 336, 363–365, 369
al-Qaeda in the Arabian Peninsula 168, 169, 172
al-Qurashi, Abu Ibrahim al-Hashimi 136, 137, 140, 147, 187
al-Shabaab (Somalia) 9, 26, 31, 262–269, 320
al-Sisi, Abdel Fattah 188–190
Ambazonia Governing Council (Cameroon) 285, 293–295, 297, 298
Ambazonia Self-Defence Council (Cameroon) 293, 294, 295
Angola 230, 280, 305
Ansarul Islam 207–213
Ansarullah (Houthi movement) 131–133, 164, 165–173
        Supreme Political Council 167, 170
Arab–Israeli War 154, 156
Arab Spring 130, 164, 186
Arakan Army (Myanmar) 352, 354, 358, 360
Arctic 32, 35, 36, 38
Arctic Council 36, 38
Argentina 67, 68, 71
Aristide, Jean-Bertrand 77, 81
Armenia 8, 102, 105, 118–127
Arunachal Pradesh (India) 36
Assam Rifles 373, 374, 379
Association of Southeast Asian Nations 352, 357–360
Aung San Suu Kyi 350, 351, 355, 356
Australia 34, 113, 348, 399
Azad Jammu and Kashmir (Pakistan) 340, 341–343
Azerbaijan 8, 102, 105, 118–127

B

Baghdad Conference for Cooperation and Partnership 152
Bahrain 155, 159, 160, 162, 189
Balochistan (Pakistan) 324, 330, 347, 362, 364, 365, 366, 367, 368, 369
Balochistan Liberation Army (Pakistan) 324, 331, 362, 364–368
Baloch Raaji Ajoi Sangar (Pakistan) 362, 365
Baloch Republican Army (Pakistan) 362, 365, 367
Bangladesh 36, 352, 362
Bangsamoro Islamic Freedom Fighters (Philippines) 391–396, 398
Barrio 18 (El Salvador) 86, 88, 89
Bashagha, Fathi 176, 179, 181, 183
Bazoum, Mohamed 207, 212, 214–217, 224
Baz Pilate 78, 80
Belarus 104–107, 109, 111–113, 127
Beltrán Leyva Organisation 48
Benin 9, 206, 208, 211, 213, 215, 217, 221, 223, 320
Bhutan 36
Bicentennial Framework for Security, Public Health, and Safe Communities 42, 45, 46, 51–54
Biden, Joe 52, 57, 63, 81, 83, 84, 87, 92, 99, 139, 141, 150, 161, 165, 172, 181, 227, 263, 269, 288, 327
bin Laden, Osama 326, 329
Biya, Paul 293
Boko Haram 26, 27, 31, 220–224, 226, 228, 282, 284, 285, 289, 290, 293, 296–298, 300, 308
Bolivia 67, 68, 73
Bolsonaro, Jair 66, 67, 71–75
Brahmaputra (river) 36, 38
Brazil 40, 43, 66–75
    Senate 73, 84
    Supreme Court 68, 72, 73, 81, 87, 88, 90, 98
Buhari, Muhammadu 222, 224–227, 284, 286–289, 297
Bukele, Nayib 86–92
Burkina Faso 12, 200, 203, 205–210, 212–218, 320
Burkina Faso Armed Forces 207, 208
Burundi 265, 267, 270–277, 279, 320

C

Calderón, Felipe 44
Cambodia 12, 352, 358
Cameroon 11, 12, 26, 200, 220–228, 231, 233, 237, 284, 285, 289, 292–294, 296–301
Cameroon Humanitarian Response Plan 300
Canada 114, 211, 213
Cartel Jalisco New Generation (Mexico) 41, 44, 47–51, 53, 58, 89, 94, 96
Caspian Pipeline Consortium 105
Castro, Xiomara 95, 98
Central African Patriotic Movement 232, 233
Central African Republic 9, 20, 24, 200, 202, 230–239, 241, 275, 298, 299, 320
    Coalition of Patriots for Change 231–238
    Central African Armed Forces 231, 232, 234–238
Chad 11–13, 20, 26, 27, 30, 31, 200, 203, 210, 220–228, 230, 232, 233, 235, 236, 239, 282, 284, 285, 289, 293, 294, 296, 298, 299, 320
Chanocha, Prayuth 383, 384
China 6, 10, 31, 32, 33–38, 40–43, 47, 48, 51, 71, 101, 113, 128, 202, 237, 238, 261, 289, 294, 317, 322–325, 331–336, 341, 343, 345, 347–350, 352, 354, 356, 359, 360, 365, 366, 369, 399
    Belt and Road Initiative 36, 324, 325, 366
    Polar Silk Road 32, 36
    People's Liberation Army Navy 325
China–Pakistan Economic Corridor 324, 341, 348, 365, 366
Chin National Front (Myanmar) 351, 355, 357
Civilian Joint Task Force (Nigeria) 222–224, 284
Climate change 5, 6, 18, 19, 21–23, 25, 27–29, 31, 32, 34–38
Cold War 108, 111, 202, 356
Colima (Mexico) 42, 47

Colombia 8, 27, 40, 43, 46, 47, 56–64, 67, 68, 70, 94, 100, 101
  National Commission for Security Guarantees 62
  National Liberation Army 57, 58, 59, 61, 63, 64, 100
  Special Circumscriptions for Peace 61
Combined Joint Task Force-Operation Inherent Resolve 139, 145–152
Communist Party of India–Maoist (India) 373, 374, 376–380
Convention on the Prohibition of Military or Any Other Hostile Use of Environmental Modification Techniques 28
Coordination Committee (India) 353, 376, 377
Coronavirus 5, 8, 9, 15, 40, 45, 51, 52, 54, 60, 62, 72, 73, 87, 88, 90, 92, 95, 97, 100, 201, 226, 237, 247, 253, 267, 293, 300, 320, 376
Costa Rica 8, 100
Côte d'Ivoire 9, 206, 208, 211, 213, 215, 217, 320
Crimea 36, 103, 105–109, 116

D

Damiba, Paul-Henri Sandaogo 206, 213
Darfur 230, 310–318
da Silva, Luiz Inácio 72, 73, 74, 75
Dbeibah, Abdul Hamid 175–177, 180, 183
Déby Itno, Mahamat Idriss 224, 225
Democratic Forces for the Liberation of Rwanda 271, 273, 275, 279
Democratic Republic of the Congo 9, 200, 202, 203, 232, 270–281, 303, 308, 320
  Armed Forces of the DRC 200, 271–280
Djibouti 200, 256, 265
Dominican Republic 77, 82, 84
Donbas (Ukraine) 8, 106, 108–112, 115, 116, 127
Donetsk People's Republic (Ukraine) 105–110, 112, 113, 116
Duarte, Gentil 57–59, 61, 63
Duque, Iván 58, 60, 61
Duterte, Rodrigo 391, 396–398

E

East African Community 276, 278, 279
Eastern Sabah Security Zone 398
East Jerusalem 154, 155, 160–162
Economic and Monetary Community of Central Africa 296
Economic Commission for Latin America and the Caribbean 97, 99, 101
Economic Community of Central African States 230
Economic Community of West African States 206, 207, 211, 213, 215, 216
Ecuador 8
Egypt 9, 130, 132, 152, 154, 159, 160, 162, 174, 181, 186–191, 198, 256, 268, 269, 317, 320
  Egyptian Armed Forces 186–190
  Operation Sinai 186
El Salvador 40
  National Assembly 89, 91
  National Civil Police 88, 91, 92
  Peace Accords 88, 89
Erdoğan, Recep Tayyip 9, 138, 148, 178, 193, 194, 196–198
Eritrea 113, 253–256, 259, 320
  Eritrean Defence Forces 255, 256
Ethiopia 9, 200, 202, 242, 244, 245, 249, 252–262, 265, 268, 269, 314, 317, 318, 320
  Ethiopian National Defence Force 253–256, 258
  Grand Ethiopian Renaissance Dam 9, 256, 257, 261, 314, 320
  Ethiopian People's Revolutionary Democratic Front 252, 254
European Union 8, 32, 33, 63, 87, 98, 104, 108, 110, 112–115, 123, 124, 127, 207, 210, 211, 214, 215, 223, 226, 228, 232, 261, 263–265, 268, 278, 303–305, 307, 308, 321, 335, 336, 346, 348, 358
  Capacity Building Mission (EUCAP) Somalia 263
  Naval Force Somalia 263
  Training Mission in Somalia 263, 268
ExxonMobil 305

F

Facebook 360, 386
Family of the North (Brazil) 66–72, 74, 75
Famine Early Warning Systems Network 83
Fatah 136, 156, 161
Fentanyl 6, 8, 40–43, 47, 51, 52, 100, 101
Financial Action Task Force 347, 349, 369
Finland 20, 36, 38, 108, 116, 143, 193, 197, 266

First Capital Command (Brazil) 66–75
France 111, 113, 184, 187, 193, 202, 203, 205–208, 210, 213–215, 217, 218, 222, 231, 232, 233, 236, 237, 239, 254, 269, 272, 284, 294
Friends of Friends (Brazil) 68, 69, 70

G

G5 Sahel Joint Force 205–212, 214, 217
G7 22
G9 Family and Allies 78, 79, 81
Gabon 230
Gadhafi, Muammar 130, 174
Gambella Liberation Front 254, 256, 258, 261
Gaza 154–159, 161, 162, 187, 188
Georgia 8, 9, 102, 104
Germany 22, 34, 38, 111, 113, 175, 184, 187, 193
Ghana 208, 213, 215
Ghani, Ashraf 327, 328
Global Environment Facility 20, 24
Gnassingbé, Faure 215
Golan Heights 154
Grand Ravine baz 78–82
Greece 196
Group to Support Islam and Muslims 205, 207–211, 213
Guadalajara Cartel 44, 47
Guatemala 47, 89, 92, 94–97, 99
Guinea 200, 215, 261
Guinea-Bissau 200
Gulf Cartel (Mexico) 47, 48, 50, 51, 100
Gulf Clan (Colombia) 56–59, 61–63
Gulf Cooperation Council 152, 159, 165
Guterres, António 32, 61, 181, 359

H

Hadi, Abd Rabbo Mansour 131, 164
Haftar, Khalifa 175
Haiti 8, 11, 40, 76–85, 99, 100
Haitian National Police (PNH) 78
Hamas 155–158, 161, 162, 188, 189, 191
Hamdok, Abdalla 311
Harris, Kamala 51
Hayat Tahrir al-Sham (Syria) 135–137, 138, 141, 142
Henry, Ariel 77, 81
Hernández, Juan Orlando 46, 60, 63, 95, 97–99
Hizbullah 136, 138, 145, 149, 156, 157, 165, 167
Hizbul Mujahideen (Kashmir) 340–342, 348
Hlaing, Min Aung 352, 356–358
Honduras 40, 89, 92, 94–99
Hungary 108, 113

I

IMF 54, 91, 92, 99, 152, 153, 203, 237, 247, 250, 267, 269, 299, 301, 315, 333, 334, 346, 360, 370
India 9, 11–13, 31–33, 36, 38, 113, 128, 322, 324, 325, 330, 338–343, 345–349, 362–364, 369, 372–380, 399
  Armed Forces Special Powers Act 339, 379, 380
  Central Reserve Police Force 340, 374, 375
Indigenous People of Biafra 283, 285, 286, 289, 294, 297
  Eastern Security Network 283–285, 287, 289
Indonesia 398
Institute for Economics and Peace 200, 203, 288
Intergovernmental Panel on Climate Change 32, 38
Interim Government of Ambazonia 293–295, 297
International Committee of the Red Cross 29, 30, 31
  Guidelines on the Protection of the Natural Environment in Armed Conflict 29, 30, 31
International Conference on the Great Lakes Region 231, 236–238, 280
International Criminal Court 28
International Energy Agency 33, 38
International Institute for Strategic Studies 6, 10, 113
International Law Commission
  Draft Principles on the Protection of the Environment in relation to Armed Conflicts 29
International Organization for Migration 228, 288, 290
International Security Assistance Force 326, 330
Iran 101, 132, 134, 136, 138–141, 143–153, 156, 157, 165, 167–169, 172,

331–337
  Islamic Revolutionary Guard Corps 136, 138–141, 143, 147, 151
Iraq 12, 18, 26, 27, 30, 130, 132, 133, 135–140, 143–154, 156, 187, 188, 192–198
  Popular Mobilisation Units 145–149, 153
Iraqi Security Forces 145–149, 151
ISIS–Libya 177, 178, 180
Islamic State 9, 11, 18, 26, 27, 31, 130, 135–140, 142, 144–151, 153, 169, 177–180, 186–188, 190, 191, 193–195, 205, 207, 208, 220, 221, 223, 228, 264, 265, 269, 271, 277, 281, 282, 293, 303, 320, 327, 329, 337, 363, 365, 370, 388, 391–395, 399
Islamic State Central Africa Province 277, 303, 304
Islamic State Khorasan Province 9, 327–334, 336, 363–370, 399
Islamic State Sahel Province 205, 207–211, 213, 214, 216, 217
Islamic State West Africa Province 27, 207, 208, 220–228, 282, 289, 293, 300
Israel 9, 12, 13, 130, 132, 133, 138, 139, 149, 151, 154, 155–162, 183, 186–191, 198

J

Jama'atu Ahlis Sunna Lidda'awati wal-Jihad (Nigeria) 220–228, 282, 293
Jammu and Kashmir (India) 338–349
Japan 33, 34, 38, 113, 348, 358, 399
Jaysh-e-Mohammad (Kashmir) 340–342, 344, 345, 348
Joint Roadmap for Peace in the CAR 236, 237
Jordan 140, 152, 154, 159, 160, 162, 198
Juárez Cartel 49
Justice and Development Party (Turkey) 197
Justice and Equality Movement (Sudan) 310, 313, 318

K

Kabila, Joseph 271
Kachin Independence Army (Myanmar) 351–353, 355, 357, 360
Kagame, Paul 270, 275, 307
Kaliningrad 106, 108, 115
Karen National Union (Myanmar) 351, 353, 355, 357, 360
Karenni Nationalities Defense Force (Myanmar) 353
Karenni National Progressive Party (Myanmar) 351, 353, 355, 357, 360
Kashmir 10, 12, 13, 322, 325, 338–349, 372, 399
Kazakhstan 103, 105, 324
Kenya 202, 245, 265, 268, 273, 280, 286
Kenyatta, Uhuru 279
Khan, Imran 368
Kharkiv 108, 109, 115
Khartoum Agreement 230, 231, 233, 237, 238
Kherson 8, 107, 108, 112, 115, 127
Kiir, Salva 240, 242
Korean Peninsula 322, 399
Kurdistan
  Kurdish Peshmerga 147–149, 151
  Kurdistan Regional Government 144, 145, 148, 151, 153, 192, 196
Kurdistan Workers' Party 132, 135–140, 143, 146, 148, 149, 153, 192–197
Kyiv 105, 107–110, 112, 115, 116, 127
Kyrgyzstan 8, 102, 105, 324

L

Lake Chad 9, 11–13, 26, 27, 30, 31, 200, 203, 220–228, 282, 285, 293, 294, 296, 298, 299, 320
Laos 36
Lashkar-e-Taiba (Kashmir) 340–342, 344, 345, 347, 348, 369
Lebanon 138, 149, 154, 156, 159
Libya 130, 132, 133, 174–184, 187, 188, 190, 191, 198, 209, 218, 298, 312, 313
  Government of National Accord 175–180, 184
  Government of National Stability 176, 179–181, 183
  Government of National Unity 175–181, 183
  High Council of State 182
  House of Representatives 175–177, 180–184
  Joint Military Commission 180, 181
  Libyan Armed Forces 175–178, 181
  Operation Dignity 174, 177
Libyan National Army 175–181, 183, 188
Line of Actual Control (India–China) 345, 348
Line of Contact (Nagorno-Karabakh) 109, 110, 119–121
Line of Control (India–Pakistan) 330, 339, 363, 364
Lithuania 108, 115
López Obrador, Andrés Manuel 42, 43, 45, 51–53
Los Angeles (US) 49, 86, 88, 96
Los Zetas 47, 48
Luhansk People's Republic (Ukraine) 106–110, 112, 113, 116
Lukashenko, Alexander 104

M

Machar, Riek 240, 243
Macron, Emmanuel 152, 213, 214
Madagascar 200
Maduro, Nicolás 64, 100
Malaysia 382–384, 388, 392, 396, 398
Mali 12, 200, 202, 203, 205–218, 261, 284, 298, 320
Malian Armed Forces 207–211
Manipur Naga People's Front 377, 379, 380
Mara Salvatrucha (El Salvador) 40, 86–92, 94, 96–99
March 23 Movement 271, 273, 275–280
Mariupol 108, 112
Maute Group (Philippines) 391–395, 397, 398
Mérida Initiative 42, 45, 46, 51, 54
Mexico 40–54, 67, 81, 84, 89, 94, 96, 99
  National Human Rights Commission 53, 54
  Secretariat of National Defence 46–53
  Secretariat of the Navy 46
Mexico City 48, 51
Michoacán 42, 46–49, 51
Michoacán Family / Knights Templar (Cárteles Unidos) 48, 49
Military Police of Rio de Janeiro 68
Modi, Narendra 10, 339, 399
Mohamed, Mohamed Abdullahi 'Farmaajo' 263
Mohamud, Hassan Sheikh 201, 263, 320
Moïse, Jovenel 11, 76, 81, 85
Moldova 102, 104, 105, 108, 114
Morena 51, 53
Morocco 155, 159, 160
Moro Islamic Liberation Front (Philippines) 390–394, 396–398
Moro National Liberation Front (Philippines) 390–394, 397
Mosul (Iraq) 26, 30
Mozambique 9, 11, 68, 74, 200, 275, 280, 302–308, 320
  Mozambican Defence Armed Forces 304
Mubarak, Hosni 130
Multinational Joint Task Force 221, 223, 228, 284, 293
Muslim Brotherhood 156, 157, 165, 177, 178, 187, 190, 191
Myanmar 9, 51, 322, 324, 325, 350, 351, 352, 354–360, 373, 376–380, 399
  National Unity Government 351, 355
  Nationwide Ceasefire Agreement 350–354, 357, 358
  Tatmadaw 350, 352–360, 373, 377, 378
Myanmar National Democratic Alliance Army/ Myanmar National Truth and Justice Party 354, 356, 357, 360

N

Nagorno-Karabakh 8, 12, 13, 102, 105, 118–127
Nagorno-Karabakh Defence Army 120, 121
National Democratic Front of the Philippines 391
National League for Democracy (Myanmar) 350–352, 355, 356
National Salvation Front–Thomas Cirillo 242–244, 246, 247
National Socialist Council of Nagaland–Khaplang (India) 373, 375–380
National Socialist Council of Nagalim–Isak Muivah (India) 373, 375
NATO 6, 22, 36, 38, 107–109, 111–113, 115, 116, 127, 136, 143, 148, 153, 174, 183, 193, 194, 197, 322, 327, 329, 330, 331, 334, 337, 364
  Enhanced Forward Presence 108
  Enhanced Opportunity Partners 108
  Tailored Forward Presence 108
Negev Summit 159, 160
Nepal 36
New People's Army (Philippines) 390–392, 394–398
Niger 12, 22, 26, 200, 205–218, 220–227, 283, 284, 286–290, 320
Niger Armed Forces 207–209
Nigeria 9, 12, 26, 27, 200, 203, 215, 220–228, 282–290, 295, 297, 298, 320
  National Livestock Transformation Plan 283, 288, 289
Nigerian Army 222, 225, 226, 228
Northern Alliance (Myanmar) 352–355
Northern Triangle 8, 100

North Korea 113
Norway 20, 34, 38, 159, 335, 336
Nyusi, Filipe 304

O

Obama, Barack 326
Ocalan, Abdullah 148, 192, 194
Odesa 102, 108
OLA-Shane (Ethiopia) 255, 257
Operation Atalanta 264, 268
Operation Barkhane 203, 205, 206, 208–214, 216, 218
Operation Safe Corridor 221, 226, 228
Organisation for Economic Co-operation and Development 23, 24, 37, 38
Organisation of Islamic Corporation 346
Organization for Security and Co-operation in Europe 106, 111, 113, 116, 119
    Normandy format 113
    Special Monitoring Mission to Ukraine 106, 116
Organization of Petroleum Exporting Countries 151
Oromo Liberation Army 254–258, 261
Oslo Accords 155, 157, 159, 160

P

Pakistan 9–11, 13, 36, 322–326, 328–349, 362–370, 399
    Federally Administered Tribal Areas 330, 363–366, 369
    Operation Radd-ul-Fasaad 331, 363, 364
    Operation Zarb-e-Azb 331, 363, 364, 369
    Pakistan Armed Forces 329, 330, 331, 340, 341, 364, 365
    Pakistani Civil Armed Forces 331, 364, 365
Palestinian Authority 155–162
Palestinian Islamic Jihad 156, 157, 162
Palestinian Liberation Organization 155, 157, 161
Palestinian Territories 9, 12, 13, 130, 154, 155, 156, 160, 161, 198
Panama 8, 59, 84, 100
Paraguay 67, 68, 71–73
Pashinyan, Nikol 120, 123
Patani Malay National Revolutionary Front (Thailand) 10, 382, 384, 385, 399
Patani United Liberation Organisation (Thailand) 382, 385, 388
People's Defence Force 9, 351–353, 355–360, 373, 377–379
People's Protection Units (Syria) 136–140, 143, 193–195
Peru 34, 67, 68, 70
Petro, Gustavo 8, 43, 61, 63, 100
Philippines 10–12, 15, 322, 342, 391, 392, 394, 395, 398, 399
    Anti-Terrorism Council 396, 397
    Armed Forces of the Philippines 391–398
    Bangsamoro Autonomous Region in Muslim Mindanao 390, 391, 393–398
    Bangsamoro Organic Law 390
    Bangsamoro Transition Authority 391, 397
    National Task Force to End Local Communist Armed Conflict 391, 392, 396
    Philippine National Police 392, 393, 394, 396, 398
Plan Colombia 56
Poland 107, 108, 114
Popular Front for the Renaissance in the Central African Republic 232, 233
Préval, René 76
Pure Third Command (Brazil) 68–70
Putin, Vladimir 103, 105–107, 109, 111–113, 115, 121, 202, 211, 234

Q

Qatar 156, 162, 178, 189, 191, 335
Quadrilateral Security Dialogue 348

R

Rapid Intervention Battalion 293, 294
Red Command (Brazil) 66–72, 74
Republic of Congo 230, 281
Resistance for the Rule of Law in Burundi (DRC) 272–275, 277, 281
Resolute Support Mission 330, 337
Revitalised ARCSS 241–249
Revolutionary Armed Forces of Colombia 27, 56–63, 100
Rio de Janeiro 66, 68, 69, 71, 72, 74, 75

Romania 108, 342
Royal Thai Army 382–385
Russia 5, 6, 8–10, 12, 13, 15, 18, 30–34, 36–38, 63, 72, 73, 101–113, 115, 116, 119–127, 136–139, 141–143, 171, 175, 176, 179, 183, 187, 190, 195, 198, 202, 207, 211, 213, 214, 216–218, 225, 227, 228, 231, 232, 234, 236–239, 256, 261, 269, 286, 288, 289, 298, 300, 317, 320, 321, 324, 333, 335, 336, 348, 349, 352, 359, 360, 399
    Armed Forces of the Russian Federation 109, 121,138
    Black Sea Fleet 108, 112
        Moskva 108, 112
    Ministry of Foreign Affairs 107
Russia–Africa Summit 202
Russia–Ukraine war 5, 12, 15, 18, 32, 33, 36, 37, 63, 72, 73, 103–105, 107, 108, 120, 124, 125, 127, 135, 136, 139, 141, 143, 152, 171, 176, 180, 183, 190, 198, 201, 216, 217, 226, 228, 238, 268, 269, 300, 320, 321, 331, 336, 348, 369, 399
Rwanda 9, 200, 202, 231, 234, 270–280, 304, 305, 307, 308, 320
Rwanda Defence Force 234, 275, 279, 280, 304, 305, 307
Rwandan Patriotic Front 270, 273

S

Sahel Alliance 215, 218
Saleh, Ali Abdullah 130, 164, 166, 167
Sall, Macky 321
Sandu, Maia 104
Santa Rosa de Lima Cartel 50, 51
Saudi Arabia 131, 132, 151, 152, 165, 166, 168, 169, 171, 172, 189, 191, 346
Second Marquetalia (Colombia) 57–60, 63
Second World War 5, 8, 102, 106
Senegal 211, 234, 321
Shanghai Cooperation Organisation 324
Shan State Army–North (Myanmar) 354
Shan State Army–South (Myanmar) 354
Sharif, Shehbaz 10, 345, 368, 399
Shekau, Abubakar 221–224, 226–228
Sinai Peninsula 154, 186–188
Sinai Province 186–190
Sinaloa Cartel (Mexico) 41, 44, 47–49, 53, 58, 89, 94, 96
Singapore 113
Sinwar, Yahya 156, 158
Six-Day War 154, 157
Slovakia 108
Solomon Islands 399
Somalia 9, 20, 21, 23, 24, 26, 27, 31, 200, 201–203, 256, 262–269, 272, 280, 320
    Transitional Federal Government 262, 263, 265
    Islamic Courts Union 262
    Transitional Federal Government 262
    Somali National Army 9, 263, 264, 269, 320
Sonora 42, 43, 44, 46, 49
South Africa 113
Southern African Development Community Standby Force Mission in Mozambique 303–305, 307, 308
Southern Cameroons Defence Force 293, 294, 295
Southern Transitional Council 165–169, 171, 172
South Ossetia (Georgia) 9, 102, 104, 105
South Sudan 200, 202, 232, 240–245, 247–250, 254, 257, 275, 310, 313, 314, 317, 320
    Transitional Government of National Unity 241–243, 250
Soviet Union 103, 107, 109, 111, 118, 120
Spain 390
SPLM/A-In Opposition 241–244, 246, 247, 249
State Administrative Council (Myanmar) 342, 352, 355, 356, 358–360
Sudan 9, 13, 155, 160, 177, 191, 200, 202, 230, 232, 233, 235, 240–245, 247–250, 253–257, 261, 275, 298, 310–318, 320
    Sovereignty Council 312, 314, 315
    Rapid Support Forces 312, 313, 315–318
    Sudanese Armed Forces 242, 311–313, 315, 317
Sudan Liberation Movement/Army-Abdel Wahid al-Nur 312, 313–315
Sudan Liberation Movement/Army-Minni Minnawi 313, 314, 318
Sudan People's Liberation Movement/Army 240–247, 249, 313, 314
Sudan People's Liberation Movement/Army–North 313, 314
Sweden 36, 38, 108, 116, 143, 193, 197
Syria 9, 20, 26, 27, 30, 130, 132–141, 143, 145–157, 159, 179, 187, 188, 192,

193–198
   Syrian Armed Forces (SAF) / The Syrian Arab Army (SSA) 136–138
Syrian Democratic Forces 9, 131, 135–141, 143, 193–198
Syrian National Army 135–138, 143, 177, 193–195

T

Ta'ang National Liberation Army (Myanmar) 352, 354, 357, 358, 360
Taiwan 10, 322, 399
Tajikistan 8, 102, 105, 324, 325, 332, 337
Taliban (Afghanistan) 9, 21, 27, 322, 323, 324, 326–337, 342, 347, 363–367, 369, 370, 399
Task Force Takuba 206, 208–214, 216, 218
Tehrik-e-Taliban Pakistan 9, 324, 329, 331, 334, 336, 347, 363–370
Thailand 10, 13, 36, 322, 342, 353, 355, 357, 360, 382, 384–388, 399
   Peace Dialogue Panel 339, 344, 383, 386, 387, 399
The Resistance Front (Kashmir) 340–342, 344, 348
Tibetan Plateau 35, 36
Ti Bois baz (Haiti) 79
Tigray People's Liberation Front (Ethiopia) 9, 200, 252–261, 320
   Tigray Defence Force 253–259
Tigris (river) 26
Tijuana Cartel (Mexico) 49
Togo 9, 211, 215, 217, 320
Tokayev, Kassym-Jomart 105
TotalEnergies 305, 306
Touadéra, Faustin-Archange 231–238
Transparency International 50, 54, 72, 75, 299, 301
Trump, Donald 139, 141, 155, 160, 161, 165, 181, 263, 327
Tshisekedi, Félix 271, 272, 276
Tunisia 130
Turkey 8, 9, 101, 111–113, 116, 119–122, 124, 127, 130, 132, 135–140, 142, 143, 146–150, 153, 175, 177, 178, 181, 184, 191–198, 202, 261, 263–266, 268, 269, 317
   Operation Eren 196
   Turkish Armed Forces 138, 148,150, 178, 179, 194

U

Uganda 11, 241, 242, 245, 246, 249, 265, 270–273, 275–279, 320
   Ugandan People's Defence Force 272, 273, 277, 278, 280
Ukraine 5–10, 12–15, 102–116, 120, 121, 124, 125, 127, 128, 135, 136, 139, 141, 143, 152, 171, 173, 176, 180, 183, 184, 190, 198
   Armed Forces of Ukraine 109, 110
   Minsk agreements 111
Union for Peace in the Central African Republic 232, 233, 236
United Arab Emirates 131, 133, 136, 141, 149, 151, 155, 159, 160, 162, 165–173, 177, 179, 187, 189, 191, 202, 256, 261, 263, 268, 269, 312, 335, 345, 346
United Front of Ethiopian Federalist and Confederalist Forces 258
United Kingdom 107, 108, 112–114, 184, 187, 193, 203, 211, 222, 223, 264, 265, 267, 284, 330, 336, 358
United Liberation Front of Asom–Independent 373, 376, 378, 380
United Nations 10, 13–15, 20, 24, 29, 32, 38, 43, 54, 60, 64, 83, 92, 97, 99, 104, 113, 114, 116, 124, 125, 131, 133, 135, 139, 141–143, 150–155, 159, 160, 162, 165, 166, 169, 170, 171, 173, 175–177, 181–184, 198, 200, 205, 210, 211, 214, 217, 218, 228, 230–237, 239, 242, 244, 247, 249, 250, 254, 256–258, 261, 263–269, 271, 272, 275, 278, 279, 281, 288, 290, 292, 293, 296, 299, 301, 310, 311, 316–318, 320, 321, 323, 325–328, 330, 334–339, 342, 346, 348, 358–360, 370
   Assistance Mission for Iraq 151
   Assistance Mission in Somalia 263, 269
   Children's Fund 124
   Climate Change Conference 32
   Development Programme 20–24, 60, 64
   Food and Agricultural Organization 321
   General Assembly 29, 104, 113, 123, 159, 320, 321, 358
   High Commissioner for Refugees 114, 116, 125, 250, 261, 267, 279, 281, 290, 336, 337
   Human Rights Council 254, 258, 261, 293
   Integrated Transition Assistance Mission in Sudan 317
   International Law Commission 29
   Military Observer Group in India and Pakistan 339, 342, 348
   Mission in the Republic of South Sudan 244
   Multidimensional Integrated Stabilization Mission in the CAR 230–234, 236–239, 275
   Multidimensional Stabilization Mission in Mali 205, 207–212, 214, 217, 218
   Office for the Coordination of Humanitarian Affairs 152, 153, 162, 198, 228, 237, 239, 268, 269, 299, 301, 359, 360
      Humanitarian Response Plan 2022 152
   Office of the High Commissioner for Human Rights 114, 116, 126
   Organization Stabilization Mission in the DRC 271–273, 275, 276, 278, 280, 281
   Security Council 13, 21–24, 29, 31, 133, 139–143, 150, 151, 153, 155, 160, 165, 170, 171, 173, 175, 177, 178, 184, 198, 210, 211, 223, 234, 237, 247, 250, 257, 264, 266, 268, 269, 275, 281, 316, 318, 325, 326, 337, 342, 359, 360, 370
   Support Mission in Libya 175, 176
United Nations-African Union (AU) Peacekeeping Force 310
United Self-Defense Forces of Colombia 56, 59
United States 8, 10, 22, 31–33, 38, 40, 42–49, 56, 71, 78, 80, 85, 87, 90, 94, 101, 107–109, 111–114, 124, 127, 131, 133, 135 153, 155 157, 159–162, 165, 166, 170–173, 176, 178, 179, 181, 184, 186–189, 192–198, 202, 203, 207, 210, 214, 215, 218, 222, 223, 225–228, 254, 256, 258, 259, 261, 263–269, 272, 273, 284, 287–290, 294, 297, 299, 303, 304, 316, 317, 322, 326–337, 346–348, 353, 356–358, 364, 365, 367–370, 384, 390, 392, 395, 398, 399
   9/11 Attacks 329
   Agency for International Development 83, 85, 266
   Cybersecurity and Infrastructure Security Agency 83
   Department of Defense 331, 337, 370
   Department of Homeland Security 299
   Department of Justice 95, 97–99
   Department of State 225, 287
   Department of the Treasury 91, 92
   Drug Enforcement Administration 42–44 , 47, 49, 84
   Special Inspector General for Afghanistan Reconstruction 331, 337
   State Department 189, 196
   Transportation Security Administration 83
   Treasury Department 335
Uppsala Conflict Data Program 11
US–China trade war 34
Uzbekistan 324, 329, 337

V

Venezuela 8, 46, 50, 57–64, 67, 68, 73, 94, 99, 100, 101
Vietnam 12, 28, 36, 325, 353
Vietnam War 28, 353

W

Wagner Group 176, 177, 179, 183, 184, 202, 207, 211, 213, 214, 217, 218, 231, 232, 234, 236, 298, 300
War On Drugs 42, 44, 52, 63
West Bank 154–159, 161, 162
Women's Protection Units (Syria) 137, 193, 195
Working Committee (India) 375, 378, 379
World Bank 20, 32, 38, 64, 83, 85, 99, 152, 153, 162, 215, 228, 247, 267, 269, 278, 299, 301, 306, 308, 315, 316, 318, 333, 334, 337, 388
World Food Programme 228, 248, 250, 264, 318

Y

Yemen 9, 130–133, 149, 164, 165–173, 198
   Presidential Leadership Council 131, 132, 166–169, 171, 172
   Stockholm Agreement 165
Yom Kippur War 154
Yusuf, Mohammed 220–224, 264

Z

Zapad 106, 111
Zaporizhzhia (Ukraine) 8
Zelaya, Manuel 95, 98
Zelenskyy, Volodymyr 107, 108, 109, 115